COLLEGE OF ALAMEDA LIBRARY
WITHDRAWN

D0871866

HC
39   Jones, Arnold
J65   The Roman economy

DATE DUE

APR 29 '81			
JUN 9 '82			
NOV 27 '82			
NOV 20 '85			
OCT 19 '89			
OCT 11 '89			

LENDING POLICY

IF YOU DAMAGE OR LOSE LIBRARY
MATERIALS, THEN YOU WILL BE
CHARGED FOR REPLACEMENT. FAIL
URE TO PAY AFFECTS LIBRARY
PRIVILEGES GRADES, TRANSCRIPTS,
DIPLOMAS AND REGISTRATION
PRIVILEGES OR ANY COMBINATION
THEREOF.

WITHDRAWN

THE ROMAN ECONOMY

THE ROMAN ECONOMY

Studies in Ancient Economic and Administrative History

A. H. M. JONES

Edited by

P. A. BRUNT

ROWMAN AND LITTLEFIELD

Totowa, New Jersey

First published in the United States 1974
by Rowman and Littlefield, Totowa, N.J.

© BASIL BLACKWELL 1974

All rights reserved. No part of this publication may
be reproduced, stored in a retrieval system, or transmitted in any form or by any means, electronic,
mechanical, photocopying, recording or otherwise,
without the prior permission of Basil Blackwell and
Mott Limited.

Library of Congress Cataloging in Publication Data

Jones, Arnold Hugh Martin, 1904–1970.
The Roman economy.

Includes bibliographical references.
CONTENTS: The cities of the Roman Empire.—The
economic life of the towns of the Roman Empire.—
Numismatics and history. (etc.)
1. Rome—Economic conditions—Addresses, essays,
lectures. 2. Rome—Politics and government—284–476—
Addresses, essays, lectures. I. Title.
HC39.J65 1973 330.9'37'6 73–5960

ISBN 0–87471–194–0

PRINTED IN GREAT BRITAIN
BY A. T. BROOME AND SON, 18 ST. CLEMENT'S, OXFORD
AND BOUND BY THE KEMP HALL BINDERY, OXFORD

PREFACE

This volume of essays by the late Professor A. H. M. Jones, who died on 9 April 1970, falls into two main parts. The first consists of general surveys, the second of papers on special problems of the later Roman Empire. With two exceptions (chapters XX and XXI in part III) the latter were written before he had completed his great history, and they are indispensable for the documentation of the views he expressed in that work on the topics concerned, since he departed from his general practice of giving the evidence there in full, when he had presented it in an article previously published. This volume should, therefore, serve as an essential supplement to Jones' *Later Roman Empire*. But his friends also felt that the opportunity should not be lost to include some of his more general papers, many of them published originally in places where they might easily be missed or where many would find them altogether inaccessible, while one (ch. VIII) was still in manuscript. Their merits should be manifest: no other historian in our time has had such a range of familiarity with the evidence for ancient history from Lycurgus of Sparta to Heraclius, and none a greater capacity for synthesis and lucid and orderly exposition.

There are certain omissions which perhaps deserve explanation. Of Jones' general surveys his *Slavery in the Ancient World* (*Econ. Hist. Rev.* IX, 1956) is already reprinted and easily accessible in *Slavery in Classical Antiquity*, edited by M. I. Finley (Heffers, 1960). One of his most recent publications, *Rome and the Provincial Cities* (*Tijdschrift voor Rechtsgeschiedenis*, 1971, 1 ff), admirable as it is, retraces much ground that he had covered in his *Greek City* and in several essays in this book; in several places I have used it to add points to these essays. Again most of what he said in his London Inaugural Lecture, *Ancient Economic History*, 1948, was developed more fully in later works, not least in chapter XXI here; his views here on the Roman census figures, a theme to which he never returned, are fully expounded in my *Italian Manpower*, 1971. In Part II, apart from some small pieces, one of his most notable essays has been omitted, *The Social Background of the Struggle between Paganism and Christianity*, but only because the volume in which it appeared, *Paganism and Christianity in the Fourth Century* (Clarendon Press, 1963, ed. A. Momigliano), must be in the hands of every serious student of late Rome.

The editorial notes to chapters VIII and IX (the latter an old article which has been supplemented from a manuscript essay on the same theme) explain the way in which I have presented these papers. Elsewhere I have given occasional cross-references and additional references, often to Jones' own *Later Roman Empire*. Attention may also be drawn to M. H. Crawford's bibliographical addendum to ch. III. These interpolations are enclosed in square brackets. Otherwise, apart from misprints and a very few corrections suggested by Jones' infrequent marginalia on his own copies, the text is that of the original publications.

Thanks are due to the editors or publishers of the various journals from which these articles are drawn, and which are named in the Contents, for consenting to their re-publication; likewise to Mouton & Cie, as well as to the École Pratique des Hautes Études, Paris, for chapter VI, to the Clarendon Press for chapter III and to Bruno Cassirer for chapter VII. The Index has been compiled by Mr. R. P. Davis of University College, Oxford. I must also express my personal gratitude for help of various kinds received from P. R. L. Brown, M. H. Crawford, J. A. Crook, G. E. M. de Ste Croix, M. I. Finley and J. M. Matthews; none has any responsibility for errors I may have made as editor, but all gladly assisted in the production of what may be regarded as a commemoration of a great scholar to whom we are greatly indebted and whose sudden death, when he was still at the height of his powers, we still lament.

P. A. BRUNT
Brasenose College,
Oxford

September 1973

NOTE ON ABBREVIATIONS

Jones adopted different abbreviations in different articles. All seem intelligible, and no attempt has been made to harmonise them. *L.R.E.* everywhere refers to his *Later Roman Empire*.

NOTE ON
WEIGHTS, MEASURES AND CURRENCY

1 *iugerum*=⅝ acre=.25 hectares.
1 *arura*=⅔ acre=.27 hectares.
1 *millena*=12½ *iugera*=7¾ acres=3.25 hectares.
1 *centuria*=200 *iugera*=125 acres=50 hectares.
24 scruples (*scripuli*)=1 Roman ounce (*uncia*).
12 *unciae*=1 Roman pound (*libra*)=11½ ounces=321 grammes.
1 *modius*=1 peck=9 litres.
1 *artaba*=3⅓ pecks=30 litres.

In gold the following denominations were used in the late Empire:
24 carats (*siliquae*)=3 *tremisses*=2 *semisses*=1 *solidus*.
72 *solidi*=1 lb gold (*libra auri*).
7,200 *solidi*=1 cwt gold (*centenarium auri*).

In the coinage of the Roman Republic and Principate:
1 *denarius*=4 sesterces (abbreviated HS).
25 *denarii*=1 aureus.
(The *denarius* is commonly equated with the Greek *drachma*, but in Roman Egypt 4 *drachmae* went to the *denarius*.)

CONTENTS

PART 3

PART I

CHAPTER ONE

THE CITIES OF THE ROMAN EMPIRE[1]

POLITICAL, ADMINISTRATIVE AND JUDICIAL INSTITUTIONS

THE early Roman provinces were groups of autonomous communities placed under the military control of a Roman magistrate. Sicily comprised sixty-five Greek or Hellenized cities; Sardinia and Corsica a few Punic towns and a number of native tribal communities; the Spanish provinces some Greek, Punic and native city states in the more civilised coastal areas and Iberian and Celtic tribes in the interior; Gaul the Greek city of Massilia and its colonies and the Gallic and Ligurian tribes up country. The kingdoms which Rome first annexed fell into the same pattern. Macedonia was already organised as a group of city states, and the parts of the Attalid kingdom formed into the province of Asia seem to have consisted of Greek or Hellenized native cities in the more civilised areas and native tribal communities in the mountains. Only the province of Africa formed an exception to the general rule. Here only the seven Punic cities which had sided with Rome in the final struggle with Carthage were allowed to subsist, and the territory of Carthage and her tributary cities was declared public land of the Roman people.

In its early experience of imperial government the Roman people thus found the districts which they annexed already divided between a number of small autonomous communities and they used these communities as the basis of the provincial administration which they established. They regulated and controlled the

---

[1] The best comprehensive book on the subject is still W. Liebenam, *Städteverwaltung im römischen Kaiserreiche*, Leipzig, 1900. F. F. Abbott and A. C. Johnson, *Municipal Administration in the Roman Empire*, Princeton, 1926 (A. and J.) contains a useful collection of documents. For the eastern half of the empire I refer to my *Cities of the Eastern Roman Provinces*, Oxford, 1937 (C.E.R.P.) and *Greek City from Alexander to Justinian*, Oxford, 1940 (G.C.). [For local government in provinces where there were few communities of the πόλις-*urbs* type see C. Jullian, *Hist. de la Gaule*, IV ch. VIII. Apart from some additional material in notes, I have amended the text in a few places from Jones's own corrections and on one detail from his article cited on p. 8].

communal governments but they had no occasion to create them. The annexation of Bithynia and Pontus presented a new problem. These two kingdoms were organised on a centralised pattern not uncommon among the minor Hellenistic monarchies; apart from a few cities, either ancient Greek colonies or royal foundations on the Greek model, the area of the kingdom was divided into prefectures, governed by royal officials. Faced with the problem of adapting them to the normal pattern of Roman provincial government, Pompey drastically reorganised them. So far as possible he used the existing cities as the basis of his scheme, assigning to them vast tracts of the kingdom to administer as their territories. In the more backward parts of Pontus, he created new city states on the local Greek model, giving Greek constitutions to the major towns, and making these new governments responsible for the surrounding areas.[2]

It is unnecessary to pursue further in detail the story of the successive provinces added to the Empire. It will suffice to say that most areas were readily adapted to the normal provincial pattern. Thus in Cilicia and Syria Pompey reorganised, and in many cases reconstituted the existing or recently destroyed cities, leaving the more backward areas under client princes, and in Gaul Caesar based the administration of the province on the Gallic tribal communities. Augustus found similar conditions and followed the same policy in the Alpine, Pannonian and Moesian districts which he annexed.

In the East Augustus established a new precedent by preserving intact the Ptolemaic centralised administration of Egypt under a Roman prefect, and this precedent was followed by himself and his immediate successors on the annexation of several minor oriental kingdoms, notably Judaea, Cappadocia and Thrace. In Thrace the experiment did not last for long; under Trajan and Hadrian a number of cities were founded and the country partitioned between them.[3] In Judaea urbanization was a more spasmodic and gradual process, and was never completed. In the course of the first three centuries A.D. a number of cities were successively founded and assigned one or more toparchies of the old kingdom as their territories, but four toparchies of the Jordan valley still survived as *regiones* in the sixth century.[4] In

---

[2] C.E.R.P., 154 ff. [3] *Ibid.*, 10 ff.
[4] *Ibid.*, 270 ff.

Cappadocia too a large area surrounding the capital Caesarea was still in the sixth century directly administered as *regiones*, although outlying districts had been organised as cities.[5] In Egypt the development of civic institutions was gradual. The country was divided into a number of administrative districts, called nomes, each governed by a *strategus* assisted by other officials appointed by the prefect. Augustus allowed a very limited degree of municipal autonomy to the metropoleis, the capital towns of the nomes, permitting their Greek or Hellenised inhabitants to elect a group of magistrates to manage the local gymnasium, regulate the market and conduct the Hellenic cults. Septimius Severus took the next step when he enrolled in each metropolis a council, which not only conducted the municipal services through the existing magistrates, but elected others to assist the *strategus* in the administration of the nome. Diocletian took the final step of formally converting each nome into a city, administered by its council, though still under the direction of an imperial official, the *strategus* of the nome being renamed the *exactor civitatis*.[6]

Outside these few areas which lacked civic institutions the imperial government had little opportunity of founding new cities. Its principal activity was in the planting of colonies of Roman citizens. A very few Roman colonies had been founded in the provinces under the republic; Narbo in Gaul is the most notable. Caesar, the triumvirs and Augustus carried out a large scale programme of colonization, mainly with the object of providing land for discharged veterans and the landless proletariat of Italy, and the process continued at a slower tempo during the early principate. Very few colonies were, however, completely new communities. Caesar's foundations at Carthage and Corinth can be considered as such, since these cities had been destroyed a century earlier, and their territories had since then been public land of the Roman people. But the great majority of Roman colonies were planted on land, obtained by confiscation or purchase, in the territory of existing communities.

The early relations of the Roman colonists to the natives are obscure, but it would appear that from the time of Augustus it was customary to grant Roman citizenship to the natives, and enrol them as members of the colony with the settlers. The main

[5] *Ibid.*, 177 ff.
[6] *Ibid.*, 316 ff.

result of the process was therefore not to increase the number of autonomous communities, but to raise the status of existing communities.[7]

From the above account it will have become clear that the term city (*civitas*, πόλις) did not in antiquity denote a town. A city was a self-governing community, membership of which depended on descent and not on domicile, occupying a defined area of land, its territory. Juridically a rural canton whose inhabitants lived scattered in villages, was a *civitas*, provided that its people met periodically to elect magistrates and vote laws. Such primitive *civitates* continued to exist in backward areas throughout the history of the empire, but normally even the most rural *civitates* developed some urban centre, and in the more civilised provinces the town had from time immemorial dominated its surrounding territory. It was however the rarest of anomalies that a *civitas* should consist of a town only, without a dependant territory: the only known case is Alexandria of Egypt and here the reason was that the Ptolemies took over the administration of 'the territory of the Alexandrians' and organised it as a nome of Egypt.[8]

Normally the native inhabitants of a *civitas* were all citizens of the community on an equal footing, whether they were domiciled in the central town or in the surrounding countryside. There were exceptions to this rule, due to exceptional circumstances. In some old Greek colonies, for instance, the descendants of the original settlers formed the citizen body, ruling over the native peasantry, and in some Hellenistic colonies similar conditions no doubt prevailed. In Bithynia the inhabitants of the royal land assigned to the cities by Pompey do not seem to have been admitted to the citizen body.[9] In the west it was a fairly common practice of the Roman government to 'attribute' backward rural communities to a neighbouring city; thus several north Italian cities had Alpine cantons attributed to them, and Nemausus in Gaul had twenty-four subject communities.[10] Such cases were, however, exceptional and by the Constitutio Antoniniana of 212 A.D., whereby all inhabitants of the empire became

---

[7] F. Vittinghoff, *Römische Kolonisation und Bürgerrechtspolitik unter Caesar und Augustus*, Wiesbaden, 1952; [P. A. Brunt, *Italian Manpower*, 1971, ch. XV].

[8] C.E.R.P., 305–6.

[9] G. C., 160–2, 172–3.

[10] *I.L.S.*, 206, 6680, Pliny, *N. H.*, III, 37, 134, 138.

Roman citizens, it is probable that all inhabitants of each city territory became *municipes* of that city.[11]

In area, population and social and economic structure there were immense contrasts between the cities of the different provinces, and between individual cities in the same province. In Britain and northern Gaul for instance, the *civitates* were tribes, occupying vast cantons whose capitals were insignificant country towns. In Africa, on the other hand, the average *civitas* was tiny in area, and the majority of the inhabitants probably lived in the town and went out daily to work in the fields; but on the coast were big towns, including Carthage, the second city of the West, ruling wide territories dotted with villages. In the East there were similar contrasts. The mountains and valleys of western and southern Asia Minor were thickly studded with small cities, while the central plateau was partitioned between a few widely scattered cities, and the majority of the population lived in the villages.

There was under the Roman empire a trend towards urban life. This trend was sometimes deliberately fostered in more backward areas by the Roman government—Agricola for instance encouraged the Britons 'to build temples, markets, and houses' in their tribal capitals, with the object, according to Tacitus, of luring them by these amenities from their warlike barbarism.[12] But in general the movement was spontaneous, a

---

[11] *J.R.S.*, 1936, p. 223. [Jones gave a revised interpretation of the Constitutio (*F.I.R.A.* 1[2] no. 88) in his *Studies in Roman Government and Law*, 1960, ch. VIII, in which he held that if the document means that the *dediticii* were excluded from the grant of citizenship, it must have been forgotten that the Egyptians and others who belonged to no *civitates* had once been classed as *dediticii*, since Egyptians undoubtedly secured the citizenship; alternatively, the *dediticii*, including Egyptians, etc.,were excepted from some subsidiary provision, which must be the local citizenship in the once peregrine *civitates*. In the latter case Egyptian villagers, for instance, did *not* become *municipes* of their local cities. Since he published this article, we have learned from the *Tabula Banasitana* (*C.R.A.I.*, 1961, 317 ff.; 1971, 468 ff.) that Marcus Aurelius granted Roman citizenship to persons from a Berber tribe 'salvo iure gentis' and 'sine diminutione tributorum et vectigalium populi et fisci'. W. Seston, the editor, persuasively suggested in 1961 that on the basis of the first phrase the lacuna in the Constitutio should be supplemented thus: δίδωμι τοί[ν]ον ἅπασιν ξένοις τοῖς κατὰ [τ]ὴν οἰκουμένην π[ολιτ]είαν ʿΡωμαίων [μ]ένοντος [τοῦ δικαίου τῶν πολιτευμ]άτων χωρ[ὶς] τῶν [δε]δειτικίων. This reading would confirm Jones' conjecture that the saving clause 'specified that the existing status of the cities should remain unaffected by the fact that all their members had become Roman citizens' (*Studies*, 136). Any class of persons previously excluded from local rights would then remain excluded, though it seems to me that the run of the sentence demands that we take the specific reference to the *dediticii* in the first of Jones' alternative senses.]

[12] Tacitus, *Agric.*, 21. [Cf. *Hist.* IV 64 f.]

product of the natural desire of the more backward peoples to assimilate themselves to the superior civilization of Greece and Rome. Thus African villages, at the same time as they petitioned for and obtained Latin and then Roman political status, equipped themselves with temples, *fora*, theatres and paved streets in the Roman manner; Spanish clans abandoned their old hill forts and built modern cities in the plains;[13] and Gallic nobles built themselves town houses in the tribal capital and sent their sons to the local grammarians and rhetoricians to receive a Latin education.[14]

STATUS OF CITIES

The cities of the empire were carefully graded in political and fiscal privilege. The vast majority belonged to the category of *civitates stipendiariae* which paid taxation in various forms to the Roman state and were subject to the unfettered jurisdiction of the Roman governor, save in so far as he was bound by the *lex provinciae*, the statute laid down for the administration of the province on its annexation, or by the instructions of the senate or the emperor. A few communities were *liberae*, having received a charter of privileges either by law or a resolution of the senate. The precise privileges varied but normally included the clause *suis legibus uti*. This clause was by the early second century at any rate narrowly interpreted to mean that the community was entitled to maintain the laws in force at the time of the grant of freedom, and the imperial government considered itself entitled to intervene in order to suppress any innovation, or any practice not expressly covered by the charter.

Under the republic such cities had normally also been *immunes*, which meant that their citizens paid no tax to Rome on the land which they held in the city territory (foreigners owning land in their territory were liable). Immunity became however an increasingly rare privilege under the empire, and the majority of free cities probably paid tribute. All these privileges, depending

---

[13] [*I.L.S.*, 6092 (A.D. 78: the initiative came from the Spaniards), 6921. Cf. for Gaul, Jullian, *Hist. de la Gaule*, IV 74 ff.; for Dalmatia J. J. Wilkes, *Dalmatia*, ch. 13.]

[14] [Tacitus, *Ann.* III 43; Jullian, o.c. VI ch. II.]

on a unilateral grant by the Roman people were both in theory and practice revocable. A small minority of free cities were in addition *foederatae*, that is, had their status guaranteed by treaty. The privileges of federate cities varied according to their position when the treaty was concluded. Some, which allied themselves with Rome as independent states, should have enjoyed a high degree of internal autonomy, others, which had merely received the ratification by treaty of a grant of freedom, had limited privileges; some appear to have paid tribute. The imperial government encroached on the liberty of federate as of free cities, and was rarely at a loss to find reasons for revoking the treaty if circumstances demanded it.[15]

An intermediate grade between the foreign cities already discussed and the communities of Roman citizens was formed by the Latin towns. Latin status was conferred by Caesar and Augustus on a considerable number of native communities in the western provinces, Sicily, Narbonese Gaul and Spain. Later emperors continued the process, granting the status both to individual communities and sometimes to entire provinces; Vespasian extended the *ius Latii* to all the stipendiary communities of Spain. A community on receiving Latin status was issued with a *lex data*, prescribing for it a constitution on the Roman model, and its citizens became subject to Roman private law. Furthermore its annual magistrates became automatically Roman citizens; if the grant were of *Latium maius* all members of the city council acquired the citizenship. This privilege, it may be noted, was granted only in the western Latin speaking parts of the empire, and was considered inappropriate to the Greek-speaking East.[16]

As has been already mentioned colonies of Roman citizens were planted in the provinces in considerable numbers from Caesar's time onwards, and the native inhabitants of the communities in which they were settled were assimilated in status to the colonists. From the beginning of the second century A.D. if

---

[15] G. C., 113 ff, 129ff. [See Tacitus, *Ann.* III 40 ff. for taxes apparently imposed on *civitates foederatae* like the Aedui, cf. XI 25.]

[16] O. Hirschfeld, *Zur Geschichte des Lateinischen Rechts* (*Kleine Schriften*). [A. N. Sherwin-White, *Roman Citizenship*, 103 ff., 170–205 *passim*, 209, 247; Vittinghoff (p. 4 n. 1) 43 ff. *Latium maius* is not attested before Hadrian nor outside Africa. The Latin right was not a step to citizenship for the whole community; most 'Latin' cities were enfranchised only by the Constitutio Antoniniana.]

B

not earlier the title and status of colony was bestowed on native communities without any settlement.[17] Caesar also initiated the practice of converting provincial communities into *municipia* of Roman citizens, and the emperors continued this policy. Colonies were planted in all parts of the empire, though more thickly in the west, and eastern as well as western cities were granted colonial status. Municipal, like Latin, status was, however, confined to Latin speaking provinces.[18]

Colonies and *municipia* received a *lex data* from the emperor prescribing their constitution. They seem originally to have enjoyed a similar immunity from the intervention of the provincial governor as did free cities; the colony of Apamea in Bithynia protested its ancient privilege when Pliny wished to audit its accounts. The Apamenes however consented to submit their accounts to Pliny 'without prejudice' and no doubt the privileged status of the communities of Roman citizens was thus gradually whittled away by administrative encroachments.[19] Fiscally some colonies and only one *municipium* (Stobi), are recorded to have enjoyed the *ius Italicum*, whereby their soil was legally assimilated to the tax free land of Italy; some colonies also enjoyed immunity without *ius Italicum*. These privileges were however the exception rather than the rule.[20]

The Constitutio Antoniniana of 212 A.D., whereby all free inhabitants of the empire were made Roman citizens, levelled out most political distinctions in theory; in practice they had already been largely obliterated. In theory all Latin, stipendiary, free and federate cities presumably became *municipia civium Romanorum*. No attempt was made, however, to provide them with new constitutions, and the traditional titles of the local magistrates continued unchanged, especially in the Greek speaking provinces. Former free and federate cities also maintained their old titles, and even strove to preserve their ancient privileges. But by the end of the third century all distinction in status between the cities of the empire had effectively vanished, though Roman colonies still clung to their title even in the fourth century.[21]

[17] [The grant to Vienna in Gaul (*I.L.S.* 212) is not later than A.D. 47; some deduce from Pliny, *N.H.* III 36 that it was Augustan.]

[18] See p. 4, n. 9, and E. Kornemann, s.v. '*Colonia*' and '*Municipium*' in *Pauly-Wissowa-Kroll*.

[19] Pliny, *Ep.* X, 47–8, cf. Pausanias, VII, xviii, 7 and Strabo, 186–7.

[20] A. von Premerstein, s.v. *Ius Italicum* in *P.W.K.*

[21] G. C., 134. [Cf. Jones, *Tijdschrift voor Rechtsgeschiedenis* 1971, 26 f.]

The fiscal privileges of the immune cities and the *coloniae iuris Italici* also vanished in the course of this century. The reason for this was the inflation of the currency, whereby the *tributum* sank progressively in real value until eventually it seems to have been abandoned. The *tributum* was replaced by new forms of taxation, the most important of which were *indictiones* or requisitions in kind and *aurum coronarium*, originally a free will offering of gold crowns to the emperor on festive occasions, now a periodical levy of gold bullion. These new forms of taxation were imposed on all cities alike, by Diocletian even on those of Italy. The *ius Italicum* was still preserved by Italy and such provincial communities as had formerly possessed it and was even granted to the new capital Constantinople. But it was now a meaningless privilege, affecting only the forms of land tenure and conveyance.[22]

IMPERIAL REPRESENTATIVES IN THE CITIES

Under the Republic and the early Empire the Roman government made no attempt to control the cities by appointing Roman officers in them. A provincial governor under the Republic occasionally imposed a military prefect on a community to ensure its obedience or extract from it its tribute or special levies,[23] but in general he relied on the local government to carry out his orders.[24] It was not until the early years of the second century A.D. that imperial commissioners began to be appointed to supervise the affairs of individual cities. The functions of these commissioners, called in Latin *curatores* and in Greek λογισταί, were primarily financial, and their appointment was provoked by the mismanagement of their local finance by the city governments. *Curatores* were at first appointed occasionally, sometimes for groups of cities, sometimes for individual cities of importance, and more particularly for *civitates liberae* and other privileged communities whose finances, being immune from inspection by the ordinary governor, were liable to be in a more involved condition. The early commissioners were persons of high standing in the empire, senators, men of equestrian rank or provincials

---

[22] *Cod. Theod.*, XIV, xiii. Cf. Soz., *H.E.*, VII, 9.

[23] Cf. Livy, XLIII, 2 *ad fin.*

[24] [Under the Principate we find military officers as *praefecti civitatium* among more or less barbarous tribes, especially on the frontiers, e.g. Tacitus, *Ann.* IV 72 'e primipilaribus regendis Frisiis impositus', *P.W.K.* XLIV 1290 ff.]

who had held the highpriesthood of the province, and were normally not members of the community concerned. During the second century such appointments became gradually more widespread and more regular, until by the end of the third century the *curator* had become a normal institution in most cities. The rank of the *curatores* inevitably sank as they became commoner and it became the practice to appoint a senior member of the community concerned. The *curator* thus tended to be assimilated to the municipal magistrates, but he differed from them in having no colleagues and in being appointed by the emperor and holding office during the Emperor's pleasure, not for a year only; the office was normally the crown of a municipal career. His powers over local finance were wide, including both the enforcement of debts to the city and the control of expenditure. The office continued to be of importance down to the sixth century A.D. In the west—in the Ostrogothic kingdom—*curatores* were still at this date appointed by royal letter. In the eastern empire the title had been changed to *pater civitatis*, and they were no longer appointed by the emperor but elected by the local community.[25]

Early in the fourth century there appear in Egypt imperial officers called *exactor civitatis*, who were responsible for the collection of the imperial taxation due from the city. These officers were evidently regarded as the successors of the *strategi* of the nomes, which had recently been abolished, and it may be that they were peculiar to Egypt in this transitional stage. During the third quarter of the century they ceased to be appointed by the imperial government and came to be elected by their city councils. At the end of the fifth century Anastasius instituted the appointment of *vindices* to collect the taxation of the several cities: the office still existed in the Eastern empire in the sixth century.[26]

Outside the sphere of finance, municipal and imperial, there was only one attempt to impose imperially nominated officials on the cities. These, the *defensores plebis* or *civitatis*, first appear in Egypt in Constantine's reign, but the office was remodelled and strengthened by Valentinian and Valens. The function of the *defensor* was to provide cheap and prompt justice for the humble classes in minor civil actions and to protect them against extortion

[25] W. Liebenam, *Philologus*, 1897, 290 ff.; E. Kornemann, s.v. *'curator'* in *P.W.K.* G. C., 136 ff., 209.
[26] G. C., 152–3.

and unfair exactions. *Defensores* were selected by the praetorian prefect, who was instructed to choose persons of high official standing, such as ex-provincial governors, palatine officials and lawyers from his own bar, and to exclude decurions of the cities and officials from his own staff or those of vicars or provincial governors, presumably because these were the classes from whose oppression the *defensor* was supposed to defend the poor. A few years later the praetorian prefects were instructed to appoint by preference candidates chosen by the cities concerned, and in 409 it was enacted by Honorius for the Western Empire that the *defensor* should be elected by the local bishop, clergy, notables and decurions and officially confirmed by the praetorian prefect: a similar enactment was issued later by Anastasius in the Eastern Empire. The *defensor* continued till the sixth century to be officially an imperial appointment, but the office had by then so sunk in esteem that it had ceased to fulfil its principal function of protecting the city against official extortion, though it was useful in providing a local court of petty jurisdiction. Justinian endeavoured to raise its prestige by compelling the local notables to hold the office in rotation, but with what success is unknown.[27]

ORGANISATION OF CIVIC GOVERNMENT

The cities of the empire were of the most diverse origins, and their institutions were correspondingly various. Common to all, however, was the general pattern of elective annual magistrates, a council and a popular assembly. The Roman government made no attempt to impose a rigidly standardised pattern of local government on all subject communities, and a considerable diversity of detail survived under the principate and even later. The titles and numbers of the principal magistrates for instance varied from district to district: vergobrets are found in Gaul, sufetes in Africa, and a great variety of titles (στρατηγοί, πρυτάνεις, ἔφοροι, ταγοί, etc.) in the Greek East.[28] The numbers of the council also varied greatly. In the West the standard Roman

27 *Ibid.*, 150–1, 209.
28 *I.L.S.*, 7040 (vergobret), 6094, 6099, 6100, 6797–9, 9395 (sufete), G. C., 174 (Greek titles). [Even in Italy old titles survived in a few towns, including Greek titles at Naples, K. J. Beloch, *Röm. Gesch.* 506 ff.]

figure of one hundred was widely adopted, but in the East much
larger councils, on the Greek model, had been customary and
this peculiarity survived even into the fourth century, when six
hundred seems to have been the standard figure in Syria.[29]

Beneath the superficial variety, however, the Roman government insisted on certain basic principles. The first was a property
qualification for magistrates and for membership of the council.
This rule was imposed even on the Greek cities which had been
liberated from Macedonian rule by Flamininus, and again on the
Achaeans and their allies by Mummius, when they were restored
their freedom after the destruction of Corinth. The rule seems to
have been universal and was no doubt incorporated in the *lex
provinciae* of every province. The second principle was that the
council should be a permanent body, whose members sat for life,
unless disqualified by the loss of their property or by misconduct.
This rule does not seem to have been applied in Greece, where
annually changing councils of the normal democratic pattern still
survived under Roman rule, but it is found in force in Cicero's
day in Sicily and in Asia. In Sicily, and probably in Asia too,
vacancies were filled by popular election, but in Bithynia Pompey
introduced a system more closely modelled on Roman practice.
Under the *Lex Pompeia* censors were periodically elected who
revised the roll of the council, striking off those who for causes
specified were disqualified and adding those who had held
magistracies and other qualified persons at their discretion. A
similar system seems to have been introduced in Cyprus and
Galatia on their annexation and no doubt in other provinces.[30]

By laying down these general regulations the Roman government secured its objective—that effective power in the cities
should be vested in the propertied class, and that their governments should thus be both stable and submissive. The popular
assemblies of the Greek and Hellenised cities continued to
function, electing magistrates and passing decrees, but their
choice of magistrates was limited by the property qualification
and their legislative activity by the fact that the council, whose
prior approval was required for all resolutions, was now no
longer an annually changing committee of the people but a
permanent body of substantial citizens. The council became

[29] Liebenam, 229, G. C., 176.
[30] G. C., 170–1.

inevitably, like the Senate at Rome on which it was modelled, the real government of the city.

In the west we know little of the local government of the *civitates stipendiariae* but it may be presumed that similar regulations were imposed. Under the principate the gradual extension of colonial, municipal and Latin status carried with it the imposition of a more or less standardised Roman constitution on the communities concerned. We possess large fragments of the *lex* granted to the Caesarian colony of Urso on its foundation and of the two *leges* granted to the Spanish cities of Malaca and Salpensa by Domitian on their acquisition of Latin status.[31] The citizen body was divided into a number of wards, usually called *curiae*, and, according to Roman practice, voting in the assembly or *comitia* was by wards, the majority in each *curia* deciding the vote of the *curia* and the majority of *curiae* carrying the day. The assembly seems to have had no other function than to elect the annual magistrates, of whom there were normally six, two *duoviri iure dicundo*, vested with jurisdiction, who were presidents of the council and assembly and in general responsible for the whole administration, two *aediles*, concerned with public works, the market, water supply and similar functions, and two *quaestores*, responsible for the treasury. The council (*ordo decurionum*) was normally one hundred strong and the list was revised and filled up at intervals of five years by the *duoviri*, who during this year bore the title of *quinquennales*: ex-magistrates had a prior right to a seat. The council was the effective governing body, and its consent was required for any important act, epecially the expenditure of public money.[32]

The one democratic feature in the civic constitutions, the popular election of the magistrates and, directly or indirectly, of the councillors, gradually fell into abeyance in the second century A.D. The history of this development is obscure, but the cause seems to have been falling off in the number of candidates presenting themselves for election. This in turn was due to the growing expensiveness of office. In the early principate election to a magistracy was considered an honour for which the successful candidate must expect to pay; it is for instance laid down in the *lex* of the colony of Urso that the *duoviri* and *aediles* must on

[31] *I.L.S.*, 6087, 6088, 6089.
[32] Liebenam, 206 ff.

election present games to the city, paying at least 2,000 sesterces out of their own pockets.[33] In many western cities there was a regular tariff of fees (*summa honoraria*) payable on admission to the several magistracies and to the council. In Greek cities such payments were less systematised, but magistrates and councillors were frequently expected to pay for their election by contributing either in cash or kind to public works in progress.[34] The expenses of a magistrate did not end here. Ambitious men who wished to make themselves popular gave feasts and entertainments to the people, adorned the streets and public places with statues and monuments, and spent on the departments under their charge out of their own pockets over and above the sums allocated from the city treasury, which they sometimes refused to accept. They thus set precedents which it was invidious for their successors not to follow and a constantly increasing scale of expenditure was expected from magistrates.

In these circumstances only the wealthiest citizens could afford office, and even amongst these the civic magistracies came to be regarded rather as an honourable obligation than as an object of ambition. As it became increasingly difficult to find a sufficient number of candidates to fill the places, it fell to the council to persuade, or even to press, its members to stand for the higher offices, which were normally held by decurions, and propose for the junior offices their sons or other qualified persons. Popular elections thus became a formality, the assembly having merely to ratify the list of candidates established by the council; this formality was still observed in Africa as late as Constantine's reign. To the council also fell the duty of filling vacancies in its own body, in so far as these were not supplied by the accession of junior magistrates to its ranks.[35]

As early as the second half of the second century there are signs that citizens qualified for magistracies and service on the council were beginning to seek means to evade office. Certain classes of persons, such as farmers of imperial taxes and lands or shippers engaged in the transport of corn for the state, were excused from civic obligations. A series of imperial constitutions

[33] *I.L.S.*, 6087, figures LXX, LXXI.
[34] Liebenam, 54–65, G. C., 247. [R. P. Duncan-Jones, *P.B.S.R.*, 1962, 47 ff. (Africa); 1965, 226 ff. (Italy). Both articles discuss local munificence generally, cf. also *P.B.S.R.* 1963, 160 ff. (Africa).]
[35] G. C., 181 ff., cf. *Cod. Theod.*, XII, v, I for popular election in Africa.

combat the misuse of such immunities; mere membership of the shippers' guild, for instance, it is noted, does not carry exemption, which is accorded only to *bona fide* shippers who have invested the major part of their wealth in the business.[36]

Persuasion was not always sufficient to fill the magistracies and vacancies in the council. Occasional difficulties had no doubt occurred from time to time, and legal provision was made for them. Thus in the Flavian charter of Malaca it is laid down that if an insufficient number of candidates make a voluntary *professio* the duumvir conducting the elections shall nominate sufficient persons to make up the requisite number, and that persons so nominated shall each be entitled to nominate one other person, and these again another: all persons thus nominated shall be deemed to have made a *professio* and the election shall then proceed on normal lines. The provisions of this law seem to be aimed at preventing unfair discrimination by the presiding magistrate rather than providing a choice of candidates for the people.[37] The principle of *nominatio* was more and more widely applied in the late second and early third centuries. The exact mode of its application varied according to the constitutions of the individual cities. In the quasi-cities of Egypt, from which most of our information comes, each college of magistrates was responsible for nominating new members of the college, while 'tribes' into which the council, like the people, was divided, seem to have taken in rotation the duty of nominating to membership of the council and to extraordinary magistracies. The person nominated was obliged to serve, unless he appealed to the courts and successfully proved that he enjoyed some legal immunity, or that he had been maliciously nominated instead of another better qualified person; his only alternative was to surrender his property less a third to his nominator. On the other hand, a nominator was responsible for his choice, and had to guarantee any financial default by his nominee.[38]

Membership of the council had from the beginning a tendency to become hereditary. The expensiveness of office early tended to limit the tenure of magistracies to a narrow circle of the richest citizens, and, therefore, as property normally passed from father to son, to a select group of families. Some families naturally

[36] G. C., 184–5, 189–90.   [37] *I.L.S.*, 6089, LI.
[38] G. C., 184–8.

became impoverished from time to time and fell out, and the new rich filled their places, but on the whole son succeeded father. The status of a decurion was an honourable one, and from the reign of Hadrian carried with it valuable legal privileges,[39] and despite the expenses involved curial families were reluctant to sink in the social scale by abandoning their rank. With the growing use of *nominatio* to fill offices and vacancies in the council, hereditary membership became *de facto* a legal obligation. The richest citizens were already members of the council and their sons, who inherited their wealth, were naturally the fittest persons to be nominated. Outsiders continued to be liable to nomination to the council, but normally only when the resources of the hereditary aristocracy were insufficient to fill the vacancies.[40]

By the reign of Diocletian the evolution was complete. Sons of decurions were automatically enrolled on attaining their majority, and service on the council (*curia*) thus became the hereditary obligation of the class known as *curiales*. A property qualification, normally in the form of land, was of course still required, and a decurion who lost his estate was struck off the roll. *Plebeii*, that is citizens below the rank of *curiales*, might still be nominated to the council, if financially qualified, and during the reigns of Diocletian and Constantine fresh blood seems to have still been introduced in this way. Julian, who made a vigorous effort to replenish the councils, encouraged them to nominate plebeians, but after this date allusions to outside recruitment are very rare, probably because the councils had already scraped the bottom of the barrel. The *curiales* thus became a closed hereditary caste.[41]

Throughout the fourth, fifth and sixth centuries the imperial government fought an unceasing battle, which was only very partially successful, to preserve the curial class and its property. The city councils were necessary not only to maintain local government but to collect and underwrite imperial taxation and to perform many other multifarious duties for the state—the levying of recruits, the maintenance of the postal service, the repair of roads and bridges. In and from the councils were

[39] [See now P. D. A. Garnsey, *Social Status and Legal Privilege in the Roman Empire*, 1970, index, s.v. decurions.]
[40] G. C., 180–1.
[41] G. C., 304–5. [For this, and what follows, cf. ch. XXI and *L.R.E.* ch. XIX.]

nominated not only the civic magistrates proper, who maintained the municipal services, but collectors of state taxes; and the councillors were jointly liable for any financial default of their nominees. If the government was to carry on, each city must have an adequate number of persons to carry out these duties, and they must possess sufficient property to cover the expenses involved and make up any deficits which might arise.[42]

The chief danger to the preservation of the councils lay in the ambition of their wealthier members to achieve a higher status which carried exemption from curial duties. During the fourth century they aspired to posts which conferred the perfectissimate or the lower grades of the equestrian order or the rank of *comes*. As these ranks carried personal immunity only and were not in theory hereditary, the imperial government did not object to decurions acquiring them by service, provided that they fulfilled their duties to their cities first; it set its face however, against decurions obtaining honorary codicils of rank. From the latter part of the fourth century, as the numbers of the imperial senates of Rome and Constantinople were expanded, decurions sought the more elevated rank of senator, which had the additional advantage of giving hereditary immunity. The imperial government was vacillating in its efforts to meet this danger, at times forbidding *curiales* all access to the senate, at others allowing them to enter provided that they left one son in their native *curia*, at others insisting that even as senators they must continue to perform their curial duties. On the whole it seems to have been unsuccessful in enforcing the law, frequently condoning past infractions of it; and most of the wealthiest curial families probably passed eventually into the senate. Decurions of less means secured posts in the imperial civil service, either in the highly lucrative palatine ministries, or in the less regarded offices of the praetorian prefects, vicars and provincial governors; others humbler still enlisted in the army. These careers were all officially banned, but the constant repetition of the ban, and the regular condonation of those who had served a considerable term, show that the law was imperfectly enforced. Other decurions took holy orders; here again the government was vacillating, sometimes forbidding the ordination of *curiales*, sometimes insisting that if ordained they must surrender their property to a relative who

[42] G. C., 152–5.

would take their place on the council, and frequently condoning past offences.[43]

Another danger to the curial class was the alienation of their property by its members, either under duress to senators or other wealthy landowners, or to raise money to purchase an official post. In 386 decurions were forbidden to sell their property except by licence of the provincial governor to pay their debts or for some other reasonable cause. In the absence of legitimate male heirs a decurion's property might pass by inheritance to an outsider; in such a case it was ruled in 428 that the *curia* might claim a quarter of the estate. A century later Justinian raised this proportion to three-quarters.[44]

By the fifth century the council of a city no longer comprised the wealthiest landed magnates of the territory. The majority of these had by now become imperial senators or had otherwise secured immunity from curial obligations. The surviving curial families were a miserable rump of medium or small landowners, who as their numbers and collective wealth gradually diminished found the burden of their functions more and more onerous. The council ceased to be representative of the city and many of its functions were successively transferred to a new body, comprising the bishop and clergy and principal landowners, to whom the decurions are sometimes added. The nomination of the *defensor civitatis* was transferred to this body as early as 409 in the West, where the decay of the city councils seems to have been more rapid than in the East. In the East it was not till a century later, in 505, that Anastasius enacted a similar measure. Anastasius made the same body responsible for civic finance, ordering them to elect the city corn-buyer when occasion demanded, and it would seem the *pater civitatis*, the regular controller of the municipal finance of the city. It was Anastasius too who appointed to each city an imperial official, the *vindex*, to take charge of imperial taxation. The cumulative effect of these changes was that the city councils ceased to function in the Eastern Empire; to Johannes Lydus, writing under Justinian, the time when the council used to administer the cities was a memory of his childhood, and Evagrius in the latter half of the sixth century looks back with nostalgia to the happy days before Anastasius when each city had its little

[43] G. C., 192–8.
[44] G. C., 199–200.

senate. The curial class still survived, and Justinian enacted stringent legislation to prevent the surviving members from changing their condition or alienating their property. But the *curiales* were by now merely a caste saddled with the hereditary liability to serve as collectors of taxes.[45] In the West the *curiae* continued to subsist under the Germanic kingdoms and in the parts of the empire recovered by Justinian, and to elect the annual magistrates, the *duoviri*, but their only recorded function was to attest conveyances and wills and to keep up to date the registers of landed property.[46]

DEFENCE AND PUBLIC ORDER

The Roman government undertook the defence of the provinces and the provincial communities were not as a rule required or permitted to maintain armed forces of their own. Under the Republic they were frequently called upon to supply contingents, which they levied and maintained themselves, to assist the legions; this practice was particularly common in the warlike Western provinces, such as Spain and Gaul, where Roman commanders depended largely on local levies for cavalry.[47] Maritime cities were also frequently required to supply warships, which they had to build, man and finance themselves.[48] Under the principate these activities lapsed when the administration of the auxiliary units was taken over by the imperial government, and permanent imperial fleets were established. Henceforth the cities had no concern with military or naval affairs. The charter of the colony of Urso includes a clause empowering the *duoviri*, after authorisation by the *ordo decurionum*, to levy the inhabitants in defence of the city territory, and giving them in such a case the disciplinary powers of a military tribune.[49] Even such emergency levies were, however, of rare occurrence.

In the maintenance of public order the cities played a larger part. In the West civic police officers are rarely recorded; at

---

[45] G. C., 208–10. Cf. *Cod. Just.* I. lv, 8 for the defensor in the West.
[46] For Italy see *Edictum Theodorici*, 52–3 and Marini, *Papiri Diplomatici*, 14, 79, 83–4, 88, etc. For Merovingian Gaul and Visigothic Spain, *Formulae*, *Mer. et Kar. aeui* (M.G.H.), Andev. I, Arvern, 1b, 2b, Turon. 3, Bitur. 6.7, Senon. 39, Visig. 25.
[47] E.g. Cic., *pro Fonteio* 3; Caesar, *B. G.*, V, 1.
[48] G. C., 126.   [49] *I.L.S.* 6087, ciii.

Nemausus there was a *praefectus armorum et vigilum* and in some other Gallic cities special commissioners for the suppression of brigandage.[50] In the East a more elaborate organisation with many local variations is traceable. In Asia and Egypt we find commanders of the night watch (νυκτοστράτηγοι) who commanded a body of nightwatchmen (νυκτοφύλακες) to patrol the streets and guard public buildings; service as a nightwatchman was a compulsory duty imposed on the humble classes. Some cities in Asia Minor had mounted frontier guards (όροφύλακες), also not professional but drawn from the gentry, who patrolled the villages of their territories under the command of civic magistrates (παραφύλακες). More important than these were the guardians of the peace (είρηνάρχαι) who seem to have been fairly general in the East. Their main function was to hunt down brigands, in which task they were supported by mounted police (διωγμῖται).[51] Civic police are still mentioned in the fourth and fifth centuries, but the government tended to rely increasingly on the army for the maintenance of public order.[52]

JUSTICE

In the administration of justice there was a great diversity of privilege. Free cities normally preserved their own courts, which administered their own law; their competence was some times limited in cases involving Roman citizens.[53] In cities of Latin and Roman status, the principal magistrates (*duoviri iure dicundo*) enjoyed, as their title implies, the right of jurisdiction, but only within a limited sphere: capital cases were referred to the provincial governor, as were civil actions of certain types or above a certain pecuniary limit.[54] The rights of the ordinary *civitas stipendiaria* varied in different provinces according to the *lex provinciae*. In Sicily, for instance, civil actions between citizens of the same city were reserved to the local courts, whereas in actions

[50] *I.L.S.* 5082, 6980, 7007.

[51] G. C., 211–3.

[52] *Ibid.*, 252.

[53] *Ibid.*, 320, n. 42.

[54] E.g., *I.L.S.* 6087, LXI, XCIV, XCV, CII, 6088, XXVIII f., 6089, LXIX. The limit of jurisdiction implied in the last clause was presumably similar to that mentioned in the Lex Rubria (Bruns, *Fontes*⁷, 16, XXII, 17).

involving citizens of different cities or Romans the governor appointed a judge according to certain rules. In Asia and Cilicia on the other hand it seems to have been left to the discretion of the governor to try any case that he pleased, and it was by their own edicts that Mucius Scaevola and Cicero renounced jurisdiction in cases between provincials, leaving them to the local courts. In Cyrenaica it was the practice for the governor to appoint Roman judges in all actions. Capital cases seem always to have been reserved to the governor, and all cases involving Roman citizens.[55]

Under the principate the jurisdiction of the civic courts steadily waned. Outside a few free cities nothing is heard of local courts in the peregrine communities, and the jurisdiction of the magistrates in Latin and Roman cities seems to have dwindled to a few formal processes. The jurisdiction of the provincial governor gradually encroached, until by the end of the third century it had absorbed all, even the most petty, litigation. This development threw a very heavy burden of work on the governor and his legates and inflicted hardship on poor litigants: it was probably one of the reasons why Diocletian increased the number and decreased the size of provinces. Julian palliated the difficulty by authorising governors to appoint *iudices pedanei* to judge minor cases.[56] A more effective reform was the institution, already mentioned, of a *defensor* in each city. Originally an imperial nominee and always formally remaining so, he was in practice from the last quarter of the fourth century appointed on the recommendation of the community, which thus regained the right of petty civil jurisdiction over its inhabitants. The *defensor* under Justinian's laws had final authority in issues not exceeding 50 solidi and was empowered to take depositions and prepare the case in more important actions reserved for the governor.[57]

CIVIC SERVICES

The services which the cities supplied for their inhabitants naturally varied according to their size and resources; there were also regional variations, notably between the areas of Greek and Roman culture. These services may be roughly classified under

---

[55] G. C., 121–3.　　　　[56] *Cod. Theod.*, I, xvi, 8.
[57] See p. 11 n. 27.

the headings of (a) religion, including not only the public cult of the city gods, but the celebration of numerous festivals and games in their honour, (b) education both physical and intellectual, (c) the control of the market and in particular of the corn supply, (d) the provision of public amenities such as streets, water supply, drainage, baths, fire services, etc., (e) public works.

Every city assumed responsibility for the public worship of the city gods. The civic magistrates *ex officio* offered certain sacrifices and took part in religious processions and celebrated games and festivals. In addition the city took a large part in building and maintaining temples and in appointing priests and other specifically religious functionaries. Here there was a great diversity of custom. Some ancient temples enjoyed a quasi-autonomous position, possessing great revenues of their own out of which the priests defrayed the expenses of the cult; in such cases the high priesthood was sometimes hereditary, sometimes sold by the city to the highest bidder (the post often carried with it substantial emoluments). More usually priests were elected or chosen by lot, either annually or for life. Cities organised on the Roman model possessed colleges of *pontifices* and *augures* elected for life, whose functions were similar to those of their Roman prototypes.[58]

A very popular feature of civic religion was the production of games in honour of the gods. In the East these took the traditional Greek form of competitions, athletic (including chariot racing) and musical (including the drama). The cities spent lavishly in order to attract the best talent from far and wide, offering large money prizes to the victors, paying salaries to the musical artists —the athletes were officially amateurs—and sending costly embassies to the emperor to persuade him to recognise their athletic games as of equal status with the four ancient festivals of Greece—in which case the victors became entitled to sundry privileges, including pensions from their native cities. The magistrates elected to conduct the games (ἀγωνοθέται) often added to their attractions from their own pockets, giving additional prizes, entertaining the competitors to banquets, and distributing wine and light refreshments to the audiences. In the western cities the Roman practice was followed whereby the principal magistrates were expected or obliged to provide spectacles—

[58] G. C., 227–30, Liebenam, 340–9.

gladiatorial combats, wild beast hunts, chariot races, plays and mimes—at their own expense in part, in part from civic funds. Under Roman influence displays of gladiators and wild beasts spread into the Hellenic East also.[59]

In education also the policy of Greek and Latin cities was different. The Greek passion for physical culture had during the Hellenistic age become diffused throughout the eastern provinces. Here every city maintained a gymnasium—the larger cities several —and provided an organised course of physical training for its young men (the ephebes) and often for the boys also. The gymnasium also served as a social club, and in larger cities separate gymnasia were provided for adults and the elders as well as for boys and youths. The director or directors of the gymnasium (gymnasiarchs) were among the most important of the civic magistrates and, although a grant was often made from civic funds towards the expenses, the office was usually a costly one, the chief burden being the provision of oil for the use of members.[60] In the Latin west ephebic training and the gymnasium did not exist, the public baths providing a substitute for the latter in its social aspect. On the other hand Latin cities sometimes provided free schools for children, a duty generally neglected in the East.[61] Higher education was supported by both Latin and Greek cities, though more vigorously by the latter, salaried professors of grammar and rhetoric being maintained from civic funds.[62]

The control of the city markets was vested in the aediles in the west and in similar officers (ἀγορανόμοι) in the East. It was their duty not only to maintain the market and to lease the shops and stalls in it, and to ensure fair dealing by testing weights and measures, controlling money changers, and enforcing contracts, but also, so far as possible, to control prices. When this could not be achieved by regulation, public spirited magistrates sometimes brought prices down by underselling the dealers.[63] To ensure a regular supply of cheap corn many if not most cities, especially in the East, operated a system of state purchase. A special fund was established and special officers (*curatores annonae*, σιτῶναι) elected, who each year bought corn with moneys drawn from the fund and then retailed it, paying back the proceeds into the fund. In

[59] G. C., 230–4, Liebenam, 113–21, 371–9.   [60] G. C., 220–6.
[61] Liebenam, 93–8 (baths). Pliny, Ep. IV, 13 (schools).
[62] G. C., 225, cf. Strabo, 181 for Gaul.   [63] G. C., 215–7, Liebenam, 362–7.

C

normal years the transaction involved no financial loss, but in shortages the magistrates had often to pay high prices and make up the loss out of their own pockets.[64]

The aediles (in Greek cities the ἀγοράνομοι or sometimes a separate board, the ἀστύνομοι) were also responsible for paving and cleaning the streets and keeping them clear of obstructions, for maintaining and cleaning the sewers and for securing a pure and adequate water supply. Lesser cities normally relied on wells and cisterns, but larger towns often built aqueducts which tapped distant springs. Street lighting seems to have been a rare luxury; in Antioch shopkeepers were compelled to maintain lamps outside their premises.[65] In precautions against fire there was a curious contrast between East and West. In most western cities there was a *collegium fabrorum* which acted as a fire brigade. In Greek cities such an institution is unknown, and Pliny was forbidden by Trajan to establish one at Nicomedia, despite a disastrous fire, on the ground that it would form a focus for political agitation. All that he was allowed to do was to provide apparatus, hitherto lacking, to be used by volunteers as occasion arose.[66] Public baths were provided both in East and West, in the former normally attached to the gymnasium. Salaried public doctors were maintained by many if not most cities, especially in the East.[67]

Large numbers of public buildings were required for the various civic activities described above, temples for the worship of the gods, theatres, stadia and amphitheatres for the games, gymnasia and baths, markets, aqueducts and fountains, besides basilicae for the administration of justice, and council chambers and offices for the magistrates. Cities took great pride in their buildings and vied with one another in architectural splendour, laying out magnificent paved streets, lined with colonnades and adorned with triumphal arches; if the city walls were sometimes neglected in times of peace, the gates were rebuilt as imposing architectural monuments. The erection of public buildings was usually entrusted to special commissioners (*curatores operum*, ἐπιμεληταὶ ἔργων) and the necessary funds were largely obtained by contributions in cash or kind from magistrates and decurions.

[64] G. C., 217–9, Liebenam, 368–71.
[65] G. C., 213–5, Liebenam, 145 ff., 402 ff.
[66] Pliny, *Ep.*, X 33–4; for *collegia fabrorum (centonariorum)* in the west see *I.L.S.*, Index XII (p. 712).
[67] G. C., 219, Liebenam, 100–04.

The building mania of the cities often led them into financial embarrassment, and the imperial government, anxious for their stability, gradually imposed restrictions on their freedom, requiring a licence for any important building project from the provincial governor.[68]

The majority of the services described above continued to be provided by the cities under the Christian empire, though on a reduced scale and somewhat irregularly. When the cult of the pagan gods was banned in the fourth century, public sacrifices and other strictly religious ceremonies ceased, and the temples were demolished, abandoned or converted to other uses. The cities continued, however, to celebrate games, which had by now lost their religious associations and become public entertainments. Theatrical shows, wild beast hunts, and above all chariot races remained a regular feature of civic life; athletic competitions were still being celebrated at the end of the fourth century in the East, but seem to have later faded out, and gladiatorial combats, first banned by Constantine, were finally suppressed in the West by Honorius. No more is heard of the gymnasium after the fourth century, but the public baths were still maintained. Rhetors, grammarians and public doctors continued to receive their salaries from civic funds. The civic magistrates still controlled the market, and civic cornbuyers were still elected—occasionally, if not regularly—to purchase corn from civic funds and retail it to the citizens. The vast public buildings erected in more prosperous times were more than sufficient for all needs, and very little new building was undertaken by the civic authorities. Indeed they found it difficult to maintain old structures, and even such essentials as walls and aqueducts fell into decay.[69]

CIVIC FINANCE

From the above account it will appear that the larger cities at any rate must have had a large annual expenditure. For the public cult, so long as it subsisted, they had to provide incense and victims for sacrifices, and in connection with the games prizes for the victors and pay for the musical artistes, as well as pensions for those of their citizens who obtained prizes in the great games. Oil

[68] G. C., 135–6, 236–8, Liebenam, 134 ff., 382 ff.   [69] G. C., 251–8.

had to be bought for the gymnasium and fuel for heating the public baths. Salaries were paid to rhetors, grammarians and doctors. The wage bill for minor public servants must also have been considerable. In cities of Roman or Latin status the magistrates were provided with a number of paid attendants, lictors, scribes, heralds and the like; a full list with rates of pay is given in the *lex* of Urso. The police in Eastern cities received pay. All cities maintained a considerable staff of public slaves who performed a variety of duties from keeping the accounts or guarding the civic gaol to stoking the baths, paving the streets and cleaning the sewers, and these were provided with regular annual allowances. Another heavy charge was the travelling allowances of envoys whom the cities frequently sent to the emperor to obtain redress of grievances, plead for privileges, or merely as a complimentary gesture. Above all the maintenance of public building must have been a heavy expense.

The financial structure of the cities was usually complicated. Besides the civic treasury which was managed by the quaestors (or ταμίαι) under the strict control of the senior magistrates and the council, there were often a number of separate funds, earmarked for special purposes and sometimes with treasurers of their own. The sacred moneys of the gods were generally thus separately managed, and so often were the cornbuying fund, the oilbuying fund, endowments for gymnasia or for celebrating certain games. Furthermore certain expenses were by local law or custom borne by the magistrates. There was an infinite variety of usage; thus in some cities there was an endowment for providing oil in the gymnasium, in others a regular grant was made to the gymnasiarch from public funds, in others the gymnasiarch was expected to provide oil at his own expense; or he might supplement the income for the endowment or the public grant from his own pocket.

The revenue from taxation available to the cities seems to have been very limited. The main direct taxes went to the Roman government. These under the Republic had taken the form either of *stipendium*, a block levy on the city, which presumably collected it as it thought fit, or *decumae* and *scriptura*, a tithe on crops and pasture dues, which were farmed to *publicani* by the Roman authorities. The city had officially no concern with these, though the city government would sometimes undertake the farm of its own territory, if auctioned separately, as in Sicily, or more generally subcontract with the *publicani*, as in Asia. Under the empire the farming of direct taxes was generally abolished, and for the old *stipendium*, *decumae* and *scriptura* was substituted a land or rather property tax (*tributum soli*) often supplemented by a poll tax (*tributum capitis*), both based on a regular census of property and population. The city governments acted as agents for the collection of these. (Cf. ch. VIII).

It was possible for the cities to levy an additional civic property tax (*tributum*, εἰσφόρα) or even a poll tax, but, apart from the fact that direct taxation of citizens was always regarded in antiquity as an exceptional measure, to be adopted in emergencies only, the double burden under Roman rule would have been severe. Levies of civic property or poll tax seem to have been not uncommon under the Republic, but they remained emergency measures, usually to meet a deficit in the quota of taxation due to Rome (p. 173 n. 71). Under the Empire such levies are not recorded.

Among indirect taxes the most important were import and export duties levied at the frontiers of the city territory. There is not much evidence for these, but they were probably fairly general. Their value would obviously have varied greatly according to the commercial importance of the city concerned: a great port like Alexandria or a caravan city like Palmyra gained a considerable revenue, but the average inland city would not collect much. Market dues of various kinds were universal, and licence taxes were often imposed on certain trades. There were in some cities taxes on the manumission of slaves and on sales. All these taxes were normally farmed. Many cities raised revenue by the lease of monopolies; in some money changing was a civic monopoly, in others fishing rights or salt. Charges were also made for certain public services; a water rate was for instance charged for a private supply. Finally fines for the breach of civic byelaws were paid into the civic treasury.

Taxes and sundry payments such as these were obviously inadequate to cover expenditure. They were probably as a rule less important than endowments.[70] These might take the form of interest on capital sums lent on mortgage, but more commonly of rent from public lands (including house and shop property): these

[70] [See for Italy and Africa Duncan-Jones' articles, cited on p. 14.]

public lands, owned by the city, are to be distinguished from the territory over which it had political jurisdiction, and did not necessarily lie in the city territory: instances are known in which cities owned land in distant provinces. In addition to public funds and lands, owned by the city corporately, there were normally sacred lands owned by the various civic gods, and endowments owned by civic corporations, such as gymnasia.

Taxes and endowments combined were still inadequate to support the lavish scale of expenditure in which the cities indulged. The deficiency was made up by contributions, legal or customary, regular or extraordinary, from the magistrates, councillors and other prominent citizens. As already stated an entrance fee (*summa honoraria*) was regularly exacted from magistrates and councillors in the West, and similar, if less regular, contributions were demanded in the East. Magistrates were, by law or custom, required to finance a part or even the whole of the expenses connected with their office. Public opinion demanded that all wealthy citizens should contribute freely to building funds and other special appeals.

The proportion of revenue derived from taxation, endowments and contributions from the magistrates varied greatly from city to city. In the metropoleis of Egypt, which could levy no taxes and, being of recent growth, were meagrely endowed, the great bulk of the expenditure fell on the magistrates. In commercial cities the local taxes must have yielded a substantial income, and some cities were lucky in possessing extensive public lands or, like Ephesus, a richly endowed goddess, whose priesthood could be sold for great sums. In general, as expenditure continued to mount, the proportion paid by the magistrates tended to rise. For taxes were a more or less fixed quantity: no new taxes could be imposed without imperial licence, which was, it seems, sparingly given.[71] And, though fresh endowments were made from time to time, they were generally earmarked for special new expenses. The bulk of the increased burden therefore fell on the civic aristocracy, and it was in their interest—since they were the ultimate guarantors of the imperial taxation—that the imperial government installed *curatores* to curb civic expenditure and eliminate waste and peculation.[72]

[71] [*I.L.S.* 6092, Pliny, *ep.* X 24, *Jahreshefte* 1954, 110 ff. (Pius); *Cod. Just.* IV lxii, 1 f. (Severus)].   [72] Liebenam, 1–173, G. C., 241–50.

In the third and fourth centuries the civic finances received a succession of heavy blows. The great inflation of the mid-third century must have swallowed up their cash endowments. The sacred lands were confiscated to the imperial *res privata* by one of the early Christian emperors, probably Constantine himself. And either Constantine or his sons also confiscated the civic lands and revenues. All were temporarily restored by Julian, but Valentinian and Valens revoked his action. The sacred lands remained thereafter imperial property, but as the pagan cult also ceased, the cities lost only such indirect profits as they made from them: the expenses of Christian worship were defrayed from church funds, and were no concern of the cities. The loss of the civic lands and revenues was a more serious matter, and Valentinian and Valens, finding that the cities could not even keep their walls in repair, restored to them a third of the revenues arising from these sources. The cities thus became dependent even for their internal revenue on the imperial government. In 401 their urban property was restored entire to the cities and, it would seem, they were given control of their third of the rural property; later, in 431, they also reacquired control of their third of the civic taxes. Justinian, however, seems to have taken back control of both lands and taxes.[73]

Gradually the cities acquired new revenues. They received some bequests of land or money, though in this period the usual beneficiary was the church, and by a series of laws they became entitled to the estates of decurions who died intestate, took orders in the church or absconded. Early in the fifth century they were empowered to impose new indirect taxes. But they were compelled to rely more on compulsory payments from their magistrates for the maintenance of their games and baths, and upon special levies for public works. In these circumstances it is not surprising that the civic services were scamped and buildings allowed to fall into disrepair.[74]

ECONOMIC ORGANISATION

In most of the cities of the empire, trade and industry played a

[73] G. C., 148–50.
[74] *Ibid.*, 251.

minor role (ch. II). This is not to deny that there were great ports, like Carthage or Aquileia, Ephesus or Alexandria, and important centres of the caravan trade, like Palmyra, where a large proportion of the population lived by trade and wealthy merchants were included in the local aristocracy. There were also large industrial towns, like Tarsus, famous for its linen fabrics, where the bulk of the population was engaged in manufacture: but it is doubtful if the local aristocracy in such towns derived their wealth from industry, which was carried on by guilds of small craftsmen. Such towns were however rare exceptions. The normal city served, of course, as a market for the surrounding country, and a distributive centre for such few imported or locally manufactured articles as the neighbouring peasantry required. Such business was however on a very small scale and carried on by very humble persons, small craftsmen and shopkeepers. The range of such trade was moreover very limited in distance. Where cities were thickly set, trade and industry was no doubt concentrated in them. But in the extensive territory of Antioch, Libanius tells us, the larger villages had their own industries and trade was carried on at rural fairs, so that the countryside was economically independent of the town. If this was the case in the neighbourhood of a great city like Antioch, small towns which ruled large territories like the Gallic *civitates*, must have had a very insignificant economic role.

Trade and manufacture played a very minor part in the economy of the Roman empire. The basic industry was agriculture; the vast majority of the inhabitants of the empire were peasants, and the wealth of the upper classes was in the main derived from rent. Fortunes might be made in trade, or more commonly in government service or in the more lucrative professions, such as rhetoric, but they were invested in land, the only form of stable capital. Decurions therefore, who were by definition men of property, were almost invariably landowners. What little evidence there is under the earlier empire points this way. In the later empire, the laws of the Codes make it perfectly plain that the property of the average decurion consisted of landed estates, and that it was very exceptional for a man whose wealth was invested in slaves to be enrolled by the council; merchants in general were of a lower social grade than decurions, and were usually admitted to the council only when they had invested their fortunes in real property.

The prosperity of the average city was based on the fact that the largest landowners of the neighbourhood resided there, and there spent, either in their private capacity or as magistrates and councillors, the rents which they drew from their country estates. The lower classes in the towns must have lived largely by serving the needs of the local aristocracy and of the city corporately, partly also by catering for the neighbouring peasantry; in small cities many of the urban population doubtless were agricultural workers who walked out daily to their fields.[75] This was probably the basic economic pattern of the great majority of cities. Other minor factors contributed to the prosperity of the cities. All were the administrative, and to a lesser extent, the judicial centres of their territories, and some, the capitals of assize districts (*conventus*) or provinces, profited by the periodic or normal presence of the Roman governor and his staff, and consequent influx of litigants, petitioners, lawyers and the like.[76] Most cities were the religious centre of a limited area and attracted crowds at their festivals; some, the patrons of famous oracles, mysteries or games, attracted tourists from far and wide. Long distance trade and large scale industry, as has already been said, enriched some. But basically the city was a social phenomenon, the result of the predilection of the wealthier classes for the amenities of urban life.

VILLAGE INSTITUTIONS

Most villages lay in the territory of a city and were subject to its administrative control. This control was however very loose. Collectors selected by and drawn from the city council exacted the imperial taxes, levied recruits for the imperial army and requisitioned supplies and transport. The city gendarmerie maintained order and in particular hunted down brigands. Otherwise the villages seem to have been left very much to themselves. In some cases, notably in western and central Asia Minor, the villages have left considerable epigraphic record of themselves. Here they are shown to have had a vigorous democratic communal life. The

[75] [Thus Cicero says that Capua was not razed in 211 B.C. 'ut aratores cultu agrorum defessi urbis domiciliis uterentur', *de leg. agr.* II 88.]
[76] [Dio Chrys. XXXV 15.]

village mass meeting (σύλλογος or ὄχλος) is never called the assembly (ἐκκλησία) but was much more active than the contemporary city assembly, not only electing the annual magistrates, but passing resolutions on such topics as the use of common lands or the disposal of trust funds.

The magistrates are known by a variety of local titles, not borrowed from the cities. A few villages had a group of elders (γερουσία) but never a council (βουλή), which was the hallmark of city states. Villages often erected public buildings—temples, baths, even occasionally theatres—and celebrated local festivals.

In a few limited areas, villages were the unit of government, and the Roman administration dealt directly with them. From one such area, Batanaea, Trachonitis and Auranitis in central Syria, a large number of inscriptions have survived. Here again a vigorous communal life survived to a late date. The villages were governed by annual elective magistrates and were active in erecting public buildings. Some of the larger villages were from time to time given the status of cities, but it is difficult to discern what the change implied save the creation of a council and a change in the titles of the magistrates.

There remain the villages in the bureaucratically administered provinces, notably Egypt. Here the situation was very different. Egyptian villages had no communal life and no elective magistrates. The village officials were appointed (by lot) by a representative of the central government from a list of qualified villagers nominated by the village scribe, who was himself similarly appointed from a list submitted by his predecessor. It is known that in Judaea under the Herods village scribes were similarly appointed by the crown. The rigid system of control survived in Egypt after the nomes had been converted by Diocletian into cities; the headman of the village now submitted nominees for appointment to the village offices to the *praepositus pagi*, the civic magistrate in charge of the district of the city territory in which the village lay.[77]

---

[77] G. C., 272–3, 286–7. [There is also some information for western provinces, see e.g. M. Rostovtzeff, *Soc. and Econ. Hist. of the Roman Empire*, index s.v. *pagi, vici*, villages, where examples will be found of oppression of villagers by the city governments.]

PROVINCIAL ORGANISATION

The Roman provinces had, in origin, no communal institutions; they were merely areas subject to a Roman magistrate. By the end of the Republic however, in a few provinces, Sicily and Asia among them, the cities had grouped themselves in a loose form of union for the celebration of festivals in honour of governors or ex-governors, and also to represent the common interests of the province.

In the reign of Augustus the development of such provincial councils (*concilia*, κοινά) received a great impetus by being associated with the cult of Rome and Augustus. They sprang up spontaneously in most eastern provinces and were actively promoted in the more barbarous western provinces such as Gaul in the West: rather later they spread to the more Latinised provinces, such as Narbonensis and Africa. These *concilia* did not always correspond exactly to a province. The *concilium Galliarum*, for instance, embraced the communities of the three administrative provinces of Belgica, Lugdunensis and Aquitania, while on the other hand the province of Lycia-Pamphylia had two κοινά, corresponding to its ethnic divisions. The *concilia* in fact tended to represent traditional groupings, which did not always coincide with provincial boundaries. The *concilium* consisted of several representatives from each city and was financed by contributions from the cities; the size of contribution, and probably the number of delegates, varied according to the importance of the city. The primary and ostensible business of the *concilium* was to celebrate the cult of Rome and Augustus with sacrifices and games, and it elected a provincial priest. The *concilia* also passed votes of thanks to popular governors, instituted judicial proceedings at Rome against those that were corrupt or extortionate, and presented petitions to the emperor on matters of common interest.

Though the worship of Rome and Augustus ceased under the Christian emperors the provincial *concilia* did not, nor did the office of high priest and the games which he celebrated. By this time the *concilium* corresponded closely to the administrative province, and *concilia* seem to have been universal, even in the newly created provinces of Italy. Their precise composition at this date is unknown, but they seem to have been composed mainly of the *honorati* of the province, that is, of senators, other imperial ex-officials and persons of equivalent honorary rank. They continued to represent the common interests of the province to the imperial government, and are often recorded to have sent delegates to the imperial court to ask for administrative reforms or remissions of taxation.[78]

After the reconquest of Italy Justinian entrusted to a similar body, the bishops and the principal landowners of the province, the right of electing, subject to imperial ratification, the provincial governor. This reform was extended by Justin II to the whole of the empire.[79]

[78] E. Kornemann, s.v. 'concilium' and κοινόν in P.W.K.; A. and J., 162–76. [J. A. O. Larsen, Representative Government in Greek and Roman History, 1955,106–61; J. Deininger, Die Provinziallandtage der röm. Kaiserzeit, 1965.]

[79] Justinian, Prag. Sanct., 12, Nov., 149.

CHAPTER TWO

THE ECONOMIC LIFE OF THE TOWNS OF THE ROMAN EMPIRE

IT is not until the period of the later Roman Empire (the fourth to the sixth centuries) that we possess any evidence whereby we can even approximately estimate the relative contribution of trade and industry on the one hand and agriculture on the other to its total wealth. During this period the fiscal structure of the empire provides a valuable clue. The main tax, the *iugatio* and *capitatio*, was assessed on the land and the rural population. It covered the heaviest item of expenditure, the rations and fodder (*annona* and *capitus*) of the army, the civil service and other state employees, such as the workers in the imperial arms factories. This tax, or supplementary levies on the same basis, also paid for public works, including roads, and the imperial postal service (*cursus publicus*). Another levy, also assessed on land and rural workers, provided uniforms for the army and the civil service. The rents of the imperial estates covered the personal expenditure of the emperors and provided a surplus for miscellaneous needs. The only other regular expense, the periodical donatives to the army (a relatively small item, averaging only a quarter to a fifth of the rations)[1] was covered by a variety of taxes. Some of these (the *gleba*, the *aurum oblaticium* and the *aurum coronarium*) were levies on particular classes of landowners—senators and decurions. But they included customs and a direct tax on traders (the *collatio lustralis* [or *chrysargyron*]).

Traders (*negotiatores*) are ill defined in the codes. The term certainly included all who made a living by buying and selling, that is merchants and shopkeepers, and also money-lenders and prostitutes.[2] Some laws draw a distinction between *negotiatores* and

[1] An *annona* was commuted for 4 or 5 solidi per annum (Valentinian III, *Nov.* XIII.3, *Cod. Just.*, I, xxvii, 1, §§ 22–38): the quinquennial donative was 5 solidi (Proc. *Anecd.* xxiv, 27–9).

[2] *Cod. Theod.*, XIII, i, 18 (money-lenders), Zosimus, II, 38, Evagrius, *Hist. Eccl.*, III, 39 (prostitutes).

plebeii or *collegiati*,[3] the members of the guilds of craftsmen, but others, which specifically exempt *coloni* who sell the produce of their land and rural smiths and potters,[4] suggest that for the purposes of the tax the net was cast fairly widely, and that urban craftsmen were included;[5] they were certainly subject to no other tax. The *collatio lustralis* then represented the whole contribution of trade and of industry, in so far as it was directly taxed at all. and this contribution was a very minor item in the imperial budget. So small an item was it, indeed, that so prudent a financier as Anastasius, who left a large surplus in the treasury, was able to abolish it altogether, making up the deficit out of the rents of the imperial estates.[6] But small though its yield was, the tax was not a light one in relation to the resources of those who had to pay it. All the ancient authorities, pagan and Christian alike, are unanimous that the *collatio lustralis* was an intolerable burden, which drove its victims even to selling their children into slavery.[7]

For the fifth and sixth centuries some precise and reliable figures are available. We know from Joshua Stylites, a contemporary, that the *collatio lustralis* levied on his native city of Edessa immediately before its abolition in 498 amounted to 140 lb. gold every four years, that is 35 lb. gold per annum.[8] From a sixth century papyrus we learn that the annual tax on Heracleopolis in Egypt, comprising the corn levy commuted into gold and the gold taxes on land, amounted to 57.500 *solidi* or very nearly 800 lb. gold.[9] Edessa was an important town, the capital of a province, and moreover lay on the great trade route whereby silk and other luxury goods from the Far East passed from the Persian frontier at Nisibis to Antioch and the West. Heracleopolis was an ordinary provincial town, possessing an extensive rural territory. The two figures are not strictly comparable, but they strongly suggest that agriculture produced something in the order of twenty times as much revenue as trade and industry in the sixth

[3] *Cod. Theod.*, VII, xxi, 3, XVI, v, 52.
[4] *Cod. Theod.*, XIII, i, 10, cf. 3.
[5] Libanius (*Or.* xlvi, 22) speaks of a cobbler, whose only asset was his knife, paying the tax at Antioch.
[6] Malalas, p. 398 (ed. Bonn.).
[7] Zosimus, II, 38, Libanius, *Or.*, xlvi, 22, Evagrius, *Hist. Eccl.*, III, 39.
[8] Josh. Styl. (ed. W. Wright), 31.
[9] *P. Oxy.*, 1909.

century. How far these conclusions would be applicable to earlier periods it is hard to say. Trade and industry had certainly shrunk in the later empire, but so also had agriculture: there is abundant evidence that large areas of once productive land had gone out of cultivation. On the whole it is likely that while the aggregate wealth of the empire had declined, the relative contribution of agriculture and of trade and industry had not changed significantly.

It would take us too far from the subject of this conference to discuss fully the reasons for the relative insignificance of trade and industry in the Roman Empire, but it may be useful to indicate briefly the more important. One was the high cost of land transport. Here Diocletian's edict on prices provides some precise figures. The authorised charge per mile for a wagon load of 1200 lb. is 20 denarii; 60 modii of wheat weigh 1200 lb; and wheat is priced at 100 denarii the modius.[10] It follows that a load of wheat would be doubled in price by a journey of three hundred miles. Sea freights as laid down in the edict are much less expensive—though it must be remembered that the risk of total loss by shipwreck was considerable. A modius of wheat could be carried, for instance, from Alexandria to Rome, some 1,250 miles, for 16 denarii,[11] a sum which would not pay for a land journey of 50 miles. This meant that it did not pay to transport heavy or bulky goods for any distance, unless they were produced near a port or inland waterway and could be sold in markets accessible by sea or navigable river. Wheat seems in fact rarely or never to have been transported any distance by land, except by the imperial government, which did not have to count the cost. In an inland town the local authorities had no resource in case of a famine save to compel the local landowners to release their stocks,[12] and conversely the landowners of inland districts such as Lydia, when Justinian suppressed the posting stations and removed the military units which had hitherto consumed the corn locally, had to let their crops rot on the threshing floor.[13] For inland regions trade was thus limited to goods of a relatively high intrinsic value.

[10] Ed. Diocl., I.1 (wheat), XVII 3 (transport), cf. PLINY, N.H., XVIII, 66 for the weight of wheat. [Cf. LRE II 841 ff.]

[11] Trans. Amer. Phil. Ass. LXXI (1940), pp. 163–5.

[12] J. R. S., XIV (1924), 180, Philostratus, Vita Apoll. Tyan., I, 15. Greg. Naz., In laud. Bas., 34–35: cf. Dio Chrys., XLVI (esp. 8).

[13] Joh. Lydus, de Mag., III, 61, Proc., Anecd., xxx, 6 and 11.

In the second place the market, especially for goods of this character, was very limited. The vast majority of the population were peasants, who were mostly very poor owing to the heavy taxes which all, and the rents which many, paid. Their needs were very simple and could mostly be satisfied by the village smith, potter and weaver. Libanius indeed, in his panegyric on Antioch, boasts that the villages of its extensive territory were not in any way economically dependent on the city; they had their own industries, and exchanged their wares in rural fairs.[14] The bulk of the urban population seem also to have been very poor. It was a problem to supply them even with their basic food, corn, at a price which they could afford, and in most cities there were official corn buyers who purchased wheat and retailed it, either direct to the public or to the bakers, often at a loss to themselves or the local exchequer.[15] It is unlikely that the urban proletariat could afford many imported goods, and they probably obtained most of their needs from local craftsmen and shopkeepers. One important potential customer, the state, rarely used the commercial market. Under the Principate the imperial government obtained the foodstuffs and clothes required by the army through compulsory purchases made through the local authorities,[16] and fed Rome with corn collected in kind as taxes or as rents on state lands. From the time of Diocletian the army, the civil service, and the population of Rome (and later Constantinople) were fed by taxes in kind; clothes for the army and civil service were supplied partly from levies in kind, partly from state factories, and arms manufactured in public armament works. As customers for the private merchant there thus remained only the landowning and professional classes.

In these circumstances industry tended to be evenly dispersed throughout the empire. Most common needs were supplied in each town, and even in villages, by local craftsmen. It was only products of a rather superior kind which commanded a wider market and were manufactured on a large scale. The *terra sigillata* of the Principate, an ornamental ware used in better class households, was, for instance exported to all the western provinces from

[14] Lib., *Or.* XI, 230, cf. Rostovtzeff, *Social and Economic History of the Roman Empire*, p. 582, n. 70.

[15] Jones, *The Greek City*, pp. 217–8.

[16] The system is best documented for Egypt (Lesquier, *L'armée romaine de l'Egypte*, pp. 350 ff). Tacitus (*Agricola*, 19, 4–5, cf. 31.2) implies a similar system in Britain.

its original place of manufacture in northern Italy; but even in this case provincial factories were soon established which could undercut the Italian product by the saving in transport costs. It was probably the textile industry that was most concentrated. We hear of a number of towns, like Patrae in Greece or Tarsus in Cilicia, where there was a large population of weavers,[17] and the Diocletianic tariff records a series of fabrics or garments named after towns or districts.[18] In this industry expense of transport rather favoured concentration, for it was more economical to weave the wool and linen in the principal sheep raising and flax growing areas and export the finished product, than to transport the bulky raw material. Even here it is difficult to estimate how far cheap clothes were produced for a wide market. On the one hand, when Pinianus at Rome in the late fourth century wished to live an ascetic life, he bought 'unbleached Antiochenes':[19] this suggests that in large towns at any rate the cheapest clothing was imported from the large centres of production. On the other hand the imperial government in the fourth century would hardly have assessed the levy of military cloaks and tunics on land on the same basis as the levies of wheat, meat, wine and oil, unless plain weaving had been generally practised throughout the country-side.[20]

It seems likely then that large scale industry was confined to a small number of towns. Large scale commerce was also probably limited to relatively few large towns. Only in the great cities, mainly the chief administrative centres, would there be a sufficient concentration of the wealthy or well-to-do classes to provide an adequate market. In the average town the local gentry probably had either to rely on the periodic visits of travelling merchants, like the dealer in shoes and clothes from Athens of whose annual visit to Cyrenaica Synesius took advantage to buy three Attic cloaks,[21] or to attend an annual fair, such as is recorded at Aegae.[22]

[17] Pausanias, VII, xxi, 14, Dio Chrys., xxxiv, 21–3.
[18] Ed. Diocl., XIX, 6, 13, 15, 16, 26 ff., XX, 3, 4, 13, XXII, 16 ff., XXVI, 13 ff., XXVII, 8 ff., XXVIII, 7 ff. Some of these are 'trade names', e.g. XIX. 27. βίρρος Λαδικηνὸς ἐν ὁμοιότητι Νερβικοῦ (cf. XX. 4), but show that the places concerned had once been famous for a speciality later imitated elsewhere.
[19] Vita S. Melaniae, 8 (Anal. Boll., VIII (1889), p. 26 for Latin version, XXII (1903), p. 13 for Greek).
[20] Cod. Theod., VII, vi, 3.
[21] Synesius, Ep. 52.
[22] Theodoret, Ep. 70, Itin. Hierosol., Theodosius, 32.

D

They also no doubt took advantage of the annual *concilia*, the gatherings of notables at the provincial or diocesan capital; the emperor Honorius in his constitution establishing an annual diocesan *concilium* at Arelate stresses the advantages of meeting at this great city, the seat of the praetorian prefecture of the Gauls, where products from all parts of the empire were available.[23] In addition to the great centres of consumption there were the major sea and river ports, which served as entrepôts for the collection and forwarding of the products of their areas, and the cities on the eastern frontier through which passed the lucrative trade in luxury articles, such as silk and spices, from the Far East.

After this rather summary and schematic discussion of the role of trade and industry in the Empire at large, we may attempt to estimate their role in the cities. The empire was a conglomeration of cities, and each city was not merely a town, but a town with a surrounding rural territory of varying extent. In the normal city there was no political distinction between the urban and the rural population, and the magistrates and council, which, *de iure* or *de facto*, were the governing body of the city, were drawn from the richest inhabitants of the whole area. Given the general economic conditions outlined above it would follow that in the average city the council would consist of the local landowners. Even in the exceptional case of the Egyptian metropoleis, where the villagers of the nome were excluded from citizenship, this was so; for substantial landowners in the nome were normally domiciled in the metropolis and registered as its citizens, and it was they who filled the civic offices in the first two centuries of the Principate and were later enrolled on the councils which Septimius Severus established. Only where rural communities were 'attributed' to a neighbouring city, that is made subject to it without being incorporated in it, were some landowners, who were members of the 'attributed' communities, excluded from the government of the city; and in these circumstances we find Tergeste petitioning Antoninus Pius to allow substantial members of the Carni and Catali to hold civic offices and thus replenish the council.[24]

It is not easy to substantiate this generalisation for the period of the Principate, when almost the only evidence available is

[23] Haenel, *Corpus legum*, p. 238 [quoted, *L.R.E.*, III, 246f.]
[24] *I.L.S*, 6680.

epigraphic. A citation in the Digest from the early third century lawyer Callistratus suggests that even in his day, when it was becoming difficult to fill the council, it was only as a last resort that persons engaged in trade would be elected. 'In fact', he writes, 'such persons (sc. 'eos qui utensilia negotiantur et vendunt') are not forbidden to be candidates for the decurionate or any office in their native city . . . nevertheless I think it degrading that such persons, who are liable to be flogged (by the *aediles*), should be received into the council, especially in those cities which have an adequate number of respectable citizens: only the fewness of men to fill public functions compels even these, if they have property, to be invited to hold municipal dignities'.[25] The inscriptions, so far as they go, in general bear out this conclusion. It is very rarely that a merchant or manufacturer on his tombstone boasts of any civic office, except in such towns as Ostia that were primarily commercial.[26] Decurions are very commonly recorded as patrons of *collegia*, the guilds of craftsmen and traders,[27] but very rarely as members or officers.[28] Decurions, of course, often owned shops which they leased to traders and craftsmen, and some of them engaged in business through slave or freedmen agents; thus the names of Umbricius Scaurus, duumvir of Pompeii, and of various of his freedmen and freedwomen are found on many pots of *garum* or fish sauce found in the town.[29] It seems likely, too, that many of the freedmen who were members of the guilds may have started life as slave agents in the same trade. Brickmaking was also a supplementary source of wealth to decurion landowners.

In the later Empire the codes provide more explicit evidence. Decurions are sharply distinguished from *negotiatores* and *collegiati*, who are often classed together as *plebeii*. By a constitution of Julian the city councils are declared to be immune from the *collatio lustralis*, 'unless perhaps it be established that a decurion is carrying on some trade'.[30] Valentinian I ruled that if a trader

[25] *Dig.*, L, ii, 12.
[26] E.g. *I.L.S*, 6169, 7033, 7481, 7529, 7592; for Ostia see below, p. 54–55.
[27] E.g. *I.L.S*, 7217, 7221, and 6595, 6616, 6634, 6645, 6678, 6681, 6686, 6691, 6726, 6744, etc.
[28] As at Alba Fucens (*ILS*, 6536). At Pompeii the duumvir Paquius Proculus (*I.L.S*, 6406, 6434) had a large bakery at the back of his house (see Tenney Frank, 'The economic life of an ancient city', *Class. Phil.*, XIII (1918), pp. 225–40).
[29] *ILS*, 6366, *CIL*, IV, 5657 ff.
[30] *Cod. Theod.*, XII, i, 50.

bought land and was enrolled on the council as the owner of some
estates, he should no longer be liable to the *collatio*.[31] Honorius
ordered that this tax was to be collected by the same body that
paid it, the *corpus negotiatorum*, and that the *curiales* were not to be
burdened with the collection of a tax which did not concern
them.[32] The laws in general assume that decurions are landowners: they are forbidden to alienate their estates without
permission,[33] or to retire to their estates to evade their duties.[34] It
is a concession to the *curiales* of the province of Moesia that they
may enrol suitable persons from the *plebs*, whose wealth consists
in slaves.[35] Persons of wealth and position sometimes dabbled
in trade as a sideline—usually through agents—but the practice
seems to have been rare, and was frowned on by the imperial
government, which in 409 forbade 'persons of noble birth or
conspicuous by imperial offices or owners of large properties to
engage in trade to the detriment of the cities, in order that the
commerce of buying and selling may be easier among commoners
and traders'.[36]

In the average city then the governing aristocracy was a group
of local landowners, resident in the town. This body naturally
tended to be hereditary in the main; from time to time, as old
families died out or became impoverished, or on the other hand
rose into the imperial aristocracy of senators, they were replaced
by the sons of men who had made fortunes in the professions or
in trade or industry and had invested them in landed property.
By the end of the third century this curial class had become legally
hereditary. After the middle of the fourth century it seems to have
received very little fresh blood from below, and as, despite all
efforts of the imperial government, the wealthier families found
their way into the senatorial order or the imperial civil service,
thereby becoming exempt from curial obligations, it dwindled in
numbers and in wealth. The landowners of the exempted classes,
the *honorati*, became the real local aristocracy, and were eventually,
in conjunction with the bishop and clergy, entrusted by the

[31] *Ibid.*, XII, i, 72.
[32] *Ibid.*, XIII, i. 17.
[33] *Ibid.*, XII, iii, 1 and 2.
[34] *Ibid.*, XII, xviii, 1 and 2.
[35] *Ibid.*, XII, i, 96. Cf. Thalassius, who owned a slave factory of knife makers
(Libanius, *Or.* XLII, 21).
[36] *Cod. Theod.*, XIII, i, 5, *Cod. Just.*, IV, lxiii, 3.

imperial government with the main responsibility for local government.[37]

Below the landed aristocracy came the merchants, shop-keepers and craftsmen, who were very commonly organised in guilds (*corpora* or *collegia* in Latin, συνεργασίαι, συντεχνίαι and a variety of other terms in Greek).[38] Under the Principate these bodies are known to us almost entirely from epigraphic sources, and we are therefore dependent on the hazard of the survival of inscriptions. Broadly speaking it may be said that in most areas where inscriptions have been found in any large numbers, guilds are attested. From Asia Minor we know of the existence—but very little more—of a considerable variety of guilds, mainly connected with the textile industry, wool and linen weavers, fullers, dyers and garment makers, but also including many miscellaneous trades, builders, smiths, potters, leatherworkers, bakers, gardeners, porters and so forth.[39] In Egypt papyri supply the place of inscriptions, and show that guilds were well nigh universal. In the Latin speaking provinces we are best informed about Italy and Gaul, where guilds are very common, but they are found in the more meagre epigraphic record of Spain and Illyricum. Africa is the only area rich in inscriptions which has failed to yield any significant evidence of guilds during the Principate, and it would seem that in this country of small agricultural towns they were rare.[40]

The Latin inscriptions reveal much about the organisation and activities of the guilds. The membership was very diverse, some-times even including slaves[41] as well as freedmen and free born citizens, and must have included a wide range of wealth, from simple craftsmen to well-to-do proprietors of big shops; many freedmen members were elected to the order of *Seviri Augustales*, an expensive honour.[42] The guilds were, formally at any rate, democratic bodies, the general meeting of members laying down the statutes, adopting patrons, and electing the officers.[43] The

[37] Jones, *The Greek City*, pp. 192–209.
[38] The standard work on Roman guilds is still Waltzing, *Corporations professionnelles chez les Romains* (1895–1900).
[39] *Economic Survey of Ancient Rome*, IV, pp. 841–4.
[40] *Ibid.*, pp. 71–3.
[41] Waltzing, I, pp. 346–7: in *I.L.S* 3127 three of the four *magistri* of the *fullones* are freedmen and one a slave.
[42] *Ibid.*, IV, pp. 576–9.
[43] Waltzing, I, pp. 368–78.

presidents, varying in number from two to six, were generally styled *magistri*, or if, as often, they held office for a five year term, *quinquennales*; subordinate to them there were in many guilds *curatores*, and treasurers, *quaestores*.[44] Some large guilds were divided into *centuriae* or more commonly *decuriae*, headed by *centuriones* and *decuriones*,[45] and in a few a committee of *decuriones* seems to have been the effective governing body.[46] Even where this was not the case the democratic character of the guilds was perhaps more formal than real, for officers had to pay a substantial contribution to the common fund (*summa honoraria*) on election and were moreover expected to entertain on a lavish scale; none therefore save the richer members could aspire to office.[47]

Many guilds possessed premises, a hall (*schola*) or a chapel (*templum*), in which they held their business meetings, conducted their cults and met for their feasts and social gatherings.[48] Every guild had its common chest (*arca*), managed by the treasurers (*quaestores*), fed by the entrance fees of new members, the *summae honorariae* of officers, and the proceeds of endowments; these latter were usually earmarked for commemorative feasts and distributions of cash (*sportulae*). On the expense side, besides maintenance of premises and staff (many guilds owned slaves), provision of feasts and support of the cult, guilds often gave funeral bounties for deceased members.[49]

So far as the evidence of the inscriptions goes the guilds seem to have been purely social bodies, unconcerned with the business activities of their members. This impression is confirmed by the fact that guilds not infrequently admitted members who practised a different trade, and that prosperous men are often members of a number of guilds simultaneously.[50] The inscriptions, however, certainly do not tell the whole story, as emerges from the following facts. A wide variety of trades and crafts are recorded sporadically, but by far the commonest in Italy and the western provinces generally are the *fabri* or *fabri tignuarii*, the builders and carpenters, the *centonarii*, the makers of patchwork rugs, and the *dendrofori*, a mysterious body associated with the worship of the

[44] *Ibid.*, pp. 383 ff.   [45] *Ibid.*, pp. 357–62.
[46] *Ibid.*, pp. 379–83.
[47] *Ibid.*, pp. 453–4.
[48] *Ibid.*, pp. 215 ff.
[49] *Ibid.*, pp. 449 ff.
[50] Waltzing, IV, pp. 248–51.

Magna Mater, probably timber merchants. These three guilds, or two of them, are very commonly found in close association. The inscriptions provide no clue either to their association or to their frequent occurrence, and it is a chance literary reference that solves the problem. Pliny, after a disastrous fire at Nicomedia, suggested to Trajan that to prevent a repetition of the misfortune, he should establish a *collegium fabrorum* in the city. It appears than that the *collegia fabrorum* served as fire brigades, and it may be inferred that the other guilds so closely associated with them shared this duty.[51] If the abundant inscriptions of the *fabri, centonarii,* and *dendrofori* are completely silent on this important side of their activities, the absence of epigraphic evidence is not conclusive proof that the guilds may not have had other practical functions of which we know nothing.

The guilds of the Principate were voluntary and private organisations. They played no part in the government of the city, and were not connected in any way with its political organization; their membership commonly included resident foreigners and even slaves as well as citizens. There is only one possible exception to this generalization. In Philadelphia of Lydia inscriptions record the 'sacred tribe of the woolworkers' and the 'sacred tribe of the leatherworkers'.[52] 'Tribe' (φυλή) is normally the designation of the official political divisions of the people, and it may be that at Philadelphia the guilds held this position. In some other Lydian and Phrygian cities, Thyatira and Hierapolis for instance,[53] guilds are frequently recorded, and tribes are not mentioned. It is possible that in this area the guilds formed the basis for the political organization of the people. It must be emphasised, however, that this is a conjecture, and, even if it be true, the phenomenon is limited to a small group of towns.

The civic authorities played no official part in establishing or even in licensing guilds. Strictly speaking all guilds, except the burial clubs of the poor and religious societies, had to be licensed by the imperial government, and according to Gaius permission was sparingly given.[54] Guilds very rarely record that they have

[51] Pliny, *Ep.* X, 33–4; Waltzing, II, pp. 193–208.

[52] Id., III nos 146 (=*I. G. R.* IV, 1632), 147.

[53] *Econ. Survey of Anc. Rome*, IV, pp. 842–3.

[54] *Dig.*, III, iv, 1 (Gaius), cf. XLVII, xxii, 1 and 3 (Marcianus); the question is discussed in Waltzing, I, pp. 114–160, and in P.W. Duff, *Personality in Roman Private Law*, chap. IV.

been officially licensed; among those that do so are the *fabri*, *centonarii*, *dendrofori*, or the *tria collegia*, and sundry guilds at Ostia connected with the *annona*.[55] It may be that only guilds which performed some direct service for the state or their city were normally licensed. The law was, however, very laxly and inter- mittently enforced, guilds being suppressed only when they caused disorders. Thus after a riot at Pompeii in A.D. 59 the senate suppressed the guilds which had been formed contrary to the law ('collegiaque quae contra leges instituerant dissoluta'),[56] and at Ephesus we find the proconsul of Asia banning the guild of bakers after a strike.[57] On Trajan's instructions Pliny in Bithynia issued an edict forbidding all guilds; here again it appears from Trajan's letter refusing permission for a *collegium fabrorum* at Nicomedia that there was much unrest in the province at the time.[58] Generally, it would seem, guilds were allowed to exist, so long as they did not cause trouble, even though they received no official license.

There is little or no evidence that the city governments were interested in fostering or protecting local trade or industry. The cities, it is true, generally provided a market, which was often a grand architectural composition, surrounded with porticoes, but this they did from civic pride in the appearance of the town, and with a view to the revenue obtained from market dues. A letter from the council of Hermopolis to Demetrius, controller of the market (ἀγοράνομος) is significant: 'The civic market is both an ornament of the city and contributes no little profit, producing revenue from those who rent places in it'.[59] Maritime cities spent considerable sums on maintaining and embellishing their harbours, but here again it may be suspected that the principal motives were civic pride and the hope of increasing the yield of harbour dues.

The main concern of the normal city in the economic sphere was to see that the basic foodstuffs, and in particular bread, were sold on the market at reasonable prices.[60] This was one of the principal duties of the aediles or ἀγοράνομοι; an interesting series

[55] *ILS*, 1164, 1367, 3399, 6172, CIL, II, 1167, X, 3699, 3700, 5198, XIV, 10.
[56] Tac., *Ann.*, XIV, 17.
[57] *Inschr. Mag. Mae*, 114, cf. W.H. Buckler, 'Labour disputes in the province of Asia', in *Anatolian Studies presented to Sir W.M. Ramsay*, pp. 30 ff.
[58] Pliny, *Ep.* X, 33–4, 96–7.
[59] Wilcken, *Chr.* I, 296.
[60] Jones, *The Greek City*, pp. 215–19.

of inscriptions from the market place of Ephesus record the prices prevailing for bread and oil under a series of successful ἀγοράνομοι 'under whom there was plenty and fair dealing'.[61] The city authorities sometimes attempted to control prices by decree; at Cyzicus, for instance, when the influx of labour due to Antonia Tryphaena's great public works had sent food prices soaring, the magistrates were instructed to support the ἀγοράνομοι in fixing prices at their old level, and shopkeepers who broke the regulation were threatened with disfranchisement if citizens and deportation if aliens.[62] Such methods, however, rarely prove effective in the long run, and cities usually tried gentler, if more expensive, methods. Ἀγοράνομοι are sometimes recorded to have undercut the dealers, themselves selling wine or oil below market price, to their own financial loss, and, as already mentioned, most cities had special funds and magistrates for the purchase of corn. But the corn had to be converted into bread before it could be placed on the market, and here an arrangement with the guild of bakers was needful. From Oxyrhynchus we have a contract between the bakers' guild and the ἀγοράνομοι whereby the former engage to grind and bake the corn provided by the latter, at a charge of 10 obols per artaba, each artaba to produce 30 two-pound loaves.[63] At Ephesus the city council seems on one occasion to have been less successful in its handling of the bakers. A strike had resulted, and the proconsul had to intervene, dissolving the bakers' guild, and ordering its members under drastic penalties 'to obey the regulations laid down in the common interest and to maintain the necessary supply of bread to the city uninterruptedly'.[64] At Oxyrhynchus at a later date it would appear that the bakers had failed the city; for we find the six eutheniarchs (the magistrates responsible for the corn supply) entering into a mutual agreement that each shall at his own expense establish a mill capable of dealing with 20 artabae a day.[65]

Requisitions of clothing by the imperial government from the cities also brought the city councils into contact with the local guilds. It is probable that in most provinces the imperial government had always used the city authorities as its intermediaries,

[61] *Forsch. Eph.*, III, 10–16.
[62] *Syll.*[3], 799.
[63] *P. Oxy.*, 1454.
[64] See n. 57
[65] *P. Oxy.*, 908.

but in Egypt, where alone we have detailed information, it dealt direct with the guilds in the first two centuries.[66] With the establishment of city councils in Egypt by Septimius Severus, however, the metropoleis took up the function which probably had been normally fulfilled hitherto by the cities of the other provinces. From the late third century we possess the unfortunately much mutilated minutes of a council meeting at Oxyrhynchus, dealing with an imperial requisition of 100 tunics. The price allowed by the imperial treasury is apparently most inadequate. The council are informed that linen yarn costs 49 denarii, and that only 11 denarii has been paid from the treasury. The councillors indignantly reply 'The linen yarn merchants must be satisfied with 19 denarii besides what is being paid by the imperial treasury'. Next a petition from the linen weavers of the city is read, in which they demand extra payment 'owing to the rise in price of materials and the increased wages of the workmen', and here again the council has to authorise a supplementary payment. The details are obscure, but it is clear that the city council, which is responsible for the delivery of the goods, has to negotiate with the guilds concerned in their manufacture, and to supplement the government payments.[67]

A law of Constantine (or perhaps one of his sons) orders that in all cities where they exist *dendrofori* are to be enrolled in the *collegia* of the *centonarii* and *fabri*, as these latter require reinforcement.[68] This is the first sign that the imperial government considered the guilds, or any rate these particular guilds, which maintained the local fire services, as of public importance, and applied compulsion to keep up their membership. A number of later laws in the Theodosian Code enforce membership of the town *collegia* on a hereditary basis, ordering that *collegiati* who had obtained posts in the provincial or palatine *officia*, joined the army, or migrated to the country and become *coloni*, must be brought back with their children to their native cities.[69] It so happens that none of these laws is earlier than 395, and that a large number fall in the next two decades. It would seem that the problem became acute at the end of the fourth century, though its

[66] *B. G. U.*, 1564.
[67] *P. Oxy.*, 1411.
[68] *Cod. Theod.*, XIV, viii, 1.
[69] *Cod. Theod.*, I, xii, 6, VI, xxx, 16–7, VII, xx, 12, xxi, 3, XII, i, 146, 156, xix, 1, 2, 3, XIV, vii, 1, 2.

origins lay further back, for some laws decide the fate of sons of *collegiati* born within the last thirty or forty years.[70] It also so happens that all this group of laws is directed to the western provinces, Italy, Africa and Gaul, and that none of them is reproduced in the Code of Justinian; in Italy on the other hand similar rules were re-enacted by Valentinian III (in 452) and Majorian (in 458) and by Theoderic in the early sixth century.[71] It may reasonably be inferred that in the eastern half of the Empire the cities never suffered from a similar migration of craftsmen, and the eastern emperors never found it necessary to enforce hereditary membership of the guilds. In the East, it would seem, where urban life was more firmly rooted and the wealthier classes continued to live in cities, the shopkeepers and craftsmen never lacked employment. In the West, on the other hand, the demand for their goods and services apparently dried up in the latter part of the fourth century, perhaps because the great landlords, in whose hands more and more of the land was concentrated, tended to move to the great cities or live in their country villas, and they were forced to migrate to the country and seek employment in agriculture.

The laws do not make it clear why the imperial government regarded the maintenance of the *collegia* as a matter of public interest. They speak vaguely of duties (*munera*) which they perform in their cities; Honorius complains that the cities of Gaul, deprived of their services, have lost their ancient splendour ('destitutae ministeriis civitates splendorem quo pridem nituerant amiserunt');[72] Majorian speaks of the *collegiati* as providing corvées (*operae*) for their native cities in rotation under the direction of the *curiales*[73]. The last phrase may be illustrated by a law which alludes to the duty incumbent on the *corporati* of Alexandria to dredge the river,[74] and by the protests of Libanius against the oppression of the shopkeepers and craftsmen of Antioch, who are compelled to replace old columns with new and to clean the drains, and must either abandon their trades to do the work themselves, or pay to hire labourers.[75] Other corvées more

[70] *Cod. Theod.*, XII, xix, 1–2.
[71] Val., *Nov.* xxxv, 3, Maj., *Nov.* vii, 2–8, *Ed. Theod.*, 64.
[72] *Cod. Theod.*, XII, xix, 1.
[73] Maj., *Nov.* vii, 3.
[74] *Cod. Theod.*, XIV, xxvii, 2.
[75] Libanius, *Or.*, xlvi, 21.

directly interested the imperial government. Valeninian I speaks
of *collegiati* being pressed into the service of the *cursus publicus* to
drive animals (*prosecutio animalium*);[76] Libanius complains of their
being obliged to furnish and serve a *mansio* of the *cursus publicus*;[77]
and a law shows that the *corporati* of Carthage were compelled to
provide materials (*species*, presumably yarn) for the local state
weaving establishment at unfair prices.[78]

The main function of the *collegiati*, it would seem then, in the
eyes of the imperial government, was the provision of corvées,
not connected with their trades, for their cities and for the central
administration. Apart from this the bakers continued to be
important in their professional capacity; Libanius has much to
say on the periodic bread crises of Antioch, and complains of the
brutal flogging of the bakers to enforce arbitrary price regulations,
and of the resulting flight of the bakers into the mountains.[79]

An inscription from Sardis[80] illustrates happier relations
between a city government and a guild. It is an agreement, dated
459 A.D., between the *defensor* of the city and the builders' guild.
The latter undertake that their members will not abandon work
on a contract, provided that the employer pays the wages mutually
agreed, and that they will supply a substitute for any member who
fails to complete a contract (except in case of sickness) and will
pay the penalties stipulated in the contract if a member obstructs
the work. Here we see the city government, in the interest of the
public, enforcing a code of commercial practices on the individual
builders through their guild, which undertakes corporate
responsibility for its members. In a law of Zeno, dated 473,
forbidding combinations of merchants and shopkeepers to keep
up prices of clothes, food and other goods, and agreements of
workmen not to complete jobs started by others and abandoned,
we find the imperial government similarly placing the responsibility for enforcing the law on the heads of the guilds concerned.[81]

The members of the Sardis guild are, it may be noted, working
builders, who personally execute the contracts which they undertake, seeing that sickness is admitted as a valid reason for delay

---

[76] *Cod. Theod.*, XI, x, 1.
[77] Libanius, *Or.*, XLVI, 19.
[78] *Cod. Theod.*, XI, i, 24.
[79] Libanius, *Or.*, I, 205 ff., 226 ff., XXIX, *passim*.
[80] *Sardis*, VII, 18, Grégoire, *I. G. C.*, 322.
[81] *Cod. Just.*, IV, lix, 2.

in the completion of the work. A law of 436[82] indicates that even the superior merchants of the provincial capitals, the bankers, jewellers, silversmiths and clothiers, who presumably catered for the gentry of the province, were modest folk. Their ambition was, it appears, to be enrolled in the provincial *officium*, that is in the lowest grade of the imperial service, whose members were hereditarily bound to their profession and expressly forbidden any promotion to the higher offices. The imperial government ordered that even this lowly service should be purged 'from such a contagion'. In the mid-fourth century Antoninus, whom Ammianus Marcellinus describes as a wealthy merchant of Mesopotamia—he was presumably engaged in the lucrative Far Eastern trade—joined the financial side of the *officium* of the *dux Mesopotamiae*, in which service he ultimately rose to be a *protector*, that is an aspirant for commissioned rank in the army. Antoninus must have been a man of rather modest station to regard this as bettering himself.[83]

Thus far I have spoken of the average city of the Roman Empire. It is now time to consider the minority which were centres of industry or commerce. Of the former class there is unfortunately very little to say, as none have left any significant records. Dio Chrysostom speaks of the linenweavers of Tarsus as being a substantial part of the population, respectable men but too poor to afford the 500 drachma fee which the city exacted for admission to political rights, and in the neighbouring great city of Anazarbus an inscription records a guild of linenworkers.[84] This suggests that the industry was in the hands of a large number of independent master craftsmen, who, no doubt, like the linen weavers of Oxyrhynchus, employed wage labour. In the later empire the chief industrial centres seem to have been the cities in which the imperial factories were situated. Sozomenus speaks of the workmen in the state weaving establishment and the mint at Cyzicus as being an important element in the population, and Gregory Nazianzen speaks similarly of the armament workers and weavers at Caesarea of Cappadocia.[85] The workers in these factories formed hereditary corporations entirely distinct from the rest of the population.

[82] *Ibid.*, XII, lvii, 12.   [83] Amm. Marc., XVIII, v, 1.
[84] *Dio. Chrys.*, XXXIV, 21–3, *I. G. R.* III, 896.
[85] Soz., *Hist. Eccl.*, V, 15, Greg. Naz., *in Laud. Bas.*, 57.

On a few commercial cities we are better informed. In the west there are substantial groups of inscriptions from Lugdunum and Arelate, and at Ostia excavation has both revealed the ruins of the ancient city and produced a huge crop of inscriptions: much of the material, however, still awaits publication. In the East the great caravan city of Palmyra has been thoroughly explored, and the results published.

Lugdunum,[86] standing at the junction of the Rhône and the Saône, and a focal point in the road system of Gaul, was the natural commercial centre of the country, for along these waterways and, to a lesser extent, roads, imports from the Mediterranean could be distributed to the interior of Gaul, and Gallic products could be forwarded to the sea. Lugdunum was also an important administrative centre, the seat of the legate who governed one of the four provinces of Gaul and of the procurator who handled the finances of two of them; it was garrisoned by an urban cohort and contained the principal mint of the western half of the empire; and it possessed the altar of Rome and Augustus at which the assemblies of the sixty cities of Gallia Comata were held. With a good local market and excellent communications one would expect considerable commercial activity at Lugdunum, and we find in fact a number of flourishing guilds of shippers and merchants. There is the *splendidissimum corpus nautarum Rhodanicorum et Araricorum*, the shippers that plied the Rhône and the Saône, sometimes united in one guild, sometimes divided into two. There is the *corpus utriclariorum Lugduni consistentium*, who navigated rafts supported by inflated skins. There are also the *negotiatores vinarii Lugduni consistentes*, probably importers of wine, since viticulture had not by this date extended north of the Massif Central.[87] We also find individual corn merchants and oil merchants (*negotiator frumentarius—olearius*) and a *negotiator corporis splendidissimi Cisalpinorum et Transalpinorum*; this guild apparently engaged in trade over the Alpine passes—another member is found at Milan. There are also a number of industrial guilds, besides the usual trio of the *fabri tignuarii, centonarii* and *dendrofori*, such as the *sagarii* or cloakmakers and the *artifices tectores* or

[86] Grenier in *Econ. Survey of Anc. Rome*, III, pp. 479–486: the inscriptions are collected in *CIL, XIII*, pp. 248 ff., nos. 1726–2445; those referring to the guilds in Waltzing, III, pp. 558–78.

[87] [It probably began in the first century A.D., Grenier, *o.c.* 580–584.]

plasterers, and many individual craftsmen and dealers (not always easy to distinguish), silversmiths, glassmakers, potters, woolcarders, linenweavers, soapmakers and so forth.

The shippers, merchants and craftsmen are a very mixed body. There are many freedmen among them, but an even larger number of foreigners, several from Augusta Trevirorum and Vienna, others from the Remi, the Vangiones, and the Velocassii: the last boasts that he was *sublectus in numerum colonorum* at Lugdunum. There was also, as the story of the Christian persecution under Marcus Aurelius shows, a considerable oriental community in the town, most of whom no doubt, like the Syrian Thaemus Julianus, whose tomb is preserved, were engaged in trade. The freedmen recorded are mostly *seviri Augustales*, and therefore men of substance. Three of the foreigners were men of rank in their native towns, one a decurion of the Treviri, another duumvir at Vienna, and Thaemus Julianus was a decurion at his native Canatha. The local men are insignificant; none boasts of being anything better than *civis Lugdunensis*. Even in this commercial centre the aristocracy of the city have no truck with trade or industry, but leave it to foreigners, freedmen and the lower orders.

Arelate[88] was the leading port of southern Gaul, where goods were transhipped from the river craft of the Rhône on to sea vessels. Here we find once again guilds of river shippers (the *corpus nautarum Druenticorum*) and of *utriclarii*, who navigated rafts. But sea transport is more important, represented by the *navicularii marini Arelatenses corporum quinque*. There was also a guild of shipbuilders (*fabri navales*), separate from the *fabri tignuarii*. The epigraphic record is poorer than at Lugdunum, but points to the same conclusions; the shippers, many of whom are freedmen, do not belong to the local aristocracy. One document is of particular interest. It is a letter from the Prefect of the Annona at Rome to a procurator,[89] perhaps the *procurator ad annonam provinciae Narbonensis et Liguriae*, whom the shippers of Arelate honour in another inscription.[90] The Prefect states that he has received a resolution of the shippers' guild, which voiced

---

[88] Grenier, *o.c.*, 473–8; inscriptions in *CIL, XII*, pp. 83 ff, nos 654–977, 5804–24; those of the guilds in Waltzing, III, pp. 524–32.

[89] *I.L.S*, 6987.

[90] *I.L.S*, 1432.

certain grievances and threatened cessation of business if they were not rectified, and orders the procurator to take appropriate measures for remedying the abuses, which were apparently connected with checking the weight of cargoes. It is noteworthy that the imperial government deals directly with the guild over the grievances of its members, and that the city of Arelate apparently took no interest in the dispute and gave the guild no support.

At Ostia,[91] the port of Rome, the situation was very different. The town had a small territory and was completely dominated by the great harbour, built by Claudius, through which poured the huge volume of goods imported by the administration of the *annona* and by private traders to meet the multifarious needs of the capital, vast quantities of corn, wine and oil to feed its teeming population, and a variety of manufactured goods, cheap clothes for the poor and luxury articles for the rich. As Ostia handled imports only, brought thither by foreign shippers and merchants, the local guild of shippers, if it existed, was unimportant; the *corpus naviculariorum* which has left one inscription only,[92] of pre-Claudian date, may well have been the guild of the as yet undifferentiated owners of river craft. Later there were several large guilds of lightermen (*lenuncularii*) and bargees (*codicarii*), who unloaded the sea going ships and carried their cargoes up the Tiber to Rome, as well as of ferrymen and miscellaneous boatmen. Other guilds connected with shipping included the *fabri navales* or shipwrights, the *stuppatores* or caulkers, the *saburrarii*, who ballasted ships going out empty, and the *curatores navium*, who guarded ships lying in port. Another important guild or group of guilds was formed by the *mensores frumentarii*, who measured the grain unloaded from the ships, stored in the warehouses and dispatched to Rome. There were also guilds of corn merchants (*mercatores frumentarii*) and wine dealers (*negotiantes fori vinari*), and an important guild of bakers (*pistores*). One of the largest and

---

[91] A useful summary is *Econ. Survey of Anc., Rome*, V, pp. 236–52; cf. F.H. Wilson, 'Studies in the Social and Economic History of Ostia', *P.B.S.R*, XIII (1935), pp. 41–68, XIV (1938), pp. 152–62. Inscriptions in *CIL*, XIV, 1–2039, 4127–75, and *Suppl.* 4279–5411; those of the guilds in Waltzing, III, pp. 593–641. The results of the new excavations still await publication, save for the *Fasti Ostienses*. [R. Meiggs, *Roman Ostia*, 1960, chapters 10, 11, 13 and 14 should now be consulted.]

[92] *ILS*, 6171; unless the *navicularii maris Hadriatici* of *ILS*, 6146 (Ostia) and 7277 Rome) are an Ostian guild.

wealthiest of the guilds was the *fabri tignuarii*, which boasted 350 members in 198 A.D.; the building trade prospered in the growing port.

The great majority of the members of these guilds were, to judge by their names, freedmen or at any rate of servile ancestry, and the bulk of them were no doubt quite humble people. But not a few of the officers of the guilds were, if freedmen, elected to the order of the *seviri Augustales*, and free-born members even rose to the decurionate; thus P. Aufidius Fortis[93] and M. Junius Faustus,[94] both corn merchants, were adlected as decurions and became duumvirs, while M. Licinius Privatus,[95] *quinquennalis* of both the *pistores* and the *fabri tignuarii*, though he himself, being apparently a freedman, received only the *ornamenta decurionatus*, could boast himself the father and grandfather of decurions. The old families which had held office in the first century in the second admitted new men who had grown rich in trade and industry, or at any rate their sons, into the municipal aristocracy, and the Lucilii Gamalae even allowed a new man, Cn. Sentius Felix,[96] who was *quinquennalis* of the *curatores navium marinarum*, as well as patron of innumerable guilds, to adopt their heir. In the exceptional circumstances prevailing at Ostia the wealth accumulated in commerce and industry competed successfully with the wealth derived from land.

Palmyra[97] is first mentioned as a wealthy town in 41 B.C. It flourished greatly in the first and still more in the second and third centuries A.D., till in 273 it was sacked by Aurelian; it never recovered from this blow. The magnificent ruins, the great temple of Bel, the colonnaded streets, and the hundreds of splendid tombs, demonstrate that the city corporately and its leading citizens individually were immensely rich, and as the town occupies a small oasis surrounded by miles of desert its wealth must have been derived entirely from trade. Palmyra seems to have owed its great prosperity to the fact it was able to attract to itself the bulk of the very lucrative trade in luxury goods from the East to the Roman Empire, so far as this was carried over land and not by the direct sea route from India to the Red Sea ports and so to Alex-

[93] *CIL*, XIV, 4620.
[94] *I.L.S*, 6140.
[95] *I.L.S*, 6165.
[96] *I.L.S*, 6146.
[97] Février, *Essai sur l'histoire politique et économique de Palmyre*; J. Starcky, *Palmyre*.

E

andria. The alternative land routes further north through Mesopotamia were in the period of Palmyra's rise to greatness little frequented, because under the lax rule of the Parthian kings political conditions were anarchic, and merchants were subject to a multitude of arbitrary tolls by local dynasts. Later the frequent wars between Rome and Parthia in this area discouraged the revival of the northern routes. The Palmyrenes were able to bypass this troubled area by running caravans direct through the desert to Babylonia and even to the ports at the head of the Persian Gulf. [See also Chapter VII.]

A number of Greek and Aramaic inscriptions throw some light on this caravan trade.[98] The famous Palmyrene tariff shows how the city profited corporately by the tolls which it levied on goods passing through. Other inscriptions mention the caravans (συνοδίαι) of merchants, who travelled to and from Volagasias in Babylonia and Spasinou Charax on the Persian Gulf, where there were establishments of Palmyrene citizens, perhaps in the nature of 'factories'. They often honour prominent citizens for their services as caravan leaders (συνοδιάρχαι). The caravan leader travelled with the merchants, and probably supplied military protection as well as guiding the party and organising its march and provisioning it. He was apparently paid for his services, since one is specially praised for remitting to his clients 300 gold denarii of expenses,[99] and another, who 'always provided security for the caravans on all the occasions when he was caravan leader', earned additional gratitude because he spent large sums from his own pocket on this account,[100] It would seem natural that the men who undertook these duties were themselves merchants, and they are probably identical with the chief merchants (ἀρχέμποροι), who are occasionally mentioned performing similar functions. The council and people of Palmyra honoured one chief merchant who escorted a caravan on its homeward journey without charge out of his own pocket.[101] Another inscription which honours Septimus Vorodes,[102] *procurator ducenarius*, *iuridicus* of the city, and former general and controller of the market, and records that he escorted back the caravans at his own expense and was thanked

[98] The most important are O.G.I., 632, 633, 638, 641, 646, I.G.R., III, 1050, S. E. G., VII, 135, 139, 142, Le Bas-Waddington, 2603. These, with some other fragments, are discussed by Rostovtzeff in *Mélanges Glotz*, II, pp. 793 ff.

[99] I.G.R III, 1050.   [100] S.E.G, VII, 139.

[101] Le Bas-Waddington, 2603.   [102] O.G.I, 646.

by the chief merchants, might be interpreted as meaning that
Vorodes had on various occasions served as caravan leader and
had in that capacity earned the gratitude of their chief merchants.
In that case the caravan leader would be a separate person from
the head of the merchants whom he escorted, and need not have
been a merchant himself; the other chief merchant who brought
back his caravan free of charge would have taken command in
exceptional circumstances. It is however perhaps more probable
that Vorodes escorted back the caravans not as an ordinary
caravan leader but as general of the city, in which case the chief
merchants would be the leaders of the caravans. The city of
Palmyra maintained its own troops to police the deserts, and a
prominent citizen, who often served as caravan leader, is also
praised for his unremitting campaigns against the Bedouin as
general.[103]

The wealth of the Palmyrene aristocracy was undoubtedly
derived from trade; the magistrates and members of the council
will have been great merchants themselves, or at any rate acquired
their money by affording protection to merchants. Palmyra was,
however, it must be remembered, a very exceptional city. Petra,
which has left no inscriptions, may have been similarly constituted,
but in Damascus, with its large and fertile territory, the merchants
are likely to have been overshadowed by the landowners.

The far eastern trade continued under the later Empire, for
silk, pepper and other oriental luxuries were still demanded by
the aristocracy (cf. chapter VII). The long sea route continued to
enrich Alexandria, but the land traffic now passed through
Mesopotamia, where it was canalised through the towns of
Nisibis on the Persian side, Callinicum on the Roman.[104] In the
maritime traffic of the Mediterranean the imperial government
played a large part, carrying large quantities of foodstuffs and
other stores from the areas where they were produced to the two
capitals and to the ports serving the armies (*expeditionales portus*)
by the agency of the guilds of shippers (*corpora naviculariorum*).
These were organised on a diocesan basis; we hear of the guilds
of the Spains, of Africa, and of Oriens, or Syria, while the fleets of
Alexandria and Carpathus represent Egypt and Asiana.[105]

[103] *S.E.G*, VII, 139.
[104] *Cod. Just.*, IV, lxiii, 4.
[105] *Cod. Theod.*, XIII, v, 7, 8, 10, 14, 32, 36–7, ix, 3, 6.

The shippers have undergone a curious transformation since the Principate; they are now a hereditary body of landowners, or to speak more accurately, the *functio navicularia* was a servitude attached to the landed estates of *navicularii*, whether these passed to their sons or to outsiders by bequest, gift or dowry.[106] The government paid freight in gold and in corn (one solidus per 1000 modii and 4 per cent of the corn carried), and also granted remission of land tax in consideration of the repair of ships (at the rate of 50 *iuga* for a ship of 10,000 modii), but frankly admits that these payments and concessions did not cover costs.[107] The *navicularii* were expected to make up the deficit out of the profits of their landed estates, and in compensation received sundry privileges, of which the most important was exemption from curial duties.[108]

It can be conjectured how the *navicularii* of the earlier Empire had undergone this curious transformation. The imperial government had from an early date found it more economical to tempt shippers into the service of the *annona* and to induce other persons of substance to enter the business by grants of privileges rather than by high freights. Claudius had begun this policy;[109] the most important privilege, *vacatio muneris publici*, which included immunity from civic *munera*, later interpreted to include civic *honores* and membership of the curia, is first mentioned under Hadrian.[110] The effect of this would have been twofold. Shippers serving the *annona*, who had invested their profits in land, tended to stay in the service, and their sons after them, to keep free from curial duties. Landowners, who would otherwise have had to become decurions, put part of their money into shipping, in order to avoid being enrolled on the curia; Hadrian, Antoninus Pius and Marcus Aurelius had to check the abuse whereby decurions or potential decurions endeavoured to secure immunity by merely joining the shipper's guild without putting a substantial part of their fortune into shipping.[111] Thus shippers built up landed estates and landowners went into the shipping business,

[106] *Ibid.*, XIII, v, 3, 19, 20, 27, vi, *passim.*

[107] *Ibid.*, XIII, v, 7, 14.

[108] *Ibid.*. XIII, v, 5, 7, 16.

[109] Suet, *Claudius*, 18–9, Gaius, *Inst.*, I, 32, Ulpian, *Frag.*, III, 6, cf. Tac., *Ann.*, XIII, 51.

[110] *Dig.*, L, ii, 9, § 1, iv, 5, v, 3, vi, 1, 5, §§ 3–9, 13.

[111] *Dig.*, L, vi, 5, §§ 6–9.

and in both cases their heirs continued in the business to conserve
the privileges. In the third century the business ceased to be
profitable, largely no doubt because the government did not
adequately raise its freights to correspond with the inflationary
rise in prices, and the shippers would have been glad to withdraw
from the service. But the government had come to regard the
navicularia functio as a public duty, for which the privileges were an
adequate compensation, and insisted on the holders of privileged
land remaining in the service.

It was probably in this way that the *navicularii* became the
peculiar class which we find existing in the fourth century, large
landowners burdened with the duty of maintaining ships for the
service of the *annona* partly at their own cost. They appear to
have been men of considerable substance. In forming a new
guild for the diocese of Oriens the praetorian prefect of the East
was instructed to enrol members from classes ranging upwards
from decurions to *honorati* (ex provincial governors) and even to
invite senators to join.[112] The rate of remission of land tax also
implies large estates; for each ship of 10,000 modii (about 75 tons)
50 iuga were excused, which in Syria was equivalent to 1000 acres
of best arable land.

There were also substantial merchants engaged in private
maritime trade. The greatest of these were undoubtedly the
merchants of Alexandria,[113] and it is therefore particularly
unfortunate that we know so little of this great city. There are
very few inscriptions or papyri of Alexandrian provenance, and
we have to rely mainly on vague literary descriptions of the city.
From these however it is plain that Alexandria was the greatest
commercial city of the empire. It was in the first place the entrepôt
through which were exported to the rest of the empire the
products of Egypt, mainly the grain grown on its proverbially
fertile soil, but also manufactured goods, notably linen. Secondly
it controlled the long sea traffic with Arabia and India. The
merchandise was landed either at Clysma (Suez) and brought
thence by Trajan's canal and the Nile, or at one of the ports on
the west coast of the Red Sea, and carried by caravan to the Nile.
Thirdly the city had considerable industries of its own, notably
glass making, linen weaving, and the manufacture of papyrus, of

112 *Cod. Theod.*, XIII, v, 14.
113 *Econ. Survey of Anc. Rome*, II, pp. 335–46.

which it held a monopoly in the Roman world; oriental products were also made up into unguents and bottled for the western market.

Some Alexandrian merchants were very rich. One of them, Firmus, who is stated to have owned ships in the Indian trade and to have much influence with the Blemmyes of the eastern and southern deserts, probably in connection with the caravan trade with north eastern Africa, and is also reputed to have held vast stocks of glass and papyrus in his warehouses, led a revolt of Egypt against Aurelian. It is unfortunate that we know of him only from so unreliable a source as the Historia Augusta, for he is the only merchant known who aspired to political power, and must have been a very great man.[114] Hagiographical sources tell us something of later merchants. Rufinus records of one, who after his final voyage with a flotilla of ships from the Thebaid (where he had doubtless been picking up oriental goods), sold all his goods and gave to the poor, that his cargo was worth 20,000 solidi (about 275 lb. gold).[115] Another, a merchant in the Spanish trade, is said to have left to his heirs 5,000 solidi (nearly 70 lb. gold) in cash besides slaves and household effects.[116] Another, whose father had been a leading man of the city, had been reduced to poverty by shipwrecks; he was set on his feet again by a gift of 50 lb. gold from the patriarch, and soon became richer than his father.[117] These stories may be apocryphal, but they at least indicate the scale of the fortunes with which the merchant princes of Alexandria were popularly credited.

When one takes into account the very high purchasing power of gold—the annual ration allowance of a soldier, which provided him with an ample diet of bread, meat, wine and oil, was four to five solidi—these fortunes are considerable. But they do not compare with those of the great territorial magnates of the empire—the senators of Rome. According to a reliable historian, Olympiodorus, a senator of moderate standing drew an annual income from his estates of from 1,000 to 1,500 lb. gold, while the richest had as much as 4,000 lb., in addition to about a third as much again in kind.[118] Once again it appears that commerce could not compete with land as a source of wealth.

[114] Hist. Aug., Firmus, 3.
[115] Rufinus, Hist. Mon., xvi (=Palladius, Hist. Laus., 65).
[116] Palladius, Hist. Laus., 15.
[117] Joh. Moschus, Prat. Spir., 193.
[118] F. H. G., IV, p. 67 (frag. 44).

CHAPTER THREE

NUMISMATICS AND HISTORY

NUMISMATICS is a science in its own right. Coins deserve study both from the technical and the artistic point of view, and must be classified topographically and chronologically. Some of this work depends upon what may be called purely numismatic expertise, the knowledge of the technical processes of striking coins and of the artistic traditions of die-cutters. But as coins have almost invariably been issued by governments, and commonly bear emblems or inscriptions (or both) of the authority which issued them, their classification depends to a very large extent on historical data. Numismatists must in fact be historians to do their own work satisfactorily, and in practice the large majority of ancient numismatists have been historians by training before they specialised in the study of coins. No more eminent example could be found of a scholar who has combined the roles of an historian and a numismatist than Harold Mattingly, to whom these studies are dedicated.

Not only do numismatists have to be historians to enable them to carry out their specialised task of classifying coins. By the classification of coins they have made a substantial contribution to history, especially in the areas and periods where the literary evidence is scanty or untrustworthy. This is a commonplace which it is hardly necessary to illustrate in detail. To take one of the many fields where Mr. Mattingly has made a special contribution, the middle years of the third century A.D. are one of the darkest periods in the history of the Roman empire. There is virtually no evidence except for a few bald chronicles of a much later date and the biographies of the *Historia Augusta*, the date of whose composition is hotly disputed, but whose historical unreliability is generally agreed. Inscriptions of this period are rare; papyri are confined to Egypt. It is a study of the abundant coins that has established a fixed chronological framework for this dark period, and given valuable indications of the areas which the various ephemeral emperors or usurpers controlled.

In better-known periods of Roman imperial history also the coins have often added precision to our chronology, for instance by fixing the dates of imperial salutations, which can be linked to victories vaguely alluded to in the literary authorities. And not only has the imperial coinage proper made its contribution to chronology. The coins issued by the cities of the empire, often dated by a local era, and also carrying the emperor's head with an appropriate inscription, may yield valuable information. By correlating the evidence of a series of coins the local era can be determined, and this often commemorates an event of more than local importance, such as the annexation of a kingdom or the creation of a province. And once the local era is fixed, it can be used to give further precision to imperial chronology.

Imperial coins carry much more than the emperor's head and titulature. They commonly also bear a brief legend and a type which has a symbolical significance. Numismatists have studied these intensively, and an historian may perhaps be permitted to say that in his opinion they have sometimes attached an exaggerated importance to them. This is a question on which there is no literary evidence: this very fact is of some significance, for, if coin legends and types had possessed the importance that some numismatists attach to them, it would seem likely that some ancient author would have commented on them. In the absence of any allusion to the matter in ancient literature, one can judge only on grounds of general probability.

The legends and types were frequently varied. Some have obviously topical significance, and some, as Professor Grant has recently argued, were issued to commemorate the jubilee, centenary, or bi-centenary of some famous event. This would suggest that the authorities who chose the legends and types— and we do not know who they were—took an interest in the coins they produced. Some of the legends and types have a fairly obvious propaganda-value, celebrating imperial victories or benefactions. No doubt they were intended to be vehicles of propaganda, though their importance can be exaggerated. Latin legends meant nothing to the eastern half of the empire, where anyone who was literate could read Greek only. In the western provinces the great bulk of the population, who spoke Celtic, Iberian, Punic, or various Illyrian tongues, would be unaffected. The educated classes had something better to read than two or three words on a denarius. It would be a matter of some interest if numismatists could try to determine, on internal evidence, within the general probabilities of the situation, at what classes the propaganda on the coins was directed. It might be hazarded that a good many legends were produced for the benefit of the army, for the bulk of the coins must have been minted for issue as pay to the troops, and the common soldier generally would have been sufficiently literate in Latin to read the legend, but not sufficiently educated to read much else except army orders.

Types are a rather different problem. We have grown unaccustomed to visual symbolism, and find it difficult to interpret. In mainly illiterate periods visual symbols were more commonly used and more generally understood. It is nevertheless questionable whether the elaborate messages which some numismatists deduce from coin types were intended to be conveyed by them, and still more questionable whether they were generally understood. In the Middle Ages we are better informed by literary sources on the significance of pictorial representations; we know that the symbolism was simple to the point of crudity. We are hardly justified in postulating a very much greater subtlety in the average inhabitant of the Roman empire. In fact we happen to know from John of Ephesus[1] that in the sixth century the familiar personification of Constantinople on the solidi was taken for a figure of Aphrodite by the general public, and, when Tiberius substituted a cross, it was inferred that his predecessor Justin II had been a cryptopagan.

If a modern analogy is to be sought for the varying types and legends of Roman imperial coins it is perhaps to be found in the similar variations in the postage stamps of many modern countries other than our own. These often show a certain propagandist tendency, depicting the famous men of the country concerned, its artistic monuments, or its principal industries. They are also sometimes topical, advertising congresses, fairs, and the like, or commemorative of great events in national history. They throw a sidelight on the history of the period, but they mainly reflect the mentality of the post-office officials. No serious historian would use them as a clue which revealed changes of government policy, even if other evidence were totally lacking. It would be better if numismatists took the coin types and legends less seriously, and

[1] iii. 14 (p. 192 in R. Payne Smith, *Ecclesiastical History of John, Bishop of Ephesus*).

if historians of the empire, instead of building fantastic history upon them, frankly admitted that the political history of periods when coins are the sole evidence is irrecoverable, apart from the bare bones of the chronology of the reigns, the areas which the various emperors effectively controlled, and any salient events which the coins directly celebrate.

The coins might be expected to throw some light on constitutional problems. Here again we are handicapped by an almost total lack of literary evidence. No ancient author says a word on any of the constitutional problems involved—whether coinage was regarded as a privilege of sovereign states, or how far politically subject communities were allowed by their suzerains to issue coins, or again, what body within a state authorised or controlled the issue of coins. This last point is of course of particular interest, under the Roman empire, where one would expect that the rights of the princeps, on the one hand, and those of the senate and people on the other would have been defined; similar questions arise in the late Republic on the rights of the government at Rome, and those of proconsuls in the provinces. There is one inscription,[2] the famous Athenian decree enforcing the exclusive use of the Athenian currency throughout the empire, which bears on the constitutional aspect of coinage. There is a decree of the city of Olbia,[3] ordering the exclusive use of Olbian coins in the city and regulating the exchange of foreign coins, one clause in the agreement between the city of Smyrna and the troops and civilians in Magnesia,[4] declaring that 'they shall accept in Magnesia the legal currency of the city', and one clause in a letter of Antiochus VII to Simon, High Priest of the Jews.[5] Finally there is a letter[6] from an official to Apollonius, the finance minister of Ptolemy II, raising questions about the new currency which was henceforth to be the exclusive legal tender in Egypt, and the calling in and restriking of old and foreign coins. No other treaty or decree mentions the question: none, for instance, of the laws or *senatus consulta* conferring freedom on, or ratifying treaties with, *civitates liberae* or *foederatae* mentions coinage as a right granted or withheld.

Prima facie this would suggest that the Greeks and Romans

[2] *A.T.L.* ii. D14 (=*S.E.G.* x. 25).   [3] *Syll.*[3] 218.
[4] *O.G.I.S.* 229, line 55.   [5] 1 Macc. xv. 6.
[6] *P. Cairo Zen*, 59021 (=Hunt and Edgar, *Select Papyri*, 409).

attached little importance to coinage as a mark of sovereignty. It may perhaps be inferred that little if any fiscal profit was derived from the mint, but this is a question which will be more conveniently discussed later with the economic aspects of numismatics.

In these circumstances the evidence of the coins themselves is difficult to interpret. Greek coins are usually stamped with the name of the issuing authority in the genitive, 'of the Syracusans' or 'of King Antigonus' for instance. This would seem to imply that they were in some rather vague and confused way thought to belong to the government which issued them, although of course individual coins were recognized as the property of their owners. The official who wrote to the finance minister, Apollonius, seems to have had this idea at the back of his mind. Owing to administrative bungling, merchants who had brought foreign gold coins with them were neither allowed to use them in Egypt nor were given facilities for having them restruck into Ptolemaic coins. The writer of the letter thought that the king's revenues were suffering loss, 'for I think that it is advantageous that as much gold as possible should be imported from abroad, and the king's currency should be always good and new, without any expense being incurred by him'. Actually Ptolemy II gained nothing— except perhaps a minting charge—by reminting gold coins imported by merchants and giving them back to them in the shape of Ptolemaic coins, but in some way it was felt that King Ptolemy was richer if there were more coins about inscribed 'of King Ptolemy'. It may be suspected that a similar idea underlay the Athenian decree. It was no doubt convenient for trade and imperial finance to have a uniform currency throughout the empire; otherwise the Athenian people gained nothing by calling in the issues of the subject cities and giving them back as Athenian tetradrachms (deducting a small minting charge); but they may have felt richer when all the silver circulating in the empire was labelled with their name and emblem.

From the coins themselves it would have been impossible to deduce the passage of this decree, as the issues of the allied cities of Athens cannot on purely numismatic evidence be sufficiently closely dated. There appears to be no distinction between 'subject', or 'tributary', and 'free' or 'naval' allies of Athens in the matter of issuing coins. In later leagues federal arrangements are sometimes reflected in the coinage. In the Achaean League, for instance, which, as we know from Polybius,[7] had a common standard of weights and measures and currency, the coins are all of the same standard and are labelled 'of the Achaean Patreans', 'of the Achaean Sicyonians', and the like. Here the coins enable us to say that the currency was not issued from a federal mint, but by the constituent cities of the league at an agreed standard. The coins enable us also to say that certain other leagues, the Lycian for instance, followed the same practice, whereas in others, like the Aetolian, no uniform currency was issued.

In the Hellenistic kingdoms the coins might be hoped to illuminate the vexed question of the relation between the royal government and the cities which the kings ruled or controlled with varying degrees of strictness, or to which they granted varying degrees of freedom, or which they recognized as free in varying degrees. It is in practice very difficult to correlate the numismatic with the literary and epigraphic evidence. The kings issued their own coins, bearing their heads and labelled with their names, from their own mints in various cities; these are identified by mint marks, or by stylistic or typological evidence. The royal mints, together with those of a few great independent cities, such as Rhodes, provided all the gold and larger silver pieces used in the Hellenistic world. Some cities, such as Ephesus, known to have been *de facto* subject to a king, issued silver coins which bear no allusion to the fact, as if they were entirely independent. And under the later Seleucids, from Antiochus IV onwards, hybrid coins, small silver and copper, probably used for local transactions, were issued by a large number of cities, labelled 'of the Hieropolitans on the Pyramus', and so forth, but bearing on the other side the king's portrait; in such cases it may be inferred that a city was licensed by the king to issue small change for local use: Antiochus VII wrote to Simon, High Priest of the Jews, 'I have allowed you to strike special issues as currency for your country'. But who provided the bullion and paid for the minting of coins labelled 'of King Antiochus: of the Sidonians'? Normally the king's head on these civic issues seems to be a mere courtesy, abandoned when the cities achieved independence—and sometimes began to issue larger silver pieces for use in foreign trade, or to pay mercenaries.

[7] ii. 37, 10.

Under the Roman empire the inscriptions and types of coins are equally ambiguous. The main currency of Asia Minor and Syria consisted of drachmae (and multiples), which passed as denarii, labelled 'of the Ephesians', 'of the Caesareans by the Argaeus' and 'of the Antiochenes'. These coins bear the emperor's head with name and titles in the nominative, sometimes the names of the proconsuls (of Asia) or legates (of Cappadocia or Syria), more often those of the local magistrates. It is generally, and probably rightly, assumed that these silver coins, which are to all appearances exactly analogous to the bronze coins issued by countless eastern cities, were in fact not issued by the cities of Ephesus, Caesarea, and Antioch, but at Ephesus, Caesarea, and Antioch by the imperial government. To add piquancy to the problem, similar bronze coins issued at Antioch are marked S(enatus) C(onsulto): it is often believed that the Roman senate should not have interfered in an imperial province. May it not be that no subtle constitutional point is involved, but that the staff of the imperial mint at Antioch, aware that bronze coins issued in the West always bore the letters SC, thought that this was a standard mark for imperial bronze?

Coins yield a good deal of political information, but their primary purpose was after all to be a medium of exchange. It might therefore be expected that they would be useful evidence for economic history. Here again we are hampered by the fact that there were practically no ancient economists—Xenophon's *Vectigalia*, and the Aristotelian Economics are almost the only works which deal primarily with the subject—and that ancient historians, lawyers, and orators rarely stopped to consider economic affairs. We have scarcely any information on some very elementary questions, such as where and how governments obtained the bullion needed for their mints, the organisation and technique of mints, and how governments put the coins they struck into circulation. Some states, like Athens, had silver mines in their territory, but even here we do not know precisely how the silver got to the mint. It is probable that the lessees of the mines had to pay 5 per cent of the gross yield of silver to the state by way of royalty.[8] The remaining 95 per cent of the silver must have belonged to the lessee, but he presumably got it minted— perhaps he was obliged to do so, though we have no evidence on

[8] Suidas, s.v. ἀγράφων μετάλλων δίκη.

this point, and perhaps he paid some commission on this. Most of the coins struck by the Athenian mint would thus have passed into circulation by the lessees of the mines spending them. A small proportion would belong to the state, and would pass into circulation by public expenditure—pay to magistrates, soldiers, and so forth. How cities like Corinth and Aegina, which had no domestic source of silver, produced their large currencies is unknown. It can only be conjectured that foreign currency or bullion received by merchants or shippers in return for exports or services was handed in to the mint and struck as Corinthian or Aeginetan staters.

By the second century B.C. the Roman republic owned important silver mines in Spain, and the treasury, Pliny[9] tells us, was well stocked with silver in bar—some presumably paid by the *publicani* who worked the mines, some the product of the war indemnities levied from Carthage, Philip, and Antiochus; these foreign silver coins were presumably melted down. By the end of Tiberius' reign[10] most important gold or silver mines had become state property by confiscation, but the method of their exploitation remains mysterious. Where they were still leased to *publicani*, it may be guessed that the lessees paid part of the bullion extracted to the state under their contract; but we do not know what happened to the rest. In the *metallum Vipascense*[11] it was possible for a contractor to buy a shaft outright from the *fiscus* for cash, or to work a shaft on a 50:50 basis; we are not told what happened to the silver which the contractor extracted under the former arrangement, nor to the half share of the contractor under the latter. In the fourth century A.D. gold-washers had to pay the state eight scruples per annum and sell the rest to the treasury;[12] we are not told in what currency the state paid for the gold, but we may guess that it was in bronze. It is, however, probable that most of the bullion used in the Roman mints consisted of the old coins received in taxation and melted down; this was certainly the case under the later empire, when the solidi received in taxation were melted down in the province in which they were collected, and sent up to the treasury in bar.[13] The treasury also usually

[9] *N.H.* xxxiii. 55.
[10] Cf. Suet. *Tib.* 49. 2, Tac. *Ann.* vi. 19.
[11] Bruns, *Fontes*[7], 113.
[12] *C.Th.* x. xix. 3.
[13] *C.Th.* xii, vi, 12, 13(=*C.J.* X. lxxii. 5).

reserved to itself gold and silver plate which formed part of confiscated properties (*bona vacantia, caduca, damnatorum*), even when the rest of the property was granted to petitioners.[14]

The mint also occasionally received windfalls of bullion, like the Dacian hoard of gold which Trajan captured, or the vast quantities of gold which Constantine confiscated from the pagan temples, where they had for centuries been sterilized in the form of dedications and cult-statues.

On the organisation of the mints and the technique of minting numismatists have given the historian much useful information derived from the study of the coins. There are, however, unsolved problems which a more intensive study might solve. Do the fifth-century imperial coins produced at the mint of Cyzicus throw any light on the curious statement of Sozomen[15] that there was a large number of persons resident with their wives and children in that town, divided into two bodies by the order of earlier emperors, who rendered each year to the government a fixed payment, the one of military tunics, and the other of freshly minted solidi? This is a curious description of a mint. Do the *officina* marks yield any information? Another point on which numismatists might be helpful to historians is in working out the theoretical weight of imperial coins. Much useful and intricate work has been done by numismatists on the various weight standards used by Greek cities and Hellenistic kings, but imperial coins, especially from the third century onwards, have not attracted much interest. From literary evidence[16] it is clear that from the first century to the sixth the directors of the mints worked on the basis that a pound of silver or gold was divided into so many coins; the pound of gold into 45 aurei from Nero's time, into 72 solidi from Constantine's time, the pound of silver into 84 denarii before Nero and 96 after him. Coins bear this out; some of Diocletian's silver is marked XCVI (96 to the pound), and some of his gold O.or $\equiv$ (70 or 60 to the pound). Normally, then, a coin should ideally weigh an integral part of a (Roman) pound. The surviving specimens do not, because they are worn, corroded or clipped. It is no easy matter to work out what an ancient coin was supposed to weigh, and it involves some statis-

[14] *C.Th.* x. ix. 2; x. 21.
[15] *Hist. Eccles.* v. 15.
[16] E.g. Pliny, *N.H.* xxxiii, 47; *C.Th.* xv. ix. 1.

tical skill: it is a task which only numismatists are qualified to perform. It would be useful to the economic historian studying the inflationary movement of the third century A.D. to know the progressive reductions in weight of the denarius, and to the historian of the fourth century A.D. to know what the silver issues in their bewildering variety were supposed to weigh—he only knows from the Theodosian Code[17] that some were 60 to the pound. Another and even more laborious service would be to work out more precisely the rate of debasement in silver content of the third-century denarius: this would involve many chemical and physical tests.

Another type of information which economic historians would greatly appreciate, and which numismatists alone might—with some difficulty, and at the cost of much work—be able to provide, is the relative volume of the various issues. This is admittedly a very tricky business. Some ancient coins are discovered in scientific excavations; the reports unfortunately do not always give the numbers of the coins discovered. Statistics of excavations, when due allowance has been made for the character of the site and the date of its occupation (often deduced from the coins, a somewhat unsafe guide, as some coins had very long lives), should, if correlated and consolidated, give some clue. Other ancient coins are found in hoards. Numismatists have devoted much useful study to these, and historians greatly appreciate the results achieved. What they would greatly value would be more comprehensive books, dealing with special periods or areas, analysing the information obtainable from all known hoards. But the vast bulk of ancient coins are in museums or private collections, or in the hands of dealers. Their history is usually quite unknown, and we cannot tell how they have survived. In special circumstances it may be that an issue which was once common is now represented by a few specimens only: certain issues may have been effectively called in and reminted, or disappeared under Gresham's law. It is on the whole probable that a smaller proportion of gold has survived than of silver, and of silver than of bronze, because the demand for the precious metals by jewellers would cause gold and silver coins to be melted down. It is likewise probable that older issues have survived in less bulk than more recent issues. It is, however, broadly true, I believe, that coins known from

[17] xv. ix. 1.

ancient literary sources to have circulated in large numbers—darics, Athenian tetradrachms, Alexanders, Roman imperial aurei and denarii, later imperial solidi—are still the commonest. It therefore seems on the whole likely that the number of surviving coins bears some rough relation to the number originally issued.

On the relative scarcity or commonness of different issues of ancient coins at the present day numismatists give virtually no information to historians—with the honourable exception of *Roman Imperial Coinage*, which under Mr. Mattingly's editorship has made a beginning by roughly classifying each issue as 'common', 'scarce', 'rare', 'very rare', and the like. Collectors and museums naturally wish to acquire a few specimens of every type, and are on the whole more interested in rare than in common coins. The catalogues which they issue usually give no clue whether a given type is a unique or very rare specimen, or can be picked up in half the junk shops of Europe or the Levant. Dealers' sale catalogues—a form of literature which ancient historians can hardly be expected to read—stress the rarities, and probably quite ignore the common types. But collectors and museum officials—and most numismatists are one or the other —know the market, and could presumably give rough estimates, which, however rough, would assist the economic historian. If I may ask a few specimen questions which would interest me; could it be estimated how many aurei and denarii were annually minted in the reigns of the successive emperors from Augustus to Septimius Severus relatively to the number of aurei and antoniniani (or denarii) minted annually from the reign of Caracalla to that of Aurelian? Was there, as the literary sources would suggest, an abnormally heavy output of aurei in the latter part of Trajan's reign? Again, what was the relative volume of Diocletian's gold and silver issues to those of Constantine? On historical grounds I should conjecture that Diocletian's issues were meagre, and that large quantities of gold and silver only began to be minted in the last years of Constantine, and under his sons. But can this conjecture be tested by the numismatic evidence? Or again did silver and bronze coins virtually cease to be issued after A.D. 395 and did solidi continue to be minted in great abundance?

Coins when minted have to be put into circulation. When privately owned bullion was brought or sent in for minting, the coins would naturally be issued to the owner of the bullion. We

F

have no direct record of this procedure, and indeed in 369 Valens ordered that if any private person was so presumptuous as voluntarily to offer his own gold to the mint, it was to be confiscated; five years later he revoked this (to us) extraordinary ruling retrospectively and allowed privately owned gold already received to be minted and issued to the owner less a charge of two ounces in the pound (one-sixth).[18] It would seem, then, that the imperial government in the fourth century A.D. normally refused to mint privately owned gold for the owner; he could, however, use it to pay his taxes, or sell it to the treasury for debased denarii. For silver the practice may have been different. Otherwise it is difficult to explain a rather curious phenomenon that numismatists have noted, that a very large number of silver coins of the fourth century minted in Gaul or even farther afield have been found in the neighbourhood of the silver mines of the Mendips. Either the mines were privately exploited, or, if they were state owned, the miners were entitled to keep a proportion of the silver extracted; the miners must have sent their own silver to the nearest mint (which was a long way away) and got it back (doubtless less minting charges) in coin.

For the coins minted from publicly owned bullion (either the product of mines, or confiscated plate, or coins received in taxation and melted down) we have no direct evidence, but, from what we know of the very simple fiscal methods of ancient governments, it is likely that most gold and silver coins were paid directly as wages and salaries to government employees, to contractors for services rendered, or to merchants for goods bought. The location of a mint, incidentally, has no necessary relation to the place where the coins were put into circulation, though mints, under the later empire at any rate, were mostly sited near the main centres of payment: one may note the concentration of mints at Constantinople and nearby (Nicomedia and Cyzicus), where there was, besides the court, a heavy concentration of officials and troops.

The circulation of the small change, of bronze, copper, or brass, presents more of a problem. Here there is a curious anomaly, which no numismatist or historian has seriously attempted to solve, that under the principate imperial (or public) mints provided the small change in the Latin-speaking provinces

[18] *C.Th.* ix. xxi. 7, 8.

of the empire, whereas in the Greek-speaking provinces city mints did so. That the imperial government made no attempt to enforce a monopoly of small change in the East is all the more surprising, because the coins of these low denominations were not intrinsically worth their face value, were in fact a token coinage, and therefore would have provided a profit for the mint. How the imperial small change was put into circulation in the West is quite unknown; we can only conjecture that money-changers bought it (with silver and gold coins). In the East the city governments minted copper, and presumably sold it to the local money-changers, who often were concessionaries enjoying a local monopoly, for imperial silver and gold, thereby making a profit for civic funds. There was, as far as we can tell, no minting profit on the gold and silver coins. This is certainly true of the later Roman empire, when the treasury was equally willing to receive gold taxes in bullion by the pound or in solidi[19] (which were weighed to make sure that they were 72 to the pound, and after A.D. 366 were melted down on receipt), and always dealt in silver by the pound. Diocletian's tariff[20] fixes the same price (in denarii) for gold in bar or coin.

The progressive debasement of the denarius (and of the antoninianus) from the period of the Severi gradually killed both the imperial bronze and copper and the civic issues. As the denarius itself became a silver-plated copper coin worth about 0.5 per cent of its second-century value, smaller change became unnecessary. When Constantine re-established a gold and silver currency, the degenerate descendants of the denarius continued to be struck (in vast quantities) by imperial mints. How these coins passed into circulation is again unknown, but probably once more mainly through money-changers: we know that at Rome the duty of the official guild of money-changers (*collectarii*) was to buy solidi from the public, at the market rate, with copper coins which they bought from a local treasury (the *arca vinaria*) with these same solidi, at a rate fixed by the government.[21] It is probable that the imperial government in the fourth century pursued a deliberate policy of buying in solidi with token money, and that this may account for the extraordinary inflation of the

[19] *C.Th.* xii. vii. 1.
[20] xxx. 1.
[21] Symmachus, *Relatio* 29.

denarius, which in Egypt exchanged with the solidus at figures like 30,000,000 to one. But this is highly speculative.[22]

How far ancient states, in particular the Roman empire, had any currency policy is very difficult to divine. The coins themselves are almost the only evidence, but great caution is needed in building any theories upon them. On the surviving evidence the economic knowledge of the ancients was childish,[23] and it is safer to postulate that the government acted upon very crude notions, e.g. that if the silver content of a denarius was diluted by 10 per cent alloy, the mint could issue 10 per cent more denarii to the pound of silver, and that the public would not notice the difference. A very eminent scholar has advanced the theory that Trajan debased the denarius, because he had minted a vast number of aurei, and thereby was disturbing the established 25:1 relation of the denarius to the aureus. This implies that Trajan or his *a rationibus* was aware of the quantity-theory of currency, which is incredible. It is, I suggest, more probable that Trajan first debased the denarius a little to get more denarii for his wars, and then, having acquired the Dacian gold, issued large numbers of aurei in *congiaria* and donatives and to pay for public works. Numismatists could perhaps settle this matter, if Trajanic denarii and aurei are sufficiently closely datable.

We may now turn to the coins when they had passed into circulation. It would be convenient for economic historians to know what the coins which we possess were called in antiquity. The question is not as simple as it sounds, for the terminology of money is and always has been complex, and very few ancient coins bear any mark of value. Even in present-day England we keep our accounts in £ s. d., but we handle and speak of half-crowns and florins as well, and doctors make up their bills in a purely notional unit of currency called a guinea: future numismatists may be puzzled to identify the twentieth-century guinea, alluded to in the literary sources. In a rather more backward country, Egypt, the current terminology is even more complex and irrational. Officially accounts are kept in the £E, which is divided into 1,000 milliemes: nothing smaller than a 5-millieme

[22] See ch. IX.

[23] For the fourth century A.D. read the naïve remarks of the *Anonymus de rebus bellicis*, ii. 1 (critical text, translation and notes in E. A. Thompson, *A Roman Reformer and Inventor*).

piece is, I believe, now minted. In ordinary speech the common terms are the pound (*Arabice* guinea) and an officially non-existent unit of 10 milliemes called by Europeans a *piastre* and by Egyptians *gursh* (the words *gursh tarifa* rather confusingly mean 5 milliemes in Arabic). This unit is also a coin (marked 10 milliemes). The coins marked 20, 50, and 100 milliemes are commonly known in Arabic as half a franc, a shilling, and half a *real* respectively.

The situation in some periods of antiquity was fully as complicated as this, with the additional difficulty that most of the coins had no names or numbers on them. The Romans during the first two centuries of the principate (perhaps later, but evidence is lacking) usually kept their accounts in sestertii, though the commonest coins were the denarius (=4 sestertii) and a gold coin (=100 sestertii). The denarius was usually known in the East as a drachma (often for old times' sake called an Attic drachma as late as the early fourth century A.D.).[24] The gold coin was usually known in Latin as an aureus, in Greek as a χρυσοῦς, in Aramaic as a denarius: this name continued to be applied to the standard imperial gold coin in Semitic tongues, being transferred to the solidus, and eventually to the Arabic gold dinar.[25] Numismatists naturally use the Latin terms, and long ago identified the relevant coins.

With the third century difficulties arise: the name and face value of the coins which numismatists call 'antoniniani', and of the coins marked XX.1, issued by Aurelian and his successors, are a matter of conjecture. From the reign of Constantine onwards the terminology of the standard gold pieces is undisputed: 'solidus' in Latin, (νόμισμα or ὁλοκοττινός) in Greek, 'denarius' in Syriac. The silver is a complete tangle, and numismatists have not helped matters by assigning to the various denominations names, some of which are certainly wrong and others conjectural. There was a silver coin called the 'milliarense', and that is all we know about it.[26] There was no coin called 'siliqua'. The siliqua

[24] *I.G.R.* i. 588; iii. 1047; iv. 182, 842, 872, 887, 1185, 1360. Eusebius, *Hist. Eccles.* ix. 8, 4. *P. Oslo*, iii. 83. *P.S.I.* 965. *P. Oxy.* 2113.

[25] This is the practice of the Aramaic inscriptions of Palmyra, of the *Lex Syro-Romana F.I.R.A.* 112, 759–98) and of Syriac hagiographers.

[26] The *milliarense* is known from (*a*) *Not. Dig. Or.* xiii. 30 and *Occ.* xi. 96 (cf. *C.Th.* VI, XXX. 7, *brevis* 10=*C.J.* XII, xxxvii, 7); (*b*) Marcus Diaconus, *Vita Porphyrii*, 100; (*c*) Johannes Moschus, *Prat. Spir.* 185; (*d*) the metrologists *passim* (see the indexes of F. Hultsch, *Metrologicorum Scriptorum Reliquiae*). (*a*) show that in the *officium* of the *comes sacrarum largitionum* there were *scrinia aureae massae, auri ad responsum,*

(Greek κεράτιον) was an accounting unit, and meant one twenty-fourth of a solidus:[27] thus a semissis=12 siliquae; a tremissis in the early and middle fourth century=9 siliquae, from Theodosius onwards=8 siliquae;[28] and a worn or clipped solidus was spoken of (in Egypt at any rate) as a solidus *minus* X siliquae (νόμισμα παρὰ X κεράτια). The bronze is an even worse tangle. Numismatists have dubbed the largest Diocletianic coin a 'follis'. What little evidence there is suggests that it was known as a 'nummus' and tariffed at 25 'denarii communes'.[29] The meaning of the term 'follis' is quite obscure; it seems in fact to have meant quite different coins (or units of account) in different provinces at different periods. The modern numismatic terms, *Aes* I, II, III, IV, are useful and not misleading for the fourth-century coins, various denominations of which were known in Latin as denarii or nummi (perhaps folles) according to local usage.

We are so used to the fixed relationship of £ *s. d.* that we find it rather difficult to believe that different denominations of one currency have not always been exchanged at fixed ratios. The literary evidence, though scanty, strongly suggests that for two centuries and more, from Augustus to Septimius Severus, a standard relation was generally accepted between the aureus, denarius, sestertius, and as (1 aureus=25 denarii; 1 denarius=4 sestertii=16 asses). But even in this monetarily stable period the papyri have revealed strange complications in the currency of

---

ab argento, a miliarensibus, and *a pecuniis*. These probably mean gold bullion, gold coin, silver bullion, silver coin, copper coin. (*b*) records a transaction in which the *milliarense* seems to be a coin of low value, probably bronze. (*c*) uses the word for a Persian (probably silver) coin current at Nisibis. (*d*) tell us that the *milliarense* was so called because it was used to pay *milites* (this is the favourite view), or because it was equal to 1,000 obols, or because it was equal to 1/1,000 lb. gold. All three statements are patently 'etymological', and probably equally worthless.

[27] My numismatic friends are shocked by this statement, but I can find no allusion to the siliqua or (κεράτιον) as a coin in the legal texts (*C.Th.* XII, iv, 1; Theod. *Nov.* xxii, 2,=*C.J.* X, xxxvi, 1; Val. *Nov.* xv, xxxiv; Maj. *Nov.* vii; *C.J.* VIII, xii, 1; IV, xxxii, 26), where it always must or may mean $\frac{1}{24}$ solidus; nor in the metrologists (Hultsch, indexes *s.v.* 'siliqua', κεράτιον), where it is always a weight, $\frac{1}{6}$ scruple; nor in the papyri, where κεράτιον is always an accounting unit, $\frac{1}{24}$ solidus (see West and Johnson, *Currency in Roman and Byzantine Egypt*, p. 129). As the pound of silver was officially valued sometimes at 4 and sometimes at 5 solidi, a silver coin could not have represented $\frac{1}{24}$ solidus (see p. 204).

[28] There is no doubt that the later coin which weighed one-third of a solidus was called a tremissis. That the older coins of 1½ scruples were also called tremisses is proved by the *Liber de Asse*, 16 (Hultsch ii, 74).

[29] [See now ch. XVI.]

Egypt.[30] Here the standard coin was called an (Alexandrian) tetradrachm, though equal in value with an (Attic) drachma (in other words a denarius); there were also smaller denominations, whose names and values the combined efforts of papyrologists and numismatists have failed to discover. Accounts were kept in drachmae and obols. In the normal Greek usage 6 obols went to a drachma, and in some accounts this rule is observed; but in others the drachma is reckoned to be worth 7 or $7\frac{1}{4}$ obols. The whole question is exceedingly complex, but the explanation would seem to be that, if someone wanted to buy a tetradrachm from a money-changer, he had to pay 28 or 29 copper obols, according to market rates, and not 24. Some clerks used the term obol as a notional unit of account ($\frac{1}{6}$ drachma or $\frac{1}{24}$ tetradrachm); some meant by an obol the actual copper piece, which in practice went 28 or 29 to the tetradrachm. A drachma similarly could be an accounting unit (4 to the tetradrachm) or 6 copper obols or a larger copper coin tariffed at 6 obols.

After the great inflation of the mid-third century A.D, the currency remained in a chaotic condition for about two centuries. Numismatists have attempted to work out neat systems of Diocletian's and Constantine's coinages, whereby one aureus or solidus was divided into so many silver coins (which they call siliquae, milliarensia, etc.), and one silver coin into so many copper coins (which they call folles, denarii, etc.). There is very good evidence that in fact there was no fixed relation between gold, silver, and copper coins, but that they exchanged at fluctuating rates according to the market, that is, what a money-changer was prepared to offer on a particular day in a particular place.[31]

Another interesting problem, to which numismatists have contributed much by the study of hoards, is that of the life of an ancient coin. This, of course varied greatly between types of coin. Some became 'favourites' in certain areas, and continued to circulate for centuries, and when the originals wore out, copies were struck: a famous modern parallel is the Maria Theresa dollar, which is still legal tender in Abyssinia. Where and when and by whom these copies were struck only numismatists can tell us, and with only provenance and typological development to guide

[30] West and Johnson, op. cit., ch. 5; cf. also *Class. Phil.* 1949, p. 236; 1951, p. 34; 1952, p. 216; and *Chron. d'Égypte*, 1953, p. 356.
[31] P. 204.

them they cannot always speak with assurance. A Palmyrene inscription[32] strongly suggests, if it does not prove, that beyond the eastern frontier the 'ancient gold denarius' (the pre-Neronian aureus) was still in A.D. 193 a 'favourite coin' which Persian merchants readily accepted, perhaps at a premium, and that Palmyrene merchants still held large stocks of them. This throws some light on the curious fact that Julio-Claudian coins are far commoner in India than later ones, and also shows how dangerous it is to argue from dated coins the dates of economic events; by themselves the coins suggest that the import of Indian goods into the Roman empire fell off markedly from about A.D. 60, but the trade may have gone on for centuries, and the old coins have been used to pay for the surplus of imports over exports. The same considerations apply to dating political events by numismatic evidence. I doubt, for instance, whether the coins will yield much evidence on the date when Britain ceased to be effectively a part of the Roman empire, until we find out a great deal more not only about the volume of coins of various denominations which the imperial mints were issuing in the relevant period, but also by what channels these coins passed into circulation, and what the 'currency habits', if I may so call them, of the public in the western dioceses of the empire were. Did people prefer old coins, which were of better quality than the new ones, either for that reason or from force of habit? Some constitutions of the Theodosian Code indicate that very occasionally the imperial government enacted that certain old (probably bronze) issues were no longer legal tender.[33] But the numismatic evidence accords with all we know about the inability of the imperial government to enforce its laws. A numismatist has recently very convincingly demonstrated that not only Diocletianic 'folles' but second-century sestertii and dupondii were still circulating in quantity in Italy and Africa in the latter part of the fifth century A.D., being tariffed by money-changers at sums like 80 or 40 contemporary 'nummi' or 'denarii'.

Coins can also yield useful information about trade. When, for instance, Roman imperial coins are found in large numbers in India, it is legitimate to deduce that by direct or indirect channels merchants in the Roman empire bought Indian goods, and that

[32] *C.I.S.* ii, 3, i, 3948 (Greek text in *I.G.R.* iii, 1050).
[33] *C.Th.* IX, xxiii, 1, 2.

the goods exported from India to the Roman empire exceeded in value the goods exported from the Roman empire to India. In this case direct trade is attested by literary and epigraphic sources, and the period when trade flourished by other objects of Roman provenance than coins found in India. The coins are in fact not very useful evidence of either the date or the channels of trade; 'favourite' coins, as I said before, might have a life of three or four centuries. Such coins might circulate for a long while over a wide area, so that, for instance, fifty Tiberian aurei used by a Palmyrene merchant to pay an Arab or Persian merchant at Spasinou Charax under Septimius Severus might subsequently be used by the heirs of that Persian or Arab merchant to pay for goods from India in A.D. 300.

The coins attest only unbalanced trade. The finds of Athenian tetradrachms over a vast area prove (what we know already from Xenophon's *Vectigalia*[34]) that the Athenians paid for imports from all quarters mainly in silver coins, of which they produced a surplus from the Laurium mines. These Attic tetradrachms were 'favourites' which circulated or were imitated in many remote parts, such as Arabia. The coins may also reflect other types of transaction than trade. The Roman emperors from time to time paid subsidies to various barbarian kings beyond the Rhine and the Danube in denarii, aurei, or later in solidi. These subsidies were fairly regular, and at times very large—between 443 and 450 the government of Theodosius II paid Attila altogether 18,600 lb. gold, or nearly 1,280,000 solidi, apart from ransoms for Roman prisoners. Many of these solidi were no doubt melted down into jewellery or plate; others returned to the empire in payment for Roman luxury goods, others may have been paid to merchants within and beyond Attila's empire. Solidi found in Norway do not necessarily attest Roman trade with that country.

If I may attempt to sum up my general conclusions, one would be that numismatists by pursuing their own science for its own sake by their normal methods produce evidence which may be and often is useful to historians. Professor Grant's discovery or identification of the coins of many Caesarian, triumviral, or Augustan colonies and municipia is a striking instance of this. But the supreme example is Mr. Mattingly's multifarious work. I can cite only a few examples, such as the correct dating of the

[34] iii, 2.

earliest Roman denarii, the five volumes of the British Museum Catalogue of Roman Imperial Coins from Augustus to Elagabalus, and six volumes of *Roman Imperial Coinage*, issued under his editorship, which so far classify the coins of the period from the beginning of the Principate to the accession of Diocletian, and from the accession of Valentinian I to the death of Theodosius II. To fix the exact date and mint of any coin, where this is possible, may well provide important historical evidence. Failing this, to range issues in chronological sequence and assign them to possible mints may be useful: but historians would like to know when the evidence is stylistic (and therefore to some degree subjective) or when it is derived from overstrikes, die-identities, mintmarks, or other technical data which yield objectively certain results. Above all historians appreciate catalogues which tabulate all available information.

If numismatists wish further to assist historians, I would suggest that they pay less attention to the political interpretation of the coins. In this once neglected sphere a vast amount of valuable work has been done by numismatists in the last thirty years, but latterly the value of the numismatic evidence has tended to be overstrained, and its interpretation has become over-subtle. I would suggest that if they wish to move out of their own field, they could do immensely valuable work for the economic historian by giving him such information as I have suggested above— estimating the relative volume of issues and the life of the various coins, investigating ancient numismatic nomenclature, the sources of bullion, the processes whereby coins were put into circulation, and the currency habits of the public. Several of the articles in this volume show that numismatists are in fact moving in this direction. The young science of ancient economic history will profit greatly by their work.

[In this essay, while paying tribute to the achievements of numismatic research, Jones seems mainly to have been preoccupied with suggesting fruitful topics for further work. It seems worthwhile to mark its re-publication by drawing attention to some recent work which has been inspired or provoked by it; an exhaustive recent bibliography may be found in the reports prepared for the Rome and Copenhagen numismatic congresses in 1961 and 1967, and select bibliographies in J. Guey, *XI Congrès Int. des Sc. Hist.*, *Stockholm* ii, 55 (Roman Empire only); P. Grierson, *Bibliographie Numismatique*, Brussels, 1966; K. Christ, *Antike Numismatik*, Darmstadt, 1967.

Jones' discussion of *the significance of coin types* provoked a reply by C. H. V. Sutherland, *J.R.S.* 1959, 46, which concentrated, however, on the intelligibility of types and did not answer Jones' main argument about their lack of effect; for well-documented scepticism about the extent to which the Emperor took thought for the selection of types, see also K. Pink, *Num. Zeit.* 1933, 20.

On the problem of *coinage and sovereignty*, the formula S.C. on Imperial bronze coins has been studied by K. Kraft, *Jahrb. Num. Geld.* 1962, 7; regal and autonomous coinages in the Hellenistic period have been the subject of a long series of studies by H. Seyrig, 'Antiquités Syriennes' in *Syria* and 'Monnaies Hellénistiques' in *Revue Numismatique*; E. Erxleben is in the process of publishing a major study of the Athenian coinage decree in *Archiv für Papyrusforschung*.

The Presidential addresses of P. Grierson to the Royal Numismatic Society, *Num. Chron.* 1963 and 1964, discuss Roman *weight standards*, J. Guey, *Rev. Num.* 1962, 73, deals with the *debasement of the Roman coinage* in the third century A.D. and C. M. Kraay and V. M. Emeleus, *The Composition of Greek Silver Coins*, Oxford, 1962, have made a promising start in the investigation of *metal sources*.

Discussion of the *relative and absolute size of issues* of coinage features in Chapter 7 of M. H. Crawford, *Roman Republican Coinage*, Cambridge, forthcoming; the effect of the availability and non-availability of coinage on the problem of debt in the late Republic is discussed by Cl. Nicolet and M. H. Crawford in *Annales* 1971, 1203; recent volumes of *Roman Imperial Coinage* continue to provide estimates of the relative size of issues, but make no attempt to provide an overall picture.

The *administrative structure of the late Roman coinage* forms the subject of three related papers by M. F. Hendy, *Univ. Birm. Hist. Journ.* 1970, 129; *Num. Chron.* 1971, 117-139; *J.R.S.* 1972, 75-82; production of coinage was throughout dictated by considerations of public finance. For a similar conclusion with regard to the Achaean League coinage, see N. Thompson, *The Agrinion Hoard*, New York, 1968.

The whole *pattern of issue and use of coinage* in the Roman world is discussed by M. H. Crawford, *J.R.S.* 1970, 40, the introduction of bronze to the Greek world by M. J. Price, in *Essays in Greek Coinage Presented to Stanley Robinson*, Oxford, 1968, 90; a very mathematical discussion of the average life of an ancient coin may be found in J. W. Müller, *Schw. Num. Rund.* 1968, 105.

Finally, the first inscription recording a monetary reform has turned up at Aphrodisias, incidentally throwing much new light on the coinage of Diocletian; see K. T. Erim, J. M. Reynolds, M. H. Crawford, *J.R.S.* 1971, 171.

M. H. CRAWFORD.]

CHAPTER FOUR

OVER-TAXATION AND THE DECLINE OF THE ROMAN EMPIRE*

R ARELY in recorded history has there been a louder and more
persistent chorus of complaint against the taxes than under
the later Roman Empire. Already under Diocletian (284–305)
Lactantius declares that the burden was intolerable, and under
Justinian (527–565) Procopius raises the same lament. Nor was
it only the taxpayers who complained. Valentinian III in 444–5
publicly admitted that 'if we claim these expenses from the
landowner in addition to what he pays already, such an exaction
will crush his last feeble strength: if again we demand them from
the merchants, they will inevitably sink under the weight of such
a burden' (*Valentiniani Novellae* XV pr.)

It would be naïve to accept without question the complaints
of taxpayers, or even the apologies of a government which is
introducing a new form of taxation—Valentinian III was imposing
a purchase tax. Taxpayers have rarely been ready to admit that
the claims of the government are moderate and reasonable. The
volume of their complaints, moreover, is usually governed not so
much by the relation of the sum demanded to their capacity to
pay, as by its relation to what they are accustomed to pay: our
great-grandfathers protested as loudly against an income tax of
threepence in the pound as we do against one of nine shillings.
Now the rate of taxation undoubtedly rose fairly steadily under
the Roman Empire. Themistius in 364 declared that it had
approximately doubled in the past forty years. This continual
rise in taxation accounts for the persistence of the complaints, but
it does not prove that they were justified. Indeed, one may
wonder whether the taxpayer under Diocletian can have been as
hard hit as Lactantius represents, when his grandson could pay

* [Evidence will be found in the more detailed expositions in chapters VIII, X, and
XIII, and in *L.R.E.*]

twice as much and survive. To Aurelius Victor, writing in 360, Diocletian's taxation was 'modestia tolerabilis' compared with the 'pernicies' of his own day [*de Caesaribus* 39, 32], and Procopius might have found the 'ruinous' rates of Constantius II very reasonable under Justinian.

The economy of the empire was primarily agricultural; the vast majority of its inhabitants were peasants, and the national income was mostly derived from the land. Its main tax, which seems to have produced over 90 per cent of the revenue, was likewise imposed on agriculture [cf. ch. II]. It was a combined land and poll tax, being assessed partly on agricultural land (*iugatio*) and partly on the rural population (*capitatio*). There are unfortunately very few figures for the rate of taxation, and it is even more difficult to estimate the relation of the tax to the yield of the land. Such information as we have dates from the 6th century. We possess a complete tax register for the Egyptian city of Antaeopolis in the reign of Justinian. The area involved was 51,655 *arurae* (roughly equivalent to 35,000 acres), nearly all arable, and the rate, including all supplementary charges, works out at about 3.2 *artabae* of wheat or $7\frac{2}{3}$ carats gold *per arura*. The average rent of good arable land in Egypt was 5 *artabae* or 12 carats *per arura*, and the rent usually represented 50 per cent of the gross yield of the land. The tax therefore comes to nearly one-third of the gross yield [*L.R.E.* 464]. A second document, also of Justinian's reign, comes from Ravenna. Here the rents of a group of estates confiscated from the Arian church and granted to the Catholic church of the city are stated to total $2,171\frac{1}{2}$ *solidi*, and the taxes payable on them amount to 1,239 *solidi* [ibid. 820]. Church lands were exempt from a number of supplementary charges, but the tax nevertheless comes to 57 per cent of the rental value, and presumably therefore, if rents were calculated on on the same basis in Italy as in Egypt, to over a quarter of the gross yield of the land.

These are the rates which taxation had reached by the 6th century. They are startling figures when compared with the *decumae* which the Roman Republic had levied in many of the provinces. Even the privileged categories of landowners paid more than twice as much in the 6th century A.D. as the provincials had in the 1st century B.C., and the ordinary landowner well over three times as much. Moreover, the tax under the later Roman

Empire did not vary with the actual annual yield of the land, as had the *decumae*, but had to be paid in bad years as in good, unless a special rebate was granted.

It may be asked if this high rate of taxation had any adverse effects on the economy of the empire. There are two ills which may be, in part at any rate, attributed to it, the progressive abandonment of the land and the resultant shrinkage of the cultivated area and of the yield of agriculture, and the depopulation of the countryside, and, therefore, since the vast bulk of its inhabitants lived on the land, of the empire as a whole.

Complaints of abandoned land (*agri deserti*) are as common as those of over-taxation and extend over as long a period. A large volume of legislation, preserved in the Theodosian and Justinian Codes, shows that they remained a perennial problem from the time of Diocletian (and even earlier yet) to that of Justinian. The government was mainly interested in the fiscal aspect of the question; it required the tax assessed on the land to be paid whether it was cultivated or not. Where possible it sold or granted abandoned lands to new owners who, encouraged by initial rebates of taxation, would bring it under cultivation again. But if this failed, it either assigned them compulsorily to owners of good land, whom it made responsible for their taxes, or distributed the tax due upon them as a surcharge on all the landowners of the village or city territory.

Here too the actual figures are scarce, but those which exist are impressive. The emperor Valens (364–78) found that in the province of Asia the civic lands comprised 6,736½ fertile *iuga* and 703 (nearly 10 per cent) 'deserted and now in bad condition and sterile'. In 451 Theodoret, bishop of Cyrrhus in N.E. Syria, complained to the government that in his city 2,500 *iuga* out of 15,000 which paid their tax in gold were registered as derelict; this works out at one-sixth. In Africa the fiscal registers in 422 showed that in the Proconsular province 5,700 centuriae of the state lands were deserted, and 9,002 in good condition, while in the southern province of Byzacena the figures were 7,615 and 7,460 respectively: that is, in the one province over a third of the lands were abandoned, and in the other more than half. High figures are officially recorded for other provinces also, 528,042 *iugera* (equivalent to 2,640 *centuriae*) for Campania in 395, and as much as 13,000 *centuriae* for Numidia in 451, but in these cases the proportion of deserted to cultivated land is not known. [See *L.R.E.* 812 ff.]

Various explanations have been offered for this phenomenon, exhaustion of the soil, shortage of agricultural labour, and the growing insecurity caused by barbarian raids. All these may well have been contributory causes in some cases, but none seem to account for the widespread and lasting character of the trouble. The exhaustion of the soil is the least convincing explanation. The same agricultural techniques had been followed for centuries before Diocletian's day, and they continued unchanged for centuries later. If they were defective the yield of the land would have sunk to the minimum below which it could sink no further long before Diocletian's time; if, as is more probable, they were sound, fertility would have been preserved. The test case for this theory is Egypt: there, under the system of basin irrigation which then prevailed, the soil was annually fertilized by the silt deposited by the flood, and continual cropping could not exhaust it. Nevertheless the papyri show that deserted lands were as great a problem here as elsewhere in the empire.

The second explanation is more plausible, for agricultural labour was undoubtedly very scarce in the later Roman Empire. But the laws show that landlords sometimes abandoned estates with agricultural slaves and sitting tenants on them. These at any rate must have had some other reason than shortage of labour.

The third explanation is valid for certain areas, and may have been a decisive factor in these. The frontier provinces along the Rhine and the Danube were constantly exposed to barbarian raiders, who carried off the stock and the people from the farms and destroyed or stole the crops. Similar conditions prevailed in the African and Syrian provinces adjacent to the desert as the control of the nomads became less efficient. These facts would help to explain the very high figure of deserted land for Byzacena, which was exposed to Moorish depredations, and for Numidia, which not only suffered from the Moors, but had in 451 been recently evacuated by the Vandals. But this explanation will not account for the abandonment of lands in such provinces as Asia, Campania or Proconsular Africa, which were beyond the reach of barbarian raiders.

Contemporaries attributed the phenomenon to the high rate of taxation; as Lactantius puts it, 'the resources of the farmers were exhausted by the outrageous burden of all the taxes, the fields were abandoned, and the cultivated land reverted to waste'. This explanation on the whole best fits the facts.

We very rarely hear of peasant proprietors abandoning their holdings, and in the few cases known there is usually a special explanation. The laws always assume that abandoned land had belonged to a landlord and had been cultivated by his tenants (*coloni*) or slaves, who at this date, it would seem, usually paid a rent for their holdings like tenants (*quasi coloni*). On such land about half the yield was retained by the tenants, and—by the 6th century—between a third and a quarter was claimed by the state. The net rent, therefore, in the case of landlords belonging to the privileged categories was somewhat less than a quarter of the gross yield, and for the ordinary landlord little more than a sixth. If the tax was fairly and accurately assessed on the actual productivity of the land, the landlord still, despite its high rate, drew an adequate profit from his estates, and it is clear that the great majority of landlords did very well. For it must not be forgotten that the government drew a very large income by way of rent from the state lands, and that the vast wealth of the church and of the senatorial aristocracy was almost entirely derived from agricultural rents. The state and church lands were, it is true, privileged, paying only the basic tax without supplementary charges, and many senators by law or by special favour enjoyed similar exemptions. But many, indeed most, ordinary landlords who paid the full rate made a comfortable income out of their estates, and there was always a strong and unsatisfied demand for land as an investment.

There were, however, cases where for some reason or another the land was over-assessed. There are frequent complaints of corruption or favouritism, whereby wealthy and influential landowners got their estates lighly assessed, with the result that those of their humbler neighbours were overburdened, for the global assessment of the city territory could not be reduced except by special imperial authorisation. The basic assessment, moreover, varied very greatly in exactitude in the different dioceses of the empire. In Oriens (Syria and Palestine) there was a very elaborate system whereby the land was classified according to its use as pasture, arable, vineyard and olive-yard, and graded by quality within these classes. But in Asiana (S.W. Asia Minor) and Egypt the system was more rough and ready, taking no account of quality, and in Africa and Italy the land was assessed simply by area, without regard to its agricultural use or quality. In these cases it can be seen that a rate of tax which left the owner of good or average land a fair margin of profit might well absorb the whole rent of land of marginal quality.

The effect of rising rates of taxation was thus that increasing areas of marginal land ceased to yield an adequate profit to their owners, and finally became a burden instead of an asset. Owners of such land naturally spent less and less on improving or maintaining their estates, and tried to put up the rents, thereby driving their tenants into overworking their land, and leaving them no margin for necessary maintenance work. The evil effects of over-taxation were most evident in areas where there was much marginal land, and the assessment took no account of variations in quality. This was the situation in Africa, and it explains the extraordinarily high figures of deserted lands recorded not only in Byzacena and Numidia, where other factors contributed, but also in the Proconsular province.

Depopulation is a much more difficult question, since in the absence of statistics most of the basic facts are disputable [cf. L.R.E. 1040 ff.] It is probable, though it cannot be proved, that by the accession of Diocletian the population of the empire had shrunk considerably owing to the continual civil wars and barbarian invasions of the mid-third century, with their attendant devastations and famines, and to the great plague which invaded the empire under Marcus Aurelius and recurred periodically during the next half-century. But from Diocletian's time no major epidemic is recorded until the appearance of the bubonic plague in 542, and relatively peaceful conditions prevailed in the western half of the empire for over a century, and until the beginning of the 7th century in the Asiatic provinces. Peasant populations normally recover rapidly after plagues and wars, since they have a very high birth rate, but so far as we can judge the population of the Roman Empire in the 4th, 5th and 6th centuries remained static at a low level, if it did not shrink. At any rate, throughout this period, as is revealed by the long series of laws tying free tenants and agricultural slaves to the soil, there was a continual shortage of agricultural labour. This shortage was not due to a flight to the towns; the laws show that

G

coloni who left their landlords normally moved to other landlords, and there are more complaints of urban craftsmen migrating to the country than of peasants seeking the towns. A contributory cause of the shortage was the conscription, which fell exclusively on the peasants; but, had the population increased normally, this should not have proved so exhausing a drain as it did.

The only explanation seems to be that the death rate amongst the peasantry was abnormally high, and this must in the ultimate analysis have been due to malnutrition. Over-taxation played its part in this, though it was not the only factor. It affected directly only the peasant proprietors, and they seem *prima facie* to have been better off than the tenants, for they had to pay in taxes only up to one-third of their produce, whereas tenants paid about one-half in rent. In actual fact the position of the peasant proprietors was not so favourable as it seems. Their holdings, having been divided and subdivided for generations by inheritance, were normally much smaller than the tenants' farms. The assessment of the tax worked out unfavourably for them, for it was calculated on the aggregate of the value of the land and of the number of persons registered on it, so that a man with a small farm and a large family might pay more than a man with a large farm and no dependants. Finally, peasants, having neither money to bribe the officials nor influence to intimidate them, were often over-assessed.

In these circumstances a peasant proprietor might well find it difficult to rear his family. But his chief difficulty was that he could accumulate no reserves, and if barbarian raiders destroyed his crops or stole his stock, or a drought or an invasion of locusts ruined the harvest, he either starved or had to borrow, with the result that his land eventually passed to his creditor. In this way an increasing number of peasant proprietors sank to the condition of tenants, whose standard of living was even lower.

These conclusions can be only tentative, but the evidence does suggest that over-taxation played a significant rôle in the decline of the empire. It can be established that the taxes rose from Diocletian's time until they absorbed a very high proportion of the yield of the land. It can plausibly be argued that the high rate of tax was the main reason for the abandonment of marginal land and the consequent impoverishment of the empire. It is at any rate probable that it was a major factor in reducing the manpower of the empire, and thereby contributed directly to its military collapse.   [See also *L.R.E.* ch. XXV.]

CHAPTER FIVE

THE GREEKS UNDER THE ROMAN EMPIRE

THE most surprising feature of Roman rule in the Greek East
is that despite its long duration it had so little effect on the
civilisation of the area. The influence was indeed in the other
direction. In Horace's much quoted phrase *Graecia capta ferum
victorem cepit*. Even in the late third century an important group
of Roman noble families became deeply imbued with Greek
culture, and as time went on every cultivated Roman came to
receive a Greek education, to read Greek literature, to study
Greek rhetoric and philosophy. Many Romans were as at home
in Greek as in Latin. Cicero in his letters often uses a Greek
phrase to convey a nuance too subtle for Latin; Marcus Aurelius
wrote his intimate memoirs in Greek. Roman aristocrats, though
they might have a low opinion of contemporary Greeks, had a
profound reverence for Greek civilisation and were deeply
imbued with its culture.

This feeling was not reciprocated. Some Greeks might
admire the political wisdom of the Romans and all were impressed
by their military power, but they never ceased to regard them
culturally as barbarians. The Greeks were supremely satisfied
with their own language and literature, and, except for a few
antiquarians like Plutarch, who were curious about Roman
history and institutions, felt no call to learn the barbarous Latin
tongue or read its uncouth and imitative literature.

The result was that the Greeks had no impulse to Romanize
themselves, and the Roman government felt no mission to impose
their civilization on the East. In the barbarian West the natives
quickly adopted Roman culture, and the government encouraged
them by appropriate grants of status. Countless communities
were converted into *municipia* of Roman citizens, and whole
provinces accorded the Latin right. Nothing of the kind happened
in the East. Nowhere was *Latinitas* granted, and the *municipia* of
the Greek world number precisely three, Stobi and Denda in
Macedonia, and Coela in the Thracian Chersonnese. There was,

moreover, relatively little Roman colonization in the East. Caesar, the triumvirs, and Augustus planted twenty odd colonies of veterans, nine or ten in Greece and Macedonia, ten in various parts of Asia Minor, and one in Syria. Later emperors added about a dozen colonies to the list. It is very unlikely that any programme of Romanisation lay behind these foundations. Some, like Corinth and Aelia Capitolina, were revivals of destroyed cities, others were perhaps designed as fortresses to control turbulent areas; this motive may explain Augustus' Pisidian group. But for the most part the founders were merely concerned to provide land for their veterans, and founded colonies where it was available; hence the large number of settlements planted by Caesar, the triumvirs, and Augustus, who had exceptionally large numbers of veterans for whom they had to provide.[1]

These colonies were gradually assimilated to their Greek environment; one can trace on their inscriptions and coins the supersession of Latin by Greek. Outside the colonies Latin can rarely have been heard. The administrative language of the Roman Empire in the eastern provinces was Greek. The emperors had a special bureau *ab epistolis Graecis* to handle their correspondence with Greek cities and provincial assemblies. Edicts were published in Greek; rescripts to Greek petitions were given in the same language; in the law courts proceedings were conducted in Greek. The proconsuls, legates, procurators, and other officials were drawn from the stratum of Roman society to which Greek was a second language. Only in the army was Latin the official language, and even here it became increasingly merely official. Regimental records and accounts were kept in Latin, and Latin was no doubt the language of command. But the eastern legions were from the beginning of the principate, and indeed earlier, largely recruited locally from men whose native language was Greek, and in their private correspondence, as we know from the papyri, the soldiers generally used that language, though they presumably had to learn enough Latin to understand their orders. In the East the army was not, as in the western provinces, a force

---

[1] Pliny, *N.H.* III. 145 (Denda), ib. IV. 34, Head, *Hist. Num.*[2], 245 (Stobi), *Année Epigr.* 1924, 82, Head, *Hist. Num.*[2], 259 (Coela). It is difficult to prove a negative, but if any other *municipia* had existed, their coins or inscriptions would probably have survived. For Roman colonization in the East see my *Greek City from Alexander to Justinian*, 60–64.

making for Romanization. The garrison towns remained Greek and no Roman *municipia* arose from the legionary *canabae*.[2]

Roman citizenship remained rare in the Greek East until the *Constitutio Antoniniana* in 212 abruptly made all free inhabitants of the Empire Romans. The only communities of citizens were the few colonies and the even fewer *municipia*. A certain number of Greeks acquired the citizenship by enrolment in the legions, or after their discharge, by service in the *auxilia*. The citizenship was also granted on a fairly liberal scale to individuals, chiefly the notables of their cities. But the proportion of Roman citizens must have been minute.

It follows that Roman law was rarely applicable in the Greek East. It was the law of the colonies and *municipia*, but the vast majority of cities followed their own codes, and Greek law prevailed in Egypt. For normal purposes the isolated Roman citizens scattered among the Greek population conformed to the local law. Only for certain aspects of family law was a Roman citizen obliged to follow Roman rules. He was, for instance, supposed to make his will in Latin. But in Egypt Roman citizens often tried to evade even this rule, and drew up their wills in Greek, adding a clause declaring that their provisions should be valid as if written in Latin; such wills were declared invalid by the Idios Logos. Here again the *Constitutio Antoniniana* in theory revolutionised the situation; Roman law was thenceforth universally applicable, and the only law of the Empire. In practice the *Constitutio* for some time made little change in the East; there were not enough notaries, barristers, or jurisconsults who knew Roman law. Documents continued to be drawn in the old Greek forms, and a clause was added to each converting it into a Roman *stipulatio*.[3]

---

[2] An imperial secretary *ad legationes et responsa Graeca* (*Année Epigr.* 1924, 78) or ἐπὶ τῶν Ἑλληνικῶν ἀποκριμάτων (Dittenberger, *Syll.*[3] 804) is recorded as early as the reign of Claudius. It is hardly necessary to cite official letters and edicts in Greek; see for instances those collected in Ehrenberg and Jones, *Documents Illustrating the Reigns of Augustus and Tiberius*, 299 ff. Imperial rescripts are often cited in Greek in the Digest (e.g. L. vi 5, §§ 2, 6). For the use of Greek in the courts we have the evidence of papyri (e.g. Mitteis, *Chrestomathie*, II. 372). For the recruitment of the eastern legions, see Parker, *The Roman Legions*, 181–3 (cf. Forni, *Il reclutamento delle legione*, for a detailed analysis). Examples of soldiers' letters in Greek are *B.G.U.* 423, 814.

[3] It is in fact only in Egypt that we have any knowledge of the law prevailing in the provinces; see Taubenschlag, *The Law of Greco-Roman Egypt in the Light of the*

So far from encouraging Romanisation the government favoured Hellenisation in the surviving backward areas of barbarism. The main evidence for this is its activity in founding Greek cities. The eastern provinces came to be littered with Sebasteias and Sebastopolises, Claudiopolises, Flaviopolises, Trajanopolises, and Hadrianopolises; scarcely an emperor was not commemorated by a city or two, and some by many more. As in the Hellenistic age, dynastic titles are tricky evidence. It is hard to tell in most cases whether the initiative came from above or from below, and what was the significance of the new name. It might be merely complimentary, an expression by the city of its devotion to an emperor, or a reward given to a city by an emperor for its loyalty. It might celebrate an imperial benefaction, such as financial aid after a fire or an earthquake. But it might be more significant, denoting the reorganisation, whether spontaneously or by imperial initiative, of a primitive tribal commune as a city, or the grant of self-government to a town which had hitherto been subject to a dynast or belonged to a centrally administered kingdom. Finally, a dynastic name might celebrate the physical creation of a new city, usually in a rural area hitherto centrally administered.

It may be doubted whether the motives of the Roman government in founding cities were always purely idealistic. Dynasts were liable to be troublesome, because they or their heirs might be incompetent or unruly; a self-governing city was a more stable and responsible unit of government. For practical reasons the Romans also disliked centralised governments, which they found difficulty in running efficiently themselves, and preferred to devolve the administration on to self-governing communities. The policy of devolution goes back to republican days, when Pompey divided the kingdom of Pontus into eleven city states, some of which were the old Greek colonies of the coast, others royal administrative centres, others again entirely new creations; to those last Pompey gave names celebrating their founder's *nomen* and *cognomen*, Pompeiopolis, Magnopolis, Megalopolis.

Papyri. For Roman wills drawn in Greek, see § 15 of the Gnomon of the Idios Logos (*B.G.U.* 1210). It has been doubted whether the *Constitutio Antoniniana* did make all free inhabitants of the Empire citizens, and whether it made them subject to Roman law, but in my view wrongly; see my *Studies in Roman Government and Law*, 129 ff. and Jolowicz, *Historical Introduction to Roman Law*,[2] 545-7. For the mechanical use of the formula of *stipulatio*, see Jolowicz, *op. cit.* 423, 546.

Under the principate the attempt was often made to preserve the bureaucratic régime of an annexed kingdom, but such attempts were never successful in the long term. Thrace, annexed under Claudius, was converted into a group of cities by Trajan and Hadrian. In Cappadocia and Judaea the area of centralised administration was gradually reduced by successive city foundations. In Egypt the Ptolemaic administrative machine, which was fiscally highly profitable if efficiently run, was preserved for over two centuries, but eventually a modified form of city government was introduced by Septimius Severus.[4]

Whatever its motives, however, the foundation of a city usually did something to promote Hellenisation. If a town was erected *de novo* it became with its gymnasium, theatre, stadium, and other urban amenities, a centre of Greek life. If a pre-existing town was granted self-government, it was thereby enabled to create such amenities for itself if they were lacking, and to improve and expand them if it possessed some or all of them already. It can, at any rate, be claimed that, either by the direct initiative of the Roman government or with its blessing and assistance, a number of small enclaves of rural barbarism were urbanised and thereby Hellenised, and several large areas, notably Thrace and northern and eastern Asia Minor, were endowed with cities which served as centres of Hellenisation.

At the same time that it was founding new cities the Roman Government was unwittingly sapping the foundations of the city state throughout the Empire. The life of the city depended on autonomy, enjoyed in the present or at least hoped for in the future, and autonomy meant, to put the matter crudely, liberty for each city to fight its neighbours whenever it wished, and liberty for the citizens to struggle with one another by constitutional means or by violence for control of the government. Both had been possible in the Hellenistic period. Most kings were not so powerful but that a combination of cities could defy them, and the cities could still exploit for their own advantage the frequent wars between rival kingdoms of rival claimants for the crown. The predominant form of constitution in the Hellenistic age was democratic, and the kings imposed their control more by means

---

[4] See my *Cities of the Eastern Roman Provinces*, 10–12 (Thrace), 157–60 (Pontus), 177–83 (Cappadocia), 274–81 (Judaea), 311–38 (Egypt).

of governors and garrisons than by constitutional restrictions on democratic liberty.

Even while the Roman republic was subduing the Hellenistic monarchies there was still hope. To us, with our knowledge of what was to come, the advance of Rome seems irresistible and inevitable, but contemporary Greeks had not the power of prophecy. Rhodes, and many of the cities of mainland Greece, hoped that the Third Macedonian war would result in a balance of power between Rome and Macedon, and trimmed their sails accordingly. In the middle of the second century the Achaean League endeavoured to assert its liberty of action and challenged Roman authority. Even in the first century most of the Greek cities of Asia, and many of those of Greece itself, must have believed that Mithridates would prevail, and actually supported him. It was only gradually—probably after Pompey's vast conquests—that it came to be realised that Rome was invincible and that her rule was universal and had come to stay. Thenceforth the Greek cities had to recognise that in their external affairs they would never again be free.[5]

The Romans distrusted democracy, and believed the government would be more stable if vested in the better sort of citizens, whom they identified with the richer. They no doubt also calculated that men of property, who had more to lose, would be less likely to take the risks involved in rebellion. They generally, therefore, imposed on cities which came under their control property qualifications for office and for membership of the council, and strengthened the council by giving its members life tenure. External forms were not altered. The popular assembly still met and elected the magistrates and passed decrees. But control passed to the propertied class. This policy goes back to Rome's earliest contact with Greece. After the Second Macedonian War Flamininus imposed the rule on the Thessalians and the other Greek peoples whom he freed from Macedonian rule. It was applied to all the rebellious cities of Greece in 146 B.C. and we find it in Asia, Bithynia and, it would seem, throughout the Greek world. Thenceforth oligarchies ruled the cities, and any attempt of the populace to challenge this dominance was 'sedition',

[5] The sentiments of the Greeks during the Third Macedonian War are well described by Polybius (xxvii. 9. 10). For the welcome given to Mithridates, see Appian, *Mith.* 20–3, 28–9.

and was, as such, forcibly repressed by the provincial governor.[6] The Greek city state thus sank to the status of a municipality, and even in its internal government all vital political activity was stifled. The spirit of civic patriotism nevertheless long survived the political demise of the city. Now that they were no longer allowed to fight one another, the cities pursued their feuds in ways which were less destructive, but were at best somewhat futile and tended to become economically unhealthy. They conducted bitter and long drawn out diplomatic battles for empty titles and points of precedence, bombarding the imperial government with embassies. But above all they strove to outshine one another in the magnificence of their public buildings and the splendour of their festivals. In their mutual rivalry they strained their economic resources, initiating huge theatres and baths which they were unable to complete, and offering extravagant prizes to attract the most celebrated athletes and artists to their games. Eventually the imperial government had to intervene; the permission of the provincial governor was required for all important building projects, iselastic games (those, that is, that carried the same privileges to victors as the Olympian and the other Panhellenic games) could be founded only by imperial authorisation; and finally imperial commissioners (*curatores* or λογισταί) were appointed, at first sporadically and temporarily, eventually as a permanent and universal institution, to control the internal finances of each city.[7]

Internal politics followed a similar evolution. An ambitious young man, as Plutarch regretfully remarks, could no longer win

---

[6] Livy, XXXIV. 51, *a censu maxime et senatum et iudices legit, potentioremque eam partem civitatum fecit cui salva tranquillaque omnia magis esse expediebat* (Flamininus), Pausanias, VII. xvi. 9, (δημοκρατίας μὲν ἔπαυε, καθίστατο δὲ ἀπὸ τιμημάτων τὰς ἀρχάς (Mummius). Life tenure of councillors in Asia is implied by Cicero, *pro Flacco*, 42 ff. For Bithynia the rules of the Lex Pompeia are cited in Pliny, *Ep.* X. 79, 112, 114. A similar system, whereby local censors enrolled the city-councils, is implied by *I.G.R.* III. 930, τιμητεύσας τὴν βουλήν, for Cyprus and by *I.G.R.* III. 179, 206, for Galatia. For the suppression of 'sedition', see Dittenberger, *Syll.*[3], 684, Cicero, *ad Quintum fratrem*, I. 1 § 25. Cf. also Cassius Dio, LII. 30.

[7] For feuds between cities, see Dio Chrysostom, *Or.* XXXIV, XXXVIII, XL. For a dispute about titles between Ephesus, Pergamum, and Smyrna, see Dittenberger, *Syll.*[3] 849; cf. also Cassius Dio, LII. 37 § 10. On competitive expenditure on buildings and games, see Dio Chrysostom, *Or.* XL. 10, Cassius Dio, LII. 30 § 3. For imperial control of buildings, see Dio Chrysostom, *Or.* XL. 6, XLV. 15, *Dig.* L. viii. 7 § 1, x. 3, 6, 7, and Pliny, *Ep.* X, *passim*; of games, Pliny, *Ep.* X. 118–9, *I.G.R.* IV. 336, 1251, 1431. On imperial *curatores*, see my *Greek City*, 136–8.

renown by leading his citizens to victory in war, by negotiating a treaty, by suppressing a tyrant or by reforming the constitution. He might, it is true, still make his name by going on an embassy to the emperor and by a brilliant speech gaining for his city the title of 'first of the province', or the privilege of being an assize town. But in general rival politicians could win popularity only by outbidding one another in their munificent expenditure on games and buildings, or on largesse to the people. Political rivalry ran so high that less opulent contestants not infrequently squandered their entire fortunes in the struggle; in which case the city was allowed, contrary to the usual rule which forbade *ex gratia* payments from public funds, to vote them a pension. Ultimately the standard of expenditure expected of aspirants to the magistracies and to seats on the council became so high that even wealthy citizens became reluctant to hold them. The rule was enforced that a candidate must accept nomination (which was automatically followed by election) unless he could plead some legal exemption, and a search for exemptions began. This development is very difficult to date and was by no means uniform. In some cities it had already begun in the first century, it became more widespread in the second, and by the early third seems, to judge by the elaborate rules laid down by the Severan lawyers, to have been generally prevalent. Long after that date, even in the fourth and fifth centuries, there were still some patriotic citizens who voluntarily accepted office and spent lavishly in producing games. But, broadly speaking, it is probably true to say that by the third century the Greek city state and the feverish patriotism which it had inspired was dead. The cities had become mere units of local administration and their government was a compulsory burden imposed on their richer citizens.[8]

Though they died politically, the cities retained, and indeed enhanced, their importance as centres of Hellenic culture. Most cities now maintained higher education from their public funds, appointing professors of grammar and rhetoric and paying them regular salaries as well as according them various immunities. A ruling of Antoninus Pius limited the number of public professors;

[8] Plutarch's *Praecepta rei publicae gerundae*, directed to a young man of modest means who wishes to enter local politics, is very revealing of the heavy demands made by the public on politicians' purses. For pensions to ruined decurions, see Pliny, *Ep.* X. 90–1, *Dig.* L. ii. 8. For the introduction of compulsion to fill the magistracies, see my *Greek City*, 181–91.

an ordinary city might have three grammarians and three rhetors, the capital of an assize district four of each, a metropolis five. In these schools a literary education was supplied according to the norm laid down in the Hellenistic age, but the curriculum became increasingly narrowed, and more and more emphasis was thrown on rhetoric. The corpus of classical literature which was taught in schools and generally used by the cultivated public tended to be more and more a selection, the seven best plays of each of three best Attic tragedians, for instance, and there was a growing use of florilegia.[9]

The expansion of education promoted by the cities was reflected in the wider diffusion of literary production to areas hitherto barren. The majority of authors naturally came from the old established centres of Hellenism, but now even Samosata on the Euphrates on the extreme eastern fringe of the Empire produced the notable satirist Lucian, and the very Syrian city of Emesa, with its archaic oriental cult of Elagabalus, the novelist Heliodorus. Oppian, the poet of fishing and hunting, came from Anazarbus in the backward hinterland of Cilicia, still under the early principate ruled by the native dynast Tarcondimotus, and in the heart of Asia Minor, Laranda of Lycaonia produced the epic poets Nestor and his son Pisander. One of the most celebrated rhetors of the second century, Aelius Aristides, hailed from the remote Mysian city of Hadrianutherae. It is at any rate a curious coincidence, if not more, that literary production corresponds closely with the development of cities. The recently urbanized areas of Pontus and Thrace were unproductive, and the few Cappadocian literary figures came from the old foundations of Ariarathes the Philhellene, Tyana and Caesarea Mazaca. In Egypt, outside Alexandria, the only notable authors were the great astronomer and mathematician Claudius Ptolemy of Ptolemais, and the author of the *Deipnosophistae*, Athenaeus of Naucratis. The metropoleis of the nomes were barren until in the third century Lycopolis gave birth to the great philosopher Plotinus.

The cities also encouraged music and drama by the many competitions which they celebrated. The theatre had, even in the Hellenistic age, been professionalised. The poets, actors, singers, and instrumentalists formed regional unions, and toured the

[9] For the numbers of civic professors, see *Dig.* XXVII. 1. 6 § 2, and for their salaries, L. ix. 4 § 2.

cities of a given area. In the Roman period, probably under Trajan, these regional unions were amalgamated into one 'holy oecumenical synod of the artists in the service of Dionysus.' They were paid for their performances, and the victor also received prizes.[10] Athletics were likewise fostered by the cities. Every city had at least one gymnasium, and some had as many as three, for boys, youths, and old men. Every city celebrated games on various scales of magnificence, comprising chariot races and the traditional athletic events. Athletes always remained in theory amateurs, but some at any rate, to judge by the immense numbers of victories which they won, seem to have become in fact professionals: they were not paid, however, though they could win large sums in prize money, and if victorious in iselastic games were entitled to a pension for life from their native cities.[11]

In the games some Roman influence penetrated into the Greek East. Gladiatorial shows and combats with wild animals were added to the repertory. The former seem never to have become common, and were abolished by Constantine. The latter became increasingly popular, and were still flourishing in Justinian's day.[12]

The cities were, moreover, the most important patrons of architecture and sculpture. They built countless temples, triumphal arches, theatres, odea, stadia, gymnasia, nymphaea, and baths, and laid out great colonnaded streets and markets. They commissioned thousands of statues of emperors, imperial officials, and local worthies, until in some cities the streets and squares became congested. On the style of these monuments I

[10] For the Dionysiac artists, see Poland, *Geschichte des griechischen Vereinwesens*, 129–47 and s.v. *technitae* in *Pauly-Wissowa*, VA, 2473 ff. Their pay is mentioned in *S.E.G.* I. 362, IV. 303, 306, 308, *I.G.* IX. i. 694, XII. ix. 207, *Syll.*³, 1077.

[11] On the gymnasia, see Oehler's article in *Pauly-Wissowa*, VII. 2004–26. For the social status of athletes, see *Rev. Arch.* 1934, pp. 55–8; examples of athletes of good family are *I.G.R.* I. 381, III. 500, 623, 625–6, IV. 844, 1344. For the pensions of victors, see Wilcken, *Chrestomathie*, I. 157.

[12] For gladiators in the East, see L. Robert, *Les gladiateurs dans l'Orient grec* (Paris, 1940). They were prohibited by *CTh* XV, xii. 1, 325, and are mentioned as a memory of childhood by Libanius (*Or.* I. 5); there is no later allusion to them in the East. For the popularity of wild beast hunts, see Libanius, *Ep.* 1399; he wrote many letters asking for their supply for games given by his friends (*Ep.* 217–9, 544, 586–8, 598–9, 1231–2, 1399, 1400). Civic beast shows are still mentioned in *C.J.* XI. xli. 5 (where 'bestias' has been interpolated by Justinian's editors into a law dealing with charioteers and horses).

will forebear to speak, since others far better qualified than I will discuss the problem later. I need only remark that oriental survivals were rare in the art of the Roman East; the Egyptian temples continued to be built in the traditional style, and in the border city of Palmyra the sculpture shows Parthian influence, and that is about all. There was much interchange of architects and sculptors between the Greek East and the Roman West, and some Roman techniques and stylistic innovations were transplanted to the East. But the main flow of men and ideas was from East to West, and in general the East seems to have maintained its Greek traditions.

The official civic cults remained as Hellenic as they had been in the Hellenistic age, and perhaps became more so. We can, at any rate, be certain that the shrines of the local gods were fully Greek in their architectural form in the Roman period, for many temples of this period survive; Zeus of Aezani in the heart of Phrygia was housed in a fine Greek temple. Even at Jerusalem Herod the Great gave the unhellenised Jehovah a great temple whose predominant effect was Greek. Only the actual sanctuary was built according to the hallowed prescription of the Scriptures; the complex of courts which surrounded it were in the Corinthian order. And Herod's temple was greatly admired by the Jewish people, suspicious as they were of anything Hellenic.[13]

But, at the same time, the Roman age saw the wide diffusion of a number of very oriental cults, the so-called mystery religions. The Egyptian worship of Isis had already begun to spread outside Egypt in the Hellenistic age and now became universal. Mithraism, a Persian cult, spread far and wide, and so also did the worship of the Phrygian Great Mother of the Gods. Judaism seems also to have become widely diffused; we hear of many proselytes in the first century. More significant for the future was the growth of Christianity. There was a steady growth of religiosity throughout the Empire, and especially in the eastern provinces, and this growing religiosity found more satisfaction in the oriental cults than in the official Hellenic or Hellenised gods. Greek philosophy also took on a more religious tone. Both the two new philosophic schools of the Roman period, Neopythagoreanism and Neoplatonism, were strongly infused with religious

[13] Josephus, *Ant. Jud.* XV. 391–420 (see especially 414 for the use of the Corinthian order).

emotion. How far this religious tone was of oriental inspiration it is difficult to say. Asceticism, contempt for the world of the senses, a craving for mystical contemplation of and union with the divine, can all be traced to a pure Hellenic source in Plato. But the strong emotional emphasis on these features of Platonism may be due to oriental influences.[14]

The Greek East imposed the Hellenistic concept of the monarchy on the Empire at large. Under the republic the Greeks were somewhat at sea. They could, and very often did, worship the goddess Roma, but so abstract a conception does not seem to have satisfied them. Alternatively they could worship their provincial governors, and this they regularly did. But the provision of temples and festivals for an annual series of proconsuls had obviously practical difficulties, especially on the financial side, and these cults were rarely enduring. Some proconsuls who had been notable benefactors to the provinces were long worshipped; the cult of Mucius Scaevola by the cities of Asia struck firm roots. But in general the worship of proconsuls became one of the many devices whereby provincial governors fleeced their subjects; a fund was raised and the new god pocketed it.[15]

Octavian's emergence as sole ruler of the Roman world was thus greeted with relief. In him the Greek East forthwith saw a king—the Greeks were not interested in the nicely adjusted republican formulae on which his authority was officially based— and they forthwith hastened to worship him. Directly after Actium the Greek cities and Bithynia asked leave of Octavian to build temples to him in their respective provinces, and to celebrate his cult in provincial festivals. Octavian insisted that Rome should be associated with himself as the object of cult, and very soon nearly every eastern province was celebrating the worship of Rome and Augustus. The cult was so obviously a useful means of focussing the loyalty of the provincials to the head of the Empire that Augustus transplanted it to the barbarian western provinces, and altars of Rome and Augustus were soon inaugurated at Lyons and Cologne, where the notables of the Gallic and

[14] See A. D. Nock's admirable chapter on 'The Development of Paganism in the Roman Empire' in the *Cambridge Ancient History*, XII. xii.

[15] On the cult of Rome, see Livy, XLIII. 6, Tacitus, *Annals*, IV. 56; on that of proconsuls Cicero, *ad Quintum fratrem*, I. i § 26, *ad Atticum*, V. 21, *ad Fam*. III. 7, *pro Flacco*, 55 ff.

German tribes met and celebrated the worship of the Emperor.[16]

To the Emperor likewise the Greeks transferred the Hellenistic philosophic doctrine of the kingship and of the royal virtues which the ideal king should cultivate. It is in fact from the Roman period that we derive the earliest extant examples of this literature in the series of orations on kingship produced by Dio Chrysostom and the other notable rhetors of the Greek East.[17]

The imperial cult and these orations, notably the great panegyric of Aelius Aristides on Rome, accurately reflect the feeling of the Greeks to the Roman Empire during this period. The Greeks were not—with a few exceptions—legally Roman citizens, full members of the commonwealth. They were, and felt themselves to be, passive beneficiaries of Roman rule. The emperor was ideally, and to a large extent in practice, their great saviour and benefactor, who with his legions protected them from the barbarians and through his governors maintained internal peace. The Romans were the aristocracy who governed and guarded the provincials under the emperor's supreme command. Under the protecting aegis of Rome the Greek cities were enabled to live their own life, developing and expanding their Hellenic culture, building yet more splendid temples to their gods, yet more schools and gymnasia wherein they perfected their intellectual and physical education, yet more theatres and stadia wherein they celebrated yet more magnificent festivals of drama, music, and athletic prowess. For all this they felt profound gratitude to Rome and the emperor, but they regarded them as external benefactors, to be worshipped and celebrated in panegyrics. Like the immortal gods the emperors needed no help in their task, they required only due honour from their subjects. The loyalty of the Greeks to the Empire was in fact completely passive, and Rome evoked no active patriotism.[18]

In the course of the late third and early fourth centuries a number of changes occurred in the Empire which had profound

---

[16] Suetonius, *Augustus*, 52, *templa, quamvis sciret etiam proconsulibus decerni solere, in nulla tamen provincia nisi communi suo Romaeque nomine recepit*; Cassius Dio, LI. 20 (Asia and Bithynia), Suetonius, *Claudius*, 2, Strabo, IV. 192 (Gaul), Tacitus, *Annals* I.59 (Germany).

[17] Dio Chrysostom, *Or.* I–IV, Aelius Aristeides, *Or.* XXVI.

[18] [See now J. Palm, *Rom. Römertum u. Imperium in der griechischen Literatur der Kaiserzeit*, 1959; he points out (p. 54) that Lucian is the first Greek writer to speak of the Romans as 'we'.]

effects on the Greek East. One of the more important of these for our purposes was the gradual decay of Greek culture among the Roman governing class. In the first place the emperors tended at this period to be military men of relatively humble origins drawn from the less cultivated areas of the Latin West, particularly from Illyricum. Such men knew no Greek themselves, and they employed as their ministers and governors men of similar origins. Constantine indeed, having spent his boyhood at Diocletian's court in the East, knew some Greek—he could understand and even intervene in the debates at Nicaea, and the Theodosian Code has preserved a fragment of the acts of the imperial consistory in which he argues with a Greek litigant. But his native language was Latin—he was born at Naissus in the Latin speaking province of Dacia—and he preferred to give his opening address to the Council of Nicaea in Latin and had the theological treatises which Eusebius of Caesarea wrote for his edification translated into Latin. For his negotiations with the eastern Christian sects he employed a bilingual Antiochene, Strategius, who became his indispensable assistant in religious affairs, and rose to become the *comes* Musonianus. Of the later emperors of the eastern parts the Pannonian Valens knew little or no Greek, nor, probably, did the Spaniard Theodosius. These Emperors moreover imported many of their own countrymen to the East. Numerous boorish and illiterate (as far as Greek went) Pannonians came in Valens' train; Libanius complains that several governors of Syria, including the notorius Festus of Tridentum, knew no Greek. Two of Theodosius' praetorian prefects of the East, Cynegius and Rufinus, were westerners, hailing from Spain and Gaul respectively; Rufinus had to have Libanius' letters to him translated into Latin. The court of Constantinople thus continued to the end of the fourth century to be predominantly Latin speaking and many high officials spoke no Greek.[19]

Apart from this social change Greek withered away in the West even in the most cultivated circles. We cannot trace the chronology of the change, but by the second half of the fourth

---

[19] For Constantine at Nicaea, see Eusebius, *Vita Constantini*, III. 13, *Theod. H.E.* I. 12; in the consistory, *CTh* VIII. xv. 1; Eusebius' works translated into Latin, Eusebius, *Vita Constantini*, IV. 35. For Strategius Musonianus, see Ammianus Marcellinus, XV. xiii. 1. That Valens knew no Greek appears from Themistius, *Or.* IX. 126b. For Festus and Rufinus, see Lib. *Or.* I. 156, *Ep.* 865.

H

century even so polished an aristocrat as Symmachus confesses that he had to rub up his schoolboy Greek to help his son in his lessons. And so learned a man as Augustine, deeply interested in Greek philosophy and theology, never mastered Greek, using translations and occasionally, it would seem, spelling out a sentence or two with the aid of a lexicon. Boys still learned Greek at school, but they ceased to read Greek literature, and soon became rusty. By this date, even cultivated Romans of the West who took up posts in the eastern parts could not speak Greek or even read it with ease.[20]

The establishment of a second capital at Constantinople thus had the rather anomalous effect of making it necessary for the Greeks of the eastern parts to learn Latin if they aspired to high imperial offices or wished to penetrate court society. Those with rather humbler ambitions also had to acquire Latin. The central imperial ministries, including the praetorian prefecture of the East, conducted their business in Latin. Latin, moreover, became more and more desirable, if not indispensable, for barristers. Proceedings in court were, it is true, still conducted in Greek, but knowledge of Roman law was coming to be expected from the bar, and the teaching of Roman law and the texts from which it was taught were all in Latin. Libanius complained that in the old days a barrister was primarily an orator who pled his client's case in eloquent Greek; if he wanted to clarify a technical point of law he went to a jurisconsult—a very inferior person—for advice. Nowadays a barrister was expected to be learned in the law himself.[21]

To Libanius these changes seemed to sound the death knell of the traditional Greek literary and rhetorical education. Parents, he bitterly lamented, sent their sons to Beirut or to Rome to learn Latin and law. Greek culture was useless for the man of ambition. He needed Latin to secure a place in the higher civil service, or to practice with success at the bar. If he had loftier ambitions, he needed Latin to gain the ear of the great men at court who controlled patronage.[22]

[20] Symm. Ep. IV. 20. For Augustine's Greek, see H. I. Marrou, Saint Augustin et la fin de la culture antique[2], 27–46, 631–7.
[21] For Latin in the praetorian prefecture of the East, see Joh. Lydus, Mag. II, 12, III. 42; for rhetors and jurisconsults, Lib. Or. II. 43–4.
[22] Libanius complains of the abandonment of Greek for Latin and the law in Or. I. 214, 234, II. 43–4, XLVIII. 22–3, Ep. 951, 957.

As a result not only the elementary but the higher teaching of Latin received a considerable impetus in the Greek East. Under Diocletian Lactantius taught Latin rhetoric at Nicomedia, then the imperial residence, and in the university of Constantinople which was founded by Theodosius II there were as many Latin as Greek grammarians—ten of each—and three Latin rhetors to five Greek.[23] One very curious result of the new situation was that Greeks sometimes wrote literary works in Latin, hoping thereby to be read in high society. Ammianus of Antioch composed his great history in Latin, and Claudian of Alexandria was the author of Latin poetry. Another result was that a number of Latin words found their way into vulgar Greek—chiefly administrative and legal terms such as (δοῦξ, κόμης, or πεκούλιον). No one who aspired to literary elegance would deign to use such words; Libanius, rather than sully his lips with βικάριος regularly uses the cumbersome periphrasis 'ruler of several peoples' (πλειόνων ἐθνῶν ἄρχων). Athanasius, who had no literary pretensions, is guilty of ἀγεντισιρήβους (agentes in rebus). But Libanius insists on 'those who carry the king's letters' (οἱ τὰ βασιλέως γράμματα φέροντες).[24]

This dominance of Latin was transitory and left little permanent effect on the Greek culture of the East. Under Arcadius and Theodosius II, who had been born and bred at Constantinople, the court became Hellenized, and after the division of the Empire in 395 few westerners migrated to the eastern parts. Cyrus, praetorian prefect of the East in the middle of the fifth century, himself a Greek poet of some distinction, abolished the use of Latin in the praetorian prefecture. Legal textbooks were compiled in Greek, and Roman law seems to have been taught in Greek by the latter years of the fifth century. Latin was required only in the sacra scrinia, since imperial constitutions were issued in Latin as

---

[23] For Lactantius, see Jerome, de viris illustribus, 88; for the university of Constantinople CTh XIV. ix. 3, 425.

[24] Athanasius is much addicted to Latinisms, being guilty not only of ἀγεντισιρή-βους (Apol. ad Const. 10) but of δοῦξ, μάγιστρος, κόμης and παλάτιον in the same chapter, βῆλον in chapter 3, and κομεντάρια in chapter 29 of the same work. Latin words are naturally most common in the administrative jargon of the civil service (they abound in John Lydus and Justinian's novels), but are also frequent in the vulgar Greek of the papyri and of John Malalas. They are sedulously avoided by Libanius, Procopius and all authors of literary pretensions. See Lib. Or. II. 58, XLVIII. 7, LXII. 14. for periphrases for agentes in rebus.

well as Greek: John Lydus learned the language with the object of entering that distinguished ministry. But John's Latin, of which he was inordinately proud, was very elementary. Constitutions were in practice drafted in Greek, and the official Latin translation is often incorrect. Despite Libanius' gloomy fears, the ancient tradition of Greek grammatical and rhetorical education was maintained unimpaired not only in the major universities— if I may use a convenient if incorrect term—of Athens, Alexandria, and Constantinople, but by the official, salaried professors which all major cities still maintained, and by many private teachers. In this period literary culture received a yet wider extension, permeating the few backward areas that still survived under the principate. The cities of Egypt at last produced historians and poets, Olympiodorus of Thebes and Nonnus of Panopolis to name only the two most distinguished, and Cappadocia produced not only Basil of Caesarea, but Gregory from the minor provincial city of Nazianzus. Even Paphlagonia gave birth to the great orator Themistius.[25]

The physical side of education languished in a Christian environment. The last ephebic games of which we know took place at Oxyrhynchus in 323, the year before Constantine's conquest of the east. A gymnasiarch last appears in 370 in the same city. Athletic contests still formed part of the Antiochene Olympia in the last years of the fourth century. Thereafter we hear of athletes no more: the church preferred the 'athletes of God', who starved their bodies into submission. Gladiatorial contests also disappeared, banned by Constantine under Christian influence. Musical games survived, and indeed flourished, in the form of the mime, whose themes were still drawn from Greek mythology. Above all, chariot racing and the Roman import of wild beast fights excited the passions of the crowd.[26]

[25] For Cyrus's reform, see John Lydus, *Mag.* II. 12, III. 42, and for the adoption of Greek in the law schools Collinet, *Histoire de l'école de droit de Beyrouth*, 211 ff. John Lydus evidently learned Latin with a view to gaining a place among the *memoriales* of the *sacra scrinia* (*Mag.* III. 26). By the end of the sixth century Gregory the Great (*Ep.* VII. 27) complained that there was no one at Constantinople who could translate Latin competently.

[26] The last ephebic games are recorded in *P.Oxy.* 42, the last gymnasiarch in *P. Oxy.* 2110. For athletes at the Antiochene Olympia, see Lib *Or.* X, *passim*, and *Ep.* 843, 1179–83, 1278–9. For gladiators and *venationes*, see *supra*, note 12. Libanius defends the mime as preserving the pagan myths in *Or.* LXIV.

Roman law gradually prevailed in the Greek East. Its acceptance in the actual practice of the courts was presumably gradual. But it seems to have been systematically enforced by Diocletian. This, at any rate, is the conclusion that I would draw from the vast mass of rescripts which that Emperor issued on often elementary points of law. Litigants by now, it would seem, were anxious to know what their rights and liabilities were under Roman law, and put their cases to the emperors. The emperor, or rather his legal secretariat, provided answers which enlightened not only the barrister conducting the case, but the judge before whom it was tried. Roman law thus came to be generally known and followed. But it underwent in the process a certain infiltration of Greek legal practices and doctrines, which either survived by tacit custom or were formally written into the law by imperial constitutions. Particularly in the realm of family law a large Greek element was thus absorbed into the Roman system; in Justinian's legislation, for instance, the Greek rules about dowries have superseded the Roman, and the Greek institution of *donatio ante nuptias* has been received into the law.[27]

Oriental influences have been postulated in the development of late Roman art. Not being an expert I hesitate to speak on this subject, but I am bound to say that I am sceptical. What we know from indubitable archaeological and historical sources is that there was during the troubled period of the third century a great falling off, one might almost say a hiatus, in monumental architecture and sculpture. As a result, architects, sculptors, and other skilled craftsmen found little employment and the inherited tradition of skill was well nigh broken. In 334 Constantine complained in one of his laws that architects were not to be found, and granted state scholarships to young men to receive training in the profession. In 337 he bestowed immunities on a large range of skilled craftsmen—sculptors, painters, mosaicists, wood carvers and the like—to encourage them to train their sons in their respective crafts. That Constantine's complaints were justified is vividly demonstrated by the absurdly childish sculptures executed for his own triumphal arch at Rome, which are surely the crude efforts of simple monumental masons to produce large compositions.[28]

[27] See Jolowicz, *Historical Introduction to Roman Law*[2], 522 ff.
[28] *CTh* XIII. iv. 1, 334 (architects), 2, 337 (craftsmen).

I am not suggesting that late Roman art continued to be primitive. What I am inclined to think is that the highly sophisticated techniques of Hellenistic and Roman art were, to a large extent, lost in the dark age of the late third and early fourth centuries, and that this loss liberated artists from a tradition which was growing sterile, and enabled them to make a fresh start. Their initial efforts were crude, but had a certain primitive vigour and dignity. With the recovery of technical expertise their work acquired refinement and delicacy, but retained the rather rigid formalism of their simple beginnings, which evidently appealed to contempoarary taste.

What I have said applies especially to sculpture and the decorative arts, which were purely traditional crafts, taught by fathers to their sons, or masters to their apprentices. Architecture, on the other hand, was a liberal art—it is worthy of note that Constantine offered his scholarships only to young men who had completed their standard literary and rhetorical education—and while it too was taught by apprenticeship, it was based on theoretical text books. Most of the buildings of the later Empire were, it is true, unambitious in design—the wooden roofed, aisled basilica which was the standard church plan is, after all structurally very simple. But the science of *mechanice*, being enshrined in books, was preserved, and *mechanici*, who ranked higher than ordinary *architecti*, could thus design complex vaulted buildings, and in Justinian's reign excelled their Hellenistic and Roman forebears in the boldness and subtlety of their vaults and domes.[29]

The greatest change which the Empire underwent in the early fourth century was, of course, the conversion of Constantine and the consequent rise of Christianity to be the dominant and eventually the sole religion of the Roman world. The change was gradual, and still not quite complete in the sixth century. John of Ephesus found many thousands of rustic pagans to baptize in Asia, Lydia, and Caria, lands where the propagation of Christianity had begun in apostolic days, and in the highest classes of society at Constantinople itself purges held under Justinian and Tiberius Constantine revealed a substantial number of crypto-pagans, especially among intellectuals. The city of Carrhae in Mesopotamia was still predominantly pagan when it passed under Arab rule, and in the coastal mountains of Syria the

[29] See the very interesting account of Anthemius of Tralles in Agathias, V. 6 ff.

sect of Nusairi to this day preserve a faith which is basically neoplatonic.[30]

By and large, however, the Greek East was conquered by a religion which was in origin and essence oriental. Christianity, it is true, assimilated many Greek elements in the course of its early history. From the first it adopted the Greek language: its Old Testament was the Septuagint, and its own holy books were initially written in Greek. In the development of its theology it made use of the concepts of Greek philosophy. But it was based on Jewish monotheism and the teaching of a Jewish Messiah.

The acceptance of Christianity inevitably affected the theory of the monarchy; a Christian emperor could no longer be a god. Here Christianity was to some extent anticipated by pagan thought. With the growth of monotheistic or pantheistic ideas in the more philosophical and intellectual levels of pagan religious thought, the emperor tended to be regarded not as God but rather as the special protegé of the supreme divinity, or as being more deeply infused with the divine element than common men. It is perhaps significant that the gods are in the coinage of the tetrarchy styled companions (*comites*) or preservers (*conservatores*) of the emperors, and that Diocletian claimed to be not Jupiter Optimus Maximus but Iovius. This concept was adopted by Christianity. Eusebius of Caesarea, in the panegyric which he delivered to celebrate the thirtieth anniversary of Constantine's accession, works out with elaborate —and to modern ears almost blasphemous—detail, the analogy between the Father and the Son, and the Son and his representative and vicegerent on earth, the emperor.[31]

This change did nothing to diminish the divine aura which surrounded the emperor's person. Everything connected with him remained sacred and divine, so much so that an imperial constitution was colloquially called a σαχρα in Greek. Any resistance to his will continued to be sacrilege. The official imperial cult continued to be celebrated in the provinces; Constantine expressly authorised the province of Umbria to build 'a temple dedicated to our name', to elect its own priest and to hold

[30] For the mission in Asia, see John of Ephesus, *Hist. Eccl.* II. 44. III. 36–7. *Lives of the Eastern Saints*, xl, xliii, xlvii; for purges among the aristocracy, Malalas, 449, Joh. Eph. H.E. III. 27 ff.; for Carrhae and the Nusairi, *Encyclopedia of Islam*, II, 270, III. 964–5.

[31] Eusebius, *de laudibus Constantini*, *passim*.

theatrical and gladiatorial games, only stipulating that his temple 'shall not be polluted with the falsehoods of any contagious superstition'. Down to the sixth century the provincial assemblies continued to meet, and under the presidency of a *sacerdos* to celebrate games in the emperor's honour; only the sacrifices were abolished.[32]

The monarchy was during this period modified by both western and eastern influences. On the one hand, Diocletian at last succeeded in achieving what Alexander the Great had attempted six centuries earlier, the introduction of Persian royal robes and ceremonies, in particular *proskynesis*, or, as it was styled in Latin, *adoratio*. On the other hand, the reception of Roman law carried with it a greatly diluted republican view of the imperial office. The emperor's will was law because the people had conferred upon him the plenitude of sovereign power. This doctrine acquired practical importance only in an interregnum, when the election of an emperor devolved upon the people, as represented by 'the palace, the senate and the army'. In the western parts, from which this doctrine originated, election was never more than the formal ratification of a usurpation. In the eastern parts genuine elections conferred the imperial power on Jovian, Valentinian, Leo, Anastasius, and Justin I.[33]

The people of the Greek East had legally become Roman citizens in A.D. 212. By the fourth century they seem to have felt themselves to be Romans, laying claim both to the cultural heritage of Greece and the political heritage of Rome. But their basic attitude to the Empire did not change. They still regarded the emperor as a divinely appointed ruler, who, with his armies, protected them against the barbarians. In return they owed him reverence, obedience—and 'the sacred taxes'. However, if the emperor's armies failed to defend them, they felt no obligation to fight for the Empire themselves, but submitted helplessly to

---

[32] Constantine's temple, *I.L.S.*, 705. That the *sacerdotium provinciae* still existed under Justinian appears from *Cod. Just.* V. xxvii. 1 where the words are explained, *id est, Phoenicarchiae vel Syriarchiae.* For the games attached to the latter office, see *Cod. Just.* I. xxxvi. 1.

[33] For *adoratio*, see Eutropius, IX. 26, Aurelius Victor, *de Caesaribus*, xxxix. 2 ff. The republican doctrine is enunciated in Just. *Inst.* I. ii. 6, cf. *Dig.* I. iv. pr. (Ulpian). Imperial elections: Amm. Marc. XXV. v, XXVI. i, Const. Porph. *Cer.* I. 91–3. In the West Majorian (*Nov.* i) claimed: *imperatorem me factum, patres conscripti, vestrae electionis arbitrio et fortissimi exercitus ordinatione cognoscite.*

barbarian rule. The Roman Empire had not yet evoked any active and positive patriotism.

Before I summarise my conclusions there is one important point that I would like to emphasise—the thinness of the veneer of Hellenism which the Near East acquired. Except in the Greek homeland and in limited areas along the western and southern coasts of Asia Minor, where Greek culture had already penetrated deeply long before Alexander's day, Hellenism remained throughout the thousand years in which the Near East was governed by Macedonian kings and philhellenic emperors an upper class monopoly. Everywhere the peasantry continued to speak their native tongues, and even in the towns the lower classes knew little Greek and normally used the indigenous language. The evidence is abundant for Syria and Egypt. To quote a few typical instances only, John Chrysostom speaks of the country folk, including the rural clergy, who flocked to Antioch for the Easter festival, as a people of alien speech. Publius of Zeugma, who founded a Greek-speaking monastery in the neighbouring desert, was approached by Syriac speaking postulants, and eventually organised a double community in which worship was conducted separately in Greek and Syriac. Procopius, the first martyr of the Diocletianic persecution in Palestine, was reader of the church of Scythopolis, whose duty it was to translate the liturgy into Syriac for the benefit of townsmen who knew no Greek. In Egypt the abbot Apollonius picked those of his monks who knew both Greek and Egyptian to accompany a party of Greek visitors on the next stage of their tour and to act as interpreters.[34]

As Christianity penetrated more and more into rural areas the church felt the need of providing the converts with version of the Scriptures and the liturgy and other Christian literature written in their native language. In Syria there was no great difficulty, for in Mesopotamia a continuous literary tradition of Syriac had been preserved. A rich Christian-Syriac literature, both translations and original works, was already in being, and could be used by the humbler converts in Syria. In Egypt, on the other hand, the demotic script had died out in the third century. The Greek alphabet, with the addition of a few demotic letters, was adapted to the Egyptian language, and the Scriptures, the liturgy, and

[34] Joh. Chrys. *Hom. ad pop. Ant.* xix. 1; Theod. *Hist. Rel.* v (Publius); Eus. *Mart. Pal.* I. i (Syriac version; Procopius); Rufinus, *Historia Monachorum*, 7 (Apollonius).

some simple hagiographical literature was thus made available to Egyptian peasants and humble townsfolk. When Syria and Egypt fell to the Arabs, Greek survived for a few generations as the administrative language, but when the Caliphs substituted Arabic for it in the government offices, Greek very soon died out. Syriac and Coptic, on the other hand, survived for centuries, as both written and spoken languages.

The evidence is less abundant for Asia Minor, but here, too, it can be proved that a number of native languages survived in the fourth, fifth, and sixth centuries. Basil of Caesarea alludes in one of his sermons to Cappadocian as a language familiar to many of his congregation. Hagiographical anecdotes of the sixth century reveal that there were still Isaurians and Lycaonians who knew no Greek and spoke only their indigenous tongues. A Galatian monk in Palestine, struck dumb, could when he first recovered his speech speak only in Celtic. In Europe Thracian survived, and in a Thracian monastery in Palestine the liturgy was conducted in the native language. At what date Asia Minor became thoroughly Greek, I do not know, but the process was far from complete in the sixth century.[35]

If I may attempt to summarise my conclusions, the principate saw the political extinction of the Greek city, but the consolidation of Greek culture. Everywhere Greek education, maintained and subsidised by the cities, flourished among the upper classes, both in its intellectual and its physical aspects. Greek musical and athletic games were widespread as never before. In every city Greek art and architecture were lavishly patronised. The legal system of the East was still Greek. Only in religion were oriental influences on the upgrade; western influence was as yet negligible.

From the fourth century the dominance of Hellenism began to wane. The Byzantine Empire as a result inherited a legal system which was basically Roman, though it incorporated many Greek elements, and a religion which was basically oriental, though its theology was framed in Greek philosophical concepts. The Hellenistic monarchy was given an oriental dress and a Roman constitutional theory. The athletic ideal of Greek culture

[35] Basil, de Spiritu Sancto, 29 (Cappadocian); Holl, Hermes xliii (1908), p. 24 ff. (Isaurian and Lycaonian); Jerome, Comm. in Ep. Gal. ii, Cyril of Scythopolis, V. Euthymii, 55 (Galatian); Gregory of Nyssa, contra Eunomium, xii, Joh. Chrys. Hom. hab. in ecclesia Pauli (P.G., LXIII. 501), Symeon Metaphrastes, V. Theodori Coenobiarchi, 9 (Thracian).

perished with the physical education and the competitive games in which it was embodied. Only chariot races survived from the ancient athletic games of Greece and with these were coupled Roman wild beast fights. The musical games survived only in the degenerate form of the mime.

On the other hand, despite the break in the tradition caused by the prolonged troubles of the third century, Hellenistic art survived in a new form; Byzantine art was, unless I am greatly mistaken, a fresh growth from the old stock. Above all, the great corpus of Greek literature, philosophy, mathematics, and science was preserved together with the grammatical and rhetorical discipline of the schools, which ensured that this great heritage continued to be read and appreciated, copied and commented, and that the Greek language, while in its spoken and vulgar forms it underwent the changes which time inevitably brings, lived on as a literary medium in all its purity.

CHAPTER SIX

ANCIENT EMPIRES AND THE ECONOMY: ROME

I. THE REPUBLIC

FROM the middle of the third century B.C. an ever-increasing
stream of coin and bullion flowed into the Roman treasury
from countries overseas. It took the form of indemnities from
conquered enemies, booty, including the sums realised from the
sale of prisoners, the proceeds of mines, and taxation from the
provinces annexed. Down to 167 B.C. we have fairly full figures
for indemnities and for the booty paid into the treasury by commanders at their triumphs. In the ten years after the First Punic
War Carthage paid 4,400 talents (28½ million denarii);[1] after the
Second Punic War she paid 10,000 talents (60 million denarii),
spread over 50 years.[2] In the twelve years following 189 B.C.
Antiochus the Great paid 15,000 talents (90 million denarii).[3] The
booty and indemnities realised from Macedonia and Greece
between 201 and 167 B.C. are calculated to have amounted to over
70 million denarii.[4] Booty from Spain during the period of
conquest (206-196), before a regular system of taxation was
introduced, came to over 20 million denarii.[5] The figures for
booty, it must be remembered, are the net returns to the treasury
at Rome, and do not include large sums spent by commanders in
the field.

After 167 B.C. there continued to be occasional windfalls of
booty, such as the Attalid treasure, and the vast sums paid in by
Pompey after the Third Mithridatic War, but reliable figures are
rare; we know that the careful Cato realised nearly 7,000 talents

---

* This paper was Jones' contribution to a symposium on 'Ancient Empires and
the Economy' at the Third International Conference of Economic History, 1965.
[1] Polyb., I, 62-3, 88.
[2] Livy, XXX, 37; Polyb., XV, 18.
[3] Livy, XXXVIII, 38.
[4] Tenney Frank, ed., *Economic Survey of Ancient Rome*, IV, 313-25.
[5] *Op. cit.*, III, 128-9.

(about 40 million denarii) from the treasure of the little kingdom of Cyprus in 58 B.C.[6] At the same time regular revenue from the mines and from provincial tribute grew. In the middle of the seond century the silver mines of New Carthage brought in to the Roman people 25,000 denarii a day, that is about 9 million a year.[7] Pompey at his triumph in 61 B.C. stated that before his conquests the revenue from tribute had been 50 million denarii per annum, and was increased by his conquests to 85 millions.[8] Caesar added 10 million by the annexation of Gaul.[9]

The chief result of this vast influx of coin and bullion was that the Roman people paid little or nothing for the initial conquest and the continued garrisoning of their expanding Empire. After 167 B.C. no *tributum* was ever levied again,[10] and even before that date it would seem that not only war loans but *tributum* levied for the wars was repaid to the citizen body.[11] Little of the money was however spent in Italy. Some was used for public works, mainly at Rome, by the censors. The Attalid treasure was allocated to grants to the Gracchan colonists for their initial expenses.[12] Caesar in 59 used the money which Pompey had paid into the treasury for the purchase of land for the settlement of his veterans.[13] From the time of Gaius Gracchus increasing sums

[6] For Pompey, Pliny (*N.H.*, XXXVII, 16) gives 200 million sesterces for the treasury, 400 million for the quaestors and legates and 6,000 H.S. for each soldier. Appian (*Mith.*, 116) gives 75,100,000 denarii (in coin) for the treasury and 16,000 talents (=96 million denarii) for the troops, 1,500 denarii for each private and officers proportionately. Plutarch (*Pompey*, 45) gives 20,000 talents (=120 million denarii) for the treasury and 1,500 denarii for each soldier. Cyprus: Plut., *Cato Min.*, 38.

[7] Strabo, III, ii, 10, p. 148 (citing Polybius).

[8] Plut., *Pomp.*, 45, πρὸς δὲ τούτοις ἔφραζε διὰ τῶν γραμμάτων ὅτι πεντακισχίλιαι μὲν μυριάδες ἐκ τῶν τελῶν ὑπῆρχον ἐκ δ' ὧν αὐτὸς προσεκτήσατο τῇ πόλει μυριάδας ὀκτακισχιλίας πεντακοσίας λαμβάνουσιν. This should mean that the revenue from the eight old provinces was 50 millions, and that Bithynia, Pontus, Cilicia and Syria yielded 85 millions, but this is scarcely credible, and Plutarch must have misunderstood the figures. [But see E. Badian, *Roman Imperialism in the Late Republic* 70 f., arguing that Pompey also exacted tribute from client states.]

[9] Suet., *Julius*, 25.

[10] Pliny, *N.H.*, XXXIII, 56. [But cf. Brunt. *Italian Manpower* 21 n. 5.]

[11] Of the war contributions made in 210 (Livy, XXVI, 36), two-thirds were repaid in 204, and 202 (Livy, XXIX, 16) and the last third settled in land in 200 (Livy, XXXI, 13). In 187 B.C. twenty-five and a half levies of *tributum simplex* were repaid (Livy, XXXIX, 7).

[12] Plut., *Tib. Gracch.*, 14.

[13] Caesar bought land at the price declared in the census, using the money ἀπό τε τῆς λείας ἣν ὁ Πομπήιος εἰλήφει καὶ ἀπὸ τῶν φόρων τῶν τε τελῶν τῶν προκαταστάντων (Cassius Dio, XXXVIII, 1), as well as distributing any surviving pub-

were spent on providing cheap and eventually free corn for the urban plebs, but in relation to the public revenues the sums involved were negligible: in 70 B.C. the annual expense was a little over 1,500,000 denarii and Cato's law raised the bill to seven and a half millions.[14] The great mass of the money was spent on wars and on the increasing regular garrisons of the provinces. Cicero in 66 B.C. stated that 'the taxes of the other provinces are such that we can scarcely be content with them for the protection of the actual provinces'.[15] and that only Asia yielded a surplus. Such surpluses as accumulated seem to have been spent on wars, and the treasury never appears to have had a large balance except immediately after a great haul of booty. This means that nearly all the income of the treasury was spent in the provinces in the form of military pay and supplies, and very little remained in Italy.

Very large sums also flowed into private hands in Italy from abroad. Common soldiers received bounties at triumphs. These rose from small sums, of the order of 25 denarii, in the early second century to 1,500 denarii at Pompey's triumph in 66 B.C.[16] The great bulk of the money, however, went to men of the upper and middle classes, senators and *equites*. At triumphs, the higher officers received far larger sums than the men; to his legates and quaestors, Pompey allocated 25 million denarii, that is about a million each, and nearly as much again, it would seem, to his tribunes and centurions: roughly half the bounty must have gone to under 600 officers, and half to over 30,000 rank and file.[17]

---

lic land, except the *ager Campanus*. He later used the *ager Campanus* also, but apparently for the plebs of Rome and not for veterans (Dio, XXXVIII, 7; cf. Suet., *Julius*, 20, 3).

[14] From Cic. *II Verr.*, III, 72, it appears that the annual issue of corn in 70 B.C. was about 2,500,000 *modii*, which at $2\frac{1}{2}$ H.S. per *modius* would have cost a little over 1,500,000 denarii. Cato's law raised the bill to 1,250 talents, that is 7,500,000 denarii (Plut., *Cat. Min.*, 26).

[15] Cic., *Pro lege Manilia*, 14. Cicero is no doubt exaggerating, since his object is to emphasize the supreme importance of Asia; Sicily and Sardinia, which were generally ungarrisoned, yielded a modest clear profit. But the military cost of the Spains and Macedonia may well have exceeded their revenues.

[16] Early donatives to the troops are listed in Tenney Frank, *op. cit.*, I, 127–37. For Pompey's donative see p. 82, n. 2 above.

[17] Pliny, *N.H.*, XXXVII, 16. Tigranes paid centurions twenty times as much as common soldiers and tribunes a hundred and twenty times as much (Appian, *Mith.*, 104; Strabo, XI, xiv, 10, 530). On this scale Pompey's donative to tribunes would have been 180,000 denarii and to centurions 30,000 denarii. Assuming that Pompey's army was eight legions, officers (48 tribunes and 480 centurions) would have received 23 million denarii. Legates, quaestors, tribunes and centurions

Commanders-in-chief seem to have been allowed, in the first century at any rate, to reserve even greater sums as *manubiae* for themselves.

Senators profited greatly from various forms of corruption and extortion. They received bribes from foreign potentates and communities for political services. As early as 129 B.C., Manius Aquillius accepted substantial bribes in his settlement of the Attalid kingdom[18] and many senators were convicted of having been corrupted by Jugurtha.[19] The sums involved were sometimes huge; Ptolemy Auletes in 59 B.C. paid 6,000 talents (36 million denarii) to the triumvirs for his recognition as king of Egypt, and promised Gabinius 10,000 talents for the reconquest of his kingdom.[20]

Extortion by provincial governors and their staffs began early; the first complaint recorded is that of the Spanish provinces in 182 B.C.[21] By 149 B.C., it had become so common a practice that a standing court was instituted for the trial of offenders.[22] It is impossible to estimate the amount of money that senators thus brought back from the provinces, but the few figures which we possess suggest that it was very substantial. Cicero in the *Verrines* claims that he could prove exactions against Verres totalling 10 million denarii during his three-year government of Sicily,[23] and it seems unlikely that he would have published his claim unless it was borne out by the official figure of damages assessed by the court. Other figures are of the same order of magnitude. Dolabella, proconsul of Cilicia in 80-79 B.C., was convicted of having made three-quarters of a million denarii under one heading alone, the requisitioning of supplies,[24] and later proconsuls of Cilicia received an annual bribe of 200 talents (1,200,000 denarii) from the cities of Cyprus to avoid having troops billeted on

---

between them would have received 48 millions, half the total bounty of 96 millions (Appian, *Mith.*, 116). The other half would have been shared between 32,000 men, which works out at 4,000 men a legion.

[18] Appian, *B.C.*, I, 22, *Mith.*, 57.

[19] Sallust, *Jug.*, 40.

[20] Suet., *Julius*, 54; Plut., *Antony*, 3. On a smaller scale Gabinius and Scaurus as legates of Pompey received 300 and 400 talents from Aristobulus of Judaea (Jos., *Ant.*, *Jud.*, XIV, iii, 2).

[21] Livy, XLIII, 2.

[22] Cic., *De Off.*, II, 75.

[23] Cic., *I Verr.*, 56.

[24] Cic., *II Verr.*, I, 95.

them.[25] Not all governors were as rapacious as Verres, but there were regular perquisites which almost all took, and most expected to make substantial sums out of their governorships.

Men of the equestrian order drew large profits from farming the provincial taxes. They farmed the customs in all provinces, but their main profits were derived from the tithe in Asia and from Pompey's time in Bithynia, Pontus, Cilicia and Syria. Here again it is impossible to estimate the sums involved, but there is no reason to think that the contractors limited their profits to the small illegal but customary commissions which they added to the amount of the tax—the *tres quinquagesimae* (6 per cent) in kind, the *accessiones* in cash.[26] The main profit came from overestimating the amount of the crop and the resultant tithe, and here Cicero produces precise figures which show that some Sicilian cities were obliged to accept *pactiones* which fixed the sum that they paid to the contractor at more than double the sum that he had bid for the tithe.[27] Not all governors were as indulgent to the tax farmers as Verres, no doubt, but few had the strength of mind to resist the pressure of the *publicani*, whose political influence was great. Cicero admits to his brother Quintus that it is impossible 'both to satisfy the *publicani*, particularly if the taxes have been bought at disadvantageous terms, and not to allow the ruin of our subjects', and suggests that he urges the provincials 'in making the *pactiones* not to regard the censorial rules but rather the convenience of finishing the business and being freed from trouble.'[28]

Another great source of profit in which both *equites* and senators shared was making loans to the provincial communities and to client kings, when they were unable to pay their taxation and the various forms of extortion to which they were subject. Governors solicitous of the welfare of the provincials endeavoured to limit the rate of interest to 12 per cent, but much higher rates were habitually charged. Brutus, as is notorious, made the Salaminians pay 48 per cent, [29] and Cicero implies that the *publicani*

    [25] Cic., *Ad. Att.*, V, 21, 7. Piso extracted 100 talents (600,000 denarii) from Achaea as *aurum coronarium* (Cic., *in Pis.*, 90). One *nobilis* expected to get 200,000 H.S. (50,000 denarii) by way of *aedilicium vectigal* from Asia (Cic., *Ad Q.f.*, I, 1, 26); this levy goes back to 179 B.C. (Livy, XL, 44).
    [26] Cic., *II Verr.*, III, 116 f.   [27] See n. 15.
    [28] Cic., *Ad Q.f.*, I, 1, 32, 35.
    [29] Cic., *Ad Att.*, V, 21, 11.

in their *pactiones* normally stipulated for considerably more than
12 per cent to be paid on arrears.[30] The indemnity of 20 thousand
talents imposed by Sulla in Asia in 84 B.C. had, by 70 B.C., been
paid twice over and yet there remained outstanding 120,000
talents of interest.[31] Here again it is impossible to estimate the
sums involved but they undoubtedly were very large. Ariobar-
zanes of Cappadocia was paying Pompey 33 talents a month
(between 2 and 3 million denarii a year) as interest on his loans,
and was unable to satisfy Brutus and other creditors.[32]

There is no evidence to estimate how much of the profits of
the provinces went to the treasury, and how much into the
pockets of the Roman upper class, but there are a number of
figures which suggest that private profits greatly exceeded public
revenue. Verres, as we have seen, made over 3 million denarii a
year out of Sicily, and the wheat tithe of Sicily, which accounted
for the bulk of the revenue, amounted to 3 million *modii*, which
at current prices, was worth under 2,000,000 *denarii*. Verres then
probably put into his own pocket considerably more than the
Roman treasury drew from Sicily.[33] Verres was no doubt a
master of extortion, but Caesar in his governorship of Hither
Spain not only paid his debts, which amounted to 5 or 6 million
denarii, but made himself a rich man.[34] As the revenues of the
eight provinces which existed before Pompey's conquests
amounted to 50 millions, the share of Hither Spain must have
come to 6 or 7 millions; for, if Sicily and Sardinia yielded less than
the average (and their revenue being mostly in corn may not have
been included in Pompey's figures), Asia yielded much above the
average. Caesar then made for himself a sum of the same order
as the public revenue, and he has never been accused of extortion.

---

[30] Cic., *Ad Att.*, VI, 1, 16.

[31] Plut., *Sulla*, 25, *Lucullus*, 20. ἦν δὲ τοῦτο κοινὸν δάνειον ἐκ τῶν δισμυρίων ταλάντων οἷς τὴν Ἀσίαν ἐζημίωσεν ὁ Σύλλας· καὶ διπλοῦν ἀπεδόθη τοῖς δανείσασι ὑπ'
ἐκείνων ἀνηγμένον ἤδη τοῖς τόκοις εἰς δώδεκα μυριάδας ταλάντων If nothing had
been repaid the rate of compound interest would be only 12 per cent.

[32] Cic., *Ad Att.*, VI, 1, 3.

[33] Verres received 9,000,000 H.S. per annum for the purchase of the second tithe
at 3 H.S. per *modius* (Cic., *II Verr.*, III, 163), and the standard price of wheat in
Sicily was 2½ H.S. per *modius* (*ib.*, 84, 173–4, 179, 189).

[34] Caesar owed 25 millions (presumably sesterces) according to Appian (*B.C.*,
II, 8), and Crassus according to Plutarch (*Caesar*, 11) went surely on this occasion
for the more pressing claims, amounting to 830 talents (20 millions H.S.). Caesar
returned a rich man (Plut., *Caesar*, 12) but is never accused of extortion. He no doubt
made his money by sale of booty, including slaves, as he later did in Gaul.

I

The profits of the tax farmers, in the cases recorded by Cicero, average 120 per cent. The cases which Cicero quotes are no doubt the worst he could find but they were not necessarily those where the contractors' profits were the highest. Verres, as Cicero admits, sold the tithe at high prices, and in some cases the bidding went so high that a profit was impossible. The case of Herbita is illuminating. In the first year the bid was 18,000 and the profit over 200 per cent; in the second year the bidding went up to 25,800 and profit dropped to only 80 per cent; in the third year the first bid was quite absurd, 48,600, and Verres had to reduce it to 45,000 to allow the contractor a modest profit of 3,600. Similarly at Therma, where the profit was only 15 per cent, the city government had bid desperately to secure the contract for itself.[35]

It would seem that, confident that governors would support their most extravagant claims, the *publicani* sometimes bid so recklessly that they found it impossible to extract enough from the provincials to make what they considered a fair profit. It is significant that such reckless bidding was not confined to Sicily under Verres. On a famous occasion the Asiatic tithe company

---

[35] Cicero gives the following figures, which he could presumably prove, in II *Verr.*, III.

Reference	City	decumae (contract price in modii)	lucrum (contractor's profit in modii)	accessio (cash bonus converted in modii)	Total profit (in modii)
75 ff.	Herbita (1)	18,000	38,800	—	38,800
—	(2)	25,800	21,000	800	21,800
—	(3)	45,000 (reduced from 48,600)	3,600	—	3,600
83	Acesta	2,000 (reduced from 5,000)	3,000	600	3,600
84	Lipara	3,600	—	12,000	12,000
89	Amestrata	4,800	5,100	600	5,700
90	Petra	18,000	—	20,800	20,800
91	Halicyae	600	—	6,000	6,000
99	Therma	48,000	7,000	800	7,800
100	Henna	49,200	18,000	1,200	19,200
110 ff.	Leontini	216,000	356,000	36,000	392,400
	Total	431,000			531,700

For Verres' boast that he sold the tithes at high prices, see II *Verr.*, III, 40.

pressed for and obtained a *demptio de capite* of $33\frac{1}{3}$ per cent.[36] These figures suggest that in some cases at any rate, the governors and the *publicani* each made as much again as, if not more than, the taxes of the provinces. To these sums must be added the interest on loans, which we have no means of calculating. We only know that debt—surety to Roman leaders—was a grave problem in the provinces, not only in Asia after Sulla but in the western provinces as well.[37]

The enormous fortunes accumulated by Roman magnates in the late Republic confirm this impression. Crassus is said to have owned 40 or 50 million *denarii*.[38] But this fortune was modest compared with that of the great conqueror Pompey, who apparently died worth 175 millions.[39]

The vast sums which came into the hands of senators and *equites* from the Empire were partly spent on luxury goods and slaves, and as these were mostly imported from abroad, much of the money returned to the provinces and other foreign countries. But luxuries did not account for the whole amount, and most of the recipients wished to put a part of their profits into the only permanent form of capital known to the ancient world, land. There was thus built up a great demand for land, primarily Italian land, which was probably the most important cause of the growth of *latifundia* at the expense of the small holdings of the peasantry In another way also the Empire contributed to this movement. The defence of the provinces demanded long term military service from the peasantry and weakened their economic position.[40]

Some efforts were made to reverse the process by resettling landless peasants on the land, but all met with determined resistance from the propertied classes, and few were successful. After the public land of Italy was exhausted, there were only two ways of obtaining allotments, by confiscation and by purchase. Sulla used the former on a large scale to settle his veterans, and Caesar

[36] Cassius Dio, XXXVIII, 7; Suet., *Julius*, 20; Appian, *B.C.*, II, 13.

[37] For Spain see Plut., *Caesar*, 12; for Gaul, Sallust, *Cat.*, 40, 4; Cic., *Pro Fonteio*, 11, for Sardinia, Livy, XXXII, 27.

[38] Pliny, *N.H.*, XXXIII, 134 (200 million H.S.); Plut., *Crassus*, 2 (7,100 talents).

[39] According to Cic., *Phil.*, XIII, 12, Sextus Pompeius was offered 700 million H.S. by the Senate in compensation for the confiscation of his father's property. Appian, *B.C.*, III, 4, makes it only 200 millions.

[40] Sallust, *Jug.*, 41; Appian, *B.C.*, I, 7.

the latter, both for Pompey's men and his own. But the expnsee of buying land was enormous, since prices were naturally high owing to heavy general demand for land, and the treasury could rarely afford it. Even Caesar found it necessary to settle many of his veterans on confiscated provincial land.[41]

Some upper class Romans also used their surplus wealth to acquire provincial lands. We know of this process only by casual references, mainly in Cicero's speeches and letters, and it is difficult to estimate its scale. In the *Verrines* Cicero mentions three *equites*, a senator and the wife of a senator who owned estates in Sicily.[42] Atticus possessed considerable estates in Epirus,[43] and we hear of two other upper class Romans who owned large properties in Africa.[44] We also hear of a number of Roman landowners in Asia.[45] Some of these owners lived on their provincial estates, but the more important were absentee landlords and their rents swelled the movement of money from the provinces to Italy.

The Empire set in motion certain important population changes. During the wars, from the first Punic War to Caesar's conquest of Gaul, vast numbers of prisoners were sold as slaves and the majority were imported into Italy, though very considerable numbers went to Sicily to work on the land, and to Spain for service in the mines. From the middle of the second century the supply of slaves was increased by kidnapping and piracy. Some regions were depopulated by this movement; Epirus had in Strabo's day not yet recovered from its ruthless treatment after the Third Macedonian War when 150,000 prisoners were sold as slaves.[46] On the numbers imported into Italy we have no figures, but they must have been very large. In the suppression of Spartacus' revolt, over 100,000 slaves are said

[41] Some idea of the cost of land settlement is given by Augustus, *Res Gestae*, 16; he spent 150 million denarii on Italian land and 65 million on provincial land in the years 30 B.C. and 14 B.C. From 7 B.C. he went over to cash payments, presumably to save money, and in five years spent 100 million. In 6 A.D. he fixed the cash bonus at 3,000 denarii (Cassius Dio, L.V., 23). Assuming that Pompey's army numbered 32,000 (see above p. 116, n. 17) and that 3,000 denarii was spent on each, Caesar's law of 59 B.C. must have involved nearly 100 million denarii, well over the total of Pompey's booty in cash (see above p. 115, n. 6).

[42] Cic., *II Verr.*, III, 36, 60, 61, 93, 97.

[43] Cic., *Ad Att.*, I, 5, 7; XVI, 16. A-F.

[44] Cic., *Pro Caelio*, 73; Nepos, *Atticus*, 12, 4.

[45] Cic., *Pro Flacco*, 51, 72 f., *Ad Fam.*, XIII, 53, 69; *I.G.R.*, IV, 1302.

[46] Livy, XLV, 34; Polyb., XXX, 15; Plut., *Aem.*, 29; Strabo, VII, vii, 3, p. 322.

to have been killed,[47] and though these figures are not trust-worthy, the difficulty which the Roman government had in suppressing the revolt shows that the numbers involved must have been very considerable.

The vast import of slaves increased the distress of the Italian peasantry, for since slaves were cheap and abundant landlords used them extensively to cultivate the estates which they had built up, and the peasantry was thus deprived not only of its land but of employment. How far imported slaves modified the racial structure of the Italian population is a much disputed point. Those engaged in domestic service were freely manumitted, and they and their descendants swelled the urban population, particularly of Rome. Rural slaves on the other hand were rarely freed, and if they lived in barracks and worked in chain gangs had little chance of propagating themselves.

There was on the other hand some migration from Italy. We hear constantly of Roman and Italian merchants and businessmen in the provinces, and numbers seem to have been large—80,000 (including wives and children and freedmen) are said to have been massacred in Asia by Mithridates.[48] It is, however, very uncertain what proportion of these businessmen settled down permanently in the provinces, and it is on the whole probable that the majority returned home when they had made their pile. Veterans discharged in the provinces seem to have settled there more commonly. Pompey in 49 B.C. was able to raise a legion 'from Crete and Macedonia from veteran soldiers who had been discharged by previous commanders and had settled in these provinces'.[49]

There were also some official colonies planted in the provinces. Gaius Gracchus initiated one at Carthage and settlers were, it seems, actually planted. Narbo was founded in Gaul in 118 B.C. Some of the Marian veterans were settled in Sardinia and Africa. It was not however until Caesar that overseas colonization was undertaken on any large scale.

The provinces were undoubtedly seriously impoverished by the rule of the Roman Republic, mainly through the illicit

[47] Livy, *Epit.*, 96–7.
[48] Memnon, fr. 22.
[49] Caesar, *B.C.*, III, 4. Cf. R. E. Smith, *Service in the Post-Marian Roman Army*, 53 ff. [See now P. A. Brunt, *Italian Manpower* ch. XIV.]

exactions of the governors and tax farmers and the exorbitant interest of the debts which they thereby incurred. This is most clearly demonstrated by the virtual cessation of civic building in this period in the provinces. Those who profited from the Empire were the senatorial and equestrian classes in Italy, but they did not use their newly acquired wealth for any economically productive purpose; they spent it either on luxury goods or on the acquisition of land. Their demand for luxuries encouraged a one-way traffic of imports into Italy, which provided employment for provincial craftsmen and profits to merchants both provincial and Italian. Their acquisition of land led to the pauperisation of many of the Italian peasantry. The Italian lower classes lost rather than gained by the Empire. Many of them lost their land and were recompensed only by cheap corn if they migrated to Rome, or meagre pay in the army.

II. THE PRINCIPATE

There can be little doubt that under the principate the flow of wealth from the provinces into Italy was greatly reduced. Extortion by provincial governors did not altogether cease, as the successful trials for *repetundae* show, and it was sometimes on a large scale; Caecilius Classicus boasted that he had made 1,000,000 denarii out of his proconsulship of Baetica—and he had at the time by no means completed his operations.[50] But it would seem that there were on the whole fewer dishonest governors and that a better check was kept upon them. The major gain of the provinces was the abolition of the tithe system and the substitution for it of a fixed tax assessed on property, since the *publicani* were thereby excluded from the collection of the direct taxes.[51] Moneylending did not cease altogether. The rebellion of Florus and Sacrovir in Northern Gaul under Tiberius was provoked by the burden of debt, owed, it would seem, to Roman *negotiatores*,[52] and Seneca is said to have lent 10,000,000 denarii at exorbitant rates of interest to the Britons.[53] But the trouble seems to have been confined to

[50] Pliny, *Ep.*, III, 9, 13, Io io, liber ad te venio; iam sestertium quadragies redegi parte vendita Baeticorum. Cf. Brunt, in *Historia*, X (1961), 189 ff. for the persistence of extortion in the Principate.

[51] Cf. pp. 165f, but also 180ff.   [52] Tac., *Ann.*, III, 40.

[53] Cassius Dio, LXII, 2; cf. Tac., *Ann.*, XIII, 42.

economically backward areas, unused to regular taxation, and in general the provincials, having to pay out less in extortion, had probably less cause to borrow.

Italy nevertheless continued to enjoy a privileged position. Its land was still immune from taxation and some part of the revenue from the provinces was spent in Italy. The Italian countryside profited from road building and the *alimenta*, but the chief gainer was Rome, whose corn supply, public works, police and municipal services in general were paid for by imperial revenue. The salaries of the central administrative offices were spent in Rome, moreover, and as most of the higher imperial administrative officers in the rest of the Empire were domiciled in Italy, their salaries were also largely spent or invested in Italy; these salaries were not inconsiderable, 75,000 or 50,000 denarii for higher grade procurators and 250,000 denarii for consular proconsuls.[54]

As under the Republic, the surplus income of the Italian upper classes was mostly spent on imported luxuries and on the acquisition of land. The demand for luxury goods stimulated their manufacture, mainly in provincial centres, and trade, especially with the Far East, in items such as silk, spices and gems. This trade was as under the Republic one-sided, the imports being paid for in money. It greatly enriched certain eastern cities through which it passed, such as Alexandria and Palmyra, whose period of great prosperity falls under the Principate. [Cf. ch. xx.]

The land hunger of the Roman aristocracy carried further the formation of large estates in Italy at the expense of the surviving small holders. It also increasingly extended to the provinces. Under Claudius, senators were allowed to visit Sicily and Narbonese Gaul in order to inspect their estates without obtaining special leave;[55] this implies that very many of them must have owned property in these neighbouring provinces, but it is not to be inferred that many did not also own land further afield. We happen to know that Sextus Marius owned considerable properties, including mines, in Spain,[56] and that Rubellius Plautus possessed ancestral lands in Asia.[57]

[54] The salary scales of procurators were *sexagenarii, centenarii, ducenarii, trecenarii*; for proconsuls see Cassius Dio, LXXIX, 22.
[55] Tac., *Ann.*, XII, 23; cf. Cassius Dio, LII, 42.
[56] Tac., *Ann.*, VI, 19; Cassius Dio, LVIII, 22.
[57] Tac., *Ann.*, XIV, 22. Sextus Pompeius owned lands in Macedonia, as well as

There thus began an increasing flow of rents from provincial estates to owners domiciled in Italy. This flow was later increased by the grant of senatorial rank to provincial landed magnates, who migrated to Italy. They were obliged to invest a part of their wealth (a third under Trajan, a quarter under Marcus Aurelius) in Italian land, but naturally retained the bulk of their provincial estates,[58]

These rents must have been considerable, a factor in the economy of the Empire comparable with the imperial revenue. It is too often assumed that because the financial qualification for the senate was a million sesterces, most senators did not own much more than that sum. The richest senators are in fact credited with fortunes of 100, 200, 300 and even 400 millions.[59] A protégé of Pliny's who aspired to the *latus clavus* was given 4 millions by his mother during her lifetime in order to enable him to make a start, and he also inherited his father's fortune, and had expectations from his stepfather, who adopted him.[60] Pliny himself, who was well off but not outstandingly wealthy, appears to have possessed about 20 millions.[61] The pittance allowed to impoverished noblemen to enable them to keep up their station was half a million a year.[62] If Pliny's income, about a million a year, be taken as an average, the total rental drawn by 600 senators would have been 150 million *denarii*, of which an increasing proportion was drawn from the provinces. We have no figures for the state revenues under the Principate but at the end of the Republic they were under 100 millions [p. 115.]

A large amount of provincial land, especially senatorial estates, passed into the imperial patrimony by bequest or confiscation. The rents of these estates were mainly spent in Rome

---

in Sicily and Campania (Ovid, *ex Ponto*, IV, v, 9 f.; xv, 15 f.). See also Pliny, *N.H.*, XVIII, 35 for Africa and the list of Egyptian estates belonging to Romans in Rostovtzeff, *Social and Economic History of the Roman Empire*, 670–1.

[58] Pliny, *Ep.*, VI, 19; S.H.A., *Ant. Phil.*, 11. Pliny notes that the sale of provincial lands by aspirants to the senate gave an opportunity to Italians to buy in the provinces cheap.

[59] Pliny, *N.H.*, XVIII, 37 (Tarius Rufus, 100 millions); Pliny, *Ep.*, II, 20 (Aquilius Regulus, 60 to 120 millions); schol. ad Juv., IV, 81 (Passienus Crispus, 200 millions); Tac., *Ann.*, XIII, 42; Cassius Dio, LXI, 10 (Seneca, 300 millions); Tac, *Dial.*, 8 (Eprius Marcellus, Vibius Crispus, 300 millions); Seneca, *De beneficiis*, II, 27, 1 (Cornelius Lentulus, 400 millions).

[60] Pliny, *Ep.*, X, 4.

[61] R. P. Duncan-Jones, *P.B.S.R.*, XXXII (1965), pp. 177-88

[62] Tac., *Ann.*, XIII, 34; Suet.,, *Nero*, 10 *Vesp.*, 17.

on the maintenance of the imperial court and the central administration.

Nonetheless the provincial communities, as is proved by the immense outburst of civic building and the foundation of numerous games, were far more prosperous than under the Republic. This was no doubt to a large extent due to the relative peace enjoyed by the Empire as a whole, after the constant foreign and civil wars of the Republic. Even in peace-time, however, the military expenditure of the Empire must have been considerable, since it maintained a standing army which was larger than the normal establishment of the late Republic, and was twice as well paid. The revival of the provinces must have been due to a large extent to decrease in extortion.

Buildings and games are evidence for the prosperity of the provincial aristocracy, the decurions, who largely financed them, but it is more doubtful if the peasantry of the provinces shared in the increased wealth of the Empire. Imperial taxation, though less oppressive than the multifarious exactions of the Republic, seems to have borne heavily on the poorer landowners at any rate. It was moreover not progressive, the humble peasant proprietor paying at the same rate as the rich landowner, and it did not vary according to the harvest, the same sum being due in bad years as in good. While not in general oppressive it could at times hit the humble class of taxpayer hard, and it no doubt forced many to mortgage or sell their land, and thus promoted the concentration of landed property in the hands of the rich.[63]

The raising and spending of the imperial revenue effected a certain re-distribution of wealth between the provinces. The bulk of the revenue was raised in the richer provinces of the Mediterranean basin, notably Africa, Asia, Syria and Egypt, but the greater part of it was spent on the army, which was mostly stationed in poorer and underdeveloped areas such as Britain, the Rhineland and the Danubian provinces. This expenditure stimulated the development of these backward areas, and in particular the growth of towns in them. The distribution of the army also initially, so long as the legions were recruited in Italy

[63]Apart from complaints of heavy taxation (e.g. Tac., *Ann.*, I, 76, III, 40) it is significant that Hadrian had to cancel 900 million sesterces of arrears of tribute (*I.L.S.*, 309). [Dio, LXXI 32 records a similar remission by Marcus Aurelius, cf. 3, 3 for his feeling that taxation had reached its limit; and *S.E.G.* XVII 755 (Domitian).]

or in other Mediterranean areas such as Narbonensis and Spain, caused a movement of population to the frontier areas, since most veterans were planted in colonies or spontaneously settled in the districts in which they had served. As however local recruitment became the rule, this movement ceased.

The slave trade, which the Republic had greatly stimulated by its wars and conquests and by its neglect of public security by sea and land, was greatly reduced under the Principate. After Augustus, wars of conquest were few and internal rebellions rare, so that the number of prisoners of war put on the market was very greatly reduced. Within the empire piracy was virtually abolished and brigandage well controlled, so that kidnapping became rare. The result was that by the second century the stock of slaves was largely dependent on breeding, and, as the demand remained high, prices rose very steeply. It ceased to be profitable to employ slave gangs in agriculture and mining, and it became usual to cultivate estates by dividing them into small holdings and leasing them to tenant farmers, and to use free indentured labour in the mines, or to lease shafts to free miners.[64] The change in agriculture was beneficial to the peasantry in that landless men could obtain employment as tenants. This is no doubt one reason why Italian recruitment in the legions fell off; there was no longer, as in the last century of the Republic, a pool of rural unemployed.

By suppressing piracy and brigandage, developing inland waterways and building roads, supplying a sound currency and levying only moderate tolls, the imperial government created conditions favourable for the development of trade. On the other hand it limited the scope of commerce in that in supplying its own needs, notably the feeding and clothing of the army and the corn supply of Rome, it made no use of merchants. Supplies were obtained not by contract or purchase from large dealers, but by taxation in kind or requisition against payment from the producers; the system was operated through the civil service and the local authorities.[65]

[64] See my article 'Slavery in the Ancient World', *Econ. Hist. Rev.*, 1956, 191 ff. (reprinted in *Slavery in Classical Antiquity*, ed. M. I. Finley).

[65] In the third century and the first half of the second B.C. contractors were often used for supplying armies overseas (e.g. Livy, XXIII, 48; XXV, 3; XXXIV, 9; XLIV, 16) but with the growth of the empire increasing use was made of corn given by subject allies (e.g. Livy, XXXI, 19; XXXII, 27) or levied in tax from the provinces or compulsorily purchased from them (e.g. Livy, XXXVI, 2; XXXVII, 2, 50; XLII, 31). In the first century B.C. corn was normally obtained by compulsory purchase from the province in which the army was operating, and so also were

In general the government of the Principate increased the overall wealth of the Empire and distributed it geographically more evenly, in effect subsidising the poorer provinces from the resources of the richer. The only exception to this tendency was Italy, which was unduly favoured at the expense of the rest of the Empire. On the other hand, by its system of taxation it tended to increase the gap between the rich and the poor and to promote the growth of large estates and the decrease of the peasant proprietors. It also encouraged the concentration of great landlords in Italy, who drew rents not only from Italian land but from extensive provincial estates. While in many ways it created ideal conditions for trade, it discouraged large-scale trade and industry by limiting the market, both by supplying directly through taxation or requisition a considerable body of potential purchasers, and by impoverishing and thus reducing the purchasing power of the vast mass of the population, the peasants. Trade was thus mainly confined to goods of a luxury character and the market to a wealthy minority.[66]

III.   THE DOMINATE

In order to withstand the greatly increased barbarian pressure on the frontiers, Diocletian and his successors had vastly to increase, probably to double, the strength of the army, which seems by the end of the fourth century to have reached about 650,000 men.[67] In order to organise the recruitment and supply of this vast force and to extract from the taxpayers the requisite levies, the government had greatly to expand the civil service, which by the fifth century had increased to over 30,000 persons,[68] and this again increased state expenditure.

---

hides, sacks, etc. (Cic., *II Verr.*, I, 95, *In Pis.*, 86–7; cf. Plut., *C. Gracchus*, 2, for clothing). For the Principate the most detailed evidence comes from Egypt (see J. Lesquier, *L'armée romaine d'Égypte*, 349–75; add *B.G.U.*, 1564, for compulsory purchase of clothing). It appears from Tac., *Agric.*, 19, 31, that corn was requisitioned in Britain. [But for the use of *navicularii* in the Roman grain trade see *L.R.E.* ch. XXI.]

[66] [In *L.R.E.* 841 ff. cf. p. 37 above, Jones also stressed the high cost of land transport as a factor powerfully limiting trade; this was true in all periods of antiquity.]

[67] *L.R.E.*, 56–60, 679–84.

[68] *L.R.E.*, III, 341-2, note 44.

In these circumstances Diocletian could not tolerate immunities, and in his new taxation system subjected Italy to the same scale of levies as the provinces.[69] Rome still retained its privileged position. Its population continued to receive 120,000 free rations of bread, to which were added pork and oil, and its public works and other civic services were financed from imperial funds. Rome, however, soon ceased to be unique in these privileges, which were extended to Constantine's new capital in the East.[70] In other ways also the profits of the empire were more evenly distributed. There were now at least two, and sometimes three or four administrative capitals, and the salaries and perquisites of the high officers of state and their staffs were thus no longer all spent in one place. Rome was moreover not normally one of these administrative centres. Milan and later Ravenna, the normal capitals of the west, and Constantinople, the capital of the east, were thus enriched, and other towns such as Trier, Sirmium and Antioch, which were temporary capitals, shared some of the profits.

The enormous incomes which the members of the senatorial aristocracy drew from rents were also more widely dispersed. Many senators in this period normally resided in the provinces, and those who were politically active lived and spent their incomes in the various centres of administration, mainly that is, Milan or Ravenna and Constantinople. The wealthiest group of senators, the members of the old Roman families, continued to reside in Rome, and to spend a large part of their incomes there. These incomes were derived from widely scattered estates—Melania owned lands not only in Italy and Sicily but in the African provinces, Spain and Britain[71]—and were on a scale comparable with the imperial revenue. The taxes of Numidia and Mauretania Sitifensis in the early fifth century can be calculated to have amounted to ten and six *centenaria* [cwts] of gold respectively[72] and the medium range of Roman senatorial income from rent is said to have been round about fifteen *centenaria*—Melania's rentroll was of about that figure.[73] The survival of Rome as a great city, when it had ceased to be the effective capital of the

[69] *L.R.E.*, III, 8, note 51.
[70] *L.R.E.*, 696 f.
[71] *Vita Melaniae Jun.*, 11–2, 19–21, 37.
[72] *L.R.E.*, p. 462–3 (based on Val. III, *Nov.*, xiii).
[73] Olympiodorus, 44; *Vita Melaniae Jun.*, 15.

Empire, seems to have been largely due to the continued presence of the wealthy senatorial families.

The imperial civil service and the army were also more widely dispersed. The army was no longer stationed almost entirely on the frontiers; the *palatini* and *comitatenses*, who amounted to about one third of the total, were distributed in various provinces of the interior, Gaul, northern Italy, Macedonia, Thrace, Asia Minor and Syria. With the multiplication of provinces, the creation of the dioceses and the growth of regional prefectures, more civil servants resided in the diocesan and provincial capitals. These factors account for the rising importance of such cities as Arles, seat of the praetorian prefecture of the Gauls, Thessalonica, where the praetorian prefect and the *magister militum* of Illyricum resided, and Antioch, the headquarters of the *comes Orientis* and the *magister militum per Orientem*.

With the great expansion of the army and the civil service, the role of the government in the economic life of the empire was correspondingly increased. For about a century from the time of Diocletian, soldiers and all other employees of the state were supplied in kind with food and clothing; soldiers were also issued with arms and horses by the state. Some of these supplies were manufactured in state factories, arms in imperial *fabricae*, a proportion of the clothing in imperial woollen and linen mills and dyeworks. The workers in these factories were state employees, supported by rations, and the raw materials and food were supplied by levies in kind. The food stuffs required were obtained by levies in kind, and so also were the horses and beasts of burden and the bulk of the clothing.[74]

All these materials were transported from the places where they were levied to their recipients by state agencies. For land transport there was the *cursus publicus*. This was directly run by the government, which built the posting stations, maintained the staff of muleteers, veterinary surgeons and cartwrights, and levied from the provincials the animals required and their fodder. For sea transport the state employed the guilds of public shippers (*navicularii*), who were landowners, who in return for certain privileges and immunities were charged with building, maintaining and operating ships; they were also paid freight—at well below commercial rates—for the cargoes which they carried.[75]

[74] *L.R.E.*, p. 834–41.   [75] *L.R.E.*, p. 827–34.

Similar methods were employed in public works. The requisite labour, both skilled and unskilled, was obtained by corvées imposed on the provincials, and much of the raw materials including timber and lime by direct levies. Stone was quarried by corvée labour, and marble supplied from the imperial quarries, which were worked by convicts.[76]

Over a considerable sector of the economy the private contractor and the merchant were thus eliminated and the state supplied its own needs and those of its numerous employees by direct levies on the producers and direct employment of labour, organized through its own administrative machine. From the end of the fourth century there was a growing tendency to commute levies and issues in kind for gold. Soldiers and civil servants thus came more and more to buy their requirements in food and clothing from money salaries, and the role of the private trader was thus increased. The field army, however, in the eastern parts at any rate, continued to receive rations in kind, and the food was obtained by levies in kind or compulsory purchase from the cultivators. Arms also continued to be produced by state factories and so did a proportion of the clothing for the army. Hired labour was substituted for corvées in public works, but the men seem to have been directly employed; contractors are not heard of.[77]

The increase in the army and the civil service necessarily involved a much greater weight of taxation, and the burden was increased by extortion, which in the western parts particularly became flagrant. Here, if the figures are rightly interpreted, the authorised fees of collectors added about a third as much again to the amount of the taxes.[78] To this must be added extortion and corruption by provincial governors which was stimulated by the sale of offices.[79] We possess very few figures, but it appears that in Egypt under Justinian the taxes (including regular fees) came to $3\frac{1}{5}$ artabae per aroura, which was about one third of the gross yield of good average arable land. This is more than three times the decumae levied under the Republic, and was a fixed rate moreover, which made no allowance for inferior land or bad crops as

[76] L.R.E., p. 837–9.
[77] L.R.E., p. 460–1, 840, 858.
[78] L.R.E., p. 467–8.
[79] L.R.E., p. 393 f.

did the tithe. Rather similar figures are attested for Italy under Justinian. Here the taxes amounted to nearly 60 per cent of the gross rental. If the rent was, as in Egypt, approximately half the gross yield, the taxes absorbed nearly a third of the yield in Italy too and the land in question was church land which enjoyed certain immunities.[80]

Such a very high rate of taxation naturally bore hardest on the peasant proprietors, and their burden was increased by the fact that they were more vulnerable to extortion, and had to pay the full rate, whereas influential landowners could secure partial exemptions, get their land under-assessed, and by postponing payment benefit by the periodical remissions of arrears. Many peasants were forced to borrow and thus lost their land. Many more surrendered their lands by some legal fiction to powerful neighbours in order to obtain their patronage. Thus large estates continued to absorb present holdings at an increasing rate. There are some figures for Egypt, an area where peasant proprietorship had been preserved on a large scale during the principate. It would appear that in the early fourth century about one-sixth of the area of Hermopolis was owned by urban landlords, and the remaining five-sixths by peasants. By the sixth century one family, the Apions, owned two-fifths of the territory of Oxyrhynchus and Cynopolis, and besides them there were many lesser landlords.[81]

The crushing burden of taxation was probably also the main cause of the progressive abandonment of cultivated land. There were no doubt other causes, the insecurity caused by barbarian raids, shortage of agricultural labour, denudation due to the reckless cutting of forests and subsequent overgrazing by goats, exhaustion of the soil by overcropping, stimulated by the pressure of rent and taxes. But in the opinion of contemporaries the heavy taxation was the main factor, and the facts would seem to bear them out. Even on good land, owners had to pay in taxes something like two-thirds of their rent. On inferior land the tax might well absorb the whole of the rent or even exceed it, if as was the case in Italy and Africa, the tax was assessed on area without taking into account the productiveness of the soil. Marginal

---

[80] *L.R.E.*, p. 820–1, based on P. Cairo, 6705, and J. O. Tjäder, *Die nicht literarischen Lat. Pap. Italiens*, no. 2.

[81] *L.R.E.*, p. 779–80, based on ch. X below, see pp. 244 ff, for Hermopolis, and *P. Oxy.*, 127 R, 1909, for the Apion estates.

lands were thus progressively abandoned as unprofitable. In some areas where conditions were particularly unfavourable the loss was catastrophic; in Africa from a third to a half of the land had been abandoned by the early fifth century. Elsewhere the loss was more moderate—in Asia one tenth in the fourth century, in Syria one sixth in the fifth century.[82]

The heavy weight of taxation may also have contributed to the depopulation of the Empire. This is a very obscure problem: the facts are difficult to establish and the causes can only be conjectured. The great plague under Marcus Aurelius, which recurred for several generations, undoubtedly greatly reduced the population. No other great epidemic is recorded until the bubonic plague under Justinian, over three centuries later. In the interval the population seems never to have recovered. There was, at any rate, a continuing shortage of manpower, particularly agricultural manpower. The main evidence of this is the imposition and maintenance and strengthening of the rules tying tenants to their farms [ch. XIII]. First, it would seem, enacted by Diocletian for fiscal purposes to facilitate the collection of the poll tax, the rules were maintained by Valentinian I and Theodosius I in areas where the poll tax was abolished, and were extended to provinces such as Palestine and Egypt where they had not been originally applied. These measures are stated to have been taken for the benefit of landlords. The shortage is also evidenced by the preference of landlords to pay a heavy commutation in gold rather than surrender a tenant as a recruit, and by the willingness of landlords to accept barbarian prisoners of war as tenants, and by the eagerness with which landlords accepted as tenants runaway tenants of their neighbours. The shortage cannot be explained by a migration of the peasantry to the towns; there is no evidence of this, and on the contrary there is evidence for the movement of miners and urban craftsman into agriculure.

The shortage was no doubt partly due to the heavier demands of the army for recruits; conscription was from Diocletian's time regularly applied to all the provinces. But it is difficult to believe that this was the sole cause. It would appear that the peasant population failed to increase, so as to make up the gap created by the plague, and perhaps even dwindled. A peasant population normally has a very high birth rate, and expands rapidly until it out-

[82] L.R.E., p. 812–23.

grows its food resources, when it is checked by a high death rate from general malnutrition and periodic famines. It would seem that under the later Roman Empire any recovery was quickly checked because the amount of food left to the peasantry after the payment of taxes, and in most cases rents also, was so meagre. This thesis cannot be proved for lack of statistical evidence, but it is significant that such figures as we have for peasant families are very low, and that in a number of recorded famines in Italy, Syria and Mesopotamia, it was the peasantry who starved and came into the towns for relief, and that in the towns there was food available in government stores and in the granaries of landlords.[83]

In the fourth, fifth and sixth centuries then, it would seem, the increased cost of defence and administration, enhanced by inefficiency and corruption, overstrained the economic resources of the empire. Taxation rose so high as to discourage the cultivation of marginal land and the cultivated area, and with it agricultural production, sank. The peasants, on whom the burden ultimately fell, were left so little of their crops that malnutrition and starvation reduced their numbers.

This prompts a reflection on the profitability of war in antiquity. Under the Republic aggressive wars, waged by armies raised for the occasion, yielded a considerable net profit. Under the Principate the defence of the Empire by a standing professional army was certainly a burden on the resources of the Empire, and under the Dominate this burden became crushing. The Roman Empire was the first state—and the only one until modern times—to maintain a permanent force sufficiently large to meet all eventualities, and, given the low technological development of the age, the effort overstrained the economy. The army was small by modern standards, but the number of man-hours of labour required to feed, clothe and arm each man and to transport the food, clothing and arms from where they were produced to the frontier was, in view of the primitive methods of production and transport, immense.

If I may venture a generalisation on the economic effects of the Roman Empire I would say that its chief effect was to promote an ever increasing concentration of land in the hands of its governing aristocracy at the expense of the population at large. It must be

[83] L.R.E., p. 1040-5.

K

remembered that throughout its history the economy of the Empire was to an overwhelming extent agricultural. The great bulk of the imperial revenue always came from the land tax [ch. II]. Wealth, however acquired, was invested in land, and the incomes of the rich were mainly derived from rents. The vast mass of the population were peasants. Taxation, being unprogressive, bore most heavily on the peasantry, and the poorest of them were constantly being forced to sell their land. The profits of Empire went for the most part to a relatively limited circle, who used them to purchase land. And most great fortunes, it may be noted, were made in politics and administration, or in the law, which was closely linked with them. Some wealth may have been accumulated in trade, but we hear little of it; the rich men of the Empire mostly made their money by booty, governmental extortion and corruption, the profits of government contracting, and to a lesser extent official salaries.

The process of accumulation was gradual and uneven, but it was cumulative and extended over centuries with very little to counteract it. In the later Republic some estates were confiscated and distributed in small holdings to landless peasants, mainly veterans, and some of the booty acquired in wars was spent in buying land for the same purpose. Under the Principate, and indeed down to the end of the fourth century, a certain number of veterans were given allotments, mainly it would seem in unoccupied or thinly populated areas in the frontier provinces. But it was rare that any accumulation of land was broken up. Estates passed by confiscation or bequest or escheat to the crown, and later by bequest or gift to the church, but this was a mere transfer of ownership, and in the later Empire much crown land returned to the aristocracy by gift, sale or the grant of perpetual leases. Individual landowners became impoverished and had to sell their estates, but the purchasers were always, so far as we know, more prosperous members of the same class who had surplus funds to invest. Noble families died out in the male line but their estates passed through heiresses or by bequest to other members of the aristocracy.

The ruling aristocracy of the Empire, which absorbed a high proportion of its profits, gradually expanded. At the beginning it consisted of a restricted group of wealthy Roman families, senatorial and equestrian. In the last years of the Republic and the early Principate it absorbed many of the leading families of Italy, and as the Principate progressed it took in an increasing number of wealthy men from the western provinces and a few from the eastern. In the later empire it came to be drawn from all the provinces. Its composition changed greatly as old families died out and new families joined the privileged group, but its accumulated property mostly remained within the group, and was constantly increased as the patrimonies of new recruits were added to it. Thus the landed wealth of the aristocracy, at first concentrated in Italy, spread out to the western provinces and finally to the whole Empire. But the greatest concentration remained always in Italy and the adjacent provinces. The imperial aristocracy thus came in time, especially in the western half of the Empire, where the process of accumulation had begun earlier, to absorb in rent a very large share of the wealth of the Empire, perhaps a larger share than the state absorbed in taxation.

POSTSCRIPT

This paper has been printed as I wrote it, with some additions made verbally when I addressed the Congress, before I heard Professor Thomsen's criticisms; notes, which were not circulated with the text, have been added. I have been allowed to reply to Professor Thomsen's major criticisms.

(*a*) I did not speak of the government's economic policy because I do not believe that it had any economic policy, save in a very rudimentary sense. The Roman government was interested in the revenue, and in acquiring precious metals and the mines which produced them, but in very little else in the economic sphere. The Senate took no steps to favour Roman traders because it was not interested in such humble persons and they had no political influence. Domitian's edict on vineyards was enacted 'ad summam quondam ubertatem vini, frumenti vero inopiam' (Suet., *Dom.*, 7, 2), that is because he feared the corn supply was being endangered by excessive conversion of arable into vineyard, and the more favourable treatment of Italy was no doubt part of the traditionally privileged status of that country, of which exemption from land tax was the principal expression; it was no doubt also due to the fact that senators would be aggrieved at having to destroy half their vineyards. Pliny (*N.H.*, XII, 84) notes the large drain of currency to the Far East, but the imperial government did nothing to check the luxury trade which caused it.

(*b*) I have not taken sufficient account of the capital investment which took the form of improving land, and especially of converting arable to vineyards and oliveyards. But I would maintain that such investment was limited in extent. In the second century B.C. the main complaint was that rich landlords made a less intensive use of their estates by going over from arable to pasture (cf. *I.L.S.* 23), and in the first century A.D. Columella in one of the very few passages in ancient literature which deal with return on capital (III, iii), produces a long argument to persuade purchasers of land to establish vineyards. Pliny the Younger, though he has much to say of his estates, never mentions agricultural improvements, and most landlords in the Principate and the later Empire seem to have been mere rentiers, collecting rent from their *coloni*; there are exceptions, like the Apion family in Egypt, who spent large sums on irrigation machinery and planting vineyards.

(*c*) I have deliberately ignored industry and trade because I think that their importance was marginal. For the later Empire, at any rate, there are figures which suggest that trade and industry combined contributed something like 5 per cent of the national income, and agriculture the remaining 95 per cent (see my *L.R.E.* 464-5), and that the capital of a great Alexandrian merchant was about a twentieth of that a typical senatorial landowner [p. 60]. The Romanization of the barbarous western provinces no doubt produced a limited and temporary demand for such Italian products as wine and olive oil and some Italian manufactured products; but the cultivation of the vine and olive soon spread as far as climate permitted, and the history of Arretine ware shows how soon local manufacture killed the Italian export trade. Even these products were semi-luxuries which did not command a mass market.

(*d*) I have said nothing of inflation, not because I am not greatly interested in the phenomenon [on which see ch. IX] but partly from lack of space, partly because I doubt if the effects of inflation were very important. Most wealth was invested in land, which maintained its real value. Since coins, however inferior in quality, had to be minted by hand, the rate of the depreciation of the currency was slow and its extent limited, until the device of retariffing coins was invented by Aurelian. Private transactions in the third century, as the papyri show, always continued to be carried on in money, and prices, wages and rents were adjusted. The main losers by the inflation were charitable trust funds, such as the *alimenta* and many civic endowments invested in mortgages or fixed rent charges. The other important loser was the imperial government, whose fiscal system was so rigid that the tribute, a money payment based on a census expressed in monetary terms, could not be raised to counterbalance the decreasing value of the currency. The state was thus forced back on to an economy in kind, paying its soldiers and civil servants mainly in food and clothing, and making levies in kind to supply its needs. This was however a temporary phase, which lasted about a century. From Constantine's time onwards a sound and abundant gold currency was built up, partly by confiscating the accumulated treasures of the temples, partly by making levies of bullion, and thus extracting gold from the hoards into which it had disappeared in the third century. By the early fifth century the Empire was on a gold economy, nearly all taxes, salaries and rents being paid in *solidi*, and all important commercial transactions being conducted in *solidi*. The evidence indeed suggests that *solidi* were in abundant supply, being used for quite minor transactions such as the payment of their rents by peasant *coloni*. [See ch. IX.]

CHAPTER SEVEN

ASIAN TRADE IN ANTIQUITY

THE period which I propose to cover is from the accession of Augustus (30 B.C.) to the Arab conquest (A.D. 633-41), over six and a half centuries. This may seem somewhat ambitious, but the sources for trade are very scarce, and there is not too much to say. The area is mainly that of the Roman empire, Syria, Palestine, Egypt, more accurately defined below, but I shall say what I know of the Hejaz, Yemen, Hadhramaut and 'Irāq. The information of the Greek and Roman authors is scanty, and I regret that I do not know the oriental sources, but they also are, I believe, scanty.

My information is drawn from the following principal authorities. Under Augustus, Strabo the geographer wrote a descriptive work, which includes Syria, Egypt and Yemen, and less adequately the lands to the east of the Arabian Desert. From the reign of Augustus also is the *Parthian Stations* of Isidore of Charax, which describes the route from northern Syria to Marv. Probably of the 1st century is the *Periplus of the Red Sea*, a mariner's and merchant's guide to the ports of the Red Sea and Indian Ocean. From the latter part of the 1st century there is much miscellaneous information scattered in Pliny's *Natural History*. From the 2nd century mainly there are a great series of inscriptions in Greek and Aramaic from Palmyra, including the customs tariff of the city (A.D. 137) and numerous honorific decrees to prominent citizens who acted as caravan leaders. From the early 3rd century there is a list of articles subject to tariff on the eastern frontier, written by a lawyer, Marcianus; it is preserved in Justinian's Digest (XXXIX, iv. 16 §7) and therefore presumably had some relevance to 6th century trade. There is then very little until Diocletian's tariff of prices issued in A.D. 302, which fixed the prices of goods of all kinds including oriental wares, and the trade regulations between the Roman and Persian empires established by the treaty of A.D. 298. From Constantius' reign (337-62) we have the *Description of the Whole World*, a short but informative work. There is then very little until Justinian's reign, when there is a brief account of the silk trade in Procopius, sundry laws on the same topic, another treaty with Persia, and the biography of two merchants in the *Lives of the Eastern Saints* by John of Ephesus. There is finally the evidence of hoards of coins throughout the whole period.

The distribution of evidence is, it may be observed, uneven, some from 30 B.C. to A.D. 150, one bit from *circa* A.D. 230, some from *circa* A.D. 300, more from *circa* A.D. 550, with huge lacunae intervening. It is also topographically very uneven. Owing to the survival of the inscriptions we know a good deal about Palmyra (during a limited period). Petra was, as its monuments show, important as a trade centre, but no inscriptions survive to document its commercial life. Bostra (Busrā or Eski Shām in the Hawrān) was important, but no epigraphical evidence survives: the same applies to Gaza and Tyre. Damascus may have been important, but the evidence has been overlaid by the Arab city. In the north we have scraps of literary evidence about the Euphrates route, but little help from archaeology. The one excavated site, Dura Europus, yielded little or nothing relevant to our theme.

A fact of primary importance to bear in mind is that there was a high customs barrier along the eastern frontier of the Roman empire. The empire under Augustus included Syria up to the Euphrates, Palestine and Egypt, with the Nabataean kingdom (capital Petra) as a dependency. The Nabataean kingdom was annexed in A.D. 106, becoming the province of Arabia, and a road was built from Damascus to 'Aqaba, which roughly formed the eastern frontier. Further north, Palmyra was annexed in A.D. 18. Further north again, the frontier was the Euphrates until the reign of Septimus Severus, who advanced it (*circa* A.D. 199) to the Khābūr (up to Nisibis). This frontier remained intact, save for the loss of Nisibis (and also Sinjār) in 363, until the Arab conquest.

In the 1st century a duty of 25 per cent was charged at this frontier on incoming goods and probably also on exports. It is attested at Leuce Come (between al-Wajh and Yanbū'). There were also local tolls, e.g. those collected by the city of Palmyra, at more modest figures. From the 4th century (perhaps as early as the mid-3rd) the rate was 12½ per cent. There were also certain prohibited exports, notably bronze and iron, from the 4th century onwards. At this period the external trade of the empire was closely controlled. There was a Minister for Trade in the Orient and Egypt (*comes commerciorum per Orientem et Aegyptum*), who controlled the frontier from the Taurus southwards. Under him a 5th century inscription suggests there were two *commerciarii*, for Mesopotamia and for Palestine and Clysma (Suez). All trade, by mutual consent of Rome and Persia, had to be channelled through certain cities. In the north these were, in Diocletian's day, Nisibis, after 363 Nisibis (Naṣībīn) in Persian, Callinicum (al-Raqqa) in Roman territory, and Artaxata in Persian Armenia. In Justinian's day the permitted trading cities were Nisibis (Persia) and Dara (just across the frontier on the Roman side). The southern points of trade were Clysma (Suez) as mentioned above, and at some periods Iotabe (an island near 'Aqaba). These of course were mainly ports for the maritime trade to Yemen, Abyssinia and India, but caravans may have come from the Hejaz and Yemen (though it is odd that no control post at 'Aqaba itself is recorded).[1]

Strabo's information east of the Roman frontier is mostly antiquated (about a century old), but in the 'unchanging East' this is immaterial. One route ran from Zeugma (Birejik) between the Tigris and Euphrates eastwards to Babylon and Seleucia. It was furnished with cisterns, and the local Bedouins (Scenite Arabs) were friendly. The Euphrates itself was avoided because of the large number of heavy tolls charged by successive shaykhs. In Augustus' reign things had changed, for Isidore of Charax describes a route thus: Zeugma, Anthemus, Ichnae, Nicephorium (al-Raqqa) and down the Euphrates. Conditions on this route may have deteriorated later, for a more southerly route, south of the Euphrates, was already before Augustus' reign being opened up by the Palmyrenes. From the west there were desert roads from Damascus, Emesa (Hims) and Epiphania (Hama); also from the Euphrates at Nicephorium (al-Raqqa). The Palmyrenes escorted caravans direct through the desert to Vologesias, Forath and Spasinou Charax at the mouth of the Euphrates, whence ships sailed to and from India.[2]

[1] 25 per cent duty: S. J. de Laet, *Portoria*, 33–39, Post at Leuce Come: *Periplus Maris Erythraei*, 19. 12½ per cent duty: A. H. M. Jones, *L.R.E.*, iii, p. 105, n. 47. *Comes commerciorum* and *commerciarii* and prohibited exports and Market towns: ibid. 272, n. 7.

[2] The Mesopotamian routes: Strabo, xvi, 748. Isidore of Charax, *Parth. Stat.* Vologesias: Steph. Byz. s.v. βολυγεσεις. Ptol. v, 19. *O.G.I.*, 632, 638, 641, etc. Forath: Pliny N.H. v, 145 O.G.I., 632, etc. Spasinou Charax. Pliny *N.H.*, v, 139. OGI 633 etc.

Strabo records other caravan routes. One ran from Arabia Felix (Yemen) to Damascus *via* Petra. From Petra caravans also went west to Rhinocolura, north-west to Gaza and north to Jericho. The people of Gerrha (on the coast opposite Bahrein) sent goods by raft up the Persian Gulf and the Euphrates, and also by caravan to Yemen. Strabo also records that large convoys of Roman ships (as many as 120 *per annum*) sailed from Myos Hermos (Qusair) to India. Naturally these convoys called at the ports of the Yemen and Hadhramaut. The author of the *Periplus* gives details of this trade and of that with Abyssinia.[3]

The objects of trade from East to West were Indian and Chinese goods, the products of 'Irāq and Īran, and those of Yemen and Hadhramaut. The first included live animals and birds (as curiosities), furs and hides, Kashmir wool, musk, ivory (but most came from Abyssinia), pearls, mother of pearl, precious and semi-precious stones, lac (red dye), and, most important of all, silk. Among vegetable products were pepper (very important), ginger, cardamon, cinnamon, cloves, spikenard, nutmegs, indigo, a little cotton, and precious woods (ebony, rosewood, sandalwood). All these were high-priced luxury articles, which would carry heavy transport charges and tariffs. Much went by long sea (by a direct voyage from Aden to Malabar or Ceylon and *vice versa*), but much was brought to Gerrha or Spasinou Charax and travelled thence by caravan.[4]

The list of Babylonian products is much shorter; embroidered stuffs, bitumen and dates; Persia exported assafoetida, precious and semi-precious stones and dates. These must have come by caravan. The products of Yemen and Hadramaut were few but most important: incense (used in every temple and, later, every church), myrrh, balsam and nard. These came either by sea or by caravan. To these must be added slaves, for which the Roman empire had an insatiable demand.[5] We know little of them, but in the tariff of Coptos (Qift), where duty was levied on imports *via* Qusair (A.D. 90), the duty on prostitutes is 27 *denarii*, and when

---

[3] Damascus and Arabia Felix: Strabo, xvi, 756. Petra: Strabo, xvi, 759 (Gaza). 779 (Jericho). 781 (Rhinocolura). Gerrha: Strabo, xvi, 766, 776. Myos Hormos: Strabo, xvi, 118, cf. xvi, 781.

[4] For objects of trade see E. H. Warmington, *The Commerce between the Roman Empire and India*, pp. 145 ff.

[5] See Warmington, *loc. cit.* Slaves; *O.G.I.* 764 (customs tariff), Philostratus, *Vita Apoll. Tyan.* i. 20.

Apollonius of Tyana arrived at Zeugma after his eastern journeys and was asked what he had to declare, he replied: 'Temperance, Virtue, Justice, Chastity, Fortitude and Industry', and the customs officer replied: 'Where are the girls?'

Another necessary import was eunuchs, who became increasingly fashionable under the empire, and had to be imported, as from Domitian's reign (A.D. 81-96) castration was forbidden within the boundaries of the empire. Later they mostly came, however, from further north, Persia, Armenia and the Caucasus.[6]

On Roman exports to Arabia we have less information, but Strabo says that Petra, the capital of the small dependent kingdom of Nabataea, imported bronze and iron, purple clothing, embossed silver plate and paintings. The author of the *Periplus* advised merchants to take to Yemen textiles of various kinds (mostly Egyptian and Syrian linen), purple stuffs (from Tyre), belts, glass ware (probably Alexandrian or Sidonian), tin, iron, saffron and a little wine (Laodicean or Italian); also for the king horses, mules, gold and silver plate, bronzes and high-grade clothing.[7]

The same author advises merchants to take a stock of silver *denarii* and gold *aurei*. This indicates that there was from the Roman point of view an adverse balance of trade. According to Pliny there was an annual drain of 100 million sesterces to India, China and Arabia; in another passage he says 55 millions to India alone. These are not very astronomical figures. The minimum property qualification for a senator was a million sesterces, and many were far richer. There was, however, a substantial export of coin. Hoards of *denarii* and *aurei* are common in India; I do not know the evidence for Yemen and 'Irāq. The debasement of the *denarius* and the disappearance of the *aureus* in the 3rd century is sometimes thought to have interrupted the Eastern trade; there are no hoards of this period. But merchants probably bought old *denarii* and *aurei* for the Eastern trade. A Palmyrene inscription praises a caravan leader for contributing 300 old gold *denarii* to the expenses of the trip in A.D. 193. From the reign of Constantine the gold *solidus* was universally acceptable; there are many hoards of *solidi* in India.[8]

---

[6] Jones, *L.R.E.* iii, 285 n. 67.
[7] Petra Strabo, xvi, 784. Yemen *Periplus Maris Erythraei*, 24.
[8] Currency drain: Pliny, *N.H.*, vi, 101; xii, 84. Old gold *denarii*, *I.G.R.* iii, 1050. For the reputation of the solidus, see Cosmas Indicopleustes, xi, 448D.

On the organisation of the caravan trade our sole information comes from the Palmyrene inscriptions, which are mostly of the 2nd and the first half of the 3rd century A.D. Palmyra was organised like a Greek city, with local magistrates and council. Its people were divided into four genuine Arab tribes. It levied customs on all goods in transit, and maintained a desert police or gendarmerie, later incorporated into the Roman army. Caravans (Greek συνοδίαι) were organised and led by caravan chiefs (συνοδιάρχαι), who were great Palmyrene notables. They were apparently entitled to a fee, which they frequently remitted, and often spent large sums out of their own pockets. They appear to be identical with the chief merchants (ἀρχέμποροι). The journey from Yemen to 'Aqaba took seventy days, from Yemen to Bahrein forty days.[9]

There was, of course, much internal trade within and between Syria, Palestine and Egypt, and much trade between this area and the West. Egypt produced very little oil and not enough wine for its needs, and so Syrian and Palestinian oil was imported, and wine from Gaza and Ascalon and as far north as Laodicea. Egyptian surplus wheat went mostly to Rome, later to Constantinople, and only by special imperial permit to neighbouring lands. Goods of international fame, which went to the west, included Tyrian purple, Sidonian glass, onions from Ascalon, dates and balsam from Jericho, asphalt from the Dead Sea, glass (especially coloured glass) and papyrus from Alexandria. Fine linen weaving is later attested in many Cilician, Syrian and Phoenician towns, and in Egypt (especially Alexandria), and was no doubt already of importance. These exports gave employment to the ports of Seleucia, Laodicea, Aradus, Tripolis, Berytus, Sidon, Ptolemais, Ascalon and Gaza, and especially Tyre; there were Tyrian 'factories' at Puteoli and Rome.[10]

Palmyra was virtually killed after Zenobia's rebellion and Aurelian's capture of the city in A.D. 273, but the trade went on

---

[9] Caravans, Rostovtsev, Mélanges Glotz ii, 793 ff.; cf. ch. II above.

[10] See *Totius Orbis Descriptio*, 22–39 (quoted below), and for Tyrian purple, Strabo, xvi, 757; Sidonian glass, Strabo, xvi, 758, Pliny, *N.H.*, v, 75–6, xxxvi, 193; Ascalonite onions, Steph Byz. s.v. 'Ασκάλων. Strabo, xvi, 759, Pliny *N.H.*, xix, 101, 105; Jericho dates and balsam, Strabo, xvi, 763; Dead Sea asphalt, Pliny *N.H.*, ii. 226, v, 72; Alexandrian industries; *S.H.A.*, *Saturninus*, 8. Linen: *Ed. Diocl.* xxvi, xxvii, xxviii. Tyrian factories: *I.G.R.*, i, 421.

via Mesopotamia, and also in Bostra, as the following extract from the *Descriptio Totius Orbis* shows:

To these are joined the race of the Saracens, who pass their life in archery and raiding, as impious and perjured as the Persians, not keeping their promises either in war or any other business. Women are said to rule them.

After them come the beginnings of our lands. You have first Mesopotamia and Osrhoene. Mesopotamia has many different cities of which the chief are Nisibis and Edessa (al-Ruhā), which have in particular excellent men of business, rich and adorned with all good things. For they themselves receive goods from Persia and sell them to all Roman territory, and buying what is necessary export it in return except bronze and iron; for it is illegal to give to the enemy these two articles, *viz.* bronze and iron. The above mentioned cities seem to stand by the guidance of God and the prudence of the emperor. They have famous walls and always break down the courage of the Persians in war, seething with goods and trading with every province.

Then there is all the region of Syria which is divided into three Syrias, Punic and Palestine and Coele, possessing various large excellent cities. First of them all is the royal city of Antioch, where the lord of the world resides, a splendid city, famous for its public works and adorned with a great population, receiving goods from everywhere and maintaining all men, abounding in all kinds of good things. There is Tyre too, a city fortunate in all things, with a closely packed population; it has citizens rich from commerce and powerful in all things. After it comes the city of Berytus, a delightful place with a law school, whereon all Roman courts of justice seem to depend. Similarly Caesarea, a most delightful city, whose four sided triumphal arch is spoken of everywhere, as it provides a unique and novel spectacle. Then Laodicea is an excellent city, which similarly receives goods and sends them to Antioch. Then there is the great city of Seleucia which receives all goods and similarly sends them itself to the above mentioned Antioch. For that reason the emperor Constantius cut through a great mountain and bringing in the sea created a fine big port where ships come and are secure. There are similarly other cities, Ascalon and Gaza, famous for their trade and abounding in all goods; they export excellent wine to the whole region of Egypt and Syria. Neapolis is a glorious and noble city. Tripolis and Scythopolis and Byblus are industrial cities. Heliopolis near Mount Lebanon breeds lovely women, called Lebanese. There are also the excellent cities of Sidon, Sarepta, Ptolemais, Eleutheropolis and Damascus.

Since then we have partly described the above mentioned cities, it seems to me necessary to indicate what each city possesses of its own, so that the reader can gain certain knowledge of them. Well, Scythopolis, Laodicea, Byblus, Tyre and Berytus all export linen to all the world. Sarepta, Caesarea, Neapolis and Lydda provide purple; all are fruitful in wine, oil and wheat. You will find the Nicolaitan palm common in Palestine, in the place called Jericho, and smaller but useful palms at Damascus, and pistaccio nuts and all kinds of fruit.

The author goes on to praise rather briefly the fertility of Egypt, which produces wheat, barley, vegetables and wine, but no oil.

Alexandria, which we have mentioned above, is a very large city, notable for its lay out, abounding in all goods and eatables; for it eats three kinds of fish, which no other province has, from the lake, the sea and the river. It carries on commerce with the Indians and barbarians and sends on to all regions spices and a variety of precious articles. It is highly praiseworthy in the fact that it alone exports papyrus to all the world, an article which is cheap but very useful and necessary. You will find it abundant in no province excepting only Alexandria. No law suit, no business can be completed without it. It performs a very useful service in supplying it to the whole world. The neighbourhood produces copious crops, being watered by the Nile: one measure yields a hundredfold. From Egypt Constantinople of Thrace and all the Orient is fed. . . . Again on the right of Syria you will find Arabia, whose largest city is Bostra, which is said to carry on a great trade, being next the Persians and Saracens. In it is a notable public building, a foursided triumphal arch. Then there is the region of Cilicia, which produces much wine and causes many provinces to rejoice. It has a fine big city called Tarsus.

The author is evidently a patriotic Syrian. He does not say much of Egypt and very little of Cilicia, but on Syria he is fairly exhaustive. It is noticeable that he represents Antioch as a centre of consumption (for the Imperial court at times, and normally for a group of high officials) and Seleucia and Laodicea as importing goods for Antioch. This is a little unjust, as there was an imperial arms factory at Antioch, and it produced cheap linen clothing which travelled as far as Egypt and Rome. It was not, however, apparently a mercantile town. The Chinese, Indian and Persian imports (which in the Diocletianic tariff include Babylonian leather and shoes and belts) apparently went due west to Cilicia, where at Aegae there was a famous fair, attested in the 5th century, frequented by western shippers from Italy and Africa.[11]

Damascus similarly is noted only for its dates and fruits; it was primarily the centre of a fertile agricultural region. Our author has again omitted an imperial arms factory, and Damascus linens and woollens are mentioned in the Diocletianic tariff. Palmyra having dropped out, no caravan route survived, it seems, south of the Euphrates until we reach Bostra. Maritime trade from Clysma (Suez) and Aila ('Aqaba) still flourished with Yemen, India, and China.[12]

Conditions were similar in the 6th and 7th centuries, except that almost continuous wars between Persia and Rome, and, it would seem, deliberate increase of export tariffs on the Persian side, greatly reduced the trade through Mesopotamia. There were wars, not always involving active hostilities, and sometimes suspended by partial truces, during 502-6, 527-61, 572-91 and 602-29. By this time, and indeed much earlier, the Bedouins of the Arabian desert were divided into Roman and Persian zones. On the Roman side there were a series of paramount shaykhs (φυλάρχαι), who received honorary titles and subsidies from the imperial government, corresponding to the military commanders (duces) of Euphratensis, Phoenice Libanensis, Arabia, and Palestine III.[13]

---

[11]Antioch arms factory: *Not. Dign. Or.* xi, 21. Antiochene linen: *Vita Melaniae Jun.* 8. *P. Fouad,* 74. Fair of Aegae: Theodoret, ep. 70. *Itin. Hierosol. Theodosius,* 32. There was also a great merchants' fair at Batnae, Amm. Marc. xiv, iii, 3. Babylonian wares: *Ed. Diocl.* viii, 1, ix, 17, 23, x, 1, 10.

[12] Damascus arms factory: *Not. Dign. Or.* xi, 20. Damascus fruits; *Ed. Diocl.* xix, 6, xxviii, 47.

[13] Phylarchs: *L.R.E.,* iii. 182–3, n. 8.

A central trans-desert route may perhaps have survived—we hear of a *commerciarius* at Tyre, who may have controlled imports into Bostra, but may have dealt with the local spinning, weaving and dyeing industry which handled silk, or with finished silk exports to the West. The Bostra route was in any case of no importance by now. Most imported oriental wares (above all silk) now entered the empire through Mesopotamia. To prevent the price being bid up by rival merchants the *commerciarius* bought all imports, and resold them to Roman merchants and manufacturers. But the price was so inflated that Justinian sought to stimulate the long sea route from Clysma (Suez), which had the further advantage of tapping the products of the Axumite kingdom (Eritrea), gold and ivory, and of the Yemen and Hadhramaut, frankincense, myrrh and nard.[14]

The Roman empire had long been in diplomatic and commercial relations with both these countries, and Justinian reinforced these ties. He sent an ambassador, Julian, to Ella Atzbaha, king of Axum, who shortly afterwards conquered Yemen and installed a client king, Abraham, a Christian. Julian urged the Axumites to trade direct with Ceylon and India, by-passing the Arabs. Procopius says that they were unsuccessful in their attempts to do so, but as Roman shippers sailed to Ceylon it is hard to see why. The most celebrated of these Roman sea captains is Cosmas, who observed the Ocean was flat as far as India and Ceylon, and wrote a book to disprove the theory that the word was spherical.[15]

It is curious that the central route through the Arabian desert *via* the Wādī Sirhān to Damascus or Bostra is mentioned once only in the ancient sources. Down to the 3rd century the northerly and southerly routes *via* Palmyra and Petra flourished, but they also declined in importance owing to the mutual suspicion of the Roman and Persian empires, which limited contact between their respective subjects to the Euphrates route, or the long sea route *via* Aden.

The trade with Arabia Felix, India and China has excited more interest both among ancient writers and modern historians owing to the exotic character of the goods which it handled, the high

---

[14] Commerciarius at Tyre: John Moschus. *Pratum Spirituale*, 186. For silk industry see pp. 361 ff.

[15] Justinian and Axum, Procopius *BP*, i, 20, 9 ff.

prices paid for them, and the romantic lands which it penetrated. Its volume, however, must have been small, since it catered for a minute, very wealthy minority. It was of sufficient importance to make Palmyra, which had no other economic resources, a wealthy city during the 1st, 2nd and early 3rd centuries. It also no doubt accounts for the wealth of Petra, which again had no other economic resources, but was certainly a rich city in the early centuries of our era. It no doubt contributed to the wealth of Alexandria; but Alexandria had many other sources of wealth, papyrus, glass and linen. The internal trade of the empire, however, was probably more important, since it dealt with objects commanding a wider market, wine, oil, papyrus, glass ware, fine linen fabrics, and even cheap linens for the working class.

Some of the merchants who were engaged in the Eastern trade were men of considerable wealth. Two of them, Odenath of Palmyra and Firmus of Alexandria, aspired to the imperial throne. But many were men of modest station. Antoninus, described by Ammianus, as an *opulentus mercator* of Mesopotamia, bettered himself by joining the provincial civil service, where he rose to the rank of *protector* or officer cadet. John of Ephesus tells the story of two brothers, Elias and Theodore, who went as agents for a Persian merchant in Mesopotamia. They at first received 5 or 6 *solidi* a year, rising to 10, 20 and 30 *solidi* in the course of 20 years' service. These rates of pay are comparable with those of privates and N.C.O.s in the contemporary Roman army. The merchant princes of Alexandria were far richer; they are credited with fortunes of 50 lbs. of gold, 5,000 *solidi*, and even 20,000 *solidi*— that is, 275 lbs. of gold. But they cannot compare with the great landed magnates of the senate; many of these enjoyed annual incomes of 1,500 lbs. of gold in rents.[16]

[16]Antoninus: Amm. Marc. xviii, v, 1. Elias and Theodore: John Eph. *Vitae Sanctorum Orientalium*, xxxi. Alexandrian merchants: Palladius, *Hist. Laus.* 14, Rufinus, *Hist. Mon.* 16. John Moschus, op. cit. 193.

CHAPTER EIGHT

TAXATION IN ANTIQUITY*

[The typescript of this essay was found among Professor Jones' papers at his death. The annotation was incomplete, and I have had to supply all the notes from n. 62 onwards, with occasional guidance from his new article cited in n. 61; there were also some lacunae in earlier notes, which I have filled, besides adding a few additional references. The text too had presumably not received final revision, but it has been left almost unchanged. Editorial alterations in the text and additions to nn. 1–61 are enclosed in square brackets. In my judgement the essay is a valuable and indeed unique introduction to the subject, but there are some points at which the evidence known to me does not seem to sustain Jones' interpretation, and while it would not have been proper to conceal or amend what he had written, perhaps with better justification than I could find, it is due to the reader that apparently discordant evidence should also be presented candidly, with indications of the conclusions it seems to require. Such evidence is presented in some of the notes, and in the Addenda. *For some abbreviations in notes see p. 185 P.A.B.]

THE Kings of Egypt, Assyria and Babylonia expected regular gifts from the peoples subject to them, and their subjects gave them as much as they thought would satisfy them. The first two Persian Kings followed the same practice. 'In the reigns of Cyrus and Cambyses', says Herodotus, 'there was nothing fixed about the tribute, but they used to collect gifts'. It was Darius who first divided the empire into satrapies and fixed the annual tribute of each in talents of silver, with occasional supplements in kind.[1] The sums are round and evidently based on the roughest of estimates of the wealth of the areas concerned. Within each satrapy the satrap apparently apportioned the tribute among the several communities, which had to collect it themselves, in a similar fashion. It was not until after the suppression of the Ionian revolt that Artaphrenes, satrap of Sardis, 'measured their territories by parasangs . . . and by this measurement fixed the

---

[1] Herod. III 89; list in 90–94.

L

tribute for each.'² This was a local and exceptional measure, and very rudimentary; a parasang is about 6 kilometres. But it was the first attempt at a scientific assessment of taxable capacity.

In assessing the tribute of their allies in the Delian League the Athenians seem to have been less scientific than Artaphrenes in Ionia. Plutarch indeed says that Aristeides was instructed to 'survey their land and revenues' before his famous assessment, but he earned his title the Just not for his accuracy but for his incorruptibility.³ There is no other hint of any census, and there would hardly have been time for one; Plutarch's words are probably an embroidery of his own. Subsequently the tribute was revised every few years,⁴ and, apart from general reassessments, like that of 425 B.C., adjustments were sometimes made in individual cases, upwards or downwards. The process was that assessors were elected to revise the tribute, and that the allied cities could appeal against their assessments to an Athenian jury.⁵ Sometimes we can infer the reason for a reduction. Cities, part of whose territory had been confiscated for Athenian settlers, had their tribute reduced; but the reduction was very rough and ready; Andros had its tribute halved (from 12 to 6 talents) Lemnos reduced from 9 to 4 talents.⁶ More often reductions were the fruit of successful appeals to the emotions of the jury. In 425 B.C. when an increase in revenue was imperative, the assessors were ordered by the people 'not to assess on any city a tribute lower than what it is now ordered to pay unless incapacity is proved, the territory being unable to contribute more'.⁷ These instructions are singularly vague, and how they could be interpreted is revealed by a fragment from Antiphon's speech on the tribute of Samothrace: 'You can see from a long way off that the island which we inhabit is mountainous and rough. The useful and workable parts of it are small, and the unproductive many, and the whole island is small.'⁸ No statistics were apparently available.

² Herod. VI 42.
³ Plut. *Arist.* 24, cf. Diod. XI 47.
⁴ Meiggs and Lewis, pp. 85 f, cf. nos 69, 75. [Athenian collectors, no. 46; local collectors, no. 68, cf. Antiphon fr. 52 Thalheim.]
⁵ Meiggs and Lewis, no. 69.
⁶ [Ibid., pp. 86, 124, 132. See Jones, *Athen. Democracy* 169 ff.]
⁷ Meiggs and Lewis, no. 69 lines 21 f.
⁸ Antiphon fr. 50.

To turn to civic finance,[9] the normal internal revenue of Athens comprised other items than taxes. There were the rents of public and sacred lands, the royalties on the mines and the sums paid for mining concessions, and judicial fines and confiscations. All these were important items in the revenue, but they fall outside my ambit. The taxes were many and various, some important, mostly insignificant. Important taxes were the 2 per cent duties on imports and exports at the Peiraeus, which under Andocides' management realised 36 talents, and the *metoikion*, the poll tax on resident aliens at 12 drachmas a head, and 6 on women who had no son who paid the tax.[10] Minor taxes included harbour dues,[11] an *octroi* at the city gates,[12] a tax on foreigners who traded in the market,[13] a prostitute tax,[14] a sales tax of [about] 1 per cent, later 2 per cent, on auction sales,[15] perhaps a slave tax[16] on moving slaves only, and two mysterious levies called the five drachmas for Theseus and the drachma for Asclepios.[17]

All these taxes, so far as we know, were farmed, or as the Greeks said 'sold', annually by auction to contractors, who collected the various taxes and paid the sums they had bid in ten instalments to the treasury.[18] The farming system is today generally condemned as the fruit of laziness. The Athenian people, it is said, did not wish to undertake themselves, as magistrates, the tedious and often invidious task of collecting

---

[9] [We are better informed about Athens than about any other Greek city, but the evidence suggests that other cities drew their revenues from sources generally similar to those of Athens, apart from *phoros*.]

[10] Andocides, *de myst.* 133 f [exceptionally low yield after Athens' collapse, cf. Dem. XXIII 110 for yield of 200 Talents from ports of the Thracian Chersonese,] see also Dem. XXI 133, XXXV 29; LIX 27, Tod, *Greek Hist. Inscriptions* no. 125, 38; 162, 24; *Etym.* Mag. s.v. πεντηκοστευόμενον. [Cf. n. 100.] Harpocration s.v. μετοίκιον.

[11] Aristophanes, *Wasps* 650, Pollux LX 30.

[12] Hesychius s.v. διαπύλιον.

[13] Dem. LVII 34.

[14] Aeschines I 119.

[15] Meiggs and Lewis 79; [see their note on p. 247;] *I.G.* II² 1579.

[16] Xenophon (*Vect.* iv 25) says that the number of slaves in the mines could be calculated from ὅσον τὸ τέλος ηὕρισκε τῶν ἀνδραπόδων.

[17] *Hesperia* V (1936) 397–404.

[18] The procedure for farming the taxes is described in Arist., *Const. Ath.* 47, 2–48, 2. Farmers are attested for the customs, *metoikion* (n. 10.), harbour dues (*Lex Seguer.* 251, 30), prostitute tax (n. 14) and the levies for Theseus and Asclepios (n. 17).

taxes, and shuffled it off on to contractors. There were, of course, obvious disadvantages in the system. Bidders might form a ring; Andocides alleges that he broke a ring led by Agyrrhius, which had kept the price of the 2 per cent tax on the Peiraeus down to 30 talents for three years.[19]

On the other hand, it seems unlikely that at Athens, where they could be sued before the people's courts, contractors often exacted more than their due. And to the state the system offered the great advantage that it knew what its revenue was going to be at the beginning of the year, and could be sure that it would be paid regularly, for contractors had to offer guarantors.[20]

There was, I think, another and more cogent reason why the Athenians—and indeed all ancient governments—farmed some taxes and not others. This may emerge from the study of an Athenian tax which was not farmed, the occasional war tax or *eisphora*.[21] The *eisphora* was a complicated and sophisticated tax, being assessed on all property—land, houses, slaves and, it would seem, personal effects and money.[22] There was probably a lower limit of 25 minae (2,500 drachmae) but taxpayers would have numbered upwards of 6,000.[23] The actual tax was a percentage of the capital valuation, usually 1 per cent or 2 per cent,[24] and had to be collected with the utmost despatch, as it was usually only voted at the opening of the campaigning season.

We know very little of how the *eisphora* was assessed and collected before the archonship of Nausinicus in 378, when the first systematic assessment was made, revealing a total of 5,750 talents,[25] and the symmories established. All taxpayers were

[19] See n. 10.

[20] Dem. XXIV 144, cf. n. 18.

[21] The latest book on the *eisphora*, Rudi Thomsen, *Eisphora*, seems to me, as to Mr. de Ste Croix (*Class. Rev.* 1966, 90–93), a baseless phantasy. For my own views see *Athen. Democracy* 23–9, 83–5, and for those of Mr. de Ste Croix, *Class. et Med.* XIV (1953), 30–70. [For *eisphorai* elsewhere cf. n. 60 and Busolt-Swoboda, 612, n. 1.]

[22] Polyb. II 62 (land, houses, other property); Isocr. XVII 49 (slaves). Demosthenes (XXVII 9–11) implies that all his father's property, including furniture and personal effects, and money on loan or on deposit, went into the assessment.

[23] Evidence, admittedly thin, in *Athen. Democracy* 28 f., 83 f.

[24] Dem. XIV 27, cf. III 4.

[25] Polyb. II 62. The total later rose to 6000 talents (Dem. XIV 19, 27; Philochorus, *F.G.H.* III no. 328 F 46). *Eisphora* is first mentioned in 434 B.C. (Meiggs and Lewis 58 B, line 17); the first recorded levy is in 428 B.C. (Thuc. III 19.) [In 411–403 it was only levied twice, Lysias XXI 1–3.] Of the original system we know only that there were elected boards of *epigrapheis*, apparently one for metics and

divided into 100 groups or symmories of approximately equal numbers and wealth—they would have had about sixty members each.²⁶ General reassessments were made occasionally²⁷ and individual assessments were revised when property changed hands.²⁸ Assessment was by self-declaration to an officer of the symmory, who kept a register of the members' property.²⁹ This may seem very trustful and there was according to the orators a good deal of evasion, particularly by concealing what the Greeks called 'non apparent property', that is cash.³⁰ But the great bulk of Athenian property consisted of land and houses, which it was impossible to conceal, and of slaves which were likewise difficult to hide. The symmory system came in useful too; members who assessed themselves honestly would hardly be human if they did not keep a sharp eye on fellow members whom they suspected of evasion. And common informers were active at Athens.

Each symmory elected from its richest members a president and a second and a third. It was their business to pay the tax for their symmory forthwith, and then to recoup themselves at leisure by exacting their quotas from the other members.³¹ The Athenians thus assessed and collected this rather complicated tax through ordinary citizens. They could take trouble when they wanted; why did they farm the other taxes?

The answer probably is that the yield of the *eisphora* was predictable and those of the other taxes were not. The amount payable in any *eisphora* by each taxpayer was known—so much percent of the assessment in the register of the symmory—and the failure of taxpayers to pay up or peculation by collectors could easily be detected and punished. But the yield of such taxes as the customs, the *octroi* or the sales tax was uncertain, and for all

---

another for citizens, who made the assessments, seemingly on each occasion a levy was made (Isocr. XVII 41; Harpocration s.v. ἐπιγραφεῖς, citing Lysias) on the basis of declarations (Isocr. XVII 49); from Pollux VIII 103 it appears that they were magistrates. The collection was made by *eklogeis* (*Lex Seguer.* 245).

²⁶ Philochorus, *F.G.H.* III no. 328 F. 41, cf. *Athen. Democracy* 141 n. 25 on Cleidemus, *F.G.H.* III no. 323 F. 8.

²⁷ Suidas, s.v. [ἀνασύνταξις]

²⁸ E.g. by Demosthenes' guardians when his father died (XVII 7 f.)

²⁹ Isocr., XVII 49; Dem., XXVII 7 f.; Harpocration s.v. διάγραμμα (citing Hyperides).

³⁰ *Athen. Democracy*, 141 n. 6.

³¹ Isaeus, VI 60; Dem. XLII 25; XVIII 103; XXI 157; XXVIII 4; Aeschines, III 222. I omit the peculiar *proeisphora* of 362 B.C., see *Athen. Democracy* 27 f.

practicable purposes so was that of the tax on resident aliens, who were a shifting population; a census in their case would have been very difficult to keep up to date, and so would a census of prostitutes. If magistrates were appointed to collect such taxes, it would be impossible to audit their accounts, and there would be no means of checking peculation, corruption or mere inefficiency. Under the farming system the contractor could be made to pay the amount of his bid, and that bid would normally, by the operation of competition, represent the highest estimate of the yield of the tax, allowing for the expenses of collection and a reasonable profit.

The same principle is observable in the collection of the land revenue in Ptolemaic Egypt. The revenue from arable land was assessed and collected by state officials, that from vineyards and orchards and gardens was farmed. The task of assessing the arable land was immensely laborious and complicated. Each village clerk had to make up annually a complete survey of the land in the village territory, with the dimensions and area of each plot and the name of its occupier. He had also to mark in the legal classification of each plot, since cleruchic land [assigned to soldiers or officials] and some other categories of land paid a fixed tax of one *artaba* of corn per *arura*, whereas the royal land was leased to royal peasants at rents (in *artabae*) which varied in rate from plot to plot. Further records had to be kept of the effects of the Nile flood. If it was a low flood, rebates would have to be allowed for unirrigated land, and if it was a high flood, for land which was waterlogged and saline. A further complication was the loan of seed corn: royal peasants—and some others— were granted a loan by the government, and this—with an additional percentage—had to be added to the rent. When the harvest arrived guards had to be posted to prevent landholders from reaping their crops surreptitiously. All grain had to be brought to the village threshing floor, and the collectors (the *sitologoi*) took and stored the government's share, and then the cultivator could remove the rest.[32]

The *apomoira* was a tax of one sixth, or in some cases one tenth, on wine, fruit and vegetables. It was an old temple tax taken over by Ptolemy Philadelphus [285-46 B.C.], and the first

[32] For the Ptolemaic corn revenue see Préaux, 117–37. I have greatly simplified the process.

operation was that all temples were required to send in returns of the vineyards, orchards and gardens which had hitherto paid tax to them, and all occupiers of vineyards, orchards and gardens had to send in returns of their land, stating to which temple they had paid their *apomoira*. This basic information having been obtained by the royal officials, the tax was sold to contractors, nome by nome. In the case of vineyards the pressing of the wine must not begin until the contractor or his agent arrived, and two royal officials, the controller and the auditor, or their representatives, had to be present all the time. If the contractor failed to appear or send an agent, the royal officials carried on without him. If there was no dispute on the quantity of the wine a double contract was drawn up giving the figures, and the sixth taken away. If there was a dispute the royal officials settled it. In the case of orchards and gardens the tax was collected in money. If the contractor and the cultivator came to an agreement on the value of the crop, a double contract was signed. If they failed to agree the contractor could sequestrate the whole crop and sell it. If the price realised exceeded the cultivator's estimate, the contractor kept the excess for himself, if it failed to reach the estimate, he had to pay the difference to the treasury. But again if he failed to present himself, the business was done by controllers and the auditors. In fact the royal officials had to supervise or if necessary perform every operation in the collection of the *apomoira*.[33]

The reason why farming was sometimes used and sometimes direct collection is by now fairly clear. The Ptolemies did not shirk the immensely laborious and complicated task of assessing and collecting the revenue from arable land—and what a huge task it was can be readily appreciated from the many rolls of papyrus which the village clerks of Tebtunis, Kerkeosiris and other villages of the Arsinoite nome covered with column upon column of closely packed and highly abbreviated entries. The Ptolemies could, one would think, have assessed and collected the *apomoira* through their officials. But in fact they preferred to farm it, and then made their officials do half the work.

The distinction is that in the grain tax, however complicated

---

[33] The regulations for the *apomoira* were first published with translation and commentary by Grenfell and Hunt, *Revenue Laws of Ptolemy Philadelphus*; revised text and bibliography in J. Bingen, *Sammelbuch gr. Urkunden aus Ägypten*, Beiheft I, 1952, Cf. Préaux, 172 ff.

and laborious its assessment was, the yield each year was fixed in advance, and the negligence or dishonesty of the officials concerned could be visited upon them if they failed to produce the proper amount. In the *apomoira* the yield, being a percentage of the actual crop, was unpredictable, and there would be no means of telling whether officials were defrauding the government. The tax was therefore sold to contractors, whose principal function was to pay to the government the highest estimate of the yield obtainable by competitive bidding. Whether they actually collected the tax was a matter of secondary importance.

The fiscal system of the Ptolemies was immensely intricate and pervasive—and to us very obscure—and no attempt can be made here to describe it in detail.[34] The land revenue included not only the levy of wheat and the *apomoira*, outlined above, but another tax of a third or a half on the crops of vineyards, which was like the *apomoira* and for the same reason farmed.[35] There were naturally customs, but on a very different scale from the 5 per cent levied by Athens and most Greek cities. The Ptolemaic dues were differential, at 20 per cent, 25 per cent, 33½ per cent or 59 per cent according to the class of merchandise.[36] There was also 'circulation tax' (*enkyklion*) on all transfers—by sale, gift, cession or mortgage—of all kinds of property—land, houses, slaves and even priesthoods and tax concessions—at rates varying from 5 per cent to 10 per cent.[37] There were also a multiplicity of minor taxes direct or indirect. Finally there were a number of monopolies, total and partial, on manufacture or on sale or on both. These monopolies included banking, papyrus, perfumes, textiles, oil, beer and salt. These were, since the yield was speculative, farmed to contractors.[38]

Monopolies are not strictly taxes, but I am tempted to give a brief account of the oil monopoly, of which the regulations

[34] There is an admirable description of the entire system in Préaux. [Wallace describes the Roman practices, which were basically similar; as usual, the Romans mainly took over what they found. The marvellously lucid account of taxation in Ptolemaic and Roman Egypt in U. Wilcken, *Gr. Ostraka* I, 1899, though in parts antiquated, remains perhaps the best introduction.]

[35] Préaux 182–4.

[36] Ibid 371–9; the long document setting out the differential rates is P. *Cairo Zenon* 59012.

[37] Ibid. 331–3.

[38] Ibid. 280–97 (banking), 190–6 (papyrus), 362–7 (perfumes), 93–116 (textiles) 65–93 (oil), 152–8 (beer), 249–52 (salt).

survive in full,[39] since it illustrates even more clearly than the *apomoira*, the role of the contractor in the Ptolemaic fiscal system. The monopoly was sold, nome by nome, to contractors, royal officials were involved in every stage of the process. The central government prescribed the number of *arurae* to be sown in each nome with oil-producing plants, and the royal officials of the nome had to see that the correct area was sown and to provide the seed; otherwise they were liable to a fine to the treasury and damages to the contractor. The contractor then bought the crop, at a price fixed by the government, from the cultivator, making out a double agreement with each cultivator on the amount. The royal officials meanwhile designated oil factories, providing the machinery and sealing all the rest, to prevent its being used by illicit manufacturers, and conveyed the crops to the factories. They also furnished workers, and paid them their wages and commission, being liable to fines to the treasury and damages to the contractor if they failed to fulfil all their functions. The royal officials then registered the retailers of oil in each town, and allocated the oil to them according to their needs, and conveyed it to them at five day intervals. The selling price of the oil was fixed by the central government. All illicit manufacture and sale of oil was visited with fines payable to the contractor, but the royal officials had to be present when searches of private premises were made.

Here again the bulk of the administrative work is done by the officials of the nome, and one may well ask what the role of the contractor was. It was to his direct advantage to keep the officials up to the mark and to suppress breaches of the monopoly, since he had to pay the crown the sum which he had bid, and would lose money by the negligence of the officials or by illicit manufacture or sale of oil. His main function was in fact to be a watch dog over the officials, and he was directly encouraged to exercise this function by being awarded damages in case of neglect.

In their overseas dominions the Ptolemies abandoned the old system of a block tribute assessed on each city and collected by the city governments. Instead they levied specific taxes on the citizens, usually through contractors. The taxes of Coele Syria and Phoenicia, if the story of Joseph the son of Tobias is to be believed, were sold annually at Alexandria,[40] and the chief men of

[39] See n. 33, cf. Edgar and Hunt. *Select Papyri* II, 302.
[40] Josephus, *Ant. Jud.* XII, 167–69.

the cities went up to Alexandria to bid for the taxes—on slaves and on cattle—which were farmed.[41] In Lycia we hear of money revenues, an octroi and a purple tax, all farmed,[42] and in Telmessus of pasture dues, a tax on fruit, and an *apomoira* of one tenth on cereals, the last certainly farmed.[43]

Elsewhere the earlier Hellenistic Kings still used the block tribute system. We find Antipater, Lysimachus, and indeed Ptolemy I, levying contributions from the Greek cities subject to them.[44] The system was used even later by the Attalids of Pergamum in backward and imperfectly pacified areas where it would have been impossible to impose specific taxes. Thus we find Attalus II remitting half a talent from the tribute of two talents which the Pisidian city of Amblada pays him.[45] In general however the Seleucids of Syria and the Attalids seem to have followed the same line as the Ptolemies. The Seleucids are recorded in an inscription to have levied a tithe on crops at Tralles in Caria.[46] In Judaea the books of Maccabees and Josephus mention a number of royal taxes, a poll tax, crowns, the price of salt, and a third of the cereal crop and half the fruit crop.[47] Even less is known of Attalid taxation. We know only of a tithe on cereals and a twentieth on vineyards, and of a tax on sheep.[48] To this rather meagre evidence for Hellenistic royal taxation may be added that of a number of civic inscriptions from Asia Minor, where the city makes a grant of immunity 'from the taxes which the city imposes' or 'which the city controls'. There were evidently royal taxes also, from which the city could not grant immunity.[49]

[41] *Aegyptus* XVI (1936), 257 ff.
[42] P. *Tebt.* 8.
[43] O.G.I. 55.
[44] O.G.I. 4; *Milet* 138 f.; S.I.G.[3] 390.
[45] O.G.I. 751.
[46] Welles, *Royal Correspondence in the Hellenistic Period*, 41. There was also some kind of royal land tax at Mylasa, Waddington, 404.
[47] I *Macc.* X 29 f.; XI 34 f.; Josephus, *Ant. Jud.* XII 142–4; XIII 49 f., 128. Seleucid taxation is discussed in Bikerman, 106–32. I do not agree with his view that the sums mentioned in 1 *Macc.* IV 8 f.; 23 f., 27 represent an annual block tribute; they seem rather to be fees or bribes for appointment as high priest. Nor do I think that the third on cereals and half of fruits were rents (the territory of the Jewish community having been confiscated on some unrecorded occasion). The rates are very high, but parallelled in Ptolemaic Egypt (see n. 35). [But see Addendum III.]
[48] Welles, *op. cit.*, 47, 51.
[49] C.I.G. 2673, 2675–7; Michel 349, 463, 519, S.E.G. II 580.

The Roman Republic was not inventive in the matter of taxation. The *tributum* or war tax, levied occasionally on citizens down to 167 B.C., closely resembled the Athenian *eisphora*. It was assessed apparently on all forms of property, land, houses, slaves, animals, personal effects and money, as declared in the quinquennial census.[50] The rate of tax, usually .01 per cent, sometimes double or treble this, seems fantastically low. A unique feature of the *tributum* was that when the war was over and the treasury was well filled it was often repaid.[51] There were also customs levied at Italian ports, and a 5 per cent tax on the manumission of slaves.[52]

In the provinces, as Cicero tells us, there were two main forms of taxation, *stipendium* or tithe (and pasture dues).[53] The original meaning of *stipendium* is military pay, and how it came to mean a provincial tax appears from Livy. In the early years of the Second Punic War the commander of the Roman army in Spain, which had received no money or supplies from Rome, wrote asking for corn and clothing; pay, he said, if the treasury was in difficulties, he would find a way of getting out of the Spaniards.[54] A few years later, [after the Roman troops had mutinied owing to arrears of pay, Scipio Africanus required money from a defeated Spanish people to pay his soldiers.][55] *Stipendium* was in fact the old arbitrarily assessed levy of money from the subject communities which the Persian Empire had employed. It was levied from the more barbarous and unruly provinces, like Spain and Gaul, where *publicani* would have found

[50] Cicero, *Flacc.* 80 (land, slaves, money). Cato the Censor assessed all luxury articles at ten times their real value (Plut. *Cato* 18; Livy, XXXIX 44, 2). [*Tributum* was levied 'pro portione census', Varro, *LL* V 181, cf. Livy I 43, 13. For registration of land cf. also Festus 50 L; Gell. VI 11, 9. Livy (VI 27, 5; 31, 2) suggests that, as at Athens (n. 22), money on loan was registered. For returns and valuations made by the citizens see *F.I.R.A.* I² no. 13, 142 ff; Festus 51 L; penalties for failure to register or for false returns, Cicero, *Caec.* 99; Dio XLVII 16.]

[51] Livy XXIII 31, 1; XXIX 15, 9; XXXIX 44, 2; Plut., *Cato Maj.* 18. Repayments, Dionysius Hal. V 47, 1; Livy XXXIX 7, 5. It is not known how the *tributum* was collected. It has been conjectured that the *tribuni aerarii*, who paid the troops in early times (Varro, *L.L.* V 181, Gell. VI 10), may have collected the *tributum* from which it was paid. Very little is known of them, but their title implies that they were state officers. [For cessation of levies p. 115 n. 10.]

[52] [Cic., *Att* II 16, 1; Livy VII 16, 7 (cf. n. 87); the customs, abolished in 60 B.C., were again levied in the Principate, see Tac., *Ann.* XIII 50 f.]

[53] Cic., *Verr.* II 3, 12. [See also n. 75.]

[54] Livy XXIII 48, 4 f.

[55] Livy XXVIII 25, 9 f.

life dangerous.[56] Since it was, as Cicero says, *certum* (fixed), it was no doubt directly collected by the quaestor or praetor—no *publicani* at any rate are found in Spain or Gaul, except for the customs. There is one exception to this rule. Cicero says that most of the Poeni, the people of the provinces of Africa, paid *stipendium*, but *mancipes stipendiorum*, contractors, are mentioned in an African inscription.[57] We know, however, that when Carthage was destroyed, the Romans imposed a poll tax and a land tax,[58] and a law of 111 B.C. refers to the grant of land to *stipendiarii* or persons who pay *stipendium*.[59] The term *stipendium* is thus in Africa used for a poll tax. If a census of the population and a cadastration of the land had been held, such taxes could have been directly collected, but the Roman republic never went to the trouble of holding provincial censuses.[60]

The Romans found the tithe already in operation in Sicily, perhaps in the Carthaginian zone which they first annexed in 241 B.C., certainly in the kingdom of Syracuse, annexed in 212 B.C. They took over the fiscal law of the Syracusan kingdom, the lex Hieronica, intact, and extended it to all Sicily.[61] The tithe was sold annually at Syracuse, city by city and crop by crop (wheat, barley, fruit),[62] and the contracts therefore normally went to Sicilians or resident Romans, sometimes to the city governments themselves.[63] The key operation was the *pactio*, the agreement on the amount of the crop between the contractor and the cultivator:

[56] *Verr.* II 3, 12. Gaul, *Caes.*, B.G. I 45; Suet. *Iul.* 25, 1; [Vell. II 39.] In Sardinia some communities apparently paid *stipendium* [Cic., *Balb.* 41; Livy XXIII 32, 9; 41, 6; XL 17, 2], most tithes [Livy XXXVI 2, 13; XXXVII 2, 12; 50, 10; XLII 31, 8; *Bell. Afr.* 98; some of these texts also attest requisitioning.]

[57] *Verr.* II 3, 12; *I.L.S.* 911; [perhaps Tac., *Ann.* IV 6.]

[58] Appian, *Bell. Pun.* 135 [cf. n. 114.]

[59] *F.I.R.A.* I² no. 8, 77 f., 80, cf. *I.L.S.* 9482 [and 901.]

[60] [Perhaps under Roman influence the Sicilian cities had censors who made quinquennial assessments on which local *tributa* could be based, *Verr.* II 2, 131; 3, 100; for *tributa* cf. Livy XXXIII 46, 9 and n. 71; see also *I.G.* V 1, 1432–3 for a local census at Messene in the first century B.C., connected with an *eisphora* to meet irregular Roman exactions. The *timetai* instituted by Pompey in Bithynia-Pontus may not have been in any way concerned with taxation, see Sherwin-White on Pliny, *ep.* X 79, 3.]

[61] *Verr.* II 2, 13; 3, 14 f. [The remaining notes are by P. A. B. For Jones' views in the Sicilian system see further pp. 119 ff., and *Tijdschrift voor Rechtsgeschiedenis* 1971, 17–20.]

[62] E.g. *Verr.* II 3, 61, 67, 72–8; 83 f.

[63] Sicilians, e.g. 77 f., 83; Romans, e.g. 54, 75, 84, 88, 90, 99, 101 f., 103; cities, e.g. 77, 99.

if they failed to settle on an agreed figure they went to special fiscal courts under the lex Hieronica.[64] The law envisaged the contractors making a separate *pactio* with each cultivator,[65] but in practice the contractors preferred, except in the case of a few important landowners, to make a block *pactio* with the city authorities,[66] who then assessed the tithe in detail and collected it themselves. According to Cicero the lex Hieronica was so ingeniously framed that a contractor could not cheat a cultivator or a cultivator a contractor even collusively.[67] We hear of no complaints in Sicily until Verres,[68] who adjudicated the contracts to men of straw, who could always outbid honest competitors in the knowledge that Verres would enforce their *pactiones* however outrageous—in return for a cut out of the profits.[69]

Gaius Gracchus in 123-2 B.C. imposed the tithe on the recently acquired province of Asia, with an important administrative change. Under the lex Sempronia the Asiatic tithe was sold *en bloc* by the censors, that is at Rome and for a period of five years.[70] The same system was applied to the eastern provinces which were annexed later, Bithynia-Pontus, Cilicia and Syria.[71] Under the system of *censoria locatio* the contracts inevitably went to companies of big Roman financiers, since the sums required for sureties were so very large,[72] and these big financiers belonged to the equestrian order, which was politically influential, and in particular usually controlled the criminal courts at Rome,

[64] 2, 32; 3, 25–30; 34 f.; 38, 3 etc.

[65] 3, 36; 92 f.; 107; 112.

[66] 66–117 *passim*; for the role of the cities in collection, 34; 70 f.; 83. *de imp. Cn. Pomp.* 15; *Flacc.* 19.

[67] 3, 20.

[68] So Cicero alleges, 2, 8.

[69] E.g. 3, 22 f.; 130–44; 147–50. According to 3, 24 Verres had virtually annulled the *lex Hieronica*.

[70] *Verr.* II 3, 12; *Att.* I 17, 9, V 13, 1; Appian, *Bell. Civ.* V 4.

[71] Bithynia, Memnon, *F.G.H.* III no. 434, 38; Appian, *Bell. Mithr*, 71, Plut., *Luc.* 7; Cic., *de leg. agr.* II 50. Cilicia, *Att.* V 13, 1; 14, 1 VI 1, 16; 2, 5. Syria, *de prov. cons.* 10; Achaea, *F.I.R.A.* 1–2 no. 36. Some of these texts show that, as in Sicily, the publicans commonly made *pactiones* with the cities (cf. also *Fam* XIII 65); the latter might then raise the lump sums required by farming out tithes to local publicans of their own (Cic., *Flacc.* 91) or by imposing their own taxes (*tributa*, Cic. *Flacc.* 20; *ad Qu. fr.* I 1, 25 and 35; *Att.* V 16, 2; *Fam.* III 8, 5) under the supervision of local magistrates, who could avail themselves of the opportunity for embezzlement (*Att.* VI 2, 5). See further, T. R. S. Broughton, *Am. Journ. Phil.* 1936, 175 f.; Jones, *Tijdschrift* nn. 53, 54, 81 concurs.

[72] Polyb., VI 17; Cic., *Verr.* II 1, 142 f.; Ps-Asconius 252 St.; *Schol. Bobb.* 106 St.; the publicans had also to furnish security in Italian lands.

including the court of extortion. Provincial governors therefore, wishing to placate the equestrian order for political reasons, and to avoid a conviction for extortion, were reluctant to protect the provincials from the *publicani*, and would approve grossly exaggerated *pactiones*.[73] Official figures cited by Cicero in the Verrines suggest that under Verres' administration the amount of corn actively collected was sometimes as much as three times the lawful tithe.[74] We have no figures for the other provinces, but conditions may have been even worse.

In the provinces where tithe was levied there was always a complementary pasture tax, called *scriptura*.[75] It was probably assessed on the numbers of cattle grazed. It may be noted that in these provinces all the taxation—except for the customs (*portoria*) discussed below—was assessed on agriculture. This was reasonable enough as agriculture produced nearly all the wealth of the empire. [See Addendum I].

It was probably Augustus who introduced the uniform and more rational system of taxation which is attested later in the empire. There were two main taxes, *tributum soli* and *tributum capitis*.[76] The first closely resembled the Athenian *eisphora*, being assessed not only, as its name might seem to imply on land, classified as arable, vineyard, oliveyard, meadow and woods but also on houses, slaves and ships (to mention only attested items).[77] The tax was a percentage of the assessed value; it is known to have been 1 per cent in Cilicia and Syria.[78] *Tributum capitis* was

[73] Cic., *adQu. fr.* I 1, 35; *de prov. cons.* 10. See further T. R. S. Broughton, *Econ. Survey of Ancient Rome* IV 535 ff; Brunt, ap. Seager, *Crisis of Roman Republic* 122 ff.
[74] *Verr.* II 3, 110–6.
[75] Sicily, *Verr.* II 2, 169 ff.; 3, 167; Africa, *F.I.R.A.* I² no. 8, 82; Asia, Cic., *de imp. Cn. Pomp.* 15; Bithynia, *Fam.* XIII 65; Cilicia, *Att.* v 15, 3; Cyrenaica, Pliny, *N.H.* XIX 39. Publicans also collected *scriptura* in Republican Italy, see e.g. *F.I.R.A.* I² no. 8, 36 f., and in Asia salt-dues, *de imp.* l.c.; *Inschr. v. Priene* 111, 12 ff., and at least tried to appropriate dues on fishing, Strabo, XIV 1, 26.
[76] *Dig.* L xv, 8, 7 (Paul).
[77] Land, *Dig.* L xv, 4 (Ulpian); Hyginus, 205 L; the classification of lands in *F.I.R.A.* III pp. 795 f. seems to go back to the 2nd century, see Déléage, 159. Liability of particular estates, *I.L.S.* 6953; *Dig.* II xiv, 42; VII i 7, 2; i 52; X i, 11; XIX i, 52; XXII iii, 10; XXV i, 13; XXX xxxix, 5; XLIX xiv, 36; xiv 46, 5; L xv, 5. Houses, Josephus, *Ant. Jud.* XIX 299, *F.I.R.A.* III no. 90 (but cf. A. von Premerstein, *R.E.* XIX 1243). Slaves, *Dig.* L xv, 4, 5 cf *CIL* VIII 23956 ('praetium servi ex forma censoria'). Ships, Tac., *Ann.* XIII 51. Moveables, *Dig.* XXXIII ii, 32, 9 (Scaevola). Note penalties for false returns, *Dig.* V i, 55; XLIII vii, 26; XLVII xv, 7; XLVIII xviii, 1, 20; *C.J.* IX xli, 1.
[78] App., *Bell. Syr.* 50, on which see Wilcken, *Gr. Ostraka* I 247.

a poll tax, levied at a flat rate on adults, from the age of 12 or 14 to 65, sometimes on males only, as in Egypt, sometimes on both sexes, as in Syria.[79]

The great advantage of the new system was that the *publicani* could now be dispensed with.[80] Regular censuses were required in all provinces both to register property and to count the population. Such censuses began under Augustus, and continued for the next two and a half centuries.[81] In Egypt the population census was taken at intervals of 14 years, because the lower age for the poll tax was 14; children down to newly born infants were counted, and brought into the poll tax lists, as they came of age. Deaths were reported by relatives.[82]

It was rightly considered a great benefit to the provinces to free them from the *publicani* [cf. n. 61]. This was achieved by altering the whole basis of taxation from a proportional levy, where yield was unpredictable, to a fixed levy based on assessed property. This new tax could be, and was, left to the provincial cities to collect.[83] Other taxes whose yield could not be deter-

[79] *Dig.* L xv, 3 (Ulpian); Egypt, Wallace 104 ff.; ibid, 116–80; 191 ff. on the nature of the various capitation taxes in Egypt. Besides the poll tax proper, payable at different rates in different nomes, and at reduced rates or not at all by certain privileged classes, there were other capitation taxes (*merismoi*) for specific purposes, and others again payable by certain classes (e.g. Jews), and also *cheironaxia*, fees to practise a trade or craft. See further n. 114.

[80] But see Addendum II.

[81] Augustan censuses in Gaul, Livy, *Per.* CXXXIV, CXXXVIII; Tac., *Ann.* I 31; *I.L.S.* 212, II 35 ff.: in Syria and Judaea, Josephus, *Ant. Jud.* XVII 355, XVIII 2; *I.L.S.* 2683; Luke II 1–3 (though his date is wrong, and he is mistaken, if he implies that the census was taken everywhere at the same time; Suidas s.v. ἀπογραφή is worthless); in Lusitania, *C.I.L.* X 680. Tiberian censuses in Narbonensis, *I.L.S.* 950; in Cappadocia, Tac., *Ann.* VI 41. Trajan took a census in Dacia on its conquest, Lactantius, *de mort. persec.* 23, 5. Senatorial and equestrian *censitores* are attested later from numerous other provinces in the Principate, and Luke was at least right in deeming the system to be universal. For the cadastre and house-to-house census in Egypt see Wallace chs. I and VII; they hardly provided models applicable elsewhere, though land surveys were certainly required where the *tributum* took the form of an *eisphora* due principally on real estate, cf. Hyginus 205 L. A new inscription in *Latomus*, 1971, 352 ff. shows Caracalla ordering a survey *ad hoc* in his march across Asia at Pessinus.

[82] See last note. In Egypt whole or part payments were due on those who died within the tax year (Wallace 124 f., cf. 106), and this practice is implied to have obtained elsewhere, see Dio (n. 114) and Lactantius (n. 81).

[83] See Addendum II. For collection by the cities through magistrates or liturgical officials such as *dekaprotoi* (E. G. Turner, *Journ. Eg. Arch.* XXII), before Diocletian see also Dio Chrys. XXXV 14; XL 10; Josephus, *B.J.* II 405, 407; Apuleius, *Apology* 101; *Dig.* L i, 17, 7 (Papinian); iv 3, 10 f. (Ulpian); *I.L.S.* 1945; *I.G.* XII 3, 326; *I.G.R.* III 739, II (cf. III 87, 7); 488; IV 259; 1290. The evidence is

mined in advance, notably the customs, were still sold to *publicani*, but their operations were controlled by imperial procurators.[84] *Publicani* had also to be used to collect Augustus' new taxes on Roman citizens. The most interesting of them was the 5 per cent tax on inheritances and legacies. This appears to have been a new invention. All fortunes over 100,000 sesterces were liable to it, except those which passed to very near relatives.[85] Augustus also enacted a 1 per cent sales tax[86] and a 4 per cent special sales tax on slaves.[87]

In the latter part of the second century the farming system gradually fades out even for [many of] these taxes. The customs of the Danube cease to be managed by contractors (*conductores publici portorii Illyrici*), who are replaced by procurators. Simultaneously the clerical staff changes from slaves of the *conductores* to imperial slaves.[88] In the inheritance tax there is a curious mixture.

---

meagre, but no other method is attested as normal, and even after Diocletian, despite the growth of the bureaucracy, the cities were generally responsible, and intermittent efforts to entrust the collection to officials failed, see *L.R.E.* 456 ff., 749, 760 f. It was an advantage to the government that the councils could be held collectively liable for arrears. As Jones points out in his *Tijdschrift* article (n. 60), 29 f., it was a consequence of this system that the central government became concerned in the solvency of the cities and prevented them from levying new taxes of their own, as under the Republic (cf. n. 71), cf. p. 28 n. 1.

[84] De Laet 370 ff.

[85] Dio, LV 25 (cf. *Res Gestae* 17); *Acta Divi Augusti*, ed. Riccobono, 219 ff., where much other evidence is quoted: J. F. Gilliam, *Amer. Journ. Phil.*, 1952, 397 ff. Pliny, *Paneg.* 37–40, attests (besides modifications in the tax made by Nerva and Trajan) that it was still collected by publicans (cf. *ep.* VII 14). See nn. 106 f.

[86] Tac., *Ann.* I 78 cf. II 42; Dio LVIII 16, LIX 9, 6; Suet., *Gaius* 16; Mattingly-Sydenham, *Rom. Imp. Coinage* I p. 118 n. 1; *Dig.* L xvi, 17, 1.

[87] Dio, LV 31, 4; *I.L.S.* 203 (under Claudius the same publicans farmed it as the tax on manumissions, cf. n. 52).

[88] De Laet, 384 ff. gives evidence fully. Since procurators are found in other regions along with tax-farmers, whose operations they presumably controlled (e.g. *I.L.S.* 1350, 1411, cf. Pflaum, pp. 1052, 1093 for other procurators in Africa and Gaul before the date at which direct collection can be assumed), the first known appearance of a procurator for the Illyrian *portoria* in 182 (*I.L.S.* 1856) would not prove that any change had been made, were it not that the same inscription shows that an imperial slave was now *vilicus vectigalis Illyrici* (cf *C.I.L.* III 8042); many other such are now found, whereas earlier the slaves employed belonged to the *conductores*. Comparable evidence for Gaul and Africa, given by de Laet, is not so precisely dateable, but seems to be rather later; the rank of the procurators in charge was raised, no doubt because their functions had been enlarged, but such higher ranking procurators are not attested before c. 242 and c. 209 respectively (Pflaum nos, 331 *bis*, 224). There is no similar evidence for other provinces; the system of direct collection certainly never became universal (cf. n. 93); and it may be that it was introduced in Illyricum after disruption of the old administration in Marcus Aurelius' Marcomannic wars, and then adopted in Gaul and Africa for special reasons that elude us.

We find men—professional civil servants—styled *procurator in urbe magister XX*—procurator at Rome and chairman of the company of the 5 per cent tax—or *procurator Augusti promagistro XX hereditatium*—procurator of Augustus and vice chairman of the 5 per cent inheritance tax (in the provinces).[89] A parallel case is M. Aurelius Mindius Matidianus Pollio, chairman of the contractors of the 2½ per cent tax at the harbours of Asia and procurator of Augustus, whose agents built a customs house at Halicarnassus.[90] We also find men becoming *conductores* in the course of an official equestrian career, usually near its beginning.[91]

The explanation of this phenomenon is probably to be found in an official letter from Egypt, dating from the late first century. Paniscus, governor of the Oxyrhynchite district to Asclepiades, chief accountant of the same district. 'At the sale of taxes held by me and you with the usual officials present, the contractors for the stamp tax and the market tax were recalcitrant on the ground that they had lost enough already and were in danger of going bankrupt. So we decided that I should write to his excellency the governor general on the matter. He has replied to me that we should inspect earlier contracts and as far as possible relieve the contractors, in case they run away if force is applied to them. I sent you a copy of the letter before for your information. When you were away the contracts were not accepted by the tax contractors and no one else made a bid though there were frequent advertisements. So I took affidavits from the contractors for the

---

[89] Pflaum pp. 1026 f. Jones' conception is not clear to me. It is usually held (on rather insubstantial grounds) that Hadrian probably substituted direct collection for tax-farming (cf. O. Hirschfeld, *Kaiserliche Verwaltungsbeamten* 98 ff). The title borne by C. Furius Sabinius AquilaTimesitheus c. 224 of *procurator in urbe magisterXX* (*I.L.S.* 1330), but not by a dozen of his post-Hadrianic predecessors in the post, might better be explained by the appearance about the same time of other *magistri* in the central bureaux at Rome (Pflaum pp. 1020, 1022) than by distant memories of a collection by publicans directed by a *magister*. As to earlier officials *pro magistro XX hereditatium* (Pflaum p. 1027), a *promagister hereditatium* is also attested under Nerva or Trajan (Pflaum no. 80), but there had never been a time when publicans collected legacies to the emperor.

[90] Pflaum no. 193. But there is no proof that this man who was *archones* of the Asian *portoria* for 30 years and held ducenarian procuratorships under Commodus performed these functions simultaneously, and he was certainly never procurator of the *portoria*.

[91] Pflaum nos. 150–1, 174. Again, though these men were both *conductores* and procurators, it is unwarranted to assume that their official posts were concerned with the Illyrian *portoria* which they farmed.

M

stamp tax. . . .' This is followed by a ruling of the Emperor Hadrian: 'it is a very inhumane practice whereby contractors for public taxes and lands are kept on, if they cannot be leased for the same sum as before; for contractors will be more easily found, if they know that they will not be kept on if they wish to leave when their five years period is finished.'[92]

Evidently Hadrian's advice was not followed, the supply of voluntary contractors dried up, and officials were ordered to collect the tax and pay in the sum reached on the previous bid. If the tax did not yield so much, the official would have to make good the deficit out of his salary, or, more probably, charge an extra percentage on the taxpayers. The customs from being an unpredictable tax varied by contractors became a fixed tax collected by officials.[93]

The Augustan system of taxation collapsed during the great inflation of the middle and late third century, in the course of which the denarius sank to about 10.5 per cent of its second century value. The ephemeral military emperors of this period neglected to raise the pay of their civil service and army, or their rates of tax. Hitherto rations, uniforms and equipment had been procured by compulsory purchase from the provincials, and issued to the troops against deductions from their pay. As the currency became almost worthless, both payments for purchases and deductions from pay became negligible and were ultimately abandoned as were the old direct taxes in money. In effect the state came to raise most of its revenue by irregular requisitions in kind, and to pay the army mainly in kind.[94]

It was Diocletian's great achievement to reorganise irregular requisitions into an elaborate system of taxation in kind. The first step was to hold new censuses throughout the empire, in

---

[92] Wilcken, *Chrestomathie* 275; *Dig.* XLIX xiv, 3, 6. See also the edict of Ti. Iulius Alexander (A.D. 68), 10 ff. (e.g. in McCrum and Woodhead, *Select Documents of the Flavian Emperors* 328); *C.J.* IV lxv, 11 (A.D. 244); *Dig.* XXXXIX iv, 9, 1, but cf. 4, 11.

[93] However, the continued use of publicans (at a time when the *portoria* in Illyricum and probably in Gaul and Africa were collected directly) is attested in *Dig.* XXXIX iv, 1; 3; 6; 12; 16, 12–14. De Laet (514 ff.) supposes that it persisted in Egypt, Syria and Judaea, but none of his evidence is clearly post-Severan, nor can I discover any other. Yet the use of publicans in the late empire (ib. 469 ff, cf *L.R.E.* 430), makes it improbable that it was everywhere abandoned and then revived. For all we know, direct collection may have been only temporarily adopted in the few regions where it is attested (n. 88).

[94] For inflation and its effects see chapter IX.

which the rural population and farm animals were counted and the land surveyed and assessed. The rules of the census differed in different areas, partly in accordance with local custom, partly because the censuses were carried out by different emperors over a considerable period of time. Thus the unit of human beings (*caput*), on which a money tax was levied, was sometimes a man (women being exempt), sometimes a man or a woman (both paying equally), sometimes a man or two women (women paying half). It was useless to value land in monetary terms, as under the principate, since the currency was so unstable, and it was assessed in ideal fiscal units, generally called *iuga*. These units also varied very much in different regions. In some they were a crude area of land. The *centuria* in Africa, for instance, was 200 *iugera* (50 hectares), whether it was rough pasture or olive groves. But in the eastern dioceses the assessment was more sophisticated. In Asia and Egypt, for instance, pasture, arable, vines and olives were rated differently, and in Syria three qualities of arable and two of olives were distinguished.[95]

The collection of the bulk of the revenue in kind had an interesting by-product. The army was naturally used to estimating its needs in advance, and it was essential to requisition enough supplies at harvest time, since they might not be available later. At the same time it was impracticable and wasteful to requisition too much, as storage space was limited, and some produce was perishable. When Diocletian systematised requisitions into an annual levy, he apparently instructed his praetorian prefects to draw up estimates of all categories of supplies required for the coming year, and by dividing the total amounts by the number of *iuga* or other fiscal units, to work out the amount of wheat, barley, meat, wine and oil that each *iugum* must pay. The requirements for uniforms, horses and recruits were similarly apportioned. These tax rates were annually published in the indiction on 1 September. He thus instituted for the first time in history a budget in which the rate of tax was calculated according to estimated expenditure.[96]

After Constantine established a sound and abundant gold currency [pp. 202 f.], levies and payments in kind were for the

[95] See chapters X and XIII and *L.R.E.* I 61 ff. for summary. Cf. n. 98.

[96] *L.R.E.* I 66, cf. for the earlier system of irregular requisitioning ib. 30; to the evidence there cited in n. 24 add *Dig.* VII i, 27, 3; XLIX xviii, 4; L iv, 14, 2; v 8, 3;

most part gradually commuted into gold. In the western empire the process seems to have been complete by the middle of the fifth century, and the government obtained what supplies it needed by compulsory purchase. In the east Anastasius (491-518) converted most of the tax into gold but levied enough in kind in limited areas to feed the local troops. Though the tax was for the most part no longer levied in kind, the annual indiction went on but seems to have been in practice stabilised at a customary level.[97]

It may be noted that under Diocletian the main direct tax of the empire was assessed entirely on agriculture, the levy in kind (*annona*) on land only, not houses or other buildings or even gardens, and the money poll tax (*capitatio*) on farm animals and the rural population, not townspeople. Very soon the assessment of persons (*capitatio*) was combined with the assessment of land (*iugatio*), one *caput* being rather arbitarily equated with one *iugum*, and the *annona* was assessed on the total of *capita* and *iuga*. This was certainly the system in the Eastern parts (chapter XIII), but in some Western dioceses there was apparently a separate money *capitatio* which included the urban population.[98]

Constantine instituted a tax, payable in gold and silver and hence called the *chrysargyron*, on merchants and manufacturers.

C.J. VIII xiii, 6 (A.D. 213); Suetonius, *Gaius* 42; *Nero* 38, 2; 44; *Titus* 7; perhaps Pliny, *Paneg.* 41, 1; Tac. *Ann.* IV 6 ('novis oneribus'); *Germ.* 29, 1; *A.É.* 1956, 90; one term used is 'indictiones'. (In his *Greek City* 143 Jones took the view that the requisition of *annona* (military supplies) became a regular routine from Septimius Severus; this view is not repeated in *L.R.E.*) The practice probably developed from requisitioning in the Republic, on which see Jones' *Tijdschrift* article (n. 60) n. 18 (from allies, Livy XLII 48, 7 f.; 55); pp. 21 f (from subjects), where he distinguished requisitions without payment (Plut. *C. Gr.* 2 and 6, Sardinia and Spain; Cic., *Font.* 3, 6 f, 16, Gaul; *Verr.* II 2, 5, Sicily, and perhaps *Verr.* II 1, 95, Cilicia; *Pis.* 86 f., 90, Macedon), and with payment (Livy XLIII 2, 12, Spain; Cic., *Verr.* II 3, 163 and 188 —163-224 *passim* are relevant—for Sicily; he writes that 'originally it would seem that Roman commanders abroad were entitled to requisition what they wanted for purposes of war, both from free and subject cities. But the senate must before 171 have ruled that the regular peace time supplies for the governor and his staff and army must be bought, and later have fixed the price'. There is a continuous history of requisitioning in kind or commutations into cash from the middle Republic to the late empire, and the abuses described in the Verrines persisted into the Principate, Tac., *Agricola* 19; Wallace, p. 22.

[97] *L.R.E.* 207 f., 235.

[98] For such a *capitatio* Déléage 208 ff. (Gaul), 277 ff. (Africa, where its persistence may explain why the assessment of land was less sophisticated; on better land there would be more payers of poll tax employed. For temporary poll taxes in the east too, and at Rome itself, *L.R.E.* I 61.

It was apparently assessed on the head of the business and his assistants—members of his family, slaves, hired workers or apprentices—and on his capital equipment—ships, wagons, oxen, donkeys in the case of merchants, and mills, tools and implements in the case of manufacturers.[99]

It remains to consider certain general features of ancient taxation. Customs duties seem always to have been levied to raise revenue, and not for the protection of domestic agriculture or industry. They were generally levies on both imports and exports, and were mostly quite low, 2 per cent or $2\frac{1}{2}$ per cent.[100] The Ptolemies, as we have seen, imposed much higher rates ranging from 20 per cent to 50 per cent, and it has been thought that some of these taxes were intended to protect Egyptian monopolies, but the highest rates were levies on goods not produced in Egypt.[101] Under the Principate, there were relatively low duties levied internally at the frontiers of certain provinces or groups of provinces, but a very high rate, 25 per cent, was apparently charged on the Eastern frontier of the empire.[102] This may have been intended to discourage the import of expensive luxury goods, which were paid for in coin, thus causing a currency drain to the East;[103] but more probably the Roman government

[99] See pp. 35 f. and *L.R.E.* (Index *s.v. collatio lustralis*).

[100] Athens, n. 10. A 2 per cent rate is attested in many other Greek cities, Busolt-Swoboda, 613 f. In 413 the Athenians imposed in lieu of tribute 5 per cent duties on the seaborne trade of their subjects (Thuc., VII 28, 4), and in 410 and 390–89 a 10 per cent toll on goods passing through the Bosphorus (Xen., *Hell.* I 1, 22; IV 8, 27 and 31; Diod., XIII 64, 2); these were extraordinary war measures. The rate levied by Rome in Italy is unknown, as in many provinces, but it was 2 or $2\frac{1}{2}$ per cent for internal *portoria* in Spain, Gaul and Asia, 5 per cent in Sicily and perhaps (de Laet 271) in Africa; probably Rome followed everywhere the prevalent practice at the time of conquest. (For Illyricum see n. 104).

[101] Préaux 371 ff., who notes 10 per cent rates in pre-Hellenistic Babylon and Egypt.

[102] De Laet 306 ff.; 333 ff.; the evidence comes from Leuke Kome on the Red Sea (*Periplous mar. Erythr.* 19) and Palmyra (*AÉ* 1947, 179 f.). It should be noted that there were some internal tolls and municipal *octrois* within the empire, as well as customs duties at the frontiers, cf. de Laet 164; 312 ff.; 341 ff.; 351 ff.; of these we know little.

[103] Pliny, *N.H.* VI 101; XII 84, cf. ch. VII. Strabo XVII i, 13 indicates the high value of the customs duties in Egypt. The rates on other external frontiers are not known, but if we read οὕτως in Strabo IV 5, 3 (which gives the best sense), he says that under Augustus a large income was obtained from the Britons, through the heavy customs duties, and that if the island were conquered and tribute imposed, it would be necessary to reduce the rates with a net loss to the treasury, taking into account the cost of maintaining a garrison of one legion. It might be inferred that the high rates on foreign trade in the east were not exceptional; in Illyricum the rate was at one time $12\frac{1}{2}$ per cent (see next note).

knew that such goods would bear a high tax and exploited this to raise more revenue. These custom dues were later, perhaps in the third century, halved, becoming an *octava* (12½ per cent).[104]

Sales taxes were common in various forms—on auction sales, on conveyances of real property, on the sale of slaves, and also on manumissions, which were often virtually sales, since the slave sometimes paid for his freedom. The rates were usually low; even the Ptolemies did not exceed 10 per cent.[105] Only one tax on inheritance is known,[106] that imposed on Roman citizens by Augustus (n. 85). Despite its low rate (5 per cent) and generous exemptions for near relatives, it was strongly resented. Caracalla (besides making all free inhabitants of the empire Roman citizens and thus liable to the tax) abolished the exemptions and raised the rate to 10 per cent. But his successor Macrinus restored the status quo and some later third century emperor abolished the tax altogether.[107] Seeing that the emperors were at this period desperately short of money, and the inheritance tax, being *ad valorem*, would have maintained its value despite the inflation, this is an extraordinary measure, and demonstrates the enduring unpopularity of the inheritance tax.

The Greeks and Romans never achieved a graduated or progressive tax. In some cases, it is true, there was a lower limit of liability. The Athenians exempted the smallest properties from the *eisphora* (n. 21) and the Roman Republic from the *tributum*;[108]

[104] De Laet, 453 ff., adopts the view that the texts he knew on the *octava* (C.J. IV lxv, 7; lxi, 7 f.; IV xlii, 2, pr.), dating from A.D. 227 to 457–65, all related to a sales tax. Since then, *A.É.* 1968, 423 (cf. *I.L.S.* 7124 f.) has shown that it represents the rate of the Illyrian *portoria* in the second century, whereas de Laet, 242 ff., had argued that the rate was 5 per cent on goods traded beyond the frontier (by uncertain inference from *I.L.S.* 1861; *C.I.L.* III 13798), but only 2½ per cent on other goods (*A.É.* 1934, 234); he rejected as corrupt testimony to a 10 per cent rate in a lost inscription (*C.I.L.* III 5120 cf. p. 2198). The new document seems to confirm Jones' view (*L.R.E.* 430, 826) that the later *octava* was a customs duty; but there remains no proof that the old 25 per cent duty in the east had been reduced by half. However, it looks as if in Illyricum different rates may have been levied at different times and on different classes of goods.

[105] For Athens see nn. 13–17; for other Greek cities Busolt-Swoboda 616, and in the Hellenistic and Roman periods Jones, *Greek City* 244 f.; for Ptolemaic Egypt, Préaux, 307–37 (*P. Columbia* 480 seems to show that up to 25 per cent was levied on registered sales of slaves); for Rome nn. 52, 86 f.

[106] But, according to Préaux 337, in Ptolemaic Egypt there was an *aparche* due from heirs to the cult of a Berenice.

[107] Dio, LXXVII 9; LXXVIII 12.

[108] Cic., *Rep.* II 40.

Augustus granted immunity from the inheritance tax to small fortunes (n. 85). There were also some special taxes on the very rich. The Athenians imposed liturgies, posts involving substantial expenditure, on the wealthiest citizens, and many Greek cities followed their example.[109] Constantine imposed a special land tax, the *gleba* or *follis*, on senators, and in the fourth century and in the first half of the fifth [special] levies of recruits and horses were imposed on *honorati*, those who received codicils of rank; these levies were often commuted for money payments and amounted to taxes. Both these taxes were abolished in the middle of the fifth century.[110]

The most inequitable of all forms of direct taxation was the poll tax, which imposed an equal burden on rich and poor alike. In classical Greece it is known only in Athens for metics,[111] in the Hellenistic period in Seleucid Judaea;[112] it is doubtful if the Ptolemies levied it.[113] The Roman Republic imposed it on Africa, perhaps following Carthaginian precedent. Augustus seems to have levied it in all provinces.[114] Diocletian limited it to the rural

[109] Jones, *Athen. Democracy* 55 ff.; *Greek City* ch. XVII. *Munera* in the western provinces of the Roman empire corresponded to liturgies in the eastern, and payments (*summa honoraria*) or contributions to the cost of games were often due from magistrates or councillors, see e.g. the largely tralatician lex Ursonensis (*I.L.S.* 6087) ch. LXX; Abbott and Johnson, *Munic. Administration in Roman Empire*, chs. VI and VIII. Duncan-Jones, cited p. 14 n. 34.

[110] *Gleba*, L.R.E. 431. Levies of recruits and horses and commutation, ib. 614–6, 625 f. Jones there makes it plain that the *honorati* were not alone affected; cities and great landowners in general were liable, see also his index, s.v. *aurum tironicum*, which goes back to the early third century, cf. M. Rostovtzeff, *J.R.S.* VIII 26 ff.

[111] See n. 10, cf. Busolt-Swoboda 295 f. for further evidence and parallels elsewhere; but in Potidaea a poll tax on the very poor is attested, Ps-Arist., *Oec.* 1347 a 18, and in Hellenistic Cos we find a tax on τὰ γυναικεῖα σώματα, *S.I.G.*³ 1000. Note Tertullian, *Apol.* 13, 6: 'sed enim agri tributo onusti viliores, hominum capita stipendio censa ignobiliora, nam hae sunt *notae captivitatis*.'

[112] Jos., *Ant.*, XII 142, XIII 50. Ps-Arist., *Oec.* 1346a 4 treats poll taxes (*epikephalaia*) and taxes on traders and craftsmen (*cheironaxia*) as normal sources of revenue for 'satraps' in the east after Alexander. On this see Rostovtzeff, *Soc. and Econ. Hist. of Hellenistic World* 440 ff.

[113] Préaux 380 ff. There is in fact clear evidence that poll taxes were levied at times (*P. Tebt.* 701, 186; *P. Petrie* III 59 b); what is lacking is documentation of the various capitation taxes copiously attested after Augustus (n. 79), though it is odd if he introduced an entirely new system, as such innovation was uncharacteristic of the Romans. On the other hand the Ptolemies did levy a *gabelle* (*halikê*) per head for the consumption of salt (Préaux, 249 ff.), which the Romans perhaps abandoned in most of Egypt (Wallace, 184).

[114] Capitation taxes are attested in Africa from 146 B.C. (App., *Bell. Pun.* 135). Syria from 63 B.C. (App., *Bell. Syr.* 50, also for Cilicia and Judaea; on the text see

population [at least in the east (see n. 98).]. Under Roman rule so far from being progressive, it was often regressive, since politically privileged categories of persons, who were usually wealthier, were wholly or partly immune. In Egypt Roman and Alexandrian citizens did not pay, and metropolites paid at a lower rate [n. 79]. In the later empire only plebeians paid. It was no doubt favoured by the government because it was simple to assess and collect, but some emperors recognised its oppressiveness, by abolishing it in poverty stricken areas—Valentinian I in Illyricum, Theodosius in Thrace; Anastasius was in process of abolishing it in the Asiatic provinces when he died.[115]

The various forms of property tax—the Athenian *eisphora*, the Roman republican *tributum*, the *tributum soli* of the Principate and the *iugatio* of the later empire, were fairer, in that the amount of tax was scaled according to the value of the property. The rate, however, was the same for the richest and the poorest, and obviously the same rate of tax was a much greater burden to a peasant living at subsistence level than to a wealthy landlord. For the great majority of taxpayers, who depended on agriculture, the major disadvantage of a property tax was that it was fixed, and did not vary according to the harvest, which especially in Mediterranean lands, can fluctuate enormously from year to year. For this reason the tithe (or other proportional taxes) was sometimes considered more equitable than a fixed land tax.[116] The trouble

---

Wilcken, *Gr. Ostraka* I 247, and cf. Mark XII 14 with Wallace 116); I know of no specific evidence, outside Judaea, for Augustus' responsibility, but for such taxes under the Principate see also Dio LXII 3, Tac., *Ann.* XII 34 (Britain); Αρχ. Δελτίον II p. 148, *Jahreshefte* 1954, 110 ff. (Macedon) *Dig.* L xv 3 (Syria); xv 8, 7 (Judaea); *I.G.* XII v 724 and 946 (Andros and Tenos); *I.G.R.* IV 181 (Lampsacus); 259 (Assos); perhaps *I.L.S.* 6960 (Ebusus in Spain); Tertullian in n. 111 (Africa); the enumeration of *libera capita* in provincial censuses in Spain (Pliny, *N.H.* III 28), Lusitania, Macedon, Bithynia and Pontus (Phlegon, *F.G.H.* II no. 257, F. 27, 1 and 47 ff.) presumably served as the basis for *capitatio*. For Egypt cf. nn. 79, 113. It cannot be assumed that capitation taxes were necessarily poll-taxes and that the *cheironaxia*, levied in Egypt at varying rates on different types of trader or craftsman, were unknown elsewhere (cf. n. 112); Josephus, *B.J.* II 383, might suggest that in Africa, as in Egypt, the taxation system was diversified, cf. Déléage, ch. X. After the destruction of Jerusalem in A.D. 70, Jews everywhere paid to the *fiscus* the didrachm that had once gone to the temple, see Josephus, *B.J.* VII 218; Origen, *ep. ad Afr.* 14 etc.; in the light of the last text we cannot generalise from the lack of evidence for collection of this tax in Egypt after Hadrian (Wallace 170 ff.); Wallace's supposition that there was an upper age limit is also contradicted by Suet., *Dom.* 12, 2.

[115] *L.R.E.* 147, 162, 237.
[116] App., *Bell. Civ.* V 4.

with tithe was that it had, for reasons stated above, to be farmed, and the disputes on the amount of the crops between tax payers and tax farmers were inevitable. If the official who in Ptolemaic Egypt controlled the contractors, and the governors who in the Roman provinces adjudicated disputes on the *pactiones*, had been impartial, all would have been well. There are in fact very few complaints of extortion by tax contractors from the Ptolemaic papyri, and Cicero states—doubtless with exaggeration—that [in Sicily] the lex Hieronica had until Verres' time operated very fairly [see n. 68]. It was only when as in the later Republic the tax farmers were politically influential that gross extortion became normal.[117] It should, moreover, be remembered that under direct collection by officials or magistrates extortion was very common in antiquity. In the later empire in particular the officials of the praetorian prefects and provincial governors and the curial collectors of the cities were very adept at inventing extra charges and fees, which under Majorian amounted to $2\frac{1}{2}$ solidi on a tax of 7 solidi per *iugum*, that is increased the nominal tax more than one third.[118]

The ancient world never achieved the notion of an income tax. Even if they had thought of it, their accounting methods were too primitive to distinguish income from capital. The result was that persons who gained their livings by wages, salaries and fees paid nothing at all.[119] Wage earners in antiquity were mostly very poor, so that their immunity was no great loss, but lawyers, rhetoricians, grammarians, doctors and higher civil servants often made very large sums in fees and salaries. Merchants

[117] Cic., *Verr.* II 3, 94; Diodorus XXXIV–V 2, 31; 25.

[118] *L.R.E.* 457 f., 467 f., 756 f. Abuses were not confined to the late empire, see for example G. Chalon, *L'Édit de Tibérius Iulius Alexander* ch. II (cf. H. I. Bell, *J.R.S.* XXVIII 1 ff.); Egypt is exceptional not only in its tax system but also in the wealth of evidence it supplies. Tacitus, *Ann.*, IV 6 ('ne provinciae novis oneribus turbarentur utque vetera sine avaritia aut crudelitate magistratuum tolerarent, providebat; corporum verbera, ademptiones bonorum aberant') suggests that abuses allegedly checked by Tiberius in A.D. 14–23 were not unfamiliar at other times in the historian's experience; the scenes graphically depicted by Lactantius, *de mort. persec.* 23, may have earlier precedents. *I.G.R.* III 488, 739 II and III (Jones, *Greek City* 327) imply that in the Principate, as later (Salvian, *Gub. Dei* V 18, 28–30), not all curial tax-collectors acted with fairness and humanity, and it is sinister that a city benefited from the amount of Roman tribute it collected (Dio Chrys., XXXV 14, cf XL 10).

[119] But see nn. 79, 112 and 114 on *cheironaxia*. The variety of rates in Egypt suggests that they were related to average profits of the trades or crafts. And note the ὠνὰ τοῦ ἰατρικοῦ in *S.I.G.*³ 1000 (Cos).

and manufacturers were also probably under taxed. The Athenian *eisphora*, it is true, and the Roman *tributum* of the republic and principate took into account property such as ships, slaves, workshops and—theoretically—liquid capital. But most merchants seem to have had little liquid capital, financing their ventures with nautical loans, and their assessable capital assets were probably low in relation to their turnover.

In the later empire, as we have seen, the main direct tax was assessed solely on agriculture, and there was a separate tax, the *chrysargyron*, on trade and industry, apparently a poll tax combined with a tax on capital assets. We do not know what the rate was, but all the ancient authorities agree that it bore very hard on the mass of small traders and craftsmen, who were driven into selling their children into slavery. The trouble was no doubt partly that rich merchants could evade the tax by concealing their liquid assets, but even more, that the rate was not graduated. Despite its oppressiveness it yielded very little revenue, about 5 per cent of the yield of the land tax, and was abolished by Anastasius, who was a prudent financier as well as a humane man. The explanation is that the volume of commerce and industry was very much smaller than that of agriculture, and the merchants and manufacturers were on the whole much poorer persons than landowners. [See chapter II.]

The reasons why taxes with an uncertain yield were sold to contractors and those whose yield was exactly predictable were collected by magistrates or officials have already been discussed. From the beginning to the end of ancient history there was a tendency in all empires to collect direct taxes from or through the cities or other communities rather than from the individual taxpayers. This was the rule with the primitive tribute of the Persian Kingdom and the Delian League and with the *stipendium* of the Roman republic, where both the repartition of the block sum required of the city and its collection and delivery to the imperial treasury were left to the city authorities. The Hellenistic kings in general abandoned block tribute, and levied taxes through contractors from individual citizens.[120] Under the Roman republic, however, there was a partial reversion to the old system, in practice if not in law, since the tax farmers normally

[120] Jones, *Greek City* 108 f. For another view of Seleucid taxes, E. Bikerman 106 ff.

subcontracted with the cities' authorities, who then assessed the tithe in detail on their citizens and collected it. Under the principate the role of the cities was reduced. The imperial government conducted the censuses on which *tributum soli* and *tributum capitis* were based. But the cities were still responsible for the collection and elected officers to perform the task. It is probable also that the cities were from the first, as they certainly were in the later empire, corporately responsible to the central government for the whole sum due from their citizens. Each collector had to make up any deficit in the total allotted to him out of his own property, and if he defaulted, all the members of the city council, which had elected him, had to make up the deficit.[121]

It is remarkable how rigid was the fiscal system of ancient states. We are used to the creation of new taxes and the constant variation, usually increase, of their rates. Most cities, it is true, had at their disposal occasional taxes, like the Greek *eisphora* or the Roman republican *tributum*, usually levied only for war. But the regular taxation normally went on unchanged from generation to generation. The 2 per cent or 2½ per cent provincial customs levied under the Roman republic were levied at the same rate in the late fourth century. Even the provincial tribute was normally static; it needed a financial crisis and a Vespasian to raise the rates in some provinces, and this is the only recorded rise during the Principate.[122] This rigidity, as we have seen, had disastrous effects, during the great inflation of the third century, and forced the government to revert to a state economy in kind.

It was not until Diocletian that a flexible budget was invented, and the effect was immediate. Hitherto governments, having a more or less fixed revenue, had to cut their coat according to their cloth. They tried to build up reserves for emergencies,[123] but if

---

[121] *Dig.* L iv 1, i; the text is Diocletianic, but the same practice is implied by Severan texts showing that tax collection was an *onus patrimonii* (L iv 3, 10 f.), falling on decurions as such (L i 17, 7), cf. also L xv 5, 2. For the obligation of *practores* or of whole communities in Egypt to make good deficiencies in the taxes see Wallace ch. XVII. It seems improbable that Caesar, who was short of cash, would have abolished the publican system in the east (see Addendum II), had he not intended that the local magnates should replace the publicans in underwriting the revenues. For the late empire cf *L.R.E.* 457 f.

[122] Suet., *Vesp.* 16, 1.

[123] For such reserves see e.g. Thuc., II 13, 3 (Athens); Arrian, *Anab.* III 13, 7 (Persia; divergent estimates in Diod., XVII 66, Plut., *Alex.* 36 and Quintus Curtius, V 2, 11); Pliny, *N.H.* XXXIII 55 ff. (Roman Republic); Suet., *Gaius* 37, 3; *Vesp.* 16,

these were exhausted they had no recourse except confiscation or debasement of the currency. Expenditure had therefore on the whole been kept down to the figure of the revenue. Now that the rate of tax could be readily varied every year it went steadily up— Themistius tells us that the indiction was doubled in the forty years from 324 to 364.[124]

In general the rates of tax in antiquity were according to modern ideas low.[125] Indirect taxes normally varied between 1 per cent and 5 per cent, the only notable exceptions being the Ptolemaic customs and imperial customs on the eastern frontier [but cf. nn. 101, 104]. The land tax was normally 10 per cent of the crop. The Seleucids and Attalids levied a tithe,[126] and the *artabieia* imposed by the Ptolemies on sacred and private land came to the same thing, since the average crop in Egypt was ten *artabae* per *arura*. The Ptolemies imposed much higher rates—up to 5 or even 6 *artabae*—(half the crop or more) on royal lands, but these were rents, not taxes. The very high rates in Seleucid Palestine may be a survival from the Ptolemaic regime, and the land may have been deemed to be royal. Under the republic again tithes were levied. Under the Principate, the 1 per cent rate of *tributum* recored in Cilicia and Syria, was probably intended to

---

3 (where *quadragies* must be read in place of *quadringenties*, as there was neither any need to create a reserve of 40,000 million H.S., nor any possibility of doing so, in view of all that we know of imperial expenses and revenues; given that expenditure had risen since Tiberius' time, 4000 million stands in a credible relation with the sum of 2700 accumulated by the frugal Tiberius, and 2900 saved by Pius, Dio LXXIII, 8, 3.)

[124] *Or.* VIII 113 c, cf. *L.R.E.* 130 f.

[125] On this paragraph see Addendum III.

[126] Seleucids: Welles, *Royal Correspondence* 41 (Tralles), I *Macc.* XI 35 (but Bikerman 117 holds that the *dekatai* here are tolls *ad valorem* on merchandise). Bikerman, 110 cf. 119, seems to think that the Seleucids collected contributions at unrecorded rates, probably in kind, from the cultivators of the soil as well as lump sums from the cities, which in turn would meet them by taxing the peasants. Attalids: Welles (n. 46), 48 D 3. The evidence for Hellenistic taxation outside Egypt is very scanty; there may have been no uniformity, and firm conclusions are unjustified, see M. Rostovtzeff, *Soc. and Econ. Hist. of the Hellenistic World*, especially pp. 440 ff., 562, 641 ff., 812 ff. On annexation Rome could sometimes afford to reduce taxes, as in Macedonia (Livy XLV 29—by half) and Cappadocia (Tacitus, *Ann.*, II 56), no doubt because expenditure was no longer incurred for a royal court and reduced for defence. Appian, *B.C.* V 4 records Antony's claim that the tithes levied by Rome were less burdensome than the taxes imposed by the Attalids. But in both Hellenistic and Roman times regular rates are no indication of the burdens that might be imposed in emergencies, see e.g. Appian, ibid., 5.

be the equivalent of a tithe, the annual value of an estate being reckoned at 10 per cent of its capital value.[127]

In the later empire, as we have seen, the indiction steadily rose until by Justinian's time it had reached 3.2 *artabae* per *arura*, or nearly a third of the crop.[128] As this was a tax on the gross return, not on the profit, it is fairly high even by modern standards. But even so high a rate, more than three times the normal rate under the Republic and the Principate, was not ruinous to the economy. There was, it is true, a continuous stream of complaints from Diocletian onwards of *agri deserti*, farms abandoned by their owners as unprofitable, and the reason given for this phenomenon by contemporaries is the mounting rate of taxation. This may not be entirely true—shortage of agricultural labour was another cause, and perhaps also over-cropping. But it is certain that substantial amounts of land were abandoned—we have official figures of 10 per cent, 17 per cent, 32 per cent, even 50 per cent from different provinces at different dates. But we must remember that most of the land continued to be cultivated and to yield substantial rents—it was from agricultural rents that the opulent senatorial class derived their huge incomes, and the endowments of the church consisted almost entirely in agricultural land. It was, it would seem, marginal land which could not bear the high taxation. Some figures may illustrate this point. In Egypt the normal yield of good average land was 10 *artabae* to the *arura*. In share cropping leases the division was normally 50/50, so that the landlord received 5 *artabae*, out of which he paid a tax of a little over 3, retaining a net profit of just under 2 *artabae*. Not all land, however, was good average, and we find some parcels being let at 4 *artabae* or 3 or even less. In the last case the landlord incurred a loss, and abandoned the land. Nor was the peasant proprietor much better off. It was apparently reckoned that he needed 5 *artabae* to keep himself and his family, so that if the gross yield sank below 8, he was approaching starvation level.[129]

ADDENDUM I

In his *Tijdschrift* article (n. 61) Jones rightly pointed out that

[127] Addendum III.
[128] *L.R.E.* 820.
[129] *L.R.E.* 812 ff., cf. 766 f.

in the Republic taxation was not the major financial burden imposed on the subjects (pp. 21 ff). Apart from illegal exactions both by governors and publicans there was extensive requisitioning of supplies which went on into the principate (n. 96 above). Billeting of troops and the *hospitium* which Roman officials could demand were also burdensome in themselves and subject to abuse. Similarly under the Principate they could sometimes be called on to build roads at their own expense and to maintain the *cursus publicus* (in the Principate more correctly called *vehiculatio*), see his *Greek City* 140 ff. for evidence; in my view the 'onera vehiculorum praebendorum' (*I.L.S.* 214) may from the first have included the provision of transport for supplies as well as for persons, as in the late empire (*L.R.E.* 830 ff.); to the evidence cited by Jones, *Greek City* 328 f. for the Principate one can now add as further documentation for the system and its abuse W. H. C. Frend, *J.R.S.* XLVI 46 ff.; *S.E.G.* XVII 755= McCrum and Woodhead, *Select Documents of the Principates of the Flavian Emperors* 466, where Domitian admits that even without illegal requisitioning of draught animals the provinces can barely meet the essential demands of the government. In the article cited Jones also refers to levies of *aurum coronarium* by Republican generals, an Oriental and Hellenistic practice (T. Klauser, *Röm. Mitteilungen* LIX, 129 ff.), forbidden by Caesar's law *de repetundis* of 59 B.C. except after the official vote of a triumph (Cic., *Pis.* 90); the prohibition shows of course that it was voluntary only in name. By the end of the Republican period even Italian towns found it prudent to offer this 'benevolence' to powerful generals, including Augustus himself, who remitted it but only to Italy (*Res Gestae* 21). For its persistence in the empire on the accession of emperors, and at other times of celebration, see *L.R.E.* 410, Kubitschek, *R.E.* s.v. One might conclude from Alexander Severus' edict of remission (Edgar and Hunt, *Select Papyri* no. 216) that it was a severe impost; emperors were always readier to remit it at least in full to the Italian towns. I mention these impositions to make Jones' survey more complete.

ADDENDUM II

Jones' account of the changes made in the system of direct taxation in the early Principate is rather summary. In the east the prevalence of *pactiones* (n. 71) had made the function of the publicans little more than that of underwriters of the imperial revenue. It was thus easy for Caesar to eliminate them in Asia and at the same time to reduce the burden of payments to the taxpayers by a third, probably without diminishing the treasury's receipts (Dio, XLII 6, 3; Appian, *B.C.* V 4); it seems probable that from the first the city governments had to assume collectively the liability to the treasury which the publicans had previously incurred (cf. Jones, *Greek City* 138 ff.) Probably Caesar also reformed the tax system in other eastern provinces on the same plan. Certainly, Josephus (*Antiquities* XIV, 201, cf. 74) attests that he forbade collection of tribute from the Jews by publicans, though A. Momigliano infers from Cicero (*prov. cons.* 10) and Dio XXXIX 56 that the change had been made in Syria and Judaea by Gabinius in 56 (*Ricerche sull' organizzazione della Givdea sotto il domino romano* 19 f.). There is no record that publicans ever again collected direct taxes in the east; the *pecunia phorikos* held by Asian publicans in Augustus' time (*AÉ* 1968, 483) can be supposed to have derived from customs or pasture tax.

Augustus is not credited with any change in the use of publicans, and a statement by Tacitus (*Annals* IV 6) that until A.D. 23 'frumenta et pecuniae vectigales, cetera publicorum fructum societatibus equitum Romanorum agitabantur' shows by its reference to 'frumenta' that some direct taxes in kind, as well as indirect taxes, were still being collected by *Roman* publican companies after his death. Where they were still active is not known. It cannot have been in Sicily, unless the system of entrusting collection to *local* publicans had been changed since Verres' day. Africa is a possibility; the 'mancipes stipendiorum' of *I.L.S.* 901 may belong to the early Principate. (For Roman publicans in Republican Africa see the *lex agraria* of 111 B.C., *F.I.R.A.* I² 70 ff.). It is commonly assumed that Tiberius eliminated publicans from the collection of all direct taxes later in his reign, but this cannot be inferred from the text cited; Tacitus does not imply that every proposition he makes of the early part of Tiberius' administration ceased to be true before his death, as can be seen from the undoubted fact that publican companies continued to collect indirect taxes long after A.D. 37. Nor can the date of the change be established *e silentio* from the absence of any later epigraphic record. With the possible exception of *I.L.S.* 901 they have left no such record even for the period between 44 B.C.

and A.D. 23. We must be content not to know. There is indeed a possibility that the employment of publicans was not wholly abandoned even in Ulpian's day; for he refers to publicans, probably including *conductores* (see p. 166), who 'tributum consequantur' (*Dig.* XXXIX iv, 1, 1). Perhaps they were retained to collect the direct taxes on private estates outside city territories, for which the city magistrates naturally had no competence; see *Dig.* XIX i, 52, *pr.* (Scaevola) for a *conductor saltus* concerned with arrears of *tributum*, and perhaps compare the *misthotai* of a Phrygian estate in A.D. 207-8 (Ramsay, *Cities and Bishoprics of Phrygia* I 286 ff.).

Jones' hypothesis that publicans could be dispensed with, because tribute no longer took the form of a proportional levy is ingenious, but hardly fits all the facts. Under Trajan quotas were still paid in some provinces, indeed fifths and sevenths (Hyginus, 205 L), and in Africa land outside the imperial *saltus* is termed 'octonarius', which suggests that it paid eighths. Within those *saltus* quotas were also paid, generally thirds, but to *conductores*, which does accord with Jones' view. See *F.I.R.A.* I² no. 100, I 19 ff.; II 8. If it be granted that in such areas publicans could still have been employed, though they have left no records of their activity, it might seem that Jones' hypothesis could still be saved. But Appian (*B.C.* V 4) does not suggest that Caesar had abolished the tithe system in Asia when he made the cities instead of the publicans responsible for tax collection; in Caesar's day the Jews still paid quotas, but not to publicans (*supra*); and Dio Chrysostom (XXXVIII 26) seems to mean that the Bithynian peasants paid tithes through the cities. Apparently even Augustus' introduction of provincial censuses did not entail the universal substitution of fixed levies for quotas, but Roman publicans were not required even for the collection of quotas. The cities could indeed employ publicans of their own for collecting their *vectigalia* (cf. Plutarch, *Mor.* 794a) as did Spanish Mulva under Titus (*Madrider Mitteilungen*, I 1960, 142 ff.), and conceivably for Roman taxes too.

The system Jones describes, which undoubtedly operated in many and perhaps in most parts of the empire, is illustrated by an interesting new inscription, probably of the first century A.D., which shows a testator providing for the annual payment to the Asian city of Nacrasus, to be made to the imperial treasury at a rate of 12 drachmae on each twelfth of a *iugerum* (*Sitzungsberichte der oesterreichischer Akad.*, 1969, 10). However it is clear, and important, that the Roman government never sought to impose uniformity in taxation on all provinces. Rome normally took over the existing tax-system, and though changes were occasionally introduced, diversity persisted even after Diocletian. In census regulations of his time the classification of lands in Asia, the Greek islands and Egypt differed, and yet another system, perhaps of the same period, is attested in Syria, while the unit of tax-assessment was not the same in Africa or in Italy as in these eastern provinces (cf. ch. X; *L.R.E.* 62). The assessment of the population similarly varied; in Egypt only males counted, in Syria and Illyricum women counted a full *caput*, but in Pontica and Asiana only half a *caput* (*L.R.E.* 63). It followed that when each *iugum* and each *caput* was required to pay so much in tax over the whole empire, the real rate of tax was heavier in one province than in another, just as in Hyginus' day. Moreover in some provinces separate poll taxes were still imposed, e.g. in Africa; this may have offset the fact that the African unit of assessment for the land-tax was so much larger than in the east. Though it was an innovation outside Egypt when Augustus introduced provincial censuses, the form each provincial census took may have varied with local conditions; the Egyptian land surveys and house-to-house returns were not the model, any more than the diversification of taxes in Egypt was adopted elsewhere; by the same token we cannot argue from the tax system of any province to any other. Even *portoria* were levied at different rates in different districts (n. 100), and when publicans ceased to collect them in one district, they were not immediately (if ever) displaced everywhere else (n. 93).

ADDENDUM III

The 1 per cent capital levy in Syria is attested only for a time after Vespasian. Suetonius in his life of that emperor (ch. 16, 1) says that he raised and sometimes doubled provincial taxes. Under Trajan we hear of fifths and sevenths paid as quotas (Hyginus 205 L) and of eighths in Africa outside the imperial *saltus*; there the *coloni* owed fourths on beans and thirds on most

N

other produce, but in their case the payments can be regarded as rents. Tenths are indeed still recorded in Bithynia (Dio Chrysostom XXXVIII 26), but the higher quotas show that we cannot assume that a capital levy of 1 per cent was taken to be equivalent of a tax of 10 per cent on gross returns. I do not know if Jones had other reasons for making this equation, but R. D. Duncan-Jones (*P.B.S.R.* 1965, 202 ff.) has collected evidence that net returns of 5 per cent or 6 per cent were often expected from estates in Italy on probably conservative estimates, and this may suggest that a 1 per cent capital levy was rather more severe than Jones supposes, quite apart from the fact that it was payable even in years when income fell below the norm. If we take it, subject to that qualification, to be equivalent to a 20 per cent income tax, and recall that it applied to medium and small properties just as much as to large, it can hardly be regarded as light even by modern standards. On Domitian's admission (quoted in Addendum I) the provinces could barely meet essential demands of the state. These of course included special *indictiones* (n. 96) and the probably heavy burdens of the *cursus publicus* or *vehiculatio* and *aurum coronarium* (Addendum I). Jones himself suggested that the remissions of arrears by Hadrian and Marcus Aurelius (*I.L.S.* 309; Dio LXIX 8; LXXI 32) might be sinister symptoms of over-taxation (*L.R.E.* 9 f.); cf. also Marcus' refusal of a donative to his soldiers, to avoid 'wringing more money from the blood of their parents and kin' (Dio LXXI 3, 3).

It is also hard to accept Jones' view that the Egyptian peasant had to pay much more under Justinian than earlier. It rests on too artificial a distinction between taxes and the rents payable to the king under the Ptolemies and then to Rome as proprietor of the land. Préaux 133 f., who also takes the average produce to be 10 *artabae per arura*, points out that under the Ptolemies *half* was due to the royal treasury under the heads ot rents and taxes; the burden was not lessened in the Principate. From the peasant's point of view, and from the revenue's, it made little difference whether payments counted as tax or rent. I suspect that where a very high proportion of the gross return was taken the payments were partly at least construed as rents, e.g. in the African *saltus* (above) and in Seleucid Palestine, *contra* n. 47. Confiscation of private land even in the provinces benefited the treasury, as it thereafter obtained the proprietor's share of the income as well as the state's. Of course, if the land confiscated was in Italy or immune in some other way from taxation, the benefit to the treasury is still more manifest. It is easy to see why an emperor might be 'inopia rapax' (Suet., *Dom.* 3, 2). Cf. p. 150.

* The following works are cited by the names of authors or short titles.

E. Bikerman, *Institutiones des Seleucides.*

Busolt-Swoboda, *Griechische Staatskunde*

S. J. de Laet, *Portorium*

A. Déléage, *La capitation du bas-empire*

R. Meiggs and D. M. Lewis, *A Selection of Greek Historical Inscriptions*

Milet. *Milet. Ergebnisse der Ausgrabungen u. Untersuchungen seit dem Jahre* 1899 (ed. C. Wiegand)

C. Préaux, *L'économie royale des Lagides*

S. L. Wallace, *Taxation in Egypt from Augustus to Diocletian*

H-G Pflaum, *Les Carrières procuratoriennes équestres sous le haut-empire romain*

Waddington. P. le Bas and W. H. Waddington, *Voyage archéologique en Grèce et en Asie Mineure.*

CORRIGENDUM

The following bibliographical note by Jones was omitted in error from page 187.

From the abundant literature which has grown up around the problems of currency and inflation in the Roman Empire I have found the following the most useful (though I disagree with many of their conclusions): A. Segrè, 'Inflation and its implications in early Byzantine times', *Byzantion*, xv (1941), 249–79; G. Mickwitz, *Geld und Wirtschaft im römischen Reich des vierten Jhdts n. Chr.* (Helsingfors, 1931), and *Die Systeme des römischen Silbergeldes im IV. Jhdt. n. Chr.* (Helsingfors, 1932); L. C. West and A. C. Johnson, *Currency in Roman and Byzantine Egypt* (Princeton, 1944); H. Mattingly, 'The monetary systems of the Roman Empire from Diocletian to Theodosius I', *Num. Chron.* vi, vi (1946), 111–20.

I am not a numismatist and for information about the actual coins I have relied on the standard works on Roman coinage, such as Mattingly and Sydenham's *Roman Imperial Coinage* and the relevant British Museum Catalogues of Coins, together with the books and articles cited above. Two numismatists who are experts on the period, Dr. Mattingly (mainly for the earlier half) and Mr. Grierson (mainly for the later half), have been kind enough to read the manuscript and have corrected some numismatic errors of which I had been guilty, and in general most generously put their expert knowledge at my disposal. I am most grateful for their help, but they cannot of course be held responsible for any factual errors which may have survived their scrutiny, still less for my theories.

PART II

CHAPTER NINE

INFLATION UNDER THE ROMAN EMPIRE[1]

1

IF a modern economist is to understand ancient inflation, he must clear his mind of all, or nearly all, the basic concepts of modern economics. He thinks in terms of banks, credit and a managed paper currency. It is true that there were institutions in antiquity which we call banks, but they were little offices in which the banker or his slave sat at a table and changed money. He also accepted deposits, which he would on instructions pay out to a third party, and made short term loans, which could be repaid to an agent overseas.

There was also credit, in the sense that people lent each other money. There were mortgages, secured on land or house property or sometimes on less permanent assets, such as slaves. There were nautical loans, in which a lender advanced money on the security of a merchant's ship or cargo or both, on condition that if the voyage was successful he got his money back with high interest, but if the ship were sunk he lost his money. This is the only form of commercial loan of which we hear. Nearly all lending was to people who were temporarily short of cash or permanently financially embarrassed. The Roman nobility seem to have lived on a succession of loans not because they were poor, but because their income and expenditure were erratic, and there were no bank overdrafts to tide over lean periods. These loans were for

---

[1] [Jones' article in *The Economic History Review*, 1953, is here reprinted with certain additions and corrections from his *Later Roman Empire* and from an unpublished typescript entitled 'Inflation in Antiquity'. The latter paper mainly repeats what he had written in the earlier article, but in less detail without documentation. However, it does include some new considerations which have been used to supplement the earlier article. Part I in the present essay is wholly derived from it; the passages in square brackets, including all the notes, are here editorial corrections or additions. In Part II square brackets indicate, except for a few references or where otherwise stated, insertions from Jones' later typescript. My aim has been to preserve all Jones' views on the subject of Roman inflation. See also 'Corrigendum', p. 186. P.A.B.].

the most part from friends and supporters, and carried no interest. On the other hand nobles and members of the equestrian order lent money at high rates of interest to client kings and provincial cities which had fallen into arrears of their tribute. It was a perfectly safe investment, because the lender could always get the support, if necessary the armed support of the provincial governor to enforce payment.

The Roman state and indeed all other states [did not normally] borrow from their citizens or subjects. [There are partial exceptions to this rule in the second Punic war,] when the Roman government was desperately short of money, and the public contractors offered to continue carrying out their contracts for the period of the war, 'provided that they were repaid at the end'; [in addition, the government later accepted contributions from senators and others which were treated in 204 as repayable.] The government eventually repaid two-thirds [of these contributions], but never repaid the last third, becoming involved in further expensive wars. Instead they assigned public lands, of which they had a plethora, . . . on condition that when they received the last instalment they would surrender the lands. So far as we know, the [lenders] and their heirs never had to surrender these lands.[2] Why the state was unwilling to borrow or the public to lend to it we do not know. The government may have thought it undignified to borrow, or preferred to confiscate. The public may have thought the investment too risky.

The currency was strictly cash. Practically all transactions whether public or private were carried out in coins of gold, silver or copper. There are some exceptions, but they are not important. A Roman provincial governor, for instance, did not always take his annual allowance out from Rome to his province in coin. He took a draft or cheque (*publica permutatio*) payable by the tax contractors in his province, who presumably had this sum deducted from their liability to the central treasury in Rome. [See

[2] [For the contractors see Livy xxiv 18, 10–15 (214 B.C.); there was a partial precedent in 215 (xxiii 48, 9 ff.). For the contributions made in 214, xxvi 36, 11 f., cf. xxix 17; xxxi 13; *F.I.R.A.* 1² no. 8, 31 f. (lex agraria of 111). I have modified Jones' account, distinguishing between the two types of loan. The instances cited are not so isolated as he apparently thought; for loans to Greek cities by their own citizens and foreigners see Busolt-Swoboda, *Gr. Staatskunde* I³ 621 ff.; given the uncertainty of repayment they were made only from patriotic fervour or under force. Brutus was authorised to make forced loans in 43, Cic., *Phil.* x 26.]

Cic., *Fam*. III 5, 4, cf. Jones, *Studies in Roman Government and Law*, 101 ff.]

Another peculiarity of ancient finance which it is necessary to grasp is the rigidity of the taxation system. We are used to annual budgets, which sometimes reduce taxes and more often increase them year by year. To the ancients to create a new tax or increase the rate of an old one was a major operation, only to be undertaken in desperate circumstances. Many taxes went on unchanged for centuries. Why the emperors were so reluctant to impose new taxes or to increase the rate of old taxes it is hard to say. In some cases it was the fear of unpopularity. Augustus was a brave man to introduce the 5 per cent tax on the inheritances of Roman citizens, for Roman citizens had come to feel themselves entitled to immunity, and the persons most affected were the aristocracy, the senators and upper *equites*. There seems less reason to have been alarmed about increasing provincial taxation, for provincials were of little account politically. But many wealthy Romans owned land in the provinces and would resent its being more heavily taxed. Taxes have never been popular, but in antiquity they seem to have aroused more resentment than today. There were persistent complaints against so mild a tax as the 1 per cent tax on auction sales, and Tiberius reduced it to 0.5 per cent, and Caligula abolished it with a flourish of trumpets. [Tac., *Ann*. I 78; II 42; Dio LIX 9, 6; Suet., *Gaius* 16; Mattingly-Sydenham, *Rom. Imp. Coinage* I 118 n. 1; Dig. L xvi 17, 1 suggests that the tax was later re-imposed.]

Finally we must never forget that ancient governments operated upon a strictly cash basis. They paid their civil servants, their soldiers, their contractors and those from whom they bought their supplies, in gold and silver coins, and they had therefore to collect enough gold and silver coins, by taxation or otherwise, to make these payments. A prudent emperor tried to build up a reserve of coins in case of emergencies, but such reserves rarely survived for long. Antoninus Pius in a peaceful reign of twenty-three years was able to accumulate 675 million denarii, but Marcus' wars quickly exhausted this sum [Dio LXXIII 8, 3].

Various measures might be taken if taxation did not produce enough coins. State property might be sold. Trajan auctioned a large number of luxurious country houses and parks which

Domitian had confiscated [Pliny, *Paneg.* 50]. Marcus Aurelius auctioned jewels, clothes and other valuables from the imperial palaces, and thus met the deficit on the Marcomannic War [S.H.A., *Marc.* 17]. Such measures might solve a temporary crisis, but obviously could not be repeated. [For other examples see Plutarch, *Galba* 5, 5; Dio LXVI 8, 4; S.H.A., *Pius* 7, 10.]

Another resource was to secure the condemnation of a number of wealthy senators for treason and confiscate their estates. This sounds very melodramatic and improbable, but the evidence is extensive and much of it contemporary and circumstantial. Nearly all the bad emperors are said to have used this method of restoring their finances—Nero, Domitian, [Commodus] Septimius Severus, Caracalla, certainly confiscated on a large scale [cf. p. 194 n. 12,] and thereby built up the small department of the *res privata* into a huge ministry, controlling estates in every province. He thus, it may be noted, increased the regular revenue of the state. [Jones, *Studies in Roman Government and Law* 112 f., though it is now known from *A.E.* 1961, 280, that the *res privata* antedated Severus.]

The last alternative was to debase the currency, that is to mix base metal with the silver or gold, and to reduce the weight of the coins, so that a larger number of coins could be produced from the same amount of the precious metals.

II

For the benefit of readers not familiar with the ancient world it may be as well to state some other basic facts about the economic structure of the Roman Empire which are relevant to a discussion of the currency. By and large the Empire formed a closed economy. External trade was mainly in luxury articles and cannot have been of significant proportions. There was some export of gold and silver coin by way of subsidies to neighbouring barbarian tribes, especially in nothern Europe, and owing to an unfavourable balance of trade with some areas, particularly with India [Pliny, *H.N.* XII 84]; but hardly on a scale to deplete the stock of precious metals in the Empire. It is extremely difficult to estimate the volume of production of gold and silver, but it does not seem to have been very high, nor to have varied greatly from period to period. Only one important change is worthy of record, the acquisition by Trajan's conquest of Dacia of a large hoard of gold and of the Transylvanian gold mines, which remained in the possession of the Empire till 270. All mines were imperial property, and newly produced gold and silver was therefore directly available for minting. It is, on the whole, probable that the Empire's stock of the precious metals would remain fairly constant, new production being balanced by wastage and export.

For two centuries the Roman Empire successfully operated a bimetallic currency. Under Augustus the standard silver coin, the denarius, was struck at 84 to the pound, the standard gold coin, the aureus, at 40-42 to the pound, and 25 denarii went to one aureus.[1] About A.D. 64 Nero slightly debased the denarius, raising the percentage of base metal to about 10 per cent and reduced the weight of both coins, the denarius to one ninety-sixth of a pound, the aureus to one forty-fifth. He thus maintained approximately the same ratio between them, and the 25 : 1 relation remained unchanged.[2] Trajan again slightly debased the denarius, reducing its silver content from 90 per cent to 85 per cent, but this change did not upset the 25 : 1 relation; the fact that the same emperor put large quantities of gold, the captured hoard of the Dacian kingdom, into circulation, no doubt slightly lowered the price of gold and thus counteracted the debasement of the denarius.[3]

It is clear that the denarius was regarded as the standard coin. Accounts, public and private, were kept in denarii or in sesterces (quarter denarii), which, though no longer issued in silver,

[1] I express the weight of coins in this way because the Roman did so—e.g. Pliny, *H.N.* xxxiii, 47: 'postea placuit * xl signari ex auri libris, paulatimque principes imminuere pondus, et novissime Nero ad xlv'; *Cod. Theod.* xv, ix, 1; 'nec maiorem argenteum nummum fas sit expendere quam qui formari solet cum argenti libra una in argenteos sexaginta dividitur'. Cf. p. 199, n. 29 and 30. The practice of the mint was no doubt to hand over to the moneyers a pound ingot, and demand delivery of the proper number of coins. [Moneyers were known to make a little on the side by striking say 74 solidi instead of 72 for a pound of gold and abstracting the odd two.] Thus the theoretical weight of a Roman coin should always work out as an integral fraction of a pound.

[2] Compare Tac. *Hist.* i, 24 with Suet. *Otho*, 4.2 and Plut. *Galba*, 20, where 100 sesterces is equated with 1 aureus; Lucian, *Pseudolog.* 30; Cassius Dio, lv, 12. 4.

[3] Mickwitz, *op. cit.* p. 32, following Heichelheim, considers that Trajan deliberately debased the denarius to adjust it to the lower price of gold. I find it difficult to believe that he (or his *procurator monetae*) was capable of such subtlety of economic thought, and think that Trajan debased the denarius to cover his heavy war expenses, and that the windfall of Dacian gold fortuitously lowered the price of gold soon after. [For Mickwitz's book see p. 186.]

remained a unit of account. Most transactions of ordinary life must have been conducted in the denarius and its bronze and copper subdivisions, since the aureus was too valuable a coin to come much into daily use. The gross annual pay of a Roman soldier, for instance, during the first century of the Empire, was 225 denarii, paid in three instalments of 75 denarii each: Domitian added a fourth instalment, thus raising the total to 300. From this, deductions were made for rations, uniform, etc., which in the pay-sheets of two legionaries at Alexandria in A.D. 83-4, totalled 130-140 denarii. A Roman private was most unlikely to handle an aureus, nine (or later, twelve) of which would have covered his gross pay for the year.[4]

In order to estimate the purchasing power of Roman coins over any length of time it is unfortunately necessary to rely on the price of one commodity only, wheat. Wheat is not an ideal commodity, since it was liable to violent seasonal fluctuations and local variations in price. The Roman Empire apparently produced barely enough for its needs and carried no reserves, so that a bad season would send prices rocketing till the next harvest brought them down to normal. Transport by land was moreover so expensive that it was scarcely ever economic to move a bulky load like corn more than one or two days' journey [cf. Ch. II at p. 37 above and L.R.E. 841 ff.], and thus one city might be paying famine prices while conditions in another were normal, and in large inland towns which had regularly to draw their supplies from a distance prices were substantially higher than elsewhere. However, wheat figures have certain advantages. Wheat was the staple diet of the vast majority of the people, and far and away the largest item in their food bill. In the second place it had no variations of quality such as bedevil any attempt to use the prices of wine, oil or meat. And thirdly its prices are quoted in relation to measures of capacity which are more or less uniform. The official modius, to which most of our prices refer, was equivalent to nine-tenths of a peck. The only other unit which comes into question, the Egyptian artaba, was for official Roman purposes equated with 3 modii.

In the reign of Domitian the governor of Galatia was asked to intervene at Antioch in Pisidia, where there was a famine, and it was complained that landowners were holding up stocks for yet

---

[4] See H. M. D. Parker, *The Roman Legions* (Oxford, 1928), pp. 214ff.

higher prices. He found on investigation that the modius of wheat had normally sold at 8 or 9 asses ($\frac{1}{2}$ to $\frac{9}{16}$ denarii), and ordered all citizens and residents to sell their surplus stocks to the civic authorities at 1 denarius.[5] What few other prices we possess from the first two centuries of the Empire accord with these figures. A number of Egyptian prices given in the papyri yield an average of 7.13 drachmae to the artaba:[6] four Egyptian drachmae were worth one denarius, so the price works out at slightly over half a denarius to the modius. From a rather earlier date (70 B.C.) Cicero cites a number of wheat prices from Sicily; he regards $2\frac{1}{2}$ sesterces ($\frac{5}{8}$ denarius) as a normal price,[7] 2 sesterces as cheap,[8] 3 sesterces as dear.[9] Finally, from Italy there is a second-century inscription which records the gratitude of a city to a local worthy for selling wheat in a shortage at one denarius the modius[10]. This price then would seem to have been regarded as a 'just price' in famine conditions. The normal price was half a denarius or a little more.

The Roman fiscal system was very rigid. The main source of revenue was the *tributum*, assessed on property in the provinces. This was supplemented by *ad valorem* customs duties, and a 5 per cent succession duty paid by Roman citizens. All these taxes were at fixed rates, and the total revenue cannot have varied greatly from year to year. It seems to have met annual expenditure but allowed for no surplus, and could only with very great difficulty be increased to meet additional charges.[11] When the State incurred additional expenditure, as for instance during wars, the government was compelled to sell public property, to confiscate private property (by encouraging informers to lay capital charges

---

[5] *J.R.S.* xiv (1924), 180.

[6] G. Mickwitz, *Aegyptus*, xiii (1933), pp. 95ff. It is at first sight rather surprising that prices in Egypt, which produced a large wheat surplus, should be the same as elsewhere in the Empire, but it must be remembered that a large proportion of the crop was taken in kind by the government and exported.

[7] Cic. *II in Verr.* iii, 84, 90, 173–4. Cicero quotes prices in sesterces (4 to the denarius) to the medimnus (= 6 modii).

[8] *Ibid.* 174.

[9] *Ibid.* 191.

[10] *C.I.L.* xi, 6117.

[11] Only one emperor is recorded to have increased the rate of *tributum*:Vespasian (Suet. *Vesp.* 16). The rigidity of the Roman fiscal system is strikingly demonstrated by S. L. Wallace, *Taxation in Egypt* (Princeton, 1938), which shows from receipts on ostraka and papyri that, with one or two insignificant exceptions, taxes continued throughout the inflationary period to be collected at the same rates.

against wealthy persons and securing their conviction),[12] or to debase the currency. Marcus Aurelius sought to relieve the financial stringency caused by his long wars by the first method,[13] but also had to resort to the third. Septimius Severus, who increased annual expenditure by raising the pay of the troops,[14] [from 300 denarii a year probably to 400] made ruthless use of the second method,[15] but again had to use the third also. Caracalla again raised the pay of the troops by 50 per cent [to 600 denarii, double the second century rate. Army pay was by far the largest item in the budget, and the effect of these increases was catastrophic.][16] Caracalla resorted to confiscations on a large scale, and also made the one recorded attempt to raise the regular revenue, by making all free inhabitants of the Empire Roman citizens and thus liable to the succession duty, whose rate he doubled.[17] The original rate was restored five years later by his successor, Macrinus.[18] But despite confiscations and increased taxation Caracalla was obliged to continue the debasement of the currency.

It was the denarius only that was debased. In Marcus's reign the silver content of the denarius sank to 75 per cent, in Severus's to 50 per cent. Caracalla issued a new coin, about 1½ times the size of the denarius, which was probably tariffed at 2 denarii; this coin has been dubbed, on rather slender grounds, the Antoninianus.[19] Meanwhile, the aureus was still issued at its original purity and weight (45 to the pound) until Caracalla, who slightly reduced it (to about 50 to the pound). The reason for this curious inconsistency was probably that the great mass of the expenditure, notably the pay of the troops, had to be made in denarii, whereas there was no pressing reason to debase the aureus used for paying higher salaries, which had not been raised. Cassius Dio, writing late in Severus's or early in Caracalla's reign, still speaks

[12] This charge is brought against most 'bad' emperors, e.g. Nero (Suet. *Nero*, 32) and Domitian (Suet. *Dom.* 12; Pliny, *Paneg.* 42), as well as those cited below.
[13] *Hist. Aug., Ant. Phil.*, 17. The same measure is recorded of Trajan (Pliny, *Paneg.* 50).
[14] Herodian, III, viii, 5.
[15] *Hist. Aug., Severus*, 12–13.
[16] Herodian, IV, iv, 7.
[17] Cassius Dio, LXXVIII, 9.4–5.
[18] Cassius Dio, LXXIX, 12.2.
[19] There is no evidence what value was put on this coin, but there would have been no object in issuing it except to increase the number of denarii that could be got out of a pound of silver; I take it therefore that it was worth 2 denarii.

of the aureus as worth 25 denarii.[20] The emperors may have hoped, at first at any rate, that the debasement of the denarius would pass unnoticed, or may have thought to maintain its value by keeping it at 25 to a still undebased aureus. This can only have been an official rate. The number of denarii circulating in the Empire must have increased considerably as a result of the successive debasements, and prices, including that of gold, must have increased substantially. Although custom would have maintained the 25:1 ratio for a while, it is hardly credible that by Dio's time there was not a black market in aurei. This is implied by an inscription dating from shortly after Caracalla's death,[21] which records that a military tribune in recognition of special merit was rewarded by receiving his salary of 25,000 sesterces in gold; he would presumably have been paid in aurei (at the official rate of 100 sesterces to the aureus), which he could change at great profit into denarii at black market rates. Even as an official rate, the 25:1 ratio can have had little meaning. For the government would not, except in such special cases as that mentioned above, pay out good gold when it could pay in bad silver; and indeed Dio complains that Caracalla used his gold to pay subsidies to barbarians (who, as hoards prove, refused the debased denarius and Antoninianus) and fobbed off his subjects with debased silver.[22] On the other hand, no citizen would pay his taxes in aurei, when he could pay them in bad silver. The government could only obtain gold through the levy of *aurum coronarium*. This was a nominally freewill offering, originally of gold crowns, but by this date of bullion, made to the emperor by the cities of the Empire on such auspicious occasions as his accession, or a triumph. Dio complains that Caracalla was continually reporting victories to serve as an excuse for a levy.[23]

[The surviving old silver coins similarly went into hoards or were melted down, or calculated for private transactions at their intrinsic value. The same even applied to the old copper pieces, the sesterces ($\frac{1}{4}$ denarius) and dupondii ($\frac{1}{8}$ denarius), which being large pieces came to command quite a high value. In Africa in the fifth century A.D. sesterces and dupondii of the second century

[20] Cassius Dio, LV, 12.4.
[21] *C.I.L.* XIII, 3162.
[22] Dio (LXXVIII, 14.3–4) actually says 'spurious silver and gold', but as Caracalla issued perfectly good gold, the last words must be a rhetorical flourish.
[23] Cassius Dio, LXXVIII, 9.2.

were still circulating, marked 83 and 42 nummi, the then prevailing monetary unit (cf. n. 124 below).

The effect of the withdrawal from circulation of nearly all the gold coins and many of the silver must have had a temporary deflationary effect. But it made it all the more necessary and the more difficult to debase the currency.]

For the next fifty years the Antoninianus, which from the middle of the century completely superseded the denarius, went from bad to worse, until [under Gallienus (260–268)] it contained less than 5 per cent of silver, as well as being substantially reduced in weight. [Not much more could be done with physical debasement.] Eventually Aurelian [270–275] carried through some reform of the coinage. In place of the many issues of variable weights then current he minted two series of silver-plated copper coins, the larger labelled xx.i or xxi or xx (in Greek κα) and the smaller vsv. The meaning of these symbols is unfortunately unknown, but it is probable that the reform was inflationary in tendency: it is therefore a plausible suggestion that xx.i means that the one new coin is equivalent to twenty old units. The interpretation of vsv is even more uncertain. It has been suggested that it means that the half (s) coin is worth ten (vv representing 5+5) units, but this seems very unnatural. A more plausible explanation is that it means vsvALIS, the regular or normal coin. The meaning then may be that the small coin was tariffed as an Antoninianus (by now the standard coin). In which case the larger coin was probably worth 20 sesterces or 5 denarii.[24] This easy way of increasing the nominal value of coins, once discovered, was naturally resorted to again. There is evidence that about thirty years later the large piece, which was known as the nummus, was tariffed at 25 denarii.[25] Gold issues became sporadic and rare, and were moreover minted at variable weights. It is probable that the gold coins were used only to distribute as donatives to the troops on accessions and other festive occasions, the gold being obtained through simultaneous levies of *aurum coronarium*. For

---

[24] Jones seems to have changed his mind, as in his later article he writes: 'As Aurelian's coins look rather better than those which preceded them this has been called a currency reform. But the coins bear the marks, XX.1 and VSV, which probably indicate that they were tariffed at 20 sesterces, i.e. 5 denarii, and 10 sesterces, i.e. 2½ denarii. The nominal value of the coins, that is to say, had been increased 150 per cent at a blow'. His earlier view is repeated in *L.R.E.* 26, citing C. H. V. Sutherland, *J.R.S.* li, 94 f. for confirmation.

[25] See below, p. 200, n. 31.

practical purposes it would seem that gold went out of circulation, being converted into plate and jewellery.[26] [A by-product of the inflation, which was probably created about this time, was the follis. Since there were by now no gold or genuine silver coins, but only the plated copper nummi, it required a very large number of coins and a great deal of tedious counting, to make any large payment. The treasury therefore provided sealed bags or purses (folles) containing, it would seem, 1,000 of Aurelian's nummi, and therefore worth nominally 5,000 denarii. When later Diocletian retariffed the nummus at 25 denarii, and then halved its value, the follis became worth 25,000 and then 12,500 denarii, at which figure it is portrayed in the mosaics of Piazza Armerina. See ch. XVI.)

Prices as reckoned in debased denarii naturally rose. [For the general public the effect seems to have been slight. The inflation had been very slow, lasting over a century, and on the whole it would seem gradual. Prices, wages and rents had been able to adjust themselves. Most people's wealth was invested in land, and it was only those who had put their money into long term mortgages who lost it; the chief sufferers were the cities which often invested their surplus income or benefactions in this way, and the alimentary foundations of the emperors. The papyri of Egypt prove that all private transactions continued to be conducted in the ever depreciating currency, and that there was no tendency towards an economy in kind. The chief sufferers were government employees (cf. further pp. 208 ff. below).] The proceeds of taxation, in so far as it was *ad valorem*, would have risen concurrently, but the *tributum*, which formed the bulk of the revenue, appears to have remained fixed at its pre-inflation figure. The government was thus unable to go on increasing its expenditure, especially military pay, in proportion to the rising cost of living. The soldiers had to be fed and clothed. The solution eventually reached was that the government requisitioned (without payment) the wheat, meat, wine, oil, textiles and leather needed to feed and clothe the troops, and issued them free. It seems unlikely that this result was achieved at one stroke.[27]

[26] Mickwitz, *Geld und Wirtschaft*, pp. 65–6, tries to prove that gold continued in circulation in this century, but fails to explain why the hoards of the inflationary period contain practically no gold.

[27] Van Berchem, *L'Annone militaire* (*Mem. Soc. Nat. Ant. de France*, 1937, pp. 117ff.), argues for the abrupt introduction of requisition without payment and free

O

Supplies for the army had always been obtained by compulsory purchase at prices which were often below market rates. The first step was doubtless to continue paying the same rates, despite the rise in prices. The soldier similarly had always drawn his rations, uniform and equipment against deductions from pay. Here again the deductions could be frozen at pre-inflation figures. Eventually, when owing to the rise in prices the payment had become nugatory, supplies were requisitioned outright, while the troops were entitled to rations, uniforms and arms, issued in kind, plus a small sum by way of money pay. The effect of this development would have been, by eliminating the currency from a large and important range of transactions, to increase the inflationary tendency.

[Thus the final result of the inflation under Diocletian was that the state, which had failed to adjust its taxes and payments, according to the changing value of money, was forced to fall back on an economy in kind. It still levied some taxes in money, the poll tax and the customs, and it still made some token payments in money to its officials and soldiers. But the great bulk of its income and expenditure was in corn, wine, meat, oil and clothes. But it was only the state which reverted to an economy in kind. Private people, who had continued to adjust their prices, wages and rents, continued to use money. . . .

An incidental but highly important result of the state's adoption of an economy in kind was the emergence of the first budget. Hitherto, as we have seen, taxes had been almost immut-

---

issue by Septimius Severus. I have expressed doubts of this thesis in my *Greek City*, pp. 329–30, nn. 94–5. [In his later paper Jones wrote that food and clothing for the army 'in the first and second centuries had been supplied by the government against deductions from pay, and obtained by the government from the producers through the city governments by compulsory purchase at low but reasonable prices. It seems likely that here too the government ignored price rises, and the payments made for most products became nugatory and were abandoned, as were small taxes. Some payment was still made for clothes under Aurelian, but it was grossly inadequate. We have a debate in the council of Oxyrhynchus, which had received an order for 100 tunics. For the linen yarn required for each tunic the treasury had paid 11 denarii. Thecity had added 19, but the yarn merchants claimed that the real price was 49.' (*P. Oxy*, 1414, cf. also *L.R.E.* 29ff.). 'By Diocletian's time a payment was still made for clothing, but nothing for anything else. Nor apparently were any deductions made from military pay for rations or clothing; in Diocletian's accounts the gross pay and ration allowance is issued to the troops' (*L.R.E.* 623). 'Diocletian regularised this position, by converting irregular requisitions (*indictiones extraordinariae*) into regular levies in kind, an annual *indictio*, assessed on the land' (cf. ch. XIII).]

able, continuing at the same rates from generation to generation and from century to century. Deficits had been filled by extraordinary measures, surpluses stored against a rainy day. Requisitions had on the other hand always been variable, calculated to feed a unit of given strength for a given period. Shortages would lead to mutinies, surpluses would have been wasteful. This attitude persisted when special requisitions were consolidated into a unified levy in kind. It was important that the troops should have enough food and clothing, but a surplus of food would be embarrassing; meat would go bad and even corn would deteriorate, especially if there were not enough storage capacity. The praetorian perfect was accordingly instructed to draw up at the beginning of each financial year (on 1st September) a calculation of all the products required for the coming year, and to divide the quantities by the number of fiscal units of land (cf. ch. XIII), and thus to establish how much each fiscal unit had to pay in modii of wheat, pounds of meat, pints of wine and oil, and in garments (cf. also *L.R.E.* 61 ff.; 451–6). The annual levy (*indictio*) was thus adjusted to the annual requirements of the state. The inevitable result of this great change was that the rate of tax began to creep up; we are told that it doubled between 324 and 364 (Themistius, *Orat.* VIII 113). The government no longer had to cut its coat according to its cloth, and yielded to the temptation.]

Diocletian endeavoured to restore a silver and gold currency. He issued a pure silver coin at 96 to the pound.[28] It name is unknown, but as it was of the same weight and purity as the old pre-inflatory denarius, it may have been called the *denarius argenteus*: this is suggested by the fact that the debased denarius is called in Diocletian's Edict of Prices the *denarius communis*. Gold coins were issued at 70, and later 60, to the pound.[29] It is not known at what rate they were intended to exchange with the silver: at the very unusual relations of the two precious metals prevailing at the time, about ten argentii would have gone to one aureus.[30] Both the silver and the gold issues are excessively rare,

[28] These coins are marked XCVI, so that there is no doubt of their theoretical weight.

[29] These coins are marked 0 (70) and Ξ (60).

[30] The aureus, at 60 to the pound of gold, would be worth 833 (50,000/60) denarii communes. The price of silver six years later than the Edict was 8,328 denarii the pound (*P.S.I.* 310): the argenteus, at 96 to the pound, would therefore be worth 86½ denarii. [See Additional Note for Jones' later view.]

and it is difficult to see how Diocletian could have found the metal to make large issues. The government's stock of gold had long vanished into private hoards, and its stock of silver had either been similarly lost or was dissipated in giving a small silver content to the vast quantities of debased denarii. It is clear from the Edict of Prices that the *denarius communis* remained the staple coin. Diocletian deflated the denarius by ordering that the current nummi (xx.i pieces), which were by then tariffed at 25 denarii, should be reduced in value by half, and by issuing a new and much heavier silver-washed copper coin, also somewhat enigmatically marked xx.i and called the nummus, to represent 25 denarii.[31] [There is vivid evidence for the deflation which halved the value of the nummus in a contemporary letter (*P. Ryl.* IV 607):—'Dionysius to Apion. The divine fortune of our Lords has ordered that the Italian coins should be reduced to half a nummus. So hurry up and spend all the Italian money you have and buy me all kinds of goods at any price you can get for them.']

The Edict [32] gives an immense list of prices, but only two are of interest for our present purposes. Wheat is tariffed at 100 denarii the modius,[33] and gold, in bar or in coins, at 50,000 denarii the pound.[34] Now it is clear from the preamble that Diocletian was endeavouring to fix normal prices, and we are told by a contemporary, Lactantius,[35] that the effect of the Edict was to drive goods off the market. The prices were therefore probably below current market level. The figure of 100 denarii is therefore comparable with the low average price of the first and second centuries, half a denarius. The price of wheat had then gone up

[31] This appears to emerge, as Segrè has divined in *Byzantion*, xv, pp. 252–5, from a combination of *P. Oslo*, iii, 83; *P.S.I.* 965; and *P. Ryl.* iv, 607. See also Additional Note.

[32] Diocletian's Edict is most conveniently consulted in Tenney Frank, *Economic Survey of Ancient Rome* (Baltimore, 1940), vol. v, Appendix. [For a new edition see S. Lauffer, *Diokletians Preisedikt*, Berlin, 1971.]

[33] *Ed. Diocl.* i, 1. The *modius castrensis*, the unit of capacity generally used in the Edict, has at last been proved by Segrè (*Byzantion*, xv, p. 277), from a papyrus published by Boak (*Harvard Studies in Classical Philology*, li, no. 4), to be none other than the ordinary modius, of which 3⅓ (nearly) went to the artaba.

[34] *Ed. Diocl.* xxx, 1. Mattingly's conjecture (*Num. Chron.* (1946), p. 113) that the figure on the stone (E) had been misread and should be restored as 10,000 (A) has been disproved on reinspection; the figure, though mutilated, is undoubtedly E. It remains a puzzle why χρυσὸς ἐνηγμένος in the next line should be valued at only 12,000 denarii. It is possible that one or other figure is an engraver's error, but more probably χρυσὸς ἐνηγμένος is a trade term for some inferior alloy.

[35] *De mortibus persecutorum*, vii, 6.

about 200 times in a century and a half. The price of gold in the second century was 1,125 denarii to the pound (25 denarii to the aureus, of which 45 went to the pound). Gold therefore in the same period had risen only about 45 times.

The figure for silver in the Edict does not survive, but a papyrus of six years later (307)[36] shows that in an official transaction it was then valued at 8,328 denarii the pound, that is 86 times the second-century price of 96 denarii to the pound. Silver thus rose less than half as much as wheat, but twice as much as gold, so that the gold: silver ratio stood at 1:6 instead of 1:11$\frac{3}{4}$.

Some scholars have endeavoured to extract from these figures a gold price index for wheat. In the early Empire, they argue, a pound of gold would buy 2,250 modii; under Diocletian it would buy only 500 modii. These facts are incontrovertible, but the implication that the real price of wheat had gone up fourfold or fivefold is false. For the Roman Empire was not on the gold standard: in it gold was a commodity whose price expressed in the normal currency, the denarius, might vary like that of wheat.

Agricultural production had undoubtedly declined since the second century; there are constant complaints of previously productive lands being left uncultivated [L.R.E. 26, 67 f., 812 ff.] The decrease in the quantity of wheat produced would thus be one factor in the rise of wheat prices. But it is clearly less important than the enormous increase in currency. Moreover, by Diocletian's time a very large proportion of the State's requirements were levied and distributed in kind, thus limiting the circulation of the coinage for the most part to private transactions. It is unfortunately impossible to evaluate the relative importance of these three factors. It is, however, suggestive that the silver content of a Neronian denarius was rather over 3 grains and that of a Diocletianic 25-denarius piece rather under $\frac{1}{2}$ grain. The same quantity of silver which went to a denarius before the inflation could produce coins to the face value of 150 denarii. This is not to say that 150 times as many (nominal) denarii were circulating in Diocletian's reign as in the second century, for large quantities of silver must have vanished into hoards.

It may be asked why in the circumstances the price of gold rose only 45 times. I can only suggest that the price of gold in the first two centuries was enhanced by the fact that a considerable

[36] P.S.I. 310.

proportion of the gold stock of the Empire was absorbed in the currency. When in the third century gold was virtually demonetised, and used for plate and jewellery only, its value would have sunk, and Diocletian's tentative attempt to recreate a gold currency was on too small a scale to affect the position. The same consideration would apply in a modified degree to silver. Much of the pure silver coinage would have been withdrawn from the currency in the inflationary period, thus increasing the stock available for plate and other luxury uses, but the debased coinage still continued to absorb a considerable quantity. Hence silver sank in real price only half as much as gold.

After Diocletian's abdication in 305 his successors continued to issue gold and silver coins. From Egypt we have some evidence of how they obtained the necessary bullion. In A.D. 306 and 307 Maximin was imposing a surcharge of silver (which was paid partly in gold coin) on the wheat tax at the rate of $1\frac{1}{2}$ oz. to 100 artabae,[37] and a similar surcharge appears again in 311 (payable in gold and silver).[38] Licinius also made compulsory purchases of gold from the cities—the allotment of Oxyrhynchus was 38 lb.[39] These measures, together with a renewed depreciation of the denarius (Diocletian's 25-denarius piece had by the early 320's sunk to less than a third of its original weight), sent the price of gold up steeply. In the compulsory purchase order the price fixed by the government is 100,000 denarii the pound, twice the rate fixed in the Edict. And by 324, when Egypt fell to Constantine, the pound of gold had reached over 300,000 denarii.[40]

Constantine from the beginning of his reign began to issue the solidus, a gold coin struck at 72 to the pound, which was to

[37] P. Oxy. 1653, P. Merton, 31, P. Cairo, 57049 (Chron. d'Égypte, 1952, p. 247).
[38] P. Thead. 33.
[39] P. Oxy. 2106. It is unfortunately impossible to date this document precisely. From the fact that Augusti and Caesars are mentioned both in the plural, it must fall either in the latter part of Diocletian's reign (293–305) or in the immediately following period (305–8) or in the latter part of Licinius's reign (317–24). It seems unlikely that Diocletian would have abandoned the price he had fixed for gold in the Edict of 301 during the next four years. On his abdication Oriens (including Egypt) came under the rule of the Caesar Maximin, while Asia Minor was ruled by Galerius Augustus. In the document the gold bought in Egypt is to be delivered at Nicomedia, and it seems improbable, however cordial their relations, that Maximin would have allowed Galerius to extract gold from his territory. The emperor in question is therefore probably Licinius, who normally resided at Nicomedia and ruled the whole of the eastern half of the Empire.
[40] P. Oxy. 1430.

remain unchanged for seven centuries. The number 72 was evidently chosen so that fractions of the pound, which was divided into 12 ounces of 24 scruples, could be readily made up in solidi, which each weighed 4 scruples. The solidus was theoretically divided into 24 siliquae (in Greek, carats, κεράτια), but no gold coins were ever issued below the semissis (12 siliquae) and tremissis (8 siliquae). [The solidus had a remarkable history, maintaining its weight and purity for over seven centuries. By the end of the fourth century solidi became so abundant that the levies and payments in kind could be commuted and all taxes and salaries paid in gold, while most private transactions except the smallest were conducted in gold. But it may be noted that it] was not in the full sense of the word a coin. Issued by the government to effect payments, it was decreed to be worth $\frac{1}{72}$ lb., and the emperors insisted that in private circulation solidi, unless clipped, should be accepted at their face value.[41] But taxes and fines were reckoned in gold bullion, and if 72 solidi did not make up a pound, they had to be supplemented. Valentinian and Valens even insisted that solidi collected in taxes must be melted down into bullion bars, whose weight and purity could be readily checked, before transmission to the treasury.[42] One of the factors which kept the solidus up to standard was no doubt the constant reminting which this procedure entailed. It is clear also that the public did not, at first at any rate, regard solidi as money in the ordinary sense. *Pecunia* in fourth-century Latin means debased denarii in contrast to *aurum* and *argentum*,[43] and people spoke of buying and selling solidi when they changed denarii for solidi or vice versa.[44] The solidus was primarily a gold unit for the use of

[41] *Cod. Theod.* ix, xxii, 1 (343).

[42] *Cod. Theod.* xii, vi, 12 (366), 13 (367).

[43] E.g. Augustine, *Sermo* 127.3: 'ad aliquid ergo magnum et pretiosum comparandum parares aurum vel argentum vel pecuniam vel fructus aliquos pecorum aut frugum qui in tua possessione nascerentur'.

[44] E.g. *Cod. Theod.* ix, xxii, 1 (343): 'omnes solidi, in quibus nostri vultus [ac] veneratio una est, uno pretio aestimandi sunt atque vendendi'; xii, vii, 2 (363): 'emptio venditioque solidorum'; Symmachus, *Relatio* 29: 'vendendis solidis . . . collectariorum corpus obnoxium est'; Augustine, *Sermo* 389.3: 'cum solidum ut assolet vendidisset centum folles ex pretio solidi pauperibus iussit erogari'; Val. *Nov.* xvi (445); *Anon. de Rebus Bellicis*, iii, 1. [This habit of mind may explain, if not excuse, a libel of Procopius in the *Secret History* xxv, 11, 12. He declares that Justinian debased the solidus, and ordered the moneychangers to exchange it for 180 folles instead of 210. The coins survive to refute this; they are of full weight and purity. On the other hand, Justinian increased the wieght of the follis, no doubt

that department of the imperial treasury (the *sacrae largitiones*) which dealt with levies and issues in the precious metals.

Constantine and his successors also issued silver on a considerable scale down to the end of the fourth century. [This was not a success, probably because the relative value of gold and silver fluctuated greatly at this period.] The coins, to judge by the surviving specimens, were struck at a bewildering variety of weights, and it remains an unsolved problem what names the various pieces bore, and what relation they were supposed to bear to the solidus or to the *denarius communis*. It is on the whole probable that gold and silver exchanged at a fluctuating rate corresponding with the relative values of the two metals. The government, when it accepted gold in lieu of silver due in taxes or fines, demanded 4 or 5 solidi to the pound, varying the rate quite arbitrarily, it would seem. In a document which probably dates from the latter part of Constantine's reign silver is commuted at an official rate of 4 solidi to the pound. In a constitution dated 397 the treasury accepts five solidi in lieu of 1 lb. silver. A constitution of 422 permits a payment of 4 solidi for 1 lb. silver. But Justinian in 528 reproduces the constitution of 397 in his Code.[45] In the circumstances a bimetallic currency can hardly have existed, and in fact the ancient sources, on the rare occasions when they speak of gold and silver in the same transaction, specify the quantity of each separately without any attempt to reduce them to a common basis.[46]

Nor does there seem to have been any fixed relation between the gold coinage and denarii. The price of gold laid down in Diocletian's Edict evidently does not envisage any regular relation, for by it the aureus (at 60 to the pound) would be worth $833\frac{1}{3}$ denarii. During the next twenty years, as we have seen, the

with the object of establishing the convenient ratio of 180 instead of 210, cf. p. 222 below. But ordinary people felt that the solidus had sunk in value in relation to real money, and Procopius, whether out of malice or because he shared their ignorance, declared that the solidus was debased.]

[45] *S.B.* 6086; *Cod. Theod.* xiii, ii, 1; viii, iv, 27; *Cod. Just.* x, lxxviii, 1.

[46] The accession donative is regularly stated to be 5 solidi and 1 lb. silver for each man (see p. 217, n. 103). The cost of Leo's Vandal expedition was 65,000 lb. gold plus 700,000 lb. silver according to John Lydus (*de mag.* iii, 43), 47,000 lb. gold from the Praetorian Prefect's treasury and 17,000 lb. gold plus 700,000 lb. silver from the *largitiones* according to Candidus (fr. 2, *F.H.G.* iv, p. 137). [But see *L.R.E.* 439 f. for the view that the government unsuccessfully aimed at bimetallism, and for further evidence.]

price of gold rose in denarii according to market conditions. A report of Symmachus, Prefect of the City, to Valentinian II in 384–5 makes the situation clear. He is writing on behalf of the *collectarii* or money-changers, a corporation among whose duties it was to buy solidi for the government. Gratian (375–83) had fixed a price, reasonable at the time, at which the government reimbursed the *collectarii* for the solidi they supplied, but, Symmachus explains, the price of the solidus had, owing to the rise in gold, gone up on the open market, and the *collectarii* were now losing on the transaction.[47]

Constantine not only levied, like his predecessors, the *aurum coronarium* at intervals of five years, and continued to impose the gold and silver tax on land like Maximin,[48] he also exacted the rent of imperial estates in gold,[49] and instituted a new tax on traders, payable in gold and silver and hence known as the *collatio auri atque argenti*, or in Greek χρυσάργυρον.[50] But his principal stroke was the confiscation, late in his reign, of the temple treasures.[51] This measure must have brought into circula tion very considerable quantities of gold and silver, and it is indeed regarded by an author writing a generation later as the basis of the new coinage. 'In the time of Constantine,' he writes, 'there was lavish expenditure; he assigned gold to mean transactions instead of bronze, which formerly used to be held of high value. The origin of this avarice is believed to have derived from the following cause. When gold and silver and a great quantity of precious stones which had been stored of old in the temples came into public use, it inflamed the desire of all for giving and possessing. And whereas the expenditure even of bronze, which, as I have said, was stamped with the face of the kings, already seemed

[47] Symmachus, *Rel.* 29, [cf. *L.R.E.* 442, 704.].

[48] *Cod. Theod.* xi, ix, 2 (337): 'si quis fundum vel mancipia ob cessationem tributorum vel etiam ob vestium auri argentique debitum quae annua exactione solvuntur occupata . . . comparaverit'. This tax appears to be different from the 'collatio auri atque argenti' which Constantius II imposed on land donated by the crown to individuals (*Cod. Theod.* xi, xx, 1, 2).

[49] *Cod. Theod.* xi, xvi, 1 (319); xii, vi, 2 (325). The rents of the estates given by Constantine to the Roman basilicas (*Liber Pontif.* 34) are all calculated in solidi, apart from special rare products.

[50] Zosimus, ii, 38. [See pp. 35 f.]

[51] Eusebius, *Vit. Const.* iii, 1, 54, *Laud. Const.* viii, ix, Julian, *Or.* vii, 228b-c, Libanius, *Or.* xxx, 6, 37, lxii, 8.

heavy and excessive, nevertheless owing to a kind of blindness there was a more lavish zeal for expenditure in gold, which is considered more valuable.'[52]

The economic thought of this anonymous fourth-century author is crude. He appears to think that using a more precious metal for the currency makes things dearer. But though the economic theory may be wrong there seems no reason to doubt that the creation of a new gold and silver currency, in addition to the existing denarius currency, out of hoards which had long been sterilised, must have had an inflationary effect. The precise influence which Constantine's monetary policy had on prices is, however, very difficult to estimate. The situation is exceedingly complex, for there were henceforth three currencies circulating simultaneously over the same area. Prices found their levels independently in gold, silver and copper (as we may now call denarii, although they continued for old times' sake to receive a silver wash), and the currencies exchanged against each other according to the market.

The gold prices of wheat are of the same order as those of the first centuries. In the second quarter of the fourth century there was a shortage one year in Egypt, and wheat stood at 5 artabae (16 modii) to the solidus. Pachomius sent out a monk to buy for his monastery, and he eventually found an obliging tax-collector who sold him corn from public stocks at 13 artabae (43 modii) to the solidus, in the expectation of postponing delivery to the government till after the harvest, when he could replace what he had—illicitly—sold. Pachomius repudiated this transaction, and wheat was ultimately bought at 5½ artabae (18 modii) to the solidus.[53] These prices are exceptionally low, and suggest that Egypt was producing a good surplus, which was not all absorbed by taxation. For the year 362-3 the emperor Julian quotes some rather high prices for Antioch. To alleviate a shortage he imported wheat from neighbouring cities and sold it at 10 modii to the solidus, and later shipped corn from Egypt, which he sold at 15 modii to the solidus. Even in normal conditions, he asks rhetorically, was wheat often sold at the latter price?[54] Wheat was doubtless normally dear at Antioch, since it was a very large

[52] Anon. de rebus bellicis, ii, 1.
[53] Patr. Or. 4. v, 'Histoire de S. Pacôme', 33–4.
[54] Misopogon, 369.

town and must have drawn its supply from considerable distances, but we may suspect that Julian is painting normal conditions rather black, to glorify his own achievement. At Carthage a few years later Hymetius, proconsul of Africa, sold wheat during a shortage from government stocks at 10 modii to the solidus (this seems to have been regarded as a 'just price' in a famine), and refilled the granaries next year, buying at the rate of 50 modii per solidus.[55] In 445 Valentinian III fixed the price of wheat in Numidia and Mauretania at 40 modii to the solidus,[56] but this, being an official rate for government purchases, may have been below market prices. The same official rate is found in sixth-century Egypt,[57] and here the market price was about the same: twenty prices given by papyri average about 12 artabae to the solidus.[58] These Egyptian prices are, however, probably below the level of the empire. Joshua Stylites[59] quotes 30 modii to the solidus as being the normal price in Mesopotamia in 495 before locusts and war created famine conditions. If 30 modii be taken as the normal quantity which a solidus would buy, the price works out approximately the same as the first- and second-century price reckoned in gold. A pound of gold in the earlier period was equal to 45 aurei, each worth 25 denarii, each of which would buy nearly 2 modii; it would therefore fetch rather less than 2,250 modii. In the later period the pound of gold, being equal to 72 solidi, each of which would buy 30 modii, would fetch 2,160 modii. As far as gold prices went, therefore, there was no inflation. On the contrary, the strong demand for gold by the government for minting sent the price of gold up from the low level recorded in Diocletian's Edict, until roughly the same relation between gold and wheat was reached as had prevailed in the first and second centuries.

This result is partially confirmed by a study of the price of another standard food, pork. Here we possess no figures for the early Empire, but in Diocletian's Edict[60] the price is fixed at 12 denarii the pound. Thus on the Diocletianic tariff a pound of gold

[55] Amm. Marc. xxviii, i, 17–18.
[56] Val. Nov. xiii, 4.
[57] P. Cairo, 67320.
[58] Wheat prices in solidi are listed in Johnson and West, Byzantine Egypt, Economic Studies (Princeton, 1949), pp. 177–8.
[59] Ch. 26.
[60] Ed. Diocl. iv, 1.

was equivalent to 4,000 pounds of pork in the fifth century (452) the standard price for Italy was 240 lb. to the solidus;[61] In Africa a lower price for meat, 270 lb. to the solidus, was set by the government in 445,[62] and in Egypt 200 was in the sixth century the standard government rate for commutation of military supplies.[63] Thus a pound of gold would purchase 14,400, 17,280 or 19,440 pounds of pork. In terms of pork, therefore, as in terms of wheat, gold has roughly quadrupled in value from the time of Diocletian.

The prices of military uniforms tell the same tale. A requisition order dated A.D. 138[64] authorised payment for one chiton and four cloaks at 24 denarii each. The Diocletianic tariff[65] price a 'military indictional chlamys (best quality)' at 4,000. In denarii the price has been multiplied by 166, in gold it has risen from 0.02 to 0.08, that is, fourfold. In the fourth century a military chlamys cost one solidus (0.014 lb. gold), three-quarters of the second-century price.[66]

The great inflation of the third century had a permanent effect in reducing the real wages and salaries of all employees of the State. The private soldier of the second century had received gross pay of 300 denarii, that is 12 aurei or $\frac{4}{15}$ lb. gold. [Under Caracalla it was 600 denarii, and from a papyrus of 299 (L.R.E. III 187 n. 31) we know that this was what legionaries still received. They now also got a ration of 200 denarii. As corn cost 100 denarii the modius and a year's ration was 40 modii, the whole of their pay and ration allowance could suffice only to buy them eight weeks' bread. Most of what they needed was supplied in kind (pp. 197 f.).) It is difficult to calculate exactly the pay of a private soldier in the fourth century, when it was made up of rations (annona), uniform (vestis), and arms issued in kind, together with pay (stipendium) in debased denarii, and a quinquennial donative in gold or silver. [L.R.E. 623 f.] By the fifth and sixth centuries the stipendium had melted away, and the issues in kind had been commuted for gold. By this time the soldier received 4 or 5 solidi a year for annona,[67] and a quinquennial donative of

[61] Val. Nov. xxxvi, 2.   [62] Val. Nov. xiii, 4.
[63] P. Cairo, 67320; cf. J.H.S. (1951), p. 271.
[64] B.G.U. 1564.   [65] XIX, 1.
[66] P. Ross. Georg. v, 61 (D5) prices 15 chlamydes at 17 solidi. The official adaeratio was raised from $\frac{2}{3}$ to 1 solidus in 396 (Cod. Theod. VII, vi, 4).
[67] Val. Nov. xiii, 3 (445, four solidi); Cod. Just. I, xxvii, 1, §§ 22–38 (five solidi): Just. Edict xiii, 18, implies four solidi.

5 solidi.[68] His allowance for *vestis* is uncertain, but as he received 1 solidus (per annum) for his chlamys,[69] and was entitled to three garments in all, chlamys, pallium and sticharium,[70] we may put it at about 3 solidi. The allowance for arms is unknown,[71] but if it be reckoned at another 3 solidi, his total emoluments would be 12 solidi, or $\frac{1}{6}$ lb. gold, that is, about two-thirds in gold value of the pay of the second-century soldier. This calculation can be checked by reckoning the surplus which a soldier might save after paying his expenses. The soldier of the fourth century had only a *stipendium* of negligible value, and one-fifth of his periodical donative—probably a solidus per annum. The fifth- and sixth-century soldier similarly had only a solidus to spare, for the commutation of *annona* and *vestis* was not on a generous scale. The soldier of the principate[72] on the other hand had 60 denarii (2.4 aurei) deducted for rations, and from 50 to 60 denarii (2 to 2.4 aurei) for uniform. Two soldiers whose pay-sheets we possess had no deduction for arms in the year in question (arms would not often require replacement), and their total outgoings including boots and sundries total only 134 to 144 denarii, or less than two-thirds of the 225 denarii (9 aurei) which the troops then—before Domitian's increase of pay—received. If deductions were not increased when the pay was raised to 300 denarii (12 aurei), soldiers of the second century would have been able to save about half their pay, 6 aurei, equivalent to about 10 solidi.

On higher officials and officers the effect of the inflation was even more severe. Equestrian officials in the second century were graded as *sexagenarii, centenarii, ducenarii* and *tricenarii,* drawing

---

[68] Proc. *Anecd.* xxiv, 27–9.

[69] *Cod. Theod.* vii, vi, 4 (396), repeated in *Cod. Just.* xii, xxxix, 3.

[70] All these garments appear in P. *Oxy.* 1905; στιχάρια and πάλλια in P. *Oxy.* 1424 and 1448; χλαμύδες in P. *Lond.* 1259; χλαμύδες, πάλλια and στολαί and πέπλα (vague terms which may cover στιχάρια) in P.R.G. v, 61. All these documents are probably concerned with military clothing. The Edict of Diocletian gives prices for χλαμὺς στρατιωτικὴ ἰνδικτιοναλία καλλίστη (xix, 1, 4,000 denarii) and στίχη ἰνδικτιοναλία (xix, 2, 2,000 denarii) under woollen garments, and for στίχων στρατιωτικῶν (xxv, 28–30, 1,500, 1,250 and 1,000 denarii according to quality) under linen garments: no figures survive for the πάλλιον, which was probably the most expensive garment.

[71] That there was a money allowance for arms may be inferred from Theophylact Simocatta, vii, 1, where the emperor Maurice ἐβούλετο τριττᾶις μοίραις συντάττεσθαι τὴν ἐπίδοσιν, δι' ἐσθῆτος καὶ χαράγματος χρυσοῦ. He appears to have been trying to restore the issue in kind of uniform and arms, hitherto commuted for gold; the suggestion was very unpopular.

[72] See p. 192, n. 4.

salaries of 60,000, 100,000, 200,000 and 300,000 sesterces, or, reckoning in gold values, $13\frac{1}{3}$, $22\frac{2}{9}$, $44\frac{4}{9}$ and $66\frac{2}{3}$ lb. gold. The highest senatorial office, the proconsulship of Africa, carried a salary of 1,000,000 sesterces, or over 220 lb. gold.[73] During the inflation the same salary scales continued to be paid in debased denarii, so that in Diocletian's reign a *magister memoriae* was still receiving 300,000 sesterces,[74] that is, 75,000 debased denarii, and even in the last decade of Constantine's reign the *praepositus* of a unit was getting only 36,000 denarii, probably not much more than twice what an officer of equivalent grade received in the second century.[75] These salaries were supplemented by multiple *annonae* and *capitus*, but what little evidence there is suggests not on a scale to compensate for the fall in the value of money. We have unfortunately no fourth- or fifth-century figures, but in the sixth Justinian states that the salary of the Augustal Prefect of Egypt was, prior to his reform of the Egyptian administrative system, 50 *annonae* and 50 *capitus*. The salary of the Dux of Libya at this date amounted to 50 *annonae* and 50 *capitus* in gold, equivalent to 400 solidi in all, and 90 *annonae* and 120 *capitus* in kind, commuted for $1,005\frac{1}{4}$ solidi.[76] It is plausible to suggest that the official salary of both these officers, who were of equal (*spectabilis*) grade, was 50 *annonae* and 50 *capitus*, and the Dux had supplemented his income by appropriating, in the fashion familiar to the later Empire, some of the *annonae* of his troops; the Augustal Prefect no doubt made up his salary by other perquisites. If so, the official salary of officers of *spectabilis* grade would have been *annonae* and *capitus* (there is no suggestion that they had any other regular and official emoluments) amounting to the value of 400 solidi, or roughly $5\frac{1}{2}$ lb. gold. The Augustal Prefect and the Dux held posts which were equivalent to those of *ducenarii* of the second century. The official salary of such officers had then, as a result of the inflation, dropped to about one-eighth of second-

---

[73] The salary grading of equestrian officials is attested by many inscriptions. For the proconsul of Africa see Cassius Dio, LXXVIII, 22.5.

[74] Eumenius, *pro Instaurandis Scholis* (*Pan. Vet.* IX (IV), 11), 'trecena illa sestertia, quae sacrae memoriae magister acceperam'.

[75] *P. Oxy.* 1047: the date on which the donative was paid (25 July) fixes the document to Constantine's reign, and it cannot be earlier than 324 when Constantine acquired Egypt. For officers' rates of pay in the principate see Brunt, *Papers of the British School at Rome*, XVIII (1950), pp. 68–9. [The assumption made there that salaries of higher officers rose *pari passu* with soldiers' pay is clearly invalid. P.A.B.]

[76] Just. *Edict.* XIII, 3 and 18.

century rates. This circumstance may help to explain, if not to excuse, the constant attempts of late Roman officials to supplement their salaries by perquisites, some of which eventually received legal sanction.

Justinian endeavoured to check these and other types of corruption by consolidating and raising salaries. Even his revised scales are, however, well below second-century levels. He normally gave about 10 lb. gold to *spectabiles*, and raised many officers to this grade.[77] But even this salary was only three-quarters of that of the most junior procurators, the *sexagenarii*. The Moderator of Arabia received 15 lb. gold[78] and the Proconsul of Cappadocia 20 lb.,[79] while the Dux of Libya kept his old salary, which amounted to about 20 lb. The post of Augustal Prefect of Egypt was united with that of Dux of Egypt and was allotted 40 lb.[80] nearly as much as a *ducenarius*. The newly created Praetorian Prefect of Africa, whose post would correspond in dignity to, and carry more onerous duties than, the old proconsulate of Africa, received 100 lb. gold, less than half the proconsul's salary.[81]

It is noteworthy that the common soldier, in theory at any rate, lost very much less by the inflation than high officials and military officers. He had to be decently fed, clothed and armed, and there was less spare to cut. When on the other hand the large cash salaries of the higher grades melted away they were replaced by allowances in kind on a much more modest scale. In practice the contrast was not so sharp, as officers regularly intercepted a proportion of the pay and allowances of their troops.

The creation of a new gold and silver currency, competing with the old copper currency for the same volume of goods, must inevitably have sent prices up in terms of denarii. But the papyri reveal that in Egypt the rise in prices was far greater than could be explained by this fact alone. The Egyptians went on reckoning in drachmae (though tetradrachms ceased to be minted in 296) and in denarii throughout the fourth and fifth centuries and even in the sixth, though by this time it was becoming more usual to keep

[77] Just. *Nov.* xxiv–xxvii (800 solidi), xxviii. 3, xxix. 2 (725 solidi), xxxi. 1 (700 solidi). *Edict* iv, 1, 2 (10 lb. =720 solidi).
[78] Just. *Nov.* cii, 2.
[79] Just. *Nov.* xxx, 6.
[80] Just. *Edict* xiii, 3.
[81] *Cod. Just.* i, xxvii, 1, §21.

accounts in fractions of the solidus. As prices rose it became customary to quote them in talents (1 talent=6,000 drachmae= 1,500 denarii) or in myriads of denarii. In 335 wheat, which had been tariffed by Diocletian at 100 denarii the modius (330 denarii the artaba), stood at 14 talents (21,000 denarii) to the artaba, and in 338 at 24 talents (36,000 denarii). A few years later the artaba stood at 50 talents (75,000 denarii), and later again at 183 talents or about 500,000 denarii.[82] Other papyri give the price of gold either by weight or in solidi. In 324, the year in which Constantine acquired Egypt, 10½ grammes of gold were valued at 7 talents 3,720 drachmae, which would make the pound of gold cost 313,488 denarii and the solidus about 4,350 denarii.[83] Other undated fourth-century documents give prices of 36 talents (54,000 denarii), 100 talents (150,000), 120 talents (180,000) and 183⅓ talents (275,000) for the solidus.[84] In the last document the price of corn is quoted as 26 talents (39,000 denarii), which suggests a date near 338; reckoned in solidi the price is unusually high (about 7 artabae to the solidus). A papyrus dated to the middle of the fourth century gives a price of gold which works out at 3,840 talents or 576 myriads of denarii to the solidus; and in another document the writer states, 'The solidus now stands at 2,020 myriads; it has gone down'.[85] Yet other papyri, dated to the late fourth century, equate the solidus to 25,000 and 30,000 talents (3,750 and 4,500 myriads).[86] Some indirect data confirm these equations and make the chronology of the inflation rather more precise. In a document dated 360 meat is priced at 7,200 myriads for 500 lb., and in another dated 390 at 105 myriads for 3½ lb., i.e. at 14⅖ and 30 myriads per lb. respectively.[87] If meat in the fourth century stood at the standard fifth-century price of 200 lb. to the solidus, the solidus was equated with 2,880 myriads in 360 and 6,000 myriads in 390.

The denarius of the papyri was not, of course, a coin. In 324 the *nummus*, the principal copper coin, had a value of 25 denarii, so that a solidus could have been bought with 174 *nummi*. During

[82] P. *Lond*. 1914; P. *Oxy*. 85; P. *Lond*. 427; P. *Princeton*, 183v.
[83] P. *Oxy*. 1430.
[84] P.E.R. 187 and 37; S.P.P. xx, 96 and 81.
[85] S.B. 7034; P. *Oxy*. 1223.
[86] P.S.I. 960–1; [L.R.E. III 114 n. 74 also cites P. *Oxy*. 2267: 3200 myriads =7 solidi (before 361).]
[87] P. *Oxy*. 1056, 1753.

the fourth century the successive issues must have been assigned higher and higher face values in denarii, while at the same time the coins tended to become smaller and smaller.

The peculiar conservatism of the Egyptians, who went on reckoning in the old units of the drachma and denarius long after they had ceased to be coins, enable us to trace the course of the inflation; it appears from the figures given above that from the time when Constantine conquered the East (324) till the reign of Julian (360–3) the inflation was extremely rapid. During these forty years the value of the denarius sank from about 4,500 to the solidus to about 30,000,000. Thereafter the movement was checked, and in the next thirty years the denarius sank only by 50 per cent.

These figures all come from Egypt, but they cannot be written off as peculiar to Egypt. The same coins circulated in Egypt as in the rest of the Empire, and it shared the same fiscal system.[88] There was certainly a vast inflation of the denarius in Egypt in the fourth century, and, unless the contrary can be proved, what happened in Egypt happened in the rest of the eastern part of the Empire at any rate. It is a more plausible hypothesis that during the periods when the Empire was divided the *comes sacrarum largitionum* in the western part may have pursued a different policy from his eastern colleague, and that the history of the denarius may therefore have followed a different course in the west than in the east. We have no information about the value of the denarius in the west during the fourth century, but there is a figure for the early fifth century which taken at its face value suggests that no inflation had taken place. In a constitution dated 419[89] the price of salt pork is fixed at 50 denarii to the pound and in another dated 452[90] that of pork at 240 lb. to the solidus.

[88] It has been argued that the fact that Alexandria alone of the imperial mints never issued solidi would account for a local inflation in Egypt. Solidi, however, came into circulation not where they were minted but where they were paid out, and it is in fact abundantly evident, both from finds and papyri, that they circulated freely in Egypt. In general, finds indicate that coins travelled widely and freely from their place of minting. There is one constitution (*Cod. Theod.* ix, xxiii, 1) of mid-fourth-century date which forbids merchants to carry copper coin from place to place beyond specified sums for travelling expenses, but other clauses of this law, prohibiting the sale of coin, make it plain that it was an emergency measure, designed to prevent speculative transactions in the copper currency at a moment when certain old issues had been declared no longer legal tender.

[89] *Cod. Theod.* xiv, iv, 10.

[90] Val. *Nov.* xxxvi.

P

In 419, then, the denarius at Rome will have stood at about 12,000 to the solidus. The figure is surprisingly low, for the western denarius could not have parted company from the eastern until 337, when on Constantine's death the Empire was divided between his sons, and by that date the Egyptian documents suggest that it had already sunk to the neighbourhood of 250,000.[91] We must in fact presume a policy of deflation in the west as against inflation in the east.

There are, however, serious grounds for questioning this conclusion. In the first place, the issues of copper coins from the western and eastern mints are, in general, uniform. There is nothing in the coins themselves to suggest that a radically different monetary policy was being pursued in the two halves of the Empire, though it is of course possible that similar coins were tariffed at entirely different rates in east and west. In the second place the Empire was not as yet permanently divided into two parts; it was only on Theodosius's death in 395 that the eastern and western parts finally parted company. It is rather difficult to conceive how in these circumstances a radically different monetary policy can have been pursued in east and west. Thirdly, there are two pieces of evidence which suggest that the denarius was rapidly depreciating in the west. In 361–3 the Consular of Numidia, fixing a scale of *sportulae* (fees payable by litigants to officials), expressed them in modii of wheat or the price thereof;[92] he would hardly have done so unless the denarius was depreciating so rapidly as to be useless as a standard of value. In 384–5 the *collectarii* of Rome protested, apparently with justice, that the official price of a solidus in denarii, recently raised by Gratian (376–83), required to be raised again to correspond with market rates.[93]

The apparent contrast between east and west is probably to be explained by a difference in terminology. The Egyptians continued to reckon in notional denarii, and not in actual coins, and thus their accounts present a faithful picture of the progress of the inflation. In the west, it would seem, the current copper coins of the day were popularly called denarii. Thus when John Cassian,[94]

[91] See p. 212, n. 84.
[92] Bruns, *Fontes*[7], 103 (=C.I.L. viii, 17896).
[93] Symm. *Rel.* 29. *Cod. Just.* xi, xi, 2 (dated by Seeck to 371–3) suggests that an attempt at deflation had recently been made, but apparently without lasting success. [Cf. p. 205.]　　　[94] *Inst. Mon.* iv, 14.

writing in the early fifth century in Latin for a western public, speaks of a cheap loaf costing 3 denarii in Egypt, he is thinking of three copper coins, which an Egyptian would have tariffed at, say, a myriad denarii each. Denarius seems to be synonymous with nummus. In 445 the rate of exchange between the solidus and the nummus was stabilized at 1:7,000–7,200.[95] Writing in about 510, Cassiodorus states that the ancients wished the solidus to be 6,000 denarii.[96]

The copper coinage issued during the fourth century does not by itself suggest a cataclysmic inflation but is not incompatible with it. There were frequent and abundant issues in various denominations in both east and west. All denominations tended to sink in weight in successive issues, and periodically a fresh start was made with a heavier coin, which in its turn dwindled in size. This in itself suggests that the currency was being steadily debased, but to account for the scale of inflation revealed by the papyri one must assume that successive issues of coins were tariffed at higher and higher values reckoned in denarii.

It might seem at first that the process of altering the nominal value of successive issues of coins without indicating this fact in any way on the coins themselves would have led to inextricable confusion. The papyri, however, prove that the Egyptians were able to cope with the situation. In general the imperial government does not seem to have tried to demonetise or withdraw old issues. Only two attempts are recorded. A mid-fourth-century constitution alludes[97] to certain types of *pecunia* as being banned, probably those issued before the new [and better] series inaugurated in 348. Another constitution of 395[98] prohibits the circulation of the *decargyrus nummus* [see *L.R.E.* 439]. It may be doubted whether these laws were very effective; to judge by hoards, coins of all different dates circulated together. It seems likely that the older coins were rated by the money changers according to their size and weight and commanded a market value based on the official valuation of the current issue. Thus the large coins

---

[95] Val. *Nov.* xvi. [In *L.R.E.* 440 Jones points also to the depreciation of the follis, cf. ch. 14; this supports his view that there was in reality no marked contrast between east and west.]

[96] Cassiodorus, *Variae*, I, 10, §5.

[97] *Cod. Theod.* IX, xxiii, 1. The date given the code (356) is rejected by Mommsen and Seeck, but on inadequate grounds.

[98] *Cod. Theod.* IX, xxiii, 2 (395).

surviving from earlier reigns would pass current as multiples of the minute nummi issued in the last years of the fourth century.[99] If this was what happened, it helps to explain the rapidity of the inflationary process: for every time the government increased the face value of a new issue, the whole of the copper coinage in circulation would be revalued in sympathy.

After the death of Theodosius the Great in 395 issues of copper almost cease, and those of silver become very rare: the coins already circulating, supplemented by unofficial imitations, had to serve for currency for eighty years in the west, and for a century in the east. In these circumstances one would expect the inflation to cease and even to recede. This seems to have been the case. In the west, the denarius or nummus stood at about 12,000 to the solidus in 419, had risen to about 7,000 in 445 (when the imperial government forbade the sale of solidi *under* that price), and later was stabilised at 6,000, if Cassiodorus be taken to mean that this figure had been official in his day for some considerable time. For the east we have unfortunately no fifth-century figures from Egypt, but by the sixth century the denarius had at any rate not greatly depreciated from the lowest values recorded in the fourth: we possess quotations of 5,200 and 7,200 myriads for the sixth century, as against 6,000 (inferred) for the end of the fourth.[100]

It remains to be considered why the denarius was inflated at so prodigious a rate in the mid-fourth century. During this period [most large private transactions were now carried out in solidi: the ever rising flood of denarii was confined to everyday market transactions.][101] Government expenditure was to a very large extent either in kind or in gold and silver, and was supplied by corresponding levies in kind and the precious metals. The heaviest item in the budget, the *annona* and *capitus* of troops and officials, was paid in foodstuffs, which were levied in kind from the provincials under the annual *indictio*. The *vestis* of soldiers and officials was also usually issued in kind; the garments needed were

[99] This conjecture is supported by the character of the reformed coinage of the late fifth century (see p. 220 below).

[100] *P. Oxy.* 1911, 2195, 1917. [Cassiod. *Variae* J, 10.]

[101] [In his later essay Jones wrote: 'I confess that I do not fully understand how and why this astronomic inflation took place but I will tentatively suggest some factors in its development'; a briefer exposition of the views in the text follows. Cf. *L.R.E.* 441ff.]

either produced in the state factories or levied from the provincials. Public works, in so far as they were not built by forced labour from requisitioned materials, seem to have been paid for in gold.[102] The other main items of expenditure, the accession and quinquennial donatives to the troops, were paid in gold and silver,[103] raised by concurrent levies of *aurum oblaticium*, *aurum coronarium* and the *collatio lustralis*. Gold was also probably used for the more casual benefactions of the emperor: the treasury of the *res privata*, fed by the gold rents of the imperial lands, supplied this need. The *navicularii* were paid partly in corn, partly in solidi.[104] The lime-burners and carters of Rome received one solidus per load.[105]

It is not easy at first sight to discern how the government expended its copper issues, or if it did not expend them, how it put them into circulation; and yet unless the government had some urgent motive for putting excessive quantities of denarii into circulation, whether by spending them or by some other method, the great inflation would not have taken place.

One use for the copper issues may have been the annual pay of the troops. Under Diocletian soldiers certainly received, in addition to their *annona*, *capitus* and *vestis* in kind, *stipendium et donativum* in *denarii communes*:[106] this *donativum* is probably to be distinguished from the accession and quinquennial donative, which seems to have been in gold and silver, and was probably an annual bonus on pay. This pay in denarii continued under Constantine: a pay statement of a *praepositus* of that reign survives, showing that he received 36,000 denarii in *stipendium* and 2,500 in *donativum*.[107] Julian, in his letter to Constantius II after his proclamation as Augustus in 360, complains that his troops had received no *annuum stipendium* during his reign as Caesar.[108] Mamertinus speaks of his anxiety when appointed *comes sacrarum largitionum* by Julian in 361 over the arrears of *stipendium*.[109] Julian

---

[102] Symm. *Rel.* 26 gives an estimate in solidi for repairing a bridge.

[103] The accession donative of 5 solidi and a pound of silver is frequently attested from Julian onwards: Amm. Marc. xx, iv, 18 (360); Const. Porph. *de caerim.* 412B (457), 432B (473), 423, 425B (491), 429B (518). The quinquennial donative of 5 solidi is recorded only by Proc. *Anecd.* xxiv, 27–9.

[104] *Cod. Theod.* xiii, v, 7 (334).   [105] *Cod. Theod.* xiv, vi, 3 (365).

[106] *Ed. Diocl.* preamble.

[107] *P. Oxy.* 1047.

[108] Amm. Marc. xx, viii, 8.

[109] *Pan. Vet.* iii (xi), 1.

found the imperial barber at Constantinople was receiving, besides 20 *annonae* and 20 *capitus*, *annum stipendium grave*.[110] Gregory Nazianzen describes how Julian, handing out royal gifts to the army, at either the regular annual distribution or one specially devised for the purpose, associated the payment with pagan sacrifice.[111] We are not told in any of these cases that the payment was in denarii, and indeed Gregory speaks of gold. But though gold may have been paid to the imperial guard—Julian could not personally have paid the whole army—the ordinary soldier must have received his meagure pay in denarii. There is only one later allusion to *stipendium*, and that not a certain one, early in the reign of Valentinian I, when the tribune and notary Palladius was sent to Africa 'ut et militi disperso per Africam praeberet stipendium debitum'; the money is subsequently called *stipendium* or *donativum* indifferently by Ammianus.[112] This might refer to a delayed accession donative, but the use of the term *stipendium* suggests that arrears of annual pay are meant. The date when annual cash pay was abolished is uncertain, but if it was for the most part paid in denarii, it would be natural to infer that it ceased when the imperial government ceased to issue copper on a large scale, on the death of Theodosius the Great.[113]

There is very little trace of the government collecting taxation in denarii after the reigns of Galerius and Maximin, who appear to have levied the *capitatio*—or at any rate the *capitatio* which they imposed on the urban population—in copper.[114] After Maximin's death the *capitatio* of the *plebs urbana* was abolished[115]—to be later replaced by a tax in gold and silver, the *collatio lustralis*—and the *capitatio* of the *plebs rustica* was paid in kind.[116] Every issue of pay

---

[110] Amm. Marc. xxii, iv, 9.

[111] *Contra Julianum* 1 (*Or.* iv), 82–4.

[112] Amm. Marc. xxxviii, vi, 12; cf. 17, 19.

[113] In marginalia Jones cites Amm. Masc. xv, vi, 3; xvii, xi, 5 f. and xxvi, viii 6, which connect payments of gold or silver with *stipendium* or *donativum*; I judge from L.R.E. 623f. that he held that they must refer to extraordinary donatives. P.A.B.

[114] Lactantius, *de mort. pers.* xxiii: 'post hoc pecuniae pro capitibus pendebantur'. Cf. Arcadius Charisius in *Dig.* L, iv, 18, §8: 'exactores pecuniae pro capitibus', and the series of receipts for ἐπικεφάλαιον πόλεως in *P.S.I.* 163, 302, 462, 780, dating from 301 to 315.

[115] *Cod. Theod.* xiii, x, 2.

[116] Riccobono, *Fontes Juris Rom. AnteJust.*, i, 83, *Année Epigr.* 1937, 232 (the Table of Brigetio, A.D. 311): 'quinque capita . . . ex censu atque a praestationibus sollemnibus annonariae pensitationis excusent eademque immunia habeant'; 'ab annonario titulo duo kapita excusent, id est tam suum quam etiam uxoris suae'.

to the troops must therefore have been newly minted coin and have been added, without any compensating withdrawal, to the denarius currency in circulation. This would lead to a steady inflation, and prices would have risen continuously as reckoned in denarii. To the government, whose finances were based on gold and on issues and levies in kind, the steady depreciation of the denarius was not of any great moment. No doubt from time to time the *stipendium* had to be raised when its value became quite derisory, but the difficulty was met by assigning higher face values to the next issue of coins.

[In general ancient governments put money into circulation by spending it. New coins were paid out to the troops, or spent on buying supplies. Since however most government payments were on a fairly large scale, and made in gold and silver, it could not put much copper into circulation in this way. What it did was to sell copper coins to money changers, who were usually licensed and sometimes held a monopoly, and were organised in guilds, and to demand payment from them in silver and gold. This benefited all parties. The public wanted small change, the government was very happy to supply a token currency if it thereby acquired gold and silver coins at a cheap rate. The government was, it seems, more eager than the public, and supplied an excess of copper. Even in the second and early third centuries denarii in Asia Minor, which were officially tariffed at 16 asses, were actually exchanged for 18 or more asses. There was evidently a glut of copper. From the last quarter of the fourth century A.D. we have explicit evidence of this policy at Rome] in the way in which Symmachus speaks of the *collectarii* of Rome: 'vendendis solidis, quos plerumque publicus usus exposcit, collectariorum corpus obnoxium est, quibus arca vinaria statutum pretium subministrat.'[117] The guild of money changers was, that is, under the obligation of selling solidi to the government, being paid in denarii at a fixed tariff from the *arca vinaria*,[118] presumably the account into which was paid the money accruing from government sales of wine in Rome; the small change thus received was of no use to the treasury, which accordingly supplied it to the

[117] *Rel.* 29.
[118] Otherwise mentioned only in *Cod. Theod.* xiv, vi, 3 (365), when a payment (in solidi) is made to the *calcis coctores* 'ex eius vini pretio . . . quod consuevit ex arca vinaria ministrari'. Cf. xiv, vi, 1 (359) for an earlier payment in actual wine, and xiv, iv, 4 (367) for a similar payment in wine to the *suarii*.

collectarii to purchase solidi on government account. We have no evidence that this technique was applied to newly minted denarii, but it is perhaps suggestive that there were 'provincial gold-buyers' (ἐθνικοὶ χρυσῶναι: the office is attested only by Egyptian papyri, but that is no reason to assume that it did not exist elsewhere).[119] These officials are only recorded to have banked taxes in gold, but their title implies a wider function, and it may be that they were responsible for buying gold from the *collectarii* against issues of denarii. If this practice was general, it would also have added to the stock of denarii in circulation without any counterbalancing withdrawal.

The technique described above would have been highly profitable to the government, which increased its stock of gold, in which it reckoned its wealth, at the cost of inflating the copper currency, which affected its finances little. It is indeed difficult to see why, if it had during the fourth century exploited this device, it should have ceased to do so in the fifth. It is, however, noticeable that by the beginning of the fifth century the gold currency seems to have been abundant, and that the government was beginning to commute the levies of *annona* into gold taxes:[120] in Africa the process seems to have been complete by 445, when Valentinian III reckons the taxes in gold, or *annona* commuted into gold, and in Italy by the time of Majorian, who in his Novels (458) assumes that all the annual *indictio* is collected in solidi;[121] in the east Anastasius made χρυσοτέλεια τῶν ἰούγων the general rule.[122] It may be that in view of the increase in its gold revenue from taxation, the government ceased to find it worth while to make further issues of denarii in order to buy solidi.

The abundance of gold may also have led to the virtual abandonment of the silver currency. It is noteworthy that for some twenty years before the silver issues fall off the government seems to have levied the *collatio lustralis* wholly in gold and no

---

[119] Wilcken, *Grundzüge*, pp. 164–5.

[120] The earliest allusion to the payment of land tax in gold seems to be the *auraria praestatio* of *Cod. Theod.* xi, i, 19 (384) in the east; for the west (Africa) see *Cod. Theod.* xi, i, 32 (412) and 34 (429). By 436 commutation into gold seems to have been a fairly commonly granted privilege in the east (*Cod. Theod.* xi, i, 37; cf. Theodoret, *Ep.* 42, who states that 15,000 of the 60,000 *iuga* of Cyrrhus became χρυστελής under Isidore, praetorian prefect of the east in 435–6).

[121] Val. *Nov.* xiii; Maj. *Nov.* ii, 3; vii, 14, 16.

[122] John Malalas, 394B.

longer in gold and silver: it would seem to have been deliberate policy to abandon silver and concentrate on gold.[123]

From the year 473 large copper coins were [again] issued at Rome bearing a mark of value, the figure XL, together with smaller pieces marked XX, X and V. Similar but rather lighter coins were issued at Carthage under the Vandal kings, marked N XLII, N XXI and N XII, presumably meaning 42, 21 and 12 nummi. It may be assumed that the units on the Roman coins also represent nummi, in which case the large pieces will have stood at 180 to the solidus, if Valentinian's III's [rate of 7,200 nummi to the solidus] was still enforced, or more probably at 150 to the solidus, if Cassiodorus's statement (n. 100) is to be referred to this period. The largest coins of each series bear an obvious resemblance in size and weight to Diocletian's nummi and to dupondii (half sesterces) of the early Empire. This suggests that the reformers took as their model old coins which were still in circulation and popular. They seem to have tariffed the new coins at the current valuation of the old coins in terms of the little nummi which formed the bulk of the copper currency: this would account for the very odd and inconvenient figure of forty-two adopted in Africa.[124]

In Africa the Vandal kings later issued small silver coins, weighing 2, 1 and $\frac{1}{2}$ a scruple (that is, at 144, 288 and 576 to the pound), marked DN C, DN L and DN XXV respectively. [The unit marked DN must have stood at 2,880 to the solidus and if, as is probable, the pound of silver was valued at 5 solidi, then, since the contemporary rate for nummi was 14,400, it must have been equivalent to 5 nummi.][125]

In 498 Anastasius followed the lead of Rome and Carthage by issuing substantial copper coins marked M (40), K (20), I (10) and E (5). These pieces were known, according to a contemporary chronicler, in Latin as terunciani, in Greek as follares.[126] There

---

[123] Cod. Theod. XIII, i, de lustrali collatione, laws 1 (356), 4 (362), 6 (364) and 8 (370) all speak, of gold and silver, whereas laws 9 (372), 11 (379), 15 (386), 17 (399), 18 (400), 19 (403), 20 (410) and 21 (418) all mention gold alone; only in I. v. 14 (405) is silver mentioned during this period as forming part of the collatio lustralis. The name χρυσάργυρον survives in Greek, but the tax was in the later fifth century certainly collected in gold only (Joshua Stylites, XXXI).

[124] [See P. Grierson, J.R.S. XLIX, 73 ff., to whom Jones expressed his debt for this suggestion.]

[125] I have substituted Jones' words in L.R.E. 444 for the original text, as he clearly changed his view.   [126] Marcellinus Comes, s.a. 498.

survive two separate series of these coins. One is rather smaller and very much lighter than the corresponding Roman coins; the other is both larger and heavier; the lighter series was issued by no later emperor. It seems likely that the two series, which are readily distinguishable at sight, were intended to be of different values, and that, therefore, the unit marked on the larger series was different from that marked on the smaller. The small M coins, which, though considerably lighter, are not much smaller than the Italian XL coins, may well have been intended to represent, like them, 40 nummi, and have been issued for use in areas where that unit was commonly used. The unit on the larger M coins may perhaps have been the myriad of denarii by the Egyptian reckoning. This is suggested by the following facts. Justinian, according to Procopius,[127] lowered the hitherto prevailing rate of 210 folles to the solidus to 180: the change is probably to be associated with his reform of the copper coinage in 538, when he raised the weight of the follis by over 25 per cent. Before 538, then, 8,400 units went to the solidus; after 538, 7,200. Now an undated papyrus of the sixth century quotes a rate of 7,200 myriads to the solidus.[128] It would seem likely therefore that the Egyptians reckoned the units on the large folles as representing a myriad. This theory involves the consequence that the follis must have depreciated very considerably since its first issue by Anastasius. For if the smaller M coins were intended to represent 40 nummi they must have been originally issued at 150 to 180 to the solidus, and the larger M coins must have been tariffed at twice this value at least, to judge by their weight and size. The large follis must therefore have dropped from about 80 to 210 between 496 and 538. In the east the follis seems to have appreciated yet further in the latter part of Justinian's reign, for a papyrus dated 557[129] reckons 5,200 myriads, that is 130 folles, to the solidus.

In Italy Justinian, during the latter part of his reign, issued small silver coins, which, to judge by their weight, were probably struck at 240 and 480 to the pound. These issues are marked CN (250) and PKE (125) respectively, and must presumably have been meant to represent 250 and 125 nummi. As the pound of silver was at this date tariffed at 5 solidi, about 12,000 nummi must have

[127] Proc. *Anecd.* xxv, 12, [cf. p. 203, n. 44.]
[128] *P. Oxy,* 1917.
[129] *P. Oxy.* 1911.

gone to the solidus; that is, the nummus must have depreciated to half its value under the Ostrogothic kings. The explanation may be that Justinian on the conquest introduced his own eastern monetary system, reckoning his *folles* as representing 40 double nummi, as Anastasius may well have reckoned his heavier series, and thereby marking down the surviving Ostrogothic xl coins to half *folles*. By this procedure, since the *follis* was tariffed after 538 at 180 to the solidus, the Italian nummus will have been halved in value.

The reformed copper currency issued in Italy under Odovacar and in Africa under the Vandal kings, and finally adopted in the eastern empire by Anastasius, was no doubt a boon to the public. There must have been a growing lack of the small change needed for everyday transactions, and the money current must have been very inconvenient to handle, a mixture of issues of varying sizes, including many unofficial imitations. That Anastasius's copper coinage was welcomed by the masses is stated by a contemporary chronicler—'nummis quos Romani teruncianos vocant, Graeci follares, Anastasius princeps suo nomine figuratis placabilem plebi commutationem distraxit'.[130] But the governments which issued the new coins may have had fiscal motives also. Anastasius, as the chronicler says, sold (*distraxit*) his new coins to the public, that is, he bought solidi with them, and bought them cheap; for the minting cost of the number of *folles* at which the solidus was tariffed must have been very substantially below a solidus. The coins show that the government from time to time succumbed to the temptation of increasing their profit by reducing the size of the *follis*—and no doubt issuing it in greater quantities. This tendency was, however, checked periodically, when the *follis* was restored to its original weight, or even made heavier than Anastasius's first issue. The exchange rates extant show considerable fluctuations, but within a reasonable range, and it would appear that the government on the whole restricted its copper issues to an amount which did not seriously disturb the balance, and were able effectively to control the exchange rate. They thus established what approximated to a fiduciary copper coinage. The copper issues, though intrinsically worth much less, were accepted as equivalent to the fraction of the solidus for which they were exchanged, a fraction which though not absolutely fixed varied only within reasonable limits.

[130] See p. 221, n. 126.

The inflation of the third century was of a normal type. It resulted from the debasement and multiplication of the standard coin of the Empire, the denarius, and its progress was relatively slow. It is interesting for four of its effects. By driving gold out of circulation it substantially reduced its price, relatively to other goods. It forced the government, whose fiscal system was too rigid to adapt itself to the rising prices, to abandon the use of money for most purposes and fall back on levies and issues in kind. It led to the introduction of an annual budget. It permanently and drastically reduced official salaries in real value. The inflation of the fourth century was more peculiar. The Empire now possessed two currencies, gold and copper. The copper currency was inflated at a speed and to a degree paralleled only in modern times, and by a method, it would seem, analogous to that of the printing press, by arbitrarily assigning ever increasing face values to the coins. At the same time the gold currency was carefully kept up to standard in weight and purity, and gradually increased in volume until the government was enabled to commute levies and issues in kind into gold payments. The government during this period seems to have made the best of both worlds. Its own finances were based on the stable gold solidus, and it was therefore indifferent to the fate of the copper denarius, which it inflated recklessly. The purpose of this inflation remains somewhat obscure, but it would appear that the government issued vast quantities of denarii partly to cover army pay and partly to buy solidi on the open market. By the end of the fourth century the denarius had sunk so low that the government abandoned its issue. But meanwhile it had built up the gold currency, bringing more and more gold into circulation by heavy taxes and, if I am right, by purchase. Eventually, towards the end of the fifth century, a new copper currency was provided for the use of the ordinary citizen, whose needs had been completely neglected during the inflationary period and during the cessation of all copper issues which followed.

[The ancients had very little idea of economics. They were aware that in a shortage of goods prices tended to go up, but they were unaware that the same thing happened if money was overabundant. To them the value of a coin depended entirely on its metal content. So when Diocletian found prices still rising despite good harvests, and this though he had recently issued silver washed copper *nummi* of superior quality, he was filled with indignation against merchants, to whose insatiable avarice he attributed the rise. It would have seemed irrelevant to him that his mints were turning out floods of new nummi.

Ancient governments ought on their own premises to have realised that debasing the coinage would cause prices to rise, but they seem to have hoped to get by with it. At any rate the emperors, as we have seen, did nothing to adjust public finance to price rises caused by debasement, raising neither taxes nor pay of government employees. This was no doubt partly because the price rises were owing to the primitive technology of the ancient world very gradual. A printing press can produce millions of notes in a few hours. A coin had to be hammered out on an anvil, even if it was a tiny copper piece, and required a piece of metal, which had to be mined. The number of mints and the number of workshops in each mint were greatly increased in the third century but even a much larger labour force could only turn out coins rather slowly.

The device of assigning higher nominal values to coins made a much more rapid expansion of the currency possible. It was first used with caution; the Antoninianus under Caracalla only raised the nominal value of the coinage by $33\frac{1}{3}$ per cent and Aurelian's nummus by 150 per cent. Here again the emperors must have been fully conscious of what they were doing, as is shown by Diocletian's devaluation of the Aurelianic nummus.

The astronomical inflation which began with Constantine and continued to the latter part of the fourth century must have been entirely caused by this technique. There is some indication that the government was occasionally shocked by the rise in prices and the miserable condition of the copper currency. A new and superior issue of copper coins was made in 348 and in 356 an attempt was made to call in all older coins. About ten years later the emperor fixed a lower exchange rate between the copper coin and the solidus and expressed the hope that the prices of goods would fall concurrently.

But the government had by now very little reason to trouble its head about the copper currency. Its own taxes and most of its outgoings were either in kind or in gold. It used denarii only for the pay of the troops, which had long been token. The incomes of the upper classes were in gold and their capital consisted of land or gold. Denarii were used mainly by the poor for day to day transactions. Ancient governments had always regarded the currency not as a medium of exchange between their citizens, but as a means of meeting state needs. They had also to pay some attention to politically important classes like the nobility and the army. These were now provided for by issues in kind and some gold and silver payments; soldiers received a donative of 5 *solidi* and a pound of silver on an accession, and 5 *solidi* every five years thereafter. The copper currency was of little interest to the government and could be allowed to run wild.]

Additional Note

As the question is important and controversial, it may be as well to outline the evidence. *P. Ryl.* 607 is a letter, dated on various grounds to about A.D. 300, from an official (who is evidently 'in the know') to a subordinate, instructing him urgently to buy goods at any price with all his (the writer's) Italian money (Ἰταλικὸν ἀργύριον), the reason being that the emperors have ordered the Italian coin to be reduced to half a nummus (προσέταξεν ἡ θεία τύχη τῶν δεσποτῶν ἡμῶν τὸ Ἰταλικόν νόμισμα εἰς ἥμισυ νούμμου καταβιβασθῆναι). It is generally agreed that τό Ἰταλικὸν νόμισμα (or ἀργύριον) means the normal imperial coinage by contrast with the local Alexandrian tetradrachms which ceased to be issued in A.D . 296, that is the Aurelianic xx.i pieces. The most natural interpretation of the phraseology would be that these pieces had hitherto been known as nummi, but were henceforth to be tariffed at half nummi.

P. Oslo, iii, 83, also dated to about A.D. 300, is unfortunately fragmentary. It contains portions of three official letters, of which the third alone concerns us. It is clearly concerned with the regulation of the currency, and alludes to the καθολικός or *rationalis*, the imperial minister who controlled the mints or his local representative in Egypt, and to a πρόγραμμα or public notice issued by some high authority (παρὰ τῆς μεγαλειότη[τος]). The first line speaks of something having reached 25 denarii (ἕως εἰς εἴκοσι πέντε Ἀττικάς) and the third of nummi (being reduced?) to 12½ denarii ([τ]ῶν δὲ νούμμων εἰς δώδεκα ἥμισυ Ἀττικάς). It is hard to resist the conclusion that this document refers to the same operation as *P. Ryl.* 607, and states that the nummus, which had previously been raised to 25 denarii is now reduced to 12½.

P.S.I. 965 is also fragmentary. The opening four lines state that the emperors have issued the *Edictum de Pretiis*, lines 5 and 6 are concerned with currency changes. Line 5 alludes to denarii ('Αττικές), line 6 (τὸ δὲ μέχρι τῆς δεῦρο ἀντὶ τοῦ δύο καὶ δέκα [καὶ ἥμισυ] may indicate that the coin hitherto current is to be valued at twelve (and a half denarii?).

It may be added that some half nummi of Licinius are marked XIIS.

[In *L.R.E.* 438 Jones takes the view that 4 aurei went to 1 lb. of silver and that 24 silver coins must therefore have gone to 1 gold. 'The larger and smaller copper coins were probably tariffed at 5 and 2 denarii respectively, and perhaps 5 of the larger copper coins went to 1 argenteus. The aureus would have been worth 600 denarii and the argenteus 25'. He refers to S. Bolin, *State and Currency in the Roman Empire to* 300 A.D., ch. XII. On this basis 1 lb. of gold=60 aurei was worth 36,000 denarii. Jones, *loc. cit.*, explains the discrepancy with the price of gold in the Edict (50,000 denarii per lb.) by the issue of vast quantities of copper coins, not even plated with silver; hence gold, coined or uncoined, as also silver, rose above its nominal value.]

CHAPTER TEN

CENSUS RECORDS OF THE LATER ROMAN EMPIRE

THERE survive from a number of places in Western Asia Minor and the islands of the Aegean inscriptions recording census registrations. They are undated, but were probably engraved in the late third or early fourth century A.D., when Diocletian and his colleagues and successors are known to have been active in carrying out censuses to serve as the basis of their new system of taxation [cf. *L.R.E.* 61 f.]. All are fragmentary, but some are of sufficient length to yield results of some statistical value on the distribution of landed property, on the density of the agricultural population, and on the proportion of slave to free labour. In view of the extreme paucity of any statistical data for the ancient world they are worth analysis.

These records are drawn up on different systems and each requires separate study. They are, however, all based on certain general principles laid down by imperial enactments. They record quantities of land and of persons and animals on the land. In some inscriptions land is recorded by its agricultural use and areas: arable, vineyard, pasture (these all in *iugera*; one *iugerum* = $\frac{5}{8}$ acre), and olives (these by the individual tree). In one small fragment from Lesbos[1] arable, vineyard, and olives are each divided into two categories according to their quality. In other inscriptions the land is recorded in *iuga*. The *iugum* was a unit of assessment and corresponded to a varying quantity of land according to its use and quality. The Syro-Roman lawbook[2] preserves the schedule established by Diocletian for Syria and still in use there in the late fifth century. Here 1 *iugum* = 20 *iugera* of 1st class arable = 40 *iugera* of 2nd class arable = 60 *iugera* of 3rd class arable = 5 *iugera* of vineyard = 220 *perticae* (= 1.1 *iugera*) of old

---

[1] *I.G.* cf. p. 230 n. 6, XII, ii, 79. This was presumably a refinement found too complicated and soon abandoned.

[2] Riccobono, *Fontes iuris Romani*[2] II (1940), pp. 795–6 (§ 121).

olive trees=450 *perticae* (= 2.25 *iugera*) of mountain olive trees. In Asia Minor the schedule in the early fourth century seems to have been very different. This emerges from an inscription of Thera[3] where an original record in *iugera* of arable and vineyard and in olive trees has been later converted into *iuga*. It is a record of farms lately, it would seem, in the possession of one Paregorius and now divided among his heirs. The original record may be tabulated as follows:

Name of Farm	Arable (*in* iugera)	Vineyard (*in* iugera)	Olive trees	Stock
Property of Euphrosyne, daughter of Paregorius				
A	40	2½ ¼	3	—
B	28½	103	67	—
C	30	—	—	—
D	18	—	27	—
Property of Paregorius according to the declaration of Lucianus				
E	3 1/30	—	30	2 oxen
				1 ass
				8 sheep
Property of the heirs of Paregorius deceased according to the registration of Scepticus: Euporia, Paregorius, Sophronius				
F	60	50	143	—
G	26	8	18	—
H	138	30	286	—
I	6	—	—	—
J	70	10 1/11	6	—

At the end of c. C, which is shorter, have been later inserted the words 'they make 1½ ⅓ $\frac{1}{46}$ *iuga* or *capita*'. At the end of e. D, which is also short, is inserted 'it makes ⅕ $\frac{1}{30}$ $\frac{1}{300}$ *iuga* or *capita*', and in the margin on the right of G and H, '8 $4\frac{1}{5}$ *iuga* or *capita*.'[4]

André Déléage, who analysed this inscription in his *Capitation dans le Bas Empire* 173 ff., failed to perceive the significance of the third entry, and thought that the first applied to farms A, B, C, and second to farm D. It is, however, more probable that each note applies to the property of one owner, the first to farms A–D, the second to farm E, and the third to farms F–J. The position of the first two notes, the one beside and the other over the property to which they respectively refer, is due to exigencies of space.

One figure, as M. Déléage observed, must be wrong, either an engraver's error or a mistake by the modern copyist. If the 103 *iugera* of vineyard in farm B is correct, no reasonable schedule of

---

[3] *I.G.* xii, iii, 343.

[4] (C) ἔχουσιν: κζ α ⟨γ′ μς : (D) ἔχι κζ ε′λ′τ′ : (G and H) $\frac{κζ}{ημε}$.

values will work; for vineyard must have been much more valuable than arable. If this figure be corrected to $9\frac{1}{3}$ (which is epigraphically plausible)[5] it is possible to make a reasonable guess at the approximate schedule. The problem may be summarised as follows:

Arable	Vineyard	Olives	Stock	iuga
$116\frac{1}{2}$ +	$12\frac{1}{12}$ +	97 +	0 =	$1\frac{1}{2}\ \frac{1}{3}\ \frac{1}{48}$ (1.8551)
$3\frac{1}{50}$ +	0 +	30 +	2 oxen	
			1 ass	
			8 sheep $= \frac{1}{15}\ \frac{1}{30}\ \frac{1}{300}$ (.2366)	
300 +	$98\frac{1}{11}$ +	453 +	0 =	$8\frac{1}{45}$ (8.0202)

If one *iugum* be equated with 100 *iugera* of arable *or* 24 *iugera* of vineyard *or* 480 olive trees, the sum works out approximately (leaving about $\frac{1}{7}$ *caput* or *iugum* for the animals on farm E), though it seems impossible to reconstruct the arithmetical processes whereby the *tabularius* reached his curious fractions. The figures must at any rate be of this order of magnitude.

The persons and animals are similarly in some inscriptions recorded individually in detail, in others converted into *capita*. The *caput* was, like the *iugum*, an ideal unit of assessment and was equal in value to the *iugum*, as is shown by one inscription in which the numbers of *iuga* (ζύγα) and *capita* (κεφαλαί) on each farm are added together to a total of *iuga vel capita* (ζυγοκεφαλαί).[6] Animals were evidently rated at small fractions if 2 oxen, 1 ass, and 8 sheep added up to about $\frac{1}{7}$ of a *caput*. Unfortunately there is only one clue in the inscriptions to indicate how many human beings went to a *caput*. A declaration from Hypaepa[7] runs: 'Aurelius Synodius son of Dracontius, Hypaepene resident in my own house—myself, aged 20: total 1.' Two early-fourth century imperial constitutions[8] clearly imply that a woman like a man was rated at a full *caput*, in the areas at any rate to which these constitutions applied, that is Illyricum and Oriens. In Egypt it would seem that according to immemorial custom only males

---

[5] The printed text gives ΡΓ; ΘΓ' would mean $9\frac{1}{3}$.

[6] *I.G.* XII, iii, 180, as read by Déléage, *La Capitation dans le Bas Empire*, pp. 190–4.

[7] Keil and Premerstein, 'Dritte Reise in Lydien', *Denkschr. Ak. Wien* 1914, no. 85.

[8] 'Table of Brigetio' (311), Riccobono, *Fontes iuris Romani* I² (1940) 93, 'ab annonario titulo duo kapita excusent, id est tam suum quam uxoris suae', *Cod. Theod.* VII, xx, 4 (325), 'duo capita excusaturis, id est suum atque uxoris'. The first was published at Brigetio in Pannonia (where the inscription was found), the second at Antioch (the title of the recipient Maximus is wrongly given as PU in the Codex: he was probably *vicarius Orientis*, see Seeck, *Regesten*, p. 118).

were registered.[9] On the other hand a constitution of 386[10] addressed to the praetorian prefect of the East announces that, whereas formerly one man or two women were reckoned as one *caput*, four women or two-and-a-half men now count as such, and orders the prefect to apply this rule to certain cities of the Pontic diocese then being reassessed by a *peraequator*. We cannot be certain what scale of values applied in our inscriptions, but it is likely to have been one *caput* = 1 man = two women. In that case, assuming the sexes were equally balanced, one *caput* would on an average represent $1\frac{1}{3}$ persons. Small chidren, down to two years old, are registered in some inscriptions[11] but it is certain that they were not technically *censiti*. The age at which they became liable to tax seems to have varied in different districts; in Syria it was 12 for females and 14 for males. There was also an upper age limit, which was 65 for both sexes in Syria.[12]

All the census records save one which are preserved are concerned with the estates of landlords who were not cultivators. It is a matter of some importance to determine what categories of persons were registered on these estates. Those recorded include rural slaves and free tenants. Rural slaves could in the early fourth century be sold apart from the land they cultivated, but it so had to be entered in the census of their new owner[13] and could not be withdrawn by the owner from agricultural employment.[14]

[9] This was the rule of the λαογραφία of the principate (Wilcken, *Grundzüge*, p. 189). That it remained the rule after Diocletian is a fairly certain inference from the fact that the nine persons declared by Aurelius Sacaon in 310 (Wilcken, *Chrestomathie* 210, cf. also *S.B.* 7673) are all males. The corresponding tax in early Arab times, ἀνδρισμός (the name is now proved by *P. Ryl.* iv, 658, to date back to the fourth century), certainly fell on males only (see Bell in the introduction to *P. Lond.* iv, 1419).

[10] *Cod. Theod.* xiii, xi, 2.

[11] *I.G.* xii, iii, 343, 346; Keil and Premerstein, l.c. (see note 7).

[12] *Dig.* l, xv, 3. This citation from Ulpian was presumably preserved by the compilers of the *Digest* because still valid. The edict of Aurelius Optatus (*S.B.* 7622) shows that Diocletian in 297 laid down lower and upper age limits for Egypt, but they are not known, save that in Aurelius Isidore's declaration (*S.B.* 7673) a boy of 3 is exempt (ἀτέλης) but in Aurelius Sacaon's (*Chr.* i, 210) one of 12 pays tax (ὑποτέλης) and a man of 55 is still liable.

[13] *Cod. Theod.* xi, iii, 2 (327), 'mancipia adscripta censibus intra provinciae terminos distrahantur, et qui emptione dominium nancti fuerint inspiciendum sibi esse cognoscant'.

[14] *Cod. Theod.* vii, i, 3 (341), 'quicumque militum ex nostra auctoritate familias suas ad se venire meruerint, non amplius quam coniugia liberos servos etiam de peculio castrensi emptos neque adscriptos censibus ad eosdem excellentia tua dirigi faciat'.

In the inscriptions they are sometimes recorded on the separate farms[15] but sometimes segregated under a special heading, either with a note of their domicile[16] or under the rubric 'on the land'.[17] From 371 rural slaves were tied to the actual land which they cultivated and could only be sold with it.[18] Free tenants (*coloni*) were registered in their landlord's census only if they owned no land of their own, and in this case the landlord was (from 371) responsible for collecting the tax due on their *capita*. If on the other hand a *colonus* owned even the smallest plot of land he was registered independently ('proprio nomine') in the census and his capitation tax was (after as before 371) collected by a public official.[19] It must therefore be borne in mind that the *capita* registered in our lists do not necessarily represent all the manpower employed on the land, since some farms are likely to have been let to adjacent small freeholders. Tenants entered on the census ('coloni adscripti censibus') of their landlord were tied to their farms, and are accordingly always entered on individual farms on the lists. Other tenants were apparently entered on their village census ('adscripti vico'),[20] but not tied to the farm they leased.

One further point needs noting. In registers which reckon in *iuga* and *capita* only the landlord's animals appear separately rated, or sometimes totalized with his slaves.[21] Tenants' animals are, as

---

[15] At Chios (Déléage, o.c., pp. 182–6) and Lesbos (*I.G.* xii, ii, 76d, 78c).

[16] At Tralles (*B.C.H.* 1880, 336–8).

[17] At Thera (*I.G.* xii, iii, 343).

[18] *Cod. Just.* xi, xlviii, 7 (371), 'quemadmodum originarios absque terra ita rusticos censitosque servos vendi omnifariam non licebit'.

[19] *Cod. Theod.* xi, i, 14 (371), 'penes quos fundorum dominia sunt, pro his colonis originalibus quos in locis isdem censos esse constabit vel per se vel per actores proprios recepta compulsionis sollicitudine implenda munia functionis agnoscant. sane quibus terrarum erit quantulacumque possessio, qui in suis conscribti locis proprio nomine libris censualibus detinentur, ab huius praecepti communione discernimus, eos enim convenit propriae commissos mediocritati annonarias functiones sub solito exactore cognoscere'.

[20] *Cod. Theod.* xi, xxiv, 6 (415).

[21] At Chios (Déléage, o.c. pp. 182–6) some farms have παροίκων κεφαλαί only (*coloni*, clearly including their animals, since they must have had some), others have παροίκων κεφαλαί and δούλων κεφαλαί and ζώων κεφαλαί. At Tralles (*B.C.H.* 1880, pp. 336–8) the figures of κεφαλαί attached to each farm clearly include animals, since they contain small fractions. Some owners record above their farms δούλων καί ζώων κεφαλαί and some ζώων κεφαλαί as well. The former are animals in charge of the slaves, the latter presumably animals supplied for the use of the *coloni*. In this list some owners have a fractional figure of ζώων κεφαλαί immediately after their names. These are presumably animals kept at the owner's residence in town. The other animals are specified as being on this or that farm.

appears from the small fractions recorded, added to the *capita* of their owners. Similarly in census lists which record individuals some animals (the landlord's) are recorded with the slaves, some with the families of the tenants.[22] Tenant's slaves, if any, would presumably be on the same principle included in their owner's *capitatio*: no such slaves appear on the detailed registers. These facts are unlikely greatly to affect the statistical value of *capita* either in reckoning the number of persons they represent or the proportion of slaves to free men, since animals were rated at very small fractions of a *caput*, and tenants, judging by the detailed records, owned few animals and no slaves.

One fact emerges at a first glance at the lists—the fragmentation of agricultural property. The landlords concerned, some considerable, some of medium wealth, do not as a rule own large continuous estates but a great number of scattered properties, ranging from large farms to small holdings. The estate of Paregorius,[23] before division between his heirs, amounted in all to 420 *iugera* of arable, 110 *iugera* of vineyard, and 580 olive trees, and was assessed at about 10 *iuga*, but it was composed of 3 largish farms, 5 smaller farms, and 2 small holdings. Another owner in Thera, whose name is lost, but who was somehow connected with one Attalus, a Roman senator,[24] owned more than 20 farms (the list is incomplete at the bottom), all fairly small: for 16 farms whose figures are more or less intact the totals are 560 *iugera* of arable, 121 *iugera* of vineyard, and about 1,500 olive trees, which would have been assessed at about 13¾ *iuga* in all. Another Theran list,[25] incomplete both at top and bottom, records 17 farms of which the 14 whose figures survive total 492½ *iugera* of arable, 72 of vineyard, and 426 olive trees: this would make up 8¾ *iuga*. From Lesbos[26] we possess another list of farms incom-

[22] At Thera (*I.G.* xii, iii, 343, 346). In Lesbos (*I.G.* xii, ii, 76) few farms have animals. Those registered without comment presumably belonged to the land-owner. Other entries of the form βοῦς δ' 'Ελπιδηφόρος· ἵππον δὲ Κυζίκιος καὶ 'Ελπιδηφόρος· presumably mean that Elpidephorus declared 4 oxen and he and Cyzicius 1 horse. Elpidephorus is known as tenant of another farm (*I.G.* xii, ii, 79) which had no pasture. He presumably kept his beasts on a farm of which he was neither owner nor tenant.

[23] *I.G.* xii, iii, 343.

[24] *I.G.* xii, iii, 345. The words at the end of line 1 should be read 'Αττάλου λαμπ (ροτάτου). Excluding the heading 16 lines survive, and some lines seem to contain two farms (ll. 9, 10, 12, and probably 2 and 3). I have omitted lines 2–3 and 14 from my calculations as their figures are incomplete.

[25] *I.G.* xii, iii, 346.   [26] *I.G.* xii, ii, 76.

plete at both ends. The 14 farms whose figures survive total 1,420 *iugera* of arable, 109 of vineyard, 5,200 olive trees, and over 925 *iugera* of pasture. Ignoring the last item, whose valuation is unknown but was probably very low, the total *iugatio* works out at about 30. Eight holdings are small, ranging from 19 to 9 *iugera* of arable and vineyard combined but well stocked with olive trees. Three are of moderate size (two of c. 125, two of c. 65, and one of 52½ *iugera*): the average is brought up by three large arable farms of 429¼, 305$\frac{7}{10}$ and 294⅞.

Turning to lists drawn up in *iuga*, Heracleides[27] of Astypalaea owned about 10½ *iuga* distributed in 8 farms of moderate size and 2 small holdings. At Tralles[28] Critias, a decurion, owned 20½ *iuga* distributed in 7 holdings, two quite small, one of nearly 2 *iuga*, two of 3½ to 4, one of nearly 5, and one of over 6. Latron, another decurion, possessed over 17 *iuga*; of his four farms two were of moderate size, under 2 *iuga* each, another of 6, and another of 8. Fulvius, a priest, owned only about 3¼ *iuga*, comprising one largish farm and one tiny holding. Tatianus, a decurion, is the wealthiest man of these lists, holding over 57½ *iuga* in 14 units. Six of these are quite small (under one *iugum*), three moderate (1½ to 3½), four substantial (just under 5 to just over 6), and one very large (just over 17½).

A similar result emerges from the list at Magnesia on the Maeander.[29] In this the farms are not grouped under their owner's names but in alphabetical order (or rather under their initial letters), with the owner's name, the *iugatio* and the *capitatio* after each. The surviving portions contain 36 farms from letter A, 36 from letter B, 9 from E, and 15 whose initials are lost. Of the 81 farms whose figures survive, 26 are under one *iugum*, 20 between one and two, 8 between two and three, 6 between three and four. There are 8 of over four and under seven, 9 of over eight and under twelve, one of thirteen odd, one of fifteen odd, and one of twenty-one odd *iuga*. Finally there is one huge estate of 75 *iuga*, the property of a Roman senator.

Of the 96 farms recorded some will no doubt have been

[27] *I.G.* xii, iii, 180, as read by Déléage, o.c., pp. 190–4. 190–4.

[28] *B.C.H.* 1880, 336–8.

[29] Kern, *Inschriften von Magnesia am Maeander*, no. 122. In the calculations which follow I have followed the editor's interpretation of the figures except as specified in note 48 below (p. 234).

individual holdings, but a fair number were parts of larger properties. It is notable that in the very small part of the alphabet surviving (and there is reason to believe that even the As and Bs are incomplete),[30] twelve owners, out of about 65 in all, own more than one farm (35 farms between them).[31] Fourteen are citizens of neighbouring cities, Ephesus, Tralles, and Colophon,[32] and almost certainly owned property in their home towns as well. Others are of such high status that they must have owned more than the small lots recorded in the surviving parts of the list. These include three men and two women of senatorial rank[33] (excluding the owner of the 75 *iuga* estate),[34] two *perfectissimi*,[35] one Asiarch,[36] and six styled Philosebasti, which probably means decurions of the city.[37] Severianus the tribune,[38] who is recorded as owning five farms, one of 13+, one of 9+, one of 2+ *iuga* and two without figures, under letters A and B, is likely to have owned some properties in other letters of the alphabet.

The great senatorial estate of 75 *iuga* would be even by modern standards considerable. If the *iugatio* was split evenly between arable on the one hand and vineyards and olives on the other, which seems by the Theran and Lesbian records fairly normal, it might have comprised say 3,200 *iugera* (2,000 acres) of arable, 400 *iugera* (225 acres) of vineyard, and 8,000 olives. This is, however, a quite exceptional estate, four or five times as big as the largest otherwise recorded, 21 *iuga* (Pollio, a decurion of Magnesia),[39]

[30] On book *b* (probably As) there are on the right the initial Bs of a lost column of farms.

[31] Valerianus son of Romus (a 1, e 17–8), Variana (a 10, b 15), Patroina (b 4, e 14, g 3), Paulus philosebastos (a 7, f 7–8, g 4), Pisticus (b 12, 18, d 16–7), Priscillianus v.c. (a 12–3), Severianus the tribune (b 1–2, 9, d 5, e 7), Tychicus son of Eugnomonius (e 4–5, f 6), Tyrannus (e 1 and 3, 12), Tyrannus the Asiarch (e 10–11), Eutychis of Ephesus (d 12, e 13), Philip of Tralles (b 7, g 1).

[32] Trallians, b 7, 14, 16, c 3, d 3; Ephesians, d 4, 8, 12, e 13, 15, f 9, h 2; Colophonian, h 5.

[33] Capitolinus (d 6), Eutychus (d 15), Priscillianus (a 12–3), Aristocleia (b 3), Hermonactiane (d 9).

[34] c 2; of his name only -NUS survives and he may be identical with Capitolinus (d 6).

[35] Maximianus (a 9), Metrodorus (a 5).

[36] Tyrannus (c 10–1).

[37] Heracleides (g 2), Mandrogenes (a 9), Paulus (a 7, f 7–8, g 4), Phanius (f 4), Pollio (d 1), Tychicus (a 8). The council of Magnesia is styled ἡ φιλοσέβαστος βουλή in nos. 179 and 193. Unless Philosebastos means member of the council, the absence of decurions would be strange.

[38] See n. 31.

[39] See n. 37.

17½ (Tatianus, decurion of Tralles),[40] 15½ (a lady named Patroina of Magnesia, who is recorded as owning two other farms, one of 10⅓ and the other of unknown size),[41] and nearly 14 (one of the five recorded holdings of Severianus the tribune).[42] Next come ten farms (nine at Magnesia and one at Tralles) ranging from 8 to under 12, and fifteen from 4 to under 7 (8 at Magnesia and 7 at Tralles). These in their turn have a greater assessable value than all but the largest farms recorded elsewhere; the two biggest farms of Lesbos would have been rated at only about 4¾ to 5.[43] One of these has a large area (430 *iugera* of arable and 240 of pasture), as it contains little vineyard or olives. The other has 250 *iugera* only, but makes up with 1,000 olive trees.

On the density of the agricultural population the detailed inscriptions unfortunately yield virtually no information. They tell us that farm G (Politike) in Paregorius' estate in Thera (26 *iugera* of arable, 8 *iugera* of vineyard, and 18 olive trees) was cultivated by one *colonus* (Theodorus, aged 30) and his wife, aged 20: he had a baby daughter, aged 2, and one ox and some (ten?) sheep.[44] His farm would be rated at ⅝ of a *iugum*, its population at 1½+if his wife was reckoned as a half. At Lesbos[45] on the other hand, a *colonus* named Dionysius (the size of his family is not recorded) leased two farms, whose total area was 105 *iugera* arable, 10⅔ vineyard, 216 plus an unknown number of olives, and 70 *iugera* of pasture. A man of the same name had a half interest in another farm containing 119 *iugera* of second class plus an unknown quantity of first class arable, 1 *iugerum* of vineyard, 138 olive trees, and 75 *iugera* of pasture. The two farms would be rated at 2 or little more *iuga*, the third at 1½ at least. Dionysius then (with his family) cultivated at least 2 and perhaps as much as 3 *iuga*. Another *colonus*, Elpidephorus (family again unknown), held a farm of 25 *iugera* of arable, more than 4 *iugera* of vineyard and 1,009 olive trees—close on 5 *iuga*. He also apparently owned four oxen and a half share in a horse, which he kept in another farm, having no pasture of his own.

We have therefore to rely on censuses which are assessed in

[40] See n. 28.
[41] See n. 31.
[42] See n. 31.
[43] *I.G.* xii, ii, 76*a*, 79.
[44] *I.G.* xii, iii, 343.
[45] *I.G.* xii, ii, 79. Elpidephorus' animals appear on no. 76e.

iuga and *capita*, and any results will depend on the validity of the conversion scale into *iuga* worked out earlier in this paper, and on the definitions of a *caput* given in the Code. On the census of Heracleides of Astypalaea[46] his eight farms are assessed first in total of *iuga+capita* (ζκ), then in *iuga* of land (γῆς ζ) and thirdly in *capita* of human beings (ἀνθρ' κ): the last heading must include animals as the entries contain fractions down to $\frac{1}{500}$, $\frac{1}{700}$, and $\frac{1}{850}$. In this list land to the value of 10½ *iuga* corresponds to about 13¼ *capita*, of which a maximum of 11½ (the sum of the integers plus halves) can represent human beings. Every farm (as opposed to the two small holdings, which were presumably worked by neighbouring freeholders) has its *capita*. These may not represent their whole agricultural manpower, for one farm of 1½ *iuga* has only ¾ *capita*. It seems unlikely that one woman (½ *caput*; the remaining ¼ is presumably animals) can have culitvated it single-handed and she may have sublet part of the farm to neighbouring freeholders or tenants of other estates, who would be registered in their villages or under other landlords; or she may have employed hired labour from similar sources. But even if two or three *capita* be added, the ratio would work out at an average of only about 1⅓ *capita* or 1¾ persons to the *iugum*.

Similar results emerge for the registers at Tralles.[47] The priest Fulvius has 4 *capita* (omitting the smaller fractions) on his 3⅕ *iuga*; curiously enough there are only 1½ on his 3 *iuga* farm, and 2½ on his tiny plot of one-fifth of a *iugum*. The great landlord Tatianus has a maximum of 65¼ human *capita* on his 51½ *iuga*. Their distribution is curious. In the village of Monnara, where he owned slightly less than one *iugum*, he registers more than 3½ *capita* of slaves and animals, nearly 4 *capita* of animals, and over 15½ *capita* of free tenants (with their animals). Monnara was evidently a centre at which Tatianus housed his tenants and slaves

[46] *I.G.* xii, iii, 180. There is a mysterious fourth column of figures on the right which Déléage (o.c., pp. 190–4) interprets as *capita animalium*. I cannot explain them, but I cannot accept Déléage's theory both for the reason given in the text and because the items are clearly labelled *iuga* $\left(\frac{\Upsilon}{Z}\right)$ or *iuga vel capita* (ZK or ΖΥΓΚ).

[47] *B.C.H.* 1880, 336–8. In Tatian's estate I read the figure of *capita* for 'Αγρός ''Αραρα (line 24) at 3 $\frac{1}{30}$ $\frac{1}{100}$ not ½ $\frac{1}{30}$ $\frac{1}{100}$ (ΓΛ'Ρ' for Γ'Λ'Ρ') as there cannot have been less than ½ a *caput* of *coloni*. In the text as printed the fact that the stone is broken away on the right towards the bottom is not obvious, but it should be noted that in lines 35 and 41 the symbol ϗ is followed by no figure and that some fractions must be missing in Latron's figures of *iugatio* to make up the total.

and stabled his plough-oxen and flocks and herds for a number of neighbouring farms. Over $4\frac{1}{4}$ *capita* of slaves and animals also are registered at the village of Paradeisus, where he is recorded to have held only two small parcels of land of $\frac{5}{8}$ and $\frac{1}{16}$ *iuga*. On the other hand the big farm of $17\frac{1}{2}$ *iuga* has only 9 *capita*, and a farm of over $1\frac{1}{2}$ *iuga* has none. The estates of Critias and Latron yield no figures, as the stone is broken away on the extreme right and most of the figures of the *capita* have vanished. The average at Tralles is again $1\frac{1}{3}$ *capita* to the *iugum*.

Some more figures come from Magnesia on the Maeander. After eliminating doubtful cases where one or other figure is missing or illegible,[48] 29 farms, totalling 183 *iuga*, are registered with *capita*, totalling 212, while 43 farms, which represent 80 *iuga*, have no *capita* at all. The former group comprises mainly large or medium farms, but it is noteworthy that some quite small holdings have large populations: one of $\frac{1}{5}$ $\frac{1}{30}$ $\frac{1}{600}$ of a *iugum* has $5\frac{1}{4}$ *capita*, another of $\frac{1}{2}$ $\frac{1}{4}$ $\frac{1}{20}$ has $9\frac{1}{2}$ $\frac{1}{10}$ and one of $1\frac{1}{4}$ $\frac{1}{50}$ has $15\frac{1}{2}$ $\frac{1}{120}$.[49] On the other hand some large farms are poorly manned. The great estate of 75 *iuga* has only 42 *capita*, the one of $15\frac{1}{2}$+only 7+, and one of $10\frac{1}{2}$+only 3+.[50] The surplus population on the small holdings no doubt worked on the larger estates which were undermanned or had no *capita* registered on them. The farms without *capita* are mostly small holdings of under one *iugum* or a little over, but include some larger farms, two of 3+, one of 4+, one of 5+, two of 6+, and one of 10+.[51]

Taking the farms with registered *capita* only, the manpower situation seems worse in Magnesia than elsewhere—only $1\frac{1}{6}$ *capita* on the average per *iugum*. If the farms without *capita* be taken into account, the average of *capita* to *iuga* falls to about four-fifths. It seems scarcely possible that these figures can represent the whole rural population. It is probable that the list

[48] These are a 1, a 12, c 1, c 4, c 6, d 1–2 (where by the position of the *iuga* figures there were probably *capita* figures following as in d 12), d 5 and 16 (where the jumble of confused symbols probably conceals *capita* figures), e 3, e 18, f 9 (where again there is a jumble of figures as in d 5 and 16), g 1, h 1. In b 18 I read Z δ < d ϰ KϘAΓ as *iuga* $4\frac{1}{2}$ $\frac{1}{4}$ $\frac{1}{20}$ *capita* $11\frac{1}{2}$ (not $91\frac{1}{3}$, which would be absurd); that is, I assume that the *capita* figure was IAΓ and the loop a fault in the stone. The following have no figures at all: b 1–6, d 17–8, e 1, 2, h 2. I read b 10, ZK′ as *iuga* $\frac{1}{30}$ (the editor wrongly writes 20) and a 5, KϛXι′ as *capita* $6\frac{1}{60}$ (not $\frac{1}{6}$ $\frac{1}{60}$ as the editor wrongly renders it).

[49] g 4, e 11, b 12. Other farms with an excessive capitation are a 5, 6, 9, b 7, e 4.
[50] c 2, e 14, c 5.   [51] d 9, f 8, f 7, e 8, h 4, e 13, e 17.

records only the estates owned by urban residents (like the Hermopolite list analysed below), and does not include villages of peasant proprietors, which were separately recorded elsewhere. A tiny fragment of a register of villages survives from Hypaepa.[52] It runs:

'Cinamura including (non-residents) owning (land) in (the village)—*iuga* . . .

Dideiphyta including (non-residents) owning (land) in (the village) . . .'

Two other blocks from Hypaepa give the detailed declarations on which such a list was based. On one block[53] are a number of entries, all very fragmentary, which seem to follow a uniform pattern: so-and-so, son of so-and-so, Hypaepene, resident in such and such a village, owner of land in Hypaepa in the village of Dideiphyta—vineyard: so many *iugera*—total: so much. These are the 'non-residents owning land in the village' on the list. On the other block[54] there are four entries of the form: 'so-and-so son of so-and-so, Hypaepene, resident in my own house—myself, aged so many years', followed by other members of the household with names, relationships and ages, and animals (if any)—total, so much. In a fifth entry the family is followed by a declaration of land—'vineyard, $3\frac{1}{5}$ *iugera*; arable, $4\frac{1}{6}$ *iugera*, olive trees . . .' and this again by a note: 'in the village of Poste olives . . . $1\frac{1}{3}$ $\frac{1}{15}$ *iugera*: declared (?)'. This block is taken by M. Déléage (o.c., 164–9) to be part of the urban register of the city of Hypaepa. This is possible. Under Diocletian the *plebs urbana* had been exempt from the *census* and the *capitatio*, but Galerius (and apparently Maximin) reversed this ruling; Licinius in 313 once again exempted the urban population and this remained the rule.[55] An urban register of Hypaepa would then have been drawn up by

[52] Keil and Premerstein, o.c., no. 87,
Κινάμουρα σὺν τοῖς ἐνκεκτημ' · ζυ . . .
Διδείφυτα σὺν τοῖς ἐυκεκτημ . . .
[53] o.c., no. 86.
[54] o.c., no. 85.
[55] Lactantius, *de Mort. Persec.* 23, 'hominum capita notabantur, in civitatibus urbanae et rusticae plebes adunatae, fora omnia gregibus familiarum referta, unusquisque cum liberis cum servis aderant' (speaking of Galerius). *Cod. Theod.* XIII, x, 2 (313): 'plebs urbana, sicut in Orientalibus quoque provinciis observatur, minime in censibus pro capitatione sua conveniatur, sed iuxta iussionem nostram immunis habeatur, sicuti etiam sub domino et parente nostro Diocletiano Seniore Augusto eadem plebs immunis fuerat' (Licinius to the governor of Lycia-Pamphylia after the fall of Maximin).

Galerius, and our inscription might record it. The small holding of cultivated land registered would then have been within the walls of the city, which is not inconceivable. On the other hand it would seem more likely that both blocks refer to the village of Dideiphyta. The declarations on the second block would make no reference to it because they would all be under the heading Dideiphyta. Those on the first block mention Dideiphyta in each case because they are extracted from declarations made in other villages by the owners; the holding of the Dideiphytene villager in the village of Poste will have been similarly transferred to the register of Poste. If our inscription is a village register, the large number of landless peasants is notable, so too is the exiguous size of the recorded holding. These facts may help to explain where the labour came from which worked the estates of the big landlords.

It is possible from this record and the Theran lists of *coloni*[56] to draw up a table of nine complete peasant households. They are as follows; the figures represent ages, a cross that the age is unknown:

	Man	Wife	Sons	Daughters	Others
(a)	+	—	—	—	Mother (48) Sister (11)
(b)	20	—	—	—	—
(c)	56	— {	3 under 3	—	{ a woman (48) a boy (under 3)
(d)	40	—	20	—	a woman (30)
(e)	30	30	3	—	2 boys (1)
(f)	—	20	—	2	—
(g)	65	+ ?	14, 11 (?), 6	12	—
(h)	60	52	+	+	—
(i)	+	—	11	—	—

The woman and boy in (c) are both labelled ο or θ, which might stand for ὄρφανος (orphan) or θρεπτός (foundling). The woman in (d), whose description, if any, has perished, might be a second wife. One day in (e) with no description may be a son: the other bears the same name as the son of 3, and is labelled προς ἀδ . . . which might mean nephew. The sample is too small to be of statistical value, but the uniformly small size of the families is suggestive and helps to explain why agricultural labour was so scanty.

If the above calculations are correct, there must have been an acute shortage of labour on the land. To a peasant family consisting of man and wife and a son and a daughter over fourteen,

[56] *I.G.* xii, iii, 343, 346.

rated at three *capita*, there corresponded land to the value of 2¼ to 2½ *iuga*. This, if entirely arable, would amount to 225 to 250 *iugera* (140 to 155 acres); if, as was more usual, partly in vineyard and olives, would represent perhaps 120 *iugera* (75 acres) of arable, 15 *iugera* (10 acres) of vineyard, and 250 to 300 olives. In the second century B.C. colonial land allotments were usually at rates of 5, 6, 8, or 10 *iugera* to each applicant (who would often have a wife and family);[57] in three colonies where land was particularly abundant, exceptional grants of 50 *iugera* were made.[58] Caesar in his consulship allotted land in farms of 10 *iugera* to married men with three or more children.[59] From 5 to 10 *iugera* was no doubt the minimum small holding which would (tax-free) support a family, whereas the *coloni* of our inscriptions had to pay heavy taxes (mostly in kind) and rent as well, but the disproportion between the figures of the second and first centuries B.C. and those of the fourth century A.D. remains striking.

A more relevant comparison is perhaps with the figures given by agricultural experts of an earlier period for the minimum labour force required to cultivate a given area for the maximum profit. Cato in the second century B.C. thought that sixteen hands were needed for a vineyard of 100 *iugera*; these with one exception, the bailiff's wife, are all adult males.[60] As against this, 4 *iuga* (96 *iugera*) of vineyard in the fourth century would on the average have carried 7 persons, including animals and children over 12 or 14. Columella in the first century A.D. recommends eight workers for 200 *iugera* of arable;[61] this area (=2 *iuga*) would in the fourth century have carried between three and four persons, again

---

[57] Livy, xxxv, 40 (10 at Vibo in 192), xxxix, 44 (6 at Potentia and Pisaurum in 184), xxxix, 55 (5 at Mutina, 8 at Parma, 10 at Saturnia in 183), xl, 29 (5 at Graviscae in 181), xlii, 4 (10 to citizens, 3 to allies in Cisalpine Gaul in 173).

[58] Livy, xxxvii, 57 (50 at Bononia in 189), xl, 34 (50 at Aquileia in 180), xli, 13 (51½ at Luna in 180). The settlers here may well have been intended to be farmers employing (slave) labour. This is suggested by the fact that at Bononia *equites* got larger plots (70) and at Aquileia centurions and *equites* got 100 and 140. At Vibo also *equites* received a double allowance (20).

[59] Suet. *Julius*, 20, 3; Cicero, *Ep. ad. Att.* ii, xvi, 1. These allotments were on the *ager Campanus* and *Stellas*, famous for their fertility.

[60] Cato, *de Agr.* 11.

[61] Columella ii, 12, 7. This is not extravagant seeing that he estimates that each *iugerum* requires 4 man-days to plough (3 times), 1 man-day to harrow, 3 to hoe, 1 to weed, 1½ to harvest (ii, 13, 1) as well as 1 man-day to cut the straw after harvest (xi, 2, 54). This work alone would occupy his 8 men 300 days in the year, without allowing for sickness or bad weather, or carting, repairs, and other odd jobs.

including women and children. The land then had well under half the labour force required for efficient cultivation. It is hardly surprising that landlords were so anxious to tie their tenants to the soil and that so much legislation is devoted to the problem of reclaiming fugitive *coloni* and punishing landlords who harboured them on their own estates.

On the proportion of servile to free labour on the land only the registers of Thera, Lesbos, and Tralles provide any data. There is also a tantilising document from Chios,[62] a list of farms with rubrics for *iuga* of land, *capita* of *coloni*, *capita* of slaves, and *capita* of animals; but unhappily the figures have never been filled in. This document only tells us that on 9 farms there were *coloni* only (whose *capita* would include their animals) and on 4 *coloni* and slaves and animals (of the owner). At Thera the register of farms which had belonged to Paregorius[63] (total value a little over 10 *iuga*) is followed by the entry 'and slaves on the land Eutychus aged 60, Polychronius aged 40, 1 ox, 1 ass, 5 sheep'. Next follows the heading 'Tenants' (πάροικοι) and the beginning of a list of *coloni* and their families and animals, starting with Theodorus of the farm Politike (v.s.); the next lines dealt with the *colonus* of farm Ophragorea (H) but are too fragmentary to be read. One can, however, be certain that there were only two slaves on this group of farms, and the rest of the population was free persons. On the general average the whole estate should have carried about 13½ *capita* or 18 persons; the ratio of slaves to free persons therefore was 1:8.

At Tralles[64] slaves and animals belonging to the landlord (reckoned in *capita*) are placed at the head of each owner's schedule, and are followed by a list of farms with their several *iugatio* and *capitatio* (*coloni* and their animals). Fulvius the priest has no slaves but $4\frac{1}{8}$ $\frac{1}{15}$ *capita* of *coloni*. Another owner whose entry is incomplete, Pausanias *alias* Achollius, has no slaves but at least 3 *capita* of *coloni*. Tatianus owns two groups of slaves and animals, of $3\frac{1}{2}$ $\frac{1}{6}$ $\frac{1}{45}$ and $4\frac{1}{4}$ $\frac{1}{20}$ $\frac{1}{150}$ *capita*, that is, a maximum of $7\frac{1}{2}$ *capita* of slaves, and $58\frac{1}{15}$ *capita* of *coloni* (and their animals), of which a maximum of 58 represent human beings. As Tatianus owned $3\frac{1}{2}$ $\frac{1}{3}$ $\frac{1}{20}$ $\frac{1}{50}$ *capita* of animals which were not registered

[62] Déléage, o.c., 182–6.
[63] *I.G.* XII, iii, 343.
[64] *B.C.H.* 1880, 336–8.

with his slaves, but apparently used by his *coloni* at Monnara, it is likely that his *coloni* owned relatively few animals, and that their *capitatio* is mainly *humana*. The proportion of slave to free labour is here about 1:8. Critias and Latron own 2(?+) and 3½+*capita* respectively of slaves and animals. Their figures for *capita* of *coloni* are incomplete, but their land, $20\frac{1}{2}$ $\frac{1}{5}$ $\frac{1}{12}$ $\frac{1}{150}$ and $17\frac{1}{3}$ $\frac{1}{80}$ respectively, would on the general average have carried about 41 *capita*. The proportion of slave to free labour is here 1:7½.

In Lesbos things were different. Here the lists of farms show slaves and animals in detail, but mention *coloni* only incidentally. One small fragment,[65] which is different from the rest in grading vineyard, arable, and olives in two qualities, places the name of the *colonus* (or *coloni*; for two of the five farms are on joint tenancies by two men) at the head of each farm; even this fragment does not, however, record the families and animals of the tenants. On the other lists the farms have no headings, and free persons are only named occasionally in connection with animals: they are probably the owners of animals grazed on farms which do not belong to them. There must presumably have been a separate register of *coloni* with their families and animals, which has not survived. The great majority of the farms (22 excluding the 5 recorded to have been worked by *coloni*) show a nil return under the slaves and animals rubric, six show animals only, but two[66] have large staffs of slaves (22 with 20 oxen and 50 sheep in the one case and 21 in the other). The first is a moderate sized farm, of 91 *iugera* of arable, 20 of vineyard, 150 of pasture, and 352 olive trees (2½ *iuga* ignoring the pasture). The other is apparently quite small, only 5 *iugera* of arable, an unknown quanity of vineyard, and 132 olive trees. These farms were evidently each a centre from which a group of farms was worked. It is unfortunately impossible, owing to the fragmentary state of the registers, to calculate even approximately how many farms were worked by free tenants and how many by these large slave establishments. The larger establishment occurs in a list of sixteen farms, broken at both ends, which otherwise shows no *capitatio humana*. The total *iugatio* of this group is about 29½ *iuga* (excluding pasture) and on the normal ratio would have a population of 37 persons. But one cannot infer that slaves were roughly two to one free person on

[65] *I.G.* xii, ii, 79.
[66] *I.G.* xii, ii, 76, 78.

this estate, as there may have been very many more farms recorded to left and right (and one of these may have housed another slave establishment). The 21 slaves figure on a small fragment carrying only seven entries, four of which are tiny plots described as gardens. All that one can safely say is that on these Lesbian estates, unlike those of Thera and Tralles, slave labour was employed on a large scale.

Certain general conclusions emerge from these documents. The average agricultural unit was very small, and even wealthy landlords as a rule owned a large number of scattered farms rather than a great estate. Slaves were sometimes employed in large gangs of 20 or so, but more often in twos and threes, and in the latter case represented from 10 per cent to 12 per cent of the registered agricultural population. Lastly, the registered agricultural population was very thin on the ground according to ancient standards, the average density being $\frac{1}{12}$ to $\frac{1}{25}$ of that of the agricultural settlements of the later Roman republic in Italy, and well under half the minimum for efficient cultivation as reckoned by agricultural experts.

There is only one other area of the empire for which documents comparable to these engraved census records survive. In Egypt the papyri have preserved a few land registers of the first half of the fourth century. These give no information on the ratio of slave to free labour—actually agricultural slaves were virtually unknown in Egypt—nor on the density of the rural population. They do, however, give fuller information than is available from other sources on the distribution of landed property between the urban and rural population, and between large, medium, and small holders, and also further illustrate the composition of large and medium estates.[67]

The most important of the Egyptian documents is *P. Flor.* 71, which can be dated by prosopographical evidence (see Johnson and West, *Byzantine Egypt: Economic studies* 19, n. 9) to the second quarter of the fourth century. Ll. 44–487 comprise a register of

[67] In what follows I have ignored fractions smaller than a half. I cannot vouch for the absolute accuracy of my arithmetic; for, apart from my incapacity for adding long columns of figures, I find Greek numerical notation troublesome, and missing or mutilated figures add to the confusion. In dealing with them I have exercised my discretion, eliminating those where the element of doubt is large, but including those where the missing figure is relatively unimportant (e.g. I have reckoned in ρπ[ ] as 180+, but ignored [ ]β).

names in the alphabetical order of their initial letters, each followed by a statement of the quantity (in *arurae*=slightly over ⅔ acre) of land, public or private, which he or she held in the several *pagi* of the territory of Hermopolis. The list is virtually complete, only 11 out of 444 lines being totally illegible, and very few individual figures, relatively to the huge total, being obliterated. The list is headed Φρουρίου Λιβός, the name of one of the four ἄμφοδα into which the town of Hermopolis was divided. The lost beginning of the roll presumably contained similar registers of the other three ἄμφοδα (the last six names of one survive in ll. 1–8). Ll. 488–800 comprise a similar list headed 'Αντινοιτικῶν ὀνομάτων. The first list evidently comprises the citizens of Hermopolis resident in the South Fort Ward who owned land in the city territory, the second the citizens of the neighbouring city of Antinoopolis who owned land in Hermopolite territory: since Antinoopolis was very near, and had, it is probable, only a small territory of its own, so many of its citizens were landowners in Hermopolis that they merited a separate schedule. Both lists, it should be noted, are confined to town dwellers. It was the administrative practice in fourth-century Egypt (and probably elsewhere) to keep separate schedules of πολιτικαὶ and κωμητικαὶ κτήσεις, the former comprising the holdings of urban residents, the latter those of villagers.[68]

The names in general present no difficulty. They are followed by a patronymic or sometimes, but rarely, an indication (usually abbreviated) of the person's profession or rank. Eighteen names are followed by several entries of land, distinguished by the words διὰ τοῦ δεινός :[69] here I take it that the names following διά are tenants or agents who registered their holding in the owner's name. In three cases an entry is followed by another headed ἐπ' ὀνόματος or καὶ ὄνομα τοῦ δεινός, the second name being out of alphabetical order.[70] In these cases I have assumed that the first

[68] This appears from P. *Princeton* 134 and P. *Strassb.* 45, discussed at the end of this paper.

[69] Ll. 143–4, 170–1, 186–9, 210–3, 235–6, 241–253, 304–8, 314–7, 424–6, 450–3, 454–7, 461–2, 536–8, 547–9, 583–8, 589–591, 596–9, 716–8.

[70] L. 88, ἐπ' ὀνόματος Διογένους Πάριδος under 'Αμμωνίων 'Αντωνίνου; l. 251, καὶ ὄνομ' Σιλβανοῦ Ἑρμαπόλλωνος under 'Ηρακλέων 'Υπερεχίου; l. 280, καὶ ὄνομ' 'Ωρίωνος under 'Ιεροκλῆς 'Ελλαδίου. Silvanus son of Hermapollon occurs elsewhere out of place, over his brother (?) Pamunis, son of Hermapollon (ll. 416–8). Another name which appears out of place is 'Ερμαπόλλων Μαικηνᾶ, who follows κλ(ηρονόμοι) Μαικηνᾶ Φιβίωνος. Σέργηνο[ς υ]ἱός follows his father in l. 782.

R

named owner had come recently into possession of the second estate, still registered under the ὄνομα of its previous owner. In eleven cases land is registered under two names jointly, presumably co-heirs of an undivided estate;[71] I have included both names in the total of landowners. Under the letter K are listed not only persons beginning with K but κληρονόμοι, sixty-six in all, of deceased owners under all letters; these are, I take it, the estates of persons recently dead whose heirs had not yet taken possession; I have counted each as one owner. Finally the Antinoite list registers under O four οὐσίαι, three of them διὰ ᾽Ανουβίωνος ἀπὸ προέδρων: two are called Οὐλπιανή (in two different *pagi*), one Πλατωνική, the fourth Στάβλου. These are probably civic estates of Antinoopolis. The Hermopolite list records five οὐσίαι πολιτικαί (presumably of Hermopolis), but includes them in the holdings of the landowners who farmed them.[72] Altogether, on the assumptions made above, there were 233 (plus perhaps half-a-dozen in the missing lines) landowners resident in the South Fort Ward, and therefore, if the four wards were of approximately the same size and character, between 900 and 1,000 landowners resident in Hermopolis. The number of Antinoites owning land in the Hermopolite territory was 208 (not counting the four civic estates).

The land holdings are classified first by the *pagus* in which they lay; there were probably eighteen *pagi* in all,[73] distinguished by numbers, and the holdings, where one owner held land in several *pagi*, are recorded according to the numerical order of the *pagi*. Within each *pagus* the land is classified as ἰδιωτική or δημοσία. In a very small minority of cases the classification has been omitted: in these cases I have assumed that the land is ἰδιωτική, since, as will appear, the overwhelming majority of unmixed holdings belong to this category. The οὐσίαι, it may be noted, do not constitute a separate legal category but are mostly classed as ἰδιωτική (one also included a small piece of δημοσία). The majority of owners in both lists hold private land only; but a substantial minority, 96 in the Hermopolite list out of 233, and 75 in the Antinoite out of 208, hold mixed estates in both categories, and this minority includes most substantial land-

---

[71] Ll. 154, 375, 463, 533, 547, 581, 611, 636, 639–640 (brothers), 755, 774.
[72] Ll. 747–752 (Antinoite); 127, 137–8, 474–5 (Hermopolite).
[73] See l. 72.

owners. There are only five holdings of public land alone, all very small.[74] The area of public land is almost invariably smaller, and usually very much smaller, than the area of private land to which it is attached. In the Hermopolite list, in the holdings in which both figures are complete, the private land totals 8,989 *arurae*, and the public 1,093. The corresponding figures in the Antinoite list are 2,950 and 249. The owners concerned held in addition parcels of unmixed private land (in other *pagi*) amounting to 1,051 and 224 *arurae*. Overall, then, owners of mixed estates held private and public land in a proportion of about 10:1.

It may be that some of the holdings of public land may have originated as voluntary leases, which had become customary tenures. It seems more probable, however, from the distribution of the holdings that the great majority arose from the practice of ἐπιβολή, compulsory assignment of public land to private owners. The figures suggest that ἐπιβολή, though a quite common procedure, was on a small scale; most sizeable estates, and many small ones, had some public land attached, but the amount in each was inconsiderable. Ἐπιβολή cannot, as has been sometimes suggested, have played any important part in the disappearance of public land as a legal category.

The grand total of private and public land recorded in both lists, including (a) the mixed holdings recorded above, (b) other mixed holdings in which one or other figure is missing, (c) the unmixed holdings of private land held by these same owners as recorded above (there is only one unmixed public holding in this category, of 6 *arurae*), (d) unmixed private estates, which total 1,490 in the Hermopolite and 2,418½ in the Antinoite list, (e) the civic οὐσίαι, comprising 130 *arurae* of private land belonging to Hermopolis, and 518½ private and 1½ public belonging to Antinoopolis, and finally (f) unmixed public tenures, which total 2½ and 10, comes to 13,480 private and 1,221 public in the Hermopolite list, and 6,377 private and 321 public in the Antinoite. If one assumes a similar pattern of land ownership in the other three wards of Hermopolis, the total private land in the Hermopolite territory held by residents in the town would be about 54,000 *arurae*, and the corresponding figure of public land about 5,000; when Antinoite owners are added in, the grand totals would be

---

[74] Ll. 111, 286, 561, 660; there is also one case (526) where an owner who holds land in several *pagi* has public land only in one *pagus*.

about 60,000 and 5,000. We do not know the proportion of land in Egypt which was public and private, but the ratio of 1:12 is hardly conceivable. It would seem probable that city dwellers in the main held private land, with small amounts of public land attached. Villagers on the other hand, though some had acquired private land, were in the main descended from δημόσιοι γεωργοί, and would hold parcels of public land. If then we possessed the κωμητικαὶ κτήσεις of the Hermopolite as well as the πολιτικαί, public land would probably be shown in a much higher ratio to private. The total area of the Hermopolite territory cannot be calculated with any approach to accuracy, but assuming that it extended northwards to include Tou, later to become a separate city as Theodosiopolis, and southwards to a line somewhat north of Cusae, which, formerly a toparchy of the Hermopolite nome, was already a separate city,[75] and that it comprised all land on the west bank, having the narrow strip on the east bank to Antinoopolis, it would have stretched about 50 miles along the river, with an average width of between 8 and 9 miles: that is, its area would have been 400–450 square miles or about 400,000 arurae. Town dwellers will have owned only about one-sixth of the land, and five-sixths will have been held by villagers.

For the distribution of landed property the Hermopolite list is more instructive than the Antinoite. Most citizens of Hermopolis would hold all or the greater part of their property within the territory of the city. Some of the wealthier citizens may have acquired estates elsewhere by marriage or inheritance, but such holdings would not be on a scale to distort the picture painted by the land register. The Antinoite list, on the other hand, records the estates of Antinoite citizens outside their own territory in the contiguous area. These estates represent only a section, and probably a small section, of the total owned by Antinoite citizens, and moreover each holding may well be, and often certainly is, only a minor part of the estate of the owner concerned, the bulk of whose property might lie in Antinoite territory, or anywhere else in Egypt. Hadrian enrolled as citizens of his new foundation 'Hellenes' from all parts of Egypt, and Antinoites are known to have owned land as far afield as the Arsinoite nome.[76] From the

[75] See A. H. M. Jones, *Cities of the Eastern Roman Provinces* 345, 482, n. 64. *SB.* 8942 has since confirmed my conjecture that Cusae was already a city.
[76] *Chr.* i, 29.

list itself it is apparent that some small holdings are in fact outliers of larger estates held elsewhere. It is for instance impossible that Harpocration, former president of the Antinoite council (ἀπὸ προέδρων), can have owned only 11½ *arurae*, and most unlikely that Anubion, another president, recorded as lessee of three large civic estates, had no land of his own. Again two former *curatores civitatis* (ἀπὸ λογιστῶν) must have owned more than 2 and 16 *arurae*.[77]

I will therefore deal first with the Hermopolite list. The list, as we have seen, records the land of each owner under the *pagi* in which it was situated. This, it should be noted, does not mean that each recorded holding was a single estate. A man might own several separate parcels of land in one *pagus*, as is proved by a few entries in which separate registrations of land are made for the same owner in the same *pagus* by two or more tenants or agents.[78] As a general rule, however, the holdings of each man in each *pagus* have been totalised in the list, and we can therefore detect scattered holdings only when they were distributed over several *pagi*.

The majority of owners, including nearly all the smaller holders, register land in one *pagus* only. There are altogether 156 entries out of 230 which total less than 30 *arurae* each. Their distribution is shown by the following tables:

	Holdings in a single pagus			*Holdings in several* pagi		
	Number of owners	*Total of* arurae	*Average holding*	*Number of owners*	*Total of* arurae	*Average holding*
All private						
Under 10 ..	66	268	4	2	10½	5¼
10–19 ..	23	316½	13¾	2	20½	10¼
20–29 ..	9	211½	23½	—	—	—
All public						
Under 10 ..	2	2½	1¼	—	—	—
Mixed						
Under 10 ..	22	97½	4½	2	11½	5¾
10–19 ..	13	173½	13¼	3	36½+	12+
20–29 ..	11	263	24	1	20	20

A few even of these small holdings, it will be noted, are dispersed over several *pagi*; of those in a single *pagus* one of 9 *arurae* consists of three blocks, under separate tenants, of 4, 2½,

[77] Ll. 521, 747–751, 566, 592.

[78] e.g. ll. 143–4, 186–9, 210–3, 304–8, 314–7, 450–3, 461–2, 583–8, 596–9.

and 2½, each subdivided into public and private land.[79] Some of these smaller holders may have worked their own land, or a part of it, though resident in the city, but the majority seem to have been absentee landlords. A number record urban occupations. Among those who own less than 10 *arurae* there are a builder, a potter, a donkey man, a fuller, three wool shearers, a doorkeeper, a letter writer, an astrologer, two *officiales*, a *beneficiarius*, and a minor official (βοηθός): another βοηθός and a money-changer own 12 each.[80]

As estates increase in size they tend more and more to be distibuted over several *pagi*, as the following tables show:

	Number of pagi	Number of arurae	
30–39 *arurae* ..	1	31	
	2	31½	Total *arurae* 168+
	2	34½+	Average holding 34
	1	36	
	2	39	
40–49 *arurae* ..	1	42	
	2	42	
	1	43½	Total *arurae* 313½
	3	44	Average holding 45
	2	45	
	1	47½	
	3	49½	
50–79	1	60	
	1	62	Total *arurae* 250
	6	62½	Average holding 62½
	1	65½	
80–99	1	81	
	2	80½ +	Total *arurae* 519½+
	4	88	Average holding 87
	2	88½	
	1	90½	
	2	91	
100–199 ..	1	113½	
	1	124	Total *arurae* 921½
	1	154	Average holding 153½
	1	155	
	1	183	
	5	192	

[79] Ll. 186–9.
[80] Ll. 77–8, 128, 159, 183, 214, 247, 267, 325, 342–3, 364, 380, 395, 438, 460.

Number of pagi   Number of arura

200-600	..	3	259	
		4	258+	Total arurae 2,919½++
		2	317	Average holding 417
		3	465+	
		6	503+	
		4	530+	
		1	587½	

Above the 190 arurae mark there is, it will be noted, only one estate, the largest of this group, containing nearly 600 arurae, which is concentrated in one pagus. There is then a considerable gap till we reach seven estates in the 1,000 arurae category. The biggest of these, of 1,370 arurae, was entirely in one pagus,[81] the other six, as the following table shows, are widely distributed:

Number of pagi   Total of arurae

8	946½
9	1,020+
9	1,027+
7	1,098
4	1,090+
10	808½++

In the last estate, that of Heracleon, a large number of figures are missing. The return made by the owner himself, which comprised land in five pagi, has perished save for one figure, 47. Land totalling 373½ arurae, distributed over four pagi, was registered in his name by Aelianus, and under his name also comes the ὄνομα of Silvanus, who held 388 arurae, all in one pagus, but in two blocks.[82]

It would appear then that, out of the 233 residents of the South Fort Ward of Hermopolis who owned land, seven men owned about half the total area (c. 7,500 out of c. 15,000), and another seven men owned close on another quarter (c. 3,000). If one may, to obtain an approximate picture of the pattern of land ownership in Hermopolis, multiply these figures by four, out of 900–1,000 urban landowners, 25–30 were in the 1,000 arurae class, owning half the total, and another 25–30 in the 250–600 arurae class, owning nearly a quarter of the total. Within the class of

[81] L. 299 (χλ' 'Αμμωνίου Ὑπερεχίου).
[82] Ll. 64 ('Ακύλας 'Ολυμπιοδώρου), 123 (Γεννάδιος Διοκλέους), 129 (Διοσκου-ρίδης Αἰλιανοῦ), 241 ('Ηρακλέων Ὑπερεχίου), 274 ('Ιεροκλῆς 'Ελλαδίου), 408 (Πινουτίων 'Ολυμπιοδώρου).

urban landowners the concentration of property is striking. But it must be remembered that, as pointed out earlier, urban landowners held only a small proportion, perhaps a sixth, of the total area of the territory, the remainder of which was held by villagers.

The Antinoite list is, as explained above, less instructive on the distribution of landed property, but, for what they are worth, the following tables analyse the information which it contains:

	Holdings in one pagus			Holdings in several pagi		
	Number of owners	Total of arurae	Average holding	Number of owners	Total of arurae	Average holding
Under 10	66	270	4	1	6½	6½
10—19	30	387½	13	2	26 +	13 +
20—29	23	548 +	24	2	40	20
30—39	9	310	34½	0	0	0
40—49	9	383 +	42½	1	45½	45½
50—99	12	811½	67½	91	609	67¾
100—200	12	1,786	149		143½	143¼

Over the 200-line there are only three holdings, one of 203 in two *pagi*, one of 292 in one *pagus*, and one of 321½ in a single *pagus* but declared by two agents. In addition there is Anubion, who leased three civic estates totalling over 500 *arurae*. In general, estates seem to be smaller and more concentrated, but it must be borne in mind that many of them may have formed parts of larger agglomerations. It is noteworthy that many of the more substantial holdings belong to civil servants or ex-civil servants. Antinoopolis was the metropolis of the Thebaid, and the governor's officials doubtless invested their savings in land in the neighbourhood. There are six *primipilares* who own 292, 179½, 116, 76, over 59, and 56 *arurae* respectively.[83] A former *praeco* (ἀπὸ πρεκόνων) has 143½ and a former procurator (ἀπὸ ἐπιτρόπων) over 130.[84] Three *beneficiarii* hold 74, 58½, and 40, and an *ab actis* (ἀβάκτης) 54.[85] The largest estate of 321½ *arurae* is held by a man described as ἀπὸ ἐξακτόρων.[86] The post of *exactor civitatis* was an imperial *dignitas*, but by this date normally bestowed on a *curialis* of the city concerned. This man will then probably have belonged

[83] Ll. 515, 612, 625, 697, 707, 714. There is also a wealthy *primipilaris* (over 206 *arurae*) at Hermopolis (l. 60). *Primipilaris* at this date, of course, means former *princeps* of the provincial *officium*.
[84] Ll. 680, 791.
[85] Ll. 509, 546, 550, 604; in the Hermopolite list (ll. 160, 380) there are another *beneficiarius* and an *actuarius*, holding 65½ and 60 *arurae*.
[86] L. 589.

to the curial aristocracy of Antinoopolis, as did Anubion, former president of the council, who leased the three civic estates.

P. Lips. 101 is a much smaller fragment containing less than fifty entries. It too is from Hermopolis, and appears to be of similar date to P. Flor. 71. It also seems to be concerned with city dwellers; the names are almost entirely Greek, most are stated to be ἀπὸ ʽΕρμουπόλεως (and a few of Antinoopolis), and four are gymnasiarchs. The land is, as in P. Flor. 71, classified as ἰδιωτική or δημοσία, but in both categories ἐσπ(αρμένη) is added. Here the resemblance between the two lists ends. In P. Lips. 101 the names are not in alphabetical order, Antionoites are mixed up with Hermopolites (both being usually labelled as such), and each name is followed by one holding only, either private, mixed, or public: there is no indication of the pagus. At the beginning of the list occurs an entry of 180½ arurae (probably private), followed by another of more than 100 arurae (presumably private), plus ¼-arura public. The preceding names (if they were names and these figures are not totals of earlier entries) are lost. The remaining entries, of which 36 preserve the figures, are all very small; only two are larger than 10 (12½ and 14), and the average is between 4 and 5. There are two holdings of public land only, five of mixed public and private (in addition to the large figure already mentioned), and twenty-nine of private; these include an οὐσία ʽΕρμοπολιτικ(ὴ) (πρότερον) Βησᾶτος (ιι, 11) and an οὐσία ταμειακὴ πρότερον ᾽Αμμωνίου of 6 arurae (ιι, 21).

It seems likely that this list represents an earlier stage in the formation of the land register of P. Flor. 71. Here, it would appear, all citizens in one pagus have been entered higgledy-piggledy as they came in, later to be sorted into ʽΕρμοπολιτικὰ ὀνόματα under the four wards and ᾽Αντινοιτικὰ ὀνόματα, arranged in alphabetical order, and consolidated with returns from other pagi. The chief importance of the fragment is in underlining the fragmentation of rural property. Apart from the two considerable estates (if they are estates) at the head of the list, the holdings are all tiny, but many were no doubt fragments of larger agglomerations: it is inconceivable that the four gymnasiarchs recorded (two αἰώνιοι) could have owned only 5 arurae private, 5 public, 6, and 1¾ private respectively (,I 4, 22, 25; II, 10). The document also confirms the earlier hypothesis about entries διὰ τοῦ δεινός. There are a number of entries in this form, in which ὁ δεῖνα is some-

254   THE ROMAN ECONOMY

times a relative, once a γεωργός (or tenant), once a προνοητής (or agent—for 14 *arurae*): the imperial estate is registered by a βοηθός.

There are unfortunately no village land registers from the Hermopolite. There appear in fact to be only three for all Egypt in this period, and of these *S.P.P* x, 221 and *P.R.G* v, 58 are too fragmentary to be of statistical value. There remains *P. Princeton* 134 which records the κωμητικὴ κτῆσις of Theadelphia in the Arsinoite in a tenth indiction early in the fourth century, probably 322. The list is certainly incomplete, being in two columns, the bottom of each of which has perished. The land is classified as βασιλική or ἰδιωτική, each class being further qualified as σπεριμή or ἄσπορος.

Owner	Royal sown	Private sown	Royal unsown	Private unsown	Total
A	$41\frac{1}{8} \frac{1}{16}$	$6\frac{1}{4} \frac{1}{16}$	—	—	$47\frac{1}{2}$
B	—	$3\frac{1}{8}$	—	—	$3\frac{1}{8}$
C	$19\frac{1}{8}$	?	—	—	$19\frac{1}{8}+$
D	$33\frac{1}{4} \frac{1}{8}$	$22\frac{3}{4} \frac{1}{8} \frac{1}{16} \frac{1}{32}$	$2\frac{1}{4} \frac{1}{16} \frac{1}{64}$	—	$58\frac{3}{4}$
E	$8\frac{1}{4}$	—	—	—	$8\frac{1}{4}$
F	—	—	$12\frac{1}{32}$	—	12
G	$6\frac{1}{12}$	$6\frac{3}{4} \frac{1}{16} \frac{1}{32}$	—	—	$12\frac{7}{8}$
H	$10\frac{1}{4}$	$16\frac{1}{4} \frac{1}{8} \frac{1}{32}$	—	—	$27\frac{1}{8}$
I	$5\frac{1}{16}$	$21\frac{1}{32}$	$2\frac{1}{16}$	$1\frac{3}{4} \frac{1}{8} \frac{1}{16} \frac{1}{32}$	$30\frac{1}{8}$
J	—	$44\frac{1}{4} \frac{1}{8}$	—	$3\frac{1}{8} \frac{1}{32}$	$47\frac{1}{2}$
K	—	$1\frac{1}{4} \frac{1}{32}$	—	—	$1\frac{1}{4}$
L	$1\frac{1}{4} \frac{1}{8}$	—	—	—	$1\frac{3}{8}$
Total	$124\frac{5}{8}$	$122\frac{3}{4}+$	$16\frac{7}{8}$	$5\frac{1}{8}$	$269+$

It will be noted that the royal land is approximately equal in extent to the private in this village; a very different proportion from that shown by the Hermopolite register. There are great anomalies between peasant holdings, which range from one of nearly 60 *arurae* and two of nearly 50 to one of 3 and two of little over 1 *arurae*.

In a petition (*P. Thead.* 17, cf. 16) addressed to Flavius Hyginus, prefect of Egypt in 332, it is stated that the taxable area (φορολογία) of the whole village was 500 *arurae*, and the registered number of its adult male inhabitants (κατ' ἄνδρα) twenty-five. Our land register therefore comprises rather over half the total. There are three other lists of about this period from Theadelphia which help to fill the gap. From a tenth indiction, probably 322 again, but later in the year (for several of the owners in the land register have recently died and are represented by their heirs) there is an εἴσπραξις σίτου κωμητῶν (P. *Thead.* 30) of 18 entries. From 314 there is a statement (P. *Flor.* 54) of amounts of seed-corn lent by the government to 16 villagers, and from 312 there is a report of the σιτολόγοι (P. *Strassb.* 45) on amounts of corn delivered to the village granary by 16 persons. Many names recur in these lists, but it is clear that none is exhaustive. Seed-corn was probably loaned only to holders of royal (public) land, and in the two documents recording receipt of corn taxes by the σιτολόγοι the names of those who had not yet paid up are absent. Allowing for this, twenty-five does not seem to be an overestimate of the adult male population.

The list of 312 is of peculiar interest in that it distinguishes between σῖτος πολιτῶν and σῖτος (and κρίθη) κωμητῶν. The latter amounts to $329\frac{3}{4}$ *artabae* of wheat and $62\frac{5}{12}$ of barley, and is delivered by 14 persons. The former totals only $33\frac{7}{12}$ *artabae* of wheat, and is delivered, through their tenants, by two persons, Masculinus ($15\frac{7}{12}$ *artabae*) and Rufina, daughter of Rufus, whose tenant is Sacaon (18 *artabae*). Nineteen years later, in 331, Sacaon rented 16 *arurae* from Aurelia Rufina, whom he describes as λαμπροτάτη (*clarissima*), wife of Claudius Lampadius, decurion of Alexandria (P. *Strassb.* 43). It is probable that this is the same holding on which in 312 he paid 18 *artabae* on his landlady's account, in which case the total of land held by urban residents in Theadelphia will have been about 30 *arurae* out of 500.

The records of Theadelphia thus confirm, for what they are worth, two inferences from the Hermopolite register. First that the proportion of public to private land was far higher than indicated by the register, and secondly that the bulk of the soil of Egypt was still in the early fourth century held by peasant proprietors. It may be added that in Theadelphia the ratio of adult males to area of land, 25 men to 500 *arurae*, is almost equivalent to Columella's optimum of 8 men to 200 *iugera*.

ADDENDUM

[In *L.R.E.* 62 Jones noted that we know little of Western censuses (for Gaul see *Pan. Lat.* V.5.): but in Africa the unit of assessment was the *centuria* of 200 *iugera* (*Cod. Theod.* XI, i, 10, 365; xxviii, 13, 422; Val. III, *Nov.* XXXIV, 431), and in Suburbicarian Italy the *millena* (*C.I.L.* X 407; Val. III, *Nov.* V 4, 440; Maj. *Nov.* VII 16, 458; Just. *App.* VII 26, 554); these presumably customary measures, in which no distinction was apparently made between different types of cultivation, were equated with *iuga*.

On the irregularity of revisions of the census after Diocletian see *L.R.E.* 454 f., 798, 814 f.]

CHAPTER ELEVEN

NOTES OF THE GENUINENESS OF THE CONSTANTINIAN DOCUMENTS IN EUSEBIUS'S LIFE OF CONSTANTINE[1]

ONE of the principal arguments against the authenticity of the Constantinian documents, and of the *Life* in which they are incorporated, has been the phrase used by Constantine in one of them[2] to describe his age at the opening of the Great Persecution in A.D. 303—τότε κομιδῇ παῖς ἔτι ὑπάρχων. According to data provided by the author of the *Life*[3]—and by other sources—Constantine was about 63 when he died in 337, and would therefore have been about 29 when the Persecution opened. A man of 29 could not possibly be described as a παῖς, and the phrase was, therefore, it was argued, evidence that the document in which it occurred was a forgery. As there is now strong presumptive evidence that the document is in fact genuine, it may be worth while to reconsider the passage.

Seeck[4] has already convincingly argued that Constantine's age at his death was exaggerated. His precise age was apparently unknown: the author of the *Life* is careful not to give an exact figure, and other writers give 62, 64, 65 and 66.[5] Phrases used by the Panegyrists suggest a considerably younger age. Nazarius would hardly have stated that Constantine was *adhuc aevi immaturus* when he mounted the throne in 306 if he was 32, nor would other orators have addressed him in 307 and 310 as *imperator adulescens*[6] if he were 33 and 36. To those who believe in the genuineness of the *Life*, the most valuable and precise piece of evidence is Eusebius's description of his first meeting with the future emperor

[1] This paper was read to the International Conference on Patristic Studies at Oxford in 1951.

[2] Eus., *Vita Constantini*, ii. 51.

[3] Ibid., i. 5, 7–8; iv. 53.

[4] *Untergang*, i. 406 ff.

[5] Victor, *Caes.*, xli. 16; *Epit.*, xli. 15; Eutropius, x. 8. 2; Zonaras, xiii. 4.

[6] *Paneg. Vet.*, iv. 16, vi. 17, vii. 5. Seeck (loc. cit.) gives other less probant examples of similar language from the Panegyrists and also cites *Firm. Mat.*, i. 10. 16 and Lactantius, *Div. Inst.*, i. 1. 14.

as he was passing through Palestine with Diocletian, probably either in 296 when Diocletian was marching to Egypt to suppress the rebellion of Achilleus, or when he was returning from Egypt in 297. Eusebius describes Constantine as ἤδη ἐκ τοῦ παιδὸς ἐπὶ τὸν νεανίαν διαβάς, that is, about 13 or 14.[7] In that case Constantine would have been about 19 when the Persecution began in 303.

Can παῖς be used to describe a youth of 19? The edict, if genuine, will have been written in Latin, and the text we possess will be the official Greek translation. It is possible that Constantine used the word *puer*, which is used to describe young men of 19 or 20 when it is desired to emphasise their youth; Cicero for instance speaks of Octavian as *puer* at 19,[8] and Silius Italicus uses the same word of Scipio Africanus at 20.[9] In that case the official translator will have mechanically rendered *puer* by παῖς. But even if Constantine had written *adulescens* the translator would probably have rendered it παῖς, for in the Greek of the period there was no half way term between παῖς and νέος or νεανίας as the phrase which I have quoted above from Eusebius indicates, and νεός was clearly inappropriate since it failed to convey the emperor's meaning that he was still immature. Παῖς was the only word available, and it was not inappropriate, for it had by the fourth century come to cover a wider range of age than in classical Greek. This is most clearly demonstrated by a passage in Libanius (*Orat.*, liii. 3–4), where he protests against the novel practice of inviting παῖδες to the banquet of the Olympia. The kind of person who should be invited is ὅστις ἐκ παίδων ἐξῆλθε καί που τις καὶ μέλλων, πατήρ τε ὢν ἤδη καὶ δεικνὺς ἐν δικαστηρίοις αὐτόν. One could thus be a father and practise at the bar while still a παῖς. He cites his own case, where according to the good old practice he was not invited at the age of 14 or 18, but only when at 22 he had begun to make a name for himself. Granted then that Constantine was about ten years younger than he represented himself to be in his latter years—a supposition supported by all the evidence contemporary with his youth—he would naturally have described himself as *puer* or *adulescens* in 303, and the official translator would naturally have rendered either word by παῖς in Greek.

[7] Eus., *V.C.*, i. 19.
[8] Cic., *ad Fam.*, x. 28.3, xii. 25. 4; *ad Att.*, xvi. 11.6, 15.3; *Phil.*, iv. 3.
[9] Sil. Ital., xv. 33, 46.

A recently published papyrus has strikingly confirmed the authenticity of one of the Constantinian edicts cited by Eusebius. The papyrus is *P. Lond.* 878 and has been published by Mr. Skeat in *Aus Antike und Orient*, 127–30.[10] Mr. Skeat selected it because it contained a reference to Britain, but was unable to elucidate its character. The text is written on the back of a petition which he has plausibly dated to 319–20, and the hand 'does not appear to be very much later than that of the recto'. It is definitely a non-literary hand. We have therefore a document (in the narrow sense, not a book), written not long after 320. Following a suggestion made by Mr. C. E. Stevens of Magdalen College, Oxford, I searched the text of Eusebius's *Life of Constantine*. The papyrus proved to be part of Constantine's letter to the provincials issued after the defeat of Licinius, and to correspond verbatim with Eusebius, *Vit. Const.*, ii. 27 and 28 with the end of 26 and the opening of 29. By a fortunate chance it contains Constantine's allusion to the pains of Hell and his definition of τὸ θεῖον as ὁ μόνον τε καὶ ὡς ὄντως ἔ[στι καὶ διαρκῆ κατὰ πάντος ἔχει τοῦ χρόνου] τὴν δύναμιν.

Col. i

(about 22 lines lost)

1. [οὐδ' ἄν ἀπὸ λόγου συμβαίνοι. Ὅσοι μὲν γὰρ μετὰ δικαίας γνώμης ἐπί τινας ἔ]ρχ[οντα]ι—

2. [πράξεις καὶ τὸν τοῦ κρίττονος φόβον διηνεκῶς ἔχουσιν ἐν νῷ, βεβαία]ν τὴ[ν περὶ]—

3. [αὐτὸν φυλάττοντες πίστιν καὶ τοὺς παρόντας φόβους τε καὶ κινδύνους οὐκ ἄγουσιν]—

4. [τῶν μελλουσῶν ἐκείνων ἐλπίδων προτιμοτέρους· κἂν εἰ πρὸς καιρὸν δυσχερῶν]—

(foot of column)

1–4. The dashes at the ends of the lines are in the original; cf. Palaeographical Note. 1. ρ is certain, and ν virtually so. 2. the fragment of the χ is a line curving upwards. This is incompatible with the normal forms of ν used in the papyrus, but a ν of this unusual type occurs medially in σεμῖολογσνθαι in col. ii, l. 20.

10 Mr. Skeat has kindly provided a revised text of the papyrus, collated with that of Eusebius, together with notes on the palaeography and restoration of the text. These are printed below.

Col. ii

1. [τινων πειραθεῖεν, τῷ μείζονας ἑαυτοῖς ἀποκεῖσθαι πιστεύειν τιμὰς ἤνεγκαν, οὐδὲ τὰ προσ-]

2. [πεσόντα βαρέως, ἀλλὰ τοσούτῳ λαμπροτέρας ἔτυχον εὐκλείας, ὅσῳ καὶ βαρυτέρων τῶν χαλεπῶν]

3. [ἐπειράθησαν. Ὅσοι δὲ ἢ τὸ δίκαιον ἀτίμως παρεῖδον ἢ τὸ κρῖττον, οὐκ ἔγνωσαν καὶ τοὺς τοῦτο]

4. [πιστῶς μετιόντας ὕβρεσι καὶ κολάσεσιν ἀνηκέστοις ὑποβαλεῖν ἐτόλμησαν, καὶ οὐχ ἑαυτοὺς μὲν]

5. [ἀθλίους ἐφ' οἷς διὰ τὰς τοιαύτας ἐκό]λαζ[ον προφάσεις ἔκριναν εὐδαίμονας δὲ καὶ μακαριστοὺς τοὺς]

6. [καὶ μέχρι τῶν τοιούτων τὴν πρὸς τὸ κρ]ῖττ[ον διασωζομένους εὐσέβειαν· τούτων πολλαὶ μὲν]

7. ἔπεσον στρατιαί, πολλαὶ δ' εἰς φυγὴν ἐ]τράπη[σαν, πᾶσα δὲ τούτων πολέμου παράταξις εἰς αἰσχίστην]

8. [ἔληξεν ἧτταν· ἐκ τῶν το]ιούτων ἀναφοίονται πόλεμ[ο]ι β[αρεῖς· ἐκ τῶν τοιούτων πορθήσεις πανώλε-]

9. θροι· ἐντεῦθεν ἐλατ]τώσις μὲν τῶν πρὸς τὰς χειρας ἀναγκ[αίων, πλῆθος δὲ τῶν ἐπηρτημένων]

10. [δεινῶν· ἐντεῦθεν οἱ τ]ῆς τοσαύτης ἀρχηςοὶ δυσσεβία[ς, ἢ ἀνατλάντες τὰ ἔσχατα, θάνατον]

11. [πανώλεθρον ἐδυστύ]χησαν ἢ ζωὴν ἐσχίστην διάγον[τες, θανάτου ταύτην βαρυτέραν ἐπέγνωσαν, καὶ]

12. [οἷον ἰσομέτρους ταῖ]ς ἀδικίαις τὰς τιμωρίας ἐκομί[σαντο. τοσοῦτον γὰρ ἕκαστος εὕραντο συμ-]

13. [φορῶν, ὅσον τις καταπ]ολεμῆσαι τὸν θεῖον, ὡς ᾤετο, ν[όμον ὑπ' ἀλογίας προήχθη· ὥστ' αὐτοῖς]

14. [μὴ] . . . [.] ρ . . [. .] . [. . εἶ]ναι βαρέα μόνον, ἀλλὰ καὶ τῶν ὑπὸ γ[ῆς κολαστηρίων χαλεπώτερον προσδοκᾶσθαι]

15. [τὸν] φόβον. τοιαύτης δὴ καὶ οὕτω βαρίας δυσσεβίας τὰ ἀνθρώ[πεια κατεχούσης, καὶ τῶν κοινῶν]

16. [οἷον] ὑπὸ νόσου λοιμώδους τινὸς ἄρδην διαφθαρῆναι κ[ινδυνευόντων, καὶ θεραπείας σωτηρίου]

17. [καὶ π]ολλῆς χρηζόντων, τ[ί]να τὸ θεῖον ἐπινοεῖ κουφισμό[ν, τίνα τῶν δεινῶν ἀπαλλαγήν; ἐκεῖνο δὲ]

18. [πάν]τως νοηταίον θεῖον, ὃ μόνον τε καὶ ὡς ὄντως ἔ[στι, καὶ διαρκῆ κατὰ παντὸς ἔχει τοῦ χρόνου]

19. τὴν δύναμιν. πάντως δὲ οὐ κόμπος τὸ τὴν π[αρὰ τοῦ κρίττονος εὐποιΐαν ὁμολογοῦντα]

20. σεμνολογῖσθαι τὴν ἐμὴν ὑπηρεσίαν πρὸς τὴν[ἑαυτοῦ βούλησιν ἐπι-
τηδείαν ἐζήτησέν τε]

21. καὶ [ἔκ]ρ[ινεν· ὁ]ς ἀπὸ τῆς Βριττανοῖς ἐκίνης θαλάττης[ἀρξάμενος,
καὶ τῶν μερῶν ἔνθα δύεσθαι]

22. τὸν ἥλ[ιον ἀνάγ]κῃ τινὶ τέτακται, κρίττ[ο]νι ἀπωθ[ούμενος καὶ
διασκεδαννὺς τὰ κατέχοντα]

23. πάντα [ἵν' ἅμ]α ἀνακαλοῖτο τὸ ἀνθρώπιον γένος τὴ[ν περὶ τὸν
σεμνότατον νόμον θεραπείαν,]

24. τῇ παρ' ἐμοῦ παιδευ[όμε]νον [ὑπ]ουργείᾳ ἅμ[α δὲ ἡ μακαριστὴ
πίστις αὔξοιτο ὑπὸ χειραγωγῷ]

25. τῷ κρίττονι. οὐ[δέποτε γὰρ ἄ]ν ἀγνώ[μων περὶ τὴν ὀφειλομένην
γενοίμην χάριν· ταύτην]

26. ἀρίστην διακονίαν, [τοῦτο κε]χαρισμέ[νον κ.τ.λ.

(foot of column)

1. 6. Read κρείττον. 8. Read ἀναφύονται. 9. Read ἐλαττώσεις, χρείας. 10. Read
ἀρχηγοί, δυσεβείας. 11. Read αἰσχίστην. 13. The letters φορον occur on a small
detached fragment which may come from the beginning of this line. If so, the papyrus omitted καὶ before καταπολεμῆσαι. 14. init. It is not clear which of the various
readings in this passage was supported by the papyrus. 15. Read βαρείας, δυσσεβείας.
17. The space seems to make it certain that καί was inserted before πολλῆς. 18. Read
νοητέον. 20. Read σεμνολογεῖσθαι. 21. Read τῆς πρὸς Βριττανοῖς ἐκείνοις. 22. Read
κρείττονι. 23. Read ἀνθρώπειον. 24. Read ὑπουργίᾳ. 25. Read κρείττονι.

I submit that we have in *P. Lond.* 878 a contemporary copy of the
Letter of A.D. 324. The papyrus proves beyond all reasonable
doubt the authenticity of one of the Constantinian documents
cited by Eusebius in the *Life,* and implies that of the rest. It does
not of course prove that the *Life* in which they are quoted is a
work of Eusebius, but I find it difficult to believe that a later
forger would have troubled to search out the originals of old
documents and copy them *in extenso.*

APPENDIX

By T. C. SKEAT
Department of Manuscripts, British Museum
Palaeographical Note.

The hand is a rapid, practised but unpretentious cursive. The
fourth century is an age of transition, in palaeography as in other
respects, and this hand is one of those which look back to the
third century rather than forward to the usual Byzantine type.

s

Professor E. G. Turner, who is editing the Abinnaeus papyri (mid 4th cent.), has given it as his opinion that the present hand in general style certainly seems to be earlier than the average hand of the Abinnaeus archive, and he suggests 330–50 as the outside limits within which the hand should be dated. This would not, of course, exclude the possibility of the papyrus being a contemporary copy of the Edict. In fact, the hand closely resembles that of P. Hamb. 21 (facsimile in Pl. VII) of a.d. 315, the similarity even extending to the long dashes at the ends of the lines, of which four are preserved in col. i.

Note on the restoration of the text.

The restoration of the last four lines of col. i rests wholly upon the identification of the four or five letters preserved. Such an identification must necessarily be somewhat precarious, but it is supported by the fact that nowhere else in the earlier part of the Edict do the same letters occur in the correct relative positions. If, then, the identification be accepted, l. 2 of col. i contained 63 letters, and the remaining lines of col. i here printed have been restored to about the same length. Col. ii, as restored, contains 26 lines. If col. i contained the same number of lines, there must be 22 lines wholly lost before the first line here printed. If these 22 lines contained 63 letters each, the total number of letters in them would be 22x63=1386. This figure is in close agreement with the number of letters in the opening part of the Edict (*i.e.* preceding the text here printed) which contains about 1350 letters. It is thus probable that the text of the Edict began at the top of col. i, and that it was not introduced by any heading or covering letter. The lines in col. ii were somewhat longer than those in col. i, the number of letters usually varying between 70 and 80. In lines 1–7 of col.ii, where little or no text is actually preserved, the text is printed *exempli gratia*, and there can of course be no certainty about either the readings of the papyrus or the exact points where the lines were divided.

CHAPTER TWELVE

THE DATE AND VALUE OF THE VERONA LIST

SINCE Bury's magistral article in this *Journal* over thirty years ago (XIII, 1923, 127 ff.) no scholar has attempted a comprehensive study of the date and value of the Laterculus Veronensis. Various historians have in passing expressed a preference for this date or that. Ernst Stein argued for 293–305 in *Rheinisches Museum* LXXVII (1925), 367, but in his *Geschichte des spätrömischen Reiches* I, 102, preferred 304–306. E. Schwartz in a rather fuller treatment (*Abh. Bayer. Akad., phil.-hist. Kl.*, 1937, 79–82) argued for a much later date, between 325 and 337 for the eastern dioceses, and under Valentinian I for the western dioceses. Others have more modestly confined themselves to certain areas. H. Nesselhauf has maintained a relatively early date (305–306) for Gaul (*Abh. Preuss. Akad., phil.-hist. Kl.*, 1938, 8 ff.), while W. Seston has argued for a date after 306 for Africa (*Dioclétien et la Tétrarchie*, I, 327–8). It may be timely to reassess the problem, particularly as some new evidence has recently emerged.

It is common ground that the Verona list contains elements which cannot be later than the early decades of the fourth century. The name of the province Diospontus is last recorded in 325 in the signatures of the Council of Nicaea[1] (and shortly before that on a milestone[2] of the latter part of Licinius' reign, 317–324); it had already been superseded by the name Helenopontus in the last years of Constantine, 333–337, as another milestone[3] witnesses. The diocese of the Moesias is elsewhere recorded only in the inscription of C. Caelius Saturninus,[4] who was its vicar some time in Constantine's reign: the later division into two, Dacia and Macedonia, was probably in force as early as 327, when Constantine addressed a constitution[5] to Acacius, *comes Macedoniae*, for all other known *comites provinciarum* ruled over dioceses. In

---

[1] I quote here and elsewhere from Gelzer, *Patr. Nic. Nom.*, lx–lxiv.
[2] *C.I.L.* III, 14184[31].   [3] *C.I.L.* III, 14184[37].
[4] *I.L.S.* 1214.   [5] *Cod. Theod.* XI, iii, 2.

Africa the list records a division of Numidia into two provinces, Cirtensis and Militiana, which appears to have existed only in the first two decades of the fourth century. The history of the African provinces at this period is obscure and complex, but for the present purpose it will suffice to say that Numidia appears to have been undivided in 303, when Valerius Florus is styled *p(raeses) p(rovinciae) N(umidiae)* and was active in both halves of the province,[6] and Aurelius Quintianus still ruled *p(rovinciam) N(umidiam)* in November;[7] that Florus was *p(raeses) p(rovinciae) N(umidiae) M(ilitianae)* under the tetrarchy, 293–305,[8] and Valerius Antoninus *p(raeses) p(rovinciae) N(umidiae) C(irtensis)* in 306;[9] that there were still two Numidias in 312–3, when Constantine directed that subsidies be granted to the clergy in all the provinces of Africa, τάς τε 'Αφρικὰς καὶ τὰς Νουμιδίας καὶ τὰς Μαυρετανίας;[10] but that before 320, when Zenophilus was *consularis*[11] (of Numidia), Iallius Antiochus was *praeses prov. Numid.*[12] A few years later Aradius Proculus enumerates the provinces of Africa as 'proconsularem et Numidiam Byzacium ac Tripolim itemque Mauretaniam Sitifensem et Caesariensem'.[13] It would seem that there were two Numidias from 304–5 to 314–320.

Finally the Verona list records the division of Aegyptus into two provinces, Iovia and Herculia. J. Lallemand has recently established by an acute analysis of the papyrological evidence, supplemented by inscriptions and ecclesiastical documents, that this division cannot have been made earlier than 312, and cannot have lasted later than 324; Aegyptus Herculia is actually attested between 315 and 322.[14]

[6] *C.I.L.* viii, 6700; Optatus, iii, 8; Augustine, *c. Cresc.* iii, xxvii, 30; *A.E.* 1942–3, 81.

[7] *I.L.S.* 644.   [8] *I.L.S.* 631–3.

[9] *I.L.S.* 651, *C.I.L.* viii, 5526, 7965, 18700. It may be noted that *C.I.L.* viii, 7067, 'Valer . . . .nus v. p. . . . diar . . . ret . . .' does not (*pace* Anderson, *J.R.S.* xxii, 1932, 30–1) prove that the Numidias were reunited immediately under the same Valer[ius Antoni]nus. The inscription probably records his promotion to be [*rationalis Numi*]*diar*[*um et Mau*]*ret*[*aniarum*], and shows that two Numidias continued to exist (contrast *I.L.S.* 691 '*rat. Numidiae et Mau*[*reta*]*niarum*' under Constantine).

[10] Eusebius, *H.E.* x, 6. 1. I take it that the Africas are Proconsularis, Byzacium, and Tripolitania, the three subdivisions of the old proconsular Africa. See Addendum, p. 279.

[11] Optatus, *App.* i.

[12] *C.I.L.* viii, 7005 (cf. 7006).

[13] *I.L.S.* 1240.

[14] *Bull. Ac. Roy. Belg.* (*Classe des lettres et sciences mor. et pol.*), 5 Série, xxxvi (1950), 387–395.

This last fact eliminates the very early datings of the list which some scholars have favoured. If the document is homogeneous in date,[15] it cannot be earlier than 312, the earliest possible date for the creation of Aegyptus Herculia, nor later than 320, the latest possible date for the amalgamation of Numidia Cirtensis and Militiana. There is nothing in the document which requires an earlier date than 312, and this *terminus a quo* may be accepted. On the other hand there are features which may be thought to point to a later—in some cases a considerably later— date than 320, and on the strength of these it has been argued that the list or parts of it have been subjected to a later revision or revisions. If this were so the list would lose most of its value as an historical document, since no individual item would be securely dated except by external evidence.

The strongest evidence for later revision is in the diocese of Viennensis, where two provinces (Prima and Secunda) of Narbonensis and of Aquitania are recorded. In both cases there is indubitable evidence that in the middle years of the fourth century there was only one province. Saturninius Secundus was *praeses provinciae Aquitaniae* about the middle of the century,[16] and a synodical letter cited by Hilary and dated 358 recognizes only one Aquitania;[17] so also does Ammianus in his survey of Gaul.[18] For Narbonensis the evidence is similar; again there is the synodical letter of 358,[19] while Ammianus mentions a *rector Narbonensis* in 359 and 361, and ignores Narbonensis II in his survey.[20] Aquitania II is first attested in the provincial list of Festus,[21] which is to be dated shortly before 369, and Narbonensis II in an ecclesiastical document of 381.[22]

The examples of Numidia and Aegyptus, however, show that

---

[15] I ignore the two overt glosses 'Paphlagonia [nunc in duas divisa]' and 'Armenia minor [nunc et maior addita]'.

[16] *I.L.S.* 1255.

[17] *De Synodis*, proem (Migne, *P.L.* x, 479), 'dilectissimis et beatissimis fratribus et coepiscopis provinciae Germaniae Primae et Germaniae Secundae et Primae Belgicae et Belgicae Secundae et Lugdunensis Primae et Lugdunensis Secundae et provinciae Aquitanicae et provinciae Novempopulanae et ex Narbonensi plebibus et clericis Tolosanis et provinciarum Britanniarum episcopis'.

[18] xv, xi, 13.

[19] See note 17.

[20] xviii, 1, 4; xxii, i, 2; xv, xi, 14.

[12] *Breviarium*, 6.

[22] Mansi, *Conc.*, iii, 615, 'dilectissimis fratribus et episcopis provinciae Viennensium et Narbonensium Primae et Secundae'.

provinces which had been divided were sometimes reunited. The same may have happened in Gaul, and there is, as Mommsen pointed out,[23] and Nesselhauf has recently emphasised,[24] good reason to believe in the case of Narbonensis that it did. It appears from the *Notitia Galliarum* that Narbonensis I occupied the western part of the province of that name, Viennensis the centre, and Narbonensis II the extreme east. Narbonensis II must in fact have been carved out of Viennensis in the latter part of the fourth century. Why then was it not called Viennensis II? The only explanation seems to be that the original Narbonensis was first bisected into Prima, the western half, and Secunda, the eastern, and that subsequently Viennensis was formed out of the western half of Secunda. Later, Narbonensis II was merged in Viennensis, the stage we find in the mid-fourth century, and finally in the late fourth century was revived under its old name.

The other evidence for a later revision lies in the Nicene signatures for the dioceses of Asiana and Oriens. There is no good reason for doubting that the provincial arrangement of the Nicene signatures is original and follows the secular boundaries.[25] The use of the name Diospontus proves an early date, for, as noted above, this name was replaced by Helenopontus before the end of Constantine's reign—and probably within a very few years of the Council, while Helena was still alive. That the bishops strictly observed the contemporary secular arrangements cannot be proved, but they certainly took account of relatively recent administrative changes, dating from the latter part of Diocletian's reign, and if they modified ecclesiastical provinces according to the official reorganisation thus far, there seems no reason why they should not have continued the process.

The Nicene list recognizes only one Phrygia, instead of the Phrygia I and II of the Verona list, and does not admit the existence of the province of Hellespontus, placing two of its cities, Ilium and Cyzicus, in Asia. In Oriens the Verona list

[23] *Ges. Schr.* v, 583.

[24] *Abh. Preuss. Ak.* (*phil.-hist. Kl.*), 1938, 9 ff.

[25] Sir William Ramsay (*Cities and Bishoprics of Phrygia*, 80 ff.) threw doubt on their value, basing his argument on Gelasius ii, 28 and 38. This is a select list of Nicene signatures in which a few bishops sign each for a group of provinces, and amongst these appear Phrygia I and II (also Hellespont). But this list is clearly a late compilation containing many anachronisms, though it incorporates some old material (e.g. the name Diospontus) taken from the genuine signatures.

records 'Arabia item Arabia Augusta Libanensis Palestina Fenice Syria Coele Augusta Eup(hr)atensis'. It thus depicts Syria as divided into three coastal provinces, Coele Syria, Phoenice, and Palestine, and three or four provinces facing on the desert, Augusta Euphratensis, Augusta Libanensis, Arabia, and probably a second Arabia. This corresponds with the arrangements known in the late fourth century, though the titles of the inland provinces differ. The Nicene signatures recognize only the old third-century provinces of Coele Syria (which includes Hierapolis and other cities of the later Euphratensis), Phoenice (which also includes cities of the later Libanensis, Emesa and Palmyra), Arabia and Palestine (which last includes Aelia, which in the Principate had been in Arabia). They also ignore Osrhoene, putting its capital, Edessa, in Mesopotamia.

Sundry documents connected with the council of Sardica[26] (343-4) give the same arrangement for Oriens—Mesopotamia, Coele Syria, Phoenice, Palestine, Arabia—but in Asiana record a separate province of Hellespont and (in some cases) two Phrygias. Ammianus in his survey of Oriens[27] (inserted in the narrative under the year 353) distinguished Osrhoene from Mesopotamia, and Euphratensis from Syria, but still makes Phoenice one province, including both the coastal cities and Damascus and Emesa, and for the rest speaks only of Palestine and Arabia. We know from a letter of Lebanius[28] that Euphratensis already existed in 358, and from another group of letters[29] that Palestine was divided in 357-8, the area which had been the southern half of Arabia becoming a separate province, known (as appears from later sources[30]) as Palestina Salutaris.

The Verona list for Asia Minor might then be dated between 325 (when Hellespont was still part of Asia, and Phrygia was undivided) and 337 (when Diospontus had become Helenopontus). For Oriens the date would have to be later than 343-4 (when the Nicene arrangement still stood), but earlier than 357-8 (when Palestine was divided).

[26] Hilary, de Synodis, 33 (Migne, P.L. x, 506–7), Opera iv (C.S.E.L.), 49, 68, Athanasius, Apol. c. Ar. i, 37, Hist. Ar. 28, Theodoret, H.E. ii, 8, Vigilius Tapsensis, c. Eutychem, v, 3 (Migne, P.L. lxii, 136), collated by Feder in Sb. Ak. Wien. CLXVI (1910), 5, 64–70, 94–100.

[27] xiv, viii, 7–13.   [28] Ep. 21.

[29] Ep. 334–5 (cf. 315, 321, 563).

[30] Not. Dig. Or. i, 87, ii, 16, xxii, 24; Jerome, Quaest. ad Gen. xvii, 30.

The Nicene list, however, recognises only one Aegyptus, and in this case we happen to know that the two provinces of Iovia and Herculia were united in 324, and that Herculia was revived in 341 under the name of Augustamnica.[31] It is at least possible that the same happened in other cases, and the fact that the provinces of the Verona list mostly bear different names from those of the late fourth century is slightly in favour of this view. Euphratensis, though called Αὐγουστοευφρατησία in ecclesiastical documents, never again officially bears the title Augusta.[32] Augusta Libanensis is replaced by Phoenice Libanensis. The second Arabia, having been joined in the interval to Palestine, becomes Palestina Salutaris. Phrygia Secunda reappears as Phrygia Salutaris (first attested under that name in 361).[33] Only Osrhoene and Hellespontus keep their old names: in the last case an inscription[34] recording Anicius Paulinus as '[pr]oconsuli prov. Asiae et Hellesponti' (before he became prefect of the city in 331) shows clearly that Asia and Hellespont had been two provinces and were reunited under Constantine.

Thus far there would seem to be no cogent reason against accepting the Verona list as a homogeneous document drawn up in the second decade of the fourth century. There remains one possible objection. Mommsen[35] observed that, while in the eastern dioceses the order of the provinces is geographical, in the western it is official, consular provinces preceding praesidial. If this observation is true, it raises the presumption that different authors produced the two halves of the list at different dates. It would have the further effect, not noted by Mommsen, that the western half could not be as early as he dated it, 297, seeing that consular provinces did not exist at that time. It would also throw some doubt on a date earlier than 320, for the rank of

---

[31] Index to the Festal Letters of St. Athanasius, 13; cf. Cod. Theod. xii, i, 34 (342).
[32] The title Augusta Euphratensis is recorded in the Acta S.S. Sergii et Bacchi (Anal. Bolland., xiv (1895), 375 ff.), whose dramatic date is 303–5: these Acta, though rhetorically embellished, seem to rest on a genuine narrative. It is used in the Acta of Constantinople (381) and Chalcedon (451). The province is called Euphratensis in Polemius, the Notitia Dignitatum, Hierocles, Georgius Cyprius, and Just. Nov. viii, Notitia: also in Cod. Theod. vii, xi, 2; xv, xi, 2; Cod. Just. viii, x, 10. Augusta Euphratensis, which evidently survived in popular usage, reappears officially in Cod. Just. xii, lix, 10 under Leo.
[33] Cod. Theod. i, vi, 1.
[34] I.L.S. 1220.
[35] Ges. Schr. v, 580 ff.

consularis seems to have been very recently established at this time, and very few provinces had governors of that rank. As the point is of interest not only for the present argument, but on general grounds, it will be as well to set out the evidence. No province which is praesidial in the Notitia Dignitatum is known to have had a governor of higher rank since the tetrarchy, and as the tendency after Diocletian was always to upgrade provinces, and never to downgrade them, it is very unlikely that any had. We can leave out of account the Italian provinces and Sicily, governed under Diocletian by *correctores*, most of whom were later upgraded to *consulares*. We thus need only consider the remaining consular provinces, which number fifteen in the East, and thirteen (excluding the later creation of Valentia) in the West. Of these nine and ten respectively can be proved to have been praesidial at one time, and in two more eastern provinces there is evidence which suggests, though it does not prove, that they were governed by equestrian *praesides*. The doubt arises from the ambiguity in the use of the term *praeses*, which was certainly still used at the beginning of Diocletian's reign in its old vague sense of 'governor' (of any grade), and does not seem to become a technical term for the lowest grade of governor (as opposed to *corrector*, *consularis* and *proconsul*), till the latter part of Constantine's reign.

PALESTINE. Eusebius speaks of τὸ περὶ τὸν ἡγεμόνα στρατιω-
τικὸν στῖφος (*Mart. Pal.*, 4, 8) and τῆς ἡγεμονικῆς τυγχάνων οἰκετίας (*Mart. Pal.*, 11, 24), but the literary usage of ἡγεμών at this date is probably not technical.

PHOENICE. *P. Ryl.* IV, page 104, 'domino suo Achillio ἡγεμ. Φοινείκης' (317–23) is perhaps not technical, but is confirmed by *Cod. Just.*, II, lvii, 1, 'Marcellino praesidi Foenice' (342); *C.I.L.* III, 6661, from Palmyra, probably refers to the governor of Augusta Libanensis.

COELE SYRIA. In *I.L.S.* 1211, 'L. Aelio Helvio Dionysio c.v. iudici sacrarum cognitionum totius Orien., praesidi Syriae Coele[s], correctori utriusque Italiae', *praeses* is clearly used untechnically, since the man was a senator; he was later in 298 proconsul of Africa (*frag. Vat.* 41), and in 301 *praefectus urbi*. *Cod. Just.*, IX, xli, 9, 'ad

Charisium praesidem Syriae' (290), is doubtful, but a tiny fragment from Aradus, *C.I.L.* iii, 185, 'in]victis A[ugg . . . v.p. pr. . . .' settles the matter.

CILICIA.　*C.I.L.* iii, 223, 'Aimilius Marcianus v.p. praes. Ciliciae' (under the tetrarchy). Cf. also *C.I.L.* iii, 13619–21, *Cod. Theod.* xi, xxx, 24 (348), ii, xxi, 1 (358).

PAMPHYLIA.　*Cod. Theod.* xiii, x, 2, 'ad Eusebium v.p. praesidem Lyciae et Pamphyliae' (311; see Seeck, *Regesten*, 52) and *I.G.R.* iii, 434, τὸν διασημότατον ἡγεμόνα Λυκίας Παμφυλίας Τερέντιον Μαρκιανόν.

BITHYNIA.　Lactantius, *de Mort. Pers.* 16, 'Hieroclem ex vicario praesidem' (of Bithynia in 303) is doubtful. Hierocles was a *v.p.* when *praeses* (of Augusta Libanensis?) in *C.I.L.* iii, 6661, and presumably as *vicarius*, since all known *vicarii* under Diocletian were *perfectissimi*.

EUROPA.　*I.G.R.* i, 789–92, ἡγεμονεύοντος τοῦ διασημοτάτου Δομιτίου Δομνείνου (tetrarchy).

THRACE.　*I.L.S.* 8944, 'Palladio v.p. praesi[de p]rovinciae Thraciae' (*c.* 340).

CRETE.　*I.G.R.* I, 1511-2, Μᾶρχος Αὐρήλιος Βύζης ὁ διασημότατος ἡγεμὼν τῆς Κρήτης (tetrarchy).

MACEDONIA.　*A.E.* 1939, 191. 'Aur. Nestor. v.p. praes. prov. Maced.' (Carinus); *Acta Agapae, Irenae, Chionae; Studi e testi*, ix (1902), 15, Δουλκίτις ἡγεμών at Thessalonica in 304.

DACIA　*Cod. Theod.* ii, xix 2, 'ad Claudium praesidem MEDITERRANEA.Daciae' (321); Dacia was at this time apparently re-united.

PANNONIA II.　*Acta Irenaei*, Knopf-Krüger, *Ausgewählte Märtyrerakten*,[3] 103, Probus *praeses Pannoniae* at Sirmium in 303–5. *I.L.S.* 1253, 'Clodio Octavian-[o], v.c., pontifici maiori, consul⟨ar⟩i Pannoniarum secundae post presides primo'. He was later proconsul of Africa under Julian and Jovian (Amm. Marc. xxix, iii, 4, *I.L.S.* 756), and

	perhaps the immediate predecessor of Africanus, consular of Pannonia, who was executed in 354 (Amm. Mar., xv, iii, 7; xvi, viii, 3).
BYZACIUM.	*A.E.* 1908, 197, '[V]arius Flavia[nu]s, v.p. p.p. Val. [Byz.]' (tetrarchy); *I.L.S.* 6111 (321), 1240. This is a test case for the technical use of *praeses*, for Aradius Proculus is described as 'praesidi provinciae Byzacenae, consulari provinciae Europae et Thraciae, consulari provinciae Siciliae', and this though he was a senator by birth: that is, *praeses* is the title of a particular grade of governorship, normally held by a *v.p.* but on occasion by a *v.c.*
NUMIDIA.	See, above, p. 264, notes 6–9 and 12.
BAETICA.	*C.I.L.* II, 2204, 'Octavius Rufus p. provinc. Baet[ic]' (Constantine), 2205, '. . . s Faustinus v.p. [praese]s prov. Baet.' (Constantine); *Cod. Theod.* XI, ix, 2, 'ad Egnatium Faustinum praesidem Baeticae' (337).
LUSITANIA.	*I.L.S.* 1218, 'Caeciliani p.v. . . . praes. Lusitaniae'; *C.I.L.* II, 5140, 'Aur. Ursinus v.p. p. provinc. Lusitaniae' (tetrarchy); 481, 'C. Sulpicius . . .s v.p. p.p. L.' (316); *I.L.S.* 5699, 'Numeri Albani v.c.p.p. L.' (336). This is another case of a senator holding the rank of *praeses*.
CALLAECIA.	*Acta Marcelli, Anal. Boll.* XLI (1923), 260, Fortunatus *praeses* at Legio. *C.I.L.* II, 4911, 'Antoninus Maximinus a nova provincia [C]al[laecia] primus consularis [ant]e praeses' (under Maximus).
VIENNENSIS.	*C.I.L.* XII, 1852, 'M. Alfius Apronianus v.p. p.p. Fl. Vienn.' (Constantine).
LUGDUNENSIS I.	*Cod. Theod.* XI, iii, 1, 'ad Antonium Marcellinum praesidem provinciae Lugdunensis primae' (319). The governor is addressed as 'vir perfectissime' in 297 by Eumenius (*Pan. Vet.*, IX, 1, 4, 6).
GERMANIA I.	*C.I.L.* VI, 1641, 'praeses [provi]nciae Germaniae superioris v.p.' (Diocletian?).

BELGICA II.   *Cod. Theod.* VII, xx, 1 and 2. This depends on
                Seeck's plausible theory (*Regesten*, p. 60) that
                law 1, addressed 'Floriano praesidi', is the
                covering letter of law 2, an edict, and that both
                were posted 'in civitate Velovocorum' in 326.
I can find no evidence for Cyprus, Hellespontus, Lydia, Galatia I,
Germania II, Belgica I, and Maxima Caesariensis. It may be
convenient also to set out the evidence for early *praesides* of other
provinces ruled under the principate by *legati Augusti pro praetore*
or proconsuls.

BRITAIN.   *I.L.S.* 5435, 'v.p. pr. [prov. Brit. pr.]'; *J.R.S.*
                XIX (1929), 214 (tetrarchy).
TARRACONENSIS. *C.I.L.* II, 4104, 'v. perf. praes. prov. Hisp. Cit.'
                (288–9), 4105, 'v.p. [p.p.] H. Tarrac.' (312),
                4106, 4108 (Constantine).
RAETIA.   *C.I.L.* III, 5785, 5862; *I.L.S.* 618 (290),
                'v.p.p.p.R.'
NORICUM.   *I.L.S.* 4197 (311); *C.I.L.* III, 5326 (Constantine),
                'v.p.p.p.N. Mt.'
PANNONIA I.   *I.L.S.* 704, 'v.p.pr.p. P. super.' (Constantine).
DALMATIA.   *I.L.S.* 5695, 'v.p. praes. prov. Del.' (280).
ARABIA.   *C.I.L.* III, 14149, 'praeses provinciae Arabiae'
                (tetrarchy), 14157, 'v.p. praes. provinc. Arabiae'
                C. H. Kraeling, *Gerasa*, nos. 105–6, 'v.p.
                praeses provinciae Arabiae' (tetrarchy), 160–1.
I know of no evidence for the Moesias and Narbonensis and
Aquitania.

To return to Mommsen's views, which still appear to receive
very wide acceptance among scholars, it is true that no official
order is perceptible in the eastern dioceses, and that in Asiana it is
obviously ignored, the proconsular province of Asia coming
fourth. It is also true that a number of geographical sequences
can be traced. But it is difficult to see any rational order, geographical or otherwise, in the opening of the Pontic list
(Bithynia, Cappadocia, Galatia) or in the end of the Asianic (Caria,
Insulae, Pisidia, Hellespontus), and many minor irregularities
occur. The order is in fact arbitrary with a geographical bias.

In the western dioceses it is impossible to make an official
order fit any given date. Mommsen evidently based his hypothesis
on the list of consular provinces in the *Notitia*, but was obliged,

in order to make it work, to assume that at the time of the Verona list some of these provinces were still praesidial. Thus in Britain the only consular province (ignoring Valentia), Maxima Caesariensis, comes third on the Verona list: Mommsen has therefore to conjecture that all four provinces were praesidial—which reduces an 'official' to a purely arbitrary order. Similarly in Gaul Lugdunensis I (consular) comes after Sequania (praesidial): therefore, it is inferred, it was still praesidial, as in fact it is recorded to be in 319. But Belgica II, second on the list, seems still to have been praesidial in 326; so that the Verona list must be more recent than that date. Viennensis, which heads the list of that diocese, was still praesidial under Constantine. In Spain Gallaecia (consular) is below Carthaginiensis (praesidial). The solution here is simple, for Gallaecia was apparently promoted by the usurper Maximus. But Lusitania, second on the list, was still praesidial in 336, and Baetica, the first, in 337: the Verona list must be brought down below that date if the official order is to be preserved at all.

In the diocese of Pannonia Clodius Octavianus, later to be proconsul of Africa in 363, was 'consul⟨ar⟩i Pannoniarum secundae post presides primo'. The order of the Verona list, where Pannonia II comes first, is therefore only official after the middle of the fourth century. In Africa, however, the first four provinces are proconsularis, Byzacium, Numidia Cirtensis, Numidia Militiana. Byzacium was still praesidial in 321, whereas Numidia had been united under a consular by 320. Here the official order is only possible before 320, and even so is reduced to putting the proconsular province first.

Any attempt to read an official order into these lists leads to confusion. Their order is in fact not much more arbitrary than that of the eastern lists. Pannonia, as Bury observed,[36] can be read equally well geographically as officially. Here and elsewhere the author shows a tendency to begin a diocese with a province of the same name (Britannia, Viennensis, (Africa) proconsularis), and where there were two provinces, Prima and Secunda, to place them together in that order (even if, like the two Narbonenses, they were not contiguous). He also tends to relegate outlying or marginal provinces to the end. Thus Tingitana comes at the end of Spain, and the Alpine provinces at the end of Gaul,

[36] *J.R.S.* 1923, 136.

Viennensis and Italy. Making allowances for these tendencies a rough geographical order is observed. Thus in Italy he goes from north to south in Italy proper, and throws in the islands and Alpine provinces at the end. In Africa he goes from east to west, in Gaul he sweeps round clockwise, in Viennensis he moves eastwards, in Spain northwards.

If the above arguments are correct, some important historical conclusions follow. Diocletian and his immediate successors pursued a very drastic policy of splitting up provinces. The Verona list represents almost the maximum of that policy. The Nicene signatures seem to indicate an advance, in that they separate Lycia from Pamphylia, whereas the Verona list has only Pamphylia. The name may represent the double province, which was still undivided in 311.[37] But it is more likely that Lycia has dropped from the text owing to its resemblance to Lydia. There is another case where the Verona list may be presumed to have once contained a name which has disappeared. The province of Tripolitania certainly existed under Maxentius (306–13)[38] and probably in the early part of his reign, if not earlier;[39] the name has presumably vanished in the corruption of the text at the end of the diocese of Africa. It may be noted, moreover, that as Bury[40] suggested, the words 'Moesia superior Margensis' are not likely to be the cumbrous title of one province, but to represent two, Moesia Superior, and an otherwise unknown Margensis; just as 'Arabia item Arabia Augusta Libanensis' probably represents three provinces, two Arabias and Augusta Libanensis. It may also well be that 'Dacias' is not a mere scribal error but means two Dacias, for there were two under Carus.[41]

[37] Cod. Theod. XIII, x, 2 (Seeck, Regesten, 52, for date).
[38] I.R.T. 465.
[39] I.L.S. 9352 shows that Aur. Quintianus, praeses of Numidia in 303 (I.L.S. 644), was praeses of Tripolitania before or after that date. It also mentions his predecessor as praeses of Tripolitania, Val. Vivianus (cf. also I.R.T. 577; C.I.L. VIII, 22763). In view of these facts I do not favour Seston's hypothesis (Dioclétien et la Tétrarchie, I, 327–31) that Numidia Militiana was the southern half of Numidia plus Tripolitania. There was a province officially called Tripolitania in the very early years of the fourth century. Seston's province would be a very awkward geographical unit. And a province the main part of which was Tripolitania would surely have been called Africa not Numidia: for although the legate of Numidia had long been responsible for policing the desert behind the three cities (I.R.T. 880), the proconsul of Africa still ruled the cities under Carus (I.R.T. 461). Moreover in 314 Tripolitania and two Numidias existed at the same time: Optatus, App. III.
[40] J.R.S. 1923, 135–6.　　　　[41] Klio, 1912, 234–9: cf. Bury, J.R.S. 1923, 135.

It also appears that Diocletian and his immediate successors had very little use for senators. The two senior proconsulates of Africa and Asia were allowed to survive, though drastically reduced in area, especially the latter. Some other proconsuls existed early in Diocletian's reign, in Crete[42] for instance, but by the early fourth century all seem to have vanished. Most were replaced by *praesides*, two by *correctores*; Sicily[43] was no doubt regarded as virtually a part of Italy, and Achaea[44] received special treatment, as so often, for sentimental reasons. The recorded *correctores* of these provinces are all senators, but in principle *viri perfectissimi* were eligible for such posts, as the record of Italian *correctores* shows.[45] A further reason for the change of title was no doubt that all proconsuls were deemed to be exempt, as the proconsuls of Africa and Asia were later,[46] from the authority of the praetorian prefects and their vicars. Diocletian was doubtless anxious to reduce this administrative inconvenience to a minimum and therefore, even if he often allowed senators to govern Sicily and Achaea, gave them a rank which brought them under the control of his prefects and vicars.

A few *legati* also existed in the early part of Diocletian's reign: one for instance is recorded in Phoenice,[47] and another in Moesia Inferior,[48] and Dionysius, the senator who is styled 'praeses Syriae Coeles', probably was a *legatus*.[49] Later the title disappears, and the provinces once ruled by *legati* all come under equestrian *praesides*. Senators were left with the two proconsulates of Africa and Asia, and the chance of being *corrector* of Sicily, Achaea, or one of the new Italian provinces.

[42] *A.E.* 1933, 101; 1934, 259.
[43] *Acta S. Eupli, Studi e Testi*, XLIX (1928), 47; *I.L.S.* 677; Eus. *H.E.* x, 5, 23; *C.I.L.* x, 7204; cf. *I.L.S.* 8843.
[44] *C.I.L.* III, 6103; cf. *B.S.A.* XXIX, 53, no. 80, and *I.G.* v, i, 538.
[45] *Clarissimi* are recorded in *I.L.S.* 614 (cf. *Cod. Just.* IX, ii, 9), 1211, 1212, 1213 (cf. *C.I.L.* x, 1655), 2941 (cf. *C.I.L.* VI, 1419, *A.E.* 1914, 249); *Frag. Vat.*, 292; *C.I.L.* x 4785; XI, 1594; *perfectissimi* in *I.L.S.* 1218; *C.I.L.* IX, 687. *Perfectissimi* are still found sporadically among the Italian *correctores* throughout the fourth century, e.g. *A.E.* 1937, 119; *I.L.S.* 734, 749, 755, 780; *C.I.L.* x, 4755.
[46] As appears from the omission of Asia in *Not. Dig. Or.* II and XXIV, and of Africa in *Not. Dig. Occ.* II and XX.
[47] *A.E.* 1939, 58.
[48] Βάσσος λήγατος appears at Durostorum in the *Acta Dasii* (*Anal. Boll.*, XVI (1897), 11). The story is dated only to Diocletian and Maximian, and may fall early in the reign, as it is a military case having no connection with the Great Persecution.
[49] See above p. 269.

Constantine, it would appear, reversed both these policies fairly sharply, reuniting divided provinces, and employing senators more freely. In the West it was certainly he who amalgamated the two Numidias, and probably the two Dacias.[50] In the East he certainly reunited Aegyptus and added Hellespontus to Asia, and, if the Nicene signatures are trustworthy, also reversed the division of Phrygia, Mesopotamia, Coele Syria, and Phoenice, and amalgamated the southern half of Arabia, made into a separate province by Diocletian, with Palestine. He also, immediately after the defeat of Licinius, appointed Aradius Proculus consular of the province of Europe and Thrace.[51] In the light of this evidence it is plausible to attribute to him the recreation of a single Aquitania and the absorption of Narbonensis II into Viennensis, and the suppression of Margensis.

Constantine promoted Achaea to be a third proconsulate; this he seems to have done directly he gained control of the province in 313, for C. Vettius Cossinius Rufinus, who is recorded to have been 'proconsuli provinciae Achaea sortito' (a curious archaism), rose to be prefect of the city in 315.[52] It is, however, noteworthy that the revived proconsulate was not accorded the constitutional privilege of the old proconsulates of Africa and Asia, but was subject to the praetorian prefects[53] (and probably to the vicar of Macedonia). It was probably also Constantine who created a fourth proconsulate, attested only after his death. In 355 and 356 Justinus and Araxius, proconsuls, read imperial messages to the Senate of Constantinople,[54] and soon after 343 a proconsul Donatus was instructed to arrest Olympius, Bishop of Aenus (in the province of Rhodope).[55] The post was evidently created to lend dignity to Constantinople, and probably therefore by its founder. It has generally been taken to be the proconsulate of the city only, but what we are told about Donatus suggests that Rhodope was under his authority, and that these men were proconsuls of the united province of Europe and Rhodope, with their seat at Constantinople.

[50] *Klio*, 1912, 234-9 (two Dacias in 283); *Cod. Theod*, ii, xix, 2 (one in 321).
[51] *I.L.S.* 1240.
[52] *I.L.S.* 1217.
[53] Achaea appears among the provinces 'sub dispositione v. ill. P.P.O. per Illyricum' in *Not. Dig. Or.* iii: the page on the vicar of Macedonia is missing.
[54] Themistius, *Or.* (*ed.* Dindorf) 502; *Cod. Theod.* vi, iv, 8, 9.
[55] Athanasius, *Apol. de fuga*, 3.

Constantine also appointed senators as *praesides*. The earliest attested instance is Aradius Proculus, who was *praeses* of Byzacium in 321.[56] Later we find Aco Catullinus, *vir consularis*, *praeses* of Gallaecia, and at the end of the reign Numerius Albinus, *v.c.*, is recorded as *praeses* of Lusitania.[57] But it was no doubt felt that the title of *praeses*, which had by now come to mean the lowest grade of governor, as opposed to proconsul or *corrector*, and was normally borne by men of equestrian rank, was inadequate for the dignity of a senator. Constantine created or revived the title of *consularis*. The title was in some sense a revival for 'legati Augusti pro praetore' had been known, semi-officially at any rate, as *consulares*: but the unanimity of the legal and epigraphical texts shows that the style *consularis* was now fully official. The first recorded instance of the title is Zenophilus, consular of Numidia in 320.[58] Some correctorial provinces were also early promoted. We find consulars of Aemilia and Liguria[59] as early as 321, of Campania[60] before 325, and of Sicily[61] soon after 321. In the East the amalgamated provinces of Europe and Thrace[62] were placed under a consular probably soon after 324, and late in Constantine's reign L. Crepereius Madalianus is styled 'consulari Ponti et Bithyniae':[63] the title is probably an archaism for Bithynia. Castrius Constans,[64] recorded in two south Phrygian inscriptions as ἡγεμών ὑπατικός or λαμπρότατος ἡγεμών, was also probably consular of reunited Phrygia in Constantine's reign, and the anonymous ὑπατικὸ[ν] ἡγεμόνα Φρυγ[ίας κὲ] Καρίας, who with grandiloquent archaism styles himself [πρ]εσβευτὴν κὲ ἀντιστρ[άτη-γον] τῶν Σεβαστῶν ὑπατ⟨ικ⟩όν, may perhaps be dated to the opening years of the joint reign of Constantine's three sons.[65] The alter-

[56] *I.L.S.* 1240; cf. 6111.
[57] *I.L.S.* 5699; *C.I.L.* ii, 2635. Under Constans a senator is *praeses* of Dalmatia (*C.I.L.* iii, 1982–3, 2771, 8710).
[58] Optatus, *App.* i, cf. *Cod. Theod.* xvi, ii, 7.
[59] *Cod. Theod.* iv, xiii, 1; xi, xvi, 2; cf. *I.L.S.* 2942.
[60] *A.E.* 1939, 151; cf. *I.L.S.* 1216, 1223–5, 2942; *Cod. Theod.* i, ii, 6.
[61] *I.L.S.* 1240; cf. 1216, 1227.   [62] *I.L.S.* 1240.   [63] *I.L.S.* 1228.
[64] *A.E.* 1940, 187 (=M.A.M.A. vi, 94); *I.L.S.* 8881. The first inscription was found at Heraclea ad Salbacum (later in the province of Caria), the second at Eumeneia.
[65] *J.R.S.* 1932, 24 (from Hierapolis and Laodicea). The area which he governed need not have comprised the whole of Phrygia and Caria; for Phrygia (Pacatiana) included some Carian cities, and was officially known under Valens as Καροφρυγία (Theodoret, *H.E.* iv, 8, 9). Castrius Constans' province included a Carian city (see Note 64).

T

native dating to the middle years of Diocletian's reign, suggested by Anderson, is also possible; the inscription would then mark an early stage in the dismemberment of Asia instead of a temporary reunion of Diocletianic provinces. The use of the old title 'legatus Augusti pro praetore consularis' may be thought to favour the earlier date, but on the other hand it seems unlikely that Diocletian, who consistently suppressed old *legati*, would have created a new one.

Constantine's policy of building up larger provinces was not carried on by his sons, and in the East Constantius II soon set about reversing it, reviving Aegyptus Herculia as Augustamnica as early as 341. By the end of his reign most of the provinces of the Verona list had been reconstituted in the East.

The other process of upgrading provinces seems to have gone on with little, if any, interruption.[66] Owing to the inadequacy of the evidence it is difficult to say how far Constantine had carried the policy before he died, and therefore how far his sons continued his policy. The *corrector* of Flaminia and Picenum was promoted to a consular about 350,[67] as was the *praeses* of Pannonia II,[68] and Baetica, still under a *praeses* in 337, was under a consular in 357.[69] Coele Syria was also a consular province in 344,[70] but may well have been so already under Constantine. Many provinces are first attested as consular in the 360's, and while a few, like Tuscia and Umbria, and Venetia and Histria,[71] can be proved to have been promoted in that period: for most there is no evidence.

---

[66] The consular governors of Phrygia or Phrygia and Caria (see notes 64 and 65) disappear in favour of *praesides* of the two Phrygias and Caria; here no doubt the break-up of the complex governed by a consular carried with it the disappearance of the *consularitas*. A doubtful case is Phoenice, which was under a *praeses* in 342 (*Cod. Just.* II, lvii, 1). Socrates (*H.E.* I, 29) speaks of Archelaus the ὑπατικός as arresting Arsenius at Tyre, but his terminology cannot be pressed. Seeck (*Regesten* 39–40) argues that the Dionysius who received two constitutions (*Cod. Theod.* IX, xxxiv, 4; VIII, xviii, 4; *Cod. Just.* VI, ix, 8) at Tyre and Heliopolis in 328–9 is identical with the Dionysius ἀπὸ ὑπατικῶν who presided at the Council of Tyre in 335 (Eus. *Vita Const.* IV, 42) and had been consular of Phoenice in 328–9. This is plausible, but not conclusive; for Dionysius is a common name; and even if the same man is meant in both cases, he might have been *praeses* of Phoenice, consular of some other province, and then president at Tyre.

[67] Contrast *C.I.L.* VI, 1772; XI, 6218–9; XIV, 3582–3, with *A.E.* 1904, 52.

[68] *I.L.S.* 1253; see above p. 270.

[69] *Cod. Theod.* IX, xlii, 3.

[70] *Cod. Theod.* XI, xxxvi, 7; cf. 8 and x, i, 6.

[71] Contrast *Cod. Theod.* IX, i, 8 with XII, i, 72; *C.I.L.* v, 8658, 8987, with *Cod. Theod.* VIII, viii, 1; XI, vii, 10.

The proconsul whose seat was at Constantinople disappeared when in 359 the city received its first prefect.[72] No more proconsulates were created till the early 380's, when three appear more or less simultaneously, Palestine[73] in the East, Campania[74] in Italy, and a third in Spain;[75] all three were suppressed after a very few years.

ADDENDUM

P. 264, par. 1, l. 6 from the end, after the word Μαυρετανίας: and in the first half of 314, when Constantine instructed Aelafius to despatch to Arles not only Caecilian (from Proconsularis) but others 'de Byzacenae, Tripolitanae Numidiarum et Mauretaniarum provinciis'. Optatus, *App.* III.

[72] Soc., *H.E.* II, 41; *Chron. Min.* I, 239.
[73] *Cod. Theod.* XI, xxxvi, 28; xxx, 42; x, xvi, 4.
[74] *I.L.S.* 5702, 1262–3, 8984; *C.I.L.* IX, 1568–9; x, 3843.
[75] Sulp. Sev. *Chron.* II, 49.

CHAPTER THIRTEEN

CAPITATIO AND IUGATIO

AMONG the many fields of Roman history which Mr. Last has illuminated the later Roman Empire is not the least, and it was he who first encouraged me to embark on its study. I hope, therefore, that he will accept this contribution to the volume dedicated to his honour both as testimony to the wide range of his interests and as a token of personal gratitude.

The problem of *capitatio* and *iugatio* has provoked much controversy and many ingenious theories have been propounded for its solution. In the limited space available it would have been impossible to traverse these theories in detail, and I have therefore thought it best simply to set out the evidence and to see how much can be deduced from it. Two general points must be premised. First, the accurate use of technical terms is not to be expected from the draftsmen of the Codes. They were more concerned with elegance than clarity and to avoid clumsy repetitions made a free use of synonyms, thereby often blurring the precise meaning of technical terms. In interpreting the Codes it is the meaning (where it can be divined) rather than the precise wording of the laws which is significant. Secondly, the system of assessing land tax and other levies on *iuga* and *capita* combined in some way, which is the problem to be investigated, was not universally applied to all parts of the empire at all times. These points will be more fully developed later. For the sake of clarity I would first set out the less equivocal evidence for the system of *iugatio vel capitatio* in those periods and those parts of the empire where it was applied.

There are in the Codes a number of laws in which *iuga* (*iugatio*) and *capita* (*capitatio*) are coupled together as the units of assessment for various taxes and levies.

(a) Cod. Theod. xi, xvi, 6 (346, 'ad vicarium Asiae'); *palatini* and citizens of Constantinople are to pay tax 'pro capitibus seu iugis suis'.

(b) xi, xxiii, 1 (361, 'ad senatum'); it is ordered that for the *protostasia* 'nec cuiusquam alterius iuga aut capita senatorum censibus adgregentur'.

(*c*) VIII, xi, 1 (364, a law of Valens to an unknown addressee); *discriptiones* are to be assessed 'pro capitatione aut iugatione'.

(*d*) XI, vii, 11 (365, *C.R.P.* of the West); taxes on imperial estates are levied 'pro iugatione vel capitatione'.

(*e*) VII, vi, 3 (377, *P.P.O. Or.*); a *vestis* is assessed in Thrace 'per viginti iuga seu capita', in Moesia and Scythia 'in triginta iugis seu capitibus', in Asiana and Pontica 'ad eundem numerum in capitibus seu iugis', but in Oriens and Egypt 'in triginta terrenis iugis'.

(*f*) XIII, x, 8 (383, 'ad populum', a western law); grants of immunity whereby 'iugatio vel capitatio' had been removed from the tax registers are cancelled.

(*g*) XV, iii, 5 (422, *P.P.O. Or.*); landowners are to contribute to the repair of the roads 'pro iugorum numero vel capitum quae possidere noscuntur'.

(*h*) XII, iv, 1 (428, *P.P.O. Or.*); a *discriptio* is levied on *possessiones* formerly belonging to *curiales* 'pro singulis earum iugis et capitibus'.

(*i*) XI, xx, 6 (430, *P.P.O. Or.*); a proportion is reclaimed for the treasury of tax abatements 'eorum iugorum sive capitum . . . quae . . . relevata sunt'.

From these laws it is plain the *iuga* and *capita* were units in the assessment of estates, and that they were of equal value; this emerges most clearly from (*e*). From (*e*) it also appears that a tax might be levied on both units combined (as was usually the case) or on one only. On the nature of *iuga* there is no question: they were units of land. This is implied in *Cod. Theod.* XI, i, 15 (366, *P.P.O. It.*), 'unusquisque annonarias species pro modo capitationis et sortium praebiturus', where *sortes* is substituted for the technical term *iugatio*, and is stated in (*e*) and in *Cod. Just.* XI, lii, 1 (c. 393, *P.P.O. Or.*), 'per universam dioecesim Thraciarum sublato in perpetuum humanae capitationis censu iugatio tantum terrena solvatur'. This law also informs us that *capitatio* covered human beings, and, since it states that as a result *coloni* were freed 'tributariae sortis nexu', shows us that *coloni* were among these human beings. Theod., *Nov.* XXII, 2, § 12 (443, *P.P.O. Or.*) amends law (*h*) by imposing the *discriptio* 'iugationibus tantum, non humanis vel animalium censibus neque mobilibus rebus'. This shows that *capita* included animals as well as human beings. Another law, *Cod. Theod.* v, xiii, 4 (368, *C.R.P.* of the West), which rules that, if a tenant improved an imperial estate, 'quidquid mancipiorum vel pecoris adcreverit capitationis aut canonis augmenta non patiatur' shows that agricultural slaves as well as *coloni* (and animals) came under the heading *capitatio*.

Similar information is contained in *Cod. Theod.* xi, xx, 6 ((*i*) above), a very complex law which requires detailed study. It first sets out the general ruling that wherever an assessment in *iuga sive capita* has been in any way reduced by special grant between 395 and the current year 430, one-fifth of the gain which has accrued to the owner thereby is to be refunded to the Treasury. Omitting all words irrelevant to our purposes the first sentence runs: 'eorum iugorum sive capitum . . . quae . . . relevata sunt . . . quinta pars commodi . . . arcae . . . societur.' There follows an exception: 'exceptis his quae in capitatione humana atque animalium diversis qualicumque [so the MS; Gothofredus emended to "qualitercumque"] concessa sunt.' There then follows a long section making the further concession that when the abatement was under 400 *iuga sive capita* the refund should be calculated upon half the figure only, and that when the abatement exceeded 400, the first 200 should not be counted. The relevant words are: 'ita ut omnium quae . . . in terrena sive animarum discriptione relevata sunt usque ad quadringentorum iugorum sive capitum quantitatem pars dimidia publicis censibus adiungatur,' etc. Omitting the exception made in the middle section, the meaning is plain enough: 'in terrena sive animarum discriptione' is a more explicit way of saying *iuga sive capita*, and emphasises that abatements in both schedules of the assessment are subject to the refund. What, then, is the meaning of the exception? At first sight it would appear that *capitatio humana atque animalium* must be something different from *animarum discriptio*, and it has been suggested the former means 'slaves and animals' and the latter *coloni*. But this runs contrary to the plain meaning of the words and to their usage in the Codes: as shown above, *humanus* is used elsewhere to cover *coloni*. My own view is that the two phrases must mean the same thing: it is very characteristic of the draftsmen to use loosely synonymous phrases to denote the same thing, and when they wish to make a distinction they usually make it explicitly. I would suggest that what were excepted were separate abatements in *capitatio*; that is, where a landlord whose human and animal stock had fallen had obtained a corresponding reduction of his *capitatio* without claiming a reduction in his *iugatio* as well (as he might well do on the ground that he could not cultivate all his land with his reduced manpower and stock), the abatement should stand. Admittedly the draftsman has not made his meaning clear, but the text, as noted above, is corrupt, and may once have been clearer: perhaps some such words as 'speciali beneficio' have dropped out after 'qualicumque'.

Further light is thrown on the problem by the epigraphic census records which I discussed in *J.R.S.* XLIII (1953) 49 ff. [ch. X above.] The register of Magnesia on the Maeander (Kern, *Inschr. Mag. Mae.* 122) is a list of estates (with the owner's name added), assessed in ζύγα and κεφαλαί, or sometimes in ζύγα only; for a farm, especially a small farm, might have no resident tenant or slaves, or stock, registered on it, but be worked by a neighbouring freeholder or tenant. The Chios register (Déléage, *La Capitation du Bas-empire*, 182–6) give a more elaborate classification. Some estates are assessed in ζύγα and παροίκων κεφαλαί (*colonorum capita*); in others δούλων κεφαλαί and ζώων κεφαλαί are added. At Tralles (*B.C.H.* 1880, 336–8) the register is by owners. Under each landlord come first δούλων καὶ ζώων κεφαλαί or ζώων κεφαλαί on various farms, and then the several farms, assessed at so many ζύγα and (in most cases) so many κεφαλαί; these last will represent *coloni* (with their animals). Lastly, at Astypalaea (*I.G.* XII, iii, 180), the property of Heracleidas is assessed: for each farm (except two which have ζύγα only) there is a figure of γῆς ζύγα and of ἀνθρώπων κεφαλαί, and these two figures are added together to form a total of ζυγοκεφαλαί (there is in some cases a fourth figure of ζύγα or ζυγοκεφαλαί which is added to the total of ζυγοκεφαλαί; it probably represents a supplementary assessment). The term ζυγοκεφαλή, it may be noted, recurs in laws of Anastasius (*Cod. Just.* x, xxvii, 2 § 8, ζευγῶν ἤτοι ζευγοκεφαλῶν) and Justinian (*Nov.* 17, 8, ζυγοκεφαλῶν ἢ ἰούγων), and in a fifth-century inscription from Mylasa (Grégoire, *I.G.C. As. Min.* I, 240, τῶν ζυγοκεφαλῶν).

The inscription from Astypalaea makes it plain that the total assessment of an estate was formed by adding together the *iuga* of land and the *capita* of persons (and animals, which are in fact, as I have argued in the article cited above, p. 237, n. 46, included in the ἀνθρώπων κεφαλαί), thus producing a total of *iuga vel* or *seu* or *et capita* (in Latin a handy portmanteau word like ζυγοκεφαλή, meaning 'assessment unit, whether *iugum* or *caput*', was never coined). Prima facie then it would seem that the assessment of an estate or farm was compiled as follows. The land was surveyed and the area of pasture, arable, vineyard, and oliveyard (or the number of olive trees) reduced to *iuga* on some such scheme as that set out in the Syro-Roman lawbook (for details see ch. X). The inhabitants (the owner, if resident, his resident *coloni*, and his and their slaves, and all their adult families) and the stock were then counted, and reduced to *capita* (for the details again see my article). The two totals were separately recorded, and also added to form the grand total of the assessment. The *annona* and other levies were normally assessed on the grand total, but payments might fall on the *iugatio* alone, as did *vestis* in Oriens and Egypt under *Cod. Theod.* VII, vi, 3, or on the *capitatio* alone, as did the levy 'annonarum et cellariensium specierum gratia' in Illyricum according to *Cod. Theod.* VII, iv, 32 (see below, pp. 289–90, for similar μερισμοί on κεφαλαί in Egypt).

If this reconstruction of the system is correct it is unlikely that there was (in the periods and areas in which it prevailed) any separate poll tax. On the other hand, since heads of population formed a part of the assessment on which taxes were levied, it was possible to reduce a taxpayer's burden by remitting his *caput* and those of his dependants. Such remissions were made to *actuarii* (*Cod. Theod.* VIII, i, 3, A.D. 333) and to soldiers and veterans (*F.I.R.*[2] I, 93, A.D. 311; *Cod. Theod.* VII, xx, 4; xiii, 6, 7, of A.D. 325, 370, and 375). Constantius II removed from the census lists the clergy with their families and servants (*Cod. Theod.* XVI, ii, 10, 14), a step which gave them immunity for the tax on their persons (cf. Basil, *Ep.* 104), but not for the tax on their land (*Cod. Theod.* XVI, ii, 15, § 2). Later, as the rural clergy grew in numbers, this immunity was curtailed. In 398 it was ruled that in villages and estates clergy 'eatenus ordinentur ut propriae capitationis onus ac sarcinam recognoscant' (*Cod. Theod.* XVI, ii, 33; cf. *Cod. Just.* I, iii, 16, of A.D. 409).

On a similar principle Constantine ruled in 332 that the receiver of a fugitive *colonus* 'super eodem capitationem temporis agnoscat' (*Cod. Theod.* V, xvii, 1). Justinian stiffened the penalty. The receiver was compelled 'omnis quidem temporis quo apud eum remoratus est publicas functiones sive terrenas sive animales pro eo inferre' (*Cod. Just.* xi, xlviii, 23, § 5): that is both the tax on the land which he should have been cultivating for his landlord, and that on his 'soul'.*

Most of the above laws are compatible with a straight poll tax, and have often been taken to allude to it. There are, however, two which strongly imply the contrary. In the Table of Brigetio (*F.I.R.*² i, 93) soldiers are allowed to excuse four (see p. 257) *capita* 'ex censu adque a praestationibus sollemnibus annonariae pensitationis', and some veterans 'ab annonario titulo duo kapita excusent, id est tam suum quam etiam uxoris suae'. This is surely explicit enough. The soldiers and veterans gain immunity for the personal *capita* of themselves and their wives (and parents), but the effect of this privilege is to reduce their liability to the regular land tax. Secondly, by *Cod. Theod.* vii, xx, 4 (325), soldiers

> suum caput, patris ac matris et uxoris, si tamen eos superstites habeant, omnes excusent, si censibus inditi habeantur. quod si aliquam ex his personis non habuerint vel nullam habuerint, tantum pro suo debent peculio excusare quantum pro iisdem, si non deessent, excusare potuissent, ita tamen ut non pactione cum alteris facta simulato dominio rem alienam excusent, sed vere proprias facultates.

A soldier is granted immunity for the *capita* of himself, his wife and parents, if they exist; but if he is an orphan bachelor he still gets immunity for the value of four *capita*, his own *caput* and three more equivalent units of his property, being only forbidden to convey his immunity to another by assuming fictive ownership of his property. These provisions strongly imply, if they do not necessarily presuppose, a consolidated tax on *capita* and other property, that is probably *iuga* of land (though the *peculium* might include animals and agricultural slaves).

The combined system is first clearly attested in the Table of Brigetio, that is in Illyricum in 311. Before that date *capitatio* is attested as a tax on *capita* of the population, but it appears to have been collected in money and to have been separate from the tax in kind on land, the *annona*. The edict of Aristius Optatus (*S.B.* 7622, A.D. 297) is inconclusive on this point, though it mentions separately payments assessed on land and payments assessed on the

---

* I take *functiones animales* to be identical with the *capitalis illatio* of the *colonus*, alluded to in the first paragraph of the law; cf. for the form of expression τυχικῆς (read ψυχικῆς) συντελείας in *Cod. Just.* x, xvi, 13, of A.D. 496.

rural population. *Cod. Just.* xi, lv, 1 (290, Syria), 'ne quis ex rusticana plebe quae extra muros posita capitationem suam detulit et annonam congruam praestat', is likewise inconclusive, though implying two separate taxes. But Lactantius (*de Mort. Pers.* 23), after describing Galerius' census of the population (presumably in Pontica), declares 'post hoc pecuniae pro capitibus pendebantur', and not taxes in kind such as were levied on the land. Arcadius Charisius (*Dig.* l, iv, 18, § 8) also distinguishes between the collector 'qui annonam suscipit vel exigit' and the 'exactores pecuniae pro capitibus' (cf. § 29, 'neque ab annona neque . . . a capitatione'). Finally, it may be noted that Galerius levied *capitatio* from the urban as well as the rural population in Asiana (*Cod. Theod.* xiii, x, 2), which implies that it was a money tax [see note 1].

There is only one Diocletianic law which links *capitatio* with land, *Cod. Just.* iv, xlix, 9 (given in 293 at Philippopolis),

> si minor a venditore . . . dicebatur capitatio praedii venditi et maior inventa sit, in tantum convenitur quanto, si scisset emptor ab initio, minus daret pretii, sin vero huiusmodi onus et gravamen functionis cognovisset, nullam adversus venditorem habet actionem.

But this may mean no more than that a landlord was responsible for the poll tax of the persons registered on his estate, as was apparently the case later in some Gallic provinces (see below, p. 287–8).

The system of *capitatio* and *iugatio* combined was applied in the fourth century to the dioceses of Thrace, Asiana, Pontica (*Cod. Theod.* vii, vi, 3), and is implied for Illyricum by the Table of Brigetio and for Oriens by *Cod. Theod.* vii, xx, 4, which was posted at Antioch: Egypt, however, as will be shown below, followed a different system. In Illyricum the system must have been abolished by Valentinian I when he suppressed the *capitatio* (*Cod. Just.* xi, liii, 1), and in Thrace by Theodosius I when he did the same there (*Cod. Just.* xi, lii, 1).

For the West the evidence is less explicit. The combination of *capitatio* and land is assumed in *Cod. Theod.* xi, i, 15, addressed to Probus, praetorian prefect of Italy, in 366. *Cod. Theod.* v, xiii, 4; xi, vii, 11, addressed to Florianus, Valentinian I's *comes rei privatae*, seems to imply the existence of the *capitatio* and *iugatio* system in the Western parts in general. *Cod. Theod.* xiii, x, 8, an edict *ad populum* issued 5th March, 383, from Milan, also seems to imply the existence of the system throughout the West. But this edict is paraphrased in a constitution issued 19th January, 383, to Probus, praetorian prefect of Italy (*Cod. Theod.* xi, xiii, 1), who is instructed to enforce it in Illyricum, Italy, the suburbicarian diocese and Africa. These two last documents reveal the danger of relying too much on the use of technical terms in imperial constitutions. In the first place the edict orders the cancellation of immunity on *iugatio vel capitatio*, while the instruction to Probus mentions only *iugatio* in the same context. Secondly, we know that in the suburbicarian diocese the fiscal unit of land was not the *iugum* but the *millena* (Déléage, o.c. 219 ff., arguing from *C.I.L.* x, 407; Just., *Prag. Sanct.* 26; Maj., *Nov.* vii; add Val., *Nov.* v) and that in Africa similarly it was not the *iugum* but the *centuria* (o.c. 228 ff. arguing from *Cod. Theod.* xi, i, 10; xxviii, 13; add Val., *Nov.* xxxiv). The imperial chancery thus used *iugatio* as a general term to cover any system of land assessment. It would be rash in view of this to infer from the use of such phrases as *iugatio vel capitatio* in general laws that the system prevailed in every diocese. There is, in fact, no specific evidence for the combined system in Italy, the suburbicarian diocese, or Africa, and in Africa there is presumptive evidence against it. *Cod. Theod.* xiii, iv, 4 (374, 'ad vicarium Africae'), very strongly implies that in Africa *capitatio* was levied on the urban population, and must therefore have been a separate poll tax, not merged in the land tax.

For the dioceses of Britain, Gaul, the Five Provinces, and Spain evidence is yet more tenuous. *Pan. Vet.* v, 5, 5, and 6, 1, prove that the *Gallicani census formula* included *hominum numerus* and *agrorum modus*, and ch. 11, 1–3, shows that the *civitas Aeduorum* was assessed at 32,000 *capita*. It has generally been assumed that this was the whole assessment, i.e. that the term *capita* denoted or included land. But ch. 12, 3, shows quite clearly that the *capita* which Constantine remitted represented human beings, and it seems much more probable that 32,000 *capita* comprised only the taxable population (males and females from, say, fourteen to sixty) of the *civitas*. Several laws addressed to the praetorian prefect of the Gauls (*Cod. Theod.* xii, i, 36; xi, xxiii, 2; xiii, x, 4 and 6, of 343, 362, and 370) mention a *capitatio plebeia*; the term does not occur elsewhere. It fell on both sexes between certain ages which are not specified; it does not appear whether it applied to the urban population. *Cod. Theod.* xi, xxiii, 2, 'prototypias et exactiones in capitatione plebeia curialium munera et quidem inferiora esse minime dubitatur', shows that it was separately levied, and therefore probably a poll tax. Another law (*Cod. Theod.* xi, i, 26) addressed to the praetorian prefect of the Gauls in 399 shows that in some provinces under his jurisdiction *certus plebis numerus* was registered on each estate, whose owner was responsible for their *munera*. This implies that in some provinces the *capitatio plebeia* was entirely divorced from the land tax, but that in others, 'in quibus haec retinendae plebis ratio adscriptioque seruatur', the landowner was somehow responsible for the fiscal obligations of *plebeii* registered on his land. But this does not prove that the combined *capitatio* and *iugatio* system prevailed: the landlord may only have had to collect a poll tax. There is one other reference which implies that in the Gallic system landlords were responsible for *capita*—Sidonius Apollinaris, *Carm*. 13, where he begs Majorian to deduct three *capita* from his assessment.

A law of Constans (*Cod. Theod.* xi, xii, 1), 'publicus ac noster inimicus diversis immunitatem dederat iugorum capitationibus et professionibus amputatis', must refer to Gaul, the dominion of Constantine II, but it is difficult to deduce anything from this gem of rhetoric. Both *iugorum* and *capitationibus* cannot be technical, for on no theory could *iuga* be assessed in *capita*. One may take *iugorum* to mean 'landed property' and translate 'cutting down the assessments of *capita* and the declarations (of land) for landed property'. Or *capitatio* may be taken very loosely as 'assessment' in general, giving 'cutting down the assessments and declarations of units of land'. This is, incidentally, the only passage which mentions *iuga* in the Gallic prefecture; it would be very unwise to draw any conclusions from the use of the term. Ammianus Marcellinus xvi, v, 14, 'quod primitus partes eas ingressus pro capitulis singulis tributi nomine vicenos quinos aureos reperit flagitari, discedens vero septenos tantum, munera universa complentes', implies the standard assessment unit (i.e. the unit of land) was called *capitulum* in Gaul.

Cod. Theod. vii, vi, 3, 'per Aegyptum et Orientis partes in triginta terrenis iugis . . . annua vestis collatio dependatur', must mean that in 377 the land of Egypt was assessed in *iuga* in the books of the praetorian prefecture of the East. The papyri prove that in the local administrative language of Egypt the term *iugum* was unknown, and assessments continued to be made by the old local unit of area, the *arura*: the unit was later officially recognised in *Cod. Theod.* XI, xxiv, 6, § 5 (415), and the Egyptian bureaucracy even coined the word ἀρουρατίων to correspond with *iugatio* (*P. Lips.* 62, VI). Men were also taxed in the late third and early fourth century, as appears from the edict of Aristius Optatus (*S.B.* 7622) and from the census declarations (*S.B.* 7673, *Chr.* I, 210). It would appear from *P. Ryl.* IV, 658 (early fourth century), ἀρουρηδοῦ καὶ ἀνδρισμοῦ, that the assessment of a village was in *arurae* and men. In *P. Thead.* 16 and 17 (332) the surviving villagers of Theadelphia state that ἡ φορολογία τῆς κώμης ἡμῶν συνάγεται εἰς πεντακοσίας ἀρούρας and that they are paying ὑπὲρ ὅλης τῆς κώμης ἀρουρῶν πεντακοσίων . . . καὶ τοῦ κατ᾽ ἄνδρα (σὺν ταμιακοῖς ἀνδράσι) εἴκοσι πέντε, that is Theadelphia was assessed at 500 *arurae* and twenty-five men.

There is no trace in the papyri of the assessment of land and men being combined in any way, and the tax on men was probably a money poll tax. It has left very little trace in the papyri. There are four receipts for ἐπικεφάλαιον πόλεως, dating between 301 and 314, from Oxyrhynchus (*P.S.I.* 163, 302, 462, 780), but this urban poll tax may be an exceptional impost levied only for a short period [see note 1]. Apart from these there is a fourth or fifth century receipt ὑπὲρ κεφαλῆς (*P. Klein Form.* 369) and a receipt and a few records in estate accounts from the fifth and sixth centuries of συντέλεια κεφαλῆς (*P. Oxy.* 1331, 1911, l. 86; 2195, ll. 34, 48; 2243 (*a*), l. 26). From the middle of the fourth century the list of κεφαλαί was also sometimes used as a basis for μερισμοί, that is irregular or supplementary levies which had to be distributed or apportioned to the taxpayers of a given district. The earliest example is *S.B.* 7756 (discussed by Déléage, o.c. 112 ff.). Here we have a receipt dated 359, giving a list of μερισμοί and similar levies, each assessed in money τῇ κεφ(αλῇ) α (*per singula capita*), and a total assessment τῇ κεφ(αλῇ) α; but the actual receipt is made out for 1⅙ *capita* (ὑπὲρ κεφ. α ϛ′) for the appropriate sum (the *per capita* assessment plus one-sixth). Déléage has argued that since the word κεφαλή here denotes an abstract unit, it is in fact the *iugum* recorded for Egypt in *Cod. Theod.* VII, vi, 3, and that henceforth the *iugatio* system prevailed in Egypt. No such sweeping conclusion can be drawn from this document. The main taxes continued to be assessed on the *arura* down to the sixth century, as in *P. Cairo Masp.* 67057, and there are to my knowledge only two other allusions (apart from the συντέλεια κεφαλῆς) to taxes or other obligations being assessed on κεφαλαί. One of these (*Chr.* I, 390, fourth century) alludes to τῶν ναυβίων τῆς κεφαλῆς αὐτοῦ, which may indicate a corvée imposed *per capita*. The other (*P. Lond.* v, 1793, A.D. 472) is a guarantee ἀποκρίνασθαι ὑπὲρ τῶν δημοσίων τῆς αὐτοῦ κεφαλῆς ἑκάστου μερισμοῦ, which shows that μερισμοί continued to be apportioned *per capita*. The fact that in *S.B.* 7756 one man is responsible for 1⅛ *capita* is explicable on a principle well established in the fiscal practice of the later Roman Empire. If, say, 35 *capita* were the registered total of a village, and there were actually only thirty persons surviving, each survivor would be rated at 1⅙ to make up the theoretical total.

To sum up my argument I would submit that there were certain areas of the Empire, including certainly Egypt and probably Africa and parts of the Gallic prefecture, where the combined system of *capitatio* and *iugatio* was not applied; but, where it was applied, it meant that the total of *iuga* was added to the total of *capita* (that is, persons and animals registered on the land) to form the assessment on which most taxes were levied. I would submit that there is no evidence to contradict this, though the laws admittedly contain many ambiguities, due mainly to the rhetorical style in which they are drafted. One stylistic trick has often caused confusion. Phrases such as *iuga vel capita, capitatio sive iugatio* are awkward and clumsy, especially if they have to be frequently repeated. Some imperial draftsmen accordingly used one or other of the technical terms to mean the combination of both. I have already noted one clear case, where in an edict to the people and a letter to the praetorian prefect on the same topic (*Cod. Theod.* XIII, x, 8; XI, xiii, 1, both early in 383), *iugatio vel capitatio* in the one corresponds to *iugatio* in the other. Another clear case is VII, xiii, 7 (375), which regulates the liability for providing a recruit. In one sentence it is stated that if the *iugatio* of the landlord is so great that he qualifies by himself to furnish a recruit, he is to do so. Another sentence states that if a money levy is to be made for a recruit, it is to be apportioned *pro modo capitationis*. There is no reason why the basis of assessment should be different in the two cases, and the suspicion that *iugatio seu capitatio* is meant in both is confirmed by *Cod. Theod.* XI, xxiii, 1, which had fourteen years before in 361 declared that this very obligation of furnishing recruits was based on *iuga aut capita*. This being so it is unscientific to build too much on the isolated use of either *iugatio* or *capitatio*. It seems likely, for instance, that in *Cod. Theod.* xi, xii, 2 (362), 'quicumque capitationis indulgentiam immunitatemque meruerunt, non solum ex annonario titulo verum etiam ex speciebus ceteris atque largitionibus excepti sunt', *capitatio* describes the whole assessment of an estate, and similarly that in *Cod. Theod.* xi, i, 33 (424), the church of Thessalonica enjoyed immunity in respect of the *iugatio* as well as the *capitatio* of its lands (if indeed after *Cod. Just.* xi, liii, 1, any landowner in Macedonia paid *capitatio*). Indeed, when the draftsman wished to make it plain that he was alluding to land only, or to men and beasts only, he usually added such words as *terrena* or *humana* to *iugatio* and *capitatio* respectively (see *Cod. Theod.* vii, vi, 3; xi, xx, 6; Theod., *Nov.* xxii, 2, § 12; *Cod. Just.* xi, xlviii, 23, § 5; lii, 1).

So much for the interpretation of the evidence. But is such a system as I have postulated historically or economically plausible? It is, I believe, an error to attribute to the emperors of the fourth century any profound economic ideas, and much ingenuity has in my view been wasted in speculating on what principles the 'value' of a man could be assessed in relation to the value of land. The emperors were practical men who wished to work out an easy and simple method of assessing levies which should at the same time be reasonably equitable. In most parts of the empire, at any rate, there were already two main forms of direct taxation, the *tributum soli*, a percentage on the assessed value of land, and *tributum capitis*, some form of poll tax. Apart from carrying out censuses, probably long neglected, of land and population, in order to provide an up-to-date basis for these taxes, Diocletian's chief contribution to the problem, it would seem, was the invention of the *iugum*, a uniform unit in which land of varying quality and use could be assessed, instead of being valued in money, which had ceased to be a stable measure. The *iugum*, as described in the Syro-Roman law book, was an equitable unit in which to assess the value of agricultural land, and the inscriptions from Asia Minor show that the valuation was carried out most meticulously down to minute fractions of the *iugum*. At the same time the *iugum* was an ideal instrument for the government to calculate the incidence of levies; if x pounds of pork were required in Palestine, and Palestine was rated at y *iuga*, it was clear that a levy of x/y pounds of pork per *iugum* would meet the case. Diocletian seems on similar principles to have evaluated men, women, and animals in uniform *capita*, which he used as the basis of a money tax. But taxes in money were not very useful, when its value was depreciating so rapidly. It was desirable that *capita* as well as *iuga* should be used as a basis for levies in kind, and the simplest way of achieving this object was to add the two together.

The system was inequitable in that it threw as large a burden on a man with a small farm and a large family as on a man with a large farm and a small family; but such anomalies are inevitable in any system which involves a poll tax, and there is no reason to believe that they were felt to be unjust. Men and land had always been taxed, and were therefore accepted as the natural units of assessment. The government did, however, in some areas mitigate the hardship by scaling down the assessment of human beings in relation to that of land. Thus, in Pontica in 386 the *caput*, which had hitherto been assessed at one man or two women, was rated at two-and-a-half men or four women (*Cod. Theod.* XIII, xi, 2). Further anomalies arose from the fact that *iugatio* was based on different scales in different dioceses (see pp. 228-9) and that in some dioceses *iugatio* was never introduced, traditional units of area such as the African *centuria* or the Italian *millena* (and perhaps the Gallic *capitulum*) being rated as *iuga*. [See note 2.] Similarly, *capitatio* was based on different scales from diocese to diocese; in Egypt only males counted, in Syria both males and females equally, in Pontica a woman counted for half. All these variations were, however, so far as we know, based on local traditional practice, and the anomalies which resulted as between one region and another would not have been felt.

[For the working of the system see further Ch. XIII and *L.R.E.* 61–68; 448 ff.; for its modifications, 108, 147 f., 237; for inequity see Chapters III and IV section III (Jones' last statement); for comparison with other ancient systems ch. VIII.]

[1 In *L.R.E.* 63 Jones inferred from Lact. *Mort. Pers.* 23, 2, *Cod. Theod.* xii, x, 2 (both cited on p. 286) and the Egyptian receipts cited on p. 289 that 'Diocletian, perhaps under Galerius' influence, did include the urban population towards the end of his reign, and that Maximin continued this practice during his reign (305–13)'; only on Galerius' death did he exempt the city population in Asia Minor, 'as is the practice in the provinces of Oriens also' and in accordance with Diocletian's system (*Cod. Theod.* xii, x, 2, 311), 'and it would seem that the urban poll tax was abolished in Egypt by Licinius after Maximin's fall'.]

[2 See Addendum to ch. X. To judge from *L.R.E.* 65, 615. Jones later gave up this conjecture on the *capitulum.*]

CHAPTER FOURTEEN

THE ROMAN COLONATE

THE problem of the late Roman Colonate has been debated since the seventeenth century. The debate still goes on, but we do not seem much nearer to answering the question, when, how, and why the *colonus* of the principate, a voluntary tenant of land, free to move when his lease expired, became the *colonus* of the later empire, a serf tied to the land by a hereditary bond.[1] The position of a *colonus* in the early third century is clearly defined by the lawyers cited in the Digest. He held a lease, normally for five years, which by the tacit consent of both parties became on expiry an annual tenancy.[2] In practice conditions varied very greatly. In Egypt short term leases, from one to four years, were normal.[3] But in many parts farms generally descended from father to son. Under Commodus the tenants of imperial lands in Africa speak of themselves as having been born and bred on the estate.[4] In the early third century other imperial tenants in Lydia threaten 'to leave the hearths of our fathers and the tombs of our ancestors' unless conditions are improved.[5] A *colonus* might, if he were, as he often was, in arrears with his rent,[6] find practical difficulty in leaving; for in such circumstances his landlord would have no hesitation in distraining on his stock. But he could leave with arrears outstanding: a case in the Digest concerns 'the arrears of *coloni* who on the conclusion of their lease, having entered into a bond, had abandoned their tenancy'.[7]

---

[1] The history of the controversy down to 1925 is summarised by R. Clausing, *The Roman Colonate*. Later discussions include C. Saumagne, *Byzantion* XII (1937), 487–581, F. L. Ganshof, *Antiquité Classique* XIV (1945), 261–77, A. Segrè, *Traditio* V (1947), 103–33, M. Pallasse, *Orient et Occident à propos du colonat romain au bas-empire* (1950).

[2] *Dig.* XIX, ii, 9 ¶ 1, 13 ¶ 11, 14, 24 ¶ 2.

[3] A. C. Johnson, *Roman Egypt* (*Economic Survey of Ancient Rome, II*), 81 ff.

[4] *C.I.L.* VIII, 10570 (=*I.L.S.* 6870), col. iii, lines 28–9.

[5] Keil and Premerstein, *Denkschr. Ak. Wien*, LVII (1914–5), 55, line 46.

[6] To judge by the frequent allusions to *reliqua colonorum* in *Dig.* XXXII, 78 ¶ 3; 91 pr. ¶ 1; 97; 101 ¶ 1; XXXIII, ii, 32 ¶ 7; vii, 20 pr. ¶ 1, 3; 27 ¶ 1.

[7] *Dig.* XXXIII, vii, 20 ¶ 3.

U

The first clear evidence that *coloni*—or at any rate some *coloni* —were tied to their farms and to their landlords is a law of Constantine dated 332: 'Any persons with whom a *colonus* belonging to some other person is found shall not only restore him to his place of origin but be liable for his poll tax for the period. It will furthermore be proper that *coloni* themselves who plan flight should be put in irons like slaves, so that they may be compelled by a servile penalty to perform the duties appropriate to them as free men'.[8] The first explicit reference to the hereditary character of the bond is in a law of 364, which orders that 'slaves and *coloni* and their sons and grandsons' who had deserted imperial estates to join the army or the civil service should be recalled.[9]

Before proceeding further it will be as well to say something of the pattern of land ownership in the later Roman empire. It is too often assumed in discussions of the colonate that the entire area of the empire was divided into large estates, each consisting of a home farm cultivated by slaves, surrounded by smaller farms worked by resident free tenants. There were many large estates, though not all were of this pattern. Many, owned by absentee landlords, were entirely divided into tenancies, the original home farm, if there had ever been one, having been let off.[10] And though in some parts of the empire, particularly in Italy and the western provinces, large estates were numerous and must have occupied a large proportion of the total area, they by no means accounted for the whole of it.

There were in the first place peasant proprietors, usually grouped in villages; in Egypt, they were predominant in the fourth century[11] and survived in substantial numbers in the sixth.[12] Villages of peasant proprietors are mentioned side by side with those owned by one landlord in Syria in the fourth and fifth

[8] *Cod. Theod.* V, xvii, 1.

[9] *Cod. Just.* XI, lxviii 3, cf. VII, xxxviii, 1 (367).

[10] In a sixth-century rent roll (J. O. Tjäder, *Die nichtliterarischen lateinischen Papyri Italiens aus der Zeit* 445–700, p. 188, *no.* 3, *col.* ii) an estate in the territory of Patavium is divided into 'locus qui adpellatur saltus Erudianus', 'colonia suprascripta' and seven other *coloniae* (besides two *paludes*). All pay rent, the first 'per Maximum vilicum', the others through *coloni*. It would seem that the original home farm, 'saltus Erudianus' had been divided into two, and half let to a group of tenants, half left in the hands of the bailiff, who leased it for a rent.

[11] A. H. M. Jones, *J.R.S.* XLIII (1953), 58–60, 63–4 [ch. X above.]

[12] There is a large mass of documents concerning Aphrodito, a village of small proprietors which was 'autopract', collecting its own taxes. Most are published in *P. Cairo Masp.* and *P. Lond.* V.

centuries.[13] In Thrace and Illyricum Justinian's legislation shows that peasant freeholders were still important in the sixth century.[14] In the West less is heard of them, but in Gaul Salvian in the middle of the fifth century still speaks of peasants whose plots are being absorbed by the great landlords,[15] while in Africa the peculiar Mancian tenures, small holdings held on perpetual and alienable leases, survived under the later Vandal kings.[16]

In the second place the estates of non-resident landlords were not always large. There were many humble townsmen who owned two or three acres, and medium landlords seem rarely to have owned a single large estate: they generally held a number of parcels of land of varying size, scattered in different villages. This is the pattern shown by the early fourth century land register of Hermopolis in Egypt.[17] The same pattern is shown in the will of Remigius, bishop of Rheims in the late fifth century.[18] Even the great landlords who owned estates big enough to hold a village, often possessed in addition many detached parcels of land. The accounts of the great Apion family in sixth century Egypt show that they owned holdings in the villages of peasant proprietors as well as entire hamlets.[19]

Many of the smaller parcels of land owned by absentee landlords had no resident tenants but were leased to villagers, either peasant proprietors whose plots were too small to maintain their families, or cottagers, who owned their houses but had no land.[20] The analysis of the rural population is thus complicated. There were the resident *coloni* of the great estates, who lived on their farms or in the estate village. There were also on the great estates persons styled *inquilini*, who are frequently coupled with the *coloni* but distinguished from them.[21] The word *inquilinus* in the

[13] Libanius, *Or.* XLVII, 11; Theodoret, *Hist. Rel.* xiv and xvii.
[14] Just. *Nov.* 32–4.
[15] Salvian, *de Gub. Dei*, V, 38–44.
[16] C. Courtois, L. Leschi, C. Perrat, *Tablettes Albertini: actes privés de l'époque vandale*.
[17] A. H. M. Jones, *J.R.S.* XLIII (1953), 52–3, 60–3 (ch. X above).
[18] *Mon. Germ. Hist., Script. rer. Merov.* III, 336–40. The authenticity of the will is upheld and its content analysed in *Rev. Belge de Philol. et d'Hist.* xxxv (1997. 356-373.
[19] E. R. Hardy, *The large estates of Byzantine Egypt*, 88–9.
[20] See below note 34.
[21] *Cod. Just.* XI, xlviii, 6 (365). 'omnes omnino fugitivos [adscripticios] colonos vel inquilinos', *Cod. Theod.* X, xii, 2 (368), 'si quis etiam vel tributarius repperitur vel inquilinus ostenditur', *Cod. Just.* XI, liii, 1 (371), 'colonos inquilinosque per Illyri-

legal language of the principate means the tenant of a house, as opposed to *colonus*, the tenant of agricultural land.[22] There is no reason to believe that the word had changed its meaning, and these *inquilini* will therefore have been cottagers on an estate, who earned their livings as craftsmen or labourers.[23] Then there were the peasant proprietors and cottagers of the independent villages, some of whom were at the same time *coloni* of detached parcels of land belonging to absentee landlords. Finally there were agricultural slaves. A few were labourers owned by more prosperous peasant freeholders or *coloni*. More were the property of absentee landlords. Some worked small parcels of land single-handed: the half dozen vineyards owned by Remigius each had its slave vine-dresser.[24] On larger estates the census registers sometimes show in addition to the *coloni* a few slaves, who perhaps worked a home farm and acted as bailiffs of the whole estate.[25] Other estates seem to have been run entirely by slave labour; we do not know if these slaves worked in gangs, or, by a practice already known to the

---

cum', *Cod. Theod.* XII, xix, 1 (400), 'inquilinas vel colonas vel ancillas', 2 (400), 'colonatus . . . aut inquilinatus quaestionem', V, xviii, 1 (419), 'colonus originalis vel inquilinus', *Cod. Just.* III, xxvi, 11 (442), 'domorum nostrarum colonus aut inquilinus aut servus', Val. *Nov.* xxvii (449), 'de originariis et colonis, inquilinis ac servis', XXXV (452), 'nullus originarius inquilinus servus aut colonus', Severus, *Nov.* ii (465), 'inquilinus vel colonus'. In *Cod. Just.* III, xxxviii, 11, 'vel colonorum adscripticiae condicionis seu inquilinorum' has been interpolated after 'servorum' of the original law (*Cod. Theod.* II, xxv, 1, 325). In *Cod. Just.* XI, xlviii, 12 (396) 'vel tributarios vel inquilinos' is also probably interpolated after 'servos'. For *tributarii*, *adscripticii*, *originales*, see below, notes 51, 53, 54.

[22] *Dig.* XIX, ii, 25 § 1, XLI, ii, 37, XLIII, xxxii, 1 § 1. Landlords under the principate were obliged to declare their *coloni* and *inquilini* in their census returns (*Dig.* L, xv, 4 § 8). In *Dig.* XXX, i, 112, 'si quis inquilinos sine praediis quibus adhaerent legaverit, inutile est legatum: sed an aestimatio debeatur, ex voluntate defuncti statuendum esse, divi Marcus et Commodus rescripserunt', *inquilinus* is used in a unique and obscure sense. The persons so described must be slaves, or they could not be left by will, but are attached to land and are only alienable with it. It has been suggested that they are barbarian prisoners of war allotted by the imperial government to landowners as agricultural labourers.

[23] They are perhaps identical with the cottagers (*casarii*) of *Cod. Theod.* IX, xlii, 7 (369), 'quotve mancipia in praediis . . . quot sint casarii vel coloni'. Their status was very similar to that of *coloni*; *Cod. Just.* XI, xlviii, 13 (400), 'inter inquilinos colonosve, quorum quantum ad originem pertinet vindicandam, indiscreta eademque paene videtur esse condicio, licet sit discrimen in nomine'.

[24] *Mon. Germ. Hist.*, *Script. rer. Merov.* III, 337, lines 13–6, 22–3; 338, lines 10, 11, 20–1; 339, lines 1–2.

[25] A. H. M. Jones, *J.R.S.* XLIII (1953), 56–7 [ch. X above]; bailiffs (*vilici* or *actores*) were commonly, as under the principate, slaves.

third century lawyers, leased farms as *quasi coloni*.[26]

Between 392 and 395 Theodosius I issued the following constitution:[27] 'Throughout the entire diocese of Thrace the census of the poll tax is abolished for ever and only the land tax will be paid. And in case it may seem that permission has been given to *coloni*, freed from the ties of their taxable condition, to wander and go off where they will, they are themselves to be bound by right of origin, and though they appear to be free born by condition are nevertheless to be held to be slaves of the land itself to which they were born, and are not to have the right to go off where they will or change their domicile. The landowners are to control them with the care of patrons and the power of masters'. An earlier law of Valentinian I,[28] dated 371, evidently alludes to a similar situation. 'We declare that *coloni* and *inquilini* throughout Illyricum and the neighbouring regions cannot have the liberty of leaving the land on which they are found to reside by virtue of their origin and descent. Let them be slaves of the land, not by tie of the tax, but under the name and title of *coloni*'.

From these two laws it is evident that *coloni* had hitherto been tied to their farms by virtue of the poll tax, or *capitatio*, which they paid, since its abolition in Thrace and Illyricum would have resulted, but for special provisions enacted, in giving freedom of movement to the *coloni* of these areas. The *capitatio* was based on censuses conducted by Diocletian and his colleagues and immediate successors in the various parts of the empire, and the tax itself under that name—there had been earlier poll taxes in many provinces—seems to have been instituted by him. The census included all the working rural population (between minimum and maximum ages) whether slaves or free, whether proprietors, tenants, or landless, and the *capitatio* was levied on all alike.[29]

From these facts two conclusions follow. The measure which tied the *coloni* to the soil cannot be earlier than Diocletian's time,

[26]A. H. M. Jones, *loc. cit*. Two Spanish landowners are said to have raised a small army in the early fifth century, 'servulos tantum suos ex propriis praediis colligentes' (Orosius, VII, 40, 6), and one of Melania's Italian estates is said to have had 'sexaginta villulas circa se, habentes quadringentos servos agricultures' (*Vita Melaniae Junioris*, Latin version, ch. 18, in *Anal. Boll.* VIII (1889) 19 ff.). For *servi quasi coloni* see *Dig*. XV, iii, 16, XXXIII, vii, 12, 3, 20, 1.

[27] *Cod. Just*. XI, lii, 1.

[28] *Cod. Just*. XI, liii, 1.

[29] See A. Déléage, *La Capitation du Bas-empire*, and A. H. M. Jones, *J.R.S.* XLVII (1957), 88–94 [ch. XIII].

and is probably to be connected with his reorganisation of the poll tax. And secondly it was primarily a fiscal measure, designed to facilitate and ensure the collection of the new poll tax, and not specifically aimed at tying tenants to their farms.

There are two facts which support the second conclusion. In the first place not only *coloni* but peasant proprietors were tied to their place of registration. In 332 the three surviving proprietors of the Egyptian village of Theadelphia complained that all their fellow villagers (the registered population of the village was twenty-five) had fled: they had tried to get them back by their own efforts but without success, and they now appealed to the prefect of Egypt to use his official powers.[30]

In the second place the rule binding the rural population to their places of registration did not in all provinces have the effect of tying *coloni* to their farms. It is expressly stated in a law of Theodosius I that in Palestine *coloni* had not hitherto been tied to their lands.[31] In Egypt there is no trace of tied tenancies until the fifth century; short term leases remain the rule as under the principate.[32] In a law addressed to the praetorian prefect of the Gauls in 399[33] a distinction is drawn between the various provinces under his jurisdiction. It is ruled that anyone who buys 'an estate on which a certain number of the humble population is registered' is to take on their fiscal obligations; but this rule is applicable only to those provinces 'in which this system of tying the humble population and this method of registration is observed'.

The explanation of this anomaly probably lies, as the last law suggests, in the different systems of registration adopted in various provinces. The census registers from western Asia Minor, which record both land and population, are drawn up under the headings of the landowner and his estates. In most lists the landowner's name comes first, followed by his several farms, each assessed at so many fiscal units (*iuga*) of land, and so many units of population (*capita*), if there was any population resident on the farm. This form of registration implies that the landowner was responsible for the *capitatio* of the population registered on his farms, and would, if the population were tied to their place of

[30] P. *Thead*. 16 and 17.
[31] *Cod. Just*. XI, li, 1.
[32] A. C. Johnson and L. C. West, *Byzantine Egypt: Economic Studies* 76, cf. note 50 below.
[33] *Cod. Theod*. XI, i, 26.

registration, have the effect of tying resident *coloni* to their farms. From the very fragmentary records surviving it would appear that peasant proprietors and landless men who owned houses were registered in their villages, and would be tied to these.[34]

In Egypt on the other hand the land register of Hermopolis gives a list of townsmen who own land, recording the size and location of their holdings but making no mention of their tenants. There are similar village lists of peasant proprietors.[35] In the surviving personal census returns villagers record details of their families, but register themselves under their village only.[36] It would seem then that in Egypt the rural population was registered by villages, without reference to whose land they cultivated, and that they were tied to their village and not to their farm or landlord. Presumably the registration system in Palestine and some provinces of the Gallic prefecture was similar and led to the same result.

It would seem, then, that the tying of the *colonus* to his farm was the by-product of a fiscal and administrative measure of wider scope. For such a measure there were partial and local precedents from the principate. In A.D. 104 C. Vibius Maximus, prefect of Egypt, issued the following edict.[37] 'Since the house to house registration is imminent it is necessary to instruct all persons who are for any reason whatsoever residing away from their district to return to their hearths in order that they may both carry out the usual procedure of the registration and may devote themselves to the agricultural work incumbent upon them'. Diocletian's more sweeping measure (if he was its author) was doubtless also primarily fiscal in motive, but may likewise have been intended to secure that the agricultural population, on whose labour the land tax depended, was kept to its task.

But if the tying of the agricultural population was in origin a measure dictated by public policy, it proved a great boon to landlords. It is evident that there was in the fourth century a general shortage of agricultural labour. The population had doubtless in many areas been reduced by the constant wars, devastations, famines and plagues of the third century, and the

---

[34]A. H. M. Jones, *J.R.S.* XLIII (1953), 49–55 [ch. X above].
[35]A. H. M. Jones, *art. cit.*, 58–64.
[36] Wilcken, *Chrestomathie*, 210, S.B. 7673.
[37] Wilcken, *Chrestomathie*, 202. cf. Luke, ii, 1.

conscription for the greatly enlarged army further depleted it. At any rate many references in contemporary laws show that tenants were hard to find, and that any who were dissatisfied with their position could readily find another landlord, willing and eager to take them on. In these circumstances landlords found the law useful in holding their tenants and reclaiming them if they left.

Since the landowning classes were predominant in governmental circles it is not surprising that the imperial government, when it abolished the *capitatio* in Illyricum and then in Thrace, specially enacted that the *coloni* of these areas should not be thereby given liberty of movement. It soon went further and introduced the tied colonate in provinces where it had not hitherto existed. Theodosius I explicitly states in whose interests he did so in Palestine. 'Whereas in other provinces which are subject to our serenity's rule a law instituted by our ancestors holds *coloni* by a sort of perpetual right, so that they may not leave the places by whose crops they are fed nor desert the fields which they have once received to cultivate: but the landowners of Palestine do not enjoy this advantage. . . .'.[38]

The dependence of tied *coloni* on their landlords was increased by successive laws. Constantine, as we have seen, authorised landlords to put their tenants in chains if they suspected them of planning flight.[39] In 365 Valens enacted that they might not alienate their own property without their landlord's consent.[40] Some years later he enacted that landlords should collect the taxes due from their registered tenants.[41] In 396 Arcadius ruled that *coloni* registered in the census, since they were virtually slaves of their landlords, should have no right of bringing civil actions against them except for raising their rent.[42] By later laws they were forbidden to join the army or the civil service,[43] or to take holy orders without their landlord's consent.[44]

While tied *coloni* were thus reduced to a quasi-servile status, agricultural slaves were converted into serfs. At first owners had been permitted to sell their agricultural slaves apart from the

[38] *Cod. Just.* XI, li, 1.
[39] *Cod. Theod*, V, xvii, 1.
[40] *Cod. Theod.* V, xix, 1.
[41] *Cod. Theod.* xi, i, 14.
[42] *Cod. Just.* XI, l, 2.
[43] *Cod. Just.* XI, xlviii, 18, XII, xxxiii, 3.
[44] *Cod. Just.* I, iii, 16 (409), Val. *Nov.* xxxv (452), *Cod. Just.* I, iii, 36 (484).

land, though they were registered on it. Constantine only prohibited sales beyond the boundary of the province, and warned purchasers that their census would be subject to revision.[45] Valentinian I assimilated registered agricultural slaves to tied tenants, and forbade their sale apart from the land.[46]

On the other hand the law, in so far as it affected peasant proprietors, seems to have been generally allowed to fall into desuetude. When the *capitatio* was abolished in Illyricum and Thrace no measures were taken to restrict the movement of the peasant freeholders, in those areas an important and numerous class, but only that of *coloni*. As against scores of laws which deal with restitution of absconding *coloni* to their masters there are only two in the Codes under which freeholders are returned to their villages. A law of Valentinian I[47] rules that if anyone petitioned the crown for the grant of a man alleged to be a vagrant and ownerless slave, an investigation should be held, and if the man were proved to be a *colonus* he should be returned to his master, if a free commoner be sent back to his place of origin. A law of 415,[48] which deals comprehensively with the problem of patronage in Egypt and aims at restoring the villages of peasant proprietors, orders that those who had left the village in which they were registered and gone to other villages or landlords should be compelled to return.

There was probably less need to enforce the law against freeholders. As a rule peasants would not wish to abandon their holdings—the case of Theadelphia was abnormal; the village lay at the end of an irrigation canal and intervening villages had intercepted the water. Normally it was to no one's interest to enforce the law: his fellow villagers or a neighbouring landlord would generally be glad to buy the holding of any peasant who wanted to leave, and would raise no complaint. It was only in the case of mass desertion, as at Theadelphia, that the surviving villagers would wish to recall the runaways, and one may doubt whether their complaints were often successful. Landlords had influence and could get a hearing for their grievances, and the provincial governor, being probably a landlord himself, would be

[45] *Cod. Theod.* XI, iii, 2 (327).
[46] *Cod. Just.* XI, xlviii, 7 (371): this rule was revoked by King Theoderic in Italy (*Ed. Theod.* 142).
[47] *Cod. Theod.* X, xii, 2 (368).
[48] *Cod. Theod.* XI, xxiv, 6 (415).

sympathetic. Villagers could exercise no effective pressure, and were unlikely to obtain a hearing, especially if, as at Theadelphia, the runaways had taken refuge on the estates of neighbouring landlords.

The tied colonate was as we have seen introduced into Palestine by Theodosius I. It appears to have been extended to Egypt before 415, for the law of that year[48] alludes to a class called locally *homologi coloni* who were tied to their landlords. But though the institution thus spread to the greater part, if not the whole, of the empire, it does not follow that all *coloni* were tied. Since *coloni* were initially bound by their census registration, only those tenants who were entered on the census under the name of a landlord and registered on one of his estates were tied to the soil. The census registers from western Asia Minor show many, mainly smaller, estates without any *capita* or units of population and these estates were presumably leased to neighbouring peasant freeholders or cottagers in the villages. The distinction is made explicit in a law of Valens,[49] which enacts that owners of estates should collect the taxes of '*coloni originales* who are registered in the same places', but that *coloni* 'who possess any piece of land however small and are registered in their own names' should pay their taxes through the public collector. In effect only the resident tenants of the larger estates were tied. This appears to have been the case on the estate of the Apion family in Egypt in the sixth century. Tied tenants (γεωργοὶ ἐναπόγραφοι) appear only on the hamlets (ἐποίκια) and estates (κτήματα) wholly owned by the family: parcels of land in the villages are let to ordinary tenants.[50]

In the third quarter of the fourth century the laws begin to make a distinction betwen ordinary tenants and tied tenants. The latter are sometimes called *tributarii*, since their landlord was responsible for their tax (*tributum*, *i.e. capitatio*).[51] In the Eastern parts they are generally distinguished by some such phrase as

[48] *Cod. Theod.* XI, i, 14 (371).

[49] *P. Oxy.* 135, 137, 1979, 1982–3, 1988–91, *P. Lond.* III 774–5, 777–8, *P.S.I.* 59, 61–2, *P. Amh.* 149: cf. *P. Oxy.* 1900, 2238 for ἐναπόγραφοὶ γεωργοί on estates of the church.

[50] *Cod. Theod.* X, xii, 2 (368), *Cod. Just.* XI, xlviii, 12, (396, but the word is probably a Justinianic interpolation, see note 21), XI, xlviii, 20, 3 (Justinian). In *Cod. Theod.* XI, vii, 2 (319) *tributarius* appears to be distinguished from *colonus*, and may mean a tax-paying (i.e. rural) slave.

'registered in the census' (*censibus adscripti*),[52] and eventually the technical term *adscripticius* was coined; it is first recorded officially in a law of 460, but the emperor Marcian used the Greek equivalent (ἐναπόγραφος) in addressing the council of Chalcedon in 451.[53] This term was never used by the Western chancellery, which preferred the words *originales* or *originarii*,[54] belonging by birth or descent to the land. The two expressions came to the same thing in fact, for the census registered a man in the place where he belonged by birth. Both conceptions are sometimes combined in a single sentence. The law of Valens cited above[55] speaks of '*coloni originales* who are registered in the same places', and in a law of Valentinian I[56] *coloni* and *inquilini* are ordered to return 'to their old homes where they are registered and were born and bred'.

The Western terminology emphasises the hereditary nature of the tie. It is evident from the census documents from western Asia Minor that from the outset registration had been conceived as hereditary. For although adults alone paid *capitatio* and were counted in the total of the village or estate, the detailed returns record children, even infants, with their ages.[57] It was evidently assumed that as they came of age they would come on to the register, filling the place of their elders as they died or reached the age of exemption. These young persons, from whom the number of the registered population was kept up, are alluded to in some laws as *adcrescentes*.[58]

The status of an *adscripticius* or *originalis* was thus hereditary: it was inherited from either parent.[59] The tie was legally unbreak-

[52] *Cod. Just.* XI, 1, 2 (396), I, iii, 16 (409), *Cod. Theod.* V, vi, 3 (409), X, xx, 17 (427), V, iii, 1 (434), Theod. *Nov.* vii, 4 (441). The phrase is applied to agricultural slaves in *Cod. Theod.* XI, iii, 2 (327), VII, i, 3 (394) and *Cod. Just.* XI, xlviii, 7 (371).

[53] *Cod. Just.* I, xii, 6 (466); Schwartz, *Act. Conc. Oec.* II, p. 353 ¶ 17. *Adscripticius* has been interpolated by the Justinianic redactors in *Cod. Just.* III, xxxviii, 11 (= *Cod. Theod.* II, xxv, 1) and XI, xlviii, 6, and even in VIII, li, 1, of A.D. 224.

[54] *Cod. Just.* XI, lxviii, 1 (325), xlviii, 7 (371), *Cod. Theod.* X, xx, 10 (380), *Cod. Just.* XI, xlviii, 11 (396), *Cod. Theod.* V, xviii, 1 (419), Val. *Nov.* xxvii (449), xxxi (451), xxxv (452), Maj. *Nov.* vii (458), *Ed. Theod.* 21, 48, 56, 63–8, 80.

[55] *Cod. Theod.* XI, i, 14.

[56] *Cod. Just.* XI, xlviii, 6.

[57] A. H. M. Jones, *J.R.S.* XLIII (1953), 53, 55–6, cf. 51, note 12 [ch. X above].

[58] *Cod. Theod.* VII, xiii, 6 (370), 'vel adfixos censibus vel (de) adcrescentibus suis obtulerint iuniores'; 7 (375), 'ex incensitis atque adcrescentibus in eorum locum, qui defensi militia fuerint, alios praecipimus subrogari'.

[59] *Cod. Just.* XI, xlviii, 16 (419), 21 (Justinian) for maternal descent. In law 24 Justinian altered the rule for paternal descent; *Nov.* liv records the old rule.

able, until in 419 the rule of thirty years' prescription was applied to it, so that if a landlord made no claim on a *colonus* for that period, he forfeited his rights over him.[60] This rule was extended by Valentinian III in 449 even to *coloni* of the crown, whose rights were normally imprescriptable. The reason he gives is interesting: high ranking civil servants were being exposed to vexatious claims that their parents or more distant forebears had been *originales*.[61] Two years later Valentinian III found the rule of thirty years' prescription was being abused by *originales* who fled from their masters to become the free tenants of other landlords. He accordingly ruled that an *originalis* who freed himself from his old landlord by thirty years' absence should become the *originalis* of his new landlord, or if he cunningly moved from farm to farm, of the landlord whom he had served for the longest period, or for the last part of the thirty years.[62] Valentinian III's legislation applied only to the Western empire. In the East the rule of thirty years' prescription survived until Justinian first restricted and then abolished it.[63] Henceforth an *adscripticius* could legally free himself only by becoming a bishop.[64]

While the hereditary character of the status meant that the descendants of an *adscripticius* or *originalis colonus* could never legally (except in so far as prescription operated) free himself, it also meant that no one not of that status by birth could be made an *adscripticius* or *originalis*. The exceptions are negligible. Sometimes barbarian prisoners of war, like the Scirae, were given to landlords as tied *coloni*:[65] sturdy beggars could be claimed as such by those who denounced them.[66] In these circumstances it is probable that the number of *adscripticii* tended to dwindle. The constant repetition of the laws against receiving runaway *coloni* shows that in fact many did leave their farms and establish themselves as free tenants elsewhere. This might well happen with the tacit consent of their landlords. It was not to the interest of a landlord to have more *coloni* than were needed to cultivate his

---

[60] *Cod. Theod.* V, xviii, 1. The rule had been applied earlier in special cases (*Cod· Theod.* XII, xix, 2 and 3).
[61] Val. *Nov.* xxvii.
[62] Val. *Nov.* xxxi.
[63] *Cod. Just.* XI, xlviii, 22 § 3–5, 23 pr.
[64] Just. *Nov.* 123 § 4.
[65] *Cod. Theod.* V, vi, 3 (409).
[66] *Cod. Theod.* XIV, xviii, 1 (382).

estate, and he would not mind if younger sons went elsewhere to seek their fortunes. Justinian envisages the case where a landlord, satisfied that one of his farms is duly cultivated by a *colonus*, allows his son to leave, and when the *colonus* dies or gets past work, finds that his claim upon the son is barred by thirty years' prescription.[67] *Adscripticii* surplus to the needs of an estate thus tended to join the ranks of free tenants. On the other hand when the number of *adiscripticii* for any reason fell below the number required, unless the landlord could fill the gaps from *adscripticii* from other estates which he owned,[68] he had to take on free tenants.

It was presumably in the interests of landlords who had such tenants that Anastasius applied the rule of thirty years' prescription in the opposite direction, enacting that a free tenant who stayed for thirty years should be tied to his farm;[69] Justinian interpreted this rule as tying his children even if they had not lived the full period on the estate.[70] Such tenants were not, however, *adscripticii*, being able to dispose of their own property freely and bring actions against their landlords and in general free from all the disabilities of adscript status except the prohibition to move.[71] Under a law of Justinian they were even entitled to move if they acquired a farm of their own sufficient to support them and requiring their full time attention.[72]

Justinian, arguing that *adscripticii* were virtually slaves, applied to mixed marriages between them and free persons the rules of law which governed the status of the offspring of free persons and slaves. The principal innovation which followed was that the children of an *adscripticius* and a free woman were no longer *adscripticii*: for it was a basic maxim of Roman law that the offspring of a 'free womb' was free, and the status of an *adscripticius* was now reckoned as servile.[73] Justinian appears to have

[67] *Cod. Just.* XI, xlviii, 22 § 3.   [68] *Cod. Just.* XI, xlviii, 13 (400).

[69] *Cod. Just.* XI, xlviii, 19. Salvian (*de Gub. Dei*, V, 43-7) declares that in his day (the mid-fifth century) in the West vagrants who settled on the estates of the rich lost their liberty and became *inquilini*, either it would seem by declaring themselves such (§ 44 'iugo se inquilinae abiectionis addicunt') or by prescription (§ 45, 'fiunt praeiudicio habitationis indigenae'). They even, he declares, became slaves (§ § 45-6). These processes were probably illegal (the second certainly was). Val. *Nov.* xxxi, 5, shows clearly that a stranger who settled on an estate (unless he were by birth a *colonus originalis* from elsewhere) could move on when he liked.

[70] *Cod. Just.* XI, xlviii, 23 § 1.

[71] *Cod, Just.* XI, xlviii, 19, 23 § 1-3, Just. *Nov.* 162 § 2.

[72] Just. *Nov.* 162 § 2.

[73] *Cod. Just.* XI, xlviii, 24.

made this ruling from mere legal purism. It was greeted by storms of protest from landlords, who complained that their estates were being deserted wholesale by tenants who claimed under the new law to be free. Justinian had hastily to enact that the rule was not retrospective, applying only to children born after the law,[74] and to enact furthermore that children who benefited from the law, though not *adscripticii*, were bound by Anastasius' law (as interpreted by himself) to remain on their farms as free persons:[75] the second of these laws was directed to the praetorian prefect of Illyricum, where protests had been most vehement. Despite these laws unrest continued, and the landowners of Africa on Justinian's death anxiously petitioned his successor Justin II for their confirmation, and on his death again petitioned his successor Tiberius Constantine to the same effect.[76]

The story shows that mixed marriages between *adscripticii* and free women, the daughters of free *coloni* or of peasant proprietors must have been very common. It follows that peasant proprietors must still have survived in substantial numbers, or that free tenants must have become numerous on the great estates.

The tied colonate was then, I would argue, originally the by-product of a measure, probably enacted by Diocletian, and mainly dictated by fiscal motives, binding all the rural population to their places of registration in the census. This measure was, owing to the general shortage of agricultural labour, found very useful by landowners who wished to hold their tenants, and was in their interest maintained by the imperial government for *coloni*, though allowed to lapse in so far as it affected freeholders, and extended to *coloni* in provinces where for technical reasons it had not hitherto tied them to their farms. The status of tied *coloni* was gradually degraded, until they were scarcely distinguishable from agricultural slaves. Not all *coloni*, however, were tied, but only those descended from resident tenants originally registered on their farms. These tended with the passage of time to diminish in number and to be replaced by free tenants. These, too, if they remained on one farm for over thirty years, were tied to it by a

---

[74] Just. *Nov.* 54, pr. ¶ 1 (537).

[75] Just. *Nov.* 162 ¶ 2 (539). Six months later in another law (Just *Nov. App.* I) addressed to the prefect of Illyricum, Justinian reversed his ruling altogether, but this measure must have been soon revoked, for the rule of *Nov.* 162 ¶ 2 is cited as a precedent in later African laws (see next note).

[76] *Corpus Iuris Civilis* (Gottofredus) II, 237.

law of Anastasius, but did not incur the other diabilities of tied
coloni. This measure was according to its author designed for the
benefit both of landlords and tenants, but was clearly more in the
interests of the former, who still feared that their estates would be
drained of agricultural labour unless they had a better hold on
their tenants. Their fears were justified, as the reaction to
Justinian's legislation proved. Shortage of agricultural manpower evidently still remained acute in the sixth century, and was
the basic cause for maintaining the tied colonate.[77]

[77] [See also for briefer statement Chapter XXI].

CHAPTER FIFTEEN

WERE ANCIENT HERESIES NATIONAL OR SOCIAL MOVEMENTS IN DISGUISE?

MOST modern historians of the later Roman Empire, whether secular or ecclesiastical, seem to agree that certain of the heresies and schisms of that period were in some sense national rather than purely religious movements.[1] They point to the fact that some heresies either were confined to certain areas, as was Donatism to Africa, or were at any rate particularly strong and persistent in some districts or among some peoples—as were Monophysitism in Egypt and Syria, or Arianism among the German tribes. They stress the fact that among these groups indigenous languages—Punic or Berber in Africa, Coptic, Syriac, or German—were adopted by the heretical or schismatic churches. Their general line of argument is that mere doctrinal differences, often of extreme subtlety, could not have engendered such powerful and enduring movements, and that their real and underlying cause must be sought in national sentiment. They often maintain that under the later Roman Empire long-dormant nationalism arose or revived in a number of areas, and was an important contributory cause in the downfall of the empire; for the dissident groups not merely stubbornly resisted the efforts of the imperial government to impose religious conformity upon them, but struggled to break away from the empire, supporting local pretenders or foreign invaders.

At the risk of a certain crudity I should like to state this thesis in more concrete terms. Did the average Copt say to himself, 'I am an Egyptian and proud of it. I hate the Roman oppressor,

[1] For a thoroughgoing statement of this thesis see E. L. Woodward, *Christianity and Nationalism in the Later Roman Empire* (London, 1916). The latest great historian of the period, E. Stein, *Geschichte des spätrömischen Reiches*, i (Vienna, 1928, *Histoire du Bas-Empire*, ii (Paris, 1949), is its strong advocate. It is also adopted by the latest history of the Church, A. Fliche and V. Martin, *Histoire de l'Église*, iii, *De la paix, Constantinienne à la mort de Théodose* (J. R. Palanque, G. Bardy, P. de Labriolle, Paris, 1945), iv, *De la mort de Théodose à l'élection de Gregoire le Grand* (P. de Labriolle, G. Bardy, L. Bréhier, G. de Plinval, Paris, 1947).

and will at the earliest opportunity cast off the alien yoke. Meanwhile I insist on speaking my native Coptic instead of Greek, the language of the foreign government, and I refuse to belong to its church. I do not know or care whether Christ has one or two natures, but as the Romans insist on the latter view, I hold the former'? This statement of the case appears to be implied by some historians, who speak of the heresies as a mere screen for nationalist aspirations. But if the last sentence seems to be too cynical even for the most private thoughts, one might substitute for it, 'The Romans anyhow are heretics, we Egyptians are clearly right in believing that Christ has one nature only. I will firmly reject any compromise which the Romans may offer, and even if they accept our view I will never be reconciled with them'.[2]

If they felt like this the heretics fairly certainly did not put their sentiments into writing. We are not, it is true, so well provided with heretical literature as we could wish: if the German Arians wrote anything, it has been lost. But we possess a considerable bulk of monophysite literature, including theological treatises, letters, and histories both ecclesiastical and secular. Some Donatist writings have been preserved, and others can be reconstructed from Augustine's elaborate refutations of them. In the vast amount of controversial literature on the orthodox side some reference would surely be found to the nationalist sentiments of their opponents if they had voiced them openly. What the sectaries actually said in public, so far as our record goes, was—to change the instance—'The Donatist church is the true Catholic church, and we will never communicate with *traditores'*, but what they thought, we are asked to believe, was: 'We are Africans and hate the Roman government; we will have nothing to do with the Romans and will maintain our African church and if possible set up our African state.'

This is a thesis which is obviously difficult to prove or to disprove, for one cannot easily read the secret thoughts of men who lived 1,500 years ago. One can only examine their written words with care, in case they have inadvertently revealed their real thoughts, or endeavour to deduce their thoughts from their actions and policies.

It could also be held that the sectaries not only said, but in their conscious thought believed, that their quarrel with the

[2] The last clause is required by Stein's view, see below, p. 317.

X

government was purely religious, but that they really held their peculiar views because they were in harmony with their national temperament or were emotionally linked with their national group, and conversely really hated the orthodox because they were foreigners, though they genuinely thought that they condemned them as heretics. On this hypothesis the conscious thought of a Copt might be: 'We Egyptians are right in believing that Christ has one nature, and I abominate the Romans as heretics and hate them as persecutors. Rather than submit to their rule I would welcome a barbarian invader'. Or he might even say no more than: 'We hold the true orthodox faith, and I abominate the government because it is heretical and persecutes us', but really hate the Romans as foreigners.

In this attenuated form the nationalist hypothesis is even more difficult to prove or disprove. One can seek to discover whether hostility to the Roman government persisted even when it accepted the theological view of the dissident groups. One can inquire whether the theological views of the sectaries show any affinity with the pre-Christian beliefs of the group which held them. One can finally inquire how far adherence to certain theological views was coterminous with national groups, defined by criteria of language or religion.

To turn from generalities to special cases I will first consider the Donatists. Donatism was confined to the African provinces, and within that area it was both widespread and persistent, at all times commanding a wide following and at some periods dominating the whole country, and surviving despite many persecutions for close on three centuries to our certain knowledge, and probably longer. Many, if not most, of its adherents were Punic- or Berber-speaking, and its greatest strength lay in the least Romanized areas, especially southern Numidia. In some of its beliefs and practices, in particular in its morbid emphasis on martyrdom, it seems to show affinities with the pagan religion of the area. Its leaders co-operated with two native pretenders, Firmus and Gildo, and some of them are alleged to have had treasonable dealings with certain Goths in the early fifth century.[3]

To take their political activities first, the Donatists were

---

[3] The evidence for these statements is well stated in Mr. W. H. C. Frend's work, *The Donatist Church* (Oxford, 1952), from which I differ only in some points of emphasis and interpretation.

certainly not anti-imperial at the beginning: they in fact appealed to the emperor against the Caecilianists.[4] When Constantine had finally rejected their cause, they raised the cry that the State should not interfere in religion[5]—as later the homoousian party did when Constantius II favoured the Arians.[6] But when Julian ordered the restoration of banished clergy and confiscated church property they were happy to accept imperial aid.[7] That they co-operated with Firmus[8] and Gildo[9] need mean no more than that the pretenders exploited local grievances to win support for their personal ambitions, and that the Donatists, who by now had little hope of obtaining what they wanted from the legitimate government, decided to risk backing a pretender who might be successful. With a good deal less excuse the Spanish bishop Ithacius, when Gratian, or rather his master of the offices, supported the Priscillianists, transferred his allegiance to the usurper Maximus;[10] and yet no one has suggested that the Catholic Ithacius was a Spanish nationalist. It may be claimed that Firmus and Gildo, unlike Maximus, were leaders of national rebellions, but beyond the fact that they came from a Moorish princely family, there is nothing to suggest that they were not usurpers of the normal type, that is, ambitious individuals seeking for personal power. The record of the members of the family certainly does not suggest zeal for any cause but their own. When Firmus rebelled, his brother Gildo took the Roman side, and received the promotion on which he had no doubt counted. When he in turn rebelled, another brother, Mascazel, led the army which crushed him. There is in fact no reason to believe that the rebellions of Firmus and Gildo were different in kind from that of Alexander the Phrygian before them, or those of Heraclian and Boniface after them.

The negotiations of the Donatists with the Goths are only known from a letter of Augustine to Count Boniface, who had inquired whether Donatism and Arianism had any points in common.[11] Augustine replied that they had none, but that

[4] Aug. *Ep.* 88; Optatus, i. 22.
[5] Optatus, iii. 3, 'quid imperatori cum ecclesia?'
[6] Hilary, *Liber I ad Constantium*, C.S.E.L., lxv, pp. 181–7.
[7] Optatus, ii. 16; Aug. *Contra Litt. Pet.* ii. 97, 224.
[8] Aug. *Ep.* 87. 10; *Contra Ep. Parm.* i. 10. 16, 11. 17; *Contra Litt. Pet.* ii. 83, 184.
[9] Frend, *op. cit.*, pp. 208 ff.
[10] Sulp. Sev. *Chron.* ii. 48–49.   [11] Aug. *Ep.* 185. 1.

'sometimes, as we have heard, some of them, wishing to conciliate the Goths to themselves, because they see that they have some power, say that they have the same beliefs as they'. It seems very unlikely that the Donatists were in touch with the Visigoths settled in Aquitania, and Boniface's interest in the matter suggests that it was his Gothic federates who were approached. If so the Donatists were merely making propaganda among influential persons in the entourage of the Comes Africae, and perhaps trying to curry favour with the Comes himself, who, we learn from a later letter of Augustine,[12] married an Arian wife. Or was Boniface himself thinking of striking an alliance with the Donatists when he put his question to Augustine? Augustine answers the question with the utmost brevity, and goes on to expiate for pages on the doctrinal and historical issues involved. It is hard to believe that if he had had any suspicion that the Donatists were plotting treason against the empire he would have dismissed the matter so lightly.

There is no evidence that the Donatists made common cause with the Vandals. All that Victor Vitensis can say against them is that one Donatist, Nicesius, was perverted to Arianism.[13] It is scarcely credible that if they had taken the Vandal side or even secured toleration from them, this would not have been trumpeted abroad by their persecuted Catholic adversaries.

There is in fact very little hint that the Donatists cherished dreams of a national African state. How far was the movement, in any national sense, African in character? It is no doubt true that a large proportion of Donatists were Punic- or Berber-speaking, and that the Donatist clergy used the indigenous languages for instruction and exhortation. But since Africa was a predominently rural country, and most rural Africans knew no Latin, it was inevitable that any church which wished to rally the mass of the population had to use the native languages. On the Catholic side Augustine too was anxious to secure Punic-speaking clergy to take charge of rural areas.[14]

Nor was Donatism by any means confined to the humble strata of society where the native languages were spoken. The leaders and apologists of the movement, men like Parmenian

---

[12] Aug. *Ep.* 220. 4.
[13] Victor Vitensis, iii. 71.
[14] Aug. *Ep.* 84; 209. 3.

(who was not even an African),[15] the learned and eloquent Tyconius,[16] the lawyer Petilian,[17] came from the cultivated and Romanised classes, and the penal law of 412 specifies appropriate penalties not only for circumcellions and plebeians, *negotiatores* and ordinary decurions, but for the higher urban aristocracy, the *principales* and *sacerdotales*, and for senators, *clarissimi, spectabiles,* and even *illustres,* the cream of Roman imperial society.[18] There is, furthermore, no suggestion that the Donatists took any pride in the indigenous languages. Their literature, or what survives of it, was all written in Latin, not only the controversial or apologetic treatises which were aimed at Catholics, but popular works, such as the Acts of Martyrs, meant for the encouragement of the faithful. The inscriptions of Donatist churches are all in Latin, even the slogans and war-cries of the circumcellions, like the famous 'Deo Laudes', were in Latin, the language of the enemy.

That Donatism may in the course of time have acquired certain African characteristics, derived from the pre-Christian beliefs of the people, may well be true. Popular Christianity everywhere tended to absorb local beliefs and customs. But I wonder whether the Donatist fixation on martyrdom may not be due as much to their quarrel with the Catholics as to any survival of primitive pagan ideas. They claimed to be the church of the martyrs as against the Catholics who were *traditores,* and martyrdom was therefore to them the touchstone of the true faith.

The Donatists certainly believed that in Africa only did the Catholic church survive, but they seem to have felt somewhat uneasy at their isolation. They apparently made abortive efforts to spread their faith in Spain. They may have negotiated with the Arians of Sardica in the hope of finding churches unsullied by *traditio* in the East. It is significant that they maintained a pope of the true faith at Rome throughout the fourth and early fifth centuries.[19] The fact, however, remained that for all practical purposes their church was confined to Africa, and they were reduced to interpreting a phrase from the Song of Songs, 'ubi pascis ubi cubas in meridie', as a prophecy that such was God's will.[20]

[15] Optatus, i. 5, ii. 7.
[16] Gennadius, *De Viris illustribus,* 18; Aug. *Contra Ep. Parm.* i. 1. 1.
[17] Aug. *Contra Litt. Pet.* iii. 16. 19.
[18] *Cod. Theod.* xvi. v. 52, cp. 54.
[19] Frend, *op. cit.,* pp. 164, 170.
[20] Aug. *Ep. ad Catholicos,* 16. 40; *Serm.* 46. 36–37, 138. 9–10.

That Donatism should have had so strong a hold throughout Africa and should have been confined to Africa can be explained by the historical circumstances in which the movement arose. It would appear that the African provinces were exceptional in that Christianity had already in the latter part of the third century captured the countryside.[21] They were also exceptional in the number of their confessors and martyrs in the Great Persecution. These two facts are not unconnected. It is clear from contemporary accounts that in both the Decian and Diocletianic persecutions upper-class Christians lapsed in very large numbers, and that the confessors and martyrs were mainly men and women of the lower orders. This was not unnatural. The upper classes feared for their property and position and could be more easily intimidated by the threat of torture, from which they were normally immune. The poor had less to lose and to them flogging was an everyday occurrence. It may be added that the poor might well hope to pass undetected if they failed to comply with the law, whereas the rich would be more likely to be denounced.

It would seem likely, then, that in Africa a larger proportion of Christians remained steadfast than in most parts of the empire. Not unnaturally they took a less charitable view of the lapsed than that which prevailed in other provinces. Throughout Africa feelings were tense, and a rupture was likely between the rigorist and the lenient groups. The dispute over the election of Caecilian fired the spark, and inevitably involved all Africa, for Carthage had for long been acknowledged as the primatial see of all the African provinces. But outside Africa the churches had no sympathy with the rigorist party, and having decided that Caecilian was the lawful bishop of Carthage they took no further interest in the affair.

Only in one other province do we hear of a similar movement. In Egypt, where as in Africa Christianity had in the third century spread to the rural areas, the resistance to the Diocletianic persecution was stubborn, and a rigorist party, the Melitians, refused to readmit the lapsed to communion.[22] But the Donatists seem never to have made contact with the Melitians; they were too far away. Melitianism remained confined to Egypt, where it lasted

[21] Frend, *op. cit.*, pp. 83 ff.
[22] Frend, *op. cit.*, p. 86. For a full account of the Melitians see H. I. Bell, *Jews and Christians in Egypt* (London, 1924), pp. 38 ff.

into the eighth century at least.[23] But it never became a dominant force there. The claim of the Melitians to be the Church of the Martyrs must have been gravely shaken when Peter of Alexandria, whose lenient views they denounced, himself died as a martyr, and the see of Alexandria was filled by a succession of able and ruthless bishops, who quickly broke the spirit of the rebels.

That Donatism survived so stubbornly is hardly a matter for surprise. Throughout history religious feuds have been long-lived, and have often survived when the original cause of quarrel has been almost forgotten. The Donatists were from the beginning a large group, which it was difficult to stamp out, and the intermittent and not very efficient persecutions which they suffered served only to embitter them—in these circumstances the blood of the martyrs was the seed of the church.

The Copts have *a priori* a stronger case to be regarded as a nation than the Africans for, whereas the inhabitants of the diocese of Africa had never formed a political unit, Egypt had in the past been a national kingdom, and long after that kingdom had fallen had cherished a strong national sentiment based on the traditions of the past and fostered by its peculiar religion. Under the later Ptolemies there had been revolts which had aimed at expelling the aliens and setting up a native dynasty, and as late as the third century A.D. copies were circulating of the Prophecy of the Potter, which holds out apocalyptic hopes of a king who should deliver Egypt from the yoke of the foreigners, and destroy 'the city beside the sea' which was 'the nurse of all men; every race of men dwelt within her'.[24] Alexandria also had its patriotic anti-Roman tradition witnessed by the Acts of the Pagan Martyrs, in which the city is represented as the champion of Hellenism against Roman tyrants and their Jewish protégés.[25] The anti-Roman movements of Egypt and Alexandria were it may be noted quite distinct and mutually hostile; the Alexandrian documents refer with contempt to Egyptians, and the Egyptian reflect hatred of Alexandria.

There is no evidence that either tradition survived the triumph of Christianity. The Egyptian tradition was closely linked with old native religion, and the Alexandrian with pagan

[23] Bell, *op. cit.*, pp. 42–43.
[24] *Hermes*, xl (1905), pp. 544 ff.
[25] Collected in H. A. Musurillo, *The Acts of the Pagan Martyrs* (Oxford, 1954).

Hellenism. Certainly in Christian Egypt no trace survived of the old antagonism between Egypt and Alexandria; Alexandria was the undisputed religious capital of Egypt. This fact seems decisive proof that there was no conscious survival of the old Egyptian nationalism in the Christian period.

The nationalist thesis in the case of Egypt is based on much the same arguments as in that of Africa.[26] It is argued that the stubborn and unanimous devotion of the Egyptians to the monophysite doctrine must have been derived from some other cause than the very subtle theological issues involved, and was in fact an expression of national Egyptian sentiment and hatred of the Roman empire. In support of this hypothesis two pieces of evidence are produced, the use of the Coptic language by the Egyptian church, and the alleged welcome given by the mono-physite Egyptians to the Persians and to the Arabs.

The linguistic point is not convincing. Coptic was the normal language of the great majority of rural Egyptians, very many of whom knew no Greek. It was naturally adopted by the church as soon as Christianity spread to the countryside, and was employed long before the Egyptian church became heretical. Long after the split the intellectual leaders of the monophysite church continued to be Greek-speaking, and the literature of the movement was written in Greek. Ultimately, it is true, the monophysite church became purely Coptic and the Orthodox purely Greek; but this was only after the Arab conquest, when Greek gradually died out in Egypt and the native church naturally abandoned its use, while on the other hand the Orthodox patriarch was a nominee of the Byzantine government, often non-resident.

In the sixth century there is no very convincing evidence that Greek-speaking Egyptians favoured Chalcedon and Copts opposed it. Alexandria, where the Greek element was strongest, was a stronghold of monophysitism: John the Almoner, when he became patriarch in the early seventh century, found only seven churches in the hands of the Chalcedonians.[27] It may well be that in periods when the penal laws were enforced, members of the

[26] For scholarly and moderate statements of the case see J. Maspero, *Histoire des patriarches d'Alexandrie depuis la mort de l'empéreur Anastase jusqu'à la réconciliation des églises jacobites, 518–616* (Paris, 1923); E. R. Hardy, 'The Patriarchate of Alexandria: a Study in National Christianity', *Church History*, xv (1946), pp. 81–100; idem, *Christian Egypt: Church and People* (New York, 1952).

[27] Sophronius, *Vita Ioh. Eleemos.* 5.

local aristocracy conformed for prudential reasons. Flavius Apion was persuaded by 'the most pious and faithful emperors', Justin and Justinian, to adopt the Chalcedonian faith: if he had not he might well have forefeited his patrician rank and his great estates. But until the change of emperors made a change of faith expedient, Flavius Apion, great aristocrat though he was, had been a monophysite,[28] and his descendants later returned to that faith.[29]

There is no hint of any anti-imperial movement, much less any rebellion, during the period of close on two centuries that elapsed between the Council of Chalcedon and the Arab conquest. The Alexandrians, of course, frequently rioted when the imperial government forced Chalcedonian patriarchs upon them, and considerable bodies of troops had to be used to suppress them. But during the periods when the emperors favoured or tolerated monophysitism, the Egyptians seem to have been content. Ernst Stein has made much of one incident.[30] When in 516 Anastasius, whose monophysite sympathies were by now quite undisguised, appointed Dioscorus II to succeed John III as patriarch of Alexandria, the people objected that he had been uncanonically installed by the secular authorities, and insisted on the clergy, who had acquiesced, going through the form of electing him again. Next day they lynched the Augustal prefect, for praising Anastasius, according to Theophanes; Malalas says that it was a food shortage that provoked the attack on the Augustal.[31] This incident, Stein argues, proves that the Egyptians were unwilling to receive a good monophysite patriarch from a monophysite emperor: they were not really interested in the theological issue but wanted a patriarch of their own choice. The story certainly shows that the people of Alexandria were jealous of the canonical rights of their church, and resented the interference of the secular authorities: but this hardly proves hostility to the imperial government.

That the Copts welcomed the Persian invaders there is no evidence. They were certainly later remembered as cruel oppressors and persecutors, as appears from a prophecy attributed

[28] *Acta Conc. Oec.* IV. ii. 170.
[29] J. B. Chabot, *Chronique de Michel le Syrien*, ii. 385 (read 'Strategios the patrician').
[30] E. Stein, *Histoire du Bas-Empire*, ii, p. 164.
[31] Theophanes, D.C. 6009; Malalas, p. 401 (Ed. Bonn.), fr. 41 (de Boor).

to Shenuda by a seventh-century biography.[32] Nor is there any good evidence that the Copts welcomed the Arabs.[33] The sources are most unreliable and confused, but from the best of them, John, bishop of Nikiu, who wrote about two generations after the event, it is evident that the rapid subjugation of Egypt by the Arabs was mainly due to the defeatism of Cyrus, the Chalcedonian patriarch and prefect, and to the dynastic disputes which paralysed the government at Constantinople after the death of Heraclius. He records, it is true, that the Arabs were encouraged not only by the weakness of the Roman troops, but by the hostility of the people to Heraclius on account of the recent persecution.[34] But the reaction of the Egyptians seems to have been confused and uncertain, some fleeing in panic, [35] others deserting to the Arabs,[36] others resisting to the best of their ability.[37] The people of Alexandria were certainly horrified when they learned that they were to be surrendered to the Arabs under the final treaty.[38]

John's own attitude is significant. He regards the Arab conquest not as a deliverance, but as a calamity, the judgement of God upon the emperor Heraclius for persecuting the orthodox. It is to him strictly comparable with the earthquakes and plagues whereby God punished the previous apostasy of Justin and Justinian. But even more significant is the whole tone of John's history. If there had been anything that could truly be called a Coptic national movement, one would have expected it to develop its own version of history, in which the Egyptian people would play a heroic or at least a central role, and its resistance to the alien oppressor would be glorified. John in fact produces a standard history of the Roman Empire, merely reversing the Chalcedonian judgements on the merits of the successive emperors. He denounces Marcian and Pulcheria, Justin and Justinian, and above all Heraclius, the arch-persecutor. But he

---

[32] M. Amélineau, *Monuments pour servir a l'histoire de l'Égypte chrétienne* (Paris, 1888); cp. idem, *Étude sur le christianisme en Égypte au septième siècle* (Paris, 1887), for a seventh-century Coptice life of Pisentios, bishop of Coptos, who fled into the desert on the advent of the Persians, and wrote to his flock, 'Because of our sins God has abandoned us: he has delivered us to the nations without mercy'.

[33] See A. J. Butler, *The Arab Conquest of Egypt*.

[34] R. H. Charles, *The Chronicle of John Bishop of Nikiu*, cxv. 9.

[35] *Op. cit.* cxiii. 6, cxv. 6, cxx. 28.

[36] *Op. cit.* cxiii. 2, cxix. 1.

[37] *Op. cit.* cxv. 1–3, 10.

[38] *Op. cit.* cxx. 24–26.

praises Anastasius, and even Tiberius who was merely tolerant of monophysitism. He betrays no hatred of the Roman Empire as such, and so far from rejoicing in its fall, laments the disasters which the apostasy of certain emperors brought upon it.

It remains true, of course, that the Egyptian church almost throughout its history maintained a remarkable solidarity, tenaciously supporting the doctrines of its chiefs, the patriarchs of Alexandria, through thick and thin; provided, of course, that these patriarchs were canonically elected and upheld the doctrines of their predecessors. To usurpers, who were intruded by an external authority and betrayed the traditions of the see, it maintained uncompromising resistance. The Egyptian church never wavered in its devotion to the homoousian doctrine enunciated by Alexander and Athanasius, and the monophysite doctrine of Dioscorus.

This monolithic solidarity may be attributed to national sentiment, but it is more simply explained by the structure and traditions of the Egyptian church. From the earliest times the bishop of Alexandria had virtually appointed all the other bishops of Egypt, and by tradition he exercised an absolute authority over them. As the Egyptian bishops at Chalcedon protested, when they were ordered to sign the statement of the dyophysite faith: 'the ancient custom has prevailed in the Egyptian diocese that all the bishops obey the archbishop of Alexandria'.[39] In these circumstances the Egytians never heard any view but that of their patriarch, and they naturally accepted it as gospel. That it was the supremacy of the patriarch and not any national spirit of unanimity which produced the solidarity of the Egyptian church is strongly suggested by the fact that when under Justinian there was for a long period no genuine patriarch in Egypt, the unity of the church broke down and rival parties formed within it.[40]

The people of Egypt—whether they spoke Greek or Coptic —naturally took great pride in the renown of their patriarchal see. The bishops of Alexandria claimed a pre-eminent position in the church and plumed themselves on being unerring champions of orthodoxy. They resented the rival pretensions of the see of Constantinople, and took a certain malicious pleasure in humbling its successive occupants—John Chrysostom, Nestorius, Flavian

[39] *Act. Conc. Oec.* ii. i. 309.
[40] See Maspero, op. cit.

—whenever they could catch them out in canonical or doctrinal deviations. The people of Egypt rejoiced in their triumphs and were bitterly chagrined at their defeats. The sullen refusal of the Egyptian church to accept any compromise on the monophysite issue was probably due not so much to the doctrinal differences involved, which were very minute, as to loyalty to Dioscorus' memory. Hence their insistence that Chalcedon, which had condemned him, must be explicitly anathematised; the Henoticon, which hedged on this point, was not satisfying to their pride. The Council's recognition of the patriarchal authority and primacy of Constantinople must also have contributed to Egyptian hatred of Chalcedon.

To turn to the Jacobite church of Syria,[41] the picture of a Syriac-speaking national monophysite church opposed to a Greek-speaking imperial orthodox church does not seem to be true for the period before the Arab conquest. In the first place the monophysite heresy was in the sixth century by no means confined to Syriac-speaking areas. John of Ephesus records that John of Hephaestopolis journeyed throughout Asia Minor, ordaining priests for the monophysite congregations, from Tralles and Ephesus in the west as far as Tarsus, and also visited Cyprus and Rhodes.[42] The journeys of James Baradaeus covered not only Syria and Armenia, but Cappadocia, Cilicia, Isauria, Pamphylia, Lycaonia, Phrygia, Lycia, Caria, and Asia, as well as Cyprus, Rhodes, Chios, and Mitylene. Of the twenty-nine sees to which he consecrated bishops thirteen were in Egypt, seven in Syria and Mesopotamia, and nine in Asia Minor, Ephesus, Smyrna, Pergamum, Tralles, Aphrodisias, Alabanda, Chios, Tarsus, and Seleucia on the Calycadnus.[43] Later John speaks of the spread of the schism in the monophysite church from Syria into Armenia, Cilicia, Isauria, Cappadocia, and Asia.[44] Elsewhere he describes the flourishing monophysite churches of Pamphylia,[45] and he incidentally mentions monophysite bishops and communities in several other cities of Asia Minor, Sardis, Chalcedon, Nicomedia, Cyzicus, Prusias, Heraclea.[46]

[41] See R. Devreesse, Le Patriarcat d'Antioche (Paris, 1945).
[42] John of Ephesus, Lives of the Eastern Saints, xxv.
[43] John of Ephesus, Lives of the Eastern Saints, l.
[44] John of Ephesus, Eccl. Hist. iv. 19, cp. i. 39 (Cappadocia), ii. 32 (Asia and Cappadocia).   [45] Op. cit. v. 6.
[46] Op. cit. i. 15 (Sardis), Lives of the Eastern Saints, xlvi (Chalcedon, etc.).

In the second place the heresy did not establish itself in all Syriac-speaking areas. In Syria itself there was, and has been ever since, a strong Chalcedonian church, and in Palestine monophysitism after initially sweeping the field was soon stamped out. Ernst Stein cites the orthodoxy of Palestine as evidence for the nationalist thesis.[47] Palestine was, he argues, a more Hellenised land than Syria, and such non-Hellenised inhabitants as it had were Jews and Samaritans who stood outside the conflict. This picture is very questionable. The Samaritans were mainly concentrated in the territory of Neapolis, though they spilled over into neighbouring cities like Caesarea and Scythopolis.[48] The Jews were dominant in Galilee, where Sepphoris and Tiberias were completely Jewish cities,[49] but seem to have been eradicated from Judaea proper after the revolt of Barcochba, and had never been particularly numerous in the coastal plain or beyond the Jordan. Palestine was no more, and probably less, Hellenised than Phoenicia and Syria, and we have evidence of Syriac-speaking Christian townsfolk, who knew no Greek, at Scythopolis[50] and Gaza,[51] the latter a great centre of Hellenic culture.

The monophysite and Syriac-speaking areas therefore by no means coincided in the sixth century. Monophysitism gradually died in Asia Minor, which remained under the control of an orthodox government, whereas it survived and prospered under the toleration accorded by the Arabs in Syria, though it never ousted orthodoxy there and never penetrated again to Palestine.

Nor until after the Arab conquest was the Syriac language particularly associated with monophysitism. East of the Euphrates Syriac had a continuous history as a literary language, and here it was used by the churches both orthodox and heretical from the fourth century onwards. In Syria and Palestine Syriac survived only as the spoken language of the lower classes, especially in the

[47] *Histoire du Bas-Empire*, ii, pp. 174 ff.
[48] This may be inferred from the story of the various Samaritan revolts, which were always confined to this area (Malalas, pp. 382–3, 445–7, 487–8 (Ed. Bonn.); Procop. *Aed.* v. vii; *Anecd.* xi. 24–30; Cyril. Scythop. *Vita Sabae*, 70).
[49] Epiphanius, *Adv. Haer.* 30. The Jewish revolt under Gallus was apparently in Galilee, its principal stronghold being Sepphoris (Soc. *H.E.* ii. 33; Soz. *H.E.* iv. 7).
[50] Eusebius, *Martyrs of Palestine*, i. 1, cited in Schürer, *Gesch. Jud. Volkes*, ii, p. 381, n. 139.
[51] Marcus Diaconus, *Vita Porphyrii*, 66–68; Jerome mentions Syriac-speaking townsfolk at Elusa (*Vita Hilarionis*, 25).

country, and Greek was normally used by the churches, though for the benefit of the lower classes some concessions were made to Syriac. At Scythopolis there were at the beginning of the fourth century readers whose duty it was to translate the service into Syriac,[52] and later Publius of Zeugma, when Syriac-speaking postulants sought admission to his Greek-speaking monastery, allowed them to sing the service in their own tongue.[53] The same linguistic division existed in the monophysite church. Those of its apologists who came from east of Euphrates, Philoxenus of Hierapolis for instance, and John of Ephesus, wrote in Syriac. Severus of Antioch, who was by origin a Pisidian,[54] wrote both his theological works and his letters in Greek, and Zacharias of Mitylene, who came from Gaza,[55] composed his ecclesiastical history and his life of Severus in that language.

There is no evidence that the monophysites of Syria were politically disaffected to the empire. The only bishop who collaborated with a rebel in these parts was Calandion, the Chalcedonian patriarch of Antioch, who accepted the support of Illus at a time when the legitimate emporer, Zeno, had by the issue of the Henoticon proclaimed his sympathy with the monophysite cause.[56] We possess very long and detailed accounts of the wars waged under Justinian, Justin II, Tiberius, and Maurice between the Persian and the Roman empires in the very areas where monophysitism was strongest, but there is no hint in them that the monophysites gave the Persians any aid or comfort, or indeed regarded them with anything but fear and detestation. Nor is there any suggestion in the monophysite historians that they ever envisaged secession from the empire, or regarded the Romans as alien oppressors. Of the attitude of the Syrian monophysites in the later Persian wars under Heraclius or during the Arab invasion we have no contemporary evidence.

The case of the Armenians is different. Armenia had been an independent kingdom down to the reign of Theodosius the Great, when it was partitioned between Rome and Persia, the latter getting the lion's share. Under alien domination the Armenians continued to feel and act as a nation. They had

[52] See p. 321, n. 50.
[53] Theodoret, Hist. Rel. 5.
[54] Zacharias, Life of Severus, Patr. Or. ii. i, p. 10.
[55] Ibid., pp. 23–24.
[56] Evagrius, H.E. iii. 16.

possessed their own church, which might truly be called national, since the early fourth century. In the middle decades of the fifth century they were involved in a struggle with Persia, which was endeavouring to impose Zoroastrianism on them, and took no part in the councils of Ephesus and Chalcedon. As late as 506 they were unaware of the issues involved, and learned of them only from certain Mesopotamian monophysites who were being persecuted, at the instigation of the Nestorians, by the Persian government. They naturally accepted the views of their fellow-sufferers, and affirmed their unity with the Romans, condemning Nestorius and the council of Chalcedon, and approving 'the letter of Zeno blessed emperor of the Romans'. When Justin and Justinian reversed Anastasius' ecclesiastical policy, they were apparently not consulted, and did not follow suit. This implied no hostility to Rome, however, for when in 572 they revolted against Persia they appealed to Justin II. He insisted on their subscribing to Chalcedon as a condition of aid, but they soon went back to their old beliefs. Maurice again attempted to impose the Chalcedonian position upon them, but the bishops of Persian Armenia refused to attend his council, and excommunicated the bishops of Roman Armenia, who had conformed. It was thus not hostility to Rome which led the Armenians into heresy; on the contrary they conformed to what was at the time the official Roman position. But having got used to this position they were unwilling to move from it, though they still regarded Rome as their natural ally and protector.[57]

The Arian German tribes are in a way a parallel case. There is, of course, no doubt that the Ostrogoths, Visigoths, Vandals, Burgundians, and Lombards were conscious national or tribal units. The Goths became Arians because they were evangelised at a time when Arianism was the official and dominant doctrine of the eastern part of the Roman Empire, and the other tribes seem to have learnt their Christianity from them. The question is why did the German tribes cling so tenaciously to their long out-moded heresy. Was it from national pride or because they believed that it was the true faith? In fact no doubt they remained Arians from mere conservatism, but they certainly were convinced that Arianism was true and pleasing to God. A remark of

[57] See V. Inglisian, 'Chalkedon und die armenische Kirche', in A. Grillmeier and H. Bacht, Das Konzil von Chalkedon (Würzburg, 1953), ii, pp. 361–417.

Sidonius Apollinaris about the Visigothic king Euric is revealing.[58] Euric was, Sidonius says, a fanatic and a persecutor, so much so that 'one might be in doubt whether he is leader of his tribe or of his sect'. 'His mistake is,' he goes on, 'that he believes that success is granted to him in his dealings and plans in virtue of true religion, whereas he really obtains it in virtue of earthly good fortune'. Euric, in other words, like most Christians of his day, believed that God rewarded with worldly success those rulers who held the true faith and stamped out heresy, and attributed his own success to his zeal in promoting Arianism and crushing the heresy of the homoousians.

Of one sect only, so far as I know, has it been claimed that it was at bottom a social movement. Donatism has been represented as a revolutionary uprising of the poor against the rich.[59] For this view there is some solid evidence. Both Augustine and Optatus depict in vivid and circumstantial terms the activities of the circumcellions.[60] They gave their protection to tenant farmers against their landlords, to debtors against their creditors, and to slaves against their masters. 'No one was allowed to be safe on his estates. The bonds of debtors lost their force, no creditor was free to exact his money at that time'. Those who dared to disobey the letters of the Leaders of the Saints suffered dire penalties. Their houses were burnt down, they themselves were forced to work at the mill like slaves, or torn from their carriages and compelled to run behind while their slaves drove.

That circumcellion bands did from time to time exercise such a reign of terror in some areas cannot be doubted. The circumcellions were recruited from the poor peasantry, and were no doubt not averse from paying off old scores against oppressive landlords and extortionate moneylenders when they had a good excuse for doing so in the name of religion. But the circumcellions must be distinguished from the Donatist church; they were the storm-troopers of the movement, whom its official leaders did not always find it easy to control, and some of whose activities they may not have approved.[61] There is, so far as I know, no evidence that the Donatist church ever proclaimed any revolutionary

[58] Sid. Apoll. *Ep.* vii. 6. 6.

[59] F. Martroye, 'Un tentative de révolution sociale en Afrique', *Rev. quest. hist.* lxxvi (1904), pp. 353-416; lxxvii (1905), pp. 1-53.

[60] Aug. *Ep.* 108. 6. 18; 185. 4. 15; Optatus, iii. 4

[61] Aug. *Contra Litt. Pet.* i. 24. 26; cp. ii. 23. 53, and *Contra Ep. Parm.* i. 11. 17.

programme of community of goods or freeing of slaves or remission of debt. In general, moreover, the activities of the circumcellions were inspired by religious zeal, and their victims were renegades who had deserted to the Catholic fold, or Catholics who had exercised pressure on Donatists to abjure their faith. There is an interesting letter of Augustine to the great senator Pammachius, who owned estates in Numidia, in which he heaps the most fulsome praise upon him for having had the courage to convert his Donatist tenants to catholicism, and expresses the hope that other senatorial landlords will be encouraged to follow his example.[62] From this it would appear that Donatist peasants were generally content to pay their rent to their landlords even if they were Catholics, and that the circumcellions would normally only take action against Catholic landlords if they tried to seduce their tenants from the faith.

The nationalist and socialist theories which I have been discussing seem to me to be based on a radical misapprehension of the mentality of the later Roman Empire. Today religion, or at any rate doctrine, is not with the majority of people a dominant issue and does not arouse major passions. Nationalism and socialism are, on the other hand, powerful forces, which can and do provoke the most intense feelings. Modern historians are, I think, retrojecting into the past the sentiments of the present age when they argue that mere religious or doctrinal dissension cannot have generated such violent and enduring animosity as that evinced by the Donatists, Arians, or Monophysites, and that the real moving force behind these movements must have been national or class feeling.

The evidence for nationalism of any kind in the later Roman Empire is tenuous in the extreme. It has been argued that when the imperial government in the fifth century tended to appoint senators of Gallic domicile to posts in Gaul, it was placating a sentiment of 'Gaul for the Gauls', which later found expression in the election of Avitus by the Gallic nobility.[63] But these facts imply no more than that Gallic senators expected their share of offices and naturally preferred to serve near home, and that in the anarchy which followed the death of Petronius they saw an opportunity of electing one of themselves to be emperor. Neither

[62] Aug. *Ep.* 58.
[63] Sundwall, *Weströmische Studien*, pp. 8-26.

Y

Avitus nor his backers had any intention of setting up a Gallic state; he intended to be emperor of the western empire. No one who has read the letters, poems, speeches, and histories which they wrote can doubt that the literate upper classes of the empire regarded themselves as Romans, as was only natural, seeing that they all shared the same cultural tradition. Of the lower classes we know little, since they were inarticulate. Very many of them spoke indigenous languages, but if they possessed any national traditions, they have not come down to us. In their actions, while they rarely displayed any positive loyalty to the empire, neither did they show any positive hostility. Usually they accepted Roman or barbarian with equal apathy.

Nor again, though there was much misery and some discontent among the lower classes, is there much sign of a class-conscious hatred of the rich. In times of famine the urban populace sometimes rioted and lynched unpopular officials or rich men who were hoarding stocks of corn, but such outbursts were sporadic and unorganised. Peasant revolts were very rare. The most notable were those of the Bacaudae in Gaul and later also in Spain.[64] Three rebellions are known in Gaul, one under Diocletian, the second under Honorius, and the third under Valentinian III. All reached formidable proportions, and required large-scale military operations to suppress them. They each lasted for a number of years, were commanded by recognised leaders, and controlled substantial areas—the two last Armorica, that is the territory between the English Channel and the Loire. Unfortunately we have very little information about their inner character save that the Bacaudae are characterised as peasants, brigands, and runaway slaves, and that Exsuperantius, who suppressed the second outbreak in 417, is said to have 'restored the laws and brought back liberty, and not suffered them to be slaves of their own servants'. Here we seem to have something more organised than sporadic jacqueries, but these revolts find no parallel in the rest of the empire.

On the other hand there is abundant evidence that interest in theology was intense and widespread. The generality of people firmly believed that not only individual salvation but the fortunes of the empire depended on correct doctrine, and it was natural that they felt passionately on the subject. Not all, of course, were

[64] The evidence is assembled by Thompson in *Past and Present*, ii (1952), pp. 11 ff.

well informed. Many humble Donatists shouted 'Deo Laudes' and denounced the Catholics as *traditores* without any clear understanding of the issues, or at best sang with gusto the songs which Parmenian had composed for their instruction.[65] Many an Egyptian monk could not have explained the subtleties of the monophysite doctrine, and was content to chant 'who was crucified for us' after the Trisagion, and to curse the Chalcedonians as Nestorians. But even uneducated people argued theological points with zest, and could cite the key texts and repeat the stock arguments. I need hardly remind you of Gregory of Nyssa's description of Constantinople during the Arian controversy. 'If you ask for your change, the shopkeeper philosophizes to you about the Begotten and the Unbegotten. If you ask the price of a loaf, the answer is "the Father is greater and the Son inferior"; if you say "Is my bath ready?", the attendant declares that the Son is of nothing'.[66] And finally thousands of people were prepared to face deportation, pecuniary loss, torture, and even death on theological issues for most of which no national or social undertones can be discovered.

I would contend that under the later Roman Empire most people felt strongly on doctrinal issues and a high proportion had sufficient acquaintance with theology to argue about them with zest if without any deep understanding. It does not, of course, follow that they adopted whatever doctrinal position they held from a rational evaluation of the arguments for and against it. As today and in all ages most people's religious beliefs were determined by a variety of irrational influences. Some were swayed by the authority of a revered theologian, or more often by that of a holy man whose orthodoxy was guaranteed by his austerities and miracles. The great majority accepted what they had been brought up to believe as children, or the dominant belief of their social milieu. Some doctrines made a special appeal to certain classes of society. It has been claimed that in Asia Minor the areas where the rigorist sects prevailed coincided with those where native

---

[65]Aug. *Ep.* 55. 18. 34; Praedestinatus, *de Haer.* 43. Other examples of popular songs for the instruction of the ignorant on theological issues are Augustine's *Psalmus contra partem Donati* and Arius' *Thaleia*. If the latter was really, as Athanasius implies (*Or. c. Arianos*, i. 4), sung in the bars of Alexandria, the proletariat of that city must have had a strong taste for theological controversy: the surviving verses (cited in Athanasius, *de Syn.* 15) are not very inspiring.

[66] Greg. Nyss., *Or. de deitate Filii et Spiritus Sancti* (*P.G.* xlvi. 557).

languages survived. This is not the whole truth, for, as we know from Socrates, there were in Constantinople, Nicomedia, Nicaea, and other great cities cultivated Novatians, like their delightful bishop Sisinnius, who when asked by censorious members of his flock why, being a bishop, he took two baths a day, replied: 'Because I have not got time for a third'.[67] But the bulk of the more fundamentalist Novatians were Phrygians and Paphlagonians, and Socrates is surely on the right lines when he explains this fact by saying that these people were naturally not addicted to the horse races and the theatre, and regarded fornication with horror.[68] He holds that the austerity of the Phrygians and Paphlagonians is due to the climate—they lie in the zone between the Scythians and Thracians, who are inclined to violent passions, and the peoples of the East, who are subject to their appetites. The truth surely is that they were simple countryfolk, whose life was necessarily somewhat austere, and that they were naturally attracted by a severe doctrine which condemned indulgences to which they were not prone. The fact that they spoke an indigenous language is an index merely of their rusticity, and not of any mysterious affinity between Novatianism and Phrygian national culture.

In brief I would maintain that when the sectaries declared, as they did on our evidence declare: 'We hold the true faith and are the true church; our opponents are heretics, and never will we accept their doctrine or communicate with them, or yield to the impious government which supports them', they meant and felt what they said. Why they held their particular beliefs we in many cases cannot divine. Who can tell why in A.D. 450 out of the 800 villages in the territory of Cyrrhus one was Arian, one Eunomian, and eight remained stubbornly faithful to the doctrines of Marcion which had been generally condemned for some three centuries?[69] In some cases the sects more or less coincided with social or regional groups, and I have endeavoured to explain how this may

----

[67] Socrates records a number of cultivated Novatian bishops of Constantinople: Marcian (iv. 9), Sisinnius (vi. 22), Chrysanthus (vii. 12), Paul (vii. 17), and also Ablabius, bisop of Nicaea, a rhetorician (vii. 12). The synod of Pazos, where the rural Novatians adopted the Quartodeciman heresy, was not attended by the leading bishops of the sect, those of Constantinople, Nicaea, Nicomedia, and Cotyaeum (iv. 28).

[68] Soc. H.E. iv. 28.

[69] Theodoret, Ep. 81, 113.

have come about. But the line of demarcation between orthodoxy and heresy never, except in the case of the Armenians and the Germans, corresponded with anything that can legitimately be called a national, as opposed to a regional, division. It was inhabitants of Egypt, and not Copts, who were monophysite, and even in Africa, though Donatism made a greater appeal, as a rigorist sect, to the Punic- or Berber-speaking peasantry, many Romanised Africans were found on the Donatist side. And finally the sects never pursued political aims, whether national or social.

CHAPTER SIXTEEN

THE ORIGIN AND EARLY HISTORY OF THE
FOLLIS

ONE of the mosaics of the villa at Piazza Armerina, which are generally dated to the early fourth century A.D., depicts in connection with a contest a table on and under which are what are evidently prizes, crowns, palms, and bags labelled $*\overline{\text{XII}}\partial$, that is 12,500 *denarii*.[1] I suggest that these bags are the *folles*, which were at this date and later units of currency. A *follis* was, as its name implies and as various metrological writers confirm,[2] a purse, and these purses, according to literary and epigraphic sources, contained bronze coins or *denarii*.[3] The *follis* is first attested in 308–9,[4] but was probably introduced at an earlier date, somewhere between the great debasement of the *antoninianus* by Gallienus and the reform of the coinage by Diocletian, when the *antoninianus* or Aurelian's piece marked XXI were the only coins in circulation and their value had sunk so low that some higher denomination was essential. If this is so, the coins which the *follis* contained cannot have been *denarii*, which had ceased to be minted, though the value of the *follis* was reckoned in *denarii*.

The curious sum of 12,500 *denarii* can be explained on the following hypothesis. Three papyrus documents between them strongly suggest that at the end of the third or the beginning of

[1] Incorrectly described on p. 42 of G. V. Gentili, *The Imperial Villa of Piazza Armerina* (1956): the correct reading of the numeral is just discernible in the photograph of the mosaic (no. 26). Other labelled money bags occur on the Constantinian mosaic floor of the church at Aquileia (Cecchelli, *La basilica di Aquileia*, pl. xxv) and in the illustrations of 'Roma', 'Constantinopolis', and Constantius Gallus in the Chronographer of 354 (*Jahrb. deutsch. Arch. Inst.*, *Ergänzungsheft* I (1888), nos. 4, 6, 35). But these are apparently bags of gold. The last is labelled $\frac{s}{\infty}$ (presumably *mille solidi*) and the others carry similar figures (∞, ∞cccc, ∞ccc; in the last two the figure disappears round the side of the bag).

[2] *Studi in onore di A. Calderini e R. Paribeni* II, 329.

[3] Hultsch, *Metrolog. Script. Rel.* I, 144–5, 267, 269, 303, 308; II, 105, 151–2.

[4] Scr. Hist. Aug., *Elag.* 22, 'centum aureos et mille argenteos et centum folles aeris'; *C.I.L.* v, 1880,' denariorum folles sexcentos'; 1973, '* fol. sescentos'; 2046, '* foll. quingentos'.

the fourth century A.D., the imperial government first raised the face value of the *nummus*, i.e. the Aurelianic piece and the similar radiate coins which succeeded it, by stages to 25 *denarii* and then cut its value by half to 12½ *denarii*.[5] The chronology is not very clear, but the last stage in the process evidently took place after the *Edictum de Pretiis* of 301. It was certainly complete in the reign of Licinius, whose radiate coins are labelled XIIГ.[6] It is then a plausible hypothesis that the *follis* was a bag of 1,000 *nummi* and was priced at the current valuation of those coins, ending up with 12,500 *denarii*.

It is not easy to determine the value of the *follis* in relation to silver or gold, since not only was its value in terms of *denarii* arbitrarily varied, as we have seen, from time to time, but the relation of the *denarius* to silver and gold changed greatly during the early fourth century. In general the *denarius* tended to sink steeply, that is the price of the precious metals in terms of *denarii* rose, owing to the reckless overissue of the copper coins and the raising of their face value in *denarii*; but the drop must have been irregular and must have been checked or reversed when their value was reduced. We possess five figures. In the *Edictum de Pretiis* of 301 gold is priced at 50,000 *denarii* to the pound.[7] In an undated Egyptian document, which may fall between 293 and 308 or between 317 and 324, the price is 100,000.[8] Two papyri, one undated, the other of 307, indicate prices of 8,000 and 8,328 *denarii* for a pound of silver,[9] which at this date was officially valued at 4 *aurei* or $\frac{1}{15}$ lb. gold;[10] this implies prices of 120,000 and 125,000 *denarii* for a pound of gold. Finally in 324 in another Egyptian document a pound of gold is valued at rather over 300,000 *denarii*.[11]

Assuming that the *follis* was already tariffed at 12,500 *denarii* in 307 and that no further change was made, it was worth $\frac{1}{10}$ lb. gold or 1½ lb. silver in 307, and had by 324 declined to less than $\frac{1}{24}$ lb. gold or ⅝ lb. silver. In coins the value of the *follis* would have

[5] *P. Ryl.* 607, *P. Oslo* III, 83, *P.S.I.* 965: their contents are summarised in *Ec. Hist. Rev.* v (1953), 317–8 (—ch. IX at p. 226 f.).

[6] *Num. Chron.* 1957, 32.

[7] *Ed. Diocl.* xxx, 1. The reading has been doubted, but is correct, p. 200 n. 34.

[8] *P. Oxy.* 2106 (cf. p. 202 n. 39.)

[9] *Archiv Pap.* xv (1953), 104; *P.S.I.* 310.

[10] *P. Thead.* 33 and *P. Oxy.* 1653, as interpreted by S. Bolin, *State and Currency in the Roman Empire to* 300 A.D., 311–13.

[11] *P. Oxy.* 1430

been at the earlier date 6 *aurei* or 144 *argentei*,[12] at the later 2½ *aurei* (or 3 *solidi*) or 60 *argentei*.

The few early references to *folles* none of them yield precise figures, but they are consonant with the range of values postulated above. A papyrus of 308–9 appears to indicate (its language is very obscure) that a fine of 5 *folles*, equivalent at that date to ½ lb. gold, was levied on villagers who left their own villages;[13] this may be compared with a law of 386 which imposed a fine of 6 oz. gold on those who harboured a runaway *colonus* of a private landlord.[14] Two constitutions dated 315 enact a fine of 30 *folles* for premature appeals;[15] by a law of 341 the penalty for the same offence is fixed at 30 lb. silver.[16] This implies a value of the *follis* intermediate between those of 307 and 324. The other references are even vaguer. In 312–3 Constantine allocated 3,000 *folles* for the relief of the African Church,[17] and shortly before that time, according to evidence submitted in 320 to Zenophilus, the consular of Numidia, Lucilla, a lady of senatorial rank, gave 400 *folles* to Silvanus, bishop of Cirta, ostensibly for the poor, but in reality to secure the election of Majorinus to the see of Carthage, and one Victor gave 20 *folles* to the same bishop to be ordained priest.[18] These figures are not unreasonable if the *follis* was worth between 1½ lb. and 1 lb. silver; the two last are perhaps rather high, but it must be remembered that they are allegations made about eight years after the event and that none of the witnesses claimed to have counted the money.

There remains the *gleba*, the surtax imposed by Constantine on senators, which was levied at the rate of 8, 4, or 2 *folles* according to the wealth of the taxpayer.[19] Hesychius of Miletus, who wrote under Justinian, about a century after the *gleba* had been abolished by Marcian, states that the tax was of 8, 4, and 2 lb. gold,[20] but this for two reasons cannot be right. In the first place the pound of gold was a common monetary unit, frequently mentioned as

[12] I give this name to the silver coins struck by Diocletian at 96 to the pound.
[13] See above, n. 2.
[14] *Cod. Theod.* v, xvii, 2.
[15] *Cod. Theod.* xi, xxxvi, 2 and 3; for the dates see Seeck, *Regesten*, 54.
[16] *Cod. Theod.* xi, xxxvi, 5.
[17] Eusebius, *Hist. Eccl.* x, 6.
[18] Optatus, *App.* 1.
[19] Zosimus ii, 19; the figures come from Hesychius (see below, n. 21), but the minimum scale of 2 *folles* is confirmed by *Cod. Theod.* vi, ii, 13.
[20] Hesychius, fr. 5; *F.H.G.* iv, 154.

such in the laws, and there is no reason why Constantine should have used the term *follis* for it, especially as *follis* had a recognised other meaning. In the second place, when the Senate complained of the burdensomeness of the tax on its humbler members, Theodosius I in 393 conceded that a new minimum scale of payment, at 7 *solidi*, should be instituted for the poorest senators, insisting that those who did not feel equal to paying this sum must resign their rank.[21] If the lowest scale hitherto had been 2 lb. gold, that is 144 *solidi*, the reduction is clearly far too great. It is plain that 2 *folles* must have been a sum exceeding, but not greatly exceeding, 7 *solidi*.

There is another puzzle about the senatorial *follis*. In this context, and in this context alone, does the *follis* appear to retain something like its original value. All other references to it indicate, as will be shown later, that in the fifty years following 324 it sank catastrophically. The clue to this puzzle is perhaps to be found in Epiphanius' treatise *de mensuris et ponderibus*. The original appears to have been a farrago of miscellaneous metrological information, Greek, Roman, and Hebrew, dating from all periods, and we only possess abstracts of the work in various versions, Greek, Latin, and Syriac.[22] The original book was, however, written in 392 and its information about the *follis* is thus more or less contemporary. In one passage Epiphanius distinguishes between two reckonings of the *follis*, one in *denarii* (κατὰ τὸν δηναρισμόν) and the other in silver or silver coins (κατὰ τὸν ἀργυρισμόν).[23] The former is equated with 2 or 2½ silver coins (the M.S. tradition varies), which are again equated to 250 *denarii*. Another passage which states that 'the *follis* makes up 125 silver coins; and it is called among the Romans a sack' must presumably refer to the *follis* reckoned in silver.[24]

I would, on the basis of these facts, suggest that Constantine, no doubt because the *follis* was rapidly depreciating, enacted that for the purposes of the *gleba* it should be reckoned in silver coins, whose value was more or less stable. If I am right in believing

---

[21] *Cod. Theod.* VI, ii, 15.

[22] Two Greek versions are printed in Hultsch, *Metrolog. Script. Rel.* I, 259–67, 267–71, with variant readings on p. 144, n. 4, and II, 151–2; the Latin version in II, 100–06. For the Syriac version see Or. Inst. Univ. Chicago, *Stud. Anc. Or. Civ.* XI (1935).

[23] Hultsch, o.c. I, 267 (§ 49); cf. 144, n. 4, and II, 151–2; Latin version, II, 105 (§ 40).   [24] o.c. I, 269 (§ 17).

that the *follis* contained 12,500 *denarii*, he based this valuation on an equation of the silver coins to 100 *denarii*, which is attested in another passage of Epiphanius, and by St. Maximus, who wrote at an unknown date a treatise 'on the value of the 30 pieces of silver which Judas received for the betrayal of Christ'.[25] The equation of the silver piece to 100 *denarii* may also explain the name *miliarense* which was—at any rate in the latter part of the fourth century—given to the standard silver coin. A coin tariffed at 100 'pieces of ten' might well be dubbed 'a piece of a thousand', which is the obvious meaning of *miliarense*.[26] The standard silver coin of Constantine's day was that struck at 96 to the pound, and a papyrus shows that some time in the fourth century after 324 the pound of silver was officially priced at 4 *solidi*, that is $\frac{1}{18}$ lb. gold.[27] The evaluation of the *follis* at 125 silver coins and the silver coin at 100 *denarii* thus implies that the price of the pound of gold was at the time 18 x 96 x 100, or approximately 175,000 *denarii*, which would fit for a date intermediate between 308, when the price was 125,000, and 324, when it was over 300,000.

The *follis* at 125 *miliarensia* would have amounted to a little over $1\frac{1}{4}$ lb. silver and been equivalent to a little over 5 *solidi*. The minimum tax of 2 *folles* would thus have been just over 10 *solidi*. The *miliarense* or standard silver coin did not remain unchanged, being reduced in 348 to $\frac{1}{144}$ lb., but this reduction was probably accompanied by an increase in the price of silver from 4 to 6 *solidi* to the pound, so that the reduced *miliarense* retained the value of a *siliqua* ($\frac{1}{24}$ *solidus*). The *follis* would thus have retained its old gold value, if it still consisted of 125 coins, though these were smaller. If on the other hand it was reckoned at the original amount of silver by weight, its gold value would have risen to $7\frac{1}{2}$ *solidi*, and the minimum tax to 15 *solidi*. In either case the lower minimum of 7 *solidi* conceded in 393 would have afforded some relief to poor senators.[28]

[25] o.c. i, 267 (§ 1), as corrected in ii, 152 (cf. i, 143–4).   [26] o.c. i, 302–3.

[27] As, owing to the rapid depreciation of the *denarius*, the equation soon ceased to be valid, the meaning of the word *miliarense* was quickly forgotten. In Epiphanius' day the current explanation was μιλιαρίσιον δὲ τὸ ἀργυροῦν, ὅ ἐστι στρατιωτικὸν δόμα· μιλιτία γὰρ ἡ στρατεία (i, 269 (§ 16)). This explanation is rightly dismissed as folk etymology, but the other, that the *miliarense* was so called because it was equivalent to $\frac{1}{1000}$ lb. gold, which depends on a nomic gloss of quite uncertain date (cited in Dindorff's edition of Epiphanius, vol. iv, pars i, 128) though scarcely more plausible, received Seeck's approval and is still widely accepted.

[28] *S.P.P.* i, 4, cf. *Num. Zeitschr.* N.F. vi (1913), 161 ff., 219 ff.

The *denarius* continued to depreciate with ever increasing speed after 324. Papyri, none of them unfortunately dated, show that the *solidus*, which in 324 was worth about 4,350 *denarii*, was later priced at 54,000; 150,000; 180,000; 275,000; 5,760,000; 20,200,000; 37,500,000; 45,000,000.[29] The *follis* reckoned in *denarii* also sank very rapidly in value, it would seem, though it is impossible to extract any very exact figures from the evidence.

Both the text and the date of *Cod. Theod.* vii, xx, 3, are corrupt. It enacts that veterans should receive either land, a pair of oxen, 100 *modii* of seed corn and 'pecuniae in nummo viginti quinque milia follium', or if they wished to go into trade, should have immune from tax 'centum follium summam'. As Seeck suggested, the word 'milia' cannot be right: on the basis of a variant manuscript reading 'militia' he proposed 'viginti quinque militiae praemium folles'. The other figure gives some clue to the contemporary value of the *follis*. In 385 the government conceded to veterans 'quindecim solidorum in mercimoniis omnibus immunitatem',[30] and in 379 gave clerical traders an immunity of 10 *solidi* in Illyricum and Italy and of 15 *solidi* in Gaul.[31] A 100 *folles* should therefore be roughly equivalent to 15 *solidi*, and the *follis* would thus be worth about $\frac{1}{7}$ *solidus* or 14 *miliarensia*. This is a sharp drop from the 3 *solidi* deduced for 324. The date 'iii Id. Oct. Constantinop. Constantino A. VI et Constantino Caes. coss.' cannot be right as Constantinople had not been founded in 320. Of the possible corrections suggested by Seeck,[32] 325 or 329, the latter year seems preferable.

Cod. Theod. xiv, xxiv, 1, of 328, which enacts that *mensae oleariae* at Rome should be sold when they fall vacant for 20 *folles*, but might not be resold for a higher sum, is not very illuminating, but 3 *solidi* is a possible sum in this context. The next law which mentions *folles* is *Cod. Theod.* vi, iv, 5, of 340, which fixes the sums to be spent on their games by the three praetors of Constantinople. They are 'viginti et quinque milium follium et quinquaginta librarum argenti' for the first, 'viginti milia follium et quadraginta libras argenti' for the second, and 'quindecim milia follium ac triginta argenti libras' for the third. It has sometimes

[29] *P.E.R.* 187, 37; *S.P.P.* xx, 96, 81; *Sb.* 7034; *P. Oxy.* 1223; *P.S.I.* 960–1.
[30] *Cod. Theod.* xiii, i, 14.
[31] *Cod. Theod.* xiii, i, 11.
[32] *Regesten,* 82.

been assumed that the sums in *folles* and those in silver are of equal value, in which case 500 *folles* would be equivalent to 1 lb. silver, and 125 therefore to a *solidus*. The assumption is, however, gratuitous, and the sums in *folles* might be considerably larger, say four or five times those in silver. But this law does suggest that the *follis* was by now worth considerably less than $\frac{1}{7}$ *solidus*.

The *follis* is next mentioned in *Cod. Theod.* IX, xxiii, 1, dated to 356.[33] It attempts to check speculation in copper coin by prohibiting its transport from place to place, but allows merchants to carry on their own animals not more than 1,000 *folles* for their expenses. In this context 1,000 *folles* is evidently a very small sum, equivalent to 1 or 2 *solidi*; the annual rations of a soldier were commuted for 4 *solidi*,[34] and a merchant, even if he had several pack-animals and a slave or two, would not have needed half that sum for the expenses of a single journey.

In a law of Julian (*Cod. Theod.* XIV, iv, 3, of 363) it is implied that the official rate at which pork required for Rome was commuted was 6 *folles* a pound. A novel of Valentinian III shows that in 452 the official price of pork bought for Rome was 240 lb. to the *solidus*.[35] There is no reason to believe that the real value of pork, as expressed in its gold price, varied greatly in the fourth and fifth centuries, and it is therefore legitimate to infer that in 363 the *follis* was worth only about $\frac{1}{1500}$ of a *solidus*.

In two passages, Augustine alludes to *folles* in terms which suggest that they were of very small value in Africa in the early fifth century. In a sermon he tells of a man of moderate means who, having sold a *solidus*, ordered 100 *folles* out of the price to be paid to the poor: a thief later stole the money 'from which a small part had been given to the poor'.[36] It may be presumed that 100 *folles* did not exceed the canonical tenth of the value of the *solidus*, and was probably less. In the *Civitas Dei*[37] he tells of Florentius, a poor cobbler of Hippo, who lost his cloak (*casula*). In his distress he prayed to the Twenty Martyrs, and some boys jeered at him 'as if he had asked the Martyrs for 500 *folles* wherewith to buy clothes'. However, as he went home he found a large fish on the

---

[33] This date has been questioned, but is probably right. Constantina of the subscription must be Arles, and Rufinus thus praetorian prefect of the Gauls.
[34] Val., *Nov.* XIII, 3 (445).
[35] Ibid., XXXVI, 2.
[36] Aug., *Serm.* 389, 3.
[37] XXII, 8.

sea shore, which he sold to a cook for 300 *folles* and planned with this money 'to buy wool so that his wife could make something for him to wear as best she could'. It appears then that a very cheap garment might be obtained for 500 *folles*, but that for 300 one could buy only the raw material. Clothes were expensive. At about this period, Pinianus, the husband of Melania the younger, obtained a very cheap suit at Rome for a *solidus* or 2 *tremisses* (the Greek and Latin versions of the *Life* differ on this point),[38] and in 395 the clothing allowance for a military cloak (*chlamys*) in Illyricum was raised from 2 *tremisses* to a *solidus*.[39] We do not know precisely what a *casula* was, but the garment which Florentius wanted to buy was probably much cheaper than a military *chlamys*. In the *Edictum de pretiis* a military *stiche* of linen is priced at 1,500 to 1,000 *denarii* and a coarse linen *stiche* 'for the use of commoners and slaves' at 750 to 500. Among woollen garments a 'best indictional *chlamys*' cost 4,000 *denarii*, whereas an African *birrus* is put at only 1,500 and an African *sagum* at as little as 500.[40] The story of Florentius thus suggests that 500 *folles* was equivalent to about a *tremissis*.

The above evidence shows that the *follis* depreciated progressively from the early years of the fourth century, and depreciated sharply. The *denarius* of the Egyptian papyri also sank progressively in value, and to a comparable degree. It is unfortunately impossible to make any exact comparison between the two, as no document gives the precise gold value of a *follis* and the documents which state the value of the *solidus* in *denarii* are none of them dated. One papyrus[41] does, however, yield a very rough cross check. It is dated 360, and indicates a price of 144,000 *denarii* for a pound of meat, as against the 6 *folles* of Julian's law of 363, which, if the *follis* consisted of 12,500 *denarii*, would be equivalent to 75,000 *denarii*. The correspondence is far from exact, but it must be remembered in the first place that the papyrus gives an actual market price, whereas the figure in Julian's law is an official commutation rate, which may well have been arbitrarily low, and in the second place that meat seems to have been dearer in Egypt than in the western provinces: the official

[38] *Vita S. Melaniae Jun.* 8; *Anal. Boll.* viii (1889), 26 (Latin), xxii (1903), 13 (Greek).
[39] *Cod. Theod.* vii, vi, 4.
[40] *Ed. Diocl.* xxvi, 28–33; xix, 1, 42, 61.
[41] *P. Oxy.* 1056.

military rate of commutation for meat was 200 lb. to the *solidus* in Egypt,[42] and 270 lb. in Africa.[43] Moreover, the exchange rate between the *solidus* and the copper currency certainly fluctuated from time to time and probably varied from province to province, according to temporary and local changes in the demand for either and the amount of either available on the market. When allowance is made for all these variables, the figures given by the papyrus of 360 and the law of 363 are not incompatible with the valuation of the *follis* at 12,500 *denarii*.

The *follis* must as it depreciated in value have soon ceased to be an actual purse of coins and it probably became, like the 'myriad of denarii' of the Egyptian papyri, a mere accounting unit. In the last quarter of the fifth century the name *follis* was applied to the large copper coins issued under the later Vandal kings in Africa and by Anastasius and his successors in the East. But the history of the *follis* in this later sense is another story.

[42] P. *Cairo* 67320.
[43] Val., *Nov.* XIII, 4.

CHAPTER SEVENTEEN

CHURCH FINANCE IN THE FIFTH AND SIXTH CENTURIES

I DO not propose in this paper to discuss the sources of ecclesi-astical revenues. It will suffice to say that, apart from a govern-ment grant, instituted by Constantine and, after its abolition by Julian, renewed by later emperors on a much more modest scale —one-third of the original amount[1]—the churches derived their income from two main sources: the offerings of the faithful, and the rents of lands and house property given or bequeathed by benefactors or more rarely purchased.[2] The offerings are some-times spoken of as first-fruits,[3] perhaps only figuratively, and were in principle voluntary, though in the late fifth or early sixth century the eastern government had to forbid the clergy to use ecclesiastical sanctions to enforce their payment.[4] Tithe seems to have been unknown save as a purely voluntary offering made by exceptionally pious Christians for the relief of the poor.[5] The

[1] Theodoret, *H.E.* i. 11, iv. 4, Soz. *H.E.* v. 5, *Cod. Just.* i. ii. 12 (451), cp. Ath. *Apol. c. Ar.* 18, *Act. Conc. Oec.* ii. i. 213, Gregory I, *Reg.* x. 8.

[2] Thiel, *Ep. Rom. Pont.*, Simplicius, *ep.* 1, 'de reditibus ecclesiae vel oblatione fidelium', Gelasius, *ep.* 14, § 27, 'tam de reditu quam de oblatione fidelium', 15, 'de reditu vero ecclesiae vel oblatione fidelium', 16, 'reditus et oblationes fidelium', cp. *Conc. Aurel.* i, *can.* 14, 15, cited p. 344 n. 24, p. 347 n. 45. In Greek *oblationes* are called καρποφορίαι, e.g. *Conc. Gangr. can.* 7, 8, *Act. Conc. Oec.* ii. i. 384, *Cod. Just.* i. iii. 38 (see n. 14 below).

[3] *Can. Apost.* 4, *Cod. Just.* i. iii. 38, *Canons of St. Athanasius*, 3, 63, 82 (ed. W. Riedel and W. E. Crum). Cp. also John Cassian and the Apostolic Constitutions, cited in note 4 below.

[4] *Cod. Just.* i. iii. 38, πρὸς τὴν τῶν καρποφοριῶν τῶν ἐν τοῖς τόποις καλουμένων ἀπαρχῶν ἤτοι προσφορῶν ἔκτισιν ὥσπερ τι τέλος μεθοδεύοντας.

[5] In *Const. Apost.* vii. 29, viii. 30, both first-fruits and tithe appear to be spoken of as a reality, but in ii. 25–26 (cp. 34–35) they are clearly referred to as part of the Old Testament dispensation, a standard from which the modern Christian ought not to fall short. John Cassian (*Coll.* xiv. vii. 1–3, xxi. i–viii) reports Egyptian peasants actually offering *primitiae* and *decimae*, not, however, to their bishop or parish priest, but to the *diaconia* of a monastery. The Canons of St. Athanasius (82–83) also speak of tithe being offered by both laity and clergy for the benefit of the poor. That tithe was not in fact paid as a normal due is proved by Joh. Chrys. *Hom. in Eph.* iv (*P.G.* lxii. 36), Jerome, *Comm. in Mal.* iii (*P.L.* xxv. 1571), Augustine, *Enarr. in Psal.* cxlvi. 17, *Serm.* ix, lxxxv. The second council of Tours in 567 ordained

greater churches seem to have derived the bulk of their revenue from endowments: John Chrysostom laments in one of his sermons that now that the church of Antioch possessed a large income derived from its own property, the laity no longer felt any obligation to make their offerings.[6] On the other hand, small and ill-endowed churches might depend largely on the offerings of the faithful: the second council of Bracara had even to legislate against founders who built chapels as a commercial speculation, sharing the offerings with the clergy fifty-fifty.[7]

What I wish to investigate is the distribution of ecclesiastical revenues, and for this purpose it is necessary to say something of the organisation of the churches. In every city there was a principal church, presided over by the bishop; in addition there were others, what may be called parochial churches, both in the town and in the villages and estates of the city territory. There were also memorial chapels of martyrs, and charitable institutions —hospitals, orphanages, almshouses for the poor and the aged, hospices for travellers and pilgrims. There were, furthermore, monasteries, but with these I shall not be concerned, as they were always financially autonomous, being supported either by the offerings of the faithful or by the labour of their inmates, or, to an increasing degree as time went on, by their own endowments.

The churches, chapels, and charitable institutions fall into two main classes. Some were annexed to the bishop's church, served by his own clergy and financed from his central fund. Others had their own separate endowments, from which their clergy were paid. This distinction is clearly made by Justinian in Novel vi[8] where he speaks on the one hand of churches whose founders had endowed them with sufficient funds for the maintenance of their staff of clergy, and on the other of cases where 'the church of the

---

a general offering of a tithe as a special measure of penitence (*M.G.H., Leg. Sect.* III. i. 136–8). The second council of Matisco in 585 made the first attempt to enforce (by excommunication) the regular payment of tithe (*can.* 6, op. cit., pp. 166–7): the claim was made on scriptural precedent, a *mos antiquus* which had admittedly fallen into complete desuetude.

[6] Joh. Chrys. *Hom. in Matth.* lxxxv (lxxxvi). 3 (*P.G.* lxviii. 761–3).

[7] *Conc. Bracar.* ii, *can.* 6 (C. W. Barlow, *Martini Bracarensis opera omnia*, p. 120), 'placuit ut si quis basilicam non pro devotione fidei sed pro quaestu cupiditatis aedificat, ut quidquid ibidem oblatione populi colligitur medium cum clericis dividat, eo quod basilicam in terra sua ipse condiderit. . . .'

[8] § 8: αὐτὴ δὲ ἡ τῆς πόλεως ἐκκλησία χορηγοίη τὰς σιτήσεις ἑαυτῇ τε καὶ ταῖς ἄλλαις ἐκκλησίαις.

city itself provides salaries for itself and the other churches'. In Novel cxx[9] he makes a similar distinction between 'the churches and other sacred institutions of which the local bishop conducts the administration in his own person or through his clergy', and 'the almshouses, hospices, hospitals and other sacred institutions' (this term, as appears later, includes 'houses of prayer' or what we should call parochial churches) 'which have their own administration'.

The same distinction existed in the West. In a letter to John, bishop of Nola, Pope Pelagius I[10] (555–61) refused him permission to sell the church plate of Suessula 'quae Nolanae ecclesiae esse videtur parochia'. His proper course is to make Suessula a 'titulus Nolanae ecclesiae', to be served 'per deputatos cardinales ecclesiae presbyteros'. The situation was evidently that the endowments of Suessula had become inadequate to pay the clergy. The remedy was to amalgamate it with the episcopal church, some of whose clergy—the *cardinales* or, as they are sometimes called, *canonici*—would be seconded to serve it. Such an amalgamated church was called a *titulus*, an independent church a *parochia* or sometimes a *diocesis*.

Independent churches were, it would seem, far more numerous than *tituli*. Most founders of churches were private benefactors, and most of them endowed the churches which they built. As time went on bishops came to realise that a new church was a doubtful blessing unless it was furnished with sufficient rents to pay for its repair and maintenance, including the lights and the salaries of the clergy. By the end of the fifth century, as we see from a letter of Pope Gelasius (492–6), the Roman see had established a rule that no bishop was to consecrate a church or chapel without verifying that it was properly endowed.[11] Justinian laid down the same rule for the East in Novel lxvii (538), and

---

[9] § 6: εἰ μὲν ἁγιώταται ὦσιν ἐκκλησίαι ἢ ἕτεροι εὐαγεῖς οἶκοι ὦν τὴν διοίκησιν ὁ κατὰ τόπον ὁσιώτατος ἐπίσκοπος ἢ δι'ἑαυτοῦ ἢ διὰ τοῦ εὐαγοῦς αὐτοῦ κλήρου ποιεῖται . . . εἰ δὲ πτωχεῖα ἢ ξενῶνες ἢ νοσοκομεῖα ἢ ἕτεροι εὐαγεῖς οἶκοι ὦσιν ἰδίαν διοίκησιν ἔχοντες. Cp. also p. 342, n. 16.

[10] S. Loewenfeld, *Ep. Pont. Rom. Ined.* 24, 'sed si tanta est ecclesie Sessulane penuria ut parrochia esse non possit, eam potius titulum Nolane ecclesie constitue, ut tali depositione habita nec de sacris quicquam ministeriis detrahatur et competentia ibidem divini cultus per deputatos cardinales ecclesie presbyteros ministeria celebrentur'.

[11] Thiel, *Ep. Rom. Pont.*, Gelasius, *ep.* 34, fr. 22; cp. Pelagius I (*P.L.*lxix. 414–15), and Gregory I, *Reg.* ii. 9, 15, ix. 58, 71, 180.

Z

in Gaul the fourth council of Orleans[12] in 541 enacted that 'if any one has or asks to have a *diocesis* on his estate he must first allot to it sufficient lands and clergy to perform their offices there'. The second council of Bracara[13] laid down the same rule for Spain in 571.

Most charitable institutions seem also to have been autonomous, having been endowed by their founders. The laws restraining alienation of church property regularly mention, besides the bishops with their οἰκονόμοι, the administrators of hospitals and similar institutions as the persons responsible.[14]

The dependent churches appear to have varied somewhat in status. Some were mere annexes of the cathedral. Thus the Great Church at Constantinople, as we learn from Justinian's third Novel,[15] comprised four buildings, Hagia Sophia itself, the Church of the Virgin built by the empress Verina (457–79) in its near neighbourhood, that of St. Theodore, built by Sporacius (consul in 452), and the old church of St. Helena. These four churches were administered as a unit, being served in rotation by one body of clergy. But in the same novel[16] Justinian speaks of two other classes of churches in Constantinople, those 'whose maintenance the Great Church undertakes', and those 'which do not have their supply and maintenance from the Great Church.' The former of these categories, he states, had been built by private founders who had laid down an establishment of clergy for them, and, he strongly implies, endowed them with revenues calculated to support this establishment. Their clergy were not enrolled on the establishment of the Great Church, and it may be that they retained some measure of control over their revenues. In Novel cxx,[17] in which Justinian regulated the grant of perpetual emphyteutic leases by churches outside Constantinople, he lays down that in the case of 'churches and other religious institutions whose administration is undertaken by the local bishop either in

---

[12] *Conc. Aurel.* iv, *can.* 33 (*M.G.H., Leg. sect.* III. i, p. 94).

[13] *Conc. Bracar.* ii, *can.* 5 (Barlow, op. cit., p. 120).

[14] *Cod. Just.* I. ii. 17, § 2, Just. *Nov.* vii, § 1, cxx, §§ 1, 5, 6, 7.

[15] § 1.

[16] § 2: ἐν δὲ ταῖς ἄλλαις ἁπάσαις ἐκκλησίαις ὧν τὴν χορηγίαν ἡ ἁγιωτάτη μεγάλη ἐκκλησία ποιεῖται . . . ἀλλ᾽ οὐδὲ ἐν ταῖς ἄλλαις ὅσαι μὴ τὴν τροφὴν καὶ χορηγίαν ἔχουσιν ἐκ τῆς ἁγιωτάτης μεγάλης ἐκκλησίας.

[17] § 6: κατὰ τὴν γνώμην αὐτοῦ (sc. τοῦ ἐπισκόπου) καὶ συναίνεσιν γίνεσθαι τὸ τοιοῦτο συνάλλαγμα, ὀμνυόντων παρόντος αὐτοῦ τῶν οἰκονόμων καὶ διοικητῶν καὶ χαρτουλαρίων τοῦ αὐτοῦ εὐαγοῦς οἴκου.

person or through his own clergy', the leases are to be granted on the authority and with the consent of the bishop, but that the *oeconomi*, administrators, and chartularies of the institution are to swear in his presence that no loss will be incurred by the institution through the lease. Here then we have religious institutions which are managed by the bishop, but nevertheless have their own financial officers and apparently separate endowments.

Western analogies may help to explain this anomalous state of affairs. A bishop may have converted a *parochia* which could not pay its way into a *titulus*, as John of Nola was ordered to do, but earmarked what endowments there were for use of the church; Suessula had some lands, which John was urged to exploit for what they were worth, so as to cover the taxes due upon them.[18] Alternatively a bishop sometimes took over *parochiae* which were over-endowed and used their surplus revenue for his own church or churches;[19] in such a case too the revenue left to the subordinate church may have been derived from certain estates which were left under the management of its own clergy.

From this evidence it would appear that *tituli* were of diverse origins. Some were no doubt built as chapels of ease of the cathedral and never had any separate endowment or clergy. Others were *parochiae* which had been absorbed but which might still retain some control over their original endowments or that portion of them which was earmarked for their use. The *tituli* of Rome mostly fell under the second category. Constantine and other founders richly endowed the churches which they built at Rome, as the records in the Liber Pontificalis show. But the popes preferred to centralise their finances, and converted them into *tituli*, thus concentrating in their own hands their vast endowments. The priests of the several *tituli*, however, retained the management of some at any rate of their estates. This appears from the rules laid down by Pope Symmachus[20] in 502 against the alienation of the property of the Roman see. This prohibition applies not only to the pope himself; 'ecclesiarum per omnes Romanae civitatis titulos qui sunt presbyteri vel quicumque

---

[18] See above, p. 341, n. 10. The passage cited continues: 'et quid est in cespite, per ecclesie Nolane homines, ut diligentius saltem fiscum solvere valeat, excolatur'.

[19] See below, p. 345, nn. 25, 26.

[20] *M.G.H., Auct. Ant.* xii, p. 450. Cp. *Cod. Can. Eccl. Afr.* 33 (early fifth century): 'item placuit ut presbyteri non vendant rem ecclesiae ubi sunt constituti . . . nec episcopo liceat matricis ecclesiae rem «nec presbytero rem» tituli sui usurpare.'

fuerint' were likewise forbidden to alienate 'quicquam de iure titulorum vel ecclesiae superius praefatae'.

The precise legal position of the bishop in regard to the property of the independent churches and institutions is not, and probably was not at the time, very clearly defined. In the East, in the sixth century at any rate, he had little control over them. Under a constitution of Anastasius[21] churches were permitted to alienate lands under certain conditions, and the authorities which could do so are said to be either the bishop with his *oeconomus* and clergy, or the administrators of almshouses, hospices, orphanages, etc., with their staff (and in the case of almshouses their inmates): in the latter case the bishop's consent was required only if it was the local custom. Justinian's Novel cxx[22] gave authority to grant perpetual leases to the majority of the clergy and the *oeconomus* in independent 'houses of prayer', and to the presidents of charitable institutions: in the latter case the financial administrator of the institution had to take an oath in the presence of the bishop that the lease would not cause it loss. Individual churches were regarded as legal personalities, capable of receiving bequests. A curious law of Justinian[23] directs how to interpret the intention of a testator who leaves a bequest to our Lord Jesus Christ or to an archangel or martyr. In the first case the church of his city or village or estate takes the bequest, in the second any church of that dedication in the city or territory, or, if there is none, in the metropolis. If there are several churches of the same dedication in the city, that which the testator most frequented, or failing that the poorest, is to benefit.

In the West it was apparently held that the bishop had over-riding control over all ecclesiastical property in his territory, and was in some sense its owner. The first council of Orleans[24] in 511 declared 'de his quae parochiis in terris vineis mancipiis atque

---

[21] *Cod. Just.* i. ii. 17: ἐπὶ δὲ τῶν πτωχείων, τοῦ διοικητοῦ καὶ τῶν ὑπουργούντων καὶ τῶν πτωχῶν, ἐπὶ δὲ τῶν ξενώνων, τοῦ διοικτοῦ καὶ τῶν εὑρισκομένων πάντων ὑπουργῶν τῆς διοικήσεως, καὶ ὁμοίως ἐπὶ τῶν ὀρφανοτροφείων, ὥστε κρατεῖν τὸ τοῖς πλείοσιν ἀρέσκον, συναινοῦντος καὶ τοῦ ἐπισκόπου τῶν τόπων ἐν οἷς τοῦτο σύνηθές ἐστι γίνεσθαι.

[22] § 6.

[23] *Cod. Just.* i. ii. 26.

[24] *Conc. Aurel.* i, *can.* 15 (*M.G.H., Leg. sect.* iii. i, p. 6), 'de his quae parochiis in terris vineis mancipiis atque peculiis quicumque fideles obtulerint, antiquorum canonum statuta serventur ut omnia in episcopi potestate consistant. De his tamen quae in altario accesserint, tertia fideliter episcopis deferatur.'

peculiis quicumque fideles obtulerint . . . ut omnia in episcopi potestate consistant'. In 527 the council of Carpentras,[25] in response to a complaint that bishops usurped 'quae a quibuscumque fidelibus parochiis conferuntur', ruled that if the church of the city was rich, what was bequeathed to *parochiae* should be spent on the clergy who served them and on the repair of their churches, but if the city church was poor, the bishop might take for it the surplus, leaving enough for the parochial clergy and repairs. The third council of Orleans[26] in 538 ruled that donations to a basilica in the city should be at the disposal of the bishop, and that it should be for him to decide what should be allocated to the repair of the basilica and the maintenance of its staff; on the other hand local custom was to be followed with regard to the property of rural churches. Gallic bishops seem to have made somewhat arbitrary use of their rights: when in 541 King Childibert founded a great hospital at Lyons, the bishop had to give an undertaking that he would not transfer its endowments to his own church.[27]

The Spanish church held a similar view of the law. The third council of Toledo in 589 remarked with disapproval 'multi contra canonum constituta sic ecclesias quas aedificaverint postulant consecrari ut dotem quam eidem ecclesiae contulerint censeant ad episcopi ordinationem non pertinere'.[28] The fourth council of Toledo (633), while condemning the practice of some bishops, who converted to their own use endowments given to newly established *parochiae*, nevertheless upheld the rule that the *dos* of a *parochia* was subject to the bishop's control.[29]

The above rules and customs applied to the capital endowments of *parochiae*. In some areas the bishops also claimed one-third of their offerings. This rule is laid down in Gaul by the council of Orleans[30] in 511, and is stated to be the ancient custom in Spain by the council of Tarraco[31] in 516: it is implied that the bishop had a countervailing obligation to repair the church. The second council of Bracara[32] in 572 strongly insisted that the bishop

[25] *Conc. Carp.* (ib., p. 41).
[26] *Conc. Aurel.* iii, *can.* 5 (ib., pp. 74–75).
[27] *Conc. Aurel.* v, *can.* 15 (ib., p. 105).
[28] *Conc. Tol.* iii, *can.* 19.
[29] *Conc. Tol.* iv, *can.* 33.
[30] *Conc. Aurel.* i, *can.* 15 (see n. 24 above).
[31] *Conc. Tarrac. can.* 8.
[32] *Conc. Bracar.* ii, *can.* 2 (see p. 346, n. 37).

should use his third of the offerings only for the repair and maintenance of the church. The fourth council of Toledo[33] in 634, however, confirmed the bishop's claim to his third without qualification. In other parts of the empire the custom is not known, and no doubt varied. According to Theodore Lector[34] until the time of the patriarch Gennadius (458–71) the whole of the offerings of the churches of Constantinople were annexed to the Great Church, but his *oeconomus*, Marcian, ruled that the clergy of the several churches should keep them.

In the West, at any rate, the bishop on his annual visitation of his parishes exacted from each a fee, called the *cathedraticum*. Pope Gelasius[35] (492–6) alludes to it as customary, and Pope Pelagius I[36] (555–61) declares that it should not exceed 2 solidi per annum. The second council of Bracara[37] (572) and the seventh council of Toledo[38] (646) also limit the *cathedraticum* to 2 solidi.

It remains to consider the distribution of ecclesiastical revenues between the various branches of expenditure. Here we have very little information save on the episcopal churches. The rule of the Roman see, which it imposed on the churches of Italy, is first mentioned in a letter of Pope Simplicius[39] dated 475. By it all the revenue, both rents and offerings, was divided into four equal parts, of which one went to the bishop, one to the clergy (of the episcopal church or churches, the *cardinales* or *canonici*), one to the maintenance of the buildings, and one to charity. Some refinements of this rule are recorded. Pope Felix IV (526–30) in his judgement on the division of the revenues of the church of Ravenna[40] ruled that while the regular rents (normally paid in

---

[33] *Conc. Tol.* iv, *can.* 33, 'episcopos its dioeceses suas regere ut nihil ex earum iure praesumant auferre sed iuxta priorum auctoritatem conciliorum tam de oblationibus quam de tributis ac frugibus tertiam consequantur'.

[34] Theodore Lector, Book i. 13 (*P.G.* lxxxvi. 172 c).

[35] Fr. 20 (ed. Thiel): 'cathedraticum etiam non amplius quam vetusti moris esse constiterit ab eius loci presbytero noveris exigendum'.

[36] Loewenfeld, op. cit. 26, 'faciemus ut non amplius de parochiis suis quam binos solidos annuos sub qualibet occasione praesumat accipere'.

[37] *Con. Bracar.* ii, *can.* 2 (Barlow, op. cit., p. 119), 'placuit ut nullus episcoporum cum per suas dioeceses ambulant praeter honorem cathedrae suae, id est duos solidos, aliquid aliud per ecclesias tollat, neque tertiam partem ex quacumque oblatione populi in ecclesiis parochialibus requirat sed illa tertia pars pro luminariis vel recuperatione servetur'.

[38] *Conc. Tol.* vii, *can.* 4.

[39] Thiel, op. cit., Simplicius, *ep.* 1: the rule is reiterated by Gelasius, *epp.* 14 § 27, 15, 16, cp. *frag.* 23, 24, and Gregory I, *Reg.* xi. 56, cp. iv. 11, v. 12, 27, 49, viii. 7, xiii. 46.   [40] Agnellus, *Lib. Pont. Eccl. Rav.* 60.

gold) should be divided, the *excepta praediorum sive accessiones* should all go to the bishop in consideration of his heavy burden of hospitality. These *excepta* or *accessiones* were additional payments in kind made by the tenants: at Ravenna according to a contemporary document they included 888 hens, 266 chickens, 8,880 eggs, 3,760 pounds of pork and 3,450 pounds of honey, besides geese and milk.[41] Gregory the Great ruled that money and foodstuffs offered by the faithful should be divided, but that other chattel should go to the bishop.[42]

It appears from another of Gregory's letters that, according to the local custom of Catana, two-thirds of the clergy's quarter share went to the priests and deacons, and one-third to the lower grades.[43] It may be suspected that some such rule lies behind the curious anomaly that in some Italian churches deacons received higher salaries than priests, and accordingly refused to be ordained to the priesthood. This would have happened, if say, one-third was allotted to the priests and one-third to the deacons, and the priests went up in numbers, whereas the deacons were restricted to the canonical seven. Gelasius, writing to a bishop named Victor, recommends that in future the priests should be better paid than the deacons, so that the latter 'convinced by this argument at least, may try to seek both the honour which they had avoided, and profit'.[44]

The Roman rule was not observed in Gaul, where the first council of Orleans[45] (511) declared that the bishop and the clergy should share the offerings half and half, but that all the estates should be at the bishop's disposal. Nor did it prevail in Spain, where the first council of Bracara[46] (561) ruled that the ecclesiastical revenues should be divided into three equal parts, one for the bishop, one for the clergy, and one for the upkeep and lighting of the churches.

In the East the principle of the dividend does not seem to have

---

[41] J. O. Tjäder, *Die nichtliterarischen lateinischen papyri Italiens*, no. 3 (pp. 186–8).

[42] Gregory I, *Reg.* xiii. 46.

[43] Ibid. viii. 7.

[44] Gelasius, fr. 10 (ed. Thiel).

[45] *Conc. Aurel.* i, *can.* 14 (*M.G.H., Leg. sect.* III, i, p. 6), 'antiquos canones religentes priora statuta credimus renovanda, ut de his quae altario oblatione fidei deferuntur medietatem sibi episcopus vindicat et medietatem dispensandam sibi secundum gradus clerus accipiat; praediis de omni commoditate in episcoporum potestate durantibus'.

[46] *Conc. Bracar.* i, *can.* 7 (Barlow, op. cit., p. 112).

applied to the revenue from endowments. Severus, patriarch of Antioch (513–18), complains in two of his letters[47] that his church was utterly impoverished, and indeed deeply in debt, owing to the large number of clergy whom he was forced to ordain under pressure from powerful patrons. Justinian[48] draws an even more lurid picture of the financial straits to which the Great Church of Constantinople had been reduced for the same reason, and ordered that no further ordinations be made until the number of the clergy had sunk to the proper establishment. Under the dividend system this could not have happened—more clergy would have meant less for each and not run the church into debt. Evidently churches paid fixed salaries to their clergy according to their grades, and had fixed establishments commensurate with their revenue. Bishops were also probably paid fixed salaries; the bishop of Anastasiapolis got 365 solidi a year,[49] which is obviously a solidus a day, and not a proportion of the total income of the church.

On the other hand, in another letter Severus of Antioch reproves the injustice of depriving aged priests, who could no longer perform their duties, of their customary share in the distribution of gifts.[50] This presumably refers to the offerings, which would have been shared out at intervals between the officiating clergy: the claims of aged absentees might thus well be neglected. Justinian in his third Novel[51] speaks of the clergy in the independent churches of Constantinople as 'sharing out the income which comes in from the pious', by which he probably means the offerings of the faithful. In the Canons of the Apostles, also, which reflect eastern practice, it is enacted that the first-fruits should be delivered to the bishops and priests, who will share them out with the deacons and lesser clergy.[52]

It would seem, then, that the dividend principle was universally applied to the offerings of the faithful, both in the East and in the West. In the West the dividend can be traced back to the

[47] E. W. Brooks, *Select Letters of Severus of Antioch*, i. 8 and 17.
[48] Just. *Nov.* iii, proem and § 1.
[49] *Vita S. Theodori Syceonitae*, 78.
[50] Brooks, op. cit. i. 57.
[51] Just. *Nov.* iii, § 2: τοὺς προσιόντας αὐτοῖς παρὰ τῶν εὐσεβῶν πόρους μεριζόμενοι.
[52] *Can. Apost.* 4: ἡ ἄλλα πᾶσα ὁπώρα εἰς οἶκον ἀποστελλέσθω ἀπαρχὴ τῷ ἐπισκόπῳ καὶ τοῖς πρεσβυτέροις ... ὁ ἐπίσκοπος καὶ οἱ πρεσβύτεροι ἐπιμερίζουσι τοῖς διακόνοις καὶ τοῖς λοιποῖς κληρικοῖς.

middle of the third century. Cyprian granted to certain confessors the honours and privileges of priests, 'ut et sportulis iisdem cum presbyteris honorentur et divisiones mensurnas aequatis quantitatibus partiantur',[53] and appears to use the same term 'quantitas' of his own episcopal income.[54] It is a plausible conjecture that the system was general in the primitive churches, which depended entirely on the offerings of the faithful: it would have been a natural and equitable system to apply to a variable and rather precarious revenue. When the churches began to acquire a more stable income from endowments, they adopted different policies. In Italy and Spain the dividend system was extended to all forms of revenues. In Gaul the bishop obtained sole control of the income from endowments and allocated it at his pleasure. In the East fixed basic stipends (supplemented by a share in the offerings) were allocated to the bishops and the various grades of clergy out of the assured income provided by rents.

[53] *Ep.* 39.
[54] *Ep.* 7: 'sumptus suggeratis ex quantitate mea propria quam apud Rogatianum compresbyterum nostrum dimisi'.

CHAPTER EIGHTEEN

THE CLOTH INDUSTRY UNDER THE ROMAN EMPIRE

W E possess lamentably little information about the weaving and clothing industry of the Roman empire. It is only in Egypt that we have any intimate knowledge of weavers, what kind of men they were and how they were organised. Here the information of the papyri,[1] scattered and scrappy though it is, extends from the annexation of the province in 30 B.C. to the Arab conquest in A.D. 641. For the rest of the empire we have to be content with casual literary allusions and a rather meagre crop of inscriptions.[2] For one moment the Edict on prices issued by Diocletian in 301[3] gives us a remarkably full and detailed schedule

[1] The following standard abbreviations are used for collections of papyri:

B.G.U.	= *Aegyptische Urkunden aus den staatlichen Museen zu Berlin: Griechische Urkunden*
Chr.	= *Grundzüge und Chrestomathie der Papyruskunde*
P. Cairo Masp.	= *Catalogue général des antiquités égyptiennes du Musée du Caire; papyrus grecs d'époque byzantine*
P. Grenf.	= *New classical fragments and other Greek and Latin papyri*
P. Lips.	= *Griechische Urkunden der Papyrussammlung zu Leipzig*
P. Lond.	= *Greek Papyri in the British Museum*
P. Mich.	= *Papyri in the University of Michigan Collection*
P. Michael.	= *Papyri Michaelidae*
P. Oxy.	= *The Oxyrhynchus Papyri*
P. Phil.	= *Papyrus de Philadelphie*
P. Ryl.	= *Catalogue of the Greek papyri in the John Rylands Library, Manchester*
P.S.I.	= *Papiri greci e latini (Publicazioni della Società Italiana)*
P. Tebt.	= *The Tebtunis Papyri*
S.B.	= *Sammelbuch griechischer Urkunden aus Aegypten*
S.P.P.	= *Studien zur Palaeographie und Papyruskunde*

[2] The following standard abbreviations are used for collections of inscriptions:

C.I.L.	= *Corpus Inscriptionum Latinarum*
I.G.	= *Inscriptiones Graecae*
I.G.R.	= *Inscriptiones Graecae ad res Romanas pertinentes*
I.L.A.	= *Inscriptions Latines d'Afrique*
I.L.S.	= *Inscriptiones Latinae Selectae*
M.A.M.A.	= *Monumenta Asiae Minoris Antiqua*
S.E.G.	= *Supplementum Epigraphicum Graecum*

[3] The best text (with translation) of the Edict of Diocletian is in Tenney Frank, *An Economic Survey of Ancient Rome*, vol. V (Baltimore, 1940). [See now the edition by S. Lauffer, *Diokletians Preisedikt*, Berlin, 1971.]

of the prices both of the raw materials, wool and linen yarn, and of a large range of garments, and also of the wages of weavers and other workers. The general scale of prices was arbitrary, but there is no reason to believe that the relation of one price to another was distorted. It may seem rash to attempt an analysis of the industry on this slender basis. Conditions in Egypt may have been different from those in the rest of the empire, and many changes may have taken place in six centuries. But the evidence on the whole suggests that the organisation of the industry was basically similar throughout the empire and that it developed little if at all throughout its history. It is on these assumptions that I base my reconstruction.

Lanificium was one of the standard virtues of the Roman matron,[4] and Augustus, to set a good example, made his wife, daughter and grand-daughter occupy themselves in weaving wool, and even went so far as to wear their products himself.[5] But this attempt to revive the good old days was not successful, and Columella, writing under Nero, complains that in his time ladies would not be bothered with weaving and bought expensive clothes instead.[6] Some domestic production of clothes went on in rich households: the *columbarium* of the Statilii Tauri records four weavers among the slaves of their town house (as well as eight spinners, two dyers and four fullers),[7] and in the Digest there are references to slave *lanificae* on rural estates, who made clothes for the *familia rustica*.[8] But such work was on a small scale: Columella advises that the *vilica* should make the slave women work on rainy days, so as to produce clothes for the *actores* and superior slaves[9]—the clothing of the ordinary workers was evidently bought. Domestic weaving in upper class households continued into the sixth century. Pope Pelagius I (555–61) instructed one of his agents, in picking slaves from an estate part of which had been bequeathed to the church, to choose agricultural workers rather than domestic servants or men who could be

---

[4] *I.L.S.* 8402, 8403, 8393, line 30.

[5] Suetonius, *Augustus*, 64, 73.

[6] Columella, *de Re Rustica*, XII, *praef.* 9–10.

[7] *C.I.L.* VI. 6213–6640; in *S.B.* 7358 an Egyptian woman in the late third century indentures herself to perform for her creditor 'weaving at which she is skilled and domestic work' (ἅπερ ἐπίσταται γερδιακά τε ἔργα καὶ οἰκιακά).

[8] *Digest*, XXXIII, vii. 12 § 6, 16 § 2, L. xvi. 203.

[9] Columella, *de Re Rustica*, XII. iii. 6.

352   THE ROMAN ECONOMY

useful in weaving ('viros qui forte gynaecaeo utiles esse possunt').¹⁰ Such household weaving, however, can have been of little economic importance. How far the poor wove their own clothes we do not know, but the majority seem to have bought their garments. Village weavers are frequently mentioned in Egypt, and the Edict of Diocletian sets prices for a wide range of inferior garments 'for the use of common people and slaves'.¹¹ An anecdote recounted by Augustine (bishop of Hippo from 395 to 430) is revealing.¹² Florentius, a poor man of Hippo, lost his *casula*. He had no money to buy another, but having prayed to the Twenty Martyrs found a large fish, which he sold for 300 *folles*. This was not enough for a *casula*, which would have cost 1000, but he bought some wool, 'so that his wife might, as best she could, make up something for him to wear'. Even a poor man normally bought ready-made clothes.

Weaving was then in the main a professional occupation, and clothing an object of trade. How far was manufacture concentrated in certain districts or towns? The Edict of Diocletian suggests that, for certain classes of garment at any rate, it was. It fixes special prices, for instance, for woollen garments styled British, Gallic, African, Norican, Raetic, Dardanian, Achaean, Phrygian, Pontic, Cappadocian, Arabian and Egyptian, and for others named after particular towns, those of the Nervii, Treviri, Ambiani and Bituriges in Gaul, Mutina and Canusium in Italy, Poetovio, Argos, Laodicea of Phrygia and Damascus.¹³ Among linen garments it specifies those of Tarsus, Laodicea, Byblos, Scythopolis and Alexandria, and mattresses and pillows from Tralles, Antinoopolis, Damascus and Cyprus.¹⁴ These are not mere trade names, for the Edict distinguishes a Modenese *chlamys* (χλαμὺς Μουτουνησία) from a Laodicene Modenese *chlamys* (χλαμὺς Λαδικηνὴ Μουτουνησία),¹⁵ and a Nervian *birrus* (βίρρος Νερβικός) from a Laodicene *birrus* in imitation of a Nervian (βίρρος Λαδικηνὸς

---

¹⁰ Pelagius I, *frag.* P. Jaffé, *Regesta Pontificum Romanorum*,² I. 956 (656).

¹¹ *Ed. Diocl.* xxvi. 10, 31, 69, 75, 96, 117, 138, xxvii. 5, 26, xxviii. 4, 13, 34, 43, 53, 56, 63, εἰς χρῆσιν τῶν ἰδιωτῶν ἤτοι φαμιλιαρικῶν.

¹²Augustine, *de civitate Dei*, XXII. viii. 9. That a *casula* cost 1000 *folles* is inferred from the youths' taunt: 'quasi a martyribus quinquagenos folles unde vestimentum emeret petivisset'. If each of the Twenty Martyrs subscribed 50 *folles*, Florentius would have got 1000.

¹³ *Ed. Diocl.* xix; cf. also xx. 3, 4, 13, xxii. 16–26.

¹⁴ *Ed. Diocl.* xxvi, xxvii, xxviii.

¹⁵ *Ed. Diocl.* xx. 3, 4.

ἐν ὁμοιότητι Νερβικοῦ),[16] and Tarsian (Ταρσικά) from Tarsian Alexandrian linens (Ταρσικὰ ʼΑλεξανδρινά),[17] and in the price litss of linen clothes distinguishes the better makes produced at named towns from those which are inferior but are made in more places.[18] Moreover some of the towns are otherwise known as important centres of the industry, Tarsus from Dio Chrysostom,[19] Scythopolis from the Theodosian Code,[20] and Alexandria from the Historia Augusta,[21] Canusium and Augusta Trevirorum from the Notitia Dignitatum.[22]

The makes of garments named after particular towns are highly priced and presumably of special excellence. This emerges most clearly from the lists of linen garments, which are very systematically arranged.[23] The towns are placed in order of merit: Scythopolis, Tarsus, Byblos, Laodicea, and Alexandria, and the products of each town are graded in three *formae*. Thus for instance tunics (στίχαι) range from first grade Scythopolitan at 7,000 denarii to third grade Alexandrian at 2,000. Below these come military tunics at 1,500, 1,250 and 1,000 and below these again tunics of rough linen for the use of common people and slaves at half these prices. Men's dalmatics similarly range from 10,000 denarii for Scythopolitan grade 1 to 2,000 for Alexandrian grade 3. Below these come those 'which are inferior to the above mentioned grade 3 but are made in more places' at 2,500, 2,000 and 1,500, and below these again those for commoners and slaves at 800, 600 and 500. Thus middle-grade garments of sound quality, such as were required for the army, were produced in many places, and cheap clothes for the poor presumably at even more. The great weaving centres produced in the main luxury garments, the best of which cost 20 times as much as those made for the poorest classes, and the cheapest of which were often dearer than the middle-grade garments suitable for the army.

The list of woollen garments is less full, less systematic and

---

[16] *Ed. Diocl.* xix, 26, 27.

[17] *Ed. Diocl.* xxvi, 13–27, 34–63, etc. That these were fabrics of Tarsian type made at Alexandria is shown by the frequent mention of Ταρσικάριοι in Egyptian papyri (see Preisigke, *Wörterbuch*, s.v.).

[18] *Ed. Diocl.* xxvi. 65.

[19] Dio Chrys. *Or.* XXXIV. 21–3.

[20] *Cod. Theod.* X. xx. 8.

[21] Scriptores Historiae Augustae, *Saturninus*, 8.

[22] *Not. Dig. Occ.* xi. 52, 58.

[23] *Ed. Diocl.* xxvi, xxvii, xxviii.

less well preserved, but there is a marked contrast between the high prices fixed for the products of certain towns and areas, and those of other areas. Thus a Nervian *birrus* cost probably over 10,000 denarii, a Laodicene imitation of a Nervian 10,000, a Norican 8,000, a British or Argolic 6,000, a Laodicene or Canusian 4,000, an Achaean or Phrygian 2,000 and an African only 1,500.[24] A Gallic *sagum* from Ambiani or Bituriges was priced at 8,000 denarii, an African at 500.[25]

The location of the great weaving towns seems to have mainly been determined by the proximity of raw material of high quality. Thus Canusium drew upon the fine wool of Apulia,[26] the *civitates Nerviorum* and *Ambianorum* on Atrebatic,[27] Laodicea on Phrygian.[28] Wool from such favoured districts is very highly priced in the Edict, Atrebatic at 200 denarii per lb., Tarentine (i.e. Apulian) at 175, Laodicene at 150 as against 'best middle wool' at 50 and 'other wool' at 25.[29] But such high-grade wools were no doubt also exported to more distant weaving centres: the very fact that they are priced in the Edict suggests that they commanded a wide market, and indeed at such high prices they would have repaid the heavy costs of transport. The rate fixed by Diocletian for camels, which carried 600 lb., was 8 denarii per mile, and for donkeys, which presumably carried half that load, 4 denarii:[30] a bale of wool priced at 150 denarii the pound could therefore be carried 100 miles for less than 1 per cent of its value. One quite high-grade wool, the Asturian (priced at 100 denarii per lb.), must have been exported, for no fine garments are known to have been produced in Spain.

Linen yarn is also steeply graded in price, the best at 1,200, 960 and 840 denarii per lb., the middling at 720, 600 and 450, and rough yarn for the use of commoners and slaves at 250, 125 and 72.[31] Linen yarn is not distinguished by its place of origin, but Egypt is known from other sources to have produced good flax,[32] and

[24] *Ed. Diocl.* xix. 26–7, 32–42.
[25] *Ed. Diocl.* xix. 60–61; cf. also xix. 47–50 for σιγγίλια, and 53–6 for *fibulatoria*.
[26] Strabo, VI. iii. 6, 9; Pliny, *Hist. Nat.* VIII. 190; Columella, *de Re Rustica*, VII. ii. 2.
[27] Strabo, IV. iv. 3.
[28] Strabo, XII. viii. 16; Pliny, *Hist. Nat.* VIII. 190; Dio Chrys. XXXV. 130.
[29] *Ed. Diocl.* xxv. 1–9.
[30] *Ed. Diocl.* xvii. 4–5.
[31] *Ed. Diocl.* xxvi. 4–12.
[32] Pliny, *Hist. Nat.* XIX. 14.

this explains the prominence of Alexandria as a weaving town.

The famous weaving towns, then, which produced high class garments from high quality material catered only for the rich; their products, since they were highly priced rarities, no doubt travelled far and commanded a widely-spread market. Were there any towns or districts which specialised in medium priced or cheap clothes for middle classes or the poor? There is very little evidence on this point. We are told that when the noble senator Pinianus took up the ascetic life at Rome at the end of the fourth century, he bought some very cheap clothes, called 'self-coloured Antiochenes'.[33] This suggests that cheap garments were produced for the Roman market in Syria. African woollens, which were notably cheaper than most others, may also have supplied the populace of Rome. But this is a mere conjecture.

A few very large towns, which like Rome had no local weaving industry, may have provided a market for cheap clothes produced elsewhere, but in general it is clear that medium priced and cheap clothing was produced locally, and that the industry was very widely dispersed. For Egypt the evidence of the Diocletianic Edict is confirmed by the papyri, which record weavers in many small towns and villages. It is also confirmed by the system of compulsory purchase whereby the Roman army supplied its needs. We possess a receipt dated A.D. 128 for 19 tunics and 5 cloaks (the latter for the army of Judaea) delivered by the wool weavers of the village of Socnupaei Nesos,[34] and an order dated A.D. 138 for payment in advance to the wool weavers of the village of Philadelphia for one chiton and four cloaks for the army of Cappadocia, and one blanket for the military hospital of Sebaste.[35] From the late third century we have an order for 100 tunics from the city of Oxyrhynchus,[36] and from A.D. 285 there is a receipt to a village for one tunic and one cloak,[37] and from A.D. 314 a payment to the village of Caranis for 24 tunics and 8 cloaks.[38] From 318 we possess a list allocating orders for tunics and cloaks between 17 villages of the Oxyrhynchite name.[39]

The army authorities would surely not have distributed their

---

[33] *Analecta Bollandiana*, VIII (1889), 26, XXII (1903), 13.
[34] P. Ryl. 189.   [35] B.G.U. 1564.   [36] P. Oxy. 1414.   [37] P. Michael. 21.
[38] *Journal of Roman Studies*, XXXVII (1947), 30–33. B.G.U. 620 is another payment of about the same date. The price of a στιχάριον is the same (4000 dr.) and the total order comes to 11 talents (66,000 dr.).
[39] P. Oxy. 1448.

orders to hundreds of villages, an undertaking which involved a heavy burden of administrative and clerical work, if they could have placed them in a few large centres. It is even more significant that the Judaean and even the Cappadocian commands placed orders in Egypt for woollen garments, which were not an Egyptian speciality. This implies that the weaving industry of Cappadocia and Judaea had little surplus capacity above local needs, and was incapable of supplying the relatively large forces stationed in these countries. The army supply authorities therefore had to distribute their orders over a wider field; Egypt with its large population and small garrison was a suitable area on which to draw.

During the fourth century the needs of the army were partly met by large state factories, *gynaecia* (for woollens) and *linyphia* (for linens), probably established by Diocletian. But the compulsory purchase or requisition of military garments also continued. This levy was apportioned on the same assessment as the levies of *annona*. A law of 377 fixes the number of *iuga* or *iuga et capita* on which a *vestis* was assessed in the dioceses of Thrace, Asiana, Pontica, Oriens and Egypt.[40] The levy must therefore have been evenly spread over the whole countryside of all provinces. The system again implies that the production of medium grade clothing was very evenly distributed throughout the empire.

In an industry of such a structure the normal unit must have been very small. The guild of woolweavers at Philadelphia, which received an army order in 138, complained next year that they could not execute it, as four of their twelve members had been sent to Alexandria.[41] At Euhemeria, a smaller village, the weavers' guild in Tiberius' reign comprised a president, secretary and at least five other members.[42] If there were twelve, or even only seven, woolweavers in a village, none of them can have had a large workshop. That similar conditions applied in ordinary towns, which were not large centres of manufacture, is implied by the existence in them also of guilds of wool and linen weavers. The evidence, which outside Egypt comes from inscriptions, is scanty but indicates that the guild organisation was everywhere normal.[43]

[40] *Cod. Theod.* VII. vi. 3.   [41] *B.G.U.* 1572, *P. Phil.* 10.   [42] *P.Ryl.* 94.
[43] *I.L.A.* 396 (*lanarii* at Carthage), *S.E.G.* VII. 827 (λίνυφοι at Gerasa), *I.G.R.*

Some rural weavers were fairly substantial men. They were in principle immune from liturgies, but we hear none the less of one who was appointed elder of his village, and in the early second century the prefect of Egypt ruled that any who were worth more than one talent (1,500 denarii) and owned private land should not be exempt.[44] But the fact that the government paid in advance for the garments which it ordered not only from the village of Philadelphia but also the city of Oxyrhynchus indicates that not only rural but urban weavers were as a rule men of very limited resources. A lease from Heracleopolis dated A.D. 246[45] is suggestive of the average size of an urban weaving establishment. A weaver leases two-thirds of a house, with the provision that he may set up three looms, and one extra if he is weaving a garment for his own use. Such a man must have had a few assistants, members of his family, apprentices, hired workers or slaves.[46] Alfius Caecilianus, duumvir of the little African town of Aptungi in 303, was apparently a prosperous weaver of this type. On the day that the edict of persecution arrived, he deposed,' I had gone to Zama to buy linen yarn with Saturninus', and later Ingentius 'came to me at my house; I was having dinner with my workmen'.[47] We do not know if his workmen (operarii) were slaves or free men.

Egyptian census returns show families in which both parents and children (of both sexes) are registered as wool or linen-weavers.[48] We have from Egypt about a dozen contracts of apprenticeship in the weaving trade,[49] and half a dozen contracts of service for one to five years.[50] Further evidence for free hired

---

IV. 1226, 1252 (λινουργοί and λανάρια at Thyateira), I.G.R. III. 896 (λινουργοί at Anazarbus), I.G.R. IV. 1632 (ἐριουργοί at Philadelphia), 863 (ἀπαλουργοί at Laodicea), Révue Archéologique, XXVIII (1874), 112 (λινουργοί at Miletus), S.E.G. IV. 541 (λεντιυφάνται at Ephesus), J. T. Wood, Discoveries at Ephesus (1857), p. 24 (λανάριοι at Ephesus), Athenische Mitteilungen, VIII (1883), 319 (λίνυφοι at Tralles).

[44] P. Phil. 1.

[45] S.P.P. XX. 53.

[46] Cf. P. Oxy. 1272 for a house at Oxyrhynchus inhabited by Heras son of Calathus, a weaver and his fellow workers (γερδίου καὶ τῶν σὺν αὐτῷ ἐργαζομένων).

[47] Optatus, de schismate Donatistarum, App. II, P. Found, 37.

[48] B.G.U. 148, 1069, P. Lond. II. 257.

[49] P. Oxy. 275, 322, 725, 1647, P. Tebt. 385, 442, P.S.I. XXII. 40, P. Mich. 170, 171, 172, 346, cf. 123 R. II. 34. (cf. P. Ryl. 654, ἔστιν γὰρ αὐτῷ (a linen weaver) σύνεργος ὁ Παῦλος οὗτος, μαθητὴς μὲν τυγχάνων, εἰς [ἄσκησι] ν δὲ τῆς τέχνης ἀφεικόμενος.

[50] P. Tebt. 384, P.S.I. 902, P. Grenf. 59, P. Mich. 121 R. II. viii, 355, c.f. 237. 7, 37.

AA

labour is provided by census returns of persons who describe themselves as 'wage earning weavers'[51] and by a petition dated A.D. 140 from a man who complains that he is poor and makes his living by wage labour in the wool-weaving trade.[52] Again in the late third century the linen-weavers of Oxyrhynchus asked the city council for a supplement to the treasury payment for 100 tunics 'because of the increased price of the materials and the increased wages of the workmen'.[53] That hired labour was commonly employed throughout the empire is suggested by the Edict of Diocletian, which fixes wage rates for *linarii* and *linyphi*. The former are paid by the pound of wool at rates varying according to its quality, the latter by the day according to the quality of their product.[54] Slaves were also sometimes employed. Five of the children apprenticed to weavers were slaves,[55] whom their owners presumably intended either to sell or to hire to a weaver,[56] or to set up in business as *institores*. A few of the weavers are freedmen,[57] who had no doubt started as *institores* or as hands of a working weaver.

On the organisation of the industry in the large centres we have only two pieces of evidence. In an Alexandrian document dated 192 A.D. one Isidore is described as 'head of a factory' or a 'chief of workshops of linen weavers, having many persons working in the trade'.[58] He must have been a man of some substance, since he was nominated to the liturgic office of sub-prefect of the Delta ward of the city. Whether he was a factory owner in the modern sense, employing hired hands, or an entrepreneur who put out work to weavers, is not clear. But it is likely that his linen-weavers were free persons. Caracalla, in his edict expelling Egyptian immigrants from Alexandria, remarks that 'genuine Egyptians can easily be distinguished from the

[51] *B.G.U.* 1069, *S.B.* 4299.
[52] *Chr.* I. 325.
[53] *P. Oxy.* 1414.
[54] *Ed. Diocl.* xxi.
[55] *S.P.P.* XXII. 40, *P. Oxy.* 1647, *P.S.I.* 241, *P. Mich.* 346. I have detected six other slave weavers (*B.G.U.* 617, *P. Grenf.* 59, *P. Oxy.* 262, *P. Lips.* 26, *S.P.P.* XXII, 36, *S.B.* 8263).
[56] As in *S.P.P.* XXII. 36 and *P. Grenf.* 59.
[57] I have detected only three, two in *B.G.U.* 1564 and one in *P. Oxy.* 984.
[58] *P. Oxy.* 2340, Ἐπίμαχος Γάνου ὑποστράτηγος Δέλτα γράμματος ἀνέδωκεν τὸν ἡμέτερον ἀνθ' αὑτοῦ ἐργαστηριάρχην ὄντα λινούφων πολλοὺς ἐργαζομένους ἐν τῇ ἐργασίᾳ ἔχοντα.

linen-weavers by their speech'.[59] From this it would appear that the bulk of the linen-weavers of Alexandria were free Egyptians, who but for special exemption might have been repatriated to their native villages: had they been slaves, the question could not have arisen.

At Tarsus in the early second century Dio Chrysostom[60] states that a large proportion of the population were linen-weavers. He represents them as poor but respectable men, who would enjoy the rights of citizenship if they could afford the registration fee of 500 drachmae. The weavers must therefore have been free men of modest means, not necessarily very poor, for 500 drachmae is a large sum, about two years pay for a legionary. This suggests an organisation in small family workshops, with a few apprentices and labourers, slave or free, as in the villages and towns of Egypt. It is also possible that the Tarsian linen-weavers were free paid employees of factory owners.

Were there then no large factories manned by slaves? We know of none except the imperial *gynaecia* and *linyphia* founded by Diocletian. These were large establishments: Sozomen in the fifth century speaks of the government wool-weavers at Cyzicus as if, with the mint workers, they formed a substantial part of the population of the town, and Gregory of Nazianzus uses similar language of the state wool-weavers and armourers at Caesarea of Cappadocia.[61] The weavers were legally state slaves. Constantine after his victory over Licinius freed Christians who had been made slaves of the treasury and drafted into *gynaecia* and *linyphia*[62] and the laws speak of the establishments as *familiae*[63] and their occupants as *mancipia*,[64] and apply to them the rules of the *Senatusconsultum Claudianum*.[65] In fact the workers in the state factories became in the fourth and fifth centuries hereditary castes, enjoying *de facto* most of the rights of free persons, marrying, rearing families and holding property.[66] On how their work was

[59] *Chr*. I. 22.
[60] Dio Chrys. *Or*. XXXIV. 21–3.
[61] Sozomen, *Hist. Eccl*. V. 15, Greg. Naz. *In laudem Basilii*, 57.
[62] Eusebius, *Vita Constantini*, II. 34.
[63] *Cod. Theod*. X. xx. 7.
[64] *tit. cit*. 2, 9.
[65] *tit. cit*. 3.
[66] *tit. cit*. 3, 16.

organised we have only one piece of evidence. Sozomen speaks of the *gynaeciarii* and *monetarii* of Cyzicus as 'a large population divided into two groups, who by the order of earlier emperors lived with their wives and families at Cyzicus, each year rendering to the treasury a stated stint of military tunics and of freshly minted coins respectively'. Analogy with the *fabricenses* and *barbaricarii*, the state armourers, suggests that the government provided them with rations[67] and with raw materials,[68] and insisted that each worker produced a fixed stint of finished articles[69] (in the armament factories a monthly quota of so many helmets per worker was laid down).

The processes prior to weaving seem to have been entirely unorganised. No one calls himself a carder or spinner on his tombstone, or registers himself as such in the census, and no guilds of carders or spinners are known. There are two apparent exceptions to this rule, the *lanarii carminatores* of Brixellum and the *lanarii pectinarii* of Brixia, who describe themselves as *sodales*.[70] But I suspect that these did not card raw wool, but teased woven fabrics. It must be presumed that the spinning was mainly done, as today in the Nearer East, by women in their spare time, who either used the flax grown on the family farm and the wool from the family flock, or, if townspeople, bought raw wool or flax. We know of one sixth century Egyptian linen-weaver who leased an *arura* of land to grow his flax.[71]

In the linen trade we hear of intermediaries between the spinners and the weavers, the linen yarn merchants (λινέμποροι): that they sold yarn and not cloth appears clearly from a papyrus from Oxyrhynchus, which is unfortunately very fragmentary.[72] The city council is debating the execution of a government order for 100 tunics. In the first fragment the president says that 'they (probably the λινέμποροι) have made the excuse that those who undertook this work and their wives are unable to spin the linen yarn; for there are few villages in your nome which have this product'. In the next bit he states that they (certainly the λινέμποροι)

---

[67] Just. *Nov.* lxxxv. 3.
[68] *Cod. Theod.* X. xxii. 2.
[69] *tit. cit.* 1.
[70] *I.L.S.* 7290, 7290a, cf. 7556b and c for a *pectinator* and a *pectinarius* from Ateste.
[71] P. *Cairo Masp.* 67116.
[72] P. *Oxy.* 1414. A guild of λινέμποροι is also known at Corycus in Cilicia (*M.A.M.A.* III. 770).

say 'that linen yarn stands at 49 denarii, and only 11 denarii have been paid them by [the fiscus]'. The council protests 'The linen yarn merchants must be content with 19 denarii besides the sum paid by the fiscus'. The debate then goes to the weavers. It would appear that the linen yarn merchants had been furnished with money from the Imperial treasury to buy yarn from the spinners, but complained that it was not nearly enough (this was a period of rapid inflation), and proposed to charge the weavers a higher sum; the latter in fact later claim a higher price for the tunics, and as one of their excuses urge the higher price of their raw material.

The finishing processes of fulling and dyeing were performed by workers who were quite distinct from one another and from the weavers. *Fullones* (γναφεῖς) and *coloratores* (βαφεῖς) formed separate trades, and were grouped in their own guilds.[73] Fullers not only finished newly woven garments but cleaned soiled ones. Dyers similarly not only dyed cloth straight from the loom, but gave a fresh lease of life to old clothes: this is clear from the Edict of Diocletian which fixes two scales of prices for the *colorator* according to whether the garment is *rudis* (*de tela*) or *ab usu*.[74] For fullers the Edict fixes only the prices for treating new clothes, carefully listing 26 types of garment.[75] It would appear that the customer normally bought his clothes straight from the loom, and had them fulled himself. The Roman army certainly, as we have seen, bought clothes direct from the weavers. If the clothes passed through the hands of a merchant, he may have got them fulled and dyed before retailing them.

What little we know of the silk industry is derived from a few laws of the later Empire, some scattered items in the Edict of Diocletian, and Procopius' story of how Justinian established an imperial monopoly of the business. Owing to the fact that the raw material was very expensive and obtainable from one source

[73] Fullers: *I.L.S.* 3127 (Spoletium), 6368 (Pompeii), 7248 (Falerio), 5594 (Mediolanum Aulercorum), 3362 (Mactar), *C.I.L.* VIII. 12575 (Carthage), *I.L.A.* 22 (Gigthis), *I.G.* XII. ii. 271 (Mitylene), *Athenische Mitteilungen*, VII (1882), 252 (Cyzicus), *I.G.R.* IV. 863 (Laodicea), 643=1696 (Acmoneia), *Journal of Hellenic Studies*, XI (1890), 236 (Cilician city), *Chr.* I. 251 (Tebtunis). Dyers: *I.G.R.* IV. 816, 822 (Hierapolis), 1213, 1239, 1242, 1250, 1265 (Thyateira), III, 360 (Sagalassus), *Bulletin de correspondence hellénique*, X (1886), 519 (Tralles), *Chr.* I. 251 (Tebtunis).

[74] *Ed. Diocl.* vii. 54–63: the first word should be restored [color]atori from the Greek κορορ[άτ]ορι.

[75] *Ed. Diocl.* xxii.

only, the government, the structure of the industry was peculiar. From the late fourth century at any rate only the *comes commerciorum* or his subordinate *commerciarii* were allowed to buy raw silk from the barbarians. A law of Justinian orders the *commerciarii* to buy silk at 15 solidi per lb. and sell it at the same rate to the *metaxarii*.[76] The object of this monopoly was then not to make a profit, but to keep the price down by preventing competitive bidding between the merchants.

Procopius' description of the industry is not very clear. It was, he says, localised at Berytus and Tyre, where the merchants (ἔμποροι) and supervisors (ἐπιδημιουργοί) and craftsmen (τεχνῖται) lived: the last were humble manual workers who, when the imperial monopoly was established, either starved or migrated to Persia, whereas the merchants were men of substance and managed to weather the storm.[77] Procopius also speaks of merchants of silk garments at Constantinople and in other towns of the empire, who seem to be different from the merchants of Tyre and Berytus. On the other hand they are said to have raised their prices because they had to pay more to the Persians (for raw silk),[78] which would imply that they handled the whole business from the purchase of the raw material to the sale of the finished product. A law of Justinian couples the *metaxarii* or raw silk merchants with the *argentarii* (silversmiths and bankers) of Constantinople as wealthy people, by implication resident in the capital, who are in the habit of buying court sinecures for themselves and their sons.[79]

It would look as if some *metaxarii* not only bought raw silk but manufactured silk garments, organising the work through 'superintendents', and sold them in the capital and other big towns: these normally resided where they sold their goods. Others may have sold the garments they produced to merchants —this would apply especially to the export trade to the west and to the distributive trade to minor cities of the empire. Others again may have sold the raw silk to 'superintendents', who may have been entrepreneurs, who organised the dyeing, spinning and weaving of the fabrics and sold them to merchants. These two last categories of *metaxarii* would naturally have resided in Phoenicia.

[76] *Cod. Just.* IV. xl. 2, Just. *Nov. App.* 5.
[77] Procopius, *Anecdota*, XXV. 14–15, 25.
[78] *op. cit.* XXV. 16, 24.   [79] *Cod. Just.* VIII. xiii. 27.

The workers in the silk industry were evidently from Procopius' description of them free persons. Whether they worked in factories or whether the work was jobbed out to them in their homes does not appear. The Edict of Diocletian gives time or piece rates for the various processes. The cocoons were apparently first dyed, if a coloured fabric was to be produced, for the Edict quotes different rates for reeling ordinary silk and dyed silk.[80] It also gives rates for spinning purple silk into pure or mixed silk thread.[81] These rates are by the ounce. Lastly the Edict gives daily rates for *sericarii* producing pure or mixed silk fabrics.[82]

It is possible that the production of very superior woollens, especially those dyed purple, was organised on similar lines to the silk industry. The Edict of Diocletian cites wage rates for spinners of first grade purple wool for smooth finished fabrics (πεξά), and for weavers of these and of *Mutinensia* and others, in the same sections as those for silk spinners and weavers.[83]

Finally a word may be said of the distribution of finished garments. In the smaller towns and villages the customer no doubt normally bought locally produced clothes direct from the weaver. In the larger towns, especially those which depended on imports, there were clothing dealers (*vestiarii*): they are frequently recorded at Rome, and occasionally elsewhere, and seem to have been humble folk, mostly freemen.[84] We also hear of *negotiatores* or *mercatores*, who seem to have been importers of higher class garments from the larger centres of production. They often were natives of the producing areas, like Q. Calusius Severinus, a *civis Gallus* who was a *negotians vestiarius* at Pola, or M. Cluvius Tertullus, a *negotiator sagarius* at Milan who came from Apulia, or another Milanese *negotiator sagarius* who was by origin a *civis Mediomatricus*.[85] In the sixth century similarly we find George of

[80] *Ed. Diocl.* xxiii, 2, τοῖς τὸ σηρικὸν λύουσιν; xxiv. 13, μεταξαβλάττην ἤτοι ἐν χρώμασιν ἀγένητον λύουσιν.
[81] *Ibid.* xxiv. 14–5, πορφύραν εἰς ὁλοσηεικὸν (συψηρικὸν) νήθουσιν.
[82] *Ibid.* xx. 9–11, σειρικαρίῳ ἐργαζομένῳ ἰς σουψειρικὸν (ὁλοσειρικον ἄσημον, ὁλοσειρικὸν σκουτλᾶτον). The context shows that weavers are in question.
[83] *Ibid.* xxiv. 16, πορφύραν εἰς πεξὰ πρωτείαν νήθουσιν, XX. 12, 13, γερδίᾳ τρεφυμένη εἱματίου πεξοῦ τῶν εἰς παράδοσιν, ἐν ἱματίοις Μουτουνησίοις ἢ τοῖς λοιποῖς τρεφομένῃ.
[84] *I.L.S.* 7568–75 (Rome), 6668 (Bononia), 6688 (Aquileia), P. *Oxy.* 2230 (Oxyrhynchus), *Forschungen in Ephesos*, III, no. 63 (Ephesus).
[85] *I.L.S.* 7576, 7578, 7579.

Antioch, a silk merchant (*holosericoprata*) at Ravenna, and in the early seventh Peter of Alexandria, a linen merchant (*negotias linatarius*) at Panormus in Sicily.[86]

There were also itinerant merchants, who went from town to town with their bale of clothes, often making a regular annual round. Early in the fifth century Synesius of Cyrene speaks of one such, an Athenian, who was evidently a familiar figure; hearing that he has arrived he asks his brother, who is down at the port, Ptolemais, to buy three Attic cloaks from him on his behalf and to do so promptly before the best items in his stock have been sold.[87] The greater merchants also employed *circitores*, agents who went round selling their wares.[88] We know something of one of them, Jacob the Jew, whom a wealthy Constantinopolitan clothing merchant employed as his salaried agent in the early seventh century. He put him on board a ship bound for Carthage with a consignment of clothes, instructing him to sell them in Africa and Gaul. Jacob, as the story shows, hawked his goods around to individual customers in each port of call.[89]

[86] J. O. Tjäder, *Die nichtliterarischen lateinischen Papyri Italiens*, no. 4–5, B. V. 13, VI. 14; *I.L.S.* 7564.

[87] Synesius, *Ep.* 52.

[88] *Digest*, XIV. iii. 5 § 4, 'sed etiam eos institores dicendos placuit quibus vestiarii vel lintearii dant vestem circumferendam et distrahendam: quos volgo circitores appellamus.'

[89] *Doctrina Iacobi nuper baptizati*, *Abh. Ges. Gött. Phil. Hist. Kl.* N.F. XII. 3 (1910), p. 90.

CHAPTER NINETEEN

THE CONSTITUTIONAL POSITION OF ODOACER AND THEODERIC

MOMMSEN in his *Ostgotische Studien* (*Ges. Schr.* vi, 362 ff.) enunciated the theory that Odoacer and Theoderic were kings of their German followers, but ruled their Roman subjects as commissaries of the emperors, holding the office of *magister militum* with certain precisely defined additional powers. Stein (*Bas-Empire* ii, 116 ff.) and Ensslin (*Theoderich der Grosse*) have considerably modified this theory, admitting that Theoderic acted as king of all his subjects. They nevertheless still maintain that he was at the same time *magister militum*, and that his powers were limited in certain respects by a formal concordat with the emperor. In my opinion Odoacer and Theoderic were kings pure and simple, in the same position as the other barbarian kings.

The received view is largely based on the fact that the consuls nominated by Odoacer and Theoderic were acknowledged in the East. It is argued that Zeno and Anastasius must have formally invested Odoacer and Theoderic with the power of nominating consuls, and thus have given them some explicit constitutional position. It is clear that Theoderic bestowed the consulship (Cass., *Var.* vi, 1, 'formula consultatus', cf. ii, 2–3; ix, 22–3, for actual appointments) and it is indubitable that the Western consuls were generally acknowledged by the emperors. But Procopius makes the Goths claim that they 'allowed the Romans each year to obtain the rank of consuls from the Emperor of the East' (*B.G.* ii, vi, 20: προσθείη δ' ἄν τις ὡς καὶ τὸ τῶν ὑπάτων ἀξίωμα Γότθοι ξυνεχώρουν Ῥωμαίοις πρὸς τοῦ τῶν ἑῴων βασιλέως ἐς ἕκαστον ἔτος κομίζεσθαι). This can only mean that the men nominated by Theoderic as consuls were not *ipso facto* acknowledged as such by the emperors, but had to obtain *codicilli* from them, if they were to be recognised in the East. Some agreement must have been reached that the emperor would leave one of the consulships open and give favourable consideration to persons nominated at Rome,

but the Emperor clearly did not give Theoderic formal authority
to appoint one consul; on the contrary he appointed both.
Eutharic's consulship in 519 was therefore not exceptional.
His son in writing to Justinian naturally stressed the fact that the
Emperor had bestowed the consulship upon him (Cass., *Var*.
VIII, 1) but this was merely in order to emphasise the friendly
relations which had prevailed between the Ostrogothic royal
family and the emperors.

It would not seem that the acknowledgment of their consuls
in the East can have been a matter of great moment to Odoacer
or Theoderic. The men they appointed would naturally be
recognised in their own kingdoms, and were in fact generally
accepted in the other barbarian kingdom of the West. The
question was important to the Roman nobility, who wished to
figure in the Fasti as legitimate consuls, and it was no doubt the
senators sent as envoys by the kings to Constantinople who
pressed the matter and negotiated the working arrangement
whereby they received a second codicil from the emperor which
made them real consuls.

We know from Malchus that Odoacer proposed to Zeno that
the latter should appoint him patrician (by which word is certainly
meant the office held by Aëtius, Ricimer, etc.) and entrust him
with the government of Italy (Malchus 10: καὶ δεῖσθαι τοῦ Ζήνωνος
πατρίκιου τε αὐτῷ ἀποστεῖλαι ἀξίαν καὶ τὴν τῶν Ἰταλῶν τούτῳ
ἐφεῖναι διοίκησιν). But from the same passage we know that
Zeno rejected the proposition; he may have given Odoacer the
rank of patrician without the office of *magister militum* (as Stein
interprets Malchus' words, καὶ βασίλειον γράμμα περὶ ὧν ἠβούλετο
πέμπων τῷ Ὀδοάχῳ πατρίκιον ἐν τούτῳ γράμματι ἐπωνόμασε, in
Bas-Empire II, 46–7), but this of course gave Odoacer no powers.
There is in fact no evidence that Zeno ever gave any kind of
official recognition to Odoacer, except that Odoacer's consuls
were acknowledged from 480 onwards, and this, I have argued,
means nothing. Odoacer is always spoken of as king in the
literary sources, and is officially so styled in the two surviving
documents of his reign, both of which concern his Roman subjects.
In his edict on papal elections the praetorian prefect Basilius is
stated to be 'agens etiam vices praecellentissimi regis Odoacris'
(*M.G.* (*A.A.*) XII, 445), and in his grant of lands to Pierius
Odoacer styles himself 'Odovacer rex' (*F.I.R.* III², 99, 1, 10)·

In this document Odoacer behaves exactly like an emperor, giving orders to 'Andromachum v.i. et magnificum magistrum officiorum, consiliario nostro' and 'Marciano v.c. notario nostro' (ib. II, 4). These officers are alluded to elsewhere in the document as 'v.c. adque magnificus magister officiorum et consiliarius d.n.' (I, 4) and 'v.c. notarium regni eius' or 'regiae sedis' or 'v.c. notarius d.n. praecellentissimi regis Odoacris' (I, 5,; II 7, 11).

The evidence about Odoacer is scanty, but for what it is worth it indicates that he was simply a barbarian king, who like the other barbarian kings assumed imperial powers and took over imperial institutions. There is much more evidence about Theoderic and one might reasonably expect to find some explicit allusion in it to the constitutional position which he is alleged to have held. According to the prevailing theory Athalaric ought not merely to have announced his accession to Justinian and asked for a continuance of the friendly relations hitherto prevailing between his grandfather and the Emperor, as he does in Cass., *Var.* VIII, 1. He surely ought to have requested the Emperor to bestow upon him the office of *patricius et magister militum* and confer other constitutional powers, such as the right to appoint magistrates; the sentence 'ut amicitiam nobis illis pactis, illis conditionibus concedatis quas cum divae memoriae domno avo nostro inclitos decessores vestros constat habuisse' can hardly cover so basic a question and must refer to normal treaty relations. Again if the Goths in their parley with Belisarius (Proc., *B.G.* II, vi) could have cited a formal treaty or grant authorising Theoderic's rule over Italy, they surely would have done so.

Of the terms on which Zeno approved of Theoderic's invasion of Italy we have only the vaguest accounts in our authorities (Jordanes, *Get.* 290–2; *Rom.* 348; Proc., *B.G.* I, i, 10–11; II, vi, 16, 23–4). The most explicit (Anon. Val. 49, 'cui Theodoricus pactuatus est, et si victus fuisset Odoacar pro merito laborum suorum loco eius dum adveniret tantum praeregnaret') suggest that Theoderic was provisionally to be king. According to Malalas (383–4) Theoderic after conquering Odoacer and becoming king in his stead was reconciled to Zeno and thereafter did everything to please him; amongst other things he 'received the codicils of his major officers from the Emperor Zeno, notifying him whom he wanted to be promoted, and he received the rods of the consuls in the presence of the Emperor himself' (καὶ τὰ κωδικίλλια μὲν τῶν αὐτοῦ ἀρχόντων τῶν μεγάλων ἀπὸ τοῦ βασιλέως Ζήνωνος ἐδέχετο, μηνύων αὐτῷ τίνα ἤθελε προαχθῆναι· καὶ τοὺς σκιπίονας δὲ τῶν ὑπάτων ἐπὶ τοῦ βασιλέως αὐτοῦ ἐλάμβανεν). The second clause may be a confused description of some such arrangement about the consuls as I have suggested. The first clause is patently untrue as a description of what actually happened, but may represent the terms which Zeno laid down. This clause is strikingly parallel to one of the conditions which Peter the patrician, as plenipotentiary of Justinian, demanded of Theodatus (Proc., B.G. I, vi, 3: ἦν δέ γέ τῶν ὑπηκόων τινὰς ἐς τὸ τῶν πατρικίων ἢ ἄλλο βουλῆς ἀξίωμα Θευδάτος ἀγαγεῖν βούληται, τοῦτο δὲ οὐκ αὐτὸν δώσειν, ἀλλὰ βασιλέα αἰτήσειν διδόναι). It is a possibility that Peter, who was, as the fragments of his works in the de Caeri- moniis show, a great man for precedents, may have used Zeno's orig- inal terms to Theoderic as a model for the terms which he offered to Theodatus. In that case Zeno intended Theoderic to be a client king, who openly acknowledged the emperor as his suzerain, and had limited rights only over Roman bishops and senators, not being allowed to execute them or confiscate their property without the Emperor's consent, and had no power to appoint to the higher offices of state, but could only make recommendations to the Emperor.

As soon as he had defeated Odoacer in 490 Theoderic sent an envoy to Zeno, 'ab eodem sperans vestem se inducere regiam' (Anon. Val. 53). For some reason this embassy achieved no result. If my previous conjecture is correct, it might be inferred that Theoderic now repudiated the rather rigid conditions on which he had been offered the crown, and that Zeno was unwilling to yield. A second embassy was sent in 493, but Zeno died while it was still at Constantinople and 'Gothi sibi confirmaverunt Theodericum regem, non expectantes iussionem novi principis' (Anon. Val. 57). Thereupon Theoderic 'privatum habitum suaeque gentis vestitum reponens insigne regii amictus quasi iam Gothorum Romanorumque regnator assumit' (Jordanes, Get. 295). Later peace was made with Anastasius 'de praesumptione regni', and the Emperor returned to Italy the 'ornamenta palatii' which Odoacer had sent to Constantinople (Anon. Val. 64).

In all this there is no mention of anything save the kingship. As Theoderic had long been king of the Ostrogoths, the kingship in question was presumably (as Jordanes states) over the Romans.

Ensslin's theory that Theoderic's title as king required reaffirmation because his original Ostrogothic subjects had by now been reinforced by other barbarians is not plausible and has been rejected by Stein. Theoderic apparently wished to receive the title from the Emperor, but not being able to get it on his own terms, allowed the Goths to proclaim him. Later, however, he secured Anastasius' recognition of his position. He appears to have attached particular importance to the right to wear the purple unlike Odoacer, who was content with the title (*Chron. Min.* II, 159, 'nomenque regis Odovacar adsumpsit cum tamen nec purpura nec regalibus uteretur insignibus'). He presumably used the imperial regalia which he persuaded Anastasius to return. He never, however, claimed to be emperor, but only king (Proc., *B.G.* I, i, 26, καὶ βασιλέως μὲν τοῦ 'Ρωμαίων οὔτε τοῦ σχήματος οὔτε τοῦ ὀνόματος ἐπιβατεῦσαι ἠξίωσεν, ἀλλὰ καὶ ῥὴξ διεβίου καλούμενος).

This, in my view, was the correct constitutional position as agreed between Anastasius and Theoderic: Italy was no longer part of the empire and Anastasius recognised Theoderic as its king. Two Roman senators do not appear to have accepted this position. In an inscription set up by Caecina Mavortius Basilius Decius (*I.L.S.* 827) Theoderic is styled 'd.n. gloriosissimus adque inclytus rex Theodericus victor ac triumfator semper Augustus'. The other inscription, set up by Valerius Florianus (*Bull. Comm. Arch. Com.* LXXIII (1949–50), 79, completing *I.L.S.* 825), begins: 'salvis dominis nostris Anastasio perpetuo Augusto et gloriosissimo ac triumfali viro Theoderico'. Both inscriptions suggest that some senators at any rate wished to believe that they were still living under the Roman empire. The first crudely makes Theoderic emperor as well as king, ignoring Anastasius. The second is more subtle. Italy is assumed to be part of the united empire and Theoderic's position is discreetly veiled; he is styled neither king nor emperor, but is coupled with Anastasius under the heading 'domini nostri' in a way which suggests that he was his colleague.

Both inscriptions must be regarded as reflecting rather the wishful thinking of the Roman aristocracy than the official constitutional doctrine. In every other document Theoderic is styled simply king, and that Italy was not, even in the most formal sense, a part of the empire under Theoderic is revealed by one of the terms on which Justinian was willing to recognise

Theodatus as king, that when the king was publicly acclaimed, the Emperor should be acclaimed before him, and when a statue was set up to the king, a statue of the Emperor should be set up on its right hand (Proc., *B.G.* I, vi, 4–5). If Anastasius had regarded Theoderic as an imperial commissary, he would surely have insisted on these acknowledgements of his sovereignty.

The theory that Theoderic was concurrently a Roman *magister militum* is based on two facts, that he never appointed a *magister militum*, and that he used as his own an *officium* which appears to have been that of the *magister militum*. Neither argument is very cogent. Theoderic may well have refrained from giving the title for political reasons; in Italy the *magistri* had been in the past overpowerful subjects, and he preferred to keep his military commanders in a subordinate role. There was evidently no constitutional difficulty since his successor Athalaric did appoint *patricii praesentales* (Cass., *Var.* VIII, 9–12; XI, 1, § 16). The second point is disputable, but I would agree that it is correct.

Theoderic, through the mouth of Cassiodorus, several times mentions 'officium nostrum'. From *Var.* VI, 13, 'formula magistri scrinii quae danda est comitiaco quando permilitat', it appears that members of the 'officium quod nostris iussionibus speciali sollicitudine famulatum est' were called *comitiaci*. In II, 28, an 'ex principe nostri officii' receives on retirement the *comitiva primi ordinis* with the rank of *spectabilis*. From VII, 21–2, it appears that there were *scriniarii nostri officii* and from VII, 31, that the *princeps cardinalis* of the *officium comitiacum* was in immediate attendance on the king (at Ravenna) and that he had a *vicarius* at Rome. From VII, 24–5, it appears the *princeps* of the *comes Dalmatiarum* was sent him 'ex officio nostro'. In IV, 40, a summons to the king's court is executed 'per officium nostrae sedis', and in I, 8 (cf. IV, 5); I, 27; II, 10; V. 6, *comitiaci* act as royal *executores*.

These data best fit the hypothesis that 'officium nostrum' was the *officium* of the *magister militum praesentalis*. His *officium* was headed by a *princeps* (*Not. Dig. Occ.* V, 276; VI, 87). It comprised *scriniarii* (implied by the *primiscrinius* of *Occ.* VI, 89; cf. *Or.* V, 72; VI, 75; VIII, 59; IX, 54; and Joh. Lydus, de mag. III, 57; τοῖς δὲ τῆς στρατηγίδος ἀρχῆς σκρινιαρίοις συναριθμούμενος). From it were seconded *principes* to the *officia* of the *comites rei militaris* and *duces* (*Not. Dig. Occ.* XXV, 38; XXVI, 22, etc.). The title *comitiacus* would seem appropriate to the officials of the *magister militum*, who was often known, particularly in the West, simply as *comes*; according to Joh. Lydus, *de mag.* II, 7, in the East also οἱ μὲν γὰρ λεγόμενοι στρατηλάται τὴν τῶν κομίτων ἔχουσιν ἐκ τῆς ἀρχαιότητος καὶ μόνην τιμήν· ταύτῃ καὶ κομιτιανοὺς τοὺς δευτεροστρατηλατιανοὺς ἡ παλαιότης οἶδε. The constitutional significance of this fact is not, however, very evident. Odoacer had no doubt taken over the *officium* of the *magister praesentalis*, since he was *de facto* commander-in-chief, and Theoderic may well have followed his example, being in the same position; alternatively he may have brought his own *officium* as *magister militum* with him when he invaded Italy and have retained it. In any case the use of this *officium* as his personal staff was a matter of administrative convenience rather than constitutional law.

It is furthermore alleged that in the 'capitulations' under which Theoderic was authorised to govern Italy two restrictions were placed on his powers. In the first place he was not authorised to enact *leges*, but only, like a praetorian prefect, to issue *edicta*. It is true that Theoderic did call his laws *edicta*, but this was probably a matter of policy. Shortly after his recognition by Anastasius Theoderic made an announcement to the Senate and People in which 'se omnia deo iuvante quod retro principes Romani ordinaverunt inviolabiliter servaturum promittit' (Anon. Val. 66). Later the Goths claimed (Proc., *B.G.* II, vi, 17), οὕτω τοίνυν παραλαβόντες τὴν τῆς Ἰταλίας ἀρχὴν τούς τε νόμους καὶ τὴν πολιτείαν διεσωσάμεθα τῶν πώποτε βεβασιλευκότων οὐδενὸς ἧσσον, καὶ Θευδερίχου μὲν ἢ ἄλλου ὁτουοῦν διαδεξαμένου τὸ Γότθων κράτος νόμος τὸ παράπαν οὐδεὶς οὐκ ἐν γράμμασιν, οὐκ ἄγραφός ἐστι. There seems no reason to doubt that Theoderic's action was, as stated, a spontaneous concession, designed to reassure and conciliate the Romans.

The second alleged restriction was that Theoderic was incapable of giving the Roman citizenship to Goths, and *a fortiori* of appointing them to Roman offices or making them senators, patricians or consuls: since Theoderic habitually appointed Goths as *comites rei militaris* and *duces*, these offices, though they carried the Roman ranks of *illustris* and *spectabilis*, are for the purpose of the theory not regarded as 'Roman', nor is the *comitiva patrimonii*, to which also Goths were sometimes appointed. It is true that Theoderic appointed no Goth as consul except his son-in-law Eutharic, and that he is not known to have created any Goth patrician: Athalaric did, however, bestow this rank on Tuluin (Cass., *Var.* VIII, 9). Tuluin took his seat in the Senate (Cass., *Var.* VIII, 10–11). It is not known if any Goths became senators under Theoderic, but many acquired the rank of *illustris*, which was the qualification for entry to the Senate (Cass., *Var.* IV, 12, 46, Marchedus; I, 40; III, 26; IV, 9; IX, 8; 9, Osuin; v, 18; IX, 13, Willia; IV, 16, 22–3, Arigern), and in one case, that of Arigern, Theoderic uses language which, taken at its face value, implies that he was a senator (Cass., *Var.* IV, 16, 'quem desideratum, sicut putamus, coetui vestro reddidimus').

It is true that Theoderic did in fact reserve the civil offices (except the *comitiva patrimonii*, which was a new creation) to Romans, and the Goths later claimed as evidence of their good rule over Italy that the Romans 'have continued to hold all the offices of state, and no Goth has participated in them' (Proc., *B.G.* II, vi, 19). But there is no evidence that this was not merely a matter of policy. All the German kings employed Romans freely in civilian posts, partly because they were alone qualified to perform their functions, and partly no doubt to conciliate public opinion.

I would maintain then that Theoderic invaded Italy as *patricius et magister militum praesentalis* of Zeno, but in 493 having conquered Odoacer abandoned this office and had himself proclaimed king (of Italy) by the Goths (in Anon. Val. 49–54, he is called *patricius* up to this date, but never thereafter). In 497 he was recognised as such by Anastasius. Having a deep admiration for Roman civilisation and wishing to conciliate his Roman subjects, and in particular the Senate, he announced that he would preserve the Roman law, thereafter modifying it only by *edicta*, maintained the existing administrative structure, and made it his consistent policy to appoint Romans to civilian offices. Goths were appointed to the military offices (and to the *comitiva patrimonii*), and given the appropriate titles of rank; if *illustres* they were perhaps enrolled in the Senate. He created no *magistri militum*, preferring to give his generals the more modest titles of *comes* or *dux*, and is not known to have conferred the patriciate on a Goth; his successor, however, did not maintain these policies. He assumed the right of nominating a consul each year, but the Emperor did not regard his nominations as valid; he did, however, informally agree himself to grant the consulship to Theoderic's nominees.

The peculiarity of Theoderic's position was not, I would maintain, the result of any formal concordat between him and the Emperor, but the fruit partly of his personal policy, partly of his exceptional position as ruler of Rome and Italy. It is evident from all our sources that he had a deep and genuine respect and admiration for Roman *civilitas*, and that he did his best to preserve it and to inculcate it among the Goths. But even if this had not been his personal preference, his practical position was very different from that of the other barbarian kings. The Vandals, Visigoths, Burgundians and Franks occupied outlying dioceses of the empire. They inherited only the provincial administration and there were relatively few senators among their subjects. Theoderic, and Odoacer before him, inherited the central government of the empire, and Rome itself, with its Senate. While the other barbarian kings improvised central governments of their own making, Odoacer and Theoderic, if only by force of inertia, maintained the ancient offices of the imperial *comitatus* and the praetorian prefecture. The other kings did not need to be over careful to placate the scattered senatorial families resident in their dominions. These senatorial families preserved, it is true, great social prestige and their members were often employed in high offices by the kings. But they did not constitute a privileged order. It is notable in the *Breviarium* of Alaric that scarcely any laws about the privileges, honours and precedence of senators are preserved. Senators are in fact mentioned only three times in the *interpretationes*. In *Cod. Theod.* II, xxxiii, 3 and 4, senators are forbidden to charge more than 6 per cent interest on loans, and in Marcian, *Nov.* v, they are permitted to marry women of low degree. In *Cod. Theod.* IX, xl, 10, where the original law gives a jurisdictional privilege to 'senatorii ordinis viri', the *interpretatio* changes this phrase to 'maiores personae aut alicuius dignitatis viri'.

Odoacer and Theoderic, on the other hand, were faced by the bulk of the senatorial order, including its most ancient and wealthiest families, and by the Senate itself, with its strong corporate tradition. It is in the circumstances hardly surprising that they should have been careful to grant to senators the offices and honours which they prized so highly, meticulously observed the

BB

protocol on which they set such store, treated the Senate as a corporation with deference, and in general avoided any unnecessary disturbance of the existing order.

PART III

CHAPTER TWENTY

COLLEGIATE PREFECTURES

AMONG the many favours for which Ausonius thanked Gratian when he wasd esignated consul in the autumn of 378 was 'ad praefecturae collegium filius cum patre coniunctus' (*Grat. Act.* 7). This favour, he goes on to say, preceded his nomination to the consulship, and was Gratian's own gift after his father's death; 'et tui tantum praefectura beneficii, quae et ipsa non vult vice simplici gratulari, liberalius divisa quam iuncta, cum teneamus duo integrum, neuter desiderat separatum' (*Grat. Act.* 11). This prefecture was apparently that of the Gauls (*Grat. Act.* 40: 'agant et pro me gratias voces omnium Galliarum, quarum praefecto hanc honorificentiam detulisti'). In later poems he alludes to his 'praefecturam duplicem' (*Protrept.* 91), in which he was, before entering upon his consulship on 1 Jan. 379, 'praefectus Gallis et Libyae et Latio' (*Epiced.* 42).

This is the only collegiate prefecture attested by any ancient source, and it was indeed an extraordinary creation. Gratian's motive is obvious, to bestow the highest honour on his tutor and at the same time to avoid overloading him with administrative duties by giving him a colleague, while keeping the profits within the family by making his son that colleague. Soon the honour was doubled by the even more extraordinary step of combining Italy with Gaul in one prefecture, jointly governed by the two colleagues Ausonius and Hesperius.

Apart from this extraordinary case there is no hint either in the literary sources or in the laws that the office of praetorian prefect was ever held by two persons as colleagues. Collegiate prefectures are an invention of modern scholars, who have sought through them to explain the not infrequent cases where two prefects (or sometimes more) appear to receive constitutions simultaneously in the same zone.

All hypotheses based on the addresses and dates of the codes are fragile, for while most laws are no doubt correctly addressed and dated, there are some which are certainly not; and while many false dates can be plausibly emended, there remain a few which look perfectly genuine but are indubitably wrong and can only be corrected by the expedient which Seeck called 'ergänzte Konsulate', that is, by postulating that the redactors of the Code, finding an undated law, arbitrarily inserted a wrong consulate.

Collegiate prefectures have been unnecessarily multiplied because the laws very rarely state a prefect's zone, and modern scholars have tended to crowd too many into Oriens and above all into Italy, despite that the lists of Gaul and Illyricum are much less crowded. They have been encouraged in this course by the assumption that an *acceptum* or *propositum* invariably gives a clue to the area which a given prefect controlled. Normally, it is true, the inference is valid; for praetorian prefects circulated the laws addressed to them only to the provincial governors under their disposition. But there are a number of cases where this rule does not work. *C.Th.* IV, 12, 5, addressed on 6 Dec. 362 to Secundus, undoubtedly praetorian prefect of the East, is 'p.p. in foro Traiani', and IX, 19, 4, addressed on 16 April 376 to Maximinus, equally certainly prefect of the Gauls, is 'p.p. Romae'. The explanation is simple. The redactors sometimes had several copies of a law circularized to the praetorian prefects, and carelessly combined the address of one with the postcript of another. *Accepta* and *proposita* must therefore be used with caution.

Another common cause of error is that men who were subsequently praetorian prefects are not infrequently given this title in laws addressed to them when holding lower offices earlier in their career. Fairly obvious instances are *C.Th.* XVI, 5, 4 (22 April 376) and VIII, 5, 34 (27 Feb. 377) which are addressed to Hesperius *P.P.O.*, though he is attested as pro-consul of Africa on 10 March 376 (XV, 7, 3) and on 8 July 377 (I, 32, 2); the error is proved in the case of VIII, 5, 34, which lays down a special order for *veredorum reparatio* 'in proconsulari provincia'.

This form of error is, I suspect, commoner than is generally admitted, and is due, I would suggest, to the sources from which the compilers draw the laws. Seeck clearly demonstrated that they found little if anything in any central files of the *comitatus*, at any rate for the fourth century, but he postulated that they used extensively the files of the praetorian prefecture. It is, however, as unlikely that the prefectures preserved massive ancient files as that the *sacra scrinia* did so. Like the *comitatus* the prefectures were migratory institutions with no permanent home. Even the praetorian prefecture of the East, which had settled down at Constantinople from the last decade of the fourth century, did not acquire an office-building of its own until the prefect Constantine built one at his own expense in the reign of Leo, probably in 471, and until then 'the man administering the office conducted business in his own premises' (Joh. Lydus, *Mag.* II, 20). He probably also, like English Cabinet Ministers down to the nineteenth century, kept his state papers with his family papers and they were passed on to his descendants. It was probably from the family papers of their descendants that the compilers obtained most of the numerous laws addressed to praetorian prefects of the fourth century, and this will explain why among the praetorian prefects of Italy Taurus and Probus are exceptionally well documented; both left distinguished descendants and those of Taurus were resident in Constantinople. These collections of papers would naturally have included some laws addressed to the prefects during their earlier careers, and it was a pardonable though careless error if the redactors of the Code added the title *P.P.O.* when the address of a given law was incomplete.

Collegiate prefectures reached their zenith under Seeck (see the tables on pp. 473–5 of the *Regesten*), but they have since been somewhat reduced in number, chiefly by Professor Palanque, who shares my aversion for them, in his *Essai sur la Préfecture du Prétoire du Bas-Empire*. I will take as my basis the latest list of praetorian prefects, that of Ensslin in *P.W.* XXII, 2495–2501. I will begin with 337, omitting the troubled problems of Constantine's prefects.

In this list we still find Domitius Leontius and Septimius Acindynus as colleagues in the East in the early years of Constantius II. If we accept Seeck's plausible emendations, Acindynus's laws fall on 27 Dec. 338, 15 Feb. 339 and 5 April 340 (he is also recorded on 14 Aug. 340 in *B.G.U.* 21), and those of Leontius fall between 11 Oct. 340 and 6 July 344, with one (*C.Th.* IX, 1, 7) on 18 Oct. 338. The consulship is impeccable ('Urso et Polemio'), but the law might have been addressed to Leontius in some lower office, such as that of vicar.

The next alleged collegiate tenure in the eastern prefecture is that of Eutropius and Neoterius at the beginning of Theodosius I's reign. Neoterius has a run of laws from 15 Jan. 380 to 16 Jan.

Consuls	Eutychianus	Aurelianus	Caesarius
Olybrio et Probino, 395			(24 June: XVI, 5, 27)[1] 30 Nov.: X, 6, 1 29 Dec.: XII, 1, 150
Arcadio IV et Honorio III, 396	24 Feb.: III, 30, 6		13 Feb.: IX, 42, 14 14 Feb.: VI, 26, 7 27 Feb.: VI, 27, 10 23 Mar.: XVI, 7, 6 24 Mar.: XV, 1, 34 17 Apr.: VII, 4, 21 21 Apr.: XVI, 5, 31, 32 25 Apr.: XV, 6, 1 9 May: VIII, 17, 1 3 Aug.: IX, 1, 18+42, 15 12 Aug.: VI, 3, 2 31 Aug.: IX, 38, 9
	8 Dec.: III, 12, 3 15 Dec.: XII, 18, 2 31 Dec.: VI, 4, 30	(6 Oct.: IV, 2, 1; V, 1, 5)[2]	7 Dec.: XVI, 10, 14
Caesario et Attico, 397	19 Feb.: XIII, 2, 1 1 Apr.: XVI, 5, 33 Anatolius P.P.O. Illyrici 17 June: XV, 8, 12 9 July: XI, 14, 3 4 Sept.: VI, 3, 4+IX, 14, 3 8 Nov.: IX, 6, 3 23 Nov.: II, 33, 3		16 Feb.: IX, 26, 1 6 Mar.: XI, 8, 1 8 Apr.: VI, 26, 9 29 Apr.: VI, 2, 19 23 June: VI, 26, 10 1 July: XVI, 8, 13 13 July: VIII, 15, 8
Honorio IV et Eutychiano, 398 Anatolius P.P.O. Illyrici 7 March.: IV, 12, 7	3 Feb.: II, 1, 10 4 Mar.: XVI, 5, 34 7 Mar.: XIII, 11, 9 23 May: VII, 4, 25 3 July: XV, 1, 38 6 July: C.J. XI, 62, 9 27 July: IX, 40, 16+45, 3+XI, 30, 57+XVI, 2, 33+C.J. 1, 4, 7		(26 July: XVI, 2, 32)[3]

Consuls	Eutychianus	Aurelianus	Caesarius
	25 Oct.: XII, 1, 159 6 Dec.: I, 2, 11 13 Dec.: XV, 1, 40		
Eutropio et Theodoro, 399	10 Mar.: XI, 24, 4 14 Mar.: XIII, 7, 1 10 Apr.: *C.J.* XI, 62, 10	(17 Jan.: IX, 40, 17)[4]	
(Tribigild's rising, spring)	25 May: XI, 24, 5 6 July: XVI, 5, 36		
(Eutropius's fall, summer)	10 July: XVI, 10, 16 25 July: IX, 40, 18		
(Gainas expels Aurelian, autumn) Anatolius P.P.O.Illyrici 12 Nov.: VI, 28, 6.		27 Aug.: II, 8, 23 2 Oct.: XV, 6, 2	
	11 Dec.: XII, 1, 163 28 Dec.: XII, 1, 164 30 Dec.: XII, 1, 165		
Stilichone et Aureliano, 400 (Gainas's flight, July 12)			8 Dec.: I, 34, 1
Vincentio et Fravitta, 401			3 Feb.: VIII, 5, 62
Arcadio V et Honorio V, 402			
Theodosio A. et Rumorido, 403			11 June: *C.J.* VII, 41, 2
Honorio VI et Aristaeneto, 404	3 Feb.: XVI, 8, 15 14 July: XV, 1, 42 18 Nov.: XVI, 4, 6		
Stilichone II et Anthemio, 405	11 June: *C.J.* V, 4, 19		

[1] With Seeck I emend to 25 Dec., as 24 June is before Rufinus's death (27 Nov.).
[2] This date is generally rejected; I would move it from 396 (*Arcadio IV et Honorio III*) to 394 (*Arcadi III et Honorio II*), and take P.P.O. to be a mistake for P.U. (as in XII, 1, 131, 132 and 138, addressed to Aurelianus P.P.O. on 27 Feb., 10 March

381. He was undoubtedly *P.P.O. Orientis*, for *C.Th.* I, 6, 10 (undated but plausibly placed by Seeck in September 380) is not only 'accepta . . . Crago' (in Lycia), but concerns the provinces of Bithynia, Paphlagonia and Phrygia Salutaris; also vii, 13, 9 (26 April 380) is 'p.p. . . . Antiochia'. This sequence is followed by another addressed to Florus, beginning on 30 July 381[5] and running on to 5 March 383. He also was apparently *P.P.O. Orientis*, for *C.Th.* v, 14, 31 (wrongly dated 389, 'Timasio et Promoto cos'., one of Seeck's 'ergänzte Konsulate') deals with imperial estates 'in Orientis regionibus'. Parallel and overlapping with these two sequences is a run of laws from 6 Jan. 380 to 28 Sept. 381, addressed to Eutropius. They contain no clues to the zone which he administered, but it was surely Illyricum. Having just received the dioceses of Dacia and Macedonia and having a war on hand in this very area, Theodosius could hardly have dispensed with a praetorian prefect of Illyricum during the first two years of his reign.

Next comes the tangle of Caesarius, Eutychianus and Aurelianus in the early years of Arcadius. The problem is best presented in tabular form (see pp. 378–9); I have given all the laws as dated in the MSS. of the Codes, bracketing those whose dates I reject.

My reconstruction is as follows. Caesarius was *P.P.O. Orientis* from Rufinus's death (Nov. 395) to July 397: this agrees with Philostorgius xi, 5: Καισαρίῳ τῷ τὴν ˊΡουφίνου διαδεξαμένῳ ἀρχήν. Eutychianus was *P.P.O. Illyrici* from Feb. 396 or earlier until April/May 397, and was promoted to Oriens in September 397 (he was certainly *P.P.O. Orientis* on 7 March and 23 May 398, as *C.Th.* xiii, 11, 9 and vii, 4, 25 deal with Hierapolis and Epiphaneia), being succeeded in Illyricum by Anatolius, who is attested as *P.P.O. Illyrici* from June 397 to November 399. On Eutropius's fall (summer 399) Eutychianus was replaced by Aurelianus, who fell from office when Gainas seized power in the autumn. Under

---

and 8 Dec. 393, when he was certainly *P.U.*).

[3] This consulship (*Honorio IV et Eutychiano*) seems sound, but can hardly be right. This law can be moved to 396, 397, 400, 401, 402 or 403 according to taste.

[4] With Seeck I emend to 17 Aug., as 17 Jan. is before the fall of Eutropius (summer 399).

[5] *C.Th.* viii, 15, 6 is correctly dated 17 June 380, but Florus' title should be *magister officiorum* as in vi, 27, 3, of 16 June 380.

the Gainas regime (autumn 399 to summer 400) Eutychianus was again *P.P.O. Orientis*, but was replaced by Caesarius on Gainas's fall. Caesarius held office for three years, and then Eutychianus came back again in 403–4. He was replaced by Anthemius in June/July 405, and Aurelianus only came back after Anthemius's long tenure of the office in 415.

This reconstruction fits Synesius's *De Providentia* rather better than Seeck's. Osiris must of course be Aurelianus. In Seeck's version Aurelianus is restored to power directly after Gainas's fall, but Synesius (*de Prov.* 125 B and C) rather lamely explains why he was not reinstated; and in my version he does not return to power until many years later. In my version Typhos is not Caesarius but Eutychianus, since he is *P.P.O.* immediately after Aurelian's fall. Typhos's previous career according to Synesius was ταμίας χρημάτων (*de Prov.* 92A), that is *comes sacrarum largitionum*, and then (ib. 92B–93B) an office in which he ruled a part of the empire with financial and judicial functions, appointing subordinates. This would be the praetorian prefecture, first of Illyricum and then of Oriens under Eutropius's domination. The prefecture of the East becomes the kingship of Egypt in the allegory when, after Eutropius's fall, it becomes the supreme office. It may be added that the career of Typhos does not correspond with that of Caesarius, who was *magister officiorum* in 386–7.

In the Italian prefecture the first alleged collegiate tenures are from 346 to 356. According to the Chronographer of 354 Ulpius Limenius held the combined offices of *P.P.O.* (of Italy) and *P.U.R.* from 12 June 347 to 8 April 349 (he is also attested on 12 Feb. and 28 March 349 in *C.Th.* ix, 21, 6 and ix, 17, 2), and after a brief interregnum Hermogenes held the same combination of offices from 19 May 349 to 26 Feb. 350. During the same period Titianus was *P.P.O. Galliarum* (attested from 30 June 343 to 12 Nov. 349). We also have to fit in Eustathius on 8 March 349 (*C.Th.* ii, 1, 1+xi, 7, 6, p.p. Romae), and Vulcacius Rufinus, who was *P.P.O.* during his consulship in 347 (*P. Oxy.* 1190, of 22 June, *P. Cairo Preis.* 39, of 22 Oct., and *P. Antin.* 31), on 28 Dec. 349 (*C.J.* vi, 62, 3) and at the time of Vetranio's rebellion in 350 (Petr. Patr. 16).

Eustathius has been made a colleague of Titianus in Gaul; the fact that his law was 'p.p. Romae' is rather against this hypothesis.

He is known to have been *C.R.P.* on 15 May 345 (*C.Th.* x, 10, 7, cf. *Philost.* III, 12) and as his law of 8 March 349 is concerned with the *res privata*, it has been suggested that his title of *P.P.O.* in this law is a mistake for *C.R.P.* This is possible, but I prefer Professor Palanque's ingenious emendation of the date from *viii id. Mart.* (8 March) to *viii id. Mai.* (8 May), which would put him in the interregnum between Limenius and Hermogenes. He was, as Professor Palanque suggests, probably made acting *P.P.O.* of Italy on Limenius's death (for such interim appointments see Amm. XXI, 8, 1).

Limenius's and Hermogenes's combination of the urban and praetorian prefectures suggests to my mind that their zone was probably limited to Italy (with Africa). Vulcacius Rufinus may then have been simultaneously prefect of Illyricum (which at that time would have included the three dioceses of Dacia, Pannonia and Macedonia). He is in fact recorded at Savaria under Constans (*I.L.S.* 727), and he was probably in Illyricum when Vetranio was proclaimed (according to Petr. Patr. 16 he alone of the four envoys of Magnentius and Vetranio was not arrested by Constantius, and soon after Mursa he is praetorian prefect in Illyricum, see below). It appears, however, from *C.Th.* XI, 1, 6 (22 May 354)—'vinum, quod ad cellarii usus ministrari solet, cuncti Italiae possessores iuxta statutum Constantis fratris mei comparent. quod ut fieri facilius possit, ab omnibus Italis nostris conferatur pecuniae quantitas ea, quam Rufini viri clarissimi et inlustris praefecti praetorio parentis amicique nostri moderatio dandam esse censuerat'—that Rufinus had included Italy in his zone sometime in Constans's reign. I would suggest that he was *P.P.O. Italiae* as successor to Placidus (recorded on 28 May 344 in *C.Th.* XII, 1, 37) and was transferred to Illyricum on Limenius's appointment on 12 June 347: whether he also ruled Illyricum in the earlier part of his prefecture one cannot say.

After Vetranio's abdication Constantius II kept Rufinus on as *P.P.O.*: the trial of Photinus at Sirmium shortly after the battle of Mursa was attended by 'Καλλικράτει ἐκσκέπτορι 'Ρουφίνου τοῦ ἐπάρχου' (Epiph., *Adv. Haer.* 71). He received at this period *C.J.* VI, 22, 5 (26 Feb. 352) and probably also *C.Th.* II, 9, 1+III, 5, 1 (12 May 352, as emended by Seeck) and perhaps other laws with suspect imperial consulates (see Mommsen's note to *C.Th.* II, 9, 1). I have in an earlier article (*Historia* IV, 1955, 229 ff.)

endeavoured to prove that his alleged colleague Philippus never held a prefecture in the West, but was finally disgraced in 351. Rufinus accompanied Constantius to Gaul, where he is found as *P.P.O.* in the spring of 354 (Amm. xiv, 10, 4). To this date probably belongs *C.Th.* ix, 23, 1 'acc. viii id. Mar. Constantina, Constantio A. viii et Iuliano Caes.' (356, to be corrected to 'Constantio A. vii et Constantio Caes. iii', 354), which Rufinus received at Arles.

Meanwhile in Italy Maecilius Hilarianus was prefect in March 354, as emerges from *C.Th.* vi, 4, 3 and 7, as emended by Seeck, and was followed by Taurus, whose long series of laws runs from 6 April 355 to 29 Aug. 361 (accepting Seeck's emendation of xii, 1, 40 and xvi, 10, 4). He has been given as colleagues Lollianus Mavortius, attested as *P.P.O.* in *C.Th.* vi, 29, 1 (22 July 355) and xi, 30, 25+36, 11 (25 July 355), and Volusianus Lampadius, attested as *P.P.O.* in *C.Th.* xi, 34, 2 (1 Jan. 355), *C.J.* vi, 22, 6 (18 Feb. 355), *C.Th.* iii, 12, 2 (30 April 355), xi, 30, 26+36, 12 (29/30 July 355); it may be noted that these two overlap one another as well as Taurus.

Both appear *prima facie* to be praetorian prefects of Italy, for xi, 30, 25 is 'p.p. Capuae' and iii, 12, 2 is 'dat. Rom.' (which must be for 'acc. Rom.' as Constantius was at Milan). *Proposita* and *accepta* are, however, as I have pointed out, not conclusive, and there is literary evidence that Lampadius was *P.P.O. Galliarum* and Mavortius *P.P.O. Illyrici*. According to Zosimus (ii, 55) Lampadius the prefect was one of those who persuaded Constantius to recall and execute Gallus, and this must have been in the summer of 354, which the emperor spent in Gaul (Amm. xiv, 10). The next year he instigated the plot against Silvanus, *magister peditum per Gallias* (Amm. xv, 5, 4–5). That Mavortius was prefect in Illyricum can be inferred from a comparison of Amm. xv, 3, 8 and xvi, 8, 5–7. In the first passage (in 354) Rufinus, 'princeps apparitionis praefecturae praetorianae', reports a treason case at Sirmium, and is rewarded with a second year of office. In the second (in 356) the same Rufinus reports another treason case, and 'iubetur Mavortius, tunc praefectus praetorio, vir sublimis constantiae, crimen acri inquisitione spectare, iuncto ad audiendi societatem Ursulo largitionum comite'; they dismiss the charge, whereupon Constantius 'missis equitibus citis Ursulum redire ad comitatum iussit'. It is clear that Ursulus was sent from the *comitatus* (at Milan) to act as assessor to Mavortius, the man on the spot, and that Mavortius was at some distance, presumbly at Sirmium.

There are no collegiate prefectures alleged for Valentinian's reign, but under Gratian they are very thick. There is of course the one attested collegiate tenure, that of Ausonius and Hesperius. The appended table will make the situation clearer; the bracketed laws have been placed in the years to which Seeck plausibly put them.

Consuls	Antonius	Hesperius	Ausonius	Siburius
376, Valente V et Valentiniano	xiii, 3, 11: 23 May, P.P.O. Gall. ix, 35, 2: 17 Sept., P.P.O. Gall.			
377, Gratiano IV et Merobaude	i, 15, 7: 16 Jan., P.P.O. i, 16, 13: 28 July, P.P.O. (ix, 40, 12: 30 Nov., P.P.O.)[6]	i, 32, 2: 8 July, Proc. Africae.		
378, Valente VI et Valentiniano II	ix, 20, 1+xi, 39, 7: 12 Jan., P.P.O. C.J. ii, 7, 2: 18 Aug., P.P.O.[8]	(i, 15, 8: 21 Jan., P.P.O.)[7] (vi, 30, 4: 6 Dec., P.P.O.)[9]	viii, 5, 35: 20 April, P.P.O.	
379, Ausonio et Olybrio		vii, 18, 2: 2 July P.P.O. xiii, 1, 11: 5 July, P.P.O. xiii, 5, 15: 21 July, P.P.O. C.J. vi, 32, 4: 30 July, P.P.O. viii, 18, 6: 31 July, P.P.O. xvi, 5, 5:		

Consuls	Antonius	Hesperius	Ausonius	Siburius
		3 Aug., P.P.O.		xi, 31, 7: 3 Dec., P.P.O.
380, Gratiano V et Theodosio		(x, 20, 10: 14 May, P.P.O.)[10]		

[6] So Seeck, *Reg.* p. 86; the law refers to Campania.
[7] So Seeck, *Reg.* p. 72.
[8] 'dat. Ravennae', which must mean p.p.
[9] So Seeck, *Reg.* p. 86.
[10] So Seeck, *Reg.* p. 102.

It will be seen that Antonius was prefect of Gaul certainly in 376, but had been transferred to Italy before 30 Nov. 377, where he remained until 18 Aug. 378 or later. Ausonius, attested *P.P.O.* (of Gaul) on 20 April 378, must have assumed this office before 30 Nov. 377 (when it had been already vacated by Antonius), and Hesperius may have been his colleague from the first (certainly by 21 Jan. 378). Ausonius's father was doubtless made *P.P.O. Illyrici* at the same time (*Epiced.* 52). Italy must have been added to Gaul after 18 Aug. 378, when Antonius was still *P.P.O. Italiae*, and before 31 Dec. 378, since the elder Ausonius lived to see his son prefect of Gaul, Italy and Africa, but not consul (*Epiced.* 46). Gaul, Italy and Illyricum are mentioned in Hesperius's law of 379 (xiii, 1, 11). Ausonius retired in favour of Siburius before 3 Dec. 379 (xi, 31, 7), and there is no reason to believe that the collegiate prefecture was continued after the retirement of its principal beneficiary. Siburius would have been *P.P.O. Galliarum* and Hesperius would have continued to govern Italy; he is still recorded as *P.P.O.* on 14 May 380 (x, 20, 10, as emended by Seeck).

We next have the alleged collegiate rule of Syagrius and Severus in Italy in 382. The data are again best presented in tabular form:

Consuls	Severus	Syagrius (1)	Syagrius (2)
Ausonio et Olybrio, 379		mag. off. 1 Oct.: vii, 12, 2	26 Aug.: i, 15, 10[11]
Gratiano V et Theodosio, 380		P.P.O. 18 June: xi, 30, 38 P.P.O. 15 July: vii 18, 4, p.p. Rom.	

Consuls	Severus	Syagrius (1)	Syagrius (2)
Syagrio (1) et Eucherio, 381			(P.P.O. 5 July: I, 10, 1)[12] P.U. 9 Oct.: VIII, 7, 15
Antonio et Syagrio (2), 382	P.U. 25 Mar.: XII, 12, 8, p.p. Karth.[13] P.U. 1 Apr.: VI, 6, 1+XIV, 6, 4 P.P.O. 2 Apr.: VII, 18, 6, p.p. Rom. P.P.O. 3 Apr.: VIII, 4, 13		
		P.P.O. 9 Apr.: XII, 1, 88, p.p. Karth.[14]	
	P.U. 20 June: XIV, 18, 1		P.P.O. 5 July, XII, I, 89[12]
	P.U. 1 Aug.: VIII, 9, 2		
			P.P.O. 30 Aug.: XI, 16, 14, lecta Capuae.

[11] Syagrius is given no title, but the content of the law shows that he was pro-consul of Africa.

[12] Both these laws are dated 'iii non. Jul. Viminacio', the former 'Syagrio et Eucherio cos.', the latter 'p.c. Syagri et Eucheri'. With Seeck I would date both to 382.

[13] This law, which was posted at Carthage on 25 March 382, was no doubt issued in Italy in the previous autumn. The content ('quaecumque civitas legatos ad sacrarium nostrum voluerit ordinare, libera ei tribuatur facultas, its tamen, ut a te probata atque elimata ad nos desideria perferantur') is obviously unsuitable to the prefect of the city and appropriate to a proconsul of Africa, and the title *P.U.* is an anticipation of Severus's next office.

[14] This law, posted at Carthage on 9 April, had doubtless also been issued to the praetorian prefect in Italy the previous autumn.

The important point to remember is that there were two Syagrii, the consuls of 381 and of 382, and that both were praetorian prefects during their consulates (*Stud. Pal.* xx, 103, A.D. 381; *P. Lips.* 21, A.D. 382). The sequence appears to be that Syagrius (1), having been *magister officiorum* in 379, was praetorian prefect in 380 and 381, but died next spring. Severus, who had been pro-consul of Africa in 381, and became *P.U.* early in 382, was appointed interim *P.P.O.*, receiving two laws as such on 2 and 3 April. Then Syagrius (2), who had been Severus's predecessor as *P.U.*, was appointed *P.P.O.*

Syagrius (2) was followed by Hypatius, who is attested from 9 Dec. 382 to 28 May 383. One of his laws falls within Syagrius's term of office, *C.Th.* xi, 16, 13, 'p.p. Karthag.id.April. post cons. Syagrii et Eucherii' (13 April 382): I suggest that it was issued in the autumn of 382, and posted at Carthage next spring—'dat. (autumn) post cons. Syagrii et Eucherii, p.p. Karthag.id.April'.

Hypatius, Atticus (attested on 13 March 384, *C.Th.* xiii, 1, 12) and Praetextatus (attested on 21 May and 9 Sept. 384, *C.Th.* vi, 5, 2 and *C.J.* i, 54, 5) are given as a colleague Petronius Probus. Probus was certainly praetorian prefect of Italy and Illyricum about this time; according to Socrates (v, 11) and Sozomen (vii, 13) he was in office at Milan at the time of the fall of Gratian (killed on 25 Aug. 383). The two laws addressed to him at this time (xi, 13, 1 and vi, 30, 6) are dated in the Code 19 Jan. 383 ('dat. xiiii kal.Feb.Med. Merobaude ii et Saturnino cos') and 26 Oct. 384 ('dat. vii kal.Nov.Med.post cons. Merobaudis et Saturnini'), but with minor emendations they can be fitted in between Hypatius's last law on 28 May 383 and Atticus's law on 13 March 384. In the first law the month Feb. could be changed to Sep., or the consulship be made a postconsulate; in the second one has only to assume that a *propositum* has fallen out, and that the law was issued on 26 Oct. 383, and posted early next year.

After Praetextatus, Principius is supposed to have been the colleague of Neoterius and then of Eusignius. The evidence is set out in the accompanying table. What emerges most clearly is that Valentinian II was resident at Milan for the first half of 385 (down to 10 July at least); and at Aquileia during the second half of 385 (from 31 August at latest to 11 December at least); and then at Milan again throughout 386 and the earlier part of 387 (from 23 January 386 at latest to 19 May 387), making one visit to Ticinum nearby. Seeck has plausibly emended the date of a law given at Verona so as to fall on the journey from Milan to Aquileia. The impression given by the table is strengthened if one consults the *Regesten*; one there sees that Valentinian is also attested at Milan on 1 Jan., 1 Feb., 15 Feb., 25 Feb. and 18 June 385; at Aquileia on 14 and 17 Sept. and 25 Nov. 385; and at Milan again on 29 March, 3 April, 6 June and 6 July 386. It is noticeable also that all Neoterius's laws fall within the first period of residence at Milan, all Eusignius's within the second period of residence at Milan, and the bulk of Principius's laws within the period of

cc

residence at Aquileia. Of the four laws of Principius which lie outside the main group the first two can be dated within it without violence. The last two cannot be so easily emended, but I find it easier to believe that their dates are wrong than that Valentinian II made two special journeys from Milan to Aquileia (some 250 miles) merely in order to issue two constitutions to Principius.

Eusignius is given another colleague in 387 in the person of Petronius Probus. This prefecture of Probus rests on Sozomen (vii, 13), who declares that Valentinian fled to Thessalonica with his mother and Probus the prefect. But this chapter of Sozomen is merely an embroidered amplification of Socrates v, 11, where Probus flees to Thessalonica, but is not given the title of prefect.

Since I have abolished this prefecture of Probus it is incumbent upon me to give my version of Probus's four prefectures. The proper method is, in my view, to consider the literary and epigraphic evidence first, and then see how the dates of his laws fit in. Ammianus (xxvii, 11, 1) states that on the death of Vulcacius Rufinus (last recorded on 19 May 367, C.Th. x, 15, 4) Probus was summoned from Rome to take up the praetorian prefecture, and from other passages (xxviii, 1, 31–3, xxix, 6, 9–11, xxx, 3, 1, 5, 4–11, Paulinus, V. Amb. 8) it is clear that his zone included both Italy and Illyricum. He still held office at the time of Valentinian II's proclamation on 22 Nov. 375 (Rufin., H.E. ii, 12). He is also, as we have seen, stated by Socrates (and Sozomen) to have been praetorian prefect (of Italy and Illyricum) in 383. In several inscriptions Probus is at the end of his career styled 'proconsuli Africae, praefecto praetorio quater Italiae Illyrici Africae Galliarum' (I.L.S. 1267–8, cf. A.E., 1934, 160), that is to say he held the prefecture four times in all and the districts that he governed in his various tenures of office included Italy, Illyricum, Africa and Gaul. On another inscription (before his fourth prefecture) he is styled 'procons. Africae, praef. praetorio Illyrici, praef. praet. Galliar. II, praef. praet. Italiae atque Africae III' (I.L.S. 1266), which can hardly mean anything else but that he governed Illyricum in his first prefecture, Gaul in his second, and Italy and Africa in his third. This appears to be contradicted by an inscription at Verona put up on 8 Aug. 378, in which he is styled 'proconsuli Africae, praefecto praetorio per Illyricum Italiam et Africam' (I.L.S. 1265). It is not, however, necessary to

Consuls	Neoterius	Principius	Eusignius
Richomere et Clearco, 384	(VIII, 5, 43, 1 Feb.)[15]	(*C.J.* 1, 48, 2, P.U. 13 Feb.)[16]	
Arcadio A.I et Bautone, 385	IX, 38, 8, 25 Feb., Med. VIII, 5, 46, 9 April, Med.[17] XI, 16, 16, 14 April, Med. II, 1, 6, 30 April, Med. XI, 22, 2, 4 May. XII, 1, 110, 28 May, Med. VIII, 4, 15, 12 June, Med. VII, 2, 2, 10 July, Med. II, 26, 4, 26 July.	(IX, 40, 14, 1 June)[18] VI, 30, 10, 31 Aug., Aquil. VIII, 7, 16, 18 Sept., Aquil. 1, 2, 9 (=XI, 1, 20), 24 Sept., Aquil. X, 20, 12, 26 Sept., Aquil. XIII, 1, 14, 4 Nov., Veronae)[19] XII, 12, 10, 5 Nov. VIII, 7, 17, 10 Dec., Aquil. XI, 16, 17, 11 Dec., Aquil.	
Honorio n.p. et Euodio, 386		I, 9, 2,[20] mag. off., pp. Hadrumeti vii id. Mart. p.c. Arcadii A.I et Bautonis v.c. (XIII, 5, 17, 20 April, Aquil.)	XVI, 1, 4, 23 Jan., Med. XII, 12, 11, 15 Feb., Ticini. VIII, 7, 18, 14 July, Med. I, 32, 5, 29 July, Med.

Consuls	Neoterius	Principius	Eusignius
		(ii, 8, 18+viii, 8, 3+xi, 7, 13, dat. or pp. 3 Nov., Aquil., acc. 26 Nov., Rom.)	
			xi, 37, 1, 18 Nov., Med.
			viii, 8, 4, 3 Dec. Med.
			xii, 1, 114, 25 Dec.
Valentiniano A.III et Eutropio, 387			i, 29, 6, 25 Jan.
			xv, 3, 3, 26 Feb.
			vi, 24, 4, 6 March, Med.
			xi, 22, 3, 14 April.
			xi, 30, 48, 19 May, Med.

[15] With Seeck I would move this law to 1 Feb. 385.

[16] Principius cannot have been *P.U.* in this period, and the law is more appropriate to a *P.P.O.* I would emend the date, which is 'd.id.Feb. Chomere' in the MSS, to 'd.id.Sep.p.c. Richomeris et Clearchi' (=13 Sep. 385).

[17] This law is addressed 'Nynegio P.P.O.', but the datum and content show that it is a western law. 'Neoterio' has been corrupted to 'Nynegio' because the preceding and following laws are addressed to Cynegius.

[18] I would emend 'kal.Iun.Arcad.A.I. et Bautone cos.' to 'kal.Ian.p.c.Arcad.A.I et Bautonis' (=1 Jan. 386).

[19] With Seeck I would move this law to 4 Aug. 385.

[20] This law must have been given in the preceding summer, before Principius became *P.P.O.*

assume that the dedicators gave his career in full; they may have preferred to ignore his first two prefectures, which were, as we shall see, brief, and to concentrate on his long third prefecture, during which he certainly governed not only Italy and Africa, but Illyricum, omitted in *I.L.S.* 1266 because the repetition of the name would be inelegant.

Most of Probus's laws fall between 12 March 368 and 3 Dec. 374, that is during his third prefecture (of Italy, Africa and Illyricum). Two, as we have seen, can be fitted into his fourth term of office in 383, when he also governed Italy, Africa and Illyricum (see *C.Th.* xi, 13, 1). There are two laws which are dated earlier than 368, *C.Th.* i, 29, 1, 'dat.v.k. Mai. divo Ioviano et Varroniano cos.' (27 April 364, dealing with Illyricum), and xi, 1, 15, 'dat.xiv kal.Jun. Remis Gratiano et Dagalaifo cos.' (19 May

366). The first date is difficult to emend without violence, and there seems no objection to accepting them both as belonging to Probus's first prefecture in Illyricum and his second in Gaul respectively. Probus may have been appointed to Illyricum by Julian or Jovian; he had been dismissed before the beginning of 365, when Mamertinus's prefecture included Illyricum as well as Italy (Amm. xxvi, 5, 5). In Gaul his prefecture (which is further attested by the undated *C.J.* vii, 38, 1) can be fitted in between Germanianus, last attested on 7 April 366 (*C.Th.* viii, 7, 9), and Florentius, attested on 3 Jun. 367 (*C.Th.* xiii, 10, 5).

There remain two laws of Probus dated 12 March and 27 June 380 (vi, 28, 2, 'p.p. iiii id.Mart.Hadrumeto dd.nn.Gratiano A.V. et Theodosio A.I cos.', and vi, 35, 10, 'dat.v.kal.Jul. Aquileia, Gratiano V et Theodosio I AA.cos.'). On any theory some of Probus's dates must be emended, and this consulship may well have been confused with one of the consulships which Gratian Augustus shared with a private person, 'Gratiano II et Probo' (371) or 'Gratiano III et Equitio' (374) or 'p.c. Gratiani III et Equitii' (375). Unless 'dat.' is emended to 'acc.' in vi, 35, 10, the last year is most plausible, as Valentinian may have passed through Aquileia on his journey from Treviri to Carnuntum that spring (Amm. xxx, 5, 1–2).

There remain only two alleged collegiate prefectures, Eusebius and Hilarius in 396 and Longinianus and Curtius in 407–8. Eusebius, attested from 19 Dec. 395[21] to 23 Dec. 396 was certainly *P.P.O. Italiae* (see Paulin., *V. Amb.* 34). Hilarius, attested 19 March to 28 Dec. 396, should be placed in Gaul, for, as Professor Palanque has argued (*Essai*, 99–100), Vincentius is not attested as *P.P.O. Gall.* until 18 Dec. 397; in *C.Th.* xv, 1, 33, of 5 July 395 the address is 'have Vincenti k.nobis' and this form of address would be equally appropriate if he were a vicar. Vincentius's immediate predecessor was Theodorus (Symm., *Ep.* ix, 25), but there is room for Hilarius, for Theodorus was still proconsul of Africa on 22 Dec. 396 (Aug., *c. Cresc.*, iii, 62) and cannot have arrived in Gaul until the spring of 397.

Longinianus is attested in the Code as *P.P.O.* (either of Italy or Gaul) on 11 Jan., 9 Feb. and 24 March 406 (*C.Th.* xiii, 7, 2,

---

[21] In *C.Th.* xv, 14, 12, he is addressed as *P.P.O.* on 18 May 395, but he was at that time *C.S.L.* (see *Regesten*, p. 117).

XIII, 11, 11, VII, 18, 15): according to Zosimus (V, 32) he was prefect of Italy when he was killed at Ticinum on 13 Aug. 408. Curtius is attested as prefect (of Italy) on 7 April 407 (XIV, 1, 5, dealing with the *decuriae urbis Romae*), 15 Nov. 407 (*Sirm*. 12 = *C.Th*. XVI, 5, 43+XVI, 10, 19, dealing with heretics, especially Donatists, and pagans) and 3 Feb. 408 (*C.Th*. I, 20, 1). It is simplest to assume that Longinianus was *P.P.O. Gall*. in 406. There is room for him between Romulianus (22 April 404 to 6 Aug. 405) and Limenius, who was killed at Ticinum on 13 Aug. 408 (Zos. V, 32), even though Petronius must also be fitted in between 402 and 408, and perhaps also Dardanus; for there are gaps between Andromachus (25 June 401) and Romulianus (22 April 404) and Longinianus (24 March 406) and Limenius (408).

I would assert that in my attempt to exorcise the ghost of the collegiate praetorian prefecture I have done less violence to the dates of the Codes than have my predecessors who were still haunted by it.

To demonstrate that I have not inadvertently created any more collegiate prefectures I append a table of praetorian prefects from 337 to 408.

PRAETORIAN PREFECTS 337–408

Year	Gaul	Italy	Illyricum	Oriens
340	Ambrosius (339–340)	Antonius Marcellinus (29 April–28 June 340) Aco Catullinus (24 June 341)		Septimius Acindynus (27 Dec. 338–14 Aug. 340) Domitius Leontius (11 Oct. 340–6 July 344)
345	Titianus (30 June 343–12 Nov. 349)	Placidus (28 May 344) Vulcacius Rufinus (344–7)		
		Limenius (12 June 347–8 Apr.	Vulcacius Rufinus (22 June 347–12	Philippus (28 July 346– summer 351)

Year	Gaul	Italy	Illyricum	Oriens
		349) (Eustathius) (8 May 349) Hermogenes (19 May 349–26 Feb. 350)	May 352)	
350				
				Thalassius (351–3 July 353) Domitianus (353/354)
	Vulcacius Rufinus (8 March 354) Volusianus Lampadius (354–30 July 355)	Maecilius Hilarianus (14 March 354)		Strategius Musonianus (25 July 354–358)
355	Honoratus (355-7) Florentius (357–360)	Taurus (5 Apr. 355–29 Aug. 361)	Lollianus Mavortius (22 July 355–356) Anatolius (23 May 357–360)	
				Hermogenes (24 Aug. 358–360)
360	Nebridius (360–361) Sallustius (361–363)		Florentius (360–361)	Helpidius (4 Feb. 360–361) Saturninius Secundus Salutius (Dec. 361–30 July 365)
		Mamertinus (22 Feb. 362–26 April 365)		
	Germanianus (18 Dec. 363–7 April 366)			
			Probus (27 April 364)	
365		Vulcacius Rufinus (21 June 365–19 May 367)		Nebridius (autumn 365) Saturninius Secundus Salutius II (2 Nov. 365–early 367)
	Probus (19 May 366) Florentius (3 June 367) Viventius (26 April 368–29 June 371)	Probus (12 March 368–22 Nov. 375)		Auxonius (1 Sept. 367–3 May 369) Domitius

Year	Gaul	Italy	Illyricum	Oriens
				Modestus (1 Aug. 369–2 Nov. 377)
370	Maximinus (13 July 371–16 April 376)			
375	Antonius (23 May 376–28 July 377)	Antonius (30 Nov. 377–18 Aug. 378)		
	Ausonius (20 Apr. 378) + Hesperius (21 Jan. 378)	Ausonius (378–379) + Hesperius (6 Dec. 378–14 May 380)	Julius Ausonius (378) Olybrius (378-9)	Aburgius (378)
	Siburius (3 Dec. 379)			Olybrius (379)
380	Mallius (380/2)	Syagrius (1) (18 June 380–382)	Eutropius (6 Jan. 380–28 Sept. 381)	Neoterius (15 Jan.380–16 Jan. 381)
		(Severus) (2–3 April 382)		Florus (30 July 381–5 March 383)
		Syagrius (2) (5 July–30 Aug. 382) Hypatius (9 Dec. 382–28 May 383)		Postumianus (6 April 383–3 Dec. 383)
	Gregorius (383)	Probus (19 Aug.–26 Oct. 383) Atticus (13 March 384) Praetextatus (21 May–9 Sept. 384)		Maternus Cynegius (18 Jan. 384– 14 March 388)
385		Neoterius (1 Feb.–26 July 385) Principius (4 Aug.–11 Dec. 385)		
	Euodius (386)	Eusignius (23 Jan. 386–19 May 387)		
	Constantianus (14 Jan.–8 Nov. 389)	Trifolius (14 June 388–19 Jan. 389)		Flavius Eutolmius Tatianus

Year	Gaul	Italy	Illyricum	Oriens
390	Neoterius (2 March–28 May 390)	Polemius (16 Jan.–22 June 390) Nicomachus Flavianus (18 Aug. 390–8 April 392) Apodemius (28 July 392–9 June 393)		(16 June 388–Sept. 392) Flavius Rufinus (10 Sept. 392–27 Nov. 395)
395		Dexter (18 March–1 Nov. 395)		Caesarius (Nov. 395–13 July 397)
	Hilarius (19 March–28 Dec. 396) Theodorus (397) Vincentius (18 Dec. 397–9 Dec. 400)	Eusebius (19 Dec. 395–23 Dec. 396) Mallius Theodorus (31 Jan. 397–20 Jan. 399) Messala (16 Feb. 399–27 Nov. 400)	Eutychianus (24 Feb. 396–1 April 397) Anatolius (17 June 397–12 Nov. 399)	Eutychianus (4 Sept. 397–25 July 399) Aurelianus (17 Aug. 399–2 Oct. 399)
400			Clearchus (402-7)	Eutychianus II (11 Dec. 399— summer 400) Caesarius II (8 Dec. 400–11 June 403)
	Andromachus (25 June 401) Dardanus? (401-4)	Hadrianus (27 Feb. 401–5 Oct. 405)		
405	Romulianus (22 April 404–6 Aug. 405) Longinianus (11 Jan.–24 March 406) Petronius? 406-8) Limenius (13 Aug. 408)	Curtius (7 April 407–3 Feb. 408) Longinianus (13 Aug. 408)	Herculius (11 April 407–26 May 410)	Eutychianus III (3 Feb. 404–11 June 405) Anthemius (10 July 405–18 April 414)

CHAPTER TWENTY-ONE

THE CASTE SYSTEM IN THE LATER ROMAN EMPIRE[1]

ONE of the most repellent features of the later Roman empire is the system of castes, whereby certain categories of persons were legally compelled to follow certain avocations, and their sons were compelled to follow in their fathers' footsteps. In this paper I shall endeavour to prove that in practice status and occupation were to a large extent hereditary under the principate, and that the later emperors did little more than give legal sanction to a system which was, through various social and economic causes, beginning to break down. I shall also try to prove that the legal caste system which was thus created was by no means all-embracing, and in practice was not rigorously enforced.

The hereditary classes fall into two main categories, those whose personal service was required by the government, such as soldiers, agricultural labourers and workers in the mints and the state factories and the public post, and those like the decurions, the shippers (*navicularii*) and the guilds of Rome, who, though they might have to perform certain personal services, were mainly required to make a financial contribution to various essential activities.

The most important and best documented instance of the second category is the decurions. Here it is important to note that no imperial constitutions are recorded making service on the city councils compulsory or hereditary. The system grew by accumulations of precedents based on certain old legal principles. Under the principate decurions were either elected by the people, or nominated by city censors, who were obliged to enrol former magistrates who had been elected by the people. There were various qualifications for office, including citizenship of the city

[1] Professor Jones read this paper in Prague, June 1967. Some references have been amended or added, misprints corrected, and one or two changes introduced in the version published in *Eirene* from Jones' own copy. Changes of substance are in square brackets.

concerned (*origo*) or, by the Severan period, residence in it (*incolatus*), and a minimum amount of property. In the first century and more of the principate, candidature for the decurionate and for the magistracies seems to have been voluntary, and there was indeed generally keen competition for these honours. From the end of the first century A.D., however, and probably earlier, there was an underlying obligation upon qualified persons to hold office if the public interest demanded. Clause 51 of the Lex Malacitana (*F.I.R.A.* i² no. 24) lays down that if there should not be a sufficient number of qualified voluntary candidates to fill the places, the presiding magistrate should nominate qualified persons, and these in turn might nominate others, and that the election should be held between these persons as if they had voluntarily professed their names. This provision may not have been often put into practice, but the legal principle existed that the city must have its magistrates—and therefore future decurions—and that qualified citizens must in the last resort serve if duly nominated and elected. *Nominatio* was henceforth the legal means of filling vacancies compulsorily both for magistracies and the council; for the decurionate was itself legally a *honor* (*Dig.* L, v. 5).

During the second century the decline of civic patriotism and the growing expenses involved in the decurionate and the magistracies made it increasingly difficult to fill them. They were no longer competed for as coveted honours, but accepted as moral obligations, or by the less conscientious evaded as burdens. Compulsion must have been used not infrequently under Marcus and Verus, who ruled that those who filled a magistracy under compulsion must provide security no less than those who voluntarily undertook office (*Dig.* L, i, 38, 6). By the Severan period it is evident from the citations from contemporary lawyers in the Digest that compulsion was regularly employed.

Membership of the council was never legally hereditary under the principate, but, as many inscriptions prove, it often was so in practice. Pliny thought this practice desirable (*Ep.* x, 79: 'quia sit aliquanto melius honestorum hominum liberos quam e plebe in curiam admitti'; since the term *plebs* includes all non-decurions, *honesti homines* must mean decurions). The hereditary tendency was reinforced by the growing expense of the decurionate. Only the wealthiest families in each city could afford it, and since wealth normally passes from father to son, so did service on the council.

Diocletian and his successors thus found a compulsory decurionate, in which membership was hereditary, but to which qualified outsiders could be added, already in being. All that they did was to stop—or try to stop—various loopholes whereby decurions and their sons freed themselves from their obligations. Service in the army was naturally incompatible with curial service so decurions were forbidden to enlist in the army, or by extension in the civil service, which was also a *militia*. Senators and members of the equestrian order had been free from the obligation to serve on their city councils; decurions were forbidden to acquire these ranks before they had completed their service to their cities. In other cases the exemption from curial duties was abolished; this was the rule from 390 for senatorial rank, and for *navicularii*, who had, since the early principate, enjoyed *publici muneris vacatio*, interpreted by Paulus as including exemption from *honores* and the decurionate. Decurions who took advantage of Constantine's exemption of the Christian clergy from the *curia* were later compelled to surrender their property to a relative who could take their place. Such legislation was not unprecedented. Ulpian had stated (*Dig.* L, iv, 4, 3): 'qui obnoxius muneribus suae civitatis nomen militiae defugiendi oneris municipalis gratia dedit, deteriorem causam reipublicae facere non potuit', and (*Dig.* L, v, 1, 2) 'qui in fraudem ordinis in honoribus gerendis . . . evitandorum maiorum onerum gratia ad colonos praediorum se transtulerint ut minoribus subicientur, hanc excusationem sibi non paraverunt'. There were also rulings against fraudulent claims. Papinian declared that only those *conductores vectigalium fisci* were exempt *qui praesentes negotium gerunt* (*Dig.* L, v, 8, 1), and Marcus and Verus had ruled that *navicularii* were immune only if they had the bulk of their capital in shipping (*Dig.* L, vi, 6, 6).

The main novelty in the legislation of Diocletian and later emperors is that they specifically mention decurions' sons and descendants or allude to the tie of *origo*. Down to the death of Constantine I have noted eight laws[2] which thus allude to the nexus of birth, but five[3] of these also specify other persons qualified for membership. After this, with one or two isolated exceptions, only sons of decurions are mentioned. I doubt if any legal conclusion is to be drawn from the language of the codes.

[2] *C.Th.* xii. i. 7, 14, 22 and the laws listed in note 3.
[3] *C.J.* xii. xxxiii. 2. *C.Th.* xii. i. 10, 13. xvi. ii. 3, 6.

The emperors naturally, when forbidding decurions or potential decurions to take up other avocations, specify the categories of persons to whom *de facto* the ban would apply. There would be, besides active decurions, their sons, who would normally succeed to their property and office, and any other persons who were financially qualified and not immune. As time went on persons of the second class became increasingly rare and cease to be mentioned except when a general round up of all possible recruits to the councils was occasionally ordered.[4]

The history of the *navicularii*, *pistores* and *suarii* is less well documented and therefore more obscure. Under the principate emperors from Claudius onwards attracted men of property into becoming shipowners in the service of the *annona* by the grant of various privileges, citizenship for Junian Latins, the *ius iv liberorum* for women, exemption from the lex Papia Poppaea (Suet. *Claudius* 18–9, Gaius, *Inst.* I, 32, Ulpian, III, 6, *C.Th.* XIII, v, 7), immunity from *tributum* for their ships (Tac. *Ann.* XIII, 51), exemption from *tutela* (*C.Th.* XIII, v, 7), and above all *publici muneris vacatio*, which was later interpreted to mean exemption from municipal *honores* and the decurionate (*Dig.* L, ii, 9, 1; iv, 5, v, 3, vi, 1, 5, 3–9 and 13). Privileges were similarly given to operators of large bakeries at Rome and to butchers; these included citizenship for Junian Latins (Gaius, *Inst.* I, 34) and exemption from *tutela* (*Frag. Vat.* 233–7). Evidently these occupations were commercially unattractive, and instead of increasing freight payments and offering better terms for baking and butchering the government rewarded those who entered these trades with privileges which cost it nothing.

The privileges applied to *navicularii* who built and operated in the service of the *annona* a ship of at least 10,000 *modii* capacity and to bakers who operated a bakery at Rome with an output of at least 100 *modii* a day (Gaius, *Inst.* I, 32, 34), but the qualification of *suarii* was that they employed at least two-thirds of their capital in the butchery business (*Frag. Vat.* 237), and a similar rule was later applied to *navicularii* (*Dig.* L, vi, 5, 6). This implies that applicants for the privileges had to submit a full return of their property, and that the privileges were in some sense attached to the property.

In the fourth century these classes still enjoyed their privileges; immunity from *tutela* and the lex Papia Poppaea and *muneris*

[4] *C.Th.* XII. i. 53, 96, 133; Val. III. *Nov.* 3, para. 4.

publici vacatio are expressly asserted for the *navicularii* (*C.Th.* XIII, v, 7), and the privileges of the *corporati urbis Romae* were frequently confirmed in general terms by successive emperors (*C.Th.* XIV, ii, 1, 2, 3, cf. Symm. *Rel.* 14). But by the beginning of Constantine's reign shippers in the state service and Roman butchers and bakers were not allowed to abandon their occupations; there is nothing in the relevant laws (*C.Th.* XIII, v, 1, 2) to suggest that the obligation was a novelty. *De facto* service seems to have been generally hereditary. The terms *origo* and *originalis* are applied to *navicularii* (*C.Th.* XIII, v, 1, 22) and an *agens in rebus* is stated to enjoy exemption from the service only 'si nec genere naviculariorum corpori cohaeret nec navarchiae obnoxias functioni retinet facultates' (*C.Th.* XIII, v, 20). The terms *origo* or *originalis* are also used of *pistores* (*C.Th.* XIV, iii, 14) and *suarii* (*C.Th.* XIV, iv, 5, 8), and it is assumed that their sons, grandsons or other relatives will succeed them (*C.Th.* XIV, iii, 3, 5; iv, 7); it is also ordered that sons-in-law must serve (*C.Th.* XIV, iii, 2, 21). But the legal obligations lay on the property, and if members alienated their lands (as they were entitled to do) the recipients were obliged to undertake the service (*C.Th.* XIII, v, 3, 19, 20, 17, vi, 1, 4, 6, 7, 8, for *navicularii*, XIII, v, 2, XIV, iii, 3, for *pistores*, XIV, iv, 1, 5, 7, 8, for *suarii*) and sons were bound as *heredes* of the property. Evidence for the other Roman guilds is scanty, but membership was certainly compulsory in the *catabolenses* (*C.Th.* XIV, iii, 9, 10) and the *mancipes salinarum* (Symm. *Rel.* 44) and the *navicularii amnici* (Symm. *Rel.* 44, *C.Th.* XIII, v, 11, 13, Val. III, *Nov.* xxix), and no doubt the same rules applied to all. A property qualification was required of the *catabolenses*, and service was hereditary in the *navicularii amnici* and alienation of property forbidden (Val. III, *Nov.* xxix).

We can only conjecture the process whereby this change came about. It seems likely that in the inflation of the third century the government payments to the shippers, bakers and butchers dropped in real value; the freight rates paid under Constantine to the *navicularii* were about a third of the commercial rate laid down by Diocletian (*C.Th.* XIII, v, 7. *A.E.* 1947, 148–9). In these circumstances, those engaged in these services may well have wished to abandon them and forfeit their privileges, but the government apparently insisted that they must carry on the essential services which they performed. The government's justification, if it felt that any justification was needed, may well have been that, since it gave privileges, it was entitled to a *quid pro quo*. This argument, as we shall see, was used in regard to soldiers, and even suggested in regard to the clergy (*C.Th*. xvi, ii, 9).

The different development of the decurions and other classes is interesting. With the latter specific properties were subject to the servitude, perhaps for the reason suggested above. Decurions had only to be persons with a certain amount of property, and the obligation was personal. It was apparently sometimes claimed that curial property carried curial obligations, but the government did not support this view (*C.J*. x, xi, 4, *C.Th*. xii, i, 52). Later it was found necessary to place restriction on decurions alienating their property to outsiders, and a complicated network of rules was framed to this end. Justinian finally made curial service a servitude on curial land (Just. *Nov*. ci).

Among the second category, the classes bound to personal labour, the workers in the mints, the public post and the state weaving and dyeing establishments present no difficulty. The *monetarii* had always been imperial slaves, and Diocletian appears to have manned the *gynaecia*, *linyphia* and *baphia* with convicts.[5] The stock of labour was maintained by breeding, and these groups came to enjoy *de facto* the normal rights of free persons, marrying and holding property. They remained, however, as the language of the codes proves, technically slaves, and their offspring therefore, if they married female imperial slaves, as they apparently usually did, were also slaves and were employed by the government in their father's jobs: if they married free women, their children could be claimed as slaves under the senatus consultum Claudianum (*L.R.E*. iii, 112, note 62, 278, note 27, 281, note 30). It is to be noted how little notice was taken of their technically servile status except to enforce their service on themselves and their descendants. As early as 317 the *monetarii* were forbidden to aspire to the equestrian order (*C.Th*. x, xx, 1), and in 424 *murileguli* were debarred from *dignitates* (*tit. cit*. 14). Julian enrolled *monetarii* in the council of Antioch (Julian, *Misopogon*, 368A), and in Justinian's reign *conchylioleguli* were intermarrying with decurions (Just. *Nov*. xxxviii, 6). In principle they were not allowed to

---

[5] [Lact. *de mort. persec*. 21; Sozomen, *H.E*. i 8: *Not. Dig. Occ*. xi 53, cf. *C.Th*. vi, ii. 5.]

alienate their property, but if they did so those who acquired it had to undertake their duties (*C.Th.* x, xx, 14, 16, Just. *Nov.* xxxviii para. 6).

The miners and goldwashers of the later Empire seem on the other hand to have been free men. Mines had ceased by the second century A.D. to be operated by companies using a large servile labour force. Quarries were still often worked by convicts, and so were some mines, but for the most part the government appears to have leased individual shafts to *coloni*, as at Vipasca (*F.I.R.A.* i,[2] no. 104). The *coloni* might have partners or employ a few slaves (sections 6, 7, 10, 13, 17) or indentured labourers (*F.I.R.A.* iii, 150), but were evidently working miners. In the later Roman Empire some mines and quarries were still worked by convicts (Eusebius, *Mart. Pal.* 8, 9, Just. *Nov.* xxii, 8) or by corvée labour (*Chr.* i, 391, P. *Thead.* 34–5, *Sb.* 2267, *S.P.P.* xx, 76, P. *Lips.* 85–6), but most mines seem to have been operated by descendants of the *coloni* of the principate. There is actually no law enforcing work in the mines on miners earlier than 369–70 A.D., when Valentinian and Valens carried out a general round up (*C.Th.* x, xix, 5–7), and no specific mention of miners' sons until 424 (*tit. cit.* 15), but all the laws assume a pre-existing obligation. Here, in default of evidence we are reduced to conjecture. Miners have in most societies tended to form closely knit hereditary groups, and this may well have been the case in the Roman empire. When Valentinian and Valens, who were greatly interested in building up stocks of gold (*L.R.E.*, p. 148) found that miners had been leaving the mines and taking up agriculture, they apparently thought it natural and proper to recall them to their traditional work.

As is shown by the increasing number of soldiers who give their origin as *castris* and are registered in the tribe Pollia, the Roman legions of the principate tended to be more and more recruited from the sons of soldiers born during service, and no doubt also from sons of veterans, who are less easily traceable.[6] The government indirectly encouraged this tendency. While many privileges were given to legionaries to encourage voluntary recruitment—the *peculium castrense*, the *testamentum militare*, generous bounties or land allotments and *publici muneris vacatio* to veterans—the government never legitimised marriages between

[6] [G. Forni, *Il Recrutamento delle legioni da Augusto a Diocleziano* 126 ff.]

soldiers in the legions and *peregrinae*, so that their sons were normally *peregrini*: but at the same time it regularly gave citizenship to peregrine recruits, especially sons of soldiers. Provincials who served in the *auxilia* and the fleets were at first given the citizenship not only for themselves but for their wives and children. Under Antoninus Pius, however, the children no longer received the citizenship and henceforth they had to join the army to acquire it.[7] The general grant of citizenship by the *Constitutio Antoniniana* destroyed this incentive to hereditary service. We do not know when military service became legally obligatory, but it is assumed to be so by Constantine in 313 (*C.Th.* vii, xxii, 1, with Seeck's date). In a later law Constantine justifies compulsion by the statement: 'We do not allow sons of veterans to be idle on account of the privileges granted to their parents' (*C.Th.* vii, xxii, 2).

Workers in the state arms factories established by Diocletian, the *fabricae*, were legally soldiers, being branded like military recruits, receiving *annonae* and rising to military non-commissioned grades. Their service was presumably from the beginning hereditary like that of soldiers, though this circumstance is not mentioned until 398 (*C.Th.* x, xxii, 4). The *bastagarii*, who operated the transport services of the *largitiones* and *res privata* were also technically soldiers (*C.Th.* x, xx, 11) and presumably tied as such.

Civil servants were also from Constantine's time graded as *milites*, but in this case Constantine specifically ruled in 331 (*C.Th.* vii, xxii, 2): 'ii qui ex officialibus quorumcumque officiorum geniti sunt, sive eorundem parentes adhuc sacramento tenentur sive iam dimissi sunt, in parentum locum procedant'. The object of this law was perhaps not to enforce hereditary service in general, but to insist on sons being enrolled in the same *officium* in which the parent had served. The government had a strong objection to migration from one department to another, since everyone tended to crowd into the favoured palatine ministries, and forbade the practice for active officials of all grades (*C.Th.*. viii, vii, 19). As there was no lack of candidates for the higher ministries, Constantine's law was not enforced in them—there is at any rate no later law referring to them—but for the officials of proconsuls,

---

[7] [For privileges and disabilities of soldiers and veterans see E. Sander, *Rh. Mus.* 1958, 152 ff., 193 ff.]

consulares, correctores and *praesides*, usually called *cohortales*, it was more stringently enacted. Such officials might not move to another office, and their sons were obliged to serve in their fathers' office (*C.Th.* viii, iv, 4, 7, 8, 13, 21, 22, etc.). The reason was no doubt mainly that the cohortal service was unpopular and could not be maintained by voluntary recruitment. A financial motive also came in. A *cohortalis* on the judicial side of the office after becoming *princeps* retired with the rank of *primipilus*, and had to perform the expensive task of the *primipili pastus* or some equivalent duty of *mancipatus*. [See *L.R.E.* 594, 831 ff.]. It was therefore important that they should be men of some substance, and the richer members of the *officium* must not be allowed to escape. We find in 361 (*C.Th.* viii, iv, 7) the same rules applied to *cohortales* who wish to take orders in the church as were applied to curial ordinands. They must first perform their *mancipatus* or *primipili pastus*, and moreover they must surrender two-thirds of their property to their sons or other relatives, or if they have none to the *officium* corporately.

It may be noted in passing that under the principate one important sector of the civil service had been hereditary—the offices filled by the slaves and freedmen of the emperor. From the large number of *Caesaris vernae* recorded, and the even larger number of *Augusti liberti* who were sons of *Augusti liberti* it is plain that though most imperial slaves were freed in their early thirties as were their wives, many of their sons and daughters were born in servitude. If, as often happened, imperial slaves intermarried the system worked automatically; if the male slaves married freedwomen or women of free birth, as they increasingly did, their children were claimed [as slaves by the emperor] under the senatus consultum Claudianum, which seems to have been devised by Pallas, freedman of Claudius, for that very purpose.[8]

These servile grades still survived at the end of Diocletian's reign, and the humblest class of them, the *Caesariani*, who served the diocesan *rationales*, continued to exist in the fourth century and later. Those in the palatine ministries were given military privileges by Constantine, and retained from their former status only certain titles such as *proximus* and *melloproximus*, and a classification by *formae*. The existence of this class of hereditary civil servants

---

[8] [Tac, *Ann.* xii 53; Pliny, ep. viii 6; Jones' view accounts for the extravagant honours bestowed on Pallas.]

may well have influenced the emperor's attitude to the military clerks.

The largest and most important class to which the hereditary obligation was applied was the agricultural population. In the principate there is no trace of compulsion, except in Egypt, but it is very probable that in practice peasants, whether they were freeholders or tenants, free or slave, tended to cultivate the same holding from generation to generation. Peasant freeholders have in every country been tenacious of their land, and there is no reason to think that those of the Roman empire differed from the rest of the world. Landlords much preferred steady, hereditary tenants, as Columella stresses: 'patris familias felicissimum fundum esse qui colonos indigenas haberet et tamquam in paterna possessione natos iam inde cunabulis longa familiaritate retineret' (*de re rustica* I, 7). That imperial *coloni* generally did cultivate their farms from generation to generation is suggested by the desperate threat of those of Lydia 'to abandon the hearths of our fathers and the graves of our ancestors and migrate to private land' (Keil and Premerstein, *Denkschr. Akad. Wien*, LVII, 1914–5, 37), and the description of themselves by those of the Saltus Burunitanus in Africa as 'rustici tui vernulae et alumni saltuum tuorum' (*I.L.S.* 6870). In Africa the grant of waste lands to squatters on the hereditary Mancian tenure must have encouraged tenants to remain and hand on their holdings to their sons.[9] Landlords also no longer bought slaves as in the Republic but preferred to breed them, as is shown by the high value attached to fertile females (Columella, *de re rustica*, I, 8, 4, *Dig.* XXXIII, vii, 12, 7 and 33, Petronius, *Satyricon*, 53). Slaves were moreover less used as labourers, and more frequently allocated permanent holdings *quasi coloni* (*Dig.* XV, iii, 16, XXXIII, vii, 12, 3, 20, 1).

There is, as I have said, no trace of the agricultural population being in any way tied to the soil except in Egypt. Here C. Vibius Maximus, the prefect, in 104 A.D. issued an edict ordering all persons to return to their homes for the census and 'to devote themselves to the agricultural work incumbent upon them' (Wilcken, *Chr.* I, 202). The return for the census was administratively desirable, as it would otherwise have been very difficult to check up with previous records and maintain reliable registers for the poll tax. The result of the rule was to create a hereditary

[9] [See e.g. T. Frank (ed.), *Econ. Survey of Ancient Rome*, IV 83 ff.]

tie to a locality, for a man's home or, to use the Greek technical term, *idia*, was determined by his first registration as an infant, in his father's *idia*. It may be doubted, however, whether the clause about agricultural work is more than a pious exhortation.

I have argued elsewhere (Chapter xiv) that the clue to the tying of *coloni* to the soil is to be found in two laws of Valentinian and Theodosius I (*C.J.* xi, lii, 1, liii, 1), which abolish the *capitatio* in Illyricum and Thrace respectively, and go on to declare that the peasants are not free to wander where they will, now that they are free from the tie of the tax ('tributario nexu', 'tributariae sortis nexibus'), but are tied by the rule of birth ('originario iure'). The original tie was fiscal, and its object was to simplify the assessment and collection of the *capitatio* or poll tax, but it was maintained for other reasons when and where the tax which occasioned it was abolished. I further argued that this rule tying the peasant to his place of origin as registered in the census probably went back to Diocletian, who initiated the new fiscal system and conducted censuses throughout the empire. The effect of the rule was from the beginning to make the attachment hereditary; for a parent's *origo* was defined by his registration in the census, and in the census infants, though not yet liable to tax, were entered. The definition of *origo* varied in different provinces according to the system of registration in the census. In some provinces such as Egypt, and it would seem Palestine and some Gallic provinces, the registration was by village only. In most areas, including Asia Minor, tenants were registered on their farms. I further argued that initially the attachment must have applied to the whole rural population, both freeholders and tenants. These arguments have since been confirmed by a papyrus document of 308–9 (*P. Cairo Isid.* 126), which cites an imperial order that strangers found in the villages must be returned to their own villages under a penalty of 5 *folles* (cf. ib. 128, a receipt by village officers for fugitive villagers returned, dated 314, and *P. Thead.* 16–7, a petition to the prefect of Egypt by villagers for the return of fugitives, dated 332).

The object of Diocletian's rule seems to have been, as I have said, like the similar but less rigid rule prevailing in Egypt under the principate, primarily fiscal—to simplify the maintenance of the poll tax registers and the collection of the poll tax. But, as in Egypt under the principate, the government was also interested in keeping the peasants on the land, in order to maintain agricultural production and thus make sure of the land tax (*iugatio* or *annona*): Diocletian speaks in a law of 290 (*C.J.* xi, lv, 1) of the 'rusticana plebe quae extra muros posita capitationem detulit et annonam congruam praestat'.

The rule binding peasants to the land proved, however, very convenient to landlords in a period of labour shortage, and in their interest it was maintained, as we have seen, in Illyricum and Thrace, when the poll tax was abolished for these areas. The two laws, it may be noted, affected tenants only and not freeholders. In those provinces in which registration was by village only, and peasants were therefore not tied to their particular farm and its owner, the rule was tightened up to achieve this end. In 386 (*C.J.* xi, li, 1) Theodosius I ruled that 'whereas in other provinces which are subject to our serenity's rule a law established by our ancestors binds tenants by a sort of perpetual bond, so that they are not allowed to leave the places by whose crops they are fed or desert fields which they have once undertaken to cultivate, but this advantage is not enjoyed by the landowners in Palestine', the more usual rule should be applied in Palestine. It was later extended to Egypt also, where adscript tenants (ἐναπόγραφοι γεωργοί) first appear in the last years of the fifth century (*P. Oxy.* 1928 of 497 A.D.). On the other hand, the Diocletianic rule was rarely enforced against freeholders. We know of two later laws only which affect them, and both deal with rather peculiar circumstances. Valentinian I ordered (*C.Th.* x, xii, 2) that if ever a petition was made to the crown from a man alleged to be an ownerless slave, his status should be investigated, and if he proved to be a *colonus* he should be returned to his landlord, if a freeholder to his place of origin. In 415 a comprehensive attempt was made to break down agricultural patronage in Egypt, and by this law (*C.Th.* xi, xxiv, 6) villages of freeholders were to be restored and their villagers compelled to return to them.

Agricultural slaves also were converted in the fourth century into a hereditary caste. Constantine ruled in 327 (*C.Th.* xi, iii, 2) that *mancipia censibus ascripta* (i.e. rural slaves) should not be sold outside their province, and that their new owners would be subject to inspection—presumably, therefore, such slaves had to be entered on their census return as rural slaves. Valentinian I definitely enacted in 371 (*C.J.* xi, xlviii, 7), 'it is completely illegal for rural slaves entered on the census to be sold without the land, as it is for *originarii* (i.e. tied *coloni*). The object of these rules was no doubt partly to maintain agricultural manpower, partly to prevent landowners from claiming tax reductions on the score that their *capitatio* had decreased.

Urban craftsmen never appear to have been hereditarily tied to their occupations in the eastern half of the empire. All the laws which impose this restriction are western, and not one of them was included in the Justinian Code. It appears from a papyrus (*P. Ryl.* 654) of the early fourth century that a boy might be compulsorily apprenticed to a given trade on the demand of the guild concerned, if they could prove that they were short of workers, but there is no indication that he had to follow his father's trade. We know, in fact, of two brothers of Lycopolis, one of whom was a dyer and the other apprenticed to a carpenter (Pall. *Hist. Laus.* xxxv). In the west at the end of the fourth century A.D. the cities of various areas complained, it would seem, that their civic services were falling into decay owing to the flight of their *collegiati* to agricultural work in the country, and the imperial government responded by ordering their landlords to restore the fugitives with their offspring—or half their offspring— born within the last forty years, to the cities. Such orders were made to the praetorian prefects of Italy and of the Gauls in 395 and 400, and during the fifth century standing rules were established whereby *collegiati* were forbidden to join the army or the civil service or to take holy orders (*C.Th.* xii, i, 146 (399); vii, xxi, 3 (396); xii, i, 156 (357); i, xvi, 6 (398); vi, xxx, 16, 17 (399); vii, xx, 12; xii, xix, 1).

The society of the principate was, as I see it, stratified and stable. There was of course some movement from class to class. There was a steady trickle of decurions into the equestrian and senatorial orders, but it must have been very small; it must be remembered that the senate numbered only 600 persons and the total of equestrian posts was still well under 200 in the Severan period. A larger number of prosperous plebeians rose to the decurionate. Soldiers might rise to the equestrian order or even the senate. But on the whole the classes were hereditary. The rich landowning families served generation after generation on the city councils. Sons of soldiers followed their fathers in the legions and the *auxilia*. Peasant proprietors cultivated their ancestral holdings, and tenants likewise.

During the late second and third centuries this static society began for a variety of reasons, demographic, economic and psychological, to break down. Civic patriotism declined and the financial burdens of the decurionate increased, so that the landed gentry were no longer willing to perform their traditional function of paying for the administration of their cities and collecting the imperial taxes. The inflation of the currency reduced the real value of the payments made by the government to the *navicularii*, who accordingly sought to abandon the service. The depopulation which resulted from the great plagues of the late second and early third centuries, and the barbarian invasions and civil wars of the third century with their resultant famines, produced a general manpower shortage, and miners were tempted to take up agriculture, soldiers' sons to cultivate their fathers' allotments instead of enlisting, tenants to abandon their old holdings and seek better farms. The manpower shortage was increased by the rising demand for recruits, which reached a climax when Diocletian doubled the size of the army.

The natural reaction of the government to the crisis was first to 'freeze' the persons engaged in each threatened occupation, next to recall to each threatened occupation those who had recently left it, and finally, as the crisis persisted, to draft their sons into it. In the last war the British government took the first two steps, and very nearly took the third. I served during the early years of the war in the Ministry of Labour and National Service, and was struck by the close resemblance of the Orders in Council issued by the government and the constitutions of the Theodosian Code. As the increasing demands of the army and the munitions industry caused labour shortages in various essential industries, the workers in agriculture, the coal mines, the merchant navy and so forth were successively 'frozen', that is forbidden to leave their jobs, and agricultural labourers, miners and seamen who had in the past decades left these occupations were 'directed' back into them. The third stage was almost reached in the coal mines, where, as the war continued, the ageing labour force began to dwindle. It was tempting to order that sons of miners—who normally went into the pits before attaining military age—should stay there, but the Minister of Labour, Ernest Bevin, refused to sanction so inequitable an order, and the vacancies in the mines were filled by a ballot from all young men who attained military age.

If a modern government reacted in this way to a crisis, it is hardly surprising that the imperial government faced by similar problems acted in a similar way. In the later Roman empire the crisis was prolonged for centuries. The pressure of the barbarians continued and a huge army had to be maintained. The economic resources of the empire gradually dwindled as marginal land went out of cultivation, and its population seems slowly to have sunk. In these circumstances much of the emergency legislation of the late third and early fourth century became permanent.

The rigidity of the system must, nevertheless, not be exaggerated. Even had the laws been strictly enforced, not all classes were hereditarily tied to their occupations. Some were throughout the period completely free, others which were initially restricted were later freed, others having been initially free were later restricted. In most cases there were some legal loopholes which allowed of a change of occupation. De facto, moreover, the government was unable to enforce its policies effectively. It had not a sufficiently numerous and efficient civil service to maintain an elaborate series of registers and a regular system of checking all changes of occupation. To enforce the system it relied either on occasional purges or round ups, or the action of interested parties; the city councils were expected to trace decurions who absconded, landlords to reclaim tenants who deserted their farms. Furthermore the administration was riddled with corruption and highly subject to the pressure of powerful persons. Those who had enough money to give generous bribes to officials or could obtain the 'interest' of great men could always defeat the law.

The smaller groups may be considered first as their story is the simplest. The workmen in the mints, the public post, the bastagae, the state weaving and dyeing establishments and the arms factories continued to be hereditary castes down into Justinian's reign, as the preservation in the Codex Justinianus of the relevant laws proves (C.Th. viii, v, 58=C.J. xii, 1, 7; C.Th. x, xx, 1, 3, 7, 9, 10, 11, 14, 15, 16, 17=C.J. xi, viii, 1, 3, 5, 6, 7, 8, 11, 12, 13, 15; C.Th. x, xxii, 4=C.J. xi, x, 3). There seems to have been no great difficulty in maintaining the rules, and indeed service in these establishments appears to have been quite popular. Men whose fathers were decurions and mothers were daughters of conchylioleguli sometimes preferred the latter service (Just. Nov. xxxviii, 6), and admission to the fabricae had to be limited to persons qualified not only by birth but by age and skill, and regulated by the issue of *probatoria* at Constantinople (*C.J.* xi, viii, 16; this Greek law taken from the Basilica appears to be in the wrong title; the σωματεῖα δημόσια to which it refers must be the *fabricae*, since they are directed by πραιπόσιτοι, not *procuratores*, and their members receive *probatoria* as soldiers). Miners also continued to be tied on similar evidence (*C.Th.* x, xix, 15=*C.J.* xi, vii, 7).

Of the classes whose property was frozen the *navicularii* and the Roman guilds presented little difficulty, since all were small bodies under the immediate supervision of high ranking ministers, the praetorian prefects and the prefect of the city. The chief difficulty with the *navicularii* was to see to it that those to whom their property was alienated undertook their share of the financial burden, but the guilds themselves had obvious motives to report such cases, and action was sometimes taken on their initiative (e.g. *C.Th.* xiii, vi, 1, issued in 326 *ad edictum naviculariorum*). With the Roman guilds, since personal service was required, it was necessary to prevent members acquiring a rank or profession which would prevent their serving, or alienating their property to such persons (e.g. *C.Th.* xiii, iii, 5, on *pistores* who become senators, 11, on those who take holy orders, 3, on those who alienate their property to senators or officials, Val. iii, *Nov.* xx, on *corporati* who obtain a *militia* or holy orders). The *navicularii* were still functioning under the old system under Justinian (*C.J.* xi, iii, 1–3=*C.Th.* xiii, vi, 5, 7, 8), the Roman guilds in the last years of Valentinian iii (Val. iii, *Nov.* xx, of 445; xxix, of 450).

It is, however, worthy of notice that no similar system of hereditary guilds was established at Constantinople; this is the necessary inference from the complete absence of any legislation on the topic in the Codex Justinianus and Justinian's Novels. As has been noted above, there is similar negative evidence that no system of hereditary compulsion was ever applied to the guilds of the Eastern cities. In the west the compulsory system initiated in the last years of the fourth century was maintained under the last emperors and under the barbarian kings, as proved by preservation of the relevant laws in the Breviarium of Alaric and the Edict of Theoderic (*Later Roman Empire*, iii, p, 243, note 112). How efficiently the law was enforced, it is very difficult to say. When it was originally introduced, *collegiati* had some of them been living in the country for over forty years, and had many of them married women who were *colonae* or *ancillae*, and produced families. In such cases the rule was laid down that their offspring should follow the father's condition if the marriage was legal, the mother being free, but the mother's if she was a slave. Majorian, enacting a round up of *collegiati* more than fifty years later, recalls these old rules (Maj. *Nov.* vii, 2–3). Evidently many *collegiati* had in the interval settled down in the country and produced families.

The sons of serving soldiers cannot have been difficult to catch for the army, but sons of veterans were a more serious problem. We can often detect the government carrying out a general round up, as did Constantine in 318, posting notices in all the cities (*C.Th.* vii, xxii, 2), or purging the *officia* of veterans' sons who preferred the *militia officialis* to the *militia armata*, and as did Valens in 365 and Valentinian I in 372 (*C.Th.* vii, xxii, 7, 8). From 318 to 333 veterans' son were given the option of military or curial service (*C.Th.* vii, xxii, 2), but in the latter year were compelled to serve in the army if fit, and otherwise enrolled in the *curia* (*tit. cit.* 5). In these purges and comb-outs quite elderly sons of veterans were often detected—they were liable for enrolment for sixteen years after attaining military age, that is up to 35 (*C.Th.* vii, xxii, 4=xii, i, 35 of A.D. 343, cf. xii, i, 18, of uncertain date, which is probably the earlier law to which the law of 343 refers), and some had reached *grandaeva senectus* before they were detected (*C.Th.* vii, xxii, 7).

The last recorded round ups of veterans' sons were by Theodosius I in 380 in the East, and by Stilicho in 398 and 400 in the West (*C.Th.* vii, xxii, 10, 12, xx, 12), and no laws on the topic are conserved in the Codex Justinianus. It must be presumed that the hereditary obligation of military service was allowed to lapse in the early fifth century. Voluntary recruitment apparently sufficed by now; the last mention of the regular annual conscription is in 403 (*C.Th.* vii, xviii, 14). For enrolment in the *limitanei* military birth was an essential qualification in the sixth century, but the service was apparently esteemed a privilege (*L.R.E.*, 669).

Sons of veterans were a very large and scattered class whom it must have been singularly difficult to catch, but sons of civil servants also presented a serious problem. As we have seen, the hereditary tie applied to—or was enforced against—*cohortales* only; but they numbered over 10,000, scattered over more than 100 provinces. The rule was relaxed in 364 by Valentinian and Valens (*C.Th.* viii, iv, 8), but was revived in 382 (*tit. cit.* 13, cf. 14), but not, it would appear, for the *apparitores* of proconsuls; these were, however, again tied in 412 (*C.Th.* viii, iv, 23). *Cohortales* and their sons were forbidden by many laws to migrate to superior *officia* or the army, but there seem to have been no effective checks on their being admitted to them, and the rule was only enforced by periodical purges, such as that ordered for the army of Mesopotamia in 349 on the suggestion of a vicar (*C.Th.* viii, iv, 4), or those of the western palatine offices and the praetorian prefecture ordered in 412 (*C.Th.* viii, iv, 23–5); later we find Florentius, praetorian prefect of the East, carrying out a general comb-out of the higher *officia* in 428 (*tit. cit.* 29). With regard to taking holy orders or admission to the bar, *cohortales* suffered restrictions parallel to those of decurions. From 361 they could take orders only if they surrendered two-thirds of their property (*C.Th.* viii, iv, 7), until Justinian introduced a severer rule that *cohortales* or their sons might be admitted to the church only if they had in infancy entered a monastery (*C.J.* i, iii, 52, of 531) or, by a later law (Just. *Nov.* cxxiii, of 546), had spent 15 years in a monastery. *Cohortales* were apparently not forbidden to practise at the bar until 435, and they were then only forbidden the highest bars, those of the urban and praetorian prefectures (*C.Th.* viii, iv, 30); this was repealed by Theodosius ii, *Nov.* x, of 439; *C.J.* ii, vii, 11, of 460, 17, of 474). It nevertheless remained the privilege of the *advocati fisci*, the senior barristers of these bars, to be excused from cohortal condition with their children (*C.J.* ii, vii, 17, 21)—a curious confession that the government knew and condoned the illegal admission of *cohortales* to the higher bars despite the strict regulations made in 460 and 474 that no one was to be admitted without being certified by the governor of his province and the provincial *officium* that he was not a *cohortalis*.

Decurions and their sons were even more numerous—there must have been about a quarter of a million of them in the empire —and were scattered over its two thousand odd cities. Some attempt was made from time to time to stop certain channels of escape systematically. Thus in 383 and 385 orders were given in the East and West respectively to military commanders to check up on all recruits and obtain certificates that they were not *curiales* (*C.Th.* vii, ii, 1, 2); these laws repealed a rule laid down under Constantine or his sons (*C.Th.* vii, xiii, 1). In 412 the same rule was laid down for applicants for the *fabricae* (*C.Th.* x, xxii, 6). But more generally the government relied on occasional purges: a thorough comb-out of the palatine offices and the higher branches of the armed forces was ordered in 357 when instructions to weed out decurions were given to the praetorian prefects, the *magistri equitum* and *peditum*, the *comes domesticorum*, the master of the offices, the *comes sacrarum largitionum* and the *castrensis* (*C.Th.* xii, i, 38). In general the government hoped that the city councils would reclaim their errant members, but for the reasons explained by Libanius in his speeches to the Council of Antioch and to Theodosius I on behalf of the councils (Or. xlviii, xlix) they were backward to do so, and had to be threatened with penalties if they failed to do so (*C.Th.* vii, ii, 2; xii, i, 110, of 385, 113 of 386, etc.). It is indisputable, in fact, that vast numbers of decurions, particularly those who were wealthy and influential enough to bribe the officials and intimidate their colleagues, did escape the net in fact, with the ultimate result that by Justinian's time 'if one should count the city councils of our empire one will find them very small, some well off neither in numbers nor in wealth, some perhaps with a few members, but none with any wealth' (Just. *Nov.* xxxviii pr.).

It would be wearisome to catalogue the various restrictive rules whereby the government attempted to keep the *curiales* in the cities. It would be more worth while to enumerate what professions were legally open to them, and by which they might hope to escape from their status. They were not during the fourth century debarred from holding equestrian offices of state, such as those of *praeses* or *rationalis*, and thereby gaining personal immunity, provided that they first performed the civic *munera*; it was shirking of *munera* and the claim to exemption by honorary offices or rank that the government resisted (*L.R.E.* iii, 236, n. 66). Entry to the senate was at first barred by the government, when in the middle of the fourth century it began to become common, but this prohibition was relaxed by Valentinian and Valens, who allowed senatorial rank to those who left a son or sons to carry on in their native cities, while they themselves enjoyed immunity and could transmit it to one son, and to any sons born after their promotion: this privilege again applied only to those who earned a seat in the senate by tenure of an office of state. This apparently remained the rule in the West, and was slightly relaxed in that decurions who obtained illustrious rank obtained exemption for all their sons. In the East, after two laws in 380 and 382 banning the senate to decurions altogether and expelling existing senators, Theodosius I in 386 allowed decurions to become senators, but made them concurrently remain decurions. This privilege was periodically withdrawn, when in 398 decurions were forbidden to become provincial governors, and in 416 to obtain codicils of the clarissimate. However, in 436 the government had withdrawn its ban, and decurions might become senators, while continuing with their descendants to perform their curial duties, except that those who had held illustrious offices were excused with their sons born thereafter. Decurions were again denied entry into the senate in 439, and codicils of illustrious rank in 444, but these were temporary measures only. The rule of 436 was restored, but the privilege of *illustres* was restricted by Zeno to the holders of the higher illustrious offices, the *gloriosi*, and this remained the rule under Justinian (*L.R.E.* iii, 236–7, nn. 67–72).

Decurions were thus always, except for a few brief periods, legally entitled to hold imperial offices of state and thereby to acquire at first equestrian and later senatorial rank; the latter could be transmitted to their descendants born after their promotion, [but did not after 386 continue to carry with it exemption from curial status except for the holders of the highest posts. But some decurions actually continued to obtain legal immunity through holding highest offices in the fifth and sixth centuries.][10]

Decurions were denied entry to the provincial *officia* as early as 325 (*C.Th.* xii, i, 11) but tolerated in the palatine offices until 341 (*tit. cit.* 5, 22, 31). Thereafter they were in principle excluded, but often confirmed in the places that they had surreptitiously obtained after varying periods of service (*L.R.E.*, iii, 237, n. 71). By a curious anomaly, those who managed to survive in the *sacra scrinia* and the *agentes in rebus* until reaching the senior posts of *proximus* and *princeps* were officially exempted with all their children from curial status (*C.J.* x, xxxii, 67); this anomalous privilege was conferred on *principes* of *agentes in rebus* in 413 (*C.Th.* vi, xxvii, 16).

[10] Amended from Jones' own copy.

In regard to the bar decurions were in the same position as *cohortales*. They could down to 436 practise in any court, provided that they fulfilled their curial *munera*. In 436 they were excluded from the high courts of the praetorian and urban prefectures, but were none the less officially granted immunity from curial status with all their sons if they managed to evade detection to the end of their careers and achieve the post of *patronus fisci* (*L.R.E.*, III, 147–8, nn. 401–2, 238, n. 76).

In the church too the position of decurions was similar to that of *cohortales*. Their entry into holy orders was forbidden by Constantine in 326 (*C.Th.* XVI, ii, 6) but before 361 this ban had been lifted provided that the curial ordinand surrendered two-thirds of his property (or the whole to his son). This rule was periodically relaxed or waived for the benefit of those who had succeeded in evading it for a stated period or had risen to high orders. Occasionally an absolute ban was re-enacted (in 398 in the East, and in 439 and 452 in the West) but never enforced for long. Justinian enacted for decurions the same rules of prior entry into a monastery that he had done for *cohortales* (*L.R.E.*, III, 239, nn. 78–80; 317, nn. 141–5).

Decurions were always free to enter the other professions, medicine and higher teaching, and on obtaining a municipal post gained personal exemption from curial duties (*L.R.E.*, III, 238, n. 77).

Recruitment into the army was banned from Diocletian's time. This rule was never officially relaxed, but illegal service, if long, was often condoned. Decurions were also always forbidden to become *fabricenses* (*L.R.E.*, III, 238, n. 74). They could always become *navicularii*, but from 390 gained no curial immunity thereby (*C.Th.* XIII, v, 5, 14, 16, 19).

The most numerous by far of the tied classes of the later Roman empire was the agricultural workers, who must have numbered many millions. Here the government relied very largely on landlords, in whose interest it was to enforce the law, and it very soon ceased to be applied to freeholders, partly because no one was interested in restraining their movements, and partly no doubt because they mostly clung to their holdings as long as they possibly could. With regard to tenants, the law was enforced with a curious legal exactitude which worked to their advantage. Only *coloni* registered in the original census and their descendants were bound to the land, and outsiders who took up tenancies later—townsmen who had migrated to the country, freeholders who had lost their land, or *coloni* who had successfully evaded their old landlords' claims—were not tied. As time went on, the category of free *coloni* became numerous, and tied tenants acquired the special name of *originales* (in the West) or *adscripticii* (in the East). This category of tied tenants was progressively more firmly tied to the land and degraded in status. They were forbidden in 365 to alienate their own property without their landlords' consent (*C.Th.* v, xix, 1), and in 396 to sue their landlords except for excessive rents (*C.J.* xi, i, 2). In 409 they were forbidden to take orders in the church without their masters' consent (*L.R.E.*, iii, 315, n. 128). Their one legal avenue of escape had in the fourth century been military service: this was denied to them in the early fifth century (*L.R.E.*, III, 184, n. 14). Free *coloni* were only tied in the West if they married daughters of *originales*; this was enacted in 451 (Val. iii, *Nov.* xxxi). In the East Anastasius tied them to the land by 30 years' prescription, but maintained their personal freedom in all other respects: this he said was to the advantage of both landlord and tenant (*C.J.* xi, xlviii, 19). Adscript status had up to Justinian's time been inherited from either father or mother, but he, apparently on grounds of legal doctrine, ruled that adscript *coloni* were virtually slaves, and that therefore the son of an adscript father and a free mother was free. The new rule had apparently a revolutionary effect, which suggests that mixed marriages must have been very common, and therefore that freeholders and free *coloni* were still a numerous class. Justinian had to explain that the rule was not retrospective, and the sons of free women were still barred by Anastasius' law, that is, tied to the land though personally free (for all the above see *L.R.E.* 797–803; Ch. xiv above).

It has already been noted that the hereditary obligation of the *fabricenses* and of soldiers in the regiments of the *limitanei* seems to have become by the sixth century a hereditary privilege. In the same period there is a tendency in other walks of life to establish hereditary rights. In the law sons of barristers had a prior claim to fill vacancies in the bar and were excused the admission fees demanded of outsiders (*C.J.* ii, vii, 11, 22, 24, 26). In the higher civil service sons of *proximi* were accorded preference in the *sacra scrinia* (*C.J.* xii, xix, 7, 11), and sons of *principes* in the *agentes in rebus* (*C.Th.* VI, xxvii, 8).

In spite of such tendencies I would venture to affirm that social mobility was greater in the later Roman empire than it had been under the principate. We know of a surprisingly large number of persons of humble status, decurions, *cohortales* and even urban workmen and peasants who rose through the law, the civil service or the army into the upper grades of the imperial aristocracy and even to the imperial throne itself. [The flood of laws which endeavour to fix various categories of persons and their descendants in their occupations itself reveals the volume of the movement which they were intended to check and goes far to prove that they failed.][11]

[11] Amended from Jones' own copy.

INDEX

Papinian, 398
papyrus, manufacturers, 59–61; trade, 145, 147, 150; monopoly, 158
Paradeisus, village near Tralles, 238
paraphylakes, 20
parasangs, tribute assessment by, 151–2
Paregorius of Thera, 229, 233, 236, 242
Parmenian, Donatist, 312–3, 327
parochia, 341–3, 345
Parthia, 56, 100
pasture land, 138
pater civitatis, 10, 18
Patrae (Greece), 39, 66
patricius, 366–7, 370, 372
patriotism, lack of, 111
Patroina of Magnesia, 236
patronage, 133
patronus fisci, 416
Paulus, jurist, 398
Pausanias of Tralles, 242
pearls, trade, 143
peasant proprietors of land, 88, 255, 294–6, 298, 301–2, 306, 405–8, 416
peasant revolt, 326
peculium, 105, 402
pecunia, meaning in fourth century, 203
pecunia phorikos, 181
Peiraeus, 153–4
Pelagius I, 341, 346
pensions, 97
pepper, 57, 143
peregrini, 403
perfectissimate, rank, 17
perfumes, 158
Pergamum, 160, 320
Periplus of the Red Sea, 140, 143–4
permutatio publica, 188

persecution, see church
Persia; Achaemenid empire, tribute, 151–2, 176; Sassanian empire, wars with Rome, 148, 322; trade, merchants, ports, 56, 78–9, 140–9, 362; products, 143; robes and ceremonies, 110; and Armenia, 323; invasion of Egypt, 316–8; Mithraism, 100
Peter, bishop of Alexandria, 315
— of Alexandria, linen merchant, 364
—, *magister officiorum*, 368
Petilian, Donatist, 313
Petra, 57, 141, 143–4, 149–50
Petronius, praetorian prefect of Gaul, 392
— Maximus, emperor, 325
— Probus, see Probus, Petronius
Philadelphia (Egypt), 355–7
Philadelphia (Lydia), 45
Philip V, of Macedon, 68
Philippus, praetorian prefect, 383
philosophy, 90, 100, 109, 113
Philoxenus of Hierapolis, 322
Phoenice, province, 267, 269, 275–6; *dux* of, 148
Phoenicia, Ptolemaic taxation, 159–60; linen weaving, 145; silk trade, 362
Photinus, 382
Phrygia, provinces, 45, 100, 182, 266–8, 276–7, 320, 328, 352, 354, 380
phylarchai, 148
Piazza Armerina, villa, 330
Pierius, 366
pillows, 352
Pinianus, 39, 337, 355
piracy, 122, 128
Pisander, epic poet, 98
Pisidia, 91